Political Science

COMPARATIVE GOVERNMENT AND POLITICS SERIES

Published

Maura Adshead and Jonathan Tonge
Politics in Ireland

Rudy Andeweg and Galen A. Irwin
Governance and Politics of the Netherlands (4th edition)

Tim Bale
European Politics: A Comparative Introduction (3rd edition)

Nigel Bowles and Robert K McMahon
Government and Politics of the United States (3rd edition)

Paul Brooker
Non-Democratic Regimes (3rd edition)

Kris Deschouwer
The Politics of Belgium: Governing a Divided Society (2nd edition)

Robert Elgie
Political Leadership in Liberal Democracies

Rod Hague, Martin Harrop and John McCormick
* Comparative Government and Politics: An Introduction (10th edition)

Paul Heywood
The Government and Politics of Spain

Xiaoming Huang
Politics in Pacific Asia

B. Guy Peters
Comparative Politics: Theories and Methods
[Rights: World excluding North America]

Tony Saich
Governance and Politics of China (4th edition)

Eric Shiraev
Russian Government and Politics (2nd edition)

Anne Stevens
Government and Politics of France (3rd edition)

Ramesh Thakur
The Government and Politics of India

Forthcoming

Tim Haughton
Government and Politics of Central and Eastern Europe

* Published in North America as **Political Science: A Comparative Introduction (8th edition)**

Comparative Government and Politics
Series Standing Order ISBN 978–0–333–71693–9 hardback
Series Standing Order ISBN 978–0–333–69335–3 paperback
(outside North America only)

You can receive future titles in this series as they are published by placing a standing order. Please contact your bookseller or, in the case of difficulty, write to us at the address below with your name and address, the title of the series and one of the ISBNs quoted above.

Customer Services Department, Macmillan Distribution Ltd,
Houndmills, Basingstoke, Hampshire, RG21 6XS, UK

8TH Edition

Political Science

A Comparative Introduction

Rod Hague

Martin Harrop

John McCormick

palgrave

First edition 1992
Second edition 1998
Third edition 2001
Fourth edition 2004
Fifth edition 2007
Sixth edition 2004
Seventh edition 2013

Published by
PALGRAVE

Palgrave Macmillan in the US is a division of St Martin's Press LLC,
175 Fifth Avenue, New York, NY 10010.

Palgrave in the UK is an imprint of Macmillan Publishers Limited,
registered in England, company number 785998, of 4 Crinan Street,
London, N1 9XW.

Palgrave is a global imprint of the above companies and is represented
throughout the world.

Palgrave® and Macmillan® are registered trademarks in the United States,
the United Kingdom, Europe and other countries.

ISBN 978–1–137–60123–0

This book is printed on paper suitable for recycling and made from fully
managed and sustained forest sources. Logging, pulping and manufacturing
processes are expected to conform to the environmental regulations of the
country of origin.

A catalogue record for this book is available from the British Library.

A catalog record for this book is available from the Library of Congress.

Printed in China

Brief contents

Detailed contents

Illustrations and features

Spotlights

Focus

Figures

Tables

Maps

Preface

Major changes to this edition

Chapter 1: Broadened to a review of the political, economic and social factors that help us compare, with an expanded section on classifying political systems.

Chapter 2: Includes new discussion of quasi-states and *de facto* states, and a new section on globalization and challenges to the state.

Chapter 3: Expanded coverage of e-democracy, liberal democracy, and civil liberties, and a new section on the contemporary problems facing democracies.

Chapter 4: Includes a new section on hybrid regimes, reorganized coverage of forms of authoritarian states, and an expanded closing section on corruption.

Chapter 5: Opens with a new section on the changing face of comparative politics.

Chapter 6: A substantial revision of the former Chapter 19 on comparative methods, with new material on empirical and normative approaches, and on political prediction.

Chapter 7: More focus on the relationship between constitutions and courts, with revised discussion on the character and durability of constitutions.

Chapter 8: Expanded discussion about the functions of legislatures, the nature of representation, and legislatures in authoritarian systems.

Chapter 9: Expanded coverage of semi-presidential and authoritarian systems, and new material on heads of state and government.

(Continued)

This is a book designed to introduce students to the study of comparative politics. The goal of the new edition is the same as that of its predecessors: to provide a wide-ranging and accessible guide for courses and modules in this fascinating and essential sub-field of political science.

As before, the book takes a thematic approach centred on liberal democracies and authoritarian states, and divides the chapters into three groups.

- The first group (Chapters 1-6) provides the foundations, with a review of key concepts followed by chapters on the state, democracies, authoritarian systems, theoretical approaches, and comparative methods.

- The second group (Chapters 7-12) focuses on institutions. It opens with a chapter on constitutions that assesses the power maps that help us make sense of how institutions work and relate to one another. This is followed by chapters on the major institutions, and a closing chapter on political culture that helps us understand the broader context within which they operate.

- The third group (Chapters 13-19) looks at wider political processes, beginning with a survey chapter on political participation and then at political communication, parties, elections, voters, and interest groups. The book ends with a chapter on the output of politics: public policy.

The addition of a new co-author inevitably results in more than the usual array of modifications. The challenge we set ourselves in this new edition was to remain true to the personality of its predecessors, and to meet the needs of students and instructors in many different settings while integrating fresh perspectives on the study of comparative politics.

There have been important changes in both content and approach:

Structure: The major structural change from the last edition lies in the ordering of the chapters: where those on institutions formerly came towards the end of the book, they have been moved to the middle, preceding the chapters on participation, communication, parties, elections, interest groups, and

Major changes to this edition (Continued)

Chapter 10: Re-ordered content, with reduced discussion of new public management to make room for expanded coverage of e-government.

Chapter 11: Expanded coverage of unitary systems comes earlier in the chapter, and a new section compares unitary and federal systems.

Chapter 12: Includes new discussion of *The Clash of Civilizations*, and of the effect of the internet on political culture.

Chapter 13: Significantly re-ordered, with new discussion of the reasons why people participate in politics.

Chapter 14: Also significantly re-ordered, with expanded discussion of the role and effects of social media.

Chapter 15: Extended section on party systems moved to the beginning of the chapter, and new material injected on parties in authoritarian regimes.

Chapter 16: Includes more detail on election types, notably majority systems and proportional representation.

Chapter 17: Includes a new section on voter choice, with expanded coverage of voter turnout and of voters in authoritarian states.

Chapter 18: Includes new coverage of think-tanks, a reorganized discussion of channels of influence, and a review of social movements.

Chapter 19: formerly a chapter titled The Policy Process, this includes new coverage of the effects of the resource curse in poorer states.

policy. We felt that it was important to begin with 'broad view' chapters before looking at institutions and at mobilization and participation. The former Chapter 19 on the comparative method has been transformed into a new and more detailed Chapter 6 on research methods, and all the chapters have been internally re-organized so as to improve their clarity.

Length: The phenomenon of textbooks that expand with each edition is well known, but *ours* remains one of the notable exceptions. The last edition was shorter than the one before, and – to sharpen the focus on key points - this new edition is again slightly reduced in length.

Features: Several improvements contribute to a clearer and more consistent presentation, including more and shorter definitions of concepts, new figures and tables designed to make complex data easier to absorb, new Focus features designed to treat stimulating topics within the text in more depth, an opening Preview and Overview for each chapter, and new summary sets of Key Arguments.

Classification of political systems: We have retained the broad division into democracies and authoritarian regimes, while providing a more nuanced breakdown of each by using the Democracy Index maintained by the *Economist*, and the Freedom House ranking *Freedom in the World*.

Case studies: As with the last edition, this one focuses on a selection of case study states, enhanced in the new edition to provide greater political, economic, social, and geographical variety. Five new cases - Brazil, Egypt, Iran, Mexico, and Nigeria - have been added in order to expand coverage of Africa and Latin America, to complete the inclusion of all five members of the BRICS group, and to add two Muslim states. The cases are as follows:

Brazil	India	South Africa
China	Iran	Sweden
Egypt	Japan	United Kingdom
European Union	Mexico	United States
France	Nigeria	Venezuela
Germany	Russia	

Writing and developing a book of this kind always involves the input and support of an extended team. The authors would particularly like to thank Steven Kennedy, who shepherded many earlier editions of the book and was the lynchpin for the changeover to a new line-up of authors; this was one of the last projects Steven worked on before his retirement in 2014, but Stephen Wenham and Lloyd Langman steered the book to completion with professionalism and good humour. The authors would also like to thank the anonymous reviewers who provided much valuable feedback on the planned changes and the finished chapters. Last but not least, John McCormick sends heartfelt love and thanks to his wife Leanne and his sons Ian and Stuart for providing a critical support system.

Guide to learning features

This book contains a range of features designed to aid learning. These are outlined below.

Overview
Each chapter includes an overview of the subject of the chapter, placing it within its broader context and introducing some of the key themes.

Preview
Each chapter begins with a 250-word outline of the contents of the chapter, designed as a preview of what to expect in the pages that follow.

Key arguments
Each chapter begins with a set of key arguments, chosen to underline some of the more important points addressed in the chapter.

Discussion questions
Each chapter closes with a set of open-ended discussion questions, designed to consolidate knowledge by highlighting major issues and to spark classroom discussions and research projects.

Further reading
An annotated list of six suggested readings is included at the end of each chapter, representing some of the most important or helpful surveys of the topic, and acting as a pointer to more detailed readings.

Key concepts
Designed to help reflect upon and memorise key concepts, a complete list of the main terms defined in boxes across the preceding pages is included at the end of each chapter.

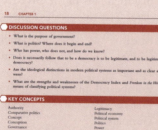

CHAPTER

1 Key concepts

PREVIEW

The best place to begin the study of any topic is with an exploration of key concepts. Most of the political terms which concern us are embedded in ordinary language; *government*, *governance*, *politics*, *power* and *authority* are all familiar terms. But – as we will see – this does not mean that they are easily defined, or that political scientists are agreed on how best to understand or apply them.

This opening chapter begins with a discussion about the meaning of *government* and *governance*, which are related terms but quite different in the ideas they convey: the first focuses on institutions while the second focuses on processes. We then go on to look at *politics*, whose core features are relatively easy to identify, but whose boundaries are not so clear: does it imply a search for a decision, or a competitive struggle for power? This is followed by a review of the meaning of *power*, *authority*, *legitimacy* and *ideology*, all of which lie at the heart of our understanding of how government and politics work.

The chapter then examines some of the core purposes of comparative politics; most fundamentally, its study helps us broaden our understanding of politics and government, taking us beyond the limitations inherent in analysing a single political system. We then look at the challenges involved in classifying political systems. Classifications help us make better sense of a large, complex and changing political world – if we could just develop a typology with which everyone could agree.

CONTENTS
- Key concepts: an overview
- Government and governance
- Politics
- Power
- The state, authority, and legitimacy
- Ideology
- Comparative politics
- Classifying political systems

KEY ARGUMENTS
- This academic study of politics requires few technical terms, but it is useful to identify both a one-sentence definition (concept) and any issues surrounding the term (conceptions).
- The concept of governance is increasingly used in political writing, emphasising the activity rather than the institutions of governing, offering a distinct focus that builds on, rather than supplanting, the more familiar notion of government.
- A precise definition of politics is difficult, because the term has multiple nuances. But it is clearly a collective activity, leading to decisions affecting an entire group.
- Power is central to politics. But here, again, conceptions are important. If we see persuasion and manipulation as forms of power, the range of the political expands considerably.
- Ideology has lost its original meaning as the science of ideas, but it remains central to all our packaging of different views about the role of government and the goals of public policy.
- Typologies are important as a means of imposing order on the variety of the world's political systems, and helping us develop explanations and rules. Unfortunately, no typology has yet won general support.

---

18   CHAPTER 1

DISCUSSION QUESTIONS
- What is the purpose of government?
- What is politics? Where does it begin and end?
- Who has power, who does not, and how do we know?
- Does it necessarily follow that to be a democracy is to be legitimate, and to be legitimate is to be a democracy?
- Are the ideological distinctions in modern political systems as important and as clear as they once were?
- What are the strengths and weaknesses of the Democracy Index and *Freedom in the World* schemes as means of classifying political systems?

KEY CONCEPTS
Authority	Legitimacy
Comparative politics	Political economy
Concept	Political system
Conception	Politics
Governance	Power
Government	Social science
Gross national income	Three Worlds system
Ideology	Typology

FURTHER READING

Crick, Bernard (2005) *In Defence of Politics*, 5th edn. A forceful exposition of the nature of politics that finds the essence of the subject in the peaceful reconciliation of interests.

Finer, S. E. (1997) *The History of Government from the Earliest Times*, three vols. Offers a monumental and, in many ways, unequalled history of government.

Heywood, Andrew (2012) *Political Ideologies: An Introduction*, 5th edn. An informative and wide-ranging textbook that successfully introduces influential political creeds and doctrines.

Lukes, Steven (2005) *Power: A Radical View*, 2nd edn. This book introduces power's third face, offering a powerful and engaging critique of conventional interpretations.

Stilwell, Frank (2011) *Political Economy: The Contest of Economic Ideas*, 3rd edn. A survey of political economy and its links with social concerns.

Woodward, Kath (2014) *Social Science: The Big Issues*, 3rd edn. A useful general survey of the social sciences and the kinds of issues they include.

---

20   CHAPTER 2

The state: an overview

Although we now take for granted the division of the world into states, we should assume neither that the state always was the dominant principle of political organization, nor that it always will be. There was a world before states and, as advocates of globalization tirelessly point out, there may be a world after them, too.

Before the modern state, government mainly consisted of kingdoms, empires and cities. These units were often governed in a personal and highly decentralized fashion, lacking the idea of an abstract political community focused on a defined territory which characterizes today's states. Even so, many of these ancient formations were substantial in area and population. For example, the ancient Chinese empire 'proved capable of ruling a population that eventually grew into the hundreds of millions over a period of millennia – albeit control was not always complete and tended to be punctuated by recurring periods of rebellion' (van Creveld, 1999: 36). Ancient history quickly dispels the idea that all modern states are larger and more stable than every traditional political system.

Yet the modern state remains distinct from all preceding political formations. They possess sovereign authority to rule the population of a specific territory, a notion which contrasts with the more personal and non-centralized rule adopted by traditional kings and emperors. It is this contrast which enables Melleuish (2002: 335) to suggest that 'the development of the modern state can be compared to the invention of the alphabet. It only happened once but once it had occurred it changed the nature of human existence for ever.'

This modern idea of the state emerged in Europe between the sixteenth and eighteenth centuries, with the use of the word *state* as a political term coming into common use towards the end of this period. The number of states grew slowly: there were only 19 in existence in 1800, and barely 30 more had been established by 1900. At a global level, the real expansion of the state system began after the Second World War as decolonization saw the end of European empires. In addition, the number of international organizations and list of international treaties began to grow. Until the Second World War, government and politics around the world had been driven mainly by the preferences and the actions of a few Western democracies, but the picture became increasingly complex as debates about sovereignty, authority, and self-determination broadened and

deepened. Where great powers such as Britain, Germany, and France had been prominent, the picture changed with the emergence of the United States and the Soviet Union as superpowers after 1945, with the independence of nearly 70 mainly African and Asian states in the 1960s and 1970s, with the final break-up of the Soviet Union in 1991, and the rise of emerging powers such as China, India, and Brazil in the 1990s.

States today have a quite different and more complex relationship with one another than they did even two generations ago. Their interactions inevitably influence domestic political and economic calculations, questions about their true independence are raised with increased frequency, and we now see a debate under way about their future: are states becoming weaker, are they as strong as they ever were, or are they simply transforming in the wake of new demands and pressures? Whatever the answer, the state remains the basis for understanding government and politics all over the world. There are sub-national units of government, to be sure, and some see the growth of governance at the global level, but when we think of government we also think of states.

What is a state?

Few terms are more central to understanding government and politics (and yet have been more often disputed) than the **state**. It is nearly impossible to proceed in any meaningful or effective fashion with the study of politics and government unless we have at least a working understanding of what states look like, because they are the world's dominant form of political organization, and the building blocks of the international system. And yet they are not easy to define.

> **State:** The legal and political authority of a territory containing a population and marked by borders. The state defines the political authority of which government is the managing authority; that authority is regarded as both sovereign and legitimate by the citizens of the state and the governments of other states.

The usual benchmark for understanding the state is the classic definition offered by the German sociologist Max Weber, who described it as 'a human community that (successfully) claims the monopoly of the legitimate use of physical force within a given territory' (quoted in Gerth and Mills, 1948: 78). When the state's monopoly

Concepts

The first time a key term is used it appears in boldface red and is separately defined. The definitions are kept as brief and clear as possible, and every term is listed at the end of the chapter in which it is first defined.

Focus

Each chapter includes two Focus features that provide in-depth treatment of a topic related to the subject of the chapter.

counterfactuals. What would the outcome have been in New Zealand had its reforming elite confronted an unsympathetic legal framework? Would public sector reform still have proceeded? What would our world

Counterfactual: A thought experiment speculating on possible outcomes if a particular factor had been absent from a process, or an absent factor had been present.

FOCUS 4.1 | Hybrid vs. authoritarian regimes

The Democracy Index makes a distinction between hybrid regimes and authoritarian regimes. The first of these groups (consisting of 39 countries in the 2014 index) has the following features: substantial irregularities that often prevent elections from being free and fair, government pressure on opposition parties and candidates, harassment of journalists, a tendency to widespread corruption, the absence of an independent judiciary, and weaknesses in political culture, the functioning of government, political participation, the rule of law, and civil society.

For their part, authoritarian regimes (of which there were 52 in the 2014 index) suffer from an absence of – or heavy limits upon – political pluralism. Many of these countries are outright dictatorships, any formal institutions of democracy having little substance. Where elections are held they are not free and fair, there is disregard for abuses and infringements of civil liberties, the media are typically state-owned or controlled by groups connected to the ruling regime, and there is repression of criticism of the government and pervasive censorship.

Distinguishing between hybrid regimes and authoritarian regimes can require fine political judgement, and it may be jarring to some to see Egypt listed as a hybrid regime, or to see Nigeria and North Korea contained within the same group of authoritarian regimes. Examples of the two types include the following:

Hybrid regimes	Authoritarian regimes
Egypt	Afghanistan
Haiti	Angola
Iraq	China
Kenya	Cuba
Libya	Iran
Pakistan	Nigeria
Singapore	North Korea
Turkey	Qatar
Ukraine	Russia
Venezuela	Saudi Arabia

Tables

These display statistics or key features of a topic in the nearby text, or summarize lists of subjects covered in the text.

TABLE 1.2: Contrasting themes of left and right

Left	Right
Peace	Armed forces
Internationalism	National way of life
Democracy	Authority, morality, and the
Planning and public	constitution
ownership	Free market
Trade protection	Free trade
Social security	Social harmony
Education	Law and order
Trade unions	Freedom and rights

Note: Based on an analysis of the programmes of left- and right-wing political parties in 50 democracies, 1945–98.

Source: Adapted from Budge (2006: 429)

Figures

A wide range of figures is used throughout the book to provide visual support to topics covered in the body of the text.

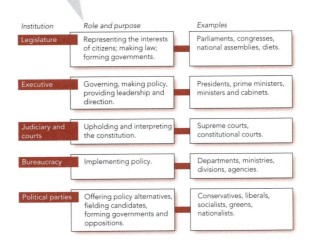

FIGURE 5.2: The formal institutions of government

Guide to spotlight feature

Spotlights provide detail on the 17 state case studies from which examples are most often quoted in the body of the text. They include a brief profile of each state (or regional organization, in the case of the European Union), brief descriptions of their political features, some key demographic and economic data (some of which is presented alongside icons which illustrate different countries' data relative to the other countries featured in the spotlights), and a short case study of each state in the context of the topic of the chapter in which the Spotlight appears.

SPOTLIGHT

SOUTH AFRICA

Brief Profile: South Africa languished for many decades under a system of institutionalized racial separation known as apartheid. This ensured privileges and opportunities for white South Africans at the expense of black, mixed race, and Asian South Africans. In the face of growing resistance, and ostracism from much of the outside world, an agreement was reached that paved the way for the first democratic elections in 1994. Much was originally expected from a country with a wealth of natural resources and the African National Congress has since won majorities at every election. Yet corruption is a growing problem, unemployment remains stubbornly high, many still live in poverty, and South Africa faces major public security challenges: it has one of the highest per capita homicide and violent assault rates in the world. Despite being the second largest economy in Africa (after Nigeria), it has only partly realized its potential as a major regional power.

Form of government ⇨ Unitary parliamentary republic. State formed 1910, and most recent constitution adopted 1997.

Legislature ⇨ Bicameral Parliament: lower National Assembly (400 members) elected for renewable five-year terms, and upper National Council of Provinces with 90 members, ten appointed from each of the nine provinces.

Executive ⇨ Presidential. A president heads both the state and the government, ruling with a cabinet. The National Assembly elects the president after each general election. Presidents limited to two five-year terms.

Judiciary ⇨ The legal system mixes common and civil law. The Constitutional Court decides constitutional matters and can strike down legislation. It has 11 members appointed by the president for terms of 12 years.

Electoral system ⇨ The National Assembly is elected by proportional representation using closed party lists; half are elected from a national list and half from provincial lists.

Parties ⇨ Dominant party. The African National Congress (ANC) has dominated since the first full democratic and multi-racial election in 1994. The more liberal Democratic Alliance, now the leading party in the Western Cape, forms the official opposition.

Population (52.5 million)

Gross National Income ($351 billion)

Per capita GNI ($7,190)

Democracy Index rating

| Not Rated | Hybrid Regime | Full Democracy |
| | Authoritarian | Flawed Democracy |

Freedom House rating

| Not Free | Partly Free | Free |

Human Development Index rating

| Not Rated | Medium | Very High |
| | Low | High |

The constitution and courts in South Africa

South Africa's transformation from a militarized state based on apartheid (institutionalized racial segregation) to a more constitutional order based on democracy was one of the most remarkable political transitions of the late twentieth century. What was the nature of the political order established by the new constitution?

In 1996, after two years of hard bargaining between the African National Congress (ANC) and the white National Party (NP), agreement was reached on a new 109-page constitution to take full effect in 1997. The NP expressed general support despite reservations that led to its withdrawal from government.

In a phrase reminiscent of the US constitution, South Africa's constitution declares that 'the Executive power of the Republic vests in the President'. As in the United States, the president is also head of state. Unlike the United States, though, presidents are elected by the National Assembly after each general election. They can be removed through a vote of no confidence in the assembly (though this event would trigger a general election), and by impeachment. The president governs in conjunction with a large cabinet.

Each of the country's nine provinces elects its own legislature and forms its own executive headed by a premier. But far more than in the United States, authority and funds flow from the top down. In any case, the ANC provides the glue linking not only executive and legislature, but also national, provincial, and municipal levels of government. So far, at least, the ruling party has dominated the governing institutions, whereas in the United States, the institutions have dominated the parties.

South Africa's rainbow nation faces some difficulties in reconciling constitutional liberal democracy with the political dominance of the ANC. The modest reduction in the size of the ANC's parliamentary majority in the 2009 elections exerted a moderating effect, reducing the ANC's desire and capacity to amend the constitution in its favour. But the country's politics, more than most, should be judged by what preceded it. By that test the achievements of the new South Africa are remarkable indeed.

Guide to Political Features

Form of government ⇨ A general description of the form of a government, including the system of administration and dates on state formation and the adoption of the most recent constitution.

Legislature ⇨ Description of the form and structure of the key institutions, including information on their terms of office and methods of election or appointment.

Executive ⇨ Description of the form and structure of the key institutions, including information on their terms of office and methods of election or appointment.

Judiciary ⇨ Description of the form and structure of the key institutions, including information on their terms of office and methods of election or appointment.

Electoral system ⇨ Description of the form and structure of executive and legislative elections.

Parties ⇨ Outline of the party system and a listing of the major parties at work in the state.

Guide to Ratings

Population ⇨ Data for 2013 on the national population, from World Bank (2015). Numbers range from a few hundred thousand in the smallest states to more than one billion in China and India.

Gross National Income ⇨ A measure of economic productivity, based on the total value of goods and services produced by a country. Numbers range from tens of billions of dollars for the smallest economies to trillions of dollars in the United States, China, and Japan. Data for 2013 from World Bank (2015).

Per capita Gross Domestic Product ⇨ Economic productivity per head of population, ranging from hundreds of dollars in the poorest economies to tens of thousands in the wealthiest. Data for 2013 from World Bank (2015).

Democracy Index rating ⇨ From the *Economist*, which divides states into full democracies, flawed democracies, hybrid regimes, and authoritarian regimes. See Focus 1.2, 3.2 and 4.1 for more information.

Freedom in the World rating ⇨ From Freedom House, which uses political rights and civil liberties to divide states into groups rated Free, Partly Free, or Not Free. See Focus 1.2, 3.2 and 4.1 for more information.

Human Development Index rating ⇨ From the United Nations Development Programme, which divides states into groups rated Very High, High, Medium and Low.

Guide to the website

This book is accompanied by a freely accessible website – located at **www.palgrave.com/politics/hague** – which provides an array of resources for students and instructors.

For students

Guide to Comparative Politics on the Internet

This guide helps students navigate their way through the multitude of resources available on the internet related to the comparative study of politics.

Flashcard Glossary

These flashcards help students to test their knowledge of the key terms highlighted and defined in each chapter.

Additional chapter on Political Economy

This online chapter explores the interdisciplinary field of Political Economy.

For instructors

Testbank

The Testbank comprises a series of pre-prepared multiple choice questions related to the coverage of each of the book's chapters.

PowerPoint Slides

A corresponding set of PowerPoint slides has been prepared for each individual chapter, ready for instructors to adapt and customize to suit their weekly lectures.

Video

New co-author John McCormick introduces the new edition and talks about the most significant changes to the book.

1 > Key concepts

PREVIEW

The best place to begin the study of any topic is with an exploration of key concepts. Most of the political terms which concern us are embedded in ordinary language; *government*, *politics*, *power* and *authority* are all familiar terms. But – as we will see – this does not mean that they are easily defined, or that political scientists are agreed on how best to understand or apply them.

This opening chapter begins with a discussion about the meaning of *government* and *governance*, which are related terms but quite different in the ideas they convey: the first focuses on institutions while the second focuses on processes. We then go on to look at *politics*, whose core features are relatively easy to identify, but whose boundaries are not so clear: does it imply a search for a decision, or a competitive struggle for power? This is followed by a review of the meaning of *power*, *authority*, *legitimacy* and *ideology*, all of which lie at the heart of our understanding of how government and politics work.

The chapter then examines some of the core purposes of comparative politics; most fundamentally, its study helps us broaden our understanding of politics and government, taking us beyond the limitations inherent in analysing a single political system. We then look at the challenges involved in classifying political systems. Classifications help us make better sense of a large, complex and changing political world – if we could just develop a typology with which everyone could agree.

CONTENTS

KEY ARGUMENTS

- The academic study of politics requires few technical terms, but it is useful to identify both a one-sentence definition (concepts) and any issues surrounding the term (conceptions).

- The concept of governance is increasingly used in political writing, emphasizing the activity rather than the institutions of governing, offering a distinct focus that builds on, rather than supplanting, the more familiar notion of government.

- A precise definition of politics is difficult, because the term has multiple nuances. But it is clearly a collective activity, leading to decisions affecting an entire group.

- Power is central to politics. But here, again, conceptions are important. If we see persuasion and manipulation as forms of power, the range of the political expands considerably.

- Ideology has lost its original meaning as the science of ideas, but it remains useful as a way of packaging different views about the role of government and the goals of public policy.

- Typologies are important as a means of imposing order on the variety of the world's political systems, and helping us develop explanations and rules. Unfortunately, no typology has yet won general support.

Key concepts: an overview

In working to understand political terms, we can distinguish between concepts and conceptions. A **concept** is an idea, term or category such as *democracy* or *power*, that is best approached with a definition restricted to its inherent characteristics. In trying to understand the features which a government must possess in order to qualify as a democracy, for example, we can probably agree that some measure of popular control over the rulers is essential; if there were no ways of holding the government to account, there could be no democracy. A good definition of democracy as a concept, in this narrow but important sense, should be clear and concise.

For its part, a **conception** builds on a concept by describing the understandings, perspectives or interpretations of a concept. We might, for instance, conceive of democracy as self-government, as direct democracy, as representative government or as majority rule. Conceptions build on definitions by moving to a fuller discussion and consideration of alternative positions.

> **Concept:** A term, idea, or category.
>
> **Conception:** The manner in which something is understood or interpreted.

The book begins with a review of several of the most important concepts involved in comparative politics; to be clear on their meanings will provide the foundations for understanding the chapters that follow. The terms *government* and *politics* are routinely used interchangeably, but are not necessarily applied correctly, and terms such as *power* come in several different forms. We also need to be clear about the definition of the state, and how it relates to authority, legitimacy, and ideology. What all these concepts have in common – apart from the fact that they are central to an understanding of the manner in which human society is organized and administered – is that the precise definition of their meanings is routinely contested. The problem of disputed meanings is found not just in political science, but throughout the social sciences, and there is even some dispute about the meaning of the term **social science**. It is used here in the context of studying and better understanding the organized relations and interactions of people within society: the institutions they build, the rules they agree, the processes they use, their underlying motives, and the results of their interactions.

> **Social science:** The study of human society and of the structured interactions among people within society. Distinct from the natural sciences, such as physics and biology.

Ultimately, we seek to better understand these concepts so as to enhance our ability to compare. Comparison is one of the most basic of all human activities, lying at the heart of almost every choice we make in our lives. No surprise, then, that it should be at the heart of research in the social sciences. In order to better understand human behaviour, we need to examine different cases, examples, and situations in order to draw general conclusions about what drives people to act the way they do. We can study government and political processes in isolation, but we can never really hope to fully comprehend them, or be sure that we have considered all the explanatory options, without comparison. Only by looking at government and politics across place and time can we build the context to be able to gain a broader and more complete understanding. Within this context, comparative politics involves the systematic study of the institutions, character, and performance of government and political processes in different societies.

Government and governance

This is a book about comparative government and politics, so the logical place to begin our review of concepts is with the term *government*. Small groups can reach collective decisions without any special procedures; thus the members of a family or sports team can reach an understanding by informal discussion, and these agreements can be self-executing: those who make the decision carry it out themselves. However, such simple mechanisms are impractical for larger units such as cities or states, which must develop standard procedures for making and enforcing collective decisions. By definition, decision-making organizations formed for this purpose comprise the **government**: the arena for making and enforcing collective decisions.

Government: The institutions and offices through which societies are governed. Also used to describe the group of people who govern (e.g. the Japanese government), a specific administration (e.g. the Putin government), the form of the system of rule (e.g. centralized government), and the nature and direction of the administration of a community (e.g. good government).

In popular use, the term *government* refers just to the highest level of political appointments: to presidents, prime ministers, legislatures, and others at the apex of power. But in a wider conception, government consists of all organizations charged with reaching and executing decisions for the whole community. By this definition, the police, the armed forces, public servants and judges all form part of the government, even though such officials are not necessarily appointed by political methods such as elections. In this broader conception, government is the entire community of institutions endowed with public authority.

The classic case for the institution of government was made in the seventeenth century by the philosopher Thomas Hobbes (see Focus 1.1). He judged that government provides us with protection from the harm that we would otherwise inflict on each other in our quest for gain and glory. By granting a monopoly of the sword to a government, we transform anarchy into order, securing peace and its principal bounty: the opportunity for mutually beneficial cooperation.

In a democracy, at least, government offers security and predictability to those who live under its jurisdiction. In a well-governed society, citizens and businesses can plan for the long term, knowing that laws are stable and consistently applied. Governments also offer the efficiency of a standard way of reaching and enforcing decisions (Coase, 1960). If every decision had to be preceded by a separate agreement on how to reach and apply it, governing would be tiresome indeed. These efficiency

FOCUS 1.1 | Hobbes's case for government

The case for government was well made by Thomas Hobbes (1588–1679) in his famous treatise *Leviathan*, published in 1651. His starting point was the fundamental equality in our ability to inflict harm on others:

> For as to the strength of body, the weakest has strength enough to kill the strongest, either by secret machination, or by confederacy with others.

So arises a clash of ambition and fear of attack:

> From this equality of ability, arises equality of hope in the attaining of our ends. And therefore if any two men desire the same thing, which nevertheless they cannot both enjoy, they become enemies; and in the way to their end, which is principally their own conservation, and sometimes their own delectation, endeavour to destroy or subdue one another.

Without a ruler to keep us in check, the situation becomes grim:

> Hereby it is manifest, that during the time men live without a common power to keep them all in awe, they are in that condition which is called war; and such a war, as is of every man, against every man.

People therefore agree (by means unclear) to set up an absolute government to escape from a life that would otherwise be 'solitary, poor, nasty, brutish and short':

> The only way to erect such a common power, as may be able to defend them from the invasion of foreigners, and the injuries of one another… is, to confer all their power and strength upon one man, or one assembly of men, that may reduce all their wills, by plurality of voices, unto one will … This done, the multitude so united is called a COMMONWEALTH.

Source: Hobbes (1651)

SPOTLIGHT

NIGERIA

Brief Profile: Although Nigeria has been independent since 1960, it was not until 2015 that it experienced a presidential election in which the incumbent was defeated by an opposition opponent. This makes an important point about the challenges faced by Africa's largest country by population, and one of the continent's major regional powers, in developing a stable political form. Nigeria is currently enjoying its longest spell of civilian government since independence, but the military continues to play an important role, the economy is dominated by oil, corruption is rife at every level of society, security concerns and poor infrastructure discourage foreign investment, and a combination of ethnic and religious divisions pose worrying threats to stability. Incursions and numerous attacks since 2002 by the Islamist group Boko Haram, an al-Qaeda ally which controls parts of northern Nigeria, have added to the country's problems.

Population (178.5 million)

Gross National Income ($522 billion)

Per capita GNI ($2,710)

Democracy Index rating

| Not Rated | Hybrid Regime | Full Democracy |
| | Authoritarian | Flawed Democracy |

Freedom House rating

| Not Free | Partly free | Free |

Human Development Index rating

| Not Rated | Medium | Very High |
| | Low | High |

Form of government ⇨ Federal presidential republic consisting of 36 states and a Federal Capital Territory. State formed 1960, and most recent constitution adopted 1999.

Legislature ⇨ Bicameral National Assembly: lower House of Representatives (360 members) and upper Senate (109 members), both elected for fixed and renewable four-year terms.

Executive ⇨ Presidential. A president elected for a maximum of two four-year terms, supported by a vice president and cabinet of ministers, with one from each of Nigeria's states.

Judiciary ⇨ Federal Supreme Court, with 14 members nominated by the president, and either confirmed by the Senate or approved by a judicial commission.

Electoral system ⇨ President elected in national contest, and must win a majority of all votes cast and at least 25 per cent of the vote in at least two-thirds of Nigeria's states. Possibility of two runoffs. National Assembly elected using single-member plurality.

Parties ⇨ Multi-party, led by the centrist People's Democratic Party and the conservative All Nigeria People's Party.

➡

gains give people who disagree an incentive to agree on a general mechanism for resolving disagreements.

Of course, establishing a government creates new dangers. The risk of Hobbes's commonwealth is that it will abuse its own authority, creating more problems than it solves. As John Locke – one of Hobbes's critics – pointed out, there is no profit in avoiding the dangers of foxes if the outcome is simply to be devoured by lions (Locke, 1690). A key aim in studying government must therefore be to discover how to secure its undoubted benefits, while also limiting its inherent dangers. We must keep in mind the question posed by Plato: 'who is to guard the guards themselves?'

➡

Government and politics in Nigeria

Many of the facets of the debate about government, politics, power, and authority are on show in Nigeria, a relatively young country struggling to develop a workable political form and national identity in the face of multiple internal divisions.

Understanding Nigeria is complicated by the lack of durable governmental patterns. Since independence in 1960, Nigerians have lived through three periods of civilian government, five successful and several attempted military coups, a civil war, and nearly 30 years of military rule. The first civilian government (1960– 66) was based on the parliamentary model, but the second and third (1979–83 and 1999–present) were based on the presidential form. Since 2007, Nigeria has twice made the transition from one civilian government to another and the long-term political prognosis has improved. Still, considerable uncertainties remain.

In part, political doubts reflect economic drift. The country's growing population is expected to double in the next 25 years, straining an infrastructure that is already woefully inadequate to support a modern economy. Nigeria's core economic problem is its heavy reliance on oil, which leaves the size and health of the economy – as well as government revenues – dependent on the fluctuating (and currently depressed) price of oil. To make matters worse, much of the oil wealth has been squandered and stolen, and there have been bitter political arguments over how best to spend the balance.

Nigeria's problems are more than just economic. In social terms, Nigeria is divided by ethnicity, handicapping efforts to build a sense of national identity. It is also separated by religion, with a mainly Muslim north, a non-Muslim south, and controversial pressures from the north to expand the reach of sharia, or Islamic law. Regional disparities are fundamental, with a north that is dry and poor and a south that is better endowed in resources and basic services. Regional tensions have been made worse by oil, most of which lies either in the southeast or off the coast, but with much of the profit distributed to political elites in other parts of the country.

In democracies, government is influenced by wider forces, such as interest groups, political parties, the media, corporations, and public opinion. In authoritarian systems, the government may lack much autonomy, effectively becoming the property of a dominant individual or clan. One way of referring to the broader array of forces surrounding and influencing government is through the concept of a **political system**.

> **Political system:** The interactions and organizations (including but not restricted to government) through which a society reaches and successfully enforces collective decisions. Interchangeably used with the term *regime*, but the latter tends to have negative connotations.

This phrase usefully extends our line of sight beyond official institutions, while still implying that political actors interact with each other and with government in a stable fashion, forming a distinct element or function within society (Easton, 1965). So, the 'Swedish political system' means more than 'Swedish government'; it is the space in which the activity of Swedish politics, or at least the bulk of it, takes place.

Another related concept that has undergone a recent revival is **governance**, which refers to the whole range of actors involved in government. But where the phrase *political system* suggests a rather static account based on organizations, the idea of *governance* highlights the process and quality of collective decision-making, with a particular focus on regulation. The emphasis is on the activity of governing, rather than on the institutions of government, so that we can – for example – speak of the governance (rather than the government) of the internet, because no single government department is in charge.

> **Governance:** The process by which decisions, laws and policies are made, with or without the input of formal institutions.

Governance directs our attention away from government's command-and-control function towards the broader task of public regulation, a role which ruling politicians in liberal democracies share with other bodies. For example, a particular sport will be run by its governing body, with the country's government intervening only in extreme situations. Hence, the need for the concept of governance as a supplement, rather than a replacement, for the notion of government.

The notion of governance has been prominent in discussions about the European Union. This 28-member regional integration association has several institutions that look much like an EU government – they include an elected European Parliament and a Court of Justice – but which are better regarded as a system of governance (McCormick, 2015). Their job is to develop policies and laws, and to oversee the implementation of those policies and laws, but they can only do as much as the foundational treaties of the EU, and the governments of its member states, allow them to do. They are better seen as servants of the process of European integration than as the leaders of the EU.

Because governance refers to the activity of ruling, it has also become the preferred term when examining the quality and effectiveness of rule. In this context, governance refers not to the institutions of government but to what they do and to how well they do it. For example, many international agencies suggest that effective governance is crucial to economic development in new democracies (World Bank, 1997). President Obama told Ghana's parliament in 2009 that 'development depends upon good governance' (BBC News, 2009). In this sense of governance, the focus is on government policies and activities, rather than the institutions of rule themselves.

Politics

In the debate over the meaning of **politics**, we can easily list and agree examples of political activity. When the president and Congress in the United States engage in their annual tussle over the budget, for example, they are clearly engaged in politics. When thousands of the residents of Hong Kong joined street protests in 2014 against the limits on self-determination and democracy imposed by the Chinese government, they, too, were taking part in politics. The political heartland, as represented by such examples, is clear enough.

> **Politics:** The process by which people negotiate and compete in the process of making and executing shared or collective decisions.

However, the boundaries of politics are less precise. When one country invades another, is it engaged in politics or merely in war? When a dictatorship suppresses a demonstration by violence, is it playing or preventing politics? When a court issues a ruling about privacy, should its judgment be read as political or judicial? Is politics restricted to governments, or can it also be found in businesses, families, and even university classrooms?

A crisp definition of politics – one which fits just those things we instinctively call 'political' – is difficult, because the term is used in so many different ways. But three aspects of politics are clear:

- It is a collective activity, occurring between and among people. A lone castaway on a desert island could not engage in politics, but if there were two castaways on the same island, they could have a political relationship.

- It involves making decisions on matters affecting two or more people, typically to decide on a course of action, or to resolve disagreements.

- Once reached, political decisions become authoritative policy for the group, binding and committing its members.

Politics is necessary because of the social nature of humans. We live in groups that must reach collective decisions about using resources, relating to others, and planning for the future. A country deliberating on whether to go to war, a family discussing where to take its vacation, a university deciding whether its priority lies with teaching or research: these are all examples of groups forming judgements impinging on all their members. Politics is a fundamental activity because a group which fails to reach at least some decisions will soon cease to exist. You might want to remove from office the current set of politicians in your country but you cannot eliminate the political tasks for which they are responsible.

Once reached, decisions must be implemented. Means must be found to ensure the acquiescence and preferably the consent of the group's members. Once set, taxes must be raised; once adopted, regulations must be imposed; once declared, wars must be fought. Public authority – and even force if needed – is used to implement collective policy, and citizens who fail to contribute to the common task may be fined or even imprisoned by the authorities. So, politics possesses a hard edge, reflected in the adverb *authoritatively* in the famous definition of a political system offered by the political scientist David Easton (1965: 21):

> A political system can be designated as the interactions through which values are authoritatively allocated for a society; that is what distinguishes a political system from other systems lying in its environment.

As a concept, then, politics can be defined as the process of making and executing collective decisions. But this simple definition generates many contrasting conceptions. Idealistically, politics can be viewed as the search for decisions which either pursue the group's common interest or at least seek peaceful reconciliation of the different interests within any group of substantial size. Alternatively, and perhaps more realistically, politics can be interpreted as a competitive struggle for power and resources between people and groups seeking their own advantage. From this second vantage point, the methods of politics can encompass violence as well as discussion.

The interpretation of politics as a community-serving activity can be traced to the ancient Greeks. For instance, the philosopher Aristotle (384–322 BCE) argued that 'man is by nature a political animal' (1962 edn: 28). By this, he meant not only that politics is unavoidable, but also that it is the highest human activity, the feature which most sharply separates us from other species. For Aristotle, people can only express their nature as reasoning, virtuous beings by participating in a political community which seeks not only to identify the common interest through discussion, but also to pursue it through actions to which all contribute. Thus, politics can be seen as a form of education which brings shared interests to the fore. In Aristotle's model constitution, 'the ideal citizens rule in the interests of all, not because they are forced to by checks and balances, but because they see it as right to do so' (Nicholson, 2004: 42).

A continuation of Aristotle's perspective can be found today in those who interpret politics as a peaceful process of open discussion leading to collective decisions acceptable to all stakeholders in society. The political theorist Bernard Crick (2005: 21) exemplifies this position:

> Politics … can be defined as the activity by which different interests within a given unit of rule are conciliated by giving them a share in power in

proportion to their importance to the welfare and the survival of the whole community.

For Crick, politics is neither a set of fixed principles steering government, nor a set of traditions to be preserved. It is instead an activity whose function is 'preserving a community grown too complicated for either tradition alone or pure arbitrary rule to preserve it without the undue use of coercion' (p. 24). Indeed, Crick regards rule by dictators, or by violence, or in pursuit of fixed ideologies, as being empty of political activity. This restriction arises because politics is 'that solution to the problem of order which chooses conciliation rather than violence and coercion' (p. 30). The difficulty with Crick's conception, as with Aristotle's, is that it provides an ideal of what politics should be, rather than a description of what it actually is.

Politics can also involve narrow concerns taking precedence over collective benefits when those in authority place their own goals above those of the wider community. So, we need a further conception, one which sees power as an intrinsic value and politics as a competition for acquiring and keeping power. From this second perspective, politics is viewed as a competition yielding winners and losers. For example, the political scientist Harold Lasswell (1936) famously defined politics as 'who gets what, when, how'. Particularly in large, complex societies, politics is a competition between groups – ideological, as well as material – either for power itself or for influence over those who wield it. Politics is anything but the disinterested pursuit of the public interest.

Further, the attempt to limit politics to peaceful, open debate seems unduly narrow. At its best, politics is a deliberative search for agreement, but politics as it exists often takes less conciliatory forms. To say that politics does not exist in Kim Jong Un's North Korea would appear absurd to the millions who live in the dictator's shadow. A party in pursuit of power engages in politics, whether its strategy is peaceful, violent or both. In the case of war, in particular, it is preferable to agree with the Prussian general Carl von Clausewitz that 'war is the continuation of politics by other means' and with Chinese leader Mao Zedong that 'war is politics with bloodshed'.

Politics, then, has many different facets. It involves shared and competing interests; cooperation and conflict; reason and force. Each conception is necessary, but only together are they sufficient. The essence of politics lies in the interaction between conceptions, and we should not narrow our vision by reducing politics to either one. As Laver (1983: 1) puts it: 'Pure conflict is war. Pure cooperation is true love. Politics is a mixture of both.'

Power

At the heart of politics is the distribution and manipulation of **power**. The word comes from the Latin *potere*, meaning 'to be able', which is why the philosopher Bertrand Russell (1938) sees power as 'the production of intended effects'. The greater our ability to determine our own fate, the more power we possess. In this sense, describing Germany as a powerful country means that it has a high level of ability to achieve its objectives, whatever those may be. Conversely, to lack power is to fall victim to circumstance. Arguably, though, every state has power, even if it is the kind of negative power involved in obliging a reaction from bigger and wealthier states; Somali pirates, Syrian refugees, and illegal migrants from Mexico may seem powerless, but all three groups spark policy responses from the governments of those countries they most immediately affect.

> **Power:** The capacity to bring about intended effects. The term is often used as a synonym for influence, but is also used more narrowly to refer to more forceful modes of influence: notably, getting one's way by threats.

Notice that the emphasis here is on power *to* rather than power *over* – on the ability to achieve goals, rather than the more specific exercise of control over other people or countries. But most analyses of power focus on relationships: on power over others. Here, the three dimensions of power distinguished by Steven Lukes (2005) are useful (Table 1.1). Lukes helps to address the question of how we can measure a

group's power, or at least establish whether one group is more powerful than another. As we move through these dimensions, so the conception of power becomes more subtle – but also, perhaps, somewhat stretched beyond its normal use.

The first dimension is straightforward: power should be judged by examining whose views prevail when the actors involved possess conflicting views on what should be done. The greater the correspondence between a person's views and decisions reached, the greater is that person's influence: more wins indicate more power. This decision-making approach, as it is called, was pioneered by the political scientist Robert Dahl (1961a) in his classic study of democracy and power in the city of New Haven, Connecticut. The approach is clear and concrete, based on identifying preferences and observing decisions, and connecting directly with the concept of politics as the resolution of conflict within groups. Even though it has now been supplemented by Lukes's other dimensions, it remains a sound initial step in studying power.

The second dimension focuses on the capacity to keep issues off the political agenda. Bachrach and Baratz (1962: 948) give the example of a discontented faculty member who rails against university policy in her office but remains silent during faculty meetings, judging that an intervention there would be ineffective and even damaging to her career. Or perhaps all the major political parties in a particular country advocate free trade, forming what amounts to an elite conspiracy to marginalize trade tariffs and quotas. In these ways, potential 'issues' (change university governance; introduce trade controls) become non-issues and the only decisions in these areas are non-decisions – successful attempts to prevent the emergence of topics which would threaten the values or interests of decision-makers.

This second dimension broadens our understanding of the political, taking us beyond the mere resolution

TABLE 1.1: Lukes's three dimensions of power

	Assessing power	Proponent
First	Who prevails when preferences conflict?	Dahl (1957)
Second	Who controls whether preferences are expressed?	Bachrach and Baratz (1962)
Third	Who shapes preferences?	Lukes (1974)

Source: Lukes (2005)

of differences and inviting us to address their suppression. In this way, Dahl's view (1961a: 164) that 'a political issue can hardly be said to exist unless and until it commands the attention of a significant segment of the political stratum' is rejected. Rather, the second dimension recognizes what Schattschneider (1960: 71) called the 'mobilization of bias':

> All forms of political organization have a bias in favour of the exploitation of some kinds of conflict and the suppression of others because organization is the mobilization of bias. Some issues are organized into politics, while others are organized out.

To deal with this second dimension, Bachrach and Baratz (1962) recommend that students of power should examine which groups gain from existing political procedures, and how powerful individuals limit the political debate to safe issues. Only then should attention turn to the question of whose views prevail on those matters that are up for debate.

The third dimension broadens our conception of power still further (some say, too far). Here, power is extended to cover the formation, rather than merely the expression, of preferences. Where the first and second dimensions assume conflicting preferences, the third dimension addresses the notion of a manipulated consensus. Hence, for example, a government may withhold information about the risks from a chemical leak, preventing those affected from taking necessary steps to protect their health. More generally, advertising may direct people's desires towards consumption and away from non-material aspects of life which could offer deeper, or at least more natural, satisfaction of genuine needs.

The implications of these examples is that the most efficient form of power is to shape people's information and preferences, thus preventing the first and second dimensions from coming into play. Lukes (2005: 24) makes this argument:

> Is it not the supreme and most insidious exercise of power to prevent people, to whatever degree, from having grievances by shaping their perceptions, cognitions and preferences in such a way that they accept their role in the existing order of things, either because they can see or imagine no alternative to it, or because they see it as natural and unchangeable, or because they value it as divinely ordained and beneficial?

The case for the third dimension of power is clearest when specific information is denied in a deliberate attempt to manipulate (Le Cheminant and Parrish, 2011). One example can be found in the selective briefings initially provided by the power company responsible for operating the Japanese nuclear power station which leaked radiation after the 2011 earthquake.

In general, though, working with power's third dimension creates difficulties of its own. In the case of advertising, who is to say that the desire for material goods is a false need? And if a materialist culture is simply an unintended and cumulative consequence of advertising, rather than an explicit aim of specific individuals, do we have an instance of power at all? In any case, does not the third face of power take us too far from the explicit debates and decisions which are at the heart of politics?

The state, authority, and legitimacy

We will consider the state in more detail in Chapter 2, but a brief preview is merited here. The world is divided into nearly 200 states (the exact number, as we will see, is debatable), each containing a population living within a defined territory, and enjoying recognition by its residents and by other states of its right to rule that territory. States are also known as countries, but the state is the more political term. The state provides the legal or formal mandate for the work of governments, allowing them to utilize the authority inherent in the state. More immediately for the purposes of comparative politics, states are the core guiding unit of comparison. We can compare government and politics at multiple levels, from the national to the local, but is the state that will provide us with our most important point of reference as we work through the complexities of comparison. The state is also intimately related to two concepts that lie at the heart of our understanding of government and politics: authority and legitimacy.

Authority is a broader concept than power and in some ways more fundamental to comparative politics. Where power is the capacity to act, authority is the acknowledged right to do so. It exists when subordinates accept the capacity of superiors to give legitimate orders, so that while an army general may exercise *power* over enemy soldiers, his *authority* is restricted to his own forces. The German sociologist Max Weber (1922: 29) suggested that, in a relationship of authority, the ruled implement the command as if they had adopted it spontaneously, for its own sake. For this reason, authority is a more efficient form of control than brute power. Yet, authority remains more than voluntary compliance. To acknowledge the authority of your state does not mean you always agree with its decisions; it means only that you accept its right to make them and your own duty to obey. In this way, authority provides the foundation for the state.

> **Authority:** The right to rule. Authority creates its own power, so long as people accept that the person in authority has the right to make decisions.

Just as there are different sources of power, so too can authority be built on a range of foundations. Almost 100 years ago, Weber distinguished three ways of validating political power: by tradition (the accepted way of doing things), by charisma (intense commitment to the leader and his message) and by appeal to legal–rational norms (based on the rule-governed powers of an office, rather than a person) (Weber, 1922). This classification remains useful, even though today legal–rational authority is pre-eminent in stable democracies.

Legitimacy builds on, but is broader than, authority. When a regime is widely accepted by those subject to it, and by other regimes with which it deals, we describe it as legitimate. Thus, we speak of the *authority* of an official but the *legitimacy* of a regime. Although the word *legitimacy* comes from the Latin *legitimare*, meaning 'to declare lawful', legitimacy is much more than mere legality. Where legality is a technical matter, referring to whether a rule was made correctly by following regular procedures, legitimacy is a more political concept. It refers to whether people accept the authority of the political system. Without this acceptance, the very existence of a state is in question.

> **Legitimacy:** The state or quality of being legitimate. A legitimate system of government is one based on authority, and those subject to its rule recognize its right to make decisions.

Legality is a topic for lawyers; political scientists are more interested in issues of legitimacy: how a political system gains, keeps, and sometimes loses public faith in its right to rule. A flourishing economy, international success, and a popular governing party will boost the legitimacy of a political system, even

though legitimacy is more than any of these things. In fact, one way of thinking about legitimacy is as the credit a political system has built up from its past successes, a reserve that can be drawn down in bad times. In any event, public opinion – not a law court – is the test of legitimacy. And it is legitimacy, rather than force alone, which provides the most stable foundation for rule.

Ideology

The concepts reviewed so far have mainly been *about* politics, but ideas also play a role *in* politics: political action is motivated by the ideas people hold about it. One way to approach the role of ideas is via the notion of **ideology**, a term which was coined by the French philosopher Antoine Destutt de Tracy during the 1790s, in the aftermath of the French Revolution, to describe the science of ideas. Its meaning has long since changed, and it now denotes packages of ideas related to different views about the role of government and the goals of public policy. An ideology is today understood as any system of thought expressing a view on:

- human nature
- the proper organization of, and relationship between, state and society
- the individual's position within this prescribed order.

> **Ideology:** A system of connected beliefs, a shared view of the world, or a blueprint for how politics, economics and society should be structured.

Which specific political outlooks should be regarded as ideologies is a matter of judgement, but Figure 1.1 offers a selection. In any case, the era of explicit ideology beginning with the French Revolution ended in the twentieth century with the defeat of fascism in 1945 and the collapse of communism at the end of the 1980s. Ideology seemed to have been destroyed by the mass graves it had itself generated. Of course, intellectual currents – such as environmental concerns, feminism, and Islamism – continue to circulate. Even so, it is doubtful whether the ideas, values, and priorities of our century constitute ideologies in the classical sense. To describe any perspective, position, or priority as an ideology is to extend the term in a manner that bears little relation to its

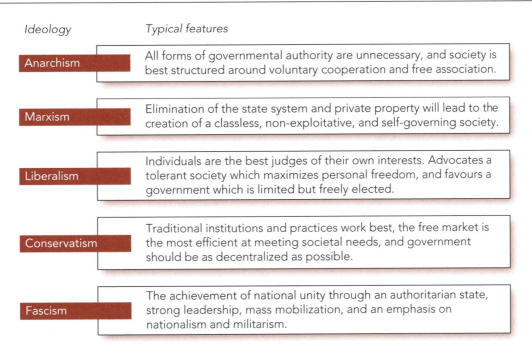

Ideology | Typical features

Anarchism
All forms of governmental authority are unnecessary, and society is best structured around voluntary cooperation and free association.

Marxism
Elimination of the state system and private property will lead to the creation of a classless, non-exploitative, and self-governing society.

Liberalism
Individuals are the best judges of their own interests. Advocates a tolerant society which maximizes personal freedom, and favours a government which is limited but freely elected.

Conservatism
Traditional institutions and practices work best, the free market is the most efficient at meeting societal needs, and government should be as decentralized as possible.

Fascism
The achievement of national unity through an authoritarian state, strong leadership, mass mobilization, and an emphasis on nationalism and militarism.

FIGURE 1.1: Five major ideologies

original interpretation as a coherent, secular system of ideas.

Even though the age of ideology may have passed, we still tend to talk about ideologies, placing them on a spectrum between left and right. The origins of this habit lie in revolutionary France, where – in the legislative assemblies of the era – royalists sat to the right of the presiding officer, in the traditional position of honour, while radicals and commoners sat to the left. To be on the right implied support for aristocratic, royal and clerical interests; the left, by contrast, favoured a secular republic and civil liberties.

The words 'left' and 'right' are still commonly encountered in classifying political parties. Hence the left is associated with equality, human rights, and reform, while the right favours tradition, established authority and pursuit of the national interest. The left supports policies to reduce inequality; the right is more accepting of natural inequalities. The left sympathizes with cultural and ethnic diversity; the right is more comfortable with national unity. (See Table 1.2 for more details.) Surveys suggest that most voters in democracies can situate themselves as being on the left or right, even if many simply equate these labels with a particular party or class (Mair, 2009: 210).

Although the terms *left* and *right* have travelled well throughout the democratic world, enabling us to compare parties and programmes across countries and time, the specific issues over which these tendencies compete have varied, and the terms are better seen as labels for containers of ideas, rather than as well-defined ideas in themselves. The blurring of the distinction can be seen in Europe, where the left (socialists and communists)

TABLE 1.2: Contrasting themes of left and right

Left	Right
Peace	Armed forces
Internationalism	National way of life
Democracy	Authority, morality, and the
Planning and public	constitution
ownership	Free market
Trade protection	Free trade
Social security	Social harmony
Education	Law and order
Trade unions	Freedom and rights

Note: Based on an analysis of the programmes of left- and right-wing political parties in 50 democracies, 1945–98.

Source: Adapted from Budge (2006: 429)

once favoured nationalization of industries and services, and the right (conservatives) supported a free market, but the widespread acceptance of the market economy has meant that the concepts of left and right have lost some bite.

Comparative politics

The core goal of **comparative politics** is to understand how political institutions and processes operate by examining their workings across a range of countries. Comparison has many purposes, including the simple description of political systems and institutions, helping us understand the broader context within with they work, helping us develop theories and rules of politics, and showing us how similar problems are approached by different societies. But two particular purposes are worth elaboration: broadening our understanding of the political world, and predicting political outcomes.

> **Comparative politics:** The systematic study of government and politics in different countries, designed to better understand them by drawing out their contrasts and similarities.

Broadening understanding

The first strength of a comparative approach is straightforward: it improves our understanding of government and politics. Through comparison we can pin down the key features of political institutions, processes and action, and better appreciate the dynamics and character of political systems. We can study a specific government, legislature, party system, social movement, or national election in isolation, but to do so is to deny us the broader context made possible by comparison. How could we otherwise know if the object of our study was unusual or usual, efficient or inefficient, the best option available or significantly lacking in some way?

When we talk of understanding, it is not only the need to comprehend other political systems, but also to understand our own. We can follow domestic politics closely and think we have a good grasp on how it works, but we cannot fully understand it without comparing it with other systems; this will tell us a great deal about the nature of our home system. Consider the argument made by Dogan and Pelassy (1990: 8):

> Because the comprehension of a single case is linked to the understanding of many cases, because we perceive the particular better in the light of generalities, international comparison increases tenfold the possibility of explaining political phenomena. The observer who studies just one country could interpret as normal what in fact appears to the comparativist as abnormal.

Comparison also has the practical benefit of allowing us to learn about places with which we are unfamiliar. This point was well-stated long ago by W. B. Munro (1925: 4) when he wrote that his book on European governments would help readers understand 'daily news from abroad'. This ability to interpret overseas events grows in importance as the world becomes more interdependent, as events from overseas have a more direct impact on our lives, and as we find that we can no longer afford to think as did Mr Podsnap in Charles Dickens's *Our Mutual Friend* when he quipped that 'Foreigners do as they do sir, and that is the end of it'.

Understanding politics in other systems not only helps us interpret the news, but also helps with practical political relationships. For instance, British government ministers have a patchy track record in negotiating with their European Union partners, partly because they assume that the aggressive tone they adopt in the chamber of the House of Commons will work as well in Brussels meeting rooms. This assumption reflects ignorance of the consensual political style found in many continental European democracies.

Predicting political outcomes

Comparison permits generalizations which have some potential for prediction. Hence a careful study of, say, campaigning and public opinion will help us better understand the possible outcome of elections. For example, we know from a study of those European countries where proportional representation is used that its use is closely tied to the presence of more political parties winning seats and the creation of coalition governments. Similarly, if we know that subcontracting the provision of public services to private agencies increases their cost-effectiveness in one country, governments elsewhere will see that this is an idea at least worth considering.

If the explanation of a phenomenon is sound, and all the relevant factors have been reviewed and considered, then it follows that our explanations should allow us to predict with at least a high degree of accuracy, if not with absolute certainty. But while the study of the natural sciences has generated vast numbers of laws that allow us to predict natural phenomena, the social sciences have not fared so well. They do not generate laws so much as theories, tendencies, likelihoods, adages, or aphorisms. A famous example of the latter is Lord Acton's that 'Power tends to corrupt, and absolute power corrupts absolutely' (see Chapter 4). While the idea contains much truth, it is not a rule or a law, and thus cannot be used either to explain or to predict with absolute certainty.

In politics, predicting is an art rather than a science, and a fallible one at that. Even so, the potential for prediction provides a starting point for drawing lessons across countries (Rose, 2005). Rather than resorting to ideology or complete guesswork, we can use comparison to consider 'what would happen if…?' questions. This function of comparative research perhaps underpinned Bryce's comment on his early study of modern democracies (1921: iv):

> Many years ago, when schemes of political reform were being copiously discussed in England, it occurred to me that something might be done to provide a solid basis for judgement by examining a certain number of popular governments in their actual working, comparing them with one another, and setting forth the various merits and demerits of each.

In fact there are some who argue that political science generally has done a poor job of helping us predict, while others argue that it should not – or cannot – be in the business of predicting to begin with. Karl Popper (1959: 280) long ago asserted that long-term predictions could only be developed in regard to systems that were 'well-isolated, stationary, and recurrent', and human society was not one of them. More recently, an opinion piece in the *New York Times* (Stevens, 2012) raised hackles when it argued that in terms of offering accurate predictions, political science had 'failed spectacularly and wasted colossal amounts of time and money'. It went on to assert that no political scientist foresaw the break-up of the Soviet Union, the rise of al-Qaeda or the Arab Spring. It quoted an award-winning study of political experts (Tetlock, 2005) which concluded that 'chimps randomly throwing darts at the possible outcomes would have done almost as well as the experts'. To be fair, however, comparative politics is still very much a discipline in the process of development, and we will see many instances throughout this book where understanding of institutions or processes is still in its formative stages.

Classifying political systems

Although the many states of the world have systems of government with many core elements in common – an executive, a legislature, courts, a constitution, parties, and interest groups, for example – the manner in which these elements work and relate to one another is often different. The results are also different: some states are clearly democratic, some are clearly authoritarian, and others sit somewhere between these two core points of reference. To complicate matters, these systems of government, and their related policies and priorities, are moving targets: they evolve and change, and often at a rapid pace. In order to make sense of this confusing picture, it is helpful to have a guide through the maze.

A **typology** is a system of classification that divides states into groups or clusters with common features. With this in hand, we can make broad assumptions about the states in each group, using case studies to provide more detailed focus, and thus work more easily to develop explanations and rules, and to test theories of political phenomena (Yin, 2013: 21). The ideal typology is one that is simple, neat, consistent, logical, and as real and useful to the casual observer as it is to journalists, political leaders, or political scientists. Unfortunately, such an ideal has proved hard to achieve; scholars of comparative politics disagree about the value of typologies, and even those who use them cannot agree on the criteria that should be taken into account, or the groups into which states should be divided. The result is that there is no universally agreed system of political classification.

Typology: A system of classification by which states, institutions, processes, political cultures, and so on are divided into groups or types with common sets of attributes.

The first such system devised – and one of the earliest examples of comparative politics at work – was Aristotle's classification of the 158 city-states of ancient Greece. Between approximately 500 and 338 BCE, these communities were small settlements showing much variety in their forms of rule. Such diversity provided an ideal laboratory for Aristotle to consider which type of political system provided what he looked for in a government: stability and effectiveness.

Aristotle based his scheme on two dimensions. The first was the number of people involved in the task of governing: one, few or many. This dimension captured the breadth of participation in a political system. His second dimension, more difficult to apply but no less important, was whether rulers governed in the common interest ('the genuine form') or in their own interest ('the perverted form'). For Aristotle, the significance of this second aspect was that a political system would be more stable and effective when its rulers governed in the long-term interests of the community. Cross-classifying the number of rulers with the nature of rule yielded the six types of government shown in Figure 1.2.

Another example of an attempt to build a typology was *The Spirit of the Laws*, a treatise on political theory written by Charles de Secondat, Baron de Montesquieu, and first published in 1748. Montesquieu identified three kinds of political system: republican systems in which the people or some of the people have supreme power, monarchical systems in which one person ruled on the basis of fixed and established laws, and despotic systems in which a single person ruled on the basis of their own priorities and perspectives.

Both typologies remain interesting as historical examples, but they reflected political realities that have long since changed. A more recent example that was current through much of the Cold War (late 1940s–early 1990s) was the **Three Worlds system**. This was less a formal classificatory template developed by political

scientists than a response to geopolitical realities, dividing the world into three groups of countries based on ideological goals and political alliances:

- First World: wealthy, democratic industrialized states, most of which were partners in the Western alliance against communism.
- Second World: communist systems, including most of those states ranged against the Western alliance.
- Third World: poorer, less democratic, and less developed states, some of which took sides in the Cold War, but some of which did not.

> **Three Worlds system:** A political typology that divided the world along ideological lines, with states labelled according to the side they took in the Cold War.

The system was simple and evocative, providing neat labels that could be slipped with ease into media headlines and everyday conversation: even today the term *Third World* conjures up powerful images of poverty, underdevelopment, corruption, and political instability. But it was always more descriptive than analytical in the Aristotelean spirit, and was dangerously simplistic: the First and Second Worlds had the most internal logic and consistency, but to consider almost all the emerging states of Africa, Asia, and Latin America as a single Third World was asking too much: some were democratic while others were authoritarian; some were wealthy while others were poor; and some were industrialized while others were agrarian. The end of the Cold War meant the end of this particular typology.

While nothing has replaced it (in the sense of having won general support), there have been many candidates. Two in particular – the Democracy Index maintained by the Economist Intelligence Unit, and the *Freedom in the World* index maintained by Freedom House – are among the most often quoted, and will be used for guidance in this book (see Focus 1.2). They are

		Rule by		
		One	*Few*	*Many*
Form	*Genuine*	Kingship	Aristocracy	Polity
	Perverted	Tyranny	Oligarchy	Democracy

FIGURE 1.2: Aristotle's classification of governments
Source: Aristotle (1962 edn, book 3, ch. 5)

FOCUS 1.2 | Two options for classifying political systems

With political scientists unable to develop and agree a single detailed classification of political systems, it has been left to the non-academic world to step into the breach. The two most compelling typologies are the following:

- The UK-based Economist Intelligence Unit (EIU, related to *The Economist*, a British weekly news magazine) maintains a Democracy Index based on sixty different ratings, giving states a score out of 10 (Norway ranks highest with 9.93 and North Korea lowest with 1.08), and dividing them into four groups: full democracies, flawed democracies, hybrid regimes, and authoritarian regimes. It achieves its rankings by considering such factors as the protection of basic political freedoms, the fairness of elections, the security of voters, election turnout rates, the freedom of political parties to operate, the independence of the judiciary and the media, and arrangements for the transfer of power. See Focus 3.2 and 4.1 for more details.
- The *Freedom in the World* index has been published annually since 1972 by Freedom House, a US-based research institute. It divides states into groups rated Free, Partly Free, or Not Free based on their records with political rights (including the ability of people to participate in the political process) and civil liberties (including freedom of expression, the independence of the judiciary, personal autonomy, and economic rights). Several countries – including Syria and North Korea – are ranked Worst of the Worst.

Table 1.3 combines the results of these typologies, focusing on the 16 cases used in this book, while also including examples of countries with the highest and lowest scores on each index.

TABLE 1.3: Comparative political ratings

	Democracy Index		Freedom in the World		
	Score	Category	Political rights	Civil liberties	Freedom rating
Norway	9.93	Full democracy	1	1	Free
Sweden*	9.73	Full democracy	1	1	Free
New Zealand	9.26	Full democracy	1	1	Free
Canada	9.08	Full democracy	1	1	Free
Germany*	8.64	Full democracy	1	1	Free
UK*	8.31	Full democracy	1	1	Free
USA*	8.11	Full democracy	1	1	Free
Japan*	8.08	Full democracy	1	1	Free
France*	8.04	Full democracy	1	1	Free
South Africa*	7.82	Flawed democracy	2	2	Free
Brazil*	7.38	Flawed democracy	2	2	Free
India*	7.92	Flawed democracy	2	3	Free
Mexico*	6.68	Flawed democracy	3	3	Partly Free
Bangladesh	5.78	Hybrid	4	4	Partly Free
Kenya	5.13	Hybrid	4	4	Partly Free
Turkey	5.12	Hybrid	3	4	Partly Free
Venezuela	5.07	Hybrid	5	5	Partly Free
Nigeria*	3.76	Authoritarian	4	5	Partly Free
Thailand	5.39	Hybrid	6	5	Not Free

(Continued)

FOCUS 1.2 | Two options for classifying political systems (Continued)

TABLE 1.3: (Continued)

	Democracy Index		Freedom in the World		
	Score	Category	Political rights	Civil liberties	Freedom rating
Egypt*	3.16	Authoritarian	6	5	Not Free
Russia*	3.39	Authoritarian	6	6	Not Free
China*	3.00	Authoritarian	7	6	Not Free
Iran*	1.98	Authoritarian	6	6	Not Free
Saudi Arabia	1.82	Authoritarian	7	7	Worst of the worst
North Korea	1.08	Authoritarian	7	7	Worst of the worst

Sources: Democracy Index (2014); *Freedom in the World* Index (2015). The latter rates states on a scale of 1–7.

* Cases used in the book. European Union is not rated.

not perfect, questions can be asked about the methodologies upon which they are based, we should take into consideration the agendas and values of the EIU and Freedom House, and we should beware the danger of taking classifications and rankings too literally; government and politics are too complex to be reduced to a single table. Nonetheless, these rankings give us a useful point of reference and a guide through an otherwise confusing world.

We will go further and also use some economic and social data to help us find our way through the maze. The relationship between politics and economics in particular is so intimate that there is an entire field of study – **political economy** – devoted to its examination. This involves looking not just at the structure and wealth of economies, but also at the influences on economic performance: good government is more likely to produce a successful economy, and bad government less so.

> **Political economy:** The relationship between political activity and economic performance.

The core measure is economic output. There are various ways of measuring this, the most popular today being **gross national income** (GNI) (see Table 1.4). This is the sum of the value of the domestic and foreign economic output of the residents of a country in a given year, and is usually converted to US dollars to allow comparison. Although the accuracy of

TABLE 1.4: Comparing economic size

	GNI (billion US$)	Per capita (US$)
European Union	18,460	35,673
United States	17,601	55,200
China	10,069	7,380
Japan	5,339	42,000
Germany	3,853	47,640
France	2,851	43,080
UK	2,754	42,690
Brazil	2,375	11,760
India	2,035	1,610
Russia	1,930	13,210
Canada	1,836	51,690
Australia	1,519	64,680
Mexico	1,235	9,980
Sweden	596	61,600
Iran	527	6,820
Nigeria	526	2,950
South Africa	367	6,800
Egypt	273	3,280
New Zealand	174	39,300
Tuvalu	57	5,840
Burundi	3	270

Source: World Bank at http://data.worldbank.org. Data are for 2014.

the data varies by country, and the conversion to dollars raises additional questions about the appropriate exchange rate, such measures are routinely used by governments and international organizations in measuring economic size. While GNI provides a measure of the absolute size of national economies, it does not take into account population size. For a more revealing comparison, we use per capita GNI, which gives us a better idea of the relative economic development of different states.

> **Gross national income:** The total domestic and foreign output by residents of a country in a given year.

Finally, we must not forget the importance of gauging the performance of political systems by looking at their relative performance in terms of providing their citizens with a good quality of life, as measured by the provision of basic needs. There are different ways of understanding 'basic needs', but at a minimum they would include adequate nutrition, education, and health care, and in this regard the most often-used comparative measure of social conditions is offered through the Human Development Index maintained by the UN Development Programme. Using a combination of life expectancy, adult literacy, educational enrolment, and per capita GNI, it rates human development for most of the states in the world as either very high, high, medium, or low. On the 2013 index, most democracies were in the top 30, while the poorest states ranked at the bottom of the table, with Niger in last place at 187 (see Table 1.5).

TABLE 1.5: Human Development Index

	Ranking	Score	Category
Norway	1	0.944	Very high
Australia	2	0.933	Very high
US	5	0.914	Very high
Germany	6	0.911	Very high
New Zealand	7	0.910	Very high
Canada	8	0.902	Very high
Sweden	12	0.898	Very high
UK	14	0.892	Very high
Japan	17	0.890	Very high
France	20	0.884	Very high
Cuba	44	0.815	Very high
Russia	57	0.778	High
Turkey	69	0.759	High
Mexico	71	0.756	High
Iran	75	0.749	High
Brazil	79	0.744	High
China	91	0.719	High
Egypt	110	0.682	Medium
South Africa	118	0.658	Medium
India	135	0.586	Medium
Pakistan	146	0.537	Low
Nigeria	152	0.504	Low
Niger	187	0.337	Low

Source: United Nations Development Programme (2015), http://hdr.undp.org/en/statistics.

Not rated: North Korea, Marshall Islands, Nauru, Somalia, South Sudan, Tuvalu.

DISCUSSION QUESTIONS

- What is the purpose of government?

- What is politics? Where does it begin and end?

- Who has power, who does not, and how do we know?

- Does it necessarily follow that to be a democracy is to be legitimate, and to be legitimate is to be a democracy?

- Are the ideological distinctions in modern political systems as important and as clear as they once were?

- What are the strengths and weaknesses of the Democracy Index and *Freedom in the World* schemes as means of classifying political systems?

KEY CONCEPTS

Authority
Comparative politics
Concept
Conception
Governance
Government
Gross national income
Ideology

Legitimacy
Political economy
Political system
Politics
Power
Social science
Three Worlds system
Typology

FURTHER READING

Crick, Bernard (2005) *In Defence of Politics,* 5th edn. A forceful exposition of the nature of politics that finds the essence of the subject in the peaceful reconciliation of interests.

Finer, S. E. (1997) *The History of Government from the Earliest Times*, three vols. Offers a monumental and, in many ways, unequalled history of government.

Heywood, Andrew (2012) *Political Ideologies: An Introduction*, 5th edn. An informative and wide-ranging textbook that successfully introduces influential political creeds and doctrines.

Lukes, Steven (2005) *Power: A Radical View*, 2nd edn. This book introduces power's third face, offering a powerful and engaging critique of conventional interpretations.

Stilwell, Frank (2011) *Political Economy: The Contest of Economic Ideas*, 3rd edn. A survey of political economy and its links with social concerns.

Woodward, Kath (2014) *Social Sciences: The Big Issues*, 3rd edn. A useful general survey of the social sciences and the kinds of issues they include.

2 > The state

PREVIEW

The standard unit of analysis in comparative politics is the state. It is by no means the only such option, because comparison can be made at any level from the local to the multinational, and can involve any political institution, process, problem, or phenomenon, but states are the most common point of reference for the comparative study of political systems. For this reason, we need to understand what states are, how they work, how they evolved, the varieties in which they can be found, and the current dynamic of the state system.

This chapter begins with a review of the features of states, with a particular focus on sovereignty. It then briefly examines the history of states, focusing on how political relationships changed both vertically (among rulers and the ruled) and horizontally (among different political communities). It then looks at the diversity that exists among states, before discussing the related concepts of *nation* and *nationalism*, ending with an analysis of today's debates over the condition and the future prospects of the state.

The state is a younger concept than most people think, and fewer than 50 were in existence at the beginning of the twentieth century. But even as the number has grown to its current total of 189, so the questions about the long-term future of states have grown. Some argue that states are as strong as ever, others argue that they are undergoing fundamental change in the face of globalization, while yet others argue that they are in decline.

CONTENTS

KEY ARGUMENTS

- The state is the most powerful and successful political organization that has ever existed. Understanding its features and evolution is essential.
- All states have four defining qualities: population, legitimacy, territory, and sovereignty.
- The modern state was born in Europe, and its form was exported to the rest of the world by imperial powers such as Britain, France, and Spain.
- States are formally equal but vary dramatically in (among other attributes) their size, economic importance, international significance and even the extent to which they control 'their' territory.
- *Nation* and *state* are central concepts in comparative politics. Although these terms are sometimes used interchangeably, they denote separate entities that can overlap in several ways.
- The condition of the modern state is open to question. Some argue that states are as strong as ever, some that they are declining, and some that they are simply evolving.

The state: an overview

Although we now take for granted the division of the world into states, we should assume neither that the state always was the dominant principle of political organization, nor that it always will be. There was a world before states and, as advocates of globalization tirelessly point out, there may be a world after them, too.

Before the modern state, government mainly consisted of kingdoms, empires and cities. These units were often governed in a personal and highly decentralized fashion, lacking the idea of an abstract political community focused on a defined territory which characterizes today's states. Even so, many of these ancient formations were substantial in area and population. For example, the ancient Chinese empire 'proved capable of ruling a population that eventually grew into the hundreds of millions over a period of millennia – albeit control was not always complete and tended to be punctuated by recurring periods of rebellion' (van Creveld, 1999: 36). Ancient history quickly dispels the idea that all modern states are larger and more stable than every traditional political system.

Yet the modern state remains distinct from all preceding political formations. They possess sovereign authority to rule the population of a specific territory, a notion which contrasts with the more personal and non-centralized rule adopted by traditional kings and emperors. It is this contrast which enables Melleuish (2002: 335) to suggest that 'the development of the modern state can be compared to the invention of the alphabet. It only happened once but once it had occurred it changed the nature of human existence for ever.'

This modern idea of the state emerged in Europe between the sixteenth and eighteenth centuries, with the use of the word *state* as a political term coming into common use towards the end of this period. The number of states grew slowly: there were only 19 in existence in 1800, and barely 30 more had been established by 1900. At a global level, the real expansion of the state system began after the Second World War as decolonization saw the end of European empires. In addition, the number of international organizations and list of international treaties began to grow. Until the Second World War, government and politics around the world had been driven mainly by the preferences and the actions of a few Western democracies, but the picture became increasingly complex as debates about sovereignty, authority, and self-determination broadened and

deepened. Where great powers such as Britain, Germany, and France had been prominent, the picture changed with the emergence of the United States and the Soviet Union as superpowers after 1945, with the independence of nearly 70 mainly African and Asian states in the 1960s and 1970s, with the final break-up of the Soviet Union in 1991, and the rise of emerging powers such as China, India, and Brazil in the 1990s.

States today have a quite different and more complex relationship with one another than they did even two generations ago. Their interactions inevitably influence domestic political and economic calculations, questions about their true independence are raised with increased frequency, and we now see a debate under way about their future: are states becoming weaker, are they as strong as they ever were, or are they simply transforming in the wake of new demands and pressures? Whatever the answer, the state remains the basis for understanding government and politics all over the world. There are sub-national units of government, to be sure, and some see the growth of governance at the global level, but almost everyone is a citizen of one state or another, and when we think of government we also think of states.

What is a state?

Few terms are more central to understanding government and politics (and yet have been more often disputed) than the **state**. It is nearly impossible to proceed in any meaningful or effective fashion with the study of politics and government unless we have at least a working understanding of what states look like, because they are the world's dominant form of political organization, and the building blocks of the international system. And yet they are not easy to define.

> **State:** The legal and political authority of a territory containing a population and marked by borders. The state defines the political authority of which government is the managing authority; that authority is regarded as both sovereign and legitimate by the citizens of the state and the governments of other states.

The usual benchmark for understanding the state is the classic definition offered by the German sociologist Max Weber, who described it as 'a human community that (successfully) claims the monopoly of the legitimate use of physical force within a given territory' (quoted in Gerth and Mills, 1948: 78). When the state's monopoly of legitimate force is threatened, as in a civil war, its very existence is at stake. As long as the conflict continues, there is no legitimate authority. But there is more to the state than physical force, and it needs to be understood more particularly in its modern context, where it is best defined as a legal and political entity with population, legitimacy, territory, and sovereignty (see Figure 2.1).

If all were neat and tidy, then every square metre of land in the world would be part of one state or another. But there are numerous parcels of territory around the world that lack one or more of these qualities, and thus cannot be considered states for the purposes of analysis: examples include Taiwan, Puerto Rico, Palestine, Western Sahara, and Hong Kong. Furthermore, there are still a few remaining colonies or overseas territories, such as Bermuda, Gibraltar, Guam, and French Polynesia, and these, too, are not normally considered as states, because they are not independent. (It should be noted that states are often described as countries, but the term *country* strictly speaking refers only to a territory and not to the mechanisms of government and power.)

How does a state differ from a government? In essence, the state defines the political community of which government is the managing agent. By successfully claiming a monopoly of authorized force, the state creates a mandate for rule which the government then puts into effect. This distinction between state and government is reflected in the characteristic separation in many countries of the roles of head of state (e.g. the monarch or non-executive president) and head of government (e.g. the prime minister) (see Chapter 9).

Since much of the theoretical justification for the state is provided by the idea of **sovereignty**, we must first unpack this related notion. As developed by the sixteenth-century French philosopher Jean Bodin, sovereignty refers to the unfettered and undivided power to make laws. In a similar vein, the eighteenth-century English jurist William Blackstone (1765–9: book 1: 68) argued that 'there is and must be in every state a supreme, irresistible, absolute and uncontrolled authority, in which the right of sovereignty resides'.

> **Sovereignty:** The ultimate source of authority in a society. The sovereign is the highest and final decision-maker within a community.

The word *sovereign* originally meant 'one seated above'. So, the sovereign body is the one institution unlimited by higher authority: the highest of the high. By definition, that body is the state. As Bodin wrote, the sovereign can 'give laws unto all and every one of the subjects and receive none from them'. Sovereignty originally developed in Europe to justify the attempt by monarchs to consolidate control over kingdoms in which authority had previously been shared with the feudal aristocracy and the Catholic Church. This is why monarchs and currencies are still known as 'sovereigns'.

However, as democracy gained ground, so too did the belief that elected assemblies acting on behalf of the people are the true holders of sovereignty. The means of acquiring sovereignty evolved, although the theoretical importance of Blackstone's 'supreme authority'

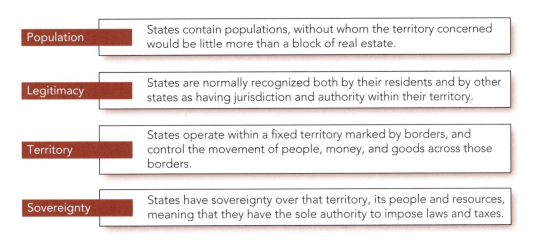

Population	States contain populations, without whom the territory concerned would be little more than a block of real estate.
Legitimacy	States are normally recognized both by their residents and by other states as having jurisdiction and authority within their territory.
Territory	States operate within a fixed territory marked by borders, and control the movement of people, money, and goods across those borders.
Sovereignty	States have sovereignty over that territory, its people and resources, meaning that they have the sole authority to impose laws and taxes.

FIGURE 2.1: The qualities of a state

remained unquestioned, especially in centralized European countries such as Britain and France. Beyond Europe, the notion of sovereignty remained weaker. In federations such as Brazil, Germany, India, and the United States, for instance, political authority is shared between the central and regional governments. In these circumstances, the idea of sovereignty is diluted, and so too is the concept of the state itself. Americans more often use the word *state* to denote the 50 states of the Union, rather than the entire United States. Limited as it is by checks and balances, the US federal government lacks the 'absolute and uncontrolled authority' which Blackstone judged so essential to the state.

The formal right to make laws does not imply that the sovereign is omnipotent, because all sovereigns are influenced by events beyond and within their borders. For this reason, claims that sovereignty has become a myth in an interdependent world should be treated with scepticism. Sovereignty always was an invention; that is its significance. Mexico, for instance, depends more on the United States than vice versa, but the two countries remain formally equal as sovereigns. A state's control over its destiny is a matter of degree but its sovereignty is, by its nature, unlimited. The essence of sovereignty lies in an unqualified legal title:

> Constitutional independence, like marriage, is an absolute condition. People are either married or not married; they cannot be 70 per cent married. The same with sovereignty: a country either has the legal title of sovereignty or it does not; there is no in-between condition. (Sørensen, 2004: 104)

Inherent in the notion of the state is the idea of the **citizen**. Just as the development of the state overrode the power of the aristocracy and the Church, so the concept of the citizen implies full and equal membership of the political community defined by the state. As Heater (1999: 1) notes: 'The title of citizen was adopted by the French revolutionaries [of 1789] to pronounce the symbolic reality of equality; the titles of aristocratic distinction were expunged.' To be a citizen is to possess both rights (such as legal protection) and duties (such as military or community service).

> **Citizen:** A full member of a state, entitled to the rights and subject to the duties associated with that status. Citizenship is typically confirmed in a document such as a passport or identity card.

Note, however, that our mental image of a state as a container for its citizens alone is a poor guide to reality. Once condemned as political polygamy, dual citizenship is now accepted by many states (Hansen and Weil, 2002). Further, international migrants – mostly living in high-income countries – made up more than 3 per cent of

---

FOCUS 2.1 | How many states are there?

This is not an easy question to answer. A benchmark point of reference is the membership roster of the United Nations, which stood at 193 in mid-2015. But this number includes 4 small European enclave states (Andorra, Liechtenstein, Monaco, and San Marino), which meet the legal definition of a state but play a minimal role in interstate relations, and are for all practical purposes parts of the larger states that surround them. Meanwhile, the UN membership list excludes several territories that function much like states but are lacking either independence and/or legitimacy; these include Kosovo, Palestine, Taiwan, and Western Sahara. Taiwan would be a member of the UN had it not been expelled in 1971 when China made it clear that it would not have diplomatic ties with any country that recognized Taiwan. In almost all respects, though, it is structured and continues to function as a state. Meanwhile, Kosovo – part of the former Yugoslavia – has been recognized diplomatically by more than 100 other states, including most of the member states of the European Union, and is a member of several key international bodies (including the World Bank and the International Monetary Fund), but cannot be considered a political and diplomatic equal of UN member states.

So while the question 'How many states are there?' is likely to elicit the response 'It depends what you mean by a state', this book opts for the number 189: the current membership of the United Nations, less the 4 European enclave states. But we should not overlook the discussion of microstates, quasi-states, and *de facto* states later in this chapter.

the world's population in 2013 (UN Population Fund, 2015). In their country of destination, legal migrants may be granted the right of permanent residence without seeking or being granted citizenship, a limitation which denies them the vote in national elections. To equate a country's adult population with its citizens is to overlook this significant inequality (Hammerstad, 2010).

Emergence of the state system

The state emerged from the embers of medieval Europe (c.1000–1500). In the Middle Ages, European governance had been dominated by the transnational Roman Catholic Church and powerful feudal lords. Sandwiched between these forces, monarchs occupied a far weaker position than do today's rulers. The process of change was long, slow, and complex. How did the modern state acquire the dominant position it occupies in the modern world? What factors drove this crucial transformation?

If there was any single force that was responsible for the transition to the modern state, it was war. As Tilly (1975: 42) wrote, 'war made the state, and the state made war'. The introduction of gunpowder in the fourteenth century transformed military scale and tactics, as organized infantry and artillery replaced the knight on horseback. The result was an aggressive, competitive, and expensive arms race in Europe, which obliged rulers to employ administrators to recruit, train, equip, and pay for standing armies, laying the foundation of modern bureaucracies. Political units became larger, and the growth of bureaucracy meant that local patterns of administration and justice became more uniform. Commerce grew more freely, and rulers began to establish formal diplomatic relations with their overseas counterparts.

Just as war-making weakened the feudal pillar of the medieval framework, so the Reformation destroyed its religious foundations. From around 1520, Protestant reformers led by Martin Luther condemned what they saw as the corruption and privileges of the organized Church. This reform movement brought profound political consequences, shattering the Christian commonwealth as antagonism developed between Protestant and Catholic rulers.

The birth of the modern state system is often tied to a single event: the 1648 Peace of Westphalia. This brought an end to both the Thirty Years' War in the Holy Roman Empire, and the Eighty Years' War between Spain and the Dutch Republic. It made several adjustments to European state borders, gave new definition to the idea of sovereignty, and helped make national secular authority superior to religious edicts from Rome, giving rise to what is often known as the **Westphalian system**. Several states predated the Peace, including England, Ireland, France, Spain, and Portugal, but it gave clearer definition to the powers of states.

> **Westphalian system:** The modern state system that many believe emerged out of the 1648 Peace of Westphalia, based on the sovereignty of states and political self-determination.

As central authority developed in Europe, so did the need for its theoretical justification. The crucial idea here was sovereignty, as later tamed by the notion of consent. The French philosopher Jean Bodin argued that, within society, a single sovereign authority should be responsible for five major functions: legislation, war and peace, public appointments, judicial appeals, and the currency. But the sovereign still needed to be subject to limits and controls, and here the English philosopher John Locke played a vital role. He argued that citizens possess **natural rights** to life, liberty, and property, and that these rights must be protected by rulers governing through law.

According to Locke, citizens agree to obey the laws of the land, even if only by tacit means such as accepting the protection which law provides. But should rulers violate citizens' natural rights, the people 'are thereupon absolved from any further Obedience, and are left to the common Refuge, which God hath provided for all Men against force and violence' – the right to resist (Locke, 1690: 412). So, in Locke's work we see a modern account of the liberal state, with sovereignty limited by consent. In theory, at least, government had become servant rather than master.

> **Natural rights:** Those rights (such as to life, liberty, and property) supposedly given to humans by God or by nature, their existence taken to be independent of government.

These ideas of sovereignty and consent were reflected, in contrasting ways, in the two most momentous affirmations of modernity: the American and

French revolutions. In America, the colonists established their independence from Britain and went on to fashion a new republic, giving substance to Locke's liberal interpretation of the state. The Declaration of Independence (1776) boldly declared that governments derive 'their just authority from the consent of the governed', while the US constitution (drafted 1787) famously begins, 'We, the People of the United States'.

But it was the French Revolution of 1789 that made the most daring attempt to reinterpret sovereignty in democratic (rather than liberal) terms. Described by Finer (1997: 1516) as 'the most important single event in the entire history of government', the French Revolution mapped out the contours of modern democracy. Where the American federal government was limited in its authority, the French revolutionaries regarded a centralized, unitary state as the sovereign expression of a national community populated by citizens with equal rights. Where the American Revolution was built on distrust of power, the French revolutionaries favoured universal suffrage and a government empowered to make decisions for the good of society as a whole.

The principles of France's modernizing revolution were articulated in the Declaration of the Rights of Man and the Citizen; this served as a preamble to the French constitution of 1791, still forms part of the country's constitution, and is considered by Finer to be 'the blueprint of virtually all modern states'. It pronounces that 'Men are born and remain free and equal in rights … These rights are liberty, property, security and resistance to oppression.' It continues: 'Law is the expression of the general will. All citizens have a right to participate in shaping it either in person, or through their representatives. It must be the same for all, whether it punishes or protects.'

The expansion of states

During the nineteenth century, the outlines of the state became more precise, especially in Europe. Borders slowly turned into barriers as maps marked out defined frontiers. Lawyers established that a country's territory should extend into the sea as far as the reach of a cannonball and, later, above its land to the flying height of a hot-air balloon. Reflecting this new concern with boundaries, passports were introduced in Europe during the First World War. To travel across frontiers became a rite of passage, involving official permission expressed in an official stamp.

Economically, too, the second half of the nineteenth century saw the end of an era of relatively liberal trade. Stimulated by economic depressions, many European states introduced protectionist trade policies. National markets gained ground against both local and international exchange, meaning that economies became more susceptible to regulation by central government. Internally, the functions performed by the state expanded to include education, factory regulation, policing, and gathering statistics (literally, 'state facts').

For most of the twentieth century, Western states bore deeper into their societies. As with the original emergence of European states, this expansion was fuelled by war. The first and second world wars were examples of **total war**, fought between entire countries, rather than just between specialized armed forces. To equip massive forces with the necessary tanks, planes and bombs demanded unparalleled mobilization of citizens, economies and societies. The ability to tax effectively and systematically – described by Bräutigam *et al.* (2008: 137) as 'the central pillar of state capacity' – grew further. Because total wars were expensive, tax revenues as a proportion of national product almost doubled in Western states between 1930 and 1945 (Steinmo, 2003: 213). The twentieth century was an era of the state because it was also an age of war.

> **Total war:** War requiring the mobilization of the population to support a conflict fought with advanced weaponry on a large geographical scale, requiring state leadership, intervention and funding.

Peace in 1945 did not initially lead to a corresponding reduction in the role of the state. Rather, Western governments sought to apply their enhanced administrative skills to domestic needs. Throughout Western Europe, the warfare state gave way to the **welfare state**, with rulers accepting direct responsibility for protecting their citizens from the scourges of illness, unemployment and old age. In this way, the European state led a post-war settlement – termed the 'Keynesian welfare state' (after the British economist John Maynard Keynes) – which integrated full employment and public welfare with an economy in which the private sector continued to play a substantial part.

> **Welfare state:** An arrangement in which the government is primarily responsible for the social and economic security of its citizens through public programmes such as incomes for the unemployed, pensions for the elderly and medical care for the sick.

THE STATE   **25**

Meanwhile, important developments were taking place further afield. Although the state was born in Europe, its form was exported to the rest of the world by imperial powers such as Britain, France, and Spain. Consequently, most states in today's world are post-colonial. As Armitage (2005: 3) points out, 'the great political fact of global history in the last 500 years is the emergence of a world of states from a world of empires. That fact fundamentally defines the political universe we all inhabit.' The few states without a history as a colony (leaving aside the ex-colonial powers themselves) include China, Ethiopia, Iran, Japan, and Saudi Arabia.

Although the term *post-colonial* is usually confined to countries achieving independence in the aftermath of the Second World War, settler societies such as Australia, Canada, New Zealand, and the United States provide early examples of states formed from colonies. In settler societies, the new arrivals ruthlessly supplanted indigenous communities, re-creating segments of the European tradition they had brought with them; as a result, the political organization of these countries remains strong and recognizably Western. By contrast,

non-settler colonies emerged into statehood in four waves spread over two centuries, the results being different from the strong European states generated in earlier centuries by military and political competition.

The first wave occurred early in the nineteenth century, in the Spanish and Portuguese territories of Latin America. Here, the early wars of independence lacked the liberal, egalitarian basis of their US predecessor. New constitutions were produced but they were neither democratic nor fully implemented. Economic exploitation of native populations, the poor, and descendants of slaves continued into the post-colonial era. The resulting inequalities created conflicts within Latin American countries which remain important even today.

The second wave of state expansion emerged in Europe and the Middle East around the end of the First World War, with the final collapse of the Austro-Hungarian, Russian, and Ottoman empires. The first of these dissolved into five separate states: Austria, Hungary, Poland, Czechoslovakia, and Yugoslavia. With the exception of Turkey, founded on the ruins of the Ottoman Empire, strong and stable states again failed to develop

TABLE 2.1: The formation of states

	Americas	Europe	Asia and Pacific	Africa	Total
Pre-1799	1	9	7	2	19
1800–49	18	4	—	1	23
1850–99	2	4	—	—	6
1900–09	1	1	1	—	3
1910–19	—	4	2	1	7
1920–29	—	2	5	1	8
1930–39	—	—	1	—	1
1940–49	—	1	13	—	14
1950–59	—	—	2	5	7
1960–69	4	2	5	32	43
1970–79	7	—	9	8	24
1980–89	3	—	3	1	7
1990–99	—	12	10	3	25
2000–09	—	—	1	—	1
2010–	—	—	—	1	1
Total	36	39	59	55	189

Notes: Includes only those states internationally recognized as sovereign and independent in January 2015. Excludes European microstates.

Source: Based on appendix in Crawford (2007)

during this wave. Instead, international politics in the shape of fascism and communism continued to intrude, preventing those countries on the European periphery from experiencing the continuous state development found in the continent's core.

The third and largest wave of state creation took place after 1945, with the retreat from empire by European states diminished by war. Asian countries, such as the Philippines (in 1946) and India (in 1947), were the first to achieve independence but many other colonies, in Africa, the Caribbean, and the Middle East, followed suit. Between 1945 and 1989, nearly 90 independent states, almost half the world's current total, were created. But most lacked any previous experience as a coherent entity, and statehood was superimposed on ethnic, regional, and religious groups that had previously coexisted in a looser arrangement. Many states continue to feel the destabilizing effects even today, including Nigeria, Iraq, and India.

The fourth and final wave of state formation occurred in the final decade of the twentieth century, triggered by the collapse of communism. The dissolution of the communist bloc previously dominated by the Soviet Union led to independence for more than a dozen Soviet satellites in Eastern Europe (e.g. Poland). In addition, the Soviet Union itself – in effect, a Russian empire – dissolved into 15 successor states (e.g. Ukraine). The experience of these new post-communist states has been mixed. The Baltic states gained economic and political stability from their proximity to, and now their membership of, the European Union. However, central Asian republics such as Uzbekistan revealed a more typical post-colonial syndrome: small size, ethnic division, a pre-industrial economy, and autocratic rule. In the successor states to the Soviet Union, these problems are, again, reinforced by the absence of pre-colonial experience as an independent state.

Overall, then, the contrasts between West European parent states and their post-colonial progeny are deep-rooted. Post-colonial states rarely possess the strength and autonomy which their European predecessors acquired during their own development. Sovereignty remains important as a title, securing international recognition and access to aid. But the label's significance is sometimes symbolic, with little to prevent the movement of people, soldiers, goods and terrorists across boundaries. In extreme but still exceptional cases, the outcome is a fragile – or even failed – state which is unable to execute its core task of securing order (see later in this chapter).

The diversity of states

The enormous contrasts of population, wealth, and power among states are often underemphasized by those analysts who concentrate on either the formal equality of states (all are equally sovereign) or their forms of government. But, clearly, neither sovereignty nor democracy matter for, say, small island states (such as Kiribati, the Maldives, and the Solomon Islands) at risk of disappearing as a result of rising sea levels brought on by climate change. Sovereignty is exercised by all states, but in varying conditions and with varying resources.

A review of the distribution of states by population, political authority, and income provides insight into these divergent political realities. In particular, it confirms that the strong form of the European state is impossible to replicate in a significant number of small, dependent post-colonial states.

Population

Although many studies in comparative politics examine large states, they are exceptional when viewed though a global lens. At one end of the distribution, China's population of 1.35 billion is greater than that of the 160 smallest countries in the world combined. At the other end, the population of most countries in the world is fewer than 10 million, with one in five falling below one million (Figure 2.2). In median position sits Switzerland (7.9 million) – a country usually presented as 'small' but which only appears as such when viewed from the perspective of larger states.

The smallest states – **microstates** – are mainly islands in the Caribbean, the Pacific or off the African coast, along with five European states, including the Vatican City. Mostly, they possess limited capacity to shape their own destiny, and must seek protection from larger patrons. But we should not assume that they are dysfunctional; several established microstates in Europe have combined political stability with economic success. As with many successful small states, Luxembourg secured its position through joining military and economic alliances, and its success continues. Helped by an economy based heavily on services, the country (population 502,000) has moved to the higher reaches of the global economic rankings, with a per capita gross national income in 2014 of more than $80,000. Many of the smallest states, however, are both people- and

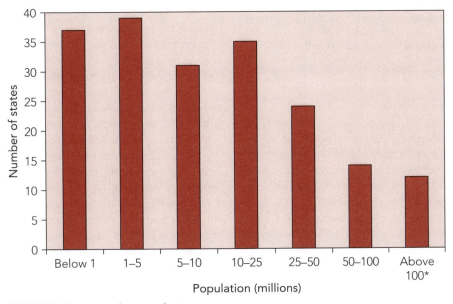

FIGURE 2.2: States by population

Source: Calculated from data listed by World Bank at http://data.worldbank.org (accessed January 2015). Figures are for 2013.

* Includes China (1.35 billion) and India (1.25 billion).

resource-poor. Several Pacific states – such as Tuvalu, Palau, the Marshall Islands, and Kiribati – have few people (Tuvalu has fewer than 10,000), little in the way of natural resources or economic opportunities, and poor trade and transport connections to the rest of the world.

> **Microstates:** States that are small in both population and territory. Andorra, Barbados, Palau, and the Maldives are examples.

Political authority

The challenge of defining a state is exemplified by the existence of several territories that fall short of all the required qualities (most notably independence and sovereignty). Some of these are what Jackson (1990: 1) calls **quasi-states**, which he defines as states that won independence from a former colonial power but have since lost control over much of their territory. They are recognized by the international community as having all the rights and responsibilities of a state, but they barely exist as a functioning entity. Somalia is a prime example: the outbreak of a civil war in 1991 led to the collapse of centralized government and the emergence of several

autonomous regions within the country. Although it has been formally a federal republic since 2012, much of northern Somalia has long functioned as either Somaliland or the Puntland State of Somalia.

> **Quasi-states:** States that exist and are recognized under international law but whose governments control little of the territory under their jurisdiction.

Other difficult cases are represented by what Pegg (1998) calls *de facto* **states**, meaning that they control territory and provide governance, but are mainly unrecognized by the international community (and thus have no legal or *de jure* existence). So while quasi-states are legitimate no matter how ineffective they are, *de facto* states are illegitimate no matter how effective they are. Key examples include Abkhazia, Nagorno-Karabakh, Transnistria, Somaliland, and the Turkish Republic of Northern Cyprus. Somaliland provides a strong contrast with Somalia; the latter has a seat in the United Nations and is recognized internationally even though it is ineffective, while the former remains unrecognized despite the fact that it has been governing the northern one-third of Somalia in relative peace since 1991.

> **De facto states:** States that are not recognized under international law even though they control territory and provide governance. They exist in fact (*de facto*) rather than under law (*de jure*).

Income

The era in which states could be classified as 'rich' or 'poor', 'developed' or 'developing', has passed. Although economic inequalities between countries remain immense, a more nuanced picture is now required, especially to capture the growth of emerging economies. The World Bank offers a useful classification, dividing states (strictly, economies) into four income groups (Table 2.2). Introduced in 1988, this scheme sought to provide an economic indicator linked to measures of well-being such as poverty and infant mortality.

The high-income category is still led by the developed economies of Europe, North America, Australasia, and parts of Asia. It is these countries which form the Organisation for Economic Co-operation and Development (OECD), the rich country club which seeks to 'build a wider consensus for market economies and democracy' (OECD, 2011). While the cultural, economic, political, and scientific resources of OECD states remain enormous, their strength was diminished by the financial crisis of 2008/09, the resulting increase in public debt, and the subsequent difficulties experienced by the eurozone currency area. Furthermore, the weight of population lies elsewhere: the United States and Japan are the only two OECD members in the world's ten most populous countries. The high-income category also includes small, oil-rich, non-democratic states such as Kuwait and Qatar, confirming, again, that scale is unnecessary for wealth.

In the upper-middle income category we find most of the fast-growing new economies; the economic dynamism and large population of some of these states has already sparked some rebalancing of world power away from the developed West. The category includes two of the BRIC countries (**B**razil, **R**ussia, **I**ndia, **C**hina), a designation invented in 2001 by an economist at the investment firm Goldman Sachs (O'Neill, 2001). The story has not been quite so happy for Brazil of late; a combination of drought, a sluggish economy, corruption and rising energy costs has led to significant economic problems.

Lower-middle income countries are found mainly in Africa and Asia. Although they have seen development, their levels of affluence and their global political weight remain limited compared to the upper-middle category. India has long been something of a puzzle: its economy is one of the world's largest, but it has suffered for many years from unmet potential, and the benefits of its economic development have not reached down to the poorest of its citizens. Root problems include the large role still played by the state in the economy, and the challenge of dealing with India's rapid population growth. Recent governments have promised to increase the pace of liberalization, but real achievements have been slow to follow. The consensus is that India is still prevented from achieving its true economic potential by continuing over-regulation and (in contrast to China) a more limited capacity to achieve policy change.

Sometimes known as the 'fourth world', the low-income countries consist mainly of African states, together with some Asian countries, such as Afghanistan, Bangladesh and Burma. In 2015, the number of countries in this group (34) was greater than the number belonging to the OECD. With average incomes of less

TABLE 2.2: States by income

	Gross national income per capita*	Number of states	Examples
High income	$39,300 or above	53	Germany, Poland, Japan, US
Upper-middle income	$7,500–39,300	54	Brazil, China, Iran, Mexico, South Africa
Lower-middle income	$2,000–7,500	49	Egypt, India, Nigeria, Philippines, Vietnam
Low income	$2,000 or below	34	Afghanistan, Ethiopia, Haiti, Somalia

Source: Calculated from data listed by World Bank at http://data.worldbank.org (accessed January 2015). Figures are for 2013.

* Rounded out.

than $2,000 per year (often substantially less), life for the vast majority of people in low-income countries remains challenging indeed.

In studying international politics, it is possible to focus on the absolute size of an economy or, alternatively, on national income per head. In comparative politics, though, we must recognize the domestic political impact of sharp inequality and mass poverty. Among many other effects, these factors create a dependence of the poor and powerless on the rich and powerful. As we will see in Chapter 3, such inequalities still create a powerful barrier to a functioning democracy.

Nations and nationalism

No discussion of states can be complete without a review of the related, overlapping, and more elusive idea of the **nation**. Where states exist under law, nations are considered by Anderson (1983) to be 'imagined communities' and are often viewed as any group that upholds a claim to be regarded as such. In two ways, though, we can be more precise. First, nations are peoples with homelands. As Eley and Suny (1996: 10) put it, a nation – like a state – implies 'a claim on a particular piece of real estate'. Here, the origin of the word *nation*, deriving from a Latin term meaning 'place of birth', is relevant. The link between nation and place is one factor distinguishing a nation from a tribe or ethnic group. Tribes can move home but a nation remains tethered to its motherland, changing shape mainly through expansion and contraction.

> **Nation:** A cultural and historical concept describing a group of people who identify with one another on the basis of a shared history, culture, language, and myths.

Second, when a group claims to be a nation, it usually professes a right to **self-determination** within its homeland. It seeks sovereignty over its land, exploiting or inventing a shared culture to justify its claim. This assertion of self-rule (not to be confused with democratic rule) gives the nation its political character. A social group becomes a nation by achieving or seeking control over its own destiny, whether through independence or devolution. To describe French-speaking Canadians as a separate nation, as opposed to a linguistic community, indicates a claim for autonomy, if not independence, for this culturally

distinct and geographically concentrated group. Similarly, the campaign for a Palestinian state since 1948 has strengthened what was previously a more amorphous Palestinian national identity.

> **Self-determination:** The ability to act without external compulsion. The right of national self-determination is the right of a people to possess its own government, democratic or otherwise.

Because the concept of nation is political, there is no necessity for nations to be united by a common language. A shared tongue certainly eases the task of cultural unification, yet in Switzerland, for example, French, German, and Italian are widely spoken. In India, 22 official languages are each spoken by more than one million people. Nationhood cannot be reduced to any other factor, linguistic or otherwise; rather, it is a subjective identity resulting from what the French philosopher Ernest Renan (1882) termed a 'daily plebiscite'.

Although scholars such as Smith (2009) view nations as creatures of antiquity, they are more often understood as attempts by peoples to assert their modern right to self-determination. Certainly, many nations have been constructed in the course of relatively recent struggles. In the nineteenth and especially the twentieth centuries, for instance, colonial peoples demanded independence under a nationalist banner. Their assertions of national identity were often artificial but they served as a rallying cry against the imperialists. It was 'the presence and power of the colonial regime that stimulated the development of a national identity as the basis of resistance' (Calhoun, 1997: 108). The nation was created through, not simply invoked in, the struggle for freedom.

To view nations as modern is to suggest that they are made, rather than found. Nations assert statehood and, since states themselves are products of modernity, so too are nations. Specifically, a national identity unites people who do not know each other but who, nonetheless, find themselves living together under common rulers and markets. A shared nationality provides an emotional bond for an increasingly rational world. In particular, it allows the losers from the emergence of a large market economy to take comfort in the progress of their country as a whole. In a similar way, national identity provides a rationalization for participation in war, encouraging people 'to die for the sake of strangers' (Langman, 2006).

Even more than nations themselves, **nationalism** is a doctrine of modernity. Like many 'isms', nationalism emerged in the nineteenth century to flourish in the twentieth. But, unlike these other 'isms', the principle of nationalism is reassuringly straightforward. It is simply the doctrine that nations have a right to determine their own destiny – to govern themselves. In this way, nationalism is a universal idea, even though each individual nation is rooted in a particular place.

> **Nationalism:** The belief that a group of people with a common national identity (usually marked by a shared culture and history) has the right to form an independent state and to govern itself free of external intervention.

The United Nations Covenant on Civil and Political Rights (UNHCR, 1966) offers a succinct statement of the principle of national self-government:

> All peoples have the right to self-determination. By virtue of that right they freely determine their political status and pursue their economic, social and cultural rights.

Nations, unlike states, do not necessarily have tidy geographical boundaries. Some national groups are spread among several states. The Kurds, for example, are found in Iran, Iraq, Syria, and Turkey, and thus form a stateless nation (see Map 2.1). Similarly, a **diaspora** is a group widely dispersed beyond its homeland. The Jews remain the primary representative case, with only a minority of the world's Jews living in their ancient homeland.

> **Diaspora:** A population that lives over an extended area outside its geographical or ethnic homeland.

An archetypal **nation–state** contains only the people belonging to its nation. The French Revolution of 1789 established the idea that the state should articulate the interests and rights of citizens bound together by a single national identity. In the nineteenth century, the English political philosopher John Stuart Mill (1861: 392) argued that 'where the sentiment of nationality exists in any force there is a *prima facie* case for uniting all the members of the nationality under the same government, and a government to themselves apart'. In today's world, Iceland is a good example of a nation-state. Its population shares such a well-documented descent from within a compact island that the state's birth records provide a perfect laboratory for genetic research. Japan is another example; while its government does not keep precise figures, it is estimated that 98.5 per cent of the population is Japanese.

> **Nation-state:** A sovereign political association whose citizens share a common national identity.

In a **multinational state**, by contrast, more than one nation is fundamental to a country's politics, and assimilation to a dominant nationality is unrealistic. International migration is moving many, perhaps most, states in this direction. Even so, we should not regard the phenomenon of multinationalism as new. Britain, for instance, has long been divided between English, Welsh, Scottish, and Irish nationals; Canada between English and French speakers; and Belgium between Dutch and French speakers. One of the more diverse states in the world is India: it has 22 official languages (with more than a hundred in regular use), and while three-quarters of the population is Hindu, there are significant Muslim, Christian, Sikh, and Buddhist minorities.

> **Multinational state:** A state consisting of multiple national groups under a single government.

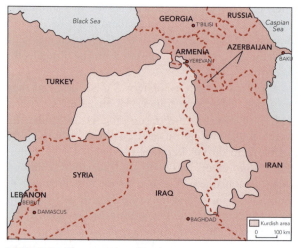

MAP 2.1: The stateless Kurds

Map showing the location of Kurds across Iran, Iraq, Syria, and Turkey.

Challenges to the state

States have never been entirely stable or fully inde-pendent: some have been involved in political disputes that have created uncertainties about their borders; oth-ers have experienced legal, economic, or political dif-ficulties that have limited their sovereignty; their levels of legitimacy vary according to the extent to which the citizens of a state (and the governments of other states) respect the powers and authority of that state; and the independence of states has always been quali-fied by external economic and political pressures, not least the need to import goods and services that they cannot provide for themselves (see Vincent, 1987 and Gill, 2003).

One school of thought argues that states are as strong as ever. They still have a monopoly over the con-trol and use of militaries, they are still the key actors in the management of economic production and interna-tional trade networks, their citizens still identify mainly with their home states and are subject to the authority and rules of the state, and the ability of states to respond to new challenges has grown thanks to technological innovation. Talk of the decline of the state, runs the argument, is premature, and the most that can be said is that its role is changing as developments in trade, international law, and modernization have changed the nature of state power, the relationship among states, and the relationship between states and citizens. (For a sur-vey of the debate, see Sørensen, 2004, and Hay *et al.*, 2006.)

On the other hand, states have long had their crit-ics, who have developed a long list of complaints (see Table 2.3). So much has the credibility and power of the state declined, argue some, that it may actually be on its way out (see, for example, Camilleri and Falk, 1992 and Ohmae, 2005), the result of four critical developments. First, public loyalty to states has long been undermined by economic, social, and political divisions. In many parts of the world, the focus of people's allegiance has changed as national minorities have become more assertive and demanded greater self-determination, and even independence in some cases, as with the Scots in Britain, the Kurds in Tur-key/Iraq/Iran, the Catalans in Spain, and the Québé-cois in Canada.

Second, international borders have been weakened by the extension of economic ties among states. Per-haps nothing today poses as much of a threat to state

TABLE 2.3: Ten criticisms of the state

1 Imposing unnecessary divisions on human society.
2 Having a history of going to war with each other.
3 Limiting the free movement of people and capital.
4 Imposing limits on trade that handicap innovation and efficiency.
5 Pursuing state interests at the expense of human interests.
6 Allowing exclusion to dominate over inclusion.
7 Promoting narrow identities at the expense of broader identities.
8 Having a poor record of working with other states to address shared problems such as terrorism, transboundary pollution, migration, and the spread of disease.
9 Being often unable to meet the demands of their residents for security, justice, prosperity, and human rights.
10 Failing to manage their economies and national resources to the benefit of all their residents.

sovereignty as **globalization**: increased economic interdependence, changes in technology and commu-nications, the rising power of multinational corpora-tions, the growth of international markets, the spread of a global culture, and the harmonization of public policies in the face of shared or common problems (see Focus 2.2). At the same time, people have become more mobile: complex new patterns of emigration have been driven by a combination of economic need and per-sonal choice, and mass tourism has broken down many of the psychological barriers among states.

Globalization: The process by which the links between people, corporations, and governments in different states become integrated through such factors as trade, investment, communication and technology.

Third, just as the number of states has grown since 1945, so has interstate cooperation on a wide range of issues, which has diluted their independent existence. States have signed bilateral and multilateral cooperative treaties, and have created a network of **intergovernmental organizations** (IGOs) responsi-ble for encouraging and monitoring cooperation on a wide range of matters. There are several hundred cur-rently in existence, including the United Nations and the World Trade Organization. Some date back to the nineteenth century (the International Telecommunica-tion Union was founded by 20 member governments

SPOTLIGHT

EUROPEAN UNION

Brief Profile: In a world of states, the European Union is an anomaly. It began in the 1950s as an effort to build a single market among its six founding members in the interests of promoting peace and economic reconstruction after the war. It has since expanded both its membership and its reach, but opinion on its political personality is much debated. It has common policies in several areas, and it encourages cooperation among its 28 member states on a wide variety of issues; most of its members have also adopted a single currency, the euro. It has treaties but no constitution, and administrative institutions that fall short of being a government of the EU. It is not a federal United States of Europe, and while some support moves in that direction, there is now widespread resistance to deeper European integration.

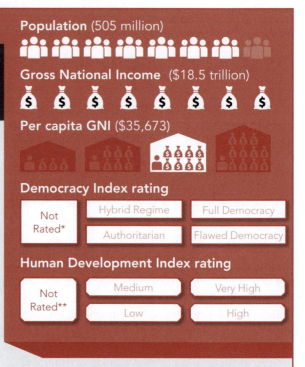

Population (505 million)

Gross National Income ($18.5 trillion)

Per capita GNI ($35,673)

Democracy Index rating

| Not Rated* | Hybrid Regime | Full Democracy |
| | Authoritarian | Flawed Democracy |

Human Development Index rating

| Not Rated** | Medium | Very High |
| | Low | High |

*12 member states are full democracies and 16 (mainly in Eastern Europe) are flawed.
**With the exception of Bulgaria and Romania – all member states rank Very High.

Form of government ⇨ Debatable. More than an intergovernmental organization, but less than a federal European superstate.

Legislature ⇨ A single-chamber European Parliament (EP) whose members are elected directly by all eligible voters of the EU member states. Its standing has increased substantially since the 1970s, though its scope still does not cover all areas of EU responsibility.

Executive ⇨ Shared between a European Council that is the meeting place of the heads of government of the member states, a Council of Ministers that is the meeting place for government ministers, and a powerful European Commission that is a cross between an executive and a bureaucracy.

Judiciary ⇨ The European Court of Justice, composed of one judge from each member state, has developed the EU's strong legal foundations, supporting the drive for European integration.

Electoral system ⇨ Members of the European Parliament are elected for renewable five-year terms using proportional representation, with member states treated as a single constituency, or divided into a number of separate constituencies.

Parties ⇨ Few political parties contest EP elections as European parties; instead, the elections are contested by national parties running in what are – effectively – 28 separate national elections.

➡

in 1865), but most were created in the twentieth century, not least in the aftermath of the world wars. IGOs include single-purpose entities, regional organizations, and universal bodies, the most important enjoy the membership of a majority of established states.

Intergovernmental organization: Cooperative bodies whose members are states that are established by treaty, possess a permanent secretariat and legal identity, and operate according to stated rules and with some autonomy.

The European Union and its meaning for the states of Europe

One of the many challenges to the modern state system has been posed by the phenomenon of **regional integration**, the process by which neighbouring states voluntarily build economic and political ties that go beyond those found in standard international organizations: they seek to reduce trade barriers, create some joint administrative institutions, and aim to develop common rules on shared interests while remaining politically sovereign. The oldest and most advanced example of regional integration is the European Union, a unique entity which has existed in one form or another since 1952 and now includes 28 countries (see McCormick, 2015, for more details). Other cases – far less ambitious in their goals – include the African Union (54 members), the Union of South American Nations (12 members), and the Association of Southeast Asian Nations (ASEAN, 10 members).

The EU's main institutions may look like a European government but are no more (and no less) than a system of shared governance. Common policies and laws are made in areas where the EU members have agreed to work together, including trade, competition, agriculture, and the environment. The result has been a reduction in the independent powers of the member states, and the development of a European identity that rests alongside the national identities of the member states. This is not a federal United States of Europe, and there is no European citizenship that replaces that of the member states, but its powers and reach have gone beyond those of any other regional body.

The expanding capacity of the EU has not been universally welcomed, and resistance to European integration has grown since the early 1990s as the ties among EU states have intensified, leading to charges that the EU is an elitist construct that threatens the traditional responsibilities of its member states. It must also be said that the powers and reach of the EU are often exaggerated. In spite of the emerging difficulties with the European model, the idea of regional integration resonates in most other parts of the world, but with a greater focus on economic rather than political objectives.

Regional integration: The process by which states build economic and political ties that result in some pooling of authority over areas of policy where they believe that cooperation is better than competition.

To the work of IGOs must be added the work and influence of non-governmental organizations (NGOs). Many of these are a form of international interest group which put pressure on government for policy change in specific areas, or carry out functions that might otherwise be the responsibility of governments; examples include Amnesty International, Doctors Without Borders, Friends of the Earth, and Oxfam. Finally, we should not ignore the global influence of multinational corporations such as Walmart, Royal Dutch Shell, Toyota, or ING. Some are sufficiently powerful as to influence policy in all countries where they do or might operate. Furthermore, the rise of multinationals from China such as Huawei and Lenovo reminds us of the growing global impact of that country, as well as the changes taking place in its economic policies.

Finally, in the face of the threat of international terrorism, many states have found themselves reasserting their power over their citizens, giving themselves broadened powers to impinge upon personal privacy and to limit the movement and the choices of those who live and travel within their borders. Monitoring by closed-circuit television, and of telephones and internet use, has offered new tools for the state to track its population, including ordinary citizens, terrorists, and terrorist suspects. This emergence of what is sometimes called the **security state** has sparked a reaction as citizens have expressed concerns about the development of a surveillance society, threats to civil liberties, and the limited accountability of intelligence services.

Security state: A state that makes efforts to follow the activities of its citizens through such means as closed-circuit television and the monitoring of phone calls and internet use.

In the most serious cases, some states have teetered on the brink of collapse, introducing the phenomenon of the failed, fragile, or **failing state** (a term that

⬡ **FOCUS 2.2** | **Globalization**

One of the most active debates in modern international politics and economics revolves around globalization, or the process by which politics, economics, culture, technology, and the provision of basic services have been integrated across state borders. The effect has been to ensure that states are impacted more than ever before by events and developments in other states, and have lost some of their powers to effect change. Politics, economics, and society have never been truly independent, because they have always been impacted to some extent by events elsewhere in the world. In this sense, globalization is not as new as many people seem to think it is (Cohen, 2007). What is different is that at no time in human history has the degree and the geographical reach of integration been as great as it is today, or have the daily lives of all of us been so significantly impacted by decisions taken in other countries and on other continents.

Globalization has both its critics and supporters (see Held and McGrew, 2007 and Bhagwati, 2007), who debate its impact on issues as varied as trade, democracy, national sovereignty, jobs, the state of the environment, culture, and working conditions. Supporters argue that it has helped promote democracy and free markets by exerting pressure on authoritarian governments, that it has reduced poverty and helped promote economic and social equality, and that it has contributed to increases in life expectancy and has helped promote technological innovation (see, for example, Goklany, 2007). Critics charge that poorer countries have suffered even further from economic competition and exploitation, that corporate interests in rich countries have profited, that income inequality has grown, that jobs have been lost in rich countries, and that the environment has suffered.

Whatever the pros and cons, emerging economies have been at the core of the changes brought by globalization. They have seen new investment, job growth, and new opportunities offered by expanded trade, even if their working and environmental conditions have not improved to the same extent. For the supporters of globalization, its disadvantages have not been unexpected, nor are they expected to be long-lasting, and parallels are drawn between the effects of rapid economic growth in today's emerging economies and those seen in the United States, Europe, and Japan when they went through their industrial revolutions. Note: see Chapter 6 for more on this theme.

overlaps with the post-colonial quasi-state considered earlier). The dimensions of state fragility are identified by Robert Rotburg (2004: 5–10)

- Authorities have difficulty keeping control and usually face insurgencies or armed revolts, which often impact large swathes of national territory, and in the worst cases become full-blown civil wars. Driven by ethnic or other inter-communal hostility, 'regimes prey on their own constituents', with rulers oppressing, extorting, and harassing their people.
- Criminal violence worsens as state authority weakens. Gangs take over the streets, arms and drug trafficking spread, the police forces lose control, and people turn to warlords and other strong figures for protection. The warlords then become the suppliers of political goods in place of the official authorities.

- Political institutions are ineffective, with all but the executive losing control or ceasing to function altogether, the court system weakening, the bureaucracy losing its sense of professional responsibility, democratic debate all but disappearing, and the military remaining as the only institution with any integrity.

Failing state: A state with weak governing institutions, often deep internal divisions, and where the basic needs of people are no longer met. Examples include Eritrea, Haiti, Somalia, Syria, and Yemen.

Estimates of the number of failing or failed states in the world vary – depending on how they are defined – from about 20 to about 60. One useful point of reference is the Failed States Index produced annually by the Fund for Peace, a Washington DC-based research body which uses a series of political, economic, and social measures to rate almost every country in the world. In its 2014 index it described most democracies as being either sustainable or very stable (Finland alone earned the label 'Very Sustainable'), it issued a warning for Brazil, high warnings for China, India, Indonesia, Mexico, and Russia, and it issued alerts for 34 mainly African and Middle Eastern states, including Egypt, Somalia, Zimbabwe, Iraq, Pakistan, and Haiti (see also discussion in Collier, 2007).

After reaching their 'commanding heights' between 1945 and 1975, argues van Creveld (1999), states have gone into decline, either forming themselves into larger communities or falling apart altogether, many of their functions being taken over by non-state actors. Strange (1996) argues that the state has become just one source of authority among several, and that the forces of world markets 'are now more powerful than the states to whom ultimate political authority over society and economy is supposed to belong'. In the opinion of former US Secretary of State Strobe Talbot (1992: 70), all states are 'social arrangements' that in spite of their seeming permanence and sacredness are in fact 'artificial and temporary'. Within the next hundred years, he suggests, states will be obsolete and we will instead 'recognize a single, global authority', giving the phrase 'citizen of the world' a new meaning.

But the future of the state may not be that uncertain or unclear. States will continue to be needed to fight international terrorism, to prepare their citizens with the education and skills needed to address global economic pressures, and to provide the driving force needed to respond to shared global problems such as disease and environmental degradation. Rather than declining, states may instead be undergoing a process of reform as they respond to the impact of globalization and the changes in political institutions and processes discussed later in this book.

DISCUSSION QUESTIONS

- How does the state make itself felt in our lives, and how do we know?

- Where does sovereignty begin and end?

- How does the life of a citizen differ from that of a legal resident of a state?

- What is the relationship between war and the state?

- How do the interests of the state differ from those of a nation?

- Is the reach of the state expanding, contracting, staying about the same, or merely being reformed?

KEY CONCEPTS

Citizen
De facto states
Diaspora
Failing state
Globalization
Intergovernmental organization
Microstates
Multinational state
Nation
Nationalism
Nation–state

Natural rights
Quasi-states
Regional integration
Security state
Self-determination
Sovereignty
State
Total war
Welfare state
Westphalian system

FURTHER READING

Chesterman, Simon, Michael Ignatieff, and Ramesh Thakur (eds) (2005) *Making States Work: State Failure and the Crisis of Governance.* An analysis not just of state failure, but also of how states can be rebuilt before they fail.

Creveld, Martin van (1999) *The Rise and Decline of the State.* A wide-ranging history of the state that also provides insight into its more recent challenges.

Jackson, Robert (2007) *Sovereignty: The Evolution of an Idea.* An accessible and concise introduction to the history and meaning of sovereignty.

Opello, Walter C. and Stephen J. Rosow (2004) *The Nation-State and Global Order: A Historical Introduction to Contemporary Politics*, 2nd edn. A wide-ranging introduction to the history of the state.

Smith, Anthony D. (2010) *Nationalism*, 2nd edn. Provides a succinct and scholarly overview of nationalism, examining conceptions, theories, histories, and prospects.

Sørensen, Georg (2004) *The Transformation of the State: Beyond the Myth of Retreat.* With exceptional clarity, this book locates the contemporary state in its international setting.

CHAPTER

3 Democratic rule

PREVIEW

Democracy is both one of the easiest and one of the most difficult of concepts to understand. It is easy because democracies are abundant and familiar, and most of the readers of this book will probably live in one, while others will live in countries that aspire to become democracies. Democracy is also one of the most closely studied of all political concepts, the ease of that study made stronger by the openness of democracies and the availability of information regarding how they work. But our understanding of democracy is made more difficult by the extent to which the concept is misunderstood and misused, by the numerous and highly nuanced interpretations of what democracy means in practice, and by the many claims that are made for democracy that do not stand up to closer examination.

This chapter begins with a review of the key features of democracy, beginning with the Athenian idea of direct democracy (an important historical concept which has regained significance with the recent rise of e-democracy and social media), before assessing and comparing the features of representative and liberal democracy. It then looks at the links between democracy and modernization, and reviews the emergence of democracy in the three waves described by Samuel Huntington, adding speculation about the possibility of a fourth wave (but noting, also, the many problems that democracies face). It ends with a discussion about the dynamics of the transition from authoritarianism to democracy, examining the different stages in the process of democratization.

CONTENTS

- Democratic rule: an overview
- Direct democracy
- Representative democracy
- Liberal democracy
- Democracy and modernization
- Waves of democracy
- Democratization

KEY ARGUMENTS

- About half the people in the world today live under democratic rule, even though there is still no universally agreed definition of democracy. Democracy is an ideal, not just a system of government.

- Studying Athenian direct democracy offers a standard of self-rule against which today's representative (indirect) democracies are often judged.

- Representative democracy limits the people to electing a government, while liberal democracy goes a stage further by placing limits on government and protecting the rights of citizens.

- The impact of modernization (notably, economic development) on democracy raises the question of whether liberal democracy is a sensible short-term goal for low-income countries lacking democratic requisites.

- Democracies emerged in three main waves that resulted in most people in the world living under democratic government, but democracies continue to face many problems, not least of which is a worrying decline in levels of trust in government.

- A more recent approach to democracy, stimulated by recent transitions from authoritarian rule, is to study how the old order collapses and the transition takes place.

Democratic rule: an overview

About half the people in the world today live under democratic rule (see Focus 3.1). This hopeful development reflects the dramatic changes that have taken place in the world's political landscape since the final quarter of the twentieth century. In the space of just over a generation, the number of democracies has more than doubled, and democratic ideas have expanded beyond their core of Western Europe and its former settler colonies to embrace Southern Europe, Eastern Europe, Latin America, and more of Asia and Africa. For Mandelbaum (2007: xi), the changes have 'a strong claim to being the single most important development in a century hardly lacking in momentous events and trends'.

This is ironic, given that there is no fixed and agreed definition of **democracy**. At a minimum, it requires representative government, free elections, freedom of speech, the protection of individual rights, and government by 'the people'. But the precise meaning of these phenomena remains open to debate, and many democracies continue to witness elitism, limits on representation, barriers to equality, and the impingement of the rights of individuals and groups upon one another.

The confusion is reflected in the lack of agreement on how many democracies there are in the world. It is hard to find a government that does not claim to be democratic, because to do otherwise would be to admit that it was limiting the rights of its citizens. But some states have stronger claims to being democratic than others, and in practical terms we find democracy in its clearest and most stable form in barely three dozen states in North America, Europe, East Asia, and Australasia. But there are many other states that are undergoing a process of **democratization**, where political institutions and processes are developing greater stability, where individual rights are built on firmer foundations, and where the voice of the people is heard more clearly.

Democracy: A political system in which government is based on a fair and open mandate from all qualified citizens of a state.

Democratization: The process by which states build the institutions and processes needed to become stable democracies.

TABLE 3.1: Features of modern democracy

- Representative systems of government based on regular, fair, and competitive elections.
- Well-defined, stable, and predictable political institutions and processes, based on a distribution of powers and a system of political checks and balances.
- A wide variety of institutionalized forms of political participation and representation, including multiple political parties with a variety of platforms.
- Limits on the powers of government, and protection of individual rights and freedoms under the law, sustained by an independent judiciary.
- An active, effective, and protected opposition.
- A diverse and independent media establishment, subject to few political controls and free to share a wide variety of opinions.

The core principle of democracy is self-rule; the word itself comes from the Greek *demokratia,* meaning rule (*kratos*) by the people (*demos*). From this perspective, democracy refers not to the election of rulers by the ruled but to the denial of any separation between the two. The model democracy is a form of self-government in which all adult citizens participate in shaping collective decisions in an atmosphere of equality and deliberation, and in which state and society become one. But this is no more than an ideal, rarely found in practice except at the local level in decentralized systems of government.

In trying to understand democracy, we should avoid the comforting assumption that it is self-evidently the best system of rule. It certainly has many advantages over dictatorship, and it can bring stability to historically divided societies provided the groups involved agree to share power through elections. But it has many imperfections, as British political leader Winston Churchill once famously acknowledged when he argued that democracy was the worst form of government, except for all the others. In coming to grips with the concept, we can distinguish among three different strands: direct democracy, representative democracy, and liberal democracy.

Direct democracy

The purest form of democracy is the type of **direct democracy** that was exemplified in the government of Athens in the fifth century BCE, and which continues to shape our assessments of modern liberal democracy. The Athenians believed that citizens were the primary agent for reaching collective decisions, and that direct

FOCUS 3.1 | How many democracies are there?

Although the precise definition of a democracy is contested, it is generally agreed that their number has more than doubled since the 1980s, thanks mainly to two developments. First, the end of the Cold War freed several Eastern European states from the centralized political and economic control of the Soviet Union. Second, an expansion of the membership of the European Union (EU) helped build on and strengthen the democratic and capitalist credentials of those Eastern European states that are now EU members, or would like to be members.

The Centre for Systemic Peace is a US-based research body that undertakes research on political violence. Its Polity IV project has gathered data for political systems dating back to 1800, the results for political change since 1945 showing how the number of democracies has grown since the end of the Cold War while the number of authoritarian regimes (specifically, autocracies) has fallen in tandem.

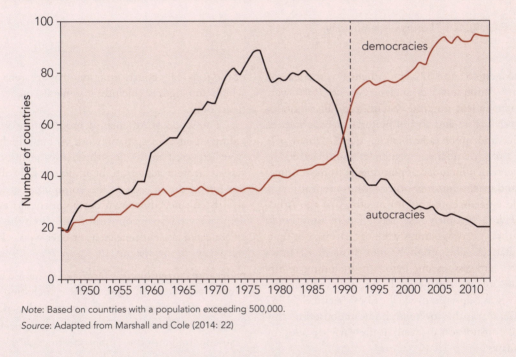

Note: Based on countries with a population exceeding 500,000.

Source: Adapted from Marshall and Cole (2014: 22)

And yet there is no universal agreement on how many democracies exist today, mainly because every assessment brings different standards to bear. Consider the following totals from the most recent editions of the three respective reports:

79	Economist Democracy Index 2014 (25 full democracies, 54 flawed democracies)
95	Centre for Systemic Peace
122	Freedom House 2015 (but only 88 are classified as Free)

popular involvement and open deliberation were educational in character, yielding confident, informed and committed citizens who were sensitive both to the public good and to the range of interests and opinions found even in small communities.

Direct democracy: A system of government in which all members of the community take part in making the decisions that affect that community.

Form   Qualities

| Direct democracy | The citizens themselves debate and reach decisions on matters of common interest. |

| Representative democracy | Citizens elect a legislature and, in presidential systems, a chief executive. Representatives are held to account at elections. |

| Liberal democracy | A form of indirect democracy in which the scope of democracy is limited by constitutional protection of individual rights, including freedom of assembly, property, religion, and speech. Free, fair, and regular elections are based on near universal suffrage. |

FIGURE 3.1: Forms of democracy

Between 461 and 322 BCE, Athens was the leading *polis* (city-community) in ancient Greece. *Poleis* were small independent political systems, typically containing an urban core and a rural hinterland. Especially in its earlier and more radical phase, the Athenian *polis* operated on democratic principles summarized by Aristotle, which included appointments to most offices by lot, and brief tenures in office with no repeat terms. All male citizens could attend meetings of the Athenian *Ekklesia* (People's Assembly), where they could address their peers; meetings were of citizens, not their representatives. The assembly met around 40 times a year to settle issues put before it, including recurring issues of war and peace. In Aristotle's phrase, the assembly was 'supreme over all causes' (Aristotle 1962 edn: 237); it was the sovereign body, unconstrained by a formal constitution or even, in the early decades, by written laws.

Administrative functions were the responsibility of an executive council consisting of 500 citizens aged over 30, chosen by lot for a one-year period. Through the rotation of members drawn from the citizen body, the council was regarded as exemplifying community democracy: 'all to rule over each and each in his turn over all'. Hansen (1999: 249) suggests that about one in three citizens could expect to serve on the council at some stage, an astonishing feat of self-government that has no counterpart in modern democracies. Meanwhile, juries of several hundred people – again, selected randomly from a panel of volunteers – decided the lawsuits which citizens frequently brought against those considered to have acted against the true interests of the *polis*. The courts functioned as an arena through which top figures (including generals) were brought to account.

The scope of Athenian democracy was wide, providing an enveloping framework within which citizens were expected to develop their true qualities. Politics was an amateur activity, to be undertaken by all citizens not just in the interest of the community at large, but also to enhance their own development. To engage in democracy was to become informed about the *polis*, and an educated citizenry meant a stronger whole. But there were flaws in the system:

- Because citizenship was restricted to men whose parents were citizens, most adults – including women, slaves, and foreign residents – were excluded.
- Turnout was a problem, with most citizens being absent from most assembly meetings even after the introduction of an attendance payment.
- The system was time-consuming, expensive, and over-complex, especially for such a small society.
- The principle of self-government did not always lead to decisive and coherent policy. Indeed, the lack of a permanent bureaucracy eventually contributed to a period of ineffective governance, leading to the fall of the Athenian republic after defeat in war.

Perhaps Athenian democracy was a dead end, in that it could only function on an intimate scale which limited its potential for expansion and, worse, increased its vulnerability to larger predators. Yet, the Athenian democratic experiment prospered for more than a century. It provided a settled formula for rule and enabled Athens to build a leading position in the complex politics of the Greek world. Athens proves that direct democracy is, in some conditions, an achievable goal.

Despite this, direct democracy is hard to find in modern political systems. It exists most obviously in the form either of referendums and initiatives (see Chapter 15), or of decision-making at the community level, for example in a village or a school where some decisions might be made without recourse to formal law or elected officials. To go any further, some would argue, would be to run the dangers inherent in the lack of interest and knowledge that many people display in relation to politics, and this would undermine effective governance. But create a more participatory social environment, respond its supporters, and people will be up to – and up for – the task of self-government. Society will have schooled them in, and trained them for, democratic politics, given that 'individuals learn to participate by participating' (Pateman, 2012: 15).

There has been some recent talk of the possibilities of electronic direct democracy, or **e-democracy**, through which those with an opinion about an issue can express themselves using the internet, via blogs, surveys, responses to news stories, or comments in social media. These are channels that are sometimes seen as a useful remedy to charges that representative government has become elitist, and while little research has yet been done on the political effects of social media, there are several early indications of its possibilities: it provides for the instant availability of more political information, it allows political leaders to communicate more often and more directly with voters (helping change the way that electoral campaigns are run), and it has been credited with helping encourage people to turn out in support of political demonstrations of the kind that led to the overthrow of the Egyptian government in 2011 and the fall of the Ukrainian government in 2014.

> **E-democracy:** A form of democratic expression through which all those with an interest in a problem or an issue can express themselves via the internet or social media.

But there are several problems with e-democracy:

- The opinions expressed online are not methodically collected and assessed as they would be in a true direct democracy; the voices that are heard tend to be those that are recorded most often, and there is often

a bandwagon effect reflected – for example – in the phenomenon of trending hashtags on Twitter.

- Many of those who express themselves via social media are either partisan or deliberately provocative, as reflected in the often inflammatory postings of anonymous internet 'trolls'. The result is to skew the direction taken by debates.

- It has led to heightened concerns about privacy, perhaps feeding into the kind of mistrust of government that has led to reduced support for conventional forms of participation (see Chapter 13).

- E-democracy relies upon having access to the internet, which is a problem in poor countries, and even, sometimes, in poorer regions of wealthy countries.

- As with other media the internet can be manipulated by authoritarian regimes, resulting in the provision of selective information and interpretation.

More broadly, the internet has provided so many sources of information that consumers can quickly become overwhelmed, advancing the phenomenon of the **echo chamber**; whatever media they use, people will tend to use only those sources of information that fit with their values and preconceived ideas, and will be less likely to seek out a variety of sources. The result: interference with the free marketplace of ideas, the reinforcement of biases and closed minds, and the promotion of myths and a narrow interpretation of events. The internet was once described as an information superhighway, but perhaps it is better regarded as a series of gated information communities.

> **Echo chamber:** The phenomenon by which ideas circulate inside a closed system, and users seek out only those sources of information that confirm or amplify their values.

Representative democracy

In its modern state form, and with barely a nod to ancient tradition, the democratic principle has transmuted from self-government to elected government, resulting in the phenomenon of **representative democracy**, an indirect form of government. To the Greeks, the idea of representation would have seemed preposterous: how can the people be said to govern themselves if a separate class of rulers exists? As late as the eighteenth century, the French philosopher Jean-Jacques Rousseau warned that 'the moment a people gives itself representatives, it

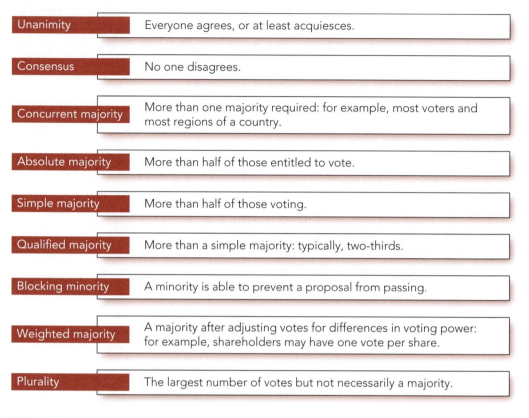

Unanimity	Everyone agrees, or at least acquiesces.
Consensus	No one disagrees.
Concurrent majority	More than one majority required: for example, most voters and most regions of a country.
Absolute majority	More than half of those entitled to vote.
Simple majority	More than half of those voting.
Qualified majority	More than a simple majority: typically, two-thirds.
Blocking minority	A minority is able to prevent a proposal from passing.
Weighted majority	A majority after adjusting votes for differences in voting power: for example, shareholders may have one vote per share.
Plurality	The largest number of votes but not necessarily a majority.

FIGURE 3.2: Degrees of democracy

is no longer free. It ceases to exist' (1762: 145). In interpreting representative government as elected monarchy, the German scholar Robert Michels (1911: 38) argued in a similar vein:

> Under representative government the difference between democracy and monarchy … is altogether insignificant – a difference not in substance but in form. The sovereign people elects, in place of a king, a number of kinglets!

> **Representative democracy:** A system of government in which members of a community elect people to represent their interests and to make decisions affecting the community.

Yet, as large states emerged, so too did the requirement for a new way in which the people could shape collective decisions. Any modern version of democracy had to be compatible with large states and electorates.

One of the first authors to graft representation on to democracy was Thomas Paine, a British-born political activist who experienced both the French and the American revolutions. In his *Rights of Man* (1791/2: 180), Paine wrote:

> The original simple democracy … is incapable of extension, not from its principle, but from the inconvenience of its form. Simple democracy was society governing itself without the aid of secondary means. By ingrafting representation upon democracy, we arrive at a system of government capable of embracing and confederating all the various interests and every extent of territory and population.

Scalability has certainly proved to be the key strength of representative institutions. In ancient Athens, the upper limit for a republic was reckoned to be the number of people who could gather together to hear a speaker. However, modern representative government allows enormous populations (such as 1.25

billion Indians and 320 million Americans) to exert some popular control over their rulers. And there is no upper limit. In theory, the entire world could become one giant system of representation. To adapt Paine's phrase, representative government has proved to be a highly convenient form.

As ever, intellectuals have been on hand to validate this thinning of the democratic ideal. Prominent among them was the Austrian-born political economist Joseph Schumpeter. In *Capitalism, Socialism and Democracy* (1943), Schumpeter conceived of democracy as nothing more than party competition: 'democracy means only that the people have the opportunity of refusing or accepting the men who are to rule them'. Schumpeter wanted to limit the contribution of ordinary voters because he doubted their political capacity:

> The typical citizen drops down to a lower level of mental performance as soon as he enters the political field. He argues and analyzes in a way that he would recognize as infantile within the sphere of his real interests. He becomes a primitive again. (1943: 269)

Reflecting this jaundiced view, Schumpeter argued that elections should not even be construed as a device through which voters elect a representative to carry out their will. Rather, the point of elections is simply to produce a government. From this perspective, the voter becomes a political accessory, restricted to choosing among broad packages of policies and leaders prepared by the parties. Modern democracy is merely a way of deciding which party will decide, a system far removed from the intense, educative discussions in the Athenian assembly:

> The deciding of issues by the electorate [is made] secondary to the election of the men who are to do the deciding. To put it differently, we now take the view that the role of the people is to produce a government. And we define the democratic method as that institutional arrangement for arriving at political decisions in which individuals acquire the power to decide by means of a competitive struggle for the people's vote. (Schumpeter, 1943: 270)

Support for indirect democracy does not require Schumpeter's scepticism about citizen quality. We might just view representation as a valuable division of labour for a specialized world. In other words, a political life is available for those who want it, while those with non-political interests can limit their attention to monitoring

government and voting at elections (Schudson, 1998). In this way, elected rulers remain accountable for their decisions, albeit after the event. To make the point more explicitly: how serious would our commitment to a free society be if we sought to impose extensive political participation on people who would prefer to spend their time on other activities?

But there are many troubling questions regarding how representation works in practice. The standard means for choosing representatives is through elections, but – as we will see in Chapter 15 – there are problems associated with the ways in which elections are structured, and therefore with the ways in which citizens are represented. Votes are not always counted in an equitable fashion or equally weighted; political parties are not always given the same amount of attention by the media; money and special interests often skew the attention paid to competing sets of policy choices; and voter turnout varies by age, gender, education, race, income, and other factors. Questions are also raised about varying and often declining rates of voter turnout, and elections can also be manipulated in numerous ways, including complex or inconvenient registration procedures, the intimidation of voters, the poor organization of polling stations, and the miscounting of ballots.

Furthermore, as we will see in Chapter 8, there are questions about the manner in which elected officials actually represent the needs and opinions of voters. Should they act as the mouthpieces of voters (assuming they can establish what the voters want), should they use their best judgement regarding what is in the best interests of society, or should they follow the lead and guidance of their political parties? And how should they guard against being influenced excessively by interest groups, big business, social movements, or the voices of those with the means to make themselves heard most loudly?

Liberal democracy

Contemporary democracies are typically labelled **liberal democracies**. The addition of the adjective *liberal* implies embracing the notion of an elected representative government while adding a concern with **limited government**. Reflecting Locke's notion of natural rights (see Chapter 2), the goal is to secure individual liberty, including freedom from unwarranted demands by the state. **Liberalism** seeks to ensure that even a representative government bows to the fundamental principle expressed by the English philosopher John Stuart Mill in *On Liberty* (1859: 68): 'the only purpose for which power can be rightfully exercised over any member of a civilized community, against his will, is to prevent harm to others'. By constraining the authority of the governing parties, the population can be defended against its rulers. At the same time, minorities can be protected from another of democracy's inherent dangers: tyranny by the majority. Another way of describing liberal democracy is majority rule with minority rights.

> **Liberal democracy:** A form of indirect democracy in which the scope of democracy is limited by constitutional protection of individual rights.

> **Limited government:** Placing limits on the powers and reach of government so as to entrench the rights of citizens.

> **Liberalism:** A belief in the supreme value of the individual, who is seen to have natural rights that exist independently of government, and who must therefore be protected from too much government.

So, in place of the boisterous debates and all-encompassing scope of the Athenian *polis*, liberal democracies offer governance by law, rather than by people. Under the principle of the rule of law (see Chapter 7), elected rulers and citizens alike are subject to constitutions that usually include a statement of individual rights. Should the government become overbearing, citizens can use domestic and international courts to uphold their rights. This law-governed character of liberal democracy is the basis for Zakaria's claim (2003: 27) that 'the Western model is best symbolized not by the mass plebiscite but by the impartial judge'.

Of course, all democracies must allow space for political opinion to form and to be expressed through political parties. As Beetham (2004: 65) rightly states, 'without liberty, there can be no democracy'. But, in liberal democracy, freedom is more than a device to secure democracy; it is valued above, or certainly alongside, democracy itself. The argument is that people can best develop and express their individuality (and, hence, contribute most effectively to the common good) by taking responsibility for their own lives. By conceiving

of the private sphere as the incubator of human development, we observe a sharp contrast with the Athenian notion that our true qualities can only be promoted through participation in the *polis*.

The protection of **civil liberties** is a key part of the meaning of liberal democracy. This is based on the understanding that there are certain rights and freedoms that citizens must have relative to government and that cannot be infringed by the actions of government. These include the right to liberty, security, privacy, life, equal treatment, and a fair trial, as well as freedom of speech and expression, of assembly and association, and of the press and religion. This is all well and good, but it is not always easy to define what each of these means and where the limitations fall in defining them. Even the most democratic of societies has had difficulty deciding where the rights of one group of citizens ends and those of another begin, and where the actions of government (particularly in regard to national security) restrict those of citizens.

> **Civil liberties:** The rights that citizens have relative to government, and that should not be restricted by government.

Take the question of freedom of speech as an example; democratic societies consider it an essential part of what makes them democratic, and yet there are many ways in which it is limited in practice. There are laws against slander (spoken defamation), libel (defamation through other media), obscenity (an offence against prevalent morality), sedition (proposing insurrection against the established order), and hate speech (attacking a person or group on the basis of their attributes). But defining what can be considered legitimate free speech, and where such speech begins to impinge upon the rights and sensibilities of others, is not easy. Should Western society – for example – respect the fact that showing the prophet Muhammad in the form of images is offensive to Muslims, or should Muslims acknowledge that many in the West consider such a limitation an infringement on their freedom of speech?

The concept of a flawed democracy contained within the Democracy Index is particularly interesting in what it suggests about the limits on rights and liberties. For example, India is often described as the world's biggest democracy, and yet it is classified in the index as flawed. At least part of the problem stems from the generalized phenomenon of **structural violence**. Originating in neo-Marxism, this term is used to describe

> **FOCUS 3.2 | Full democracies vs. flawed democracies**
>
> *The Economist*'s Democracy Index makes a distinction between what it calls full democracies and flawed democracies. The former group (consisting of 25 countries in the 2014 index) is characterized by the efficient functioning of government with an effective system of checks and balances, respect for basic political freedoms and liberties, a political culture that is conducive to the flourishing of democracy, a variety of independent media, and an independent judiciary whose decisions are enforced. For their part, flawed democracies (of which there were 54 in the 2014 index) enjoy most of these features but experience weaknesses such as problems in governance, an underdeveloped political culture, and low levels of political participation. Examples of the two types include the following:
>
> | Full democracies | Flawed democracies |
> | --- | --- |
> | Australia | Brazil |
> | Canada | Chile |
> | Germany | France |
> | Japan | Ghana |
> | Netherlands | Greece |
> | Norway | India |
> | South Korea | Indonesia |
> | Sweden | Italy |
> | United Kingdom | Mexico |
> | United States | South Africa |

intangible forms of oppression, or the 'violence' concealed within a social and political system. Hence the oppression of women is a form of structural violence perpetrated by male-dominated political systems, and extreme poverty is a form of violence perpetrated by one part of society on another. In India, structural violence can be found in the effects of poverty and caste oppression. These deep-rooted inequalities carry over to the political sphere, and impact on the way Indians relate to their political system.

> **Structural violence:** A term used to describe the social economic and political oppression built into many societies.

Some democracies emphasize the *liberal* in liberal democracy more than others, and here we can contrast the United States and the United Kingdom. In the US, the liberal component is entrenched by design. The founding fathers wanted, above all, to forestall a dictatorship of any kind, including tyranny by the majority. To prevent any government – and, especially, elected ones – from acquiring excessive power, the constitution set up an intricate system of **checks and balances**. Authority is distributed not only among federal institutions themselves (the executive, legislative, and judicial branches), but also between the federal government and the 50 states. Power is certainly dispersed; some would say dissolved.

> **Checks and balances:** An arrangement in which government institutions are given powers that counter-balance one another, obliging them to work together in order to govern and make decisions.

Where American democracy diffuses power across institutions, British democracy emphasizes the sovereignty of Parliament. The electoral rules traditionally ensured a secure majority of seats for the leading party, which then forms the government. This ruling party retains control over its own members in the House of Commons, enabling it to ensure the passage of its bills into law. In this way, the hallowed sovereignty of Britain's Parliament is leased to the party in office.

SPOTLIGHT

INDIA

Population (1,267 million)

Gross National Income ($1,877 billion)

Per capita GNI ($1,570)

Democracy Index rating

| Not Rated | Hybrid Regime | Full Democracy |
| | Authoritarian | **Flawed Democracy** |

Freedom House rating

| Not Free | Partly free | **Free** |

Human Development Index rating

| Not Rated | **Medium** | Very High |
| | Low | High |

Brief Profile: Often described as the world's largest democracy, India is also one of the most culturally and demographically varied countries in the world, and has the second biggest population after that of China (with which it is rapidly catching up). After centuries of British imperial control (some direct, some indirect), India became independent in 1947. While it has many political parties, it spent many decades dominated by a single party (Congress), which has recently lost much ground to the Hindu nationalist Bharatiya Janata Party. India has a large military and is a nuclear power, but its economy remains notably staid, with many analysts arguing that its enormous potential is held back by excessive state intervention as well as endemic corruption. It also suffers from religious and cultural divisions that have produced much communal strife, and has had difficulties addressing its widespread poverty.

Form of government ⇨ Federal parliamentary republic consisting of 25 states and seven union territories. State formed 1947, and most recent constitution adopted 1950.

Legislature ⇨ Bicameral Parliament: lower Lok Sabha (House of the People, 545 members) elected for renewable five-year terms, and upper Rajya Sabha (Council of States, 250 members) with most members elected for fixed six-year terms by state legislatures.

Executive ⇨ Parliamentary. The prime minister selects and leads the Council of Ministers (cabinet). The president, indirectly elected for a five-year term, is head of state, formally asks a party leader to form the government, and can take emergency powers.

Judiciary ⇨ Independent Supreme Court consisting of 26 judges appointed by the president following consultation. Judges must retire at age 65.

Electoral system ⇨ Elections to the Lok Sabha are by single-member plurality. The Election Commission of India, established by the constitution, oversees national and state elections.

Parties ⇨ Multi-party, with a recent tradition of coalitions. The two major parties are the Bharatiya Janata Party and the once dominant Congress Party. Regional parties are also important.

Except for the government's sense of self-restraint, the institutions that limit executive power in the United States – including a codified constitution, a separation of powers and federalism – are absent in Britain. Far more than the United States, Britain exemplifies Schumpeter's model of democracy as an electoral competition between organized parties. 'We are the masters now', trumpeted a Labour MP after his party's triumph in 1945. And his party did indeed use its power to institute substantial economic and social reforms.

But even Britain's representative democracy has moved in a more liberal direction. The country's

➡

Democracy in India

India is the great exception to the thesis that stable liberal democracy is restricted to affluent states. In spite of enormous poverty and massive inequality, democracy is well-entrenched in India, begging the question of how it has been able to consolidate liberal democracy when most other poor post-colonial countries initially failed.

Part of the answer lies in India's experience as a British colony. The British approach of indirect rule allowed local elites to occupy positions of authority, where they experienced a style of governance which accepted some dispersal of power and often permitted the expression of specific grievances. The resulting legacy favoured pluralistic, limited government.

More important still was the distinctive manner in which the colonial experience played out in India. Its transition to independence was more gradual, considered, and successful than elsewhere, avoiding a damaging rush to statehood. The Indian National Congress, which led the independence struggle and governed for 30 years after its achievement, was founded in 1885. Over a long period, Congress built an extensive, patronage-based organization which proved capable of governing a disparate country after independence.

In particular, Congress gained experience of elections as participation widened even under colonial rule. By 1946, before independence, 40 million people were entitled to vote in colonial elections, providing the second largest electorate in the non-communist world (Jayal, 2007: 21). These contests functioned as training grounds for democracy.

But perhaps the critical factor in India's democratic success was the pro-democratic values of Congress's elite. Democracy survived in India because that is what its leaders wanted. Practices associated with British democracy – such as parliamentary government, an independent judiciary, and the rule of law – were seen as worthy of emulation. So in India, as elsewhere, the consolidation of liberal democracy was fundamentally an elite project.

The quality of India's democracy is inevitably constrained by inequalities in Indian society. Political citizenship has not guaranteed social and economic security yet such assurance is needed for democracy to deepen. Such limitations contribute to the Democracy Index's rating of India as a flawed democracy. But the openness of the political system at least allows low status groups to express their interests. Jayal (2007: 45) sums up: 'the singular merit of Indian democracy lies in its success in providing a space for political contestation and the opportunity for the articulation of a variety of claims'.

---

judiciary has become more active and independent, stimulated in part by the influence of the European Court of Justice. Privatization has reduced the state's direct control over the economy. Also, the electoral system is now less likely to deliver a substantial majority for a single party. But, from a comparative perspective, a winning party (or even coalition) in Britain is still rewarded with an exceptionally free hand. The contrast with the United States remains.

To conclude this section, we need to clarify the relationship between representative democracy and liberal democracy. In truth, the terms cover the same group of states and the qualifier used is largely a matter of preference. Still, the changing popularity of the two phrases does tell a story about how democracy is implicitly conceived:

- Representative democracy (or government) is the older phrase, emerging at a time when indirect democracy was establishing itself as a practical alternative to direct democracy. The phrase does not imply limits on elected authority, other than those needed for free and fair elections, and in the twentieth century tended to find particular favour with those supporting a strong role for party-based governments, such as socialists supporting public ownership of industry.

- Liberal democracy is the more recent term, acquiring greater currency in the second half of the twentieth century and continuing to grow in popularity today. In the name of individual liberty, it directs attention to the constitutional constraints on elected governments and places limits on the decision-making scope of representatives. So liberal democracy is a more natural phrase for those who favour a market economy with its limitations on the scope of government.

Democracy and modernization

Why are some countries democratic and others not? What, in other words, are the economic and social requisites of sustainable democracy? A frequent answer is that liberal democracy flourishes in **modern** conditions: in high-income industrial or post-industrial states with an educated population. By contrast, middle-income states are more likely to be flawed democracies, and low-income countries will tend to be authoritarian.

> **Modern:** A term used to characterize a state with an industrial or post-industrial economy, affluence, specialized occupations, social mobility, and an urban and educated population.

Linking modernity and democracy carries important policy implications. It suggests that advocates of democracy should give priority to economic development in authoritarian states such as China, allowing political reform to emerge naturally at a later date. First get rich, then get a democracy, runs the logic. Russia tried it the other way around, and found that democracy did not take root as hoped, and that wealth drifted into the hands of the few rather than the many. But if we accept this advice, controversial policy implications will arise. Should we really follow Apter (1965) in applying the notion of 'premature democratization' to low-income countries? Do we want to encourage modernizing dictatorships? And if not, why not?

The political sociologist Seymour Martin Lipset (1959) provided the classic statement of the impact of **modernization**, suggesting that 'the more well-to-do a [country], the greater the chances that it will sustain democracy'. Using data from the late 1950s, Lipset found strong correlations between affluence, industrialization, urbanization and education, on the one hand, and democracy, on the other. Much later, Diamond (1992: 110) commented that the relationship between affluence and democracy remained 'one of the most powerful and stable … in the study of national development'. In an analysis of all democracies existing between 1789 and 2001, Svolik (2008: 166) concluded that 'democracies with low levels of economic development … are less likely to consolidate'. Boix (2011) agrees, with the qualification that the effect of affluence on democracy declines once societies have achieved developed status.

> **Modernization:** The process of acquiring the attributes of a modern society, or one reflecting contemporary ideas, institutions, and norms.

Inevitably, there continue to be exceptions to the rule, both apparent and real. The record of the oil-rich kingdoms of the Middle East suggests that affluence, and even mass affluence, is no guarantee of democracy. But these seeming counter-examples show only that modernity consists of more than income per head; authoritarian monarchs in the Middle East rule societies that may be wealthy, but are also highly traditional. A more important exception is India, a lower-middle-income country with a consolidated, if distinctive, democracy (see Spotlight).

So, why does liberal democracy seem to be the natural way of governing modern societies? Lipset (1959) proposed several possible answers:

- Wealth softens the class struggle, producing a more equal distribution of income and turning the working class away from 'leftist extremism', while the presence of a large middle class tempers class conflict between rich and poor.
- Economic security raises the quality of governance by reducing incentives for corruption.
- High-income countries have more interest groups to reinforce liberal democracy.
- Education and urbanization also make a difference. Education inculcates democratic and tolerant values, while towns have always been the wellspring of democracy.

Lipset's list, like the relationship between modernity and democracy itself, has stood the test of time. However, recent contributions offer a more systematic treatment (Boix, 2003). Vanhanen (1997: 24), for instance, suggests that a relatively equal distribution of power resources in modern societies prevents a minority from becoming politically dominant:

> When the level of economic development rises, various economic resources usually become more widely distributed and the number of economic interest groups increases. Thus the underlying factor behind the positive correlation between the level of economic development and democracy is the distribution of power resources.

Modernity has been an effective incubator of liberal democracy, but we should be careful about projecting this relationship forward. Today's world contains many more liberal democracies than it did when Lipset was writing in the 1950s, suggesting that democracy can consolidate at lower, pre-modern levels of development. That threshold may continue to decrease, delivering a world that is wholly democratic before it becomes wholly modern. Alternatively, a few authoritarian regimes, such as China, may succeed in creating modern societies without becoming democracies.

Waves of democracy

When did modern democracies emerge? As with the phases of decolonization discussed in Chapter 2, so today's democracies emerged – argues political scientist Samuel Huntington (1991) – in a series of distinct **waves of democratization** (see Figure 3.3). And just as each period of decolonization deposited a particular type of state on the political shore, so too did each democratic wave differ in the character of the resulting democracies. Not everyone agrees with Huntington's analysis (see Munck, 1994, for example, and Doorenspleet, 2000, who argues that Huntington's distinction between democracies and authoritarian regimes was too vague), but it is an interesting point of departure.

> **Waves of democratization:** A group of transitions from non-democratic to democratic regimes that occurs within a specified period of time and that significantly outnumbers transitions in the opposite direction during that period.

First wave

The earliest representative democracies emerged during the longest of these waves, between 1828 and 1926. During this first period, nearly 30 countries established at least minimally democratic national institutions, including Argentina, Australia, Britain, Canada, France, Germany, the Netherlands, New Zealand, the Scandinavian countries, and the United States. However, some backsliding occurred as fledgling democracies were overthrown by fascist, communist or military dictatorships during what Huntington describes as the 'first reverse wave' from 1922 to 1942.

A distinctive feature of many first-wave transitions was their slow and sequential character. Political competition, traditionally operating within a privileged elite, gradually broadened as the right to vote extended to the wider population. Unhurried transitions lowered the political temperature; in the first wave, democracy was as much outcome as intention. In Britain, for example, the expansion of the vote occurred gradually (see Figure 3.4), with each step easing the fears of the propertied classes about the dangers of further reform.

In the United States, the idea that citizens could only be represented fairly by those of their own sort gained ground against the founders' view that the republic should be led by a leisured, landed gentry. Within 50 years of independence, nearly all white men had the vote (Wood, 1993: 101), but women were not given the vote on the same terms as men until 1919, and the franchise for black Americans was not fully realized until

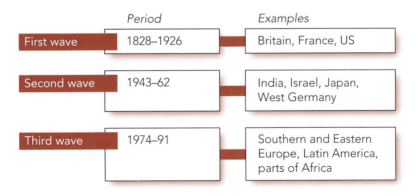

FIGURE 3.3: Huntington's waves of democratization

Note: The first wave partly reversed between 1922 and 1942 (e.g. in Germany and Italy) and the second wave between 1958 and 1975 (e.g. in much of Latin America and post-colonial Africa). Many such reversals have now themselves reversed.

Source: Huntington (1991)

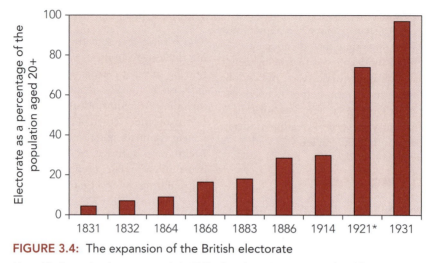

FIGURE 3.4: The expansion of the British electorate

Notes: The last major change was made in 1969, when the voting age was reduced from 21 to 18.
* In 1918, the vote was extended to women over 30.
Source: Adapted from Dahl (1998: figure 2)

the Voting Rights Act of 1965. In that sense, America's democratic transition was also a prolonged affair.

Second wave

Huntington's second wave of democratization began during the Second World War and continued until the 1960s. As with the first wave, some of the new democracies created at this time did not consolidate; for example, elected rulers in several Latin American states were quickly overthrown by military coups. But established democracies did emerge after 1945 from the ashes of defeated dictatorships, not just in West Germany, but also in Austria, Japan, and Italy. These post-war democracies were introduced by the victorious allies, supported by local partners. The second-wave democracies established firm roots, helped by an economic recovery which was nourished by US aid. During this second wave, democracy also consolidated in the new state of Israel and the former British dominion of India.

Political parties played a key role in the transition. First-generation democracies had emerged when parties were seen as a source of faction, rather than progress. But by the time of the second wave, parties had emerged as the leading instrument of democracy in a mass electorate. As in many more recent constitutions, Germany's Basic Law (1949) went so far as to codify

their role: 'political parties shall take part in forming the democratic will of the people'. In several cases, though, effective competition was reduced by the emergence of a single party which dominated government for a generation or more: Congress in India, the Christian Democrats in Italy, the Liberal Democrats in Japan, and Labour in Israel. Many second-wave democracies took a generation to mature into fully competitive party systems.

Third wave

This was a product of the final quarter of the twentieth century. Its main and highly diverse elements were:

- The ending of right-wing dictatorships in Greece, Portugal, and Spain in the 1970s.
- The retreat of the generals in much of Latin America in the 1980s.
- The collapse of communism in the Soviet Union and Eastern Europe at the end of the 1980s.

The third wave transformed the global political landscape, providing an inhospitable environment for those non-democratic regimes that survive. Even in sub-Saharan Africa, presidents subjected themselves to re-election (though rarely to defeat). With the end of the Cold War and the collapse of any realistic alternative to democracy, the European Union and the United

States also became more encouraging of democratic transitions while still, of course, keeping a close eye on their own shorter-term interests.

Fourth wave, or a stalling of democracy?

While Huntington stopped with three waves, it is worth extending the logic of his arguments and looking in more detail at what has happened since 1991. Inspired by the end of the Cold War and the speed of the democratic transition in Eastern Europe, the political economist Francis Fukuyama was moved in 1989 to borrow from Hegel, Marx and others in declaring the **end of history**, or the final triumph of democracy:

> What we may be witnessing is not just the end of the Cold War, or the passing of a particular period of post-war history, but the end of history … That is, the end point of mankind's ideological evolution and the universalization of Western liberal democracy as the final form of human government. (Fukuyama, 1989)

End of history: The idea that a political, economic or social system has developed to such an extent that it represents the culmination of the evolutionary process.

An attractive thought, to be sure, if we think of liberal democracy in its ideal form. But it was soon clear that Fukuyama had spoken too soon, and many of today's political conversations are not about the health or the spread of democracy but about the difficulties it faces even within those states we consider to be firmly liberal democratic. Among the concerns: social disintegration, voter alienation, the tensions between individual rights and democracy, and the manner in which competitive politics and economics can undermine the sense of community. In some cases, such as Brazil, France, India, and South Africa, the problems are sufficiently deep that the Democracy Index classifies them as flawed democracies. The more specific challenges that democracies face include the following:

- Women have less political power and opportunity than men, do not earn as much as men for equal work, and are still prevented from rising to positions of political and corporate power as easily as men.

- Racism and religious intolerance remain critical challenges, with minorities often existing on the margins of society, and denied equal access to jobs, loans, housing, or education.

- There is a large and sometimes growing income gap between the rich and the poor, and levels of unemployment and poverty often remain disturbingly high. With both comes reduced political influence, and sometimes political radicalization.

Opinion polls show declining faith in government and political institutions in many countries, reflecting less a concern with the concept of democracy than with the manner in which democracy is practised. Many see government as being dominated by elites, have less trust in their leaders, feel that government is doing a poor job of dealing with pressing economic and social problems, and – as a result – are voting in smaller numbers and switching to alternative forms of political expression and participation. As we will see in Chapter 12, trust in government has been falling in most liberal democracies.

Despite these concerns, democracy has been stable and lasting, and no country with a sustained history of liberal democracy has ever freely or deliberately opted for an alternative form of government. Neither have any liberal democracies gone to war with one another. The broad goals of the liberal democratic model – including freedom, choice, security, and wealth – are widely shared, and while the practice of liberal democracy is rarely clean or simple, as Churchill implied, the system still provides a uniquely stable and successful formula for achieving these important objectives.

Democratization

One of the most dramatic waves of political change of recent decades was the Arab Spring, a series of mass demonstrations, protests, riots, and civil wars that broke in Tunisia in late 2010, and quickly spread through much of the Arab world. Rulers were forced from power in Egypt, Libya, Tunisia, and Yemen, a civil war erupted in Syria, and there were mass protests or uprisings in Algeria, Bahrain, Jordan, Kuwait, and other countries. It was widely hoped that this remarkable protest wave would bring lasting democratic change to North Africa and the Middle East, where many of the world's surviving authoritarian states are concentrated. However, the momentum of change had largely faded by mid-2012, with the actions of many governments in the region creating new uncertainties. Libya, for example, was in many ways in a more desperate situation by 2015 than it had been before the Arab Spring, with instability and political violence bringing death, destruction, and economic disruption. A critical point confirmed by the experience of the Arab Spring was that a transition *from* an authoritarian regime did not entail an immediate or even medium-term transition *to* liberal democracy: alternative outcomes include the replacement of one authoritarian order with another, or the emergence of a failed state.

For one point there is much supporting evidence: it is extraordinarily hard to impose democracy by force. It was a key part of US foreign policy throughout the Cold War to protect its allies from the threat of communist domination, and a goal since the end of the Cold War to bring peace to the Middle East through the promotion of democracy. But the record has not been a good one. For example, a 2003 Carnegie Endowment study (Pei, 2003) found that of 16 nation-building efforts in which the United States had engaged militarily during the twentieth century, only 4 (Germany, Japan, Grenada, and Panama) were successful in the sense that democracy remained ten years after the departure of US forces. Britain and France have shown no better average returns in their military interventions, and countries neighbouring those in which interventions have occurred have often shown more progress towards democracy than the target countries.

Why is this? De Mesquita and Downs (2004) blame US, British, and French policy, which they argue 'has been motivated less by a desire to establish democracy or reduce human suffering than to alter some aspect of the target state's policy'. Despite official claims,

promoting democracy is rarely the most important goal. The chances of success are increased in cases where a multinational coalition takes action with the backing of the international community (or at least the bulk of the membership of the United Nations), but to assume that authoritarian regimes can be bullied or bombed into democracy is misguided, because democracy needs time to put down roots and to grow organically out of society, particularly in deeply divided states such as Afghanistan or Iraq.

Figure 3.5 offers a model of the stages in the process of successful democratization (O'Donnell *et al.*, 1986). However, this framework was developed in the 1980s out of research on the successful transitions in Southern Europe and Latin America, rather than the more varied outcomes from the later collapse of the Soviet Union, or the more recent experience of the Arab Spring. Even so, the model remains useful in identifying stages in a successful transition.

The first step in the process comes with the liberalization of the authoritarian regime. Much as we would like to believe in the power of public opinion, transitions are rarely initiated by mass demonstrations against a united dictatorship. Rather, democracy is typically the outcome – intended or unintended – of recognition within part of the ruling group that change is inevitable, or even desirable. As O'Donnell and Schmitter (1986: 19) assert:

> There is no transition whose beginning is not the consequence – direct or indirect – of important divisions

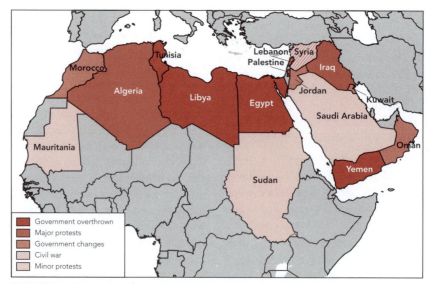

MAP 3.1: The Arab Spring, 2011–

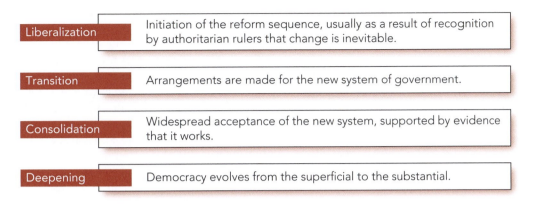

FIGURE 3.5: Stages of democratization

within the authoritarian regime itself, principally along the fluctuating cleavage between hardliners and softliners … In Brazil and Spain, for example, the decision to liberalize was made by high-echelon, dominant personnel in the incumbent regime in the face of weak and disorganized opposition.

So, for example, a military regime might lose a sense of purpose once the crisis that propelled it into office is resolved. In the more liberal environment that emerges, opportunities increase to express public opposition, inducing a dynamic of reform.

In the fraught and often lengthy transition to democracy, arrangements are made for the new system of government. Threats to the transition from hardliners (who may consider a military coup) and radical reformers (who may seek a full-scale revolution, rather than just a change of regime) need to be overcome. Constitutions must be written, institutions designed and elections scheduled. Negotiations frequently take the form of round-table talks between rulers and opposition, often leading to an elite settlement. During the transition, the existing rulers will look for political opportunities in the new democratic order. For example, military rulers may seek to repackage themselves as the only party capable of guaranteeing order and security. In any event, the current elite will seek to protect its future by negotiating privileges, such as exemption from prosecution. The transition is substantially complete with the installation of the new arrangements, most visibly through a high turnout election which is seen as the peak moment of democratic optimism (Morlino, 2012: 85–96).

The consolidation of democracy only occurs when new institutions provide an accepted framework for political competition, or – as Przeworski (1991: 26) puts it – 'when a particular system of institutions becomes the only game in town and when no-one can imagine acting outside the democratic institutions'. It takes time, for example, for the armed forces to accept their more limited role as a professional, rather than a political, body.

While consolidation is a matter of attitudes, its achievement is measured through action and, in particular, by the peaceful transfer of power through elections. The first time a defeated government relinquishes office, democracy's mechanism for elite circulation is shown to be effective, contributing further to political stability. So, consolidation is the process through which democratic practices become habitual – and the habit of democracy, as any other, takes time to form (Linz and Stepan, 1996). Transition establishes a new regime but consolidation secures its continuation.

Finally, the deepening of democracy refers to the continued progress (if any) of a new democracy towards full liberal democracy. This term emerged as academic awareness grew that many third-wave transitions had stalled midway between authoritarianism and democracy, with accompanying popular disenchantment. As we saw earlier, democracy in flawed democracies is 'superficial rather than deep and the new order consolidates at a low level of "democratic quality"' (Morlino, 2012: pt III). So, the point of the term 'deepening' is not so much to describe a universal stage in transitions as to acknowledge that the outcome of a transition, especially in less modern countries, may be a democracy which is both consolidated and superficial.

The political changes witnessed by Mexico since the 1990s offer an example of these four stages at work.

It had been governed without a break since 1929 by the centrist Institutional Revolutionary Party (PRI), which was able to maintain control in part because of its ability to incorporate key sectors of Mexican society, offering them rewards in return for their support. But as Mexicans became better educated, and with PRI unable to blame anyone else for the country's growing economic problems in the 1990s, the pressures for democratic change began to grow.

Presidents had long been chosen as a result of a secretive process through which the incumbent effectively named his own successor, who was sure to win because of PRI's grip on the electoral process. An attempt was made in 1988 to make the nomination process more democratic, a dissident group within PRI demanding greater openness in selecting presidents. When it failed, one of its leaders – Cuauhtémoc Cárdenas – broke away and ran against Carlos Salinas, the anointed PRI candidate. Heading a coalition of parties on the left, Cárdenas was officially awarded 31 per cent of the vote, although most independent estimates suggest that he probably won. Salinas was declared the winner, but with the slimmest margin of any PRI candidate for president (50.7 per cent) and only after a lengthy delay in announcing the results, blamed on a 'breakdown' in the computers counting the votes (Preston and Dillon, 2004, ch. 6).

Salinas's successor in 1994 was Ernesto Zedillo, who ordered a review of the presidential selection process, which resulted in the use of open party primaries. Meanwhile, more opposition political parties were on the rise, changes had been made to the electoral system, more seats were created in Congress, and elections were subject to closer scrutiny by foreign observers. In 1997, PRI lost its majority in the Chamber of Deputies, and in 2000 lost its majority in the Senate and – most remarkable of all – lost the presidency of Mexico to the opposition National Action Party (PAN). PAN won the presidency again in 2006, and PRI won it back in 2012, but the changes of the 1990s – sparked by the realization among PRI's leaders that change was inevitable – have created a healthier democratic system in which three parties compete for power, albeit against a still-troubled background of widespread poverty, a bloody drug war that has been under way since 2006, and ongoing corruption.

Mexico is today listed as a flawed democracy in the Democracy Index, and as Partly Free by Freedom House. As with so many recent transitions, the Mexican case shows the importance of distinguishing between the collapse of an authoritarian system, on the one hand, and the consolidation or deepening of its more democratic successor, on the other.

DISCUSSION QUESTIONS

- Is democracy – in practice – truly government by the people, or have other voices come to be heard more loudly?

- Does the internet allow the recreation of Athenian-style direct democracy in today's states?

- Do you agree with Schumpeter's doubts about the political capacity of ordinary voters? Does your answer affect your judgement of democracy's value?

- What conditions are needed in order for democracy to flourish?

- How close are we to the end of history?

- What can we learn from the evidence that democracy can rarely be spread by force?

KEY CONCEPTS

Checks and balances
Civil liberties
Democracy
Democratization
Direct democracy
Echo chamber
E-democracy
End of history

Liberal democracy
Liberalism
Limited government
Modern
Modernization
Representative democracy
Structural violence
Waves of democratization

FURTHER READING

Alonso, Sonia, John Keane, and Wolfgang Merkel (eds) (2011) *The Future of Representative Democracy*. A wide-ranging collection of essays examining trends in representative democracy.

Dahl, Robert A. (1998) *On Democracy*. An accessible primer on democracy by one of its most influential academic proponents.

Haerpfer, Christian W., Patrick Bernhagen, Ronald F. Inglehart, and Christian Welzel (eds) (2009) *Democratization*. A comprehensive text, covering actors, causes, dimensions, regions and theories.

Held, David (2006) *Models of Democracy*, 3rd edn. A thorough introduction to democracy from classical Greece to the present.

Morlino, Leonardo (2012) *Changes for Democracy: Actors, Structures, Processes*. An extensive review of the academic literature on democratization, including hybrid regimes.

Rosanvallon, Pierre (2008) *Counter-Democracy: Politics in an Age of Distrust*. An original (if abstract) interpretation, viewing democracy as consisting in informal mechanisms through which the public can express confidence in, or mistrust of, its representatives.

4 Authoritarian rule

PREVIEW

Even though democratic ideas have spread to many parts of the world since 1945, and many people now live in democracies, many states remain authoritarian, with strong rulers and limits placed on the ability of citizens to participate in government. As Brooker (2009: 1) puts it, 'non-democratic government, whether by elders, chiefs, monarchs, aristocrats, empires, military regimes or one-party states, has been the norm for most of human history'. Certainly, the twentieth century will be remembered at least as much for the dictatorships it spawned – including Hitler's Germany, Stalin's Russia, Mao's China, and Pol Pot's Cambodia – as for the democratic transitions at its close. And in spite of the spread of democracy, the most prominent authoritarian states remain internationally significant, whether judged by their economic reach (China), as incubators of terrorism (Afghanistan), by their natural resources (Russia), or by their actual or seemingly intended possession of nuclear weapons (Pakistan and Iran).

This chapter follows the lead of the Democracy Index by looking at non-democracies as hybrid and authoritarian regimes. It begins with a survey of those hybrid regimes that give some of the appearances of being democratic, but where institutions are manipulated to keep rulers in power. It goes on to look at authoritarian regimes, breaking them down into several different types: absolute monarchy, ruling presidents, ruling parties, military government, and theocracy. It ends with a review of the particular problem of corruption, which is so much a part of the political landscape in authoritarian systems.

CONTENTS

- Authoritarian rule: an overview

- Hybrid regimes

- Authoritarian regimes

- Forms of authoritarian rule

- The political impact of corruption

KEY ARGUMENTS

- Identifying the dynamics of authoritarian regimes provides a useful contrast to our understanding of democracy, and vice versa.

- The concept of hybrid regimes offers an intermediate position between authoritarianism and democracy.

- The exploitation of the military, the use of patronage, and control of the media are key elements in the maintenance of authoritarian regimes.

- One key to understanding authoritarian regimes is to recognize that few are absolute tyrannies; many of their leaders are in a weaker political position than their liberal democratic equivalents.

- Establishing hard and fast rules for authoritarian regimes, and defining templates, is more difficult than is the case for democracies, partly because their formal structures are weak and partly because they vary in their source of power.

- Although we can find corruption wherever there are people willing to abuse the offices they hold for private gain, it plays a particularly telling role in authoritarian regimes. It is both a cause and effect of the misuse of power.

Authoritarian rule: an overview

We saw in the previous chapter that the meaning of democracy is contested, and that democracies come in different types. In much the same fashion, the meaning of authoritarianism is also contested, and there is no single model of an authoritarian regime. In studying them, we should avoid falling into the trap of associating them too readily with the kind of despotism and rule through fear and surveillance that most easily comes to mind when thinking about non-democracies.

Authoritarian rulers operate within unspoken limits, recognizing the need to strike deals with other power-holders such as business, the military, or regional bosses. Just as democratic leaders need to retain electoral support, so authoritarian rulers must convince their allies to continue supporting the existing regime. Furthermore, government typically takes the form not of a single dominant leader but, rather, of an elite group within which there is considerable internal jockeying for power. Ideology and policy are often absent. Rulers seek to maintain their control (and increase their wealth) by limiting mass participation, rather than by mobilizing the population. Ordinary people are unlikely to experience a knock on the door at midnight as long as they keep away from politics. In such a situation, governance is an uneasy combination of formally unlimited authority and considerable political vulnerability.

Since non-democratic leaders so clearly stand above the law, the constitutional architecture (if any) is a poor guide. Laws are vague and contradictory, creating a pretext for bringing any chosen troublemaker to court. Special courts, such as military tribunals, are often used for sensitive cases. The legislature and the judiciary are under-resourced, unprofessional and ineffective. Civil liberties are poorly respected and the state often requires private organizations to be licensed. The absence of constitutional constraint leads to callous treatment of the powerless, including women, minority groups, non-nationals, and prisoners. With no enforceable legal framework to protect private property rights, authoritarian rule is often associated with economic stagnation. The price of the rulers securing a large slice of the pie is that the pie itself fails to grow, generating more political vulnerability.

In the wake of the dramatic collapse of communism at the end of the 1980s and the Arab Spring of 2011, it is tempting to view any remaining non-democratic

TABLE 4.1: Features of authoritarian rule

- The absence of record on representative government, with elections – where they are held – often accompanied by fraud, manipulation, and violence.
- Weak, immature, or poorly defined political institutions and processes, with power in the hands of leaders and elites, and occasionally the establishment of dictatorships.
- A limited selection of forms of political participation and representation, and no guarantees that the voices of citizens will be heard effectively.
- Relatively few limits on the powers of government, and a mixed record on the protection of individual rights and freedoms under the law, with no independent judiciary.
- An opposition that is constrained, and subject to threats and even violence.
- A limited and controlled media establishment, subject to political controls and free to share only officially sanctioned opinions.

regimes as historical anomalies which will soon be vanquished by the Facebook generation. But we saw in Chapter 3 that such optimism is both sweeping and premature. It fails to recognize that ousting one authoritarian leader may just lead to another – or to a failed state or invasion. The collapse of communism has not brought democracy to Belarus, Kazakhstan, or Uzbekistan, and the long-term prognosis for Egypt, Libya, Tunisia, and Yemen remains questionable. In fact, Way (2011: 17) judges that a comparison with the communist collapse suggests that more Arab autocrats will hang on, 'and that those [Arab] countries which do witness authoritarian collapse will be less likely to democratize than their European counterparts were'.

That there are different shades of authoritarianism is reflected in the distinction made in the Democracy Index between hybrid regimes and authoritarian regimes. The first of these blend democracy and authoritarianism, with some of the indicators of democracy, but substantial weaknesses in the way it is conducted and expressed. Authoritarian regimes, meanwhile, contain all the features that we normally associate with the least democratic systems, such as strong leaders, centralized political control, and limits on popular participation.

Hybrid regimes

The **hybrid regimes** described by the Democracy Index overlap with a category described by Levitsky and Way (2010) as competitive authoritarian regimes. They define these as states in which 'formal democratic institutions are widely viewed as the principal means of obtaining and exercising political authority … [but where] incumbents violate those rules so often and to such an extent … that the regime fails to meet conventional minimum standards for democracy'. In the Democracy Index, hybrid regimes are described as suffering weaknesses both in political culture and in the functioning of government and political participation. Elections are held, but are undermined by irregularities that often prevent them from being both free and fair, and government pressure on opposition parties and candidates can be common. Corruption tends to be widespread, civil society and the rule of law are weak, the judiciary lacks independence, and journalists are typically harassed.

Hybrid regimes: Political systems that have some of the appearances of being democratic, but where institutions, processes, laws, and policies are manipulated to keep rulers or elite groups in power.

In a hybrid regime, leaders or ruling parties are elected, but they use state resources and their influence over the media to determine the outcome of elections long before campaigns begin. Ballot-stuffing is only needed if a defeat is in the offing. Once elected, the government shows only a limited sense of constitutional restraint; such concepts as fair play, a loyal opposition, and individual rights barely register. In this kind of system, notes O'Donnell (1994: 59), whoever wins the election 'is thereby entitled to govern as he or she sees fit, constrained only by the hard facts of existing power relations and by a constitutionally limited term of office'. The result is what Huntington (1991: 306) once described as 'democracy without turnover and competition without alternation'. If liberal democracy 'is a system in which parties lose elections' (Przeworski, 1991: 10), competitive authoritarianism is a system in which they do not. Rather, change at the top usually results from a constitutional limit on tenure, or the occasional resignation.

Singapore offers an example. While it has multiple political parties, a vibrant high-technology economy and one of the world's highest standards of living, it is classified in the Democracy Index as a hybrid regime. This is mainly because the People's Action Party has governed the island state since 1959, routinely winning more than 60 per cent of the vote, maintaining an electoral system that allowed it to win 93 per cent of legislative seats in 2011 with only a 60:14 per cent share of

the vote, and directing investment to districts that vote for the party.

Hybrid regimes are normally founded on a powerful leader or political party, rather than on strong institutions. In return for taking care of the needs of the people, leaders claim their respect, deference, and support. Because the judiciary is under-resourced, it is unable to enforce the individual rights documented in the constitution. The law is used selectively, as a tool of power, so that while political opponents are subject to detailed legal scrutiny, supporters find that the law rarely intrudes on their activities: 'for my friends, everything; for my enemies, the law,' said Getúlio Vargas, twice president of Brazil. The state intervenes in the market, with political connections influencing economic rewards. Yet, in contrast to pure authoritarian regimes, the leader often provides effective governance, thus earning – as well as manipulating – popular support.

The form is particularly common in states that are poor, that suffer deep internal divisions (whether ethnic, religious, or economic), and that face real or constructed external threats. In these circumstances, a national father figure or dominant party can be presented as an engine of development, as a bulwark against domestic disintegration, and as a protector against external threats. The head, it is claimed, must be allowed to rule the body politic.

For most of its post-communist history, Ukraine has offered a representative case. A former republic of the Soviet Union, it became independent in 1991, but remains poor (with a per capita GNI of just under $4,000 in 2013), and finds itself torn between Western and Russian circles of influence. The efforts made by President Leonid Kuchma to control the media, manipulate the political system, side Ukraine with Russian economic interests, and then rig presidential elections sparked the 2004 'Orange Revolution' and new elections. These were won by a pro-Western alliance of political groups which elevated Viktor Yushchenko to the presidency. Democratic reform followed, but the country remained divided between pro-Western and pro-Russian forces, and when Viktor Yanukovych won the 2010 presidential election, he took the country firmly in the Russian direction.

Yanukovych enriched himself and his political supporters, reinforcing his country's status as one of the world's most corrupt. For ordinary people, the need to bribe public officials was a fact of political life, alienating them from their supposedly democratic government. Neither civil society nor the judiciary provided an effective check on power. When Yanukovych's government dropped plans in 2013 to sign a trade agreement with the European Union, mass demonstrations ensued and the government fell. The deposed leader fled to Russia, which then annexed the Crimean peninsula. Fighting broke out in the eastern part of the country, reinforcing historic divisions and threatening the ability of the Ukrainian national government to establish effective governance.

To the extent that hybrid regimes are personal in character, they might be expected to be unstable in the long run. Huntington (1991: 137), for example, claims that 'this half-way house cannot stand'. Similarly, Levitsky and Way (2010: 20) note that such regimes are marked by an 'inherent tension' in which oppositions can develop a serious challenge to the existing power structure. These threats force rulers either to submit (and democratize), or to repress (and revert to cruder authoritarian rule).

Yet, we cannot wish these regimes out of existence by just describing them as transitional. Some (especially those far from Western zones of influence) have provided a stable method of governing poor and unequal societies, particularly since the end of communism rendered blatant dictatorship less defensible. Once set, a hybrid regime can be a strong amalgam, not least in Islamic settings where liberal democracy can be equated with Western permissiveness. Writing on sub-Saharan Africa, Herbst (2001: 359) judges that 'it is wrong to conclude that African states are travelling between democracy and authoritarianism simply because a majority of them belong to neither category. Rather, the current condition of African states could well prevail for decades.' Such thinking led Case (1996: 464) to conclude that hybrid regimes are not 'a mere way station on the road to further democracy'.

Haiti provides a particularly disturbing case of a hybrid state. It has been independent since 1804 but has never been able to settle on a durable and stable political model, and stands out as the most troubled country in the western hemisphere. In theory it is a unitary presidential republic with three branches of government, but in reality it is whatever its incumbent administration is able to fashion from the wreckage of instability, civil unrest and corruption. It does not help that the country has suffered numerous natural disasters, ranging from hurricanes to earthquakes, but a failure to build adequate infrastructure has made it less able to withstand such problems. In 2006, however, the advent of a new government did encourage Freedom House to upgrade Haiti from a ranking of Not Free to Partly Free. But then came the January 2010 earthquake, which killed

an estimated 230,000 people and left government, the economy, infrastructure, and the social fabric in ruins. On the 2014 Human Development Index it ranked 168th out of the 187 countries on the list.

Authoritarian regimes

In this section, we look at states with the features we most readily associate with authoritarianism: strong leaders, centralized political control, and weak records in popular participation, civil liberties, and civil rights. As we will see, however, **authoritarian regimes** come in different forms, ranging from states where power rests with a ruling party or the military to systems revolving around a single individual, with the wielding of power rising and falling with the fortunes of the leader.

> **Authoritarian regimes:** Regimes based on submission to authority, characterized by ruling elites, limited political pluralism, centralized political control, intolerance of opposition, and human rights abuses.

Absolute monarchies apart, the absence of a clear succession procedure is a central weakness of authoritarian regimes, providing much of their political dynamic. Because there are no competitive elections to refresh the leadership, authoritarian leaders may continue in post until well past their sell-by dates, as with the ageing autocrats finally overthrown in the Arab revolts of 2011 (Table 4.2). As those uprisings show, changing the leader in an authoritarian regime is generally a more difficult process than in a democracy. The pattern in China, where since the 1990s the Communist Party has changed its top leaders on a ten-year cycle, is exceptional; it contributes to the party's continued hold on power.

A decline into **despotism** is an inherent danger of authoritarian regimes. In the case of Libya, Muammar Gaddafi came to power in 1969 as the result of a military coup, and claimed that it was his goal to unite the Arab world. He imposed his own ideology on Libya (contained within his Green Book), and exercised total control over his government and the people of Libya. Even Gaddafi did not prove invulnerable. Inspired by the Arab Spring, an uprising against him in 2011 led to a brief civil war that resulted in his brutal death at the hands of rebels. But no agreement on a post-Arab Spring settlement has emerged, resulting in fighting among competing factions. As the example of Gaddafi

FOCUS 4.1 │ Hybrid vs. authoritarian regimes

The Democracy Index makes a distinction between hybrid regimes and authoritarian regimes. The first of these groups (consisting of 39 countries in the 2014 index) has the following features: substantial irregularities that often prevent elections from being free and fair, government pressure on opposition parties and candidates, harassment of journalists, a tendency to widespread corruption, the absence of an independent judiciary, and weaknesses in political culture, the functioning of government, political participation, the rule of law, and civil society.

For their part, authoritarian regimes (of which there were 52 in the 2014 index) suffer from an absence of – or heavy limits upon – political pluralism. Many of these countries are outright dictatorships, any formal institutions of democracy having little substance. Where elections are held they are not free and fair, there is disregard for abuses and infringements of civil liberties, the media are typically state-owned or controlled by groups connected to the ruling regime, and there is repression of criticism of the government and pervasive censorship.

Distinguishing between hybrid regimes and authoritarian regimes can require fine political judgement, and it may be jarring to some to see Egypt listed as a hybrid regime, or to see Nigeria and North Korea contained within the same group of authoritarian regimes. Examples of the two types include the following:

Hybrid regimes	Authoritarian regimes
Egypt	Afghanistan
Haiti	Angola
Iraq	China
Kenya	Cuba
Libya	Iran
Pakistan	Nigeria
Singapore	North Korea
Turkey	Qatar
Ukraine	Russia
Venezuela	Saudi Arabia

shows, authoritarian rulers can be removed by upstarts at any time, meaning that they must devote constant attention to shoring up their position. In this effort, they normally exploit three key control devices: the military, patronage, and the media.

> **Despotism:** The exercise of absolute power, often characterized by the abuse of the powers of office, arbitrary choices, and the use of violent intimidation. It can be used to describe the actions of an individual or a group, and the term is interchangeable with *dictatorship*, *tyranny*, and *autocracy*.

TABLE 4.2: Leaders overthrown in the Arab Spring, 2011

	Leader	Age at which overthrown	Number of years in power
Libya	Muammar Gaddafi	69	42
Egypt	Hosni Mubarak	82	30
Tunisia	Zine El Abidine Ben Ali	74	22
Yemen	Ali Abdullah Saleh	69	22

Note: Before becoming president of Yemen in 1990, Saleh was president of North Yemen for 12 years.

A strong military and security presence, and a willingness by authoritarian leaders to use this resource, is essential. The Arab Spring generally moved further and faster in those countries where the regime lost the support of the organs of violence, or showed an unwillingness to use them – though government repression did not prevent violence in Libya and Syria. High spending on the armed forces, often made possible by revenues from natural resources, is an investment that helps rulers buy off potential opposition, and provides the means for suppressing domestic dissent. Even when the military does not itself rule, it still provides a key support base for the political executive. Lavish treatment of the armed forces is therefore inevitable, producing a drag on economic performance. Authoritarian regimes lack the separation of military and political spheres which characterizes liberal democracy.

The second device is an unofficial **patronage** network in which other holders of power are incorporated by providing them with resources (such as control over jobs, natural resources, and access to money-making opportunities) which they distribute, in turn, to their own supporters. In this way, direct allegiance to one's patron, and indirectly to the regime, becomes the key to a successful career. These patron–client pyramids extend throughout society, providing a web of allegiances which overrides the public–private divide. As long as the clients are politically sound, their patrons will ignore shady behaviour, a fact which helps explain why corruption is so widespread in authoritarian regimes. Institutions are weak, while pragmatic alliances are strong, holding the regime together. But there is a high price to pay: corruption corrodes whatever public support the regime may possess, increasing potential instability.

> **Patronage:** Support, encouragement, access, and privileges bestowed by one individual on another. In the case of authoritarian regimes, the term describes the use of state resources by leaders to reward those providing support to the regime.

The third device used by authoritarian leaders is control of the media to ensure favourable coverage for their achievements, and criticism – or neglect – of their opponents. Censorship is implemented by catch-all offences such as threatening the dignity and effectiveness of the state. In Iran, there is a mixture of public and private ownership of the media, and a wide variety of options from which to choose, but the Islamic Revolutionary Court monitors reports and actions that might be deemed as threats to the state. These are sufficiently vaguely defined as to allow a wide range of charges, which might lead to closure, suspension, or imprisonment of the publication in question. Many Iranians circumvent official censorship by relying on the internet, satellite television, and mobile phones.

Aggression and belligerence are often driven by fear and vulnerability, and this is also true of authoritarian rule. Communication is opaque, trust is lacking, government spending is misused, corruption is endemic, laws are ignored, economics and obedience come before private initiative, and foreign investors are cautious. In many cases, the outcome is a static society, an underperforming economy, and a cynical population. Even so, authoritarian rule can sometimes generate rapid economic growth. China is the notable example: its economic growth between 1978 and 2009 far exceeded that of democratic India (Madhukar and Nagarjuna, 2011; Sen, 2011). There is evidence to suggest that authoritarian rule can generate early-stage economic development in particular; industrialization requires massive investments in infrastructure (such as transport, communications, and education), and authoritarian rulers can generate the surplus for this investment by resisting short-term, electoral pressures for immediate consumption. Simply put, they can kick-start development because they can ignore the complaints of those whose consumption is initially limited.

Although a few non-democratic regimes initiate economic take-off, most do not. Many traditional rulers, such as the ruling families in the Middle East, continue to resist modernization. Other dictators – for example, Nigeria's military 'lootocrats' – set back economic development by decades through gross mismanagement. A statistical study by Przeworski *et al.* (2000: 271) found that, even in those cases where authoritarian regimes have achieved growth, this increase has depended primarily on expanding the labour force. Democracies, by contrast, make more productive use of their inputs, a form of growth which can, in principle, continue indefinitely.

Forms of authoritarian rule

Because there is such a large element of opportunism involved in authoritarian rule, with strong leaders and/or ruling groups either exploiting opportunities

TABLE 4.3: Forms of authoritarian rule

Absolute monarchy	A ruling sovereign exerts control, with other members of the royal family in key political and military posts.	Bahrain, Kuwait, Oman, Qatar, Saudi Arabia, United Arab Emirates
Ruling presidents	The presidency dominates government and the media, with opponents kept off-guard and the opposition marginalized.	Several former Soviet republics, Angola, Zimbabwe
Ruling parties	Rule by a single party, often combined with a strong president.	Communist states, and many African states in the decades after independence
Military rule	Government by the military, often ruling through a junta comprising the leaders of each branch of the armed forces.	Many African, Asian and Latin American countries in the decades following the Second World War. Less common today
Theocracy	A rare form of rule in which religious leaders govern directly.	Iran

that come their way, or being brought to power by accident, or simply falling into bad habits, authoritarianism has few of the standard templates that we find when we study democracy. It is important to note that the most common tool of authoritarian rule is not repression but co-option, and not just of rival elites but of whole segments of the population. We will see this as we review five different strands that give us more insights into the personality of authoritarian government: absolute monarchy, ruling presidents, ruling parties, military rule, and theocracy (see Table 4.3).

Absolute monarchy

While undemocratic, an **absolute monarchy** can provide a stable framework for the exercise of traditional authority, in which rulers show paternalistic concern for their subjects. In contrast to the constitutional monarchies of Europe, where kings and queens survive only as figureheads with few significant powers (see Chapter 9), absolute monarchs still wield unlimited power. They are particularly important in the Middle East, their major oil and natural gas reserves giving several of them – such as Bahrain, Kuwait, Oman, Qatar, Saudi Arabia, and the United Arab Emirates – considerable global influence.

> **Absolute monarchy:** A form of government in which a monarch wields absolute power over a state, and in which all other institutions of government are marginal. Should not be confused with the limited powers of a constitutional monarchy.

We need to be careful in our use of the term *monarchy* (literally, 'rule by one') to describe the traditional political systems found in the Persian Gulf, for three main reasons:

- The titles taken by Arab 'monarchs' reflect tribal or Islamic tradition, as in *emir* (leader or commander), *sheikh* (revered leader of the tribe), or *sultan* (a leader who possesses authority).

- The leading members of the ruling dynasty, rather than a single monarch, often exercise authority. These countries are run by family businesses, rather than sole traders.

- While the king typically designates a crown prince as his preferred successor, custom requires that a clan council meets after the monarch's death to confirm or change this appointment. In most European monarchies, by contrast, succession is based on inheritance by the first-born.

Authority in these male-dominated Arab dynasties is owed to the ruler, rather than to a more abstract entity such as a state or party; the ruler is constrained neither by law nor by competitive election. In some cases these systems have shown remarkable staying power. In Oman, for example, the Al Bu Said dynasty has ruled since 1749, longer than the United States has existed as an independent country. According to its 1996 constitution, the person of the Sultan 'is inviolable and must be respected and his orders must be obeyed'.

Several kingdoms, notably Kuwait, have now established consultative assemblies, but this reform is unlikely to presage a transition to a constitutional monarchy (Herb, 2005). Because the ruler is expected to take responsibility for his people, the right of ordinary people to petition on individual matters is well established. However, the petitioner requests benevolent treatment, not the implementation of constitutional rights. The abstract idea of a state linking rulers and citizens is weak, as are such modern concepts as constitutions, rights, interest groups, the separation of powers, and the rule of law. Politics is based on intrigue at the palace, with little distinction between public and private sectors.

Saudi Arabia offers an example of an absolute monarchy. The country's political style reflects the influence of King Abdul Aziz Ibn Saud, who led the Saudi state from its inception in 1902 until his death in 1953. In true patrimonial style, Ibn Saud ran his kingdom as a gigantic personal household, using marriage as a vital political tactic. Saudi Arabia's sprawling royal family, led by an influential group of several hundred princes, still constitutes the government's core.

Family members occupy the key positions on the Saudi Council of Ministers, serving as a bridge between the government, the military, and the active security forces. This large ruling family, itself divided into factions, populates and controls the leading institutions of state, providing a form of dispersed collective leadership and a barrier to radical change. At the same time, the ruling family does not monopolize wealth, instead leaving space for lower-tier families.

Political parties are still banned but some mechanisms of representation have emerged, adding an institutional veneer to a traditional regime. The Basic Law of 1992, an innovation in itself, introduced a Consultative Council, with a non-princely and technocratic membership, to 'advise the King on issues of importance'. The Council is a strengthened form of a body which dates back to 1927 – yet it remains, at most, a proto-legislature. Rulers also keep an eye on, and sometimes act upon, the issues raised on social media.

In Saudi Arabia, as elsewhere in the Middle East, ruling monarchies have proved resilient. They survived the Arab Spring, though not without protests in some kingdoms – notably, Bahrain. In contrast to regime-toppling rebellions elsewhere, few demonstrators in the Gulf explicitly sought political transformation. Many sought economic change (more jobs, less corruption) and political reform (widening the suffrage where representative institutions already existed), rather than abolition of the monarchy. A combination of some repression and tactical reforms, such as more handouts to the people, contained the protests. Even if times have

become less certain, traditions of personal, paternalistic, and princely rule remain entrenched.

Ruling presidents

Although many authoritarian leaders derive their power from a source external to the executive office, such as family or ethnic connections, the office of president (or, less often, prime minister) can itself occasionally be the power base. A president in an authoritarian system occupies a unique position, possessing a visibility which can be invested in an attempt to transfer personal authority to an executive post, typically by establishing a direct relationship through the media with the people. In an absolute monarchy, the office outlasts the incumbent and is passed on through an assured line of succession. In the case of a ruling president, the office also outlasts the incumbent, but there is no line of succession (even if the occasional authoritarian president will try to keep power within the family).

While several former Soviet republics became democracies (the prime examples being the Baltic states of Estonia, Latvia, and Lithuania), many did not, and one element these non-democratic successor regimes have shared since becoming independent in 1991 is a ruling president. Azerbaijan, Belarus, Kazakhstan, Tajikistan, Turkmenistan, and Uzbekistan all come to mind, as well – of course – as Russia.

In the case of Belarus, Alexander Lukashenko has maintained a grip on power since winning office in 1994. While his western neighbours have been moving towards free-market democracy, Lukashenko maintains Soviet-era policies, including state ownership of key industries. He has been the target of US and EU sanctions for human rights violations, maintains close relations with Putin's Russia, and has been described as Europe's last dictator. He began his fourth term in 2011 after allegedly winning nearly 80 per cent of the vote on 90 per cent turnout, figures that are too high to be credible.

Further east, the politics of Uzbekistan reveals a similar pattern. Here, Islam Karimov, a former first secretary of the Uzbek Communist Party, won the 1991 presidential election, establishing a dictatorship via a coup against the party he led. In 1994, Karimov resigned from the communist successor party, claiming that only a non-partisan head of state could guarantee constitutional stability. By this route, he instituted a gradual change in the nature of authoritarian rule in his country: from a party-based regime to a presidency-based regime.

To forestall opposition, Karimov regularly dismisses ministers and replaces regional leaders. He keeps tight control of the media, uses a traditional institution of local governance (the *mahalla*) as an instrument of social control, and relies on the National Security Service for surveillance. As with other leaders of secular regimes in Islamic societies, Karimov has sought to prevent the mosque from becoming an explicit site of opposition, banning parties based on religion or ethnicity.

Elsewhere, many African states have experienced long periods of rule by powerful leaders around whom political systems revolve. A prime example is Zimbabwe, ruled by Robert Mugabe since 1980. He has proved adept at wrong-footing his opponents (using land confiscated from white farmers as a tool for rewarding his supporters), has marginalized and divided the political opposition, and along the way has driven the economy into the ground. Inflation was running at more than 230 million per cent in 2008 when it was decided to abandon the Zimbabwe dollar and use the US dollar instead. As advancing age began to impact Mugabe's health, rumours began to circulate that his wife Grace – 41 years younger than him, and nicknamed 'Gucci Grace' because of her expensive tastes and spending habits – was wielding growing power behind the scenes.

One possibility inherent in a ruling presidency is a **cult of personality**, through which the president comes to dominate the consciousness of the people. He (no dictator in the modern era has been a woman) is often the first item on the daily news headlines, his picture or image is omnipresent, he provides whatever energy the regime possesses, and the stability of the political system depends heavily on his control. Rarely does the president's reach extend as far as it did in the totalitarian regimes of the twentieth century – such as Nazi Germany or the USSR under Stalin – or as it exists even today in North Korea, but a cult of personality remains an important part of the manner in which many ruling presidents maintain their control.

> **Cult of personality:** An arrangement in which authoritarian leaders use the media, propaganda, and political institutions to make sure that they dominate how the wider population relates to a political system.

Ruling parties

The twentieth century saw the birth, ossification, and disintegration of party-based dictatorships (communist, fascist, and nationalist) which monopolized public authority in the name of economic modernization, social transformation, and national revival. While they are now relatively rare, they are still found in the last few remaining communist states, with some non-communist varieties.

Communist parties. At the time of the collapse of the communist order in the late 1980s and early 1990s, 23 regimes claiming Marxist inspiration ruled more than 1.5 billion people: about one in three of the world's population (Holmes, 1997: 4). Today there are just five 'communist' states remaining (China, North Korea, Vietnam, Laos, and Cuba), but most are undergoing the kind of free-market economic change that might well lead to further political changes. (see Table 4.4).

Although vastly different in size, China, Vietnam, and Laos comprise a coherent regional group; they are traditionally poor, agricultural societies in which ruling communist parties have loosened their direct control

TABLE 4.4: The five last communist party states

	Communist rule established	Key features
North Korea	1948	A brutal totalitarian regime led by the Kim family for three generations. Strong military influence. The official ideology stresses national independence and self-reliance.
China	1949	The Communist Party retains tight political control while leading substantial and successful economic reform.
Cuba	1961	Long dominated by Fidel Castro and now led by his younger brother Raúl. A new opening to the United States since 2015 promises to bring change.
Laos	1975	Laos's partly liberalized economy has grown significantly, albeit from a low base.
Vietnam	1976 (North Vietnam 1954)	As in China, the Communist Party has initiated economic reform while retaining a political monopoly.

over the economy, while keeping a firm grip on political power. This strategy has delivered substantial if uneven growth, most significant in China and Vietnam. By unleashing entrepreneurial initiative, ruling parties have averted the inertia which led to the fall of communism in the Soviet Union and Eastern Europe, and their position remains intact and largely unchallenged.

From the beginning, Chinese communism possessed distinct national characteristics, so that while power is exerted through the Chinese Communist Party (CCP), the party itself has been controlled by elite factions which have embraced nationalism. Like Vietnam, China has not so much a market economy as a highly politicized economy in which not only party members, but also local bureaucrats and army officers, can advance themselves alongside more conventional entrepreneurs. Business people must focus not only on market opportunities, but also on creating strong ties to local officials that will provide access to those prospects.

China faces numerous problems, including inequality between regions and between individuals, the inefficient allocation of capital, an ageing population, poor social services, massive population movements into the cities, and severe environmental degradation. But the party elite has shown exceptional skill in managing these challenges. A combination of growth, propaganda, reform, and repression has forestalled mass public demands for democracy, and the nationalist narrative of China rising continues to resonate. China's success in entering the world economy has established the world's dependence on its goods, reducing international pressures for democratization. Even though its Marxist legacy has faded, China continues to offer a model of development without democratization.

Other ruling parties. Occasionally, single ruling parties other than those that are communist provide the basis for authoritarian rule, but they are increasingly rare. Until the late 1980s, most African states (including Ethiopia, Kenya, Malawi, Tanzania, and Zambia) were run on this basis, but almost all have now switched to competitive multi-party systems. We are now more likely to find dominant-party systems, such as those in Angola, the Democratic Republic of Congo, Mozambique, and Sudan.

It is important in these instances to distinguish between the supports of power and power itself. Often, the party is the vehicle rather than the driver, with real authority resting with a dominant president, military ruler, or political elite. The supposed ruling party is an arena within which particular elite groups express and perpetuate their control. When the elite goes, so does the party.

The case of the National Democratic Party (NDP) in Egypt is illustrative. Until the Arab Spring, the party formed part of an established structure of power based on a strong presidency and an extended bureaucracy. Within this framework, however, the NDP was the junior partner: 'the NDP has failed to serve as an effective means to recruit candidates into the elite. Rather, persons who are already successful tend to join the party in order to consolidate their positions' (Lesch, 2004: 600). With its close links to the state, the NDP was an arena for furthering political and business careers, but not a major policy-making force. Even so, its headquarters were destroyed during the Egyptian revolt of 2011 and the party itself was outlawed.

Military government

Military governments are far less common than they once were; during the second half of the twentieth century they could be found in many parts of Africa, Latin America, and parts of Asia. Today, we are more likely to speak of leaders who came to power in a military coup and then transformed themselves into civilian leaders, or of regimes in which the military influences civilian governments from behind the scenes. Since a bloodless coup in Thailand in 2006, for example, the country has experienced phases of both military and civilian rule, with the latter often using the military to contain anti-government protests. While currently rare, military government remains a variety of authoritarian rule that is still worth studying.

Usually ushered in by a **coup d'etat**, or an illegal seizure of power, military rule typically involves the suspension of all other key political institutions except the bureaucracy, the courts and the police, and is based on the military principles of hierarchy and the absence of negotiation. Coups are generally easier to stage in smaller countries where the state remains underdeveloped, and government institutions and media outlets are focused in the capital city. An ambitious general may just need a few tanks, commanded by a handful of discontented officers, to seize the presidential palace and begin broadcasting from the radio and TV stations. Once in power, military governments are typically headed by a ruling council made up of the leader of each branch of the armed forces, with one emerging as the dominant figure.

SPOTLIGHT

CHINA

Population (1,370 million)

Gross National Incme ($9,240 billion)

Per capita GNI ($6,560)

Democracy Index rating

| Not Rated | Hybrid Regime | Full Democracy |
| | Authoritarian | Flawed Democracy |

Freedom House rating

| Not Free | Partly free | Free |

Human Development Index rating

| Not Rated | Medium | Very High |
| | Low | High |

Brief Profile: China is the world's largest state by population, the second biggest by economic output, and has been undergoing a process of political and economic reform which is changing the world order. It has one of the world's oldest cultures, but is normally reviewed only in terms of the changes it has seen since the institution of communist rule in 1949. Until 1976 it was under the idiosyncratic and hard-line control of Mao Zedong, since when several generations of leaders have overseen pro-market changes that have helped China become the world's fastest-growing economy. Political reform has not moved as quickly, however, and China remains under the watchful control of the Chinese Communist Party. Dissent and opposition are controlled and limited, corruption is a persistent problem, China's human rights record is poor, and in spite of the changes it has undergone, it ranks low on most comparative political, economic and social rankings.

Form of government ⇨ Unitary communist republic. State formed 1949, and most recent constitution adopted 1982.

Legislature ⇨ Unicameral National People's Congress of nearly 3,000 members, chosen indirectly through local and provincial congresses. Meets only for brief periods, its work carried out when in recess by a 150-member Standing Committee.

Executive ⇨ The State Council, headed by the premier, is the top executive body, supervising the work of the ministries. A president serves a maximum of two five-year terms as ceremonial head of state. Ultimate power rests, however, in the top leaders of the CCP.

Judiciary ⇨ No independent constitutional court. Rule through law has strengthened but the judicial system remains underdeveloped.

Electoral system ⇨ Elections have been introduced to many of China's villages and to some townships. However, elected officials still operate under the party's supervision. Indirect election is usual at higher levels.

Parties ⇨ Single-party. The Chinese Communist Party (CCP) remains the dominant political force, its leadership being a parallel government within which most real power is focused.

Coup d'etat: An illegal seizure of political power by the military. Although the term conjures up images of a violent and unwelcome capture of power from civilian rulers, many coups replace one military regime with another, involve little loss of life, and some are even welcomed by citizens.

In many African cases, military leaders have justified coups by arguing that the civilians are doing a poor job of governing, and claiming that power will be returned to the civilians once a new and more effective system of government is established. But then the new military leaders often decide to stay on indefinitely, or

Authoritarian rule in China

Dickson (2007: 828) argues that 'China has become a prime example of how authoritarian governments can employ strategic action to survive indefinitely despite rapid economic development'. How has it managed to do this?

Part of the answer lies in the skills of the Chinese Communist Party in both maintaining its monopoly position (supervising the government, the justice system and the mass media) while also becoming less intrusive and more supervisory. The crucial reform has been the reduction of central control from Beijing. In local communities, informal networks of power-holders now determine 'who gets rich first' – a political market, rather than a free market. These alliances are composed not only of well-placed party members, but also of officials in the bureaucracy, local government, and the army. Local officials provide favoured businesses (including their own) with contracts, land, sympathetic regulations, information, supplies, transport, and other subsidies.

So political and economic reform does not necessarily imply a shift towards a market economy operating within the rule of law. Reform empowers local elites to create a state-sponsored business class, whose members include public officials and party members. In this way, the newly rich remain dependent on the political system and do not seek to change it.

The loosening of central political control has led to an explosion of corruption. In the new environment, public employees are quick to recognize opportunities to earn extra money from their official position: 'Li Gang paid 300,000 for his post but within two years netted five million. The return is 1500 per cent. Is there any other profession as profitable as this under heaven?' (an official from the Central Discipline Inspection Commission, quoted in McGregor, 2010: 70). Here, perhaps, is one of the party's major dilemmas: it can only attract members by offering opportunities to acquire resources, but the dubious manner in which these are obtained increases the distance between party and society.

Like China itself, the party faces considerable challenges in the years ahead. Its prospects must depend on its ability to sustain strong economic growth and expand its international significance. Yet the possibility remains that achieving these goals will itself eventually initiate calls for a freer, and perhaps more democratic, China.

---

try to reinvent themselves as civilian politicians. Such transitions to a more civilian status may be real or purely for appearances; in either case, the armed forces usually remain a significant political actor.

Nigeria is a representative case, having spent nearly 30 years under military government since independence in 1960. Civilians were removed in a coup in 1983 amid charges that political parties were becoming too ethnically based and, ironically, that the government was becoming more authoritarian. The new military leader – Major General Ibrahim Babangida – oversaw the transition to a new civilian system of government based on a new constitution. But he refused to hand over power to a new president in 1993, claiming that the election had been fraudulent. The resulting outcry forced him to step down, and he was soon replaced by Brigadier Sani Abacha, who made no bones about his desire to be elected as a civilian president, and actively looted Nigeria's oil profits along the way. He died of a supposed heart attack in June 1998 (an event popularly described as the 'coup from heaven'), and a new military leader completed the return to civilian government in 1999. In 2015, Nigeria experienced its first transition from one civilian government to another as the result of the defeat of an incumbent running for re-election. Nonetheless, the military remains a powerful force in the background, and Nigeria faces enormous internal divisions that even today might encourage soldiers to retake power if they feel that civilians are not doing a good job.

Attempted military coups are hard to count precisely, for several reasons: many fail or are badly organized, many are only alleged to have happened, and in many cases it is uncertain who is implicated (some apparent coups are in fact assassinations of leaders rather than efforts to change a government). An exhaustive study by Powell and Thyne (2011) found that between 1950 and 2010 just over 450 coups were attempted in a total of 94 states, of which just under half were successful. About one-third occurred in Africa, another third took place in Latin America, with the balance divided between Asia and the Middle East. The number of coups has tailed off from an average of about ten annually in the 1960s to about three to five annually between 2000 and 2010.

Part of the explanation for the changing numbers lies with the changing attitudes of the great powers. During the Cold War, the United States and the Soviet Union were more concerned with the global chessboard than with how their client countries governed themselves; hence ruling generals could survive through the political, economic, and military backing of a superpower even though they lacked support in their own country. The end of the Cold War meant the end of superpower sponsorship, with aid and technical assistance flowing to civilian regimes adopting democratic forms and offering at least some commitment to civil rights. In recent times, military coups have been rare and sometimes short-lived affairs in smaller countries – see Table 4.5.

What role does the military now play in authoritarian regimes? In most cases, it remains an important element in the civilian ruler's support base. For example, the stance of the military was decisive in determining the success of the Arab uprisings of 2011. Where the army remained loyal to the regime, as in Syria, the government could fight the disparate opposition. But where the military declined to repress protestors, as in Egypt, the regime fell. So the relative rarity of military rule does not signal the end of political influence by the armed forces. When new civilian rulers are unable to limit the generals to a professional military role, the armed forces will continue to dominate, supervise, or constrain the government, compromising its democratic credentials.

Theocracy

As with military rule, government by religious leaders is rare, but that does not mean that religion has ceased to be a factor in authoritarian governance (or even, in some countries, in democratic governance). A religious society may be quite different from a clerical government, and even Muslim countries typically separate religious and civil leadership within the context of an overall commitment to Islam. Indeed, in much of the Middle East the mosque has become a source of opposition to authoritarian rulers, a divide which would not be possible if religious and civil leadership belonged in the same hands.

At least since the end of Taliban rule in Afghanistan in 2001, the Islamic Republic of Iran stands alone as an example of a constitutional **theocracy**. Afghanistan, Pakistan, and Mauritania also consider themselves to be **Islamic republics**, but religious leaders are less prominent. Even in Iran, rule by religious leaders (*ayatollahs* and *mullahs*) possesses limited legitimacy, especially among the young and educated. Public demonstrations in Iran disputing the result of the 2009 presidential election confirmed not only popular disaffection with the political system, but also divisions between reformers and hardliners within the ruling elite itself. Further protests during the Arab Spring in 2011 were contained by a vigorous security response, but this did not stop the victory in the 2013 presidential election of the relatively reformist Hassan Rouhani.

TABLE 4.5: Recent examples of military rule

	Circumstances
Niger, 2010–11	President Mamadou Tandja suspended the constitution and assumed emergency powers following his failed 2009 efforts to change the constitution to allow him to run for a third term. He won a fresh period in office but was overthrown in a 2010 coup. A new constitution was agreed and civilians returned to power in 2011.
Guinea, 2008–10	Following the death of Lansana Conté, who had seized power in a 1984 coup, and against the background of a rebel insurgency, Moussa Dadis Camara seized power in 2008. He was forced to step down by public protests, and in 2010 the country held its first open elections since 1958.
Burma, 1962–2011	Burma was long ruled by a military government notorious for its human rights abuses. A civilian government came to power in 2011, but the 2008 constitution ensured substantial political influence for the military.
Fiji, 2006–14	When the military protested plans to set up a commission to look into compensation for victims of an earlier coup, the civilian government was forced out of office in 2006. Military chief Frank Bainimarama won an open general election in 2014.

FOCUS 4.2 | Totalitarianism

Totalitarian regimes demanding rigid support for a supreme leader were rare even in the twentieth century, and there is only one left today (North Korea). In spite of its rarity, totalitarianism cannot be ignored as a political type, and it is worth reviewing if only as the benchmark for the most extreme form of political control we have seen in the modern era. Its features include a dominating leader portrayed as working in the benevolent interests of the people, and a single guiding ideology based on a pessimistic view of human nature and the supposed attempt to build an ideal society in the face of external and internal opposition (see Goodwin, 2007).

The archetypal totalitarian regime was that dominated by Joseph Stalin in the Soviet Union between the late 1920s, when he came to power, and his death in 1953. Under his iron fist, the USSR moved away from Marxist ideals towards an absolutist and unyielding dictatorship that demanded unquestioning support for the state, the party, and its leaders. Stalin used systematic and calculated oppression to enforce his reforms, in the process of which perhaps as many as 20 million people died from famine, execution, or war, and many millions more were purged, or exiled to concentration camps. Stalinism also meant the elimination of human rights and the use of a cult of personality, and of a secret police to identify and remove rivals.

Stalin also established a command economy in which all the decisions that are driven by the free market in a liberal democracy were made by state planners: they decided what should be produced, when it should be produced, where it should be delivered, and at what prices it should be sold. As a result, the Soviet bureaucracy became both massive and massively inefficient. A series of five-year plans set ambitious targets such as industrialization, with the goal of strengthening the country's weak international position. The Communist Party infiltrated every part of Soviet life, creating a new class of privileged political leaders and dashing any remaining hope of achieving Marx's vision of a classless society.

Today, North Korea reveals many of the same qualities: rule by a leader who sits at the apex of the system, human rights abuses, the consolidation of political and military power, close supervision of the lives of citizens, domination by the ruling Worker's Party, elections in which there is only one candidate in each district, and an inflexible economic system that has led not just to stagnation but also to mass starvation.

Totalitarianism: The most absolute form of authoritarian rule, based either on a guiding ideology or the goal of major social change, with total control exercised by a leader, state, or party over all aspects of public and private life.

Theocracy: Government by religious leaders.

Islamic republic: A state based on an Islamic constitution and full application of Islamic law (sharia), although the precise role of the latter is sometimes ambiguous.

Iran's theocracy was a child of the 1979 revolution, the last great insurrection of the twentieth century, in which Ayatollah Khomeini, a 76-year-old cleric committed to Islamic fundamentalism, overthrew the pro-Western Shah of Iran. The revolutionaries advocated a traditional Islamic republic free from foreign domination; 'neither East nor West' was the slogan.

In power, the *ayatollah*s created a unique Islamic state in which they mainly govern indirectly through secular rulers; there is a directly elected president and legislature, but Iran remains authoritarian, real power lying with the clerics. The most senior of these is the Supreme Leader, who has a lifetime appointment as head of state, must be an expert in Islamic law, and has many executive powers, including control of foreign and economic policy. Meanwhile, a 12-member Council of Guardians certifies that all legislation and candidates for office conform to Islamic law. Government is based on strictly enforced traditional, male-dominated Islamic codes, the Interior Ministry still makes extensive use of informants, and the state employs arbitrary arrests as a form of control through fear.

As with many authoritarian regimes, Iran's rulers offer no clear direction on such practical matters as economic development, monetary policy, and overseas trade. Their nuclear programme and sponsorship of international terrorism attracts international sanctions, thereby limiting economic growth, oil revenues notwithstanding. Instead, the clerics have grown wealthy by establishing *bonyads* – tax-exempt 'charitable' trusts – for their personal benefit. These foundations – and the public sector, generally – dominate an inefficient economy. The result is that Iran's theocratic establishment consists of competing factions of middle-aged to elderly men exploiting the revolutionary heritage in a successful effort to build and retain power and wealth. Neither a strong party nor a royal family exist to impose overall direction.

Unsurprisingly in a country where the median age was just 29 years in 2015, rule by this theocratic elite has intensified generational divisions. Well-educated young people, including many female graduates, chafe at the restrictions imposed by the religious establishment. This desire for freedom is not necessarily rooted in a secular outlook; rather, it reflects opposition to the cultural repression imposed by a religious leadership lacking a positive vision of the country's future (Gheissari, 2009).

The political impact of corruption

Corruption is far from unique to authoritarian systems, and can be found at every level of government and administration in every society where people are willing to abuse public office for private gain. It can be found in the most stable and successful democracies, as well as – more often – flawed democracies. However, corruption plays a particularly telling role in hybrid and authoritarian regimes, being both a cause and effect of the kind of power that authoritarian leaders wield. In the famously cynical observation of the nineteenth-century British politician Lord Acton:

> Power tends to corrupt, and absolute power tends to corrupt absolutely. Great men are almost always bad men, even when they exercise influence and not authority: still more when you superadd the tendency or the certainty of corruption by authority. (Acton, quoted in Figgis and Laurence, 1907)

Corruption: The abuse of office for private gain. It occurs for example when an official allocates a benefit in exchange for a bribe, rather than on the basis of entitlement. The bribe may persuade officials to do what they should have done anyway, or to do it promptly.

Most worryingly, corruption can undermine the quality of governance and the efficiency of an economy. It replaces efforts to promote the public good with efforts to promote the private good, diverts limited resources away from those who most need them, discourages foreign investment, and places the interests of those willing and able to break the law above the interests of the population as a whole.

Political corruption comes in many different forms, including the following:

- *Electoral fraud* involves manipulating the outcome of elections, whether by the design of electoral districts, by making it difficult for voters to cast their ballots, by intimidating opposition candidates and their supporters, or by artificially expanding the electoral roll (by double-counting voters or adding fake or dead voters).
- The giving of a *bribe* to a government official or a police officer.
- *Influence peddling*, where someone sells their influence in government to benefit a third party. For example, officials may use their office to ensure that a particular company is awarded a public contract, or to ensure that a friend or associate is chosen to fill a vacancy.
- *Patronage* was discussed earlier, and in many forms is legitimate, but becomes corrupt when it involves leaders selecting less qualified over more qualified candidates for office in return for their political support.
- *Nepotism* involves favouring relatives, while cronyism involves favouring personal friends, for example in being selected as candidates in elections, in being appointed to important government office, or in being awarded government contracts.
- *Embezzlement* involves the theft of public funds, as in the infamous cases of Nigerian military leaders who during the 1990s used their offices to siphon off enormous sums from oil profits into foreign bank accounts.
- *Kickbacks* occur when government officials use their position to offer a contract for public work to a company in return for a share of the payment made to the company.

Measuring and quantifying corruption is not easy, mainly because it is – by definition – an illegal and underground activity. In terms of making comparisons, the best guide we have comes in the form of the reports published by Transparency International, an organization headquartered in Berlin that works to limit corruption and promote transparency. It publishes an annual Corruption Perceptions Index which uses a variety of governmental and non-governmental sources to rank perceptions of corruption around the world. The key word here is *perceptions*; the index reflects how countries are regarded by those who know them, rather than providing a direct and objective measure of corruption itself. The index is based on a compilation of information from banks, foundations, and interest groups. The overlap with forms of political rule is close, the least corrupt countries corresponding with full democracies, and the most corrupt overlapping with authoritarian regimes (see Figure 4.1).

That even the most advanced democracies experience corruption is reflected in the cases of Denmark and New Zealand, which sit at the top of the Transparency International rankings (although this does not mean that they are the least corrupt countries so much as those where corruption is less evident). The report notes that Denmark lacks transparency in political and campaign financing, has outdated laws on freedom of information, and provides insufficient protection to whistle-blowers, while New Zealand is criticized for its failure to ratify the United Nations Convention Against Corruption.

These are minor concerns when compared with the situation in North Korea and Somalia, which tied for last place in the 2014 Corruption Perceptions Index. In the case of North Korea, information is gleaned mainly from defectors, whose reports suggest that a culture of corruption has infiltrated the entire society. Bribery, notes Lankov (2013: 89–91), has become a matter of basic survival, given the country's food shortages, lack of basic resources, and harsh penalties for any actions that might be defined as threatening the governing regime. Somalia experiences comparable problems, with the addition of even more high-level corruption involving patronage and the misappropriation of public funds.

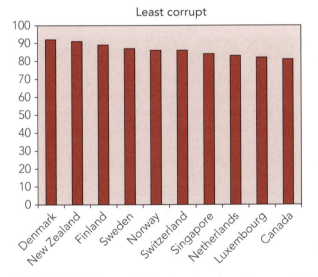
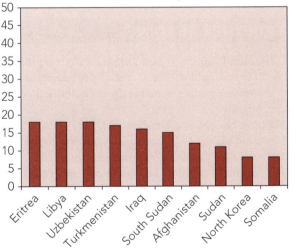
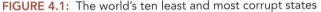

FIGURE 4.1: The world's ten least and most corrupt states

Note: Numbers indicate scores out of 100

Source: Transparency International, Corruption Perceptions Index 2014

DISCUSSION QUESTIONS

- Which is preferable: a stable dictatorship or the instability that often arises in poor and deeply divided societies with no experience of democracy?

- How does patronage differ in its democratic and authoritarian forms?

- Where does Western criticism of non-Western authoritarianism cease to be helpful and evolve into cultural or political imperialism?

- Mao Zedong once suggested that political power grows out of the barrel of a gun. So why, then, are the armed forces not in charge everywhere?

- Does military rule necessarily involve the occupation by military officers of the key institutions of government?

- Why are so many authoritarian regimes corrupt?

KEY CONCEPTS

Absolute monarchy
Authoritarian regime
Corruption
Coup d'etat
Cult of personality
Despotism

Hybrid regime
Islamic republic
Patronage
Theocracy
Totalitarianism

FURTHER READING

Brooker, Paul (2009) *Non-Democratic Regimes: Theory, Government and Politics*, 2nd edn. A comprehensive analysis of the main types of authoritarian regime.

Ezrow, Natasha and Erica Frantz (2011) *Dictators and Dictatorships: Understanding Authoritarian Regimes and Their Leaders*. A crisp summary of the academic literature on non-democratic governments.

Heywood, Paul M. (ed.) (2015) *Routledge Handbook of Political Corruption*. A review of the meaning and causes of corruption, with chapters offering cases from different parts of the world.

Levitsky, Steven and Lucan A. Way (2010) *Competitive Authoritarianism: Hybrid Regimes After the Cold War*. A detailed account of the rise and diverging fate of competitive authoritarian regimes since 1990.

Saich, Tony (2015) *Governance and Politics of China*, 4th edn. An informative guide to the world's most important authoritarian regime.

Svolik, Milan W. (2012) *The Politics of Authoritarian Rule*. A survey of the dynamics of dictatorship, and of the problems faced by dictators.

5 Theoretical approaches

PREVIEW

So far we have looked at comparative government and politics in broad terms, and it is probably already clear that it is a field of complexity and of conflicting analyses. It is tangled enough at the level of the individual state, but when we add multiple political systems to the equation, the challenges of achieving an understanding are compounded. Theory comes to the rescue by pulling together what might otherwise be a cluster of unstructured observations and facts into a framework that can be tested and applied in different places and at different times.

A theoretical approach is a simplifying device or a conceptual filter that helps us decide what is important in terms of explaining political phenomena. In other words, it can help us sift through a body of facts, decide which are primary and which are secondary, enable us to organize and interpret the information, and develop complete arguments and explanations about the objects of our study.

This chapter offers some insights into the theoretical approaches used by political scientists. There are so many that it is impossible in a brief chapter to be comprehensive; instead, we focus here on five of the most important: the institutional, behavioural, structural, rational, and interpretive approaches. The chapter begins with a brief review of the changing face of comparative politics and a sampling of the debates about theory, then goes through each of the five key approaches in turn, explaining their origins, principles, and goals, and offering some illustrative examples.

CONTENTS

- Theoretical approaches: an overview

- The changing face of comparative politics

- The institutional approach

- The behavioural approach

- The structural approach

- The rational choice approach

- The interpretive approach

KEY ARGUMENTS

- Theoretical approaches are ways of studying politics, and help in identifying the right questions to ask and how to go about answering them.

- The institutional perspective has done most to shape the development of politics as a discipline and remains an important tradition in comparative politics.

- The behavioural approach examines politics at the level of the individual, relying primarily on quantitative analysis of sample surveys.

- The structural approach focuses on networks, and looks at the past to help understand the present. In this way, it helps bridge politics and history.

- The rational choice approach seeks to explain political outcomes by exploring interactions between political actors as they pursue their particular interests and goals.

- The interpretive approach, viewing politics as the ideas people construct about it in the course of their interaction, offers a contrast to more mainstream approaches.

Theoretical approaches: an overview

Theory is a key part of the exercise of achieving understanding in any field of knowledge. For comparative politics, it means developing and using principles and concepts that can be used to explain everything from the formation of states to questions of national identity, the character of institutions, the process of democratization, and the dynamics of political instability, political participation, and public policy.

> **Theory:** An abstract or generalized approach to explaining or understanding a phenomenon.

Unfortunately, there are several complicating factors. First, the field of comparative politics is so broad that it includes numerous theoretical explanations, ranging from the broad to the specific. For some, there are so many choices that diversity can sometimes seem to border on anarchy (Verba, 1991: 38), prompting comparative politics to lose (or even lack) direction. For others, the variety is good because it gives comparativists a wide array of options, and allows them to be 'opportunists' who can use whatever approach works best (Przeworski, in Kohli *et al.*, 1995: 16).

Second, comparative political theory has been criticized for focusing too much on ideas emerging from the Western tradition. As comparison takes a more global approach – pressed by the influence of globalization – there have been calls for it to be more inclusive. This trend will further expand the already substantial range of theoretical approaches.

Third, comparative political theory suffers the standard problem faced by political theory more generally of being the victim of fad and fashion. For every new theory that is proposed or applied, there is a long line of critics waiting to shoot it down and propose alternatives. It can sometimes seem as though the debate about theory is more about competing explanations than about their practical, real-world applications.

Finally, the place of theory in the social sciences more generally is based on shaky foundations. Many natural sciences have a strong record of developing theories that are well supported by the evidence, are broadly accepted, and can be used to develop laws and make predictions. The social sciences suffer greater uncertainties (if only because they focus more on trying to understand human behaviour), with the result that they generate theories that are subject to stronger doubts, and that have a weaker track record in generating laws and predicting outcomes.

In this chapter, we focus on the major theoretical approaches to the comparative study of politics. By 'approaches' we mean ways of understanding, or 'sets of attitudes, understandings and practices that define a certain way of doing political science' (Marsh and Stoker, 2010: 3). They are schools of thought that influence how we go about political research, that structure the questions we ask, that offer pointers on where we should seek an answer, and that help us define what counts as a good answer.

Five such approaches are worth close study. We will take them in an order that reflects the historical evolution of politics as an academic discipline, but for clarity will avoid the many subdivisions, crossovers, and reinventions within each perspective. We will argue that the institutional approach is the most important, but that the other frameworks provide important additional insights. We will also make the point that comparative political theory needs to take a more inclusive approach by bringing non-Western perspectives into the picture.

The changing face of comparative politics

Although comparison lies at the heart of all research, the sub-field of comparative politics is relatively young, and so is its theoretical base. As a systematic endeavour, it can be dated back to the formal origins of political science in the late nineteenth century, but it long lagged behind the study of domestic politics, and still lacks a well-developed identity. Comparative political theory is even younger, although Dallmayr may have overstated the case when he described it in 1999 as 'either non-existent or at most fledgling and embryonic'.

We saw in Chapter 1 how Aristotle is credited with the first attempt to classify political systems, but his work was mainly descriptive and did not establish principles that had much staying power. And while both comparative politics and comparative political theory owe much to some of the biggest names in political science and philosophy – from Machiavelli to Montesquieu and

Marx – none of them took a systematically comparative approach to understanding government and politics as we would define the task today.

Most other early examples of comparison were historicist in the sense that they tried to understand past events as determinants of the future, and so were only tangentially comparative; the German writer Johann Wolfgang van Goethe even once quipped that 'only blockheads compare' (von Beyme, 2011). The English philosopher John Stuart Mill, best known for his treatise *On Liberty*, made an early contribution to systematic comparison with his 1843 work *A System of Logic*. This outlined his five principles of inductive reasoning, which included methods of agreement and difference that are reflected in the most different and most similar system designs used today in comparative politics (see Chapter 6).

Not only was the systematic study of politics and government still in its formative phase in the nineteenth century, but there were also few cases available to compare, and scholars in most countries were more interested in studying their home political systems than in taking a broader view. For European scholars, the differences among European states were not seen to be particularly profound or interesting, so it is perhaps unsurprising that the birth of modern comparative politics took place in the United States (see Munck, 2007), where American scholars began to study 'foreign' political systems as distinct from their own. There remained a view, however, that Americans had little to learn from other systems, thanks to a deeply held belief that the American system was superior (Wiarda, 1991: 12). The few scholars who studied other systems focused mainly on Western Europe, with the Soviet Union and Japan added later, and their comparisons were more often descriptive than analytical.

Attitudes changed after the Second World War, when the foreign policy interests of the United States broadened, and the Cold War made American scholars and policy-makers more interested in understanding both their allies and their enemies. Eventually, this perspective extended to potential allies and enemies in Latin America, Asia, and Africa (Lim, 2010: 7–11). The end of the colonial era also saw a near-doubling in the number of sovereign states, from just over 70 in 1945 to more than 130 in 1970 (see Table 2.1). As well as a new interest in emerging states, there was also a change in the approach taken by comparative political scientists, whose past work had been often

criticized for being too parochial, too descriptive, too lacking in theory, and not even particularly comparative (Macridis, 1955). As part of what became known as the 'behavioural revolution', comparativists became interested in studying processes as well as institutions, in explaining as well as describing, and in taking a more scientific approach to the development of theory and methods.

While most of the famous names of comparative politics until this time had been American – including Charles Merriam, Gabriel Almond, Seymour Martin Lipset, Lucien Pye, and Samuel Huntington – new influence was asserted by scholars with European backgrounds and interests, including Giovanni Sartori, Stein Rokkan, Philippe Schmitter, Maurice Duverger, and Arend Lijphart. There was also more transfer of ideas between the study of domestic and comparative politics, and new interests were added with the break-up of the Soviet Union, the end of the Cold War, the emergence of the European Union, and the growing importance of states such as Brazil, China, India, Mexico, and South Africa.

Just as quickly, there was a reaction against the focus by behaviouralists on the scientific method and their attempts to develop a **grand theory** of comparative politics. A difference of opinion also developed between scholars favouring a quantitative approach (based on data analysis and emphasizing breadth over depth) and those favouring a qualitative approach (focused more on cases, history, and culture, and emphasizing depth over breadth) (see Chapter 6 for more details). More differences emerged as rational choice approaches began to win support within the sub-field, further promoting the use of mathematical modelling. The divisions reached a point in the late 1990s and early 2000s where there was something of a rebellion among American political scientists against what they described as the 'mathematicization of political science', and the particular marginalization of comparative politics. An informal 'Perestroika movement' emerged that pressed for multiple methods and approaches, and for new efforts to broaden political science in search of greater relevance (Monroe, 2005).

Grand theory: A broad and abstract form of theorizing that incorporates many other theories and tries to explain broad areas of a discipline rather than more concrete matters.

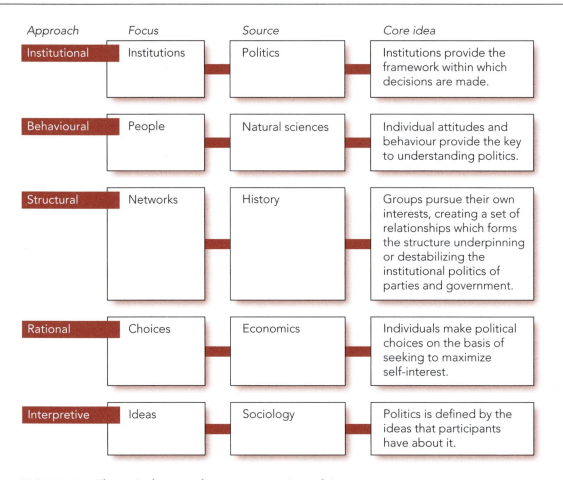

Approach	Focus	Source	Core idea
Institutional	Institutions	Politics	Institutions provide the framework within which decisions are made.
Behavioural	People	Natural sciences	Individual attitudes and behaviour provide the key to understanding politics.
Structural	Networks	History	Groups pursue their own interests, creating a set of relationships which forms the structure underpinning or destabilizing the institutional politics of parties and government.
Rational	Choices	Economics	Individuals make political choices on the basis of seeking to maximize self-interest.
Interpretive	Ideas	Sociology	Politics is defined by the ideas that participants have about it.

FIGURE 5.1: Theoretical approaches to comparative politics

The last 30 to 40 years have seen both a dramatic increase in interest in comparative politics and new efforts to make it more systematic. But the development of theories of comparative politics has lagged behind, more often borrowing from other sub-fields of political science – or even other subjects entirely – than developing its own distinctive approaches. The importance of institutions has been a consistent theme throughout, but behaviouralism was inspired by the natural sciences, structuralism is influenced by history, rational choice approaches came out of economics, and interpretive approaches owe something to sociology. And in spite of decades of hard work, it is hard to find theories that have both won general support and produced lasting results.

Consider, for example, the critical question of what causes democratization. Finding an answer might be considered the Holy Grail of political research;

armed with such knowledge, we might be able to reproduce the conditions needed and move the world more rapidly and sustainably towards a democratic future. But in her review of research on the question, Geddes (2007) is only able to point to some tendencies and to rule out others: richer countries are more likely to be democratic (but development does not cause democratization, although modernization might), as are countries that were once British colonies, but reliance on oil reduces the chances, as does having a large Muslim population. And every one of these arguments has been challenged. 'Given the quality and amount of effort expended on understanding democratization', Geddes concludes, 'it is frustrating to understand so little.'

The most recent problem identified with theories of comparative politics (and of politics and government in general) is their long history of association with

Western ideas. This was a phenomenon noted by Parel (1992) when he argued that the scholarship of political theory was so focused on Western political thought that there was a prevailing assumption that modern Western texts were 'products of universal reason itself'. But he also argued that Western claims of universality were being questioned by other cultures, and argued that comparative political philosophy meant taking an approach that paid more attention to cultural and philosophical pluralism. This point was later taken up by Dallmayr (1999):

> Only rarely are practitioners of political thought willing (and professionally encouraged) to transgress the [Western] canon and thereby the cultural boundaries of North America and Europe in the direction of genuine comparative investigation.

The sub-field of comparative politics today is broader and more eclectic than ever before, with new concepts and ideas regularly shaking up old assumptions. But it has sometimes been slow to catch up with the evolving realities of government and politics around the world, including the changing role of the state, the rise of new economic powers, the impact of new technology and globalization, the new political role of Islam, and the impact of failed and failing states. The changes within the sub-field have been positive and productive, and it employs a greater diversity of approaches than before, but much remains to be done.

The institutional approach

The study of governing **institutions** is a central purpose of political science in general, and of comparative politics in particular; hence the mantra often seen in studies of politics that 'institutions matter'. **Institutionalism** provides the original foundation of the discipline and lies at the core of the discipline, and of this book.

Institutions: In the political sense, these are formal organizations or practices with a political purpose or effect, marked by durability and internal complexity. The core institutions are usually mandated by the constitution.

Institutionalism: An approach to the study of politics and government that focuses on the structure and dynamics of governing institutions.

What, then, is an institution? In politics, the term traditionally refers to the major organizations of national government, particularly those specified in the constitution such as the legislature, the judiciary, the executive, and, sometimes, political parties (see Figure 5.2). Since they often possess legal identity, acquiring privileges and duties under law, these bodies are treated as literal 'actors' in the political process. However, the concept of an institution is also used more broadly to include other organizations which may have a less secure constitutional basis, such as the bureaucracy and local government. It is also used more widely to denote virtually any organization (such as interest groups) or even any established and well-recognized political practice. For instance, scholars refer to the 'institutionalization' of corruption in Russia or Nigeria, implying that the abuse of public office for private gain in these countries has become an accepted routine of political life – an institution – in its own right. When the concept of an 'institution' is equated with any and every political or social practice, however, it risks over-extension (Rothstein, 1996).

Institutional analysis assumes that positions within organizations matter more than the people who occupy them. This axiom enables us to discuss roles rather than people: presidencies rather than presidents, legislatures rather than legislators, the judiciary rather than judges. The capacity of institutions to affect the behaviour of their members means that politics, as other social sciences, is more than a branch of psychology.

Institutional analysis can be static, based on examining the functioning of, and relationships between, institutions at a given moment. But writers within this approach show increasing interest in institutional evolution and its effects. Institutions possess a history, culture and memory, frequently embodying traditions and founding values. In a process of **institutionalization**, they grow 'like coral reefs through slow accretion' (Sait, 1938: 18). In this way, many institutions thicken naturally over time, developing their internal procedures and also becoming accepted by external actors as part of the governing apparatus. In other words, the institution becomes a node in a network and, in so doing, entrenches its position.

Institutionalization: The process by which organizations build stability and permanence. A government department, for example, is institutionalized if it possesses internal complexity, follows clear rules of procedure, and is clearly distinguished from its environment.

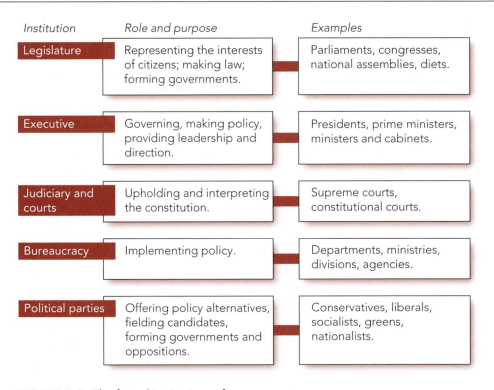

Institution	Role and purpose	Examples
Legislature	Representing the interests of citizens; making law; forming governments.	Parliaments, congresses, national assemblies, diets.
Executive	Governing, making policy, providing leadership and direction.	Presidents, prime ministers, ministers and cabinets.
Judiciary and courts	Upholding and interpreting the constitution.	Supreme courts, constitutional courts.
Bureaucracy	Implementing policy.	Departments, ministries, divisions, agencies.
Political parties	Offering policy alternatives, fielding candidates, forming governments and oppositions.	Conservatives, liberals, socialists, greens, nationalists.

FIGURE 5.2: The formal institutions of government

As particular institutions come to provide an established and accepted way of working, they acquire resilience and persistence (Pierson, 2004). For example, uncertainty abounded in 1958 when France adopted a new constitution with a semi-presidential system of government, greatly strengthening the powers of the executive relative to those of the legislature. Just a generation later, though, it would have been hard to find anyone favouring a switch back to the inefficiencies and uncertainties of the old parliamentary system. So, as with constitutions, institutions are devices through which the past constrains the present. Thus, the study of institutions is the study of political stability, rather than change. As Orren and Skowronek (1995: 298) put it:

> Institutions are seen as the pillars of order in politics, as the structures that lend the polity its integrity, facilitate its routine operation and produce continuity in the face of potentially destabilizing forces. Institutional politics is politics as usual, normal politics, or a politics in equilibrium.

Institutions are particularly central to the functioning of liberal democracies, because they provide a settled framework for reaching decisions, In addition, they enable long-term commitments which are more credible than those of any single employee, thus building trust. For example, governments can borrow money at lower rates than are available to individual bureaucrats. Similarly, a government can make credible promises to repay its debt over a period of generations, a commitment that is beyond the reach of any individual debtor.

Institutions also offer predictability. When we visit a government office, we do so with expectations about how the members of staff will behave, even though we know nothing about them as individuals. A shared institutional context eases the task of conducting business between strangers. In and beyond politics, institutions help to glue society together, extending the bounds of what would be possible for individuals acting alone.

At the same time, an institutional approach, like all others, can become inward-looking. Two particular problems should be highlighted. First, some institutions are explicitly created to resolve particular problems. For example, in the wake of the global financial crisis of 2007–10, and of the debt crisis that broke in the eurozone in 2009, European Union governments agreed to create new institutions designed to improve financial supervision and to encourage more consistent regulation of banking. We should perhaps focus more on these key historical moments which spark institutional creativity. Although uncommon, they help us to view institutions as a product of, rather than just an influence on, political action by individuals.

Second, governing institutions rarely act independently of social forces, especially in poorer, less complex, and authoritarian states. Sometimes, the president is the presidency, and the entire superstructure of government is a facade behind which personal networks and exchanges continue to drive politics. In the extreme case of communist party states, for instance, the formal institutions of government were controlled by the ruling party. Government was the servant, not the master, and its institutions carried little independent weight.

Even in liberal democracies, it is always worth asking whose interests benefit from a particular institutional set-up. Just as an institution can be created for specific purposes, so too can it survive by serving the interests of those in charge. For example, the arrangement in the United States by which electoral districts are designed by the dominant political parties in each state, allowing them to manipulate the outcome of elections in a

process known as 'gerrymandering', is a distortion of democracy, but it suits the interests of the Republicans and the Democrats. In addressing the collective benefit that institutions deliver, we should remember that the support of powerful political and economic interests provides additional stability (Mahoney and Thelen, 2010: 8).

Overall, the institutions of government must be seen as central to liberal democratic politics, and we must look not just at their definition and origins, but also at their purpose, effects, and character (see Figure 5.3). They are the apparatus through which political issues are shaped, processed, and sometimes resolved. They provide a major source of continuity and predictability, and they shape the environment within which political actors operate and, to an extent, structure their interests, values, and preferences. The institutional approach offers no developed theory but does provide observations about institutional development and functioning which can anchor studies of specific cases.

New institutionalism

The manner in which theories and approaches tend to go in and out of fashion (or, at least, to evolve) is reflected in what happened to institutionalism in the

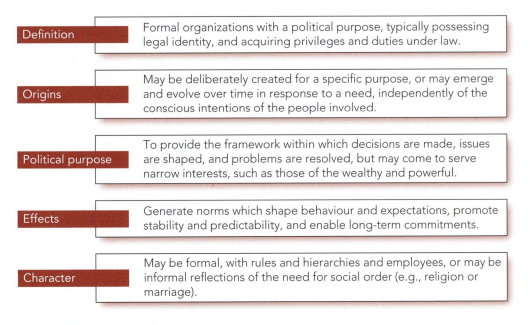

Definition — Formal organizations with a political purpose, typically possessing legal identity, and acquiring privileges and duties under law.

Origins — May be deliberately created for a specific purpose, or may emerge and evolve over time in response to a need, independently of the conscious intentions of the people involved.

Political purpose — To provide the framework within which decisions are made, issues are shaped, and problems are resolved, but may come to serve narrow interests, such as those of the wealthy and powerful.

Effects — Generate norms which shape behaviour and expectations, promote stability and predictability, and enable long-term commitments.

Character — May be formal, with rules and hierarchies and employees, or may be informal reflections of the need for social order (e.g., religion or marriage).

FIGURE 5.3: Understanding political institutions

1950s and 1960s, when new approaches such as behaviouralism won support. The institutional approach was criticized for being too descriptive and for looking at the formal rules of government at the expense of politics in its many different forms, and fell out of favour. But then the 1980s saw new research on social and political structures and a new interest in the reform of institutions in developing countries. The result was the birth of what became known as **new institutionalism** (March and Olsen, 1984).

> **New institutionalism:** A revival of institutionalism that goes beyond formal rules and looks at how institutions shape decisions and define interests.

This looks not just at the formal rules of government but also at how institutions shape political decisions, at the interaction of institutions and society, and at the informal patterns of behaviour within formal institutions. This lent itself well to comparative politics as researchers undertook cross-national studies, many of them interested in better understanding the process of democratization. Revealing just how many variations there can be on a theoretical theme, Peters (1999) identifies seven strands of new institutionalism, ranging from the historical to the international and the sociological.

The institutional approach offers two main reasons for supposing that organizations shape behaviour. First, because institutions provide benefits and opportunities, they shape the interests of their staff. As soon as an organization pays salaries, its employees acquire interests, such as ensuring their own personal progress within the structure and defending their institution against outsiders. March and Olsen (1984: 738) suggest that institutions become participants in the political struggle:

> The bureaucratic agency, the legislative committee and the appellate court are arenas for contending social forces but they are also collections of standard operating procedures and structures that define and defend interests. They are political actors in their own right.

Second, sustained interaction among employees encourages the emergence of an institutional culture, which can weld the organization into an effective operational unit. Institutions generate norms which, in turn, shape behaviour. One strength of the institutional approach is this capacity to account for the origins of interests and cultures, rather than just taking them for granted. As Zijderveld writes (2000: 70), 'institutions are coercive structures that mould our acting, thinking and feeling'.

The new institutional approach suggests that much political action is best understood by reference to the contrasts between the **logic of appropriateness** and the **logic of consequences**. The former sees human action as driven by the rules of appropriate behaviour, and hence institutions shape activity simply because it is natural and expected, not because it has any deeper political motive. For instance, when prime ministers visit an area devastated by floods, they are not necessarily seeking to direct relief operations, or even to increase their public support, but may just be doing what is expected in their job. In itself, the tour achieves the goal of meeting expectations arising from the actor's institutional position. 'Don't just do something, stand there', said Ronald Reagan, a president with a fine grasp of the logic of appropriateness. When an institution faces an obligation to act, its members are as likely to be heard asking 'What did we do the last time this happened?' as 'What is the right thing to do in this situation?' They seek a solution *appropriate* for the organization and its history.

> **Logic of appropriateness:** The actions which members of an institution take to conform to its norms. For example, a head of state will perform ceremonial duties because it is an official obligation.

> **Logic of consequences:** The actions which members of an institution take on the basis of a rational calculation of altruism or self-interest.

This emphasis within the institutional framework on the symbolic or ritual aspect of political behaviour contrasts with the view of politicians and bureaucrats as rational actors who define their own goals independently of the organization they represent. In other words, their actions are shaped by consequences, or the political returns they expect to achieve from those actions; they are faced with a problem, they look at the alternatives and at their personal values, and they choose the option that provides the most efficient means to achieving their goals. In short, institutions provide the rules of the game within which individuals pursue their objectives (Shepsle, 2006).

FOCUS 5.1 | Empirical versus normative approaches

One of the more important debates in political research concerns the differences between **empirical** and **normative** perspectives; one uses facts to ask what happened and why (descriptive), while the other uses judgements or prescriptions to ask what should have happened or what ought to happen (evaluative) (see Gerring and Yesnowitz, 2006). Take electoral systems, for example: the statement that 'proportional representation encourages multi-party systems' is empirical, while the statement that 'proportional representation should be used to encourage multiple parties' is normative.

Most political research tries to be empirical in the sense that it asks why things are the way they are in a manner that tries to be value-neutral, as when a researcher looks into the causes of war in a purely objective and scientific fashion. But other research takes a more normative approach by asking what should be done in order to achieve a desired outcome, such that the researcher questions the phenomenon of war in a more value-driven and philosophical manner, asking – for example – whether and in what circumstances war is ever justified.

The empirical and normative approaches are not mutually exclusive, and there has been renewed demand for the idea of making political science more relevant by combining the two. Consider the argument made by Gerring and Yesnowitz (2006):

Empirical study in the social sciences is meaningless if it has no normative import … It matters, or may matter, but we do not know how. Likewise, a normative argument without empirical support may be rhetorically persuasive or logically persuasive, but it will not have demonstrated anything about the world out there. It has no empirical ballast. Good social science must integrate both elements; it must be empirically grounded, and it must be relevant to human concerns.

Many of the towering figures in the history of political thought trod lightly between the two perspectives, the cases of Machiavelli and Marx illustrating this point:

- Niccolò Machiavelli (1469–1527) was a writer and historian whose masterpiece *The Prince* looked at the qualities of power and the means used by rulers to win, keep, and manipulate it. On the one hand, his book can be seen as an empirical (and even cynical) analysis of the nature and exercise of power in the real world. On the other hand, it can also be understood as normatively endorsing the sometimes brutal tactics rulers need to, or indeed should, follow to sustain their position.
- Karl Marx (1818–83) wrote a vast body of empirical work presenting history as a class struggle between the owners of the means of production and the labourers, arguing that states were run in the interests of the owners. He concluded that capitalism created internal tensions which ensured that it was sowing the seeds of its own inevitable destruction. But underlying this empirical analysis was a normative concern to accelerate capitalism's overthrow so as to create the possibility of a new classless society. In Marx's work, empirical research was motivated by normative goals.

Empirical: Conclusions or inferences based on facts, experience or observation.

Normative: Reaching judgements and prescriptions about what ought to be done.

The behavioural approach

The major problem faced by political science in its early decades was the doubt that it was a science at all (Dahl, 1961b). This began to change in the 1960s as the theoretical focus moved away from institutions and towards individual behaviour, particularly in American political science; in other words, there was a switch from electoral systems to voters, from legislatures to legislators, and from presidencies to presidents. The central tenet of **behaviouralism** was that 'people matter', meaning not specific people so much as the individual as the level or unit of analysis. The aim was to use scientific methods to develop generalizations about political attitudes and behaviour by studying what people actually do, rather than studying constitutions, institutions and organizational charts. Rather than implying an exclusive concern with action, the word *behaviour* expressed a focus on observable political reality, rather than official discourse; on individuals rather than institutions; and on scientific explanation rather than the loose descriptions of the institutionalists.

> **Behaviouralism:** An approach to the study of politics that emphasizes people over institutions, studying the attitudes and behaviour of individuals in search of scientific generalizations.

The shift can be traced back to the work of the political scientist Charles Merriam at the University of Chicago in the 1920s. He argued the importance of moving beyond the study of formal rules and looking at the behaviour of individuals, but his ideas took some time to become more widely adopted. In part, the eventual shift grew out of the influence of decolonization. In newly independent states, government institutions proved to be of little moment as presidents, and then ruling generals, quickly dispensed with the elaborate constitutions written at independence. A fresher and wider approach – one rooted in social, economic, and political realities, rather than constitutional fictions – was needed to understand politics in the developing world.

In the United States, meanwhile, the post-war generation of political scientists was keen to apply innovative social science techniques developed during the Second World War – notably, interview-based sample surveys of ordinary people. In this way, the study of politics could be presented as a social science and become eligible for research funds made possible by that designation. The study of legislatures, for example, moved away from formal aspects (e.g. the procedures by which a bill becomes law) towards legislative behaviour (e.g. how members defined their job). Researchers delved into the social backgrounds of representatives, their individual voting records, their career progression, and their willingness to rebel against the party line.

Similarly, scholars who studied judiciaries began to take judges, rather than courts, as their unit of analysis, using statistical techniques to assess how the social background and political attitudes of judges shaped their decisions and their interpretations of the constitution. This level of inquiry tended to focus on 'the backgrounds, attitudes and ideological preferences of individual justices rather than on the nature of the Court as an institution and its significance for the political system' (Clayton and Gillman, 1999: 1). In fact, the institutional setting was often just taken for granted.

Although the behavioural approach could target elites, it earned its spurs in the study of ordinary people. Survey analysis yielded useful generalizations about voting behaviour, political participation and public opinion. Unlike institutional analysis of government, these studies located politics in its social setting, showing – for example – how race and class impinged on whether, how, and to what extent people took part in politics. In this way, the behavioural revolution broadened our outlook.

The behavioural approach provided the research foundation for several chapters in this book. There have been 'few areas in political science', claim Dalton and Klingemann (2007: vii), 'where scholarly knowledge has made greater progress in the past two generations'. Yet, as a model for the entire discipline, the behavioural revolution eventually ran its course. Its focus on individual political behaviour took the study of politics away from its natural concern with the institutions of government. Its methods became more technical and its findings more specialized.

Behaviouralism produced a political science with too much science and too little politics. Amid the political protests of the late 1960s, behaviouralists were criticized for fiddling while Rome burned. Rather like the institutional approach before it, behaviouralism seemed unable to address current political events. The strategy of developing generalizations applying across space and time was ill-suited to capturing the politics of any particular moment. In short, the research programme had become orthodox, rather than progressive; it was time for something new.

The structural approach

Structuralism is an approach to political analysis that focuses on relationships among parts rather than the parts themselves. In other words, it involves examining the 'networks, linkages, interdependencies, and interactions among the parts of some system' (Lichbach and

Zuckerman, 1997: 247). The central tenet here is that 'groups matter', in the sense that the structural approach focuses on powerful groups in society, such as the bureaucracy, political parties, social classes, churches, and the military. These groups possess and pursue their own interests, creating a set of relationships which forms the structure underpinning or destabilizing the institutional politics of parties and government. Each group within the structure works to sustain its political influence in a society which is always developing in response to economic change, ideological innovations, international politics and the effects of group conflict itself. It is this framework which undergirds, and ultimately determines, actual politics, because human actions are shaped by this bigger structural environment.

> **Structuralism:** An approach to the study of politics that emphasizes the relationships among groups and networks within larger systems. The interests and positions of these groups shape the overall configuration of power and provide the dynamic of political change.

A structure is defined by the relationships between its parts, with the parts themselves – including their internal organization and the individuals within them – being of little interest. As Skocpol (1979: 291) put it, structuralists 'emphasize objective relationships and conflicts among variously situated groups and nations, rather than the interests, outlooks, or ideologies of particular actors'. For example, the relationship between labour and capital is more important than the internal organization or the leaders of trade unions and business organizations. The assumption is that capital and labour will follow their own real interests, regardless of who happens to lead the organizations formally representing their concerns. Individuals are secondary to the grand political drama unfolding around them.

But *real interests* and *social actors* are, of course, terms imposed by the researcher. Who is to say where a group's true interests lie? How can we refer to the 'actions' of a group, rather than a person? In execution, the structural approach is broad-brush, making large if plausible assumptions about the nature of conflict in a particular society and using them to make inferences about causes without always paying great attention to the detailed historical record.

We can draw a clear contrast between structuralism and the cultural analysis covered in Chapter 12. While, for example, a structural explanation of poverty would emphasize the contrasting interests and power positions of property-owners and the working class, a cultural analysis would place more weight on the values of poor people themselves, showing how, for example, limited aspirations trap the poor in a cycle of poverty that can persist across generations. For the structuralist, the important factor is the framework of inequality, not the values that confine particular families to the bottom of the hierarchy. This point, and the overall thrust of structuralism, is summarized by Mahoney (2003: 51):

> At the core of structuralism is the concern with objective relationships between groups and societies. Structuralism holds that configurations of social relations shape, constrain and empower actors in predictable ways. Structuralism generally downplays or rejects cultural and value-based explanations of social phenomena. Likewise, structuralism opposes approaches that explain social outcomes solely or primarily in terms of psychological states, individual decision-making processes, or other individual-level characteristics.

The best-known structural work in politics has adopted an explicitly historical style, seeking to understand how competition between powerful groups over time leads to specific outcomes such as a revolution, democracy, or a multi-party system. The authors of such studies argue that politics is about struggle rather than equilibrium, and they favour comparative history, giving us another contrast with the non-historical generalizations favoured by behaviouralists and the sometimes static descriptions of the institutionalists.

One of the leading figures in the field – who not only exemplifies the structural approach but helped to define it – was the American sociologist Barrington Moore. His 1966 book *Social Origins of Dictatorship and Democracy: Lord and Peasant in the Making of the Modern World* did more than any other to shape this format of historical analysis of structural forces. In trying to understand why liberal democracy developed earlier and more easily in France, Britain, and the United States than in Germany and Japan, he suggested that the strategy of the rising commercial class was the key. In countries such as Britain, where the bourgeoisie avoided entanglement with the landowners in their battles with the peasants, the democratic transition was relatively peaceful. But where landlords engaged the commercial classes in a joint campaign against the peasantry, as in Germany, the result was an authoritarian regime which delayed the onset of democracy.

Although later research qualified many of Moore's judgements, his work showed the value of studying structural relationships between groups and classes as they evolve over long periods (Mahoney, 2003). He asked important comparative questions and answered them with an account of how and when class relationships develop and evolve.

The structural approach asks big questions and, by selecting answers from the past, it interrogates history without limiting itself to chronology. Many authors working in this tradition make large claims about the positions adopted by particular classes and groups; specifically, interests are often treated as if they were actors, leading to ambitious generalizations which need verification through detailed research. Even so, the structural approach, in the form of comparative history, has made a distinctive contribution to comparative politics.

The rational choice approach

Like behaviouralism, **rational choice** approaches are focused on people, but instead of examining actions they try to explain the calculations behind those actions. They argue that politics consists of strategic interaction between individuals, with all players seeking to maximize the achievement of their own particular goals. The central tenet here is that objectives matter. The assumption is that people 'are rational in the sense that, given goals and alternative strategies from which to choose, they will select the alternatives that maximize their chances of achieving their goals' (Geddes, 2003: 177). Where behaviouralists aim to explain political action through statistical generalization, the rational choice approach focuses on the interests of the actors. And where the structural perspective is rooted in historical sociology, the rational choice approach comes out of economics.

Rational choice: An approach to the study of politics based on the idea that political behaviour reflects the choices made by individuals working to maximize their benefits and minimize their costs.

The potential value of rational choice analysis lies in its ability to model the essentials of political action, and hence make predictions, without all-encompassing knowledge of the actors. We simply need to identify the goals of the actors and how their objectives can best be advanced in a given situation. Then, we can predict what

they will do. All else, including the accounts actors give of their own behaviour, is detail. The aim is to model the fundamentals of human interaction, not to provide a rich account of human motives.

Neither are rational choice analysts concerned to provide an accurate account of the mental process leading to decisions; the test is whether behaviour is correctly predicted. The underlying philosophy – that explanation is best sought in models that are both simple and fundamental – is a distinctive feature of the approach, reflecting its origins in economics. More than any other approach, the rational choice approach values parsimonious explanations. To appreciate the style of rational choice thinking, it is crucial to recognize how simplifying assumptions can be seen as a strength in building models and generating predictions.

What goals can people pursue within the rational choice framework? Most analysts adopt the axiom of self-interest. This was defined long ago by John C. Calhoun, the American politician and one-time vice president, in his *Disquisition on Government* (1851) as the assumption that each person 'has a greater regard for his own safety or happiness, than for the safety or happiness of others: and, where they come into opposition, is ready to sacrifice the interests of others to his own'.

At the cost of increased complexity, we can broaden the range of goals. We can imagine that people take satisfaction from seeing others achieve their ends, or we can even permit our subjects to pursue altruistic projects. Yet, just as markets are best analysed by assuming self-interest among the participants, so too do most rational choice advocates believe that the same assumption takes us to the essence of politics. As Hindmoor (2010: 42) puts it, 'if people are rational and self-interested it becomes possible to explain and even predict their actions in ways that would allow rational choice theorists to claim a mantle of scientific credibility'.

Rational choices are not necessarily all-knowing. Operating in an uncertain world, people need to discount the value of going for a goal by the risk they will fail to achieve it. In situations of uncertainty, they may prefer to eliminate the risk of a bad outcome, rather than go for broke by staking all on a single bet. Thus, a rational choice needs to be distinguished from a knowledgeable one.

Consider, for example, the task of working out which party to vote for. As voters, we might well find that the cost of research on all the candidates exceeds the benefits gained, leading us to use shortcuts such as relying on expert opinion. It is not always rational to be fully informed, a fact that brings the approach closer to the real world. However, the full rational model – the version which allows us to predict most easily – assumes that actors are knowledgeable as well as rational and self-interested.

In the study of politics, the rational choice framework is often extended from the individual to the larger units that are most often studied by comparativists. So rational choice analysts sometimes apply their techniques to political parties and interest groups, treating them as if they were individuals. In his analysis of political parties, for example, Downs (1957: 28) imagined that all party members 'act solely in order to attain the income, prestige, and power which come from being in office'. For ease of analysis, he treated parties as if they were unitary actors, in the same way that students of international politics often regard states. In both cases, the aim is accurate prediction, not a detailed reconstruction of the actual decision process.

A major contribution of the approach lies in highlighting **collective action problems**. These arise in coordinating the actions of individuals so as to achieve the best outcome for each person. For instance, many people persist in living a polluting lifestyle, arguing that their behaviour will make no decisive difference to overall environmental quality. Yet, the outcome from everyone behaving in this way is climate change that is damaging to all. In other words, individual rationality leads to a poor collective result.

> **Collective action problem:** Arises when rational behaviour by individuals produces a negative overall outcome. The issue typically arises when people seek to free ride on the efforts of others in providing public goods.

Similarly, during the global financial crisis, many investment bankers made high-risk investments in order to increase their bonuses; their employers, too, were happy enough as long as their corporate profits continued to grow. When these investments eventually turned bad, the effect was a problem not only for the original investors, but also – and more importantly – a threat to the stability of the Western financial system. Clearly, some form of coordination is needed if private actions are to be made compatible with desirable collective outcomes – in this case, governments imposed stricter regulation of banks by governments. More than any other framework, the rational choice approach encourages to

us to recognize that individual preferences and collective outcomes are two different things; a government is needed to bridge the gap.

Paradoxically, the rational choice approach can be useful even when it is inaccurate. Its value lies not merely in the accuracy of its predictions, but also in identifying what appears to be irrational behaviour. If people behave in a surprising way, we have identified a puzzle in need of a solution. Perhaps we have misunderstood their preferences, or the situation confronting them. Or perhaps their actions really are irrational. At the international level, Government A might judge that Government B's interests lie in pursuing policy X. If Government B actually adopts policy Y, then Government A has some thinking to do. Has it misunderstood B's goals, or has B simply made a mistake?

Yet the rational choice approach, as any other, takes too much for granted. It fails to explain the origins of the goals that individuals hold; it is here, in understanding the shaping of preferences, that society re-enters the equation. Our aspirations, our status, and even our goals emerge from our interactions with others, rather than being formed beforehand. Certainly, we cannot take people's goals and values as given.

Also, since the rational choice approach is based on a universal model of human behaviour, it has limited relevance in understanding variation across countries. Just as individual goals are taken for granted, so too should be the different national settings which determine the choices available to individuals and within which they pursue their strategies. Still, even though the rational choice approach does not always generate accurate predictions, it provides one lens, among several, for analysing political processes.

The interpretive approach

The focus of the **interpretive approach** is on the interpretations within which politics operates, including assumptions, codes, constructions, identities, meanings, norms, narratives, and values. In other words, people do some things and avoid others because of the presence of social constructs that filter the way they see the world (hence the approach is also sometimes known as 'constructivism'). This approach takes us away from the behaviouralist search for scientific laws and towards a concern with the ideas of individuals and groups, and how their constructs define and shape political activity. The starting point is that we cannot take the actor's goals and definition of the situation for granted, as the rational actor approach does; instead, we must look at the way those goals and definitions are constructed.

> **Interpretive approach:** An approach to the study of politics based on the argument that politics is formed by the ideas we have about it.

In its strongest version, the interpretive approach argues that politics consists of the ideas participants hold about it. There is no political reality separate from our mental constructions, and no reality which can be examined to reveal the impact of ideas upon it. Rather, politics is formed by ideas themselves. In short, 'ideas matter' and there is nothing but ideas.

In a more restrained version, the argument is not that ideas comprise our political world but, rather, that they are an independent influence upon it, shaping how we define our interests, our goals, our allies, and our enemies. We act as we do because of how we view the world; if our perspective differed, so would our actions. Where rational choice analysis focuses on how people go about achieving their individual objectives, the interpretivist examines the framing of objectives themselves and regards such interpretations as a property of the group, rather than the individual (hence interpretivists take a social rather than a psychological approach).

Because ideas are socially constructed, many interpretivists imagine that we can restructure our view of the world and, so, the world itself. For instance, there is no intrinsic reason why individuals and states must act (as rational choice theorists imagine) in pursuit of their own narrow self-interests. To make such an assumption is to project concepts onto a world that we falsely imagine to be independent of our thoughts. Finnemore (1996: 2), for example, suggests that interests 'are not just "out there" waiting to be discovered; they are constructed through social interaction'. Also, ideas come before material factors because the value placed on material things is itself an idea (although Marxists and others would disagree).

For example, states are often presented as entities existing independently of our thoughts. But the state is not a physical entity such as a building or a mountain; it is an idea built over a long period by political thinkers, as well as by practical politicians. Borders between blocs of land were placed there not by nature but by people. There are no states when the world is viewed from outer space, as astronauts frequently tell us. Or, more

accurately, the maps construct their own reality. It is this point Steinberger (2004) has in mind when he says that his idea of the state is that the state is an idea. True, the consequences of states, such as taxes and wars, are real enough, but these are the effects of the world we have made, and can remake.

Similarly, the class relationships emphasized by the structuralists, and the generalizations uncovered by the behaviouralists, are based not on physical realities but on interpretations that can, in principle, be changed. For instance, a behavioural observation about the under-representation of women in legislatures can generate a campaign that leads to an increase in the number of legislators who are women, thus altering the observation itself.

For this reason, interpretivists often focus on historical narratives, examining how understandings of earlier events influence later ones. Take the study of revolutions as an example. Where behaviouralists see a set of cases (French, Russian, Iranian, and so on) and seek common causes of events treated as independent, interpretivists see a single sequence and ask how later examples (such as the Russian Revolution) were influenced by the ideas then held about earlier revolutions (such as the French). Alternatively, take the study of elections. The meaning of an election is not given by the results themselves but by the narrative that the political class later establishes about it: for example, 'the results showed that voters will not tolerate high unemployment' (see Chapter 17 for more about this).

Parsons (2010: 80) provides a useful definition of the interpretive approach:

> People do one thing and not another due to the presence of certain 'social constructs': ideas, beliefs, norms, identities or some other interpretive filter through which people perceive the world. We inhabit 'a world of our making' (Onuf, 1989) and action is structured by the meanings that particular groups of people develop to interpret and organise their identities, relationships and environment.

The interpretive approach sees the task of explanation as that of identifying the meaning which itself helps to define action. The starting point is not behaviour but action – that is, meaningful behaviour. Geertz (1973: 5) argues that, since we are suspended in webs of meaning that we ourselves have spun, the academic study of social and political affairs cannot be a behavioural science seeking laws but must instead be an interpretive one seeking meaning. Wendt (1999: 105) further illustrates this notion of explanation through meaning:

If we want to explain how a master can sell his slave then we need to invoke the structure of shared understandings existing between master and slave, and in the wider society, that makes this ability to sell people possible. This social structure does not merely describe the rights of the master; it explains them, since without it those rights by definition could not exist.

In politics, as in other disciplines concerned with groups, most interpretivists consider how the meanings of behaviour form, reflect, and sustain the traditions and discourses of a social group or an entire society. The concern is social constructs, rather than just the specific ideas of leaders and elite groups. For example, by acting in a world of states – where we apply for passports, support national sports teams, or just use the word *citizen* – we routinely reinforce the concept of the state. By practising statehood in these ways, as much as by direct influence through education and the media, the idea itself is socially reinforced or, as is often said, 'socially constructed'. These understandings can also be socially contested ('Why should I need a visa each time I visit this country?'), leading to gradual changes in the ideas themselves.

There is a clear and useful lesson here for students of politics, and of comparative politics especially. When we confront a political system for the first time, our initial task is to engage in political anthropology: to make

---

FOCUS 5.2   The interpretive approach: mass killings and genocide

As an example of the independent impact of ideas in politics, consider the book *Final Solutions*, Benjamin Valentino's prize-winning 2004 study of mass killing and genocide in the twentieth century. Valentino suggests that the mass murder of civilians is a product of the ideas of the instigators, designed to accomplish their most important ideological and political objectives (2004: 67). Valentino is a student of elite ideas, which he takes to include both goals and assessments of how to achieve them; he is less concerned with structural relationships or government institutions:

> To identify societies at high risk for mass killing, we must first understand the specific goals, ideas and beliefs of powerful groups and leaders, not necessarily the broad social structures or systems of government over which these leaders preside. (p. 66)

Valentino contends that 'mass killing occurs when powerful groups come to believe it is the best available means to accomplish certain radical goals, counter specific types of threat or solve difficult military problems' (p. 66). Unlike rational choice thinkers, he does not assume that politicians are accurate in their perceptions of their environment. Their understandings are what matter, even if these are misunderstandings:

> An understanding of mass killing does not imply that perpetrators always evaluate objectively the problems they face in their environment, nor that they accurately assess the ability of mass killings to resolve these problems. Human beings act on the basis of their subjective perceptions and beliefs, not objective results. (p. 67)

But it is not just ideas and perceptions that are Valentino's concern. Rather, he examines how leaders are driven by actual and perceived changes in the political environment to regard mass killing as the final solution for achieving their ends. Thus, his approach is not purely interpretive but, instead, consists of a fruitful examination of the interaction over time between political realities, on the one hand, and elite ideas and perceptions, on the other.

Valentino carries through his interest in ideas to a consideration of how we can best prevent future occurrences of mass killing. He rejects the relevance of behavioural and structural generalizations suggesting that mass killings only occur in dictatorships or war. Rather, he suggests that leaders in any type of structure or political system may come to see mass killing as the best, most effective or sole method of achieving their goals. Effective prevention therefore requires us to return once more to leaders' ideas: 'if we hope to anticipate mass killing, we must begin to think of it in the same way its perpetrators do' (p. 141).

sense of the activities that comprise the system. What are the moves? What do they mean? What is the context that provides this meaning? And what identities and values underpin political action? Behaviour which has one meaning in our home country may possess a different significance, and constitute a different action, elsewhere. For example, offering a bribe may be accepted as normal in one place, but be regarded as a serious offence in another. Casting a vote may be an act of choice in a democracy, but of subservience in a dictatorship. Criticizing the president may be routine in one country, but sedition in another. Because the recognised consequences of these acts vary, so does their meaning.

So far, so good. Yet, in studying politics we want to identify patterns that abstract from detail; we seek general statements about presidential, electoral, or party systems which go beyond the facts of a particular case. We want to examine relationships between such categories so as to discover overall associations. We want to know, for instance, whether a plurality electoral system always leads to a two-party system. Through such investigations we can acquire knowledge which goes beyond the understandings held by the participants in a particular case.

We must recognize, also, that events have unintended consequences: the Holocaust was certainly a product of Hitler's ideas, but its effects ran far beyond his own intentions. With its emphasis on meaning, an interpretive approach misses the commonplace observation that much social and political analysis studies the unintended consequences of human activity. In short, unpacking the meaning of political action is best regarded as the start, but not the end, of political analysis. It provides a practical piece of advice: we must grasp the meaning of political behaviour, thus enabling us to compare like with like. Yet, it would be unsatisfactory to regard a project as complete at this preliminary point.

Compared with the other approaches reviewed in this chapter, the interpretive approach remains more aspiration than achievement. Some studies conducted within the programme focus on interesting but far-away cases when meanings really were different: when states did not rule the world; when lending money was considered a sin; or when the political game consisted of acquiring dependent followers, rather than independent wealth.

Yet, such studies do little to confirm the easy assumption that the world we have made can be easily dissolved. As the institutionalists with whom we began this chapter are quick to remind us, most social constructs are social constraints, for institutions are powerfully persistent. Our ability to imagine other worlds should not bias how we go about understanding the world as it is.

DISCUSSION QUESTIONS

- Why is there so much disagreement among political scientists (or comparativists) about the best theoretical approach, and why are grand theories so elusive?

- How far can we understand politics and government by focusing only – or mainly – on institutions?

- Which matter more to an understanding of government and politics: institutions or people?

- What does 'rational' mean and do people behave rationally?

- What influences have been most important in shaping how you view the political world? Which of the approaches in this chapter is most useful in comparative politics?

KEY TERMS

Behaviouralism
Collective action problem
Empirical
Grand theory
Interpretive approach
Institutionalism
Institutionalization
Institutions

Logic of appropriateness
Logic of consequences
New institutionalism
Normative
Rational choice
Structuralism
Theory

FURTHER READING

Boix, Carles and Susan C. Stokes (eds) (2009) *The Oxford Handbook of Comparative Politics*. A survey of the field of comparative politics, including a section on theory and methodology.

Green, Daniel M. (ed.) (2002) *Constructivism and Comparative Politics*. Examines the value of the interpretive approach in comparative politics.

Lichbach, Mark Irving and Alan S. Zuckerman (eds) (2009) *Comparative Politics: Rationality, Culture and Structure*, 2nd edn. Detailed essays on the rational, cultural, and structural approaches to comparative politics.

Mahoney, James and Dietrich Rueschemeyer (eds) (2003) *Comparative Historical Analysis in the Social Sciences*. A thorough presentation of structural analysis as expressed in comparative history.

Marsh, David and Gerry Stoker (eds) (2010) *Theory and Methods in Political Science*, 3rd edn. Includes essays on most of the approaches introduced in this chapter.

Peters, B. Guy (2011) *Institutional Theory in Political Science*, 3rd edn. A survey of the different facets of institutional theory, and its potential as a paradigm for political science.

CHAPTER

6

Comparing government and politics

PREVIEW

So far we have looked at the conceptual and theoretical aspects of comparative politics. But these only begin to have meaning when we put comparison into practice, for which reason we now turn to the practicalities of comparison: the kinds of questions that need to be asked, the methods that can be used, the options for designing a comparative research project, and the pitfalls to be avoided. This chapter is intended in part to be a survey of methods and in part to be a practical *How To* guide to the comparative process, giving more insight into the dynamics of that process. The goal is not to cover the details of specific techniques such as interviewing or statistical analysis so much as to provide strategies that will help students working on comparative projects of their own.

The chapter begins with a discussion about the number and the use of cases chosen in comparison; these range from one to many, the research methods used being different for single-case studies, those involving a small number of cases (small-N studies), and those involving a large number of cases (large-N studies). The chapter then reviews the features of qualitative and quantitative research methods, and considers some of the challenges faced by comparison, including the troubling problem of too few cases and too many variables. It ends with an assessment of the historical method, which can be useful in offsetting some of the limitations inherent in the case study method.

KEY ARGUMENTS

- There is a wide range of options when it comes to conducting comparative political research. It is important to be aware of the potential of comparison (Chapter 1) as well as the alternatives and limitations (this chapter).

- Researchers have choices to make that include the unit of analysis, the level of analysis, and the variables to be studied.

- The three main research methods are the case study, the qualitative approach to a small selection of cases, and the quantitative approach to large numbers of cases.

- Comparative research will have different approaches and results according to whether it is empirical or normative in approach, or quantitative or qualitative.

- When comparative projects seek to examine the relationship between two or more factors, it is worth considering the relative strengths of the most similar and most different system designs.

- History is arguably under-used in comparative political research. Current cases can be compared with past examples, and developments over time can be compared across countries.

Comparing government and politics: an overview

The direction and outcome of scientific study both depend on how we undertake our research, and thus **methodology** is critical. We saw in Chapter 5 that there are different theoretical approaches to comparison, and now we will see that there are also many research methods, and differing opinions about the best way of realizing the potential of comparison (Munck and Snyder, 2007). The options begin with the **unit of analysis**, whether states, institutions, processes, movements, themes, policies, or individuals. A related decision concerns the **level of analysis**, which can be anything from the relations among and between states down through groups or social classes to politics at the level of the individual.

> **Methodology:** The systematic analysis of the methods used in a given field of enquiry. Also used to describe the body of methods used in a discipline, or the means used to reach a particular set of conclusions.

> **Unit of analysis:** The object of study in comparative politics.

> **Level of analysis:** The level of study in comparative politics, ranging from the political system level to the individual level.

Researchers are then faced with a number of additional choices: the case or cases they wish to study, the particular combination of such cases, the particular **variable** that interests them, and the question of whether to use quantitative or qualitative research methods. Even if they opt for the most popular approach – the case study method – they are faced with several subsidiary questions regarding the number of cases they use, and whether the cases they use are representative of a type, or not.

> **Variable:** A changeable feature, factor, quantity, or element.

Lijphart (1971) made a distinction between three different approaches to political research: the experimental method uses experimental and control groups to isolate the effects of different stimuli, the statistical method uses empirically observed data to tease out relationships among variables, and the **comparative method** is exactly the same as the statistical method except that it focuses on drawing conclusions from the study of a small number of cases.

> **Comparative method:** Comparing a small number of cases in order to better understand their qualities, and to develop and investigate hypotheses, theories, and concepts.

Comparison is one of the oldest tools of political science, found in the work of Aristotle. Some have even argued that the scientific study of politics is unavoidably comparative (Almond, 1966; Lasswell 1968), and that 'comparison is the methodological core of the scientific study of politics' (Powell *et al.*, 2014). The 'method' is usually taken to mean the study of a few carefully selected cases using a middle level of analysis (rather than the more intensive analysis possible with a few cases, or the more abstract analysis necessary with many cases) (Landman, 2008: 29), but it can take different forms according to the number of cases being studied.

Comparative research methods

The methods available for the comparative study of politics and government are many and varied. The choice among them, argues Landman (2008: 24) depends on a combination of the research question being asked, the time and resources available, the method with which the researcher is most comfortable, and the epistemological preferences of the researcher; that is, how they believe that understanding is best acquired. At the heart of most comparison is the case study method, which comes with many subsidiary choices: how many cases are appropriate, what selection of cases are appropriate, and are they best approached using qualitative, quantitative, or historical methods? There are also many pitfalls involved in assessing cases, all of which must be factored in to planning and design.

The key question in choosing cases is that of how many there should be, in which regard there are three main options:

- The case study method typically involves a single case, and thus might not seem to be comparative at first glance, but a case is necessarily comparative because it needs to be an example of something larger, against which it can then be juxtaposed. Single cases are not as widely used as they once were, but they have the advantage of depth, and other researchers can use two or more single-country studies to explore broader similarities and differences, and single cases can usefully be compared with an ideal type or a typology.

- The qualitative method is what we usually associate with the comparative method, and involves comparing anything from two to a dozen or more cases (otherwise known as small-N, for the number of cases). It has the advantage of going beyond a single case while also remaining manageable, but many questions arise in regard to the number and the choice of cases.

- The quantitative method tends to be more abstract, involves more cases (that is, large-N studies), and is also better suited to statistical analysis. It will take more time and resources, is more likely to suffer from the variable quality and availability of data from multiple cases, the results will offer more breadth than depth, and it might ultimately have to be checked against single case or small-N studies.

In the pages that follow we will look at each of these in turn, reviewing their features and dynamics, and their advantages and disadvantages. But it must be said in anticipation that they are not divorced from one another, and there is much overlap. In reviewing quantitative and qualitative approaches, for example, King *et al.* (1994: 3–4) note that the two traditions 'appear quite different; indeed they sometimes seem to be at war', but conclude that the differences are mainly of style and technique. The first uses numbers and statistical methods, and 'abstracts from particular instances to seek general description or to test causal hypotheses … [or] measurements and analyses that are easily replicable by other researchers'. The second covers a wide range of approaches, none of which relies primarily on numerical measures.

Case study method

The **case study method** is one of the most widely used strategies in research, being at the heart of political science and widely used also in subjects as diverse as anthropology, business, economics, education, psychology, and sociology. It usually involves an in-depth study of a single example, which might be an event, a policy, or a political institution or process, and an effort is made to use the case to illustrate a wider point applying to other cases. Such studies combine a qualitative investigation of a specific topic, using all the techniques appropriate for

that subject, with a link to wider themes in the study of politics. The greatest advantage is that it offers a real-world understanding of a phenomenon, a clearly defined example that helps to illustrate a wider principle.

> **Case study method:** A research method involving the detailed study of a particular object (a person, institution, country, phenomenon, etc.) as well the context within which it exists.

Yin (2013: 16–17) points out that case studies must be understood in terms of both their scope and their features. In terms of scope, they look in depth at a phenomenon within its actual context; case studies are different from experiments, for example, because the latter separate the phenomena to be studied from their context. In terms of features, case studies help address the phenomenon of too many variables and not enough cases (discussed later in this chapter), and are broadranging in that they rely on multiple sources of evidence.

One key to a successful case study is to be clear what the case represents, and how a case differs from a study. By its nature, a case is an instance of a more general category, such that to examine a case is to undertake an investigation with significance beyond its own boundaries. An account of the Japanese general election of 2012 which does not venture beyond the topic itself is a study, not a case study. But an analysis which takes this election as an example of the return to power of a previously dominant party (the Liberal Democrats) is a case study. A case study adds value by offering a detailed illustration of a theme of wider interest.

By their nature, case studies are multi-method, using a wide range of techniques, including the following:

- Reading the academic literature.
- Examining primary and secondary sources.
- Conducting interviews with participants and other observers in the unit.
- Experiencing and visiting the unit.

As King *et al.* (1994: 38) put it, scholars of cases engage in 'soaking and poking, marinating themselves in minutiae'. They aim to provide a description which is both rounded and detailed, a goal which Geertz (1973) called 'thick description'. This multiple-methods approach contrasts with a more specific and explicit approach using a single lens, such as a statistical analysis, or an experiment. Unlike statistical analysis, which seeks to identify relationships between variables

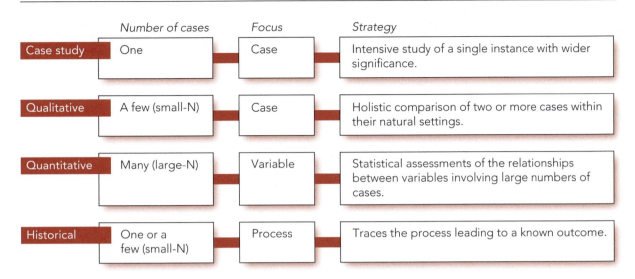

FIGURE 6.1: Political science research methods

Note: N means the number of cases.

measured across a series of observations, case analysis aims to identify how a range of factors interact in the context of the example being studied.

Figure 6.2 outlines five types of case study, of which the representative case is the most common. It is the work-horse of case studies, as useful as it is undramatic. Often researchers will use their own country as a representative example. For instance, researchers may be interested in the formation of coalition governments in general, but

choose to study in detail how governments form in their homeland. The home country is the research site but the hope is that the results will contribute to broader under-standing. A collection of representative case studies can go on to provide the raw material for comparative generali-zation by other scholars taking a wider approach.

By contrast, a prototypical case is chosen not because it is representative but because it is expected to become so. 'In other words, their present is our future'

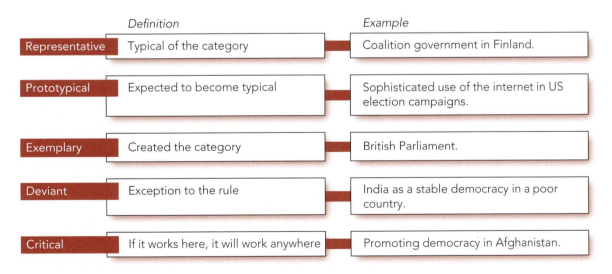

FIGURE 6.2: Five types of case study

Further reading: Yin (2013)

FOCUS 6.1 | Hypotheses and variables

At the heart of research in almost every field of study is the formulation and testing of a **hypothesis**. This is a proposed explanation for a phenomenon that can be supported (confirmed) or refuted (falsified) through observation or experimentation. Hypotheses should not be confused with theories, which are explanatory frameworks from which hypotheses might flow, and which can in turn be tested in order to support or refute theories (see Chapter 5). Examples of hypotheses include the following:

- Plurality electoral systems always produce a two-party system (otherwise known as Duverger's law – see Chapter 15).
- The wealthier a country, the more likely it is to sustain a stable democracy.
- The violent end to a dictatorial regime is more likely to bring chaos than democracy.
- Colonialism is the root cause of the problems of the world's poorest states.

We have also seen how variables play a key role in research, particularly in comparison. The object is usually to explore the extent to which variables or factors co-vary with one another, such that knowing a country's score on one variable (for instance, literacy) allows us to predict its score on another (for instance, electoral turnout). In such analyses, one variable is **dependent**, in the sense that it is the one we want to better understand, while the others are **independent**, in the sense that we believe that they may explain or impact the dependent variable. For example:

- Higher participation in politics may be driven by factors such as greater wealth and higher education.
- The incidence of military coups may be tied to poverty, social division, and the past incidence of coups.
- An assertive foreign policy may be driven by a high sense of mission, the power of the defence industry, fear of the foreign, or (as in the case of Putin's Russia) a desire to reassert lost influence.

Hypothesis: Proposed explanation for a phenomenon that can be confirmed or falsified through observation or experimentation.

Dependent variable: The factor or element we wish to explain.

Independent variable: The factor or element believed to influence the dependent variable. There are often many such variables.

(Rose, 1991: 459). The point here is that studying a pioneer can help us understand a phenomenon which is growing in significance elsewhere. One famous early example of a prototypical case study was *Democracy in America*, written by the French politician Alexis de Tocqueville as a product of his travels in the United States in 1831 to 1832. He had been sent by the French government to study the American prison system, but the book he wrote became a broader analysis of democracy and representative government, using the US as a case. De Tocqueville regarded the United States as a harbinger of democracy and therefore a guide to Europe's own future (1835, ch. 1). More recent examples of prototypical cases would be Tunisia as the first instance of the Arab Spring, or Egypt and Ukraine as cases of the political impact of social media in mobilizing mass demonstrations.

Where the study of prototypical cases aims to reveal how similar cases may evolve in the future, exemplary cases are the archetypes that are considered to have generated the category of which they are taken as representative. For instance, the parliamentary system was born in Britain, and thus a study of the features of the British Parliament will give us insights into the manner in which legislatures and executives work in all those countries using this system. In similar fashion, the US presidency does far more than illustrate the presidential system of government: it is the model which influenced later political systems, notably in Latin America. While an exemplar is often defined as a case to be emulated, in research design the term refers more neutrally to an influential example which illustrates the essential features of a phenomenon. An exemplary case is often, but need not be, prototypical.

The purpose of a deviant case study is to seek out the exceptional and the untypical, rather than the norm: the few countries which remain communist, or which are still governed by the military, or which seem to be immune from democratizing trends. Deviant cases are often used to tidy up our understanding of exceptions and anomalies. Why does India contradict the thesis that democracy presupposes prosperity? Why did tiny Switzerland adopt a federal architecture when many federations are found in large countries? Why has voter turnout stayed high in Denmark even as it has fallen elsewhere (Elkit *et al.*, 2005)? Deviant cases always attract interest and, by providing a contrast with the norm, enhance our understanding of representative examples. But since the exceptional tends to the exotic, the danger is over-study. Comparative politics should be more than a collection of curios.

Finally, a critical case (also known as a 'crucial case') enables a proposition to be tested in the circumstances least favourable to its validity. The logic is simple: if it is true here, then it is true everywhere. For instance, if we were to find that most Germans opposed further European integration, we could anticipate that the same would hold true in other EU countries such as Britain which have historically been more suspicious of the European project. In this way, critical case studies can be highly efficient, providing exceptional returns on the research investment; by studying just one country, we can generalize to others. However, the pay-off comes with risk: a critical case design builds a potential for generalization into a single investigation but involves a bet that the relevant proposition will, in fact, be confirmed in the conditions least favourable to its validity.

In the absence of overarching theory, case studies are the building blocks from which we construct our understanding of the political world. In a similar way to judges in common law systems, political scientists (and politicians more so) usually proceed by comparing cases, rather than by making deductions from first principles. In consequence, much comparative political analysis takes the form not of relating cases to abstract theory but, rather, of drawing analogies between the cases themselves. For instance, how did the process of state-building differ between the states of early modern Europe and the post-colonial states of the twentieth century? What are the similarities and differences

between the Russian, Chinese, and Iranian revolutions? Why does the plurality electoral system produce a two-party system in the United States but a multi-party system in India? As we will see in the next section, a comparison of cases can create space for a broader understanding.

Qualitative method

Implementing a comparative design involves making either qualitative or quantitative comparisons, or a blend of the two. The **qualitative method** is most often used in research that falls between single-case and large-N studies, and concentrates on the intensive examination of two cases (a paired or binary comparison), three cases (a triangular comparison), or more. Cases are usually selected to introduce variation into the dependent variable, thus overcoming an inherent limit of the single case study.

> **Qualitative method:** A research method that typically uses a small number of cases to understand a phenomenon holistically and within its natural setting, with an emphasis on values, opinions, behaviour, and context.

The qualitative approach has the following features:

- A limited number of cases are studied in depth.
- It is descriptive rather than predictive.
- An effort is made to understand the interaction of multiple variables.
- Meaning is allowed to emerge from the objects of study.
- Observation is the main means of data collection.
- Phenomena are studied within their natural setting.

To illustrate the technique, consider the controversial conclusions of Jeremy Rifkin in his 2004 study *The European Dream* which compared and contrasted the priorities and values of Americans and Europeans. He began with the notion of the 'American dream', an idea usually credited to the historian James Truslow Adams in his book *The Epic of America* (1931). Although never clearly defined, it is usually taken to mean that Americans living the dream are being allowed to pursue their goals in life through hard work and free choice, regardless of race, gender, age, religion, or class.

Rifkin was critical of the notion, arguing that it was centred more on personal material advancement than on concern with broader human welfare. He contrasted it with a 'European dream' that emphasized 'quality of life over the accumulation of wealth', as well as:

> community relationships over individual autonomy, cultural diversity over assimilation … sustainable development over unlimited material growth, deep play over unrelenting toil, universal human rights and the rights of nature over property rights, and global cooperation over the unilateral exercise of power. (p. 3)

He concluded that the European Union had been developing a new social and political model better suited to the needs of the globalizing world of the new century, and that the 'European dream' was – as a result – eclipsing the American dream. Ironically, Rifkin was writing just before the onset of the global financial crisis in 2007 and the eurozone crisis in 2009, which would strike severe blows to dreams on both sides of the Atlantic.

The selection of cases is important, and there are two core strategies involved (Przeworski and Teune, 1970). The most common – known as the **most similar system** (MSS) design – involves selecting those cases which are as similar as possible except in regard to the object of study (the dependent variable). The underlying logic is that 'the more similar the units being compared, the more possible it should be to isolate the factors responsible for differences between them' (Lipset, 1990: xiii). If the states being studied are similar in, say, their history, culture, and government institutions, it should be possible to rule out such common factors as explanations for the particular difference being studied.

An example of the MSS method at work might be a study of attitudes towards membership of the European Union among its six founding states, or a selection of Western European members, or a selection of Eastern Europeans members. Attitudes towards integration differ among countries within each group, even though the countries might appear to have much else in common, so the goal would be to tease out the differences that accounted for the variation in levels of support for the EU within an otherwise similar group.

Most similar system: A research design based on using cases that are as similar as possible, in effect controlling for the similarities and isolating the causes of differences.

Most different system: A research design based on using cases that are as different as possible, in effect controlling for the differences and isolating the causes of similarities.

However, even with an MSS design, many factors will remain as possible explanations for an observed difference and, usually, there will be no decisive way of testing among them. The problem of too many variables and too few countries (see later in chapter) cannot be sidestepped; in practice, much of the value of a qualitative comparison (using an MSS design) lies in the journey, rather than the destination.

The **most different system** (MDS) design follows the opposite track. Here, we seek to test a relationship between two factors by discovering whether it can be observed in a range of countries with contrasting histories, cultures, and so on. If so, our confidence that the relationship is real, and not due to the dependence of both factors on an unmeasured third variable, will increase (Peters, 1998). A well-known example of this approach is the historical analysis by Theda Skocpol (1979) of revolutions in France, Russia, and China. These three cases had quite different political economic and social systems, so she set out to ask what they had in common that would produce a similar political outcome. She concluded that regimes which were internationally weak and domestically ineffective became vulnerable to insurrection when well-organized agitators succeeded in exploiting peasant frustration with an old order to which the landed aristocracy offered only limited support.

Another example is provided by Rothstein (2002), who examined the evolution of social and political trust in two contrasting democracies, Sweden and the United States, assuming that any trends shared between these two countries should also be observable in other democracies. In a similar way, if we were to find that the plurality method of election is associated with a two-party system in each of the diverse group of countries employing that electoral system, our confidence in the robustness of the relationship between plurality elections and a two-party system would increase.

Quantitative method

Where the qualitative method takes an intensive approach approach to understanding political phenomena, using small-N cases in their natural setting, the **quantitative method** takes a narrower approach based on a large number of cases, more variables, and statistical analysis. It typically tries to quantify data and to generalize the results to a larger population, and generates information through experiments and survey research. It is also heavily statistical,

TABLE 6.1: Comparing qualitative and quantitative approaches

	Qualitative	Quantitative
Goal	To understand underlying reasons and motivations in the setting of a phenomenon	To quantify data and generalize results from a sample to the population of interest
Method	Exploratory or 'bottom-up'; hypotheses and theory generated from data	Confirmatory or 'top-down'; hypotheses and theory tested with data
View of human thought and behaviour	Contextual, personal and unpredictable	Regular and predictable
Context	Natural setting	Controlled conditions
Sample size	Small	Large
Core principles	Interpretive, exploratory	Scientific, conclusive
Types of information	Open-ended, narrative, non-numerical, words, images, themes	Statistical, numerical
Information collection	Interviews, focus groups, case studies, observation	Experiments, audits, survey research, rating scales
Results	Particularistic, respondent-framed	Generalizable, researcher-framed
Advantages	Best where ideas cannot be reduced to numbers	Allows for large-scale studies
Disadvantages	Can be difficult to analyse, generating conflicting conclusions	Ideas and political phenomena cannot always be expressed in numbers

Note: These should be regarded as tendencies rather than absolutes. There is much overlap between the two methods.

Source: Adapted from Johnson and Christensen (2014, ch. 2)

demanding a familiarity with approaches and methods that are technical and involve their own specialized language. (It should be emphasized, though, that quantitative sources can also be used within small-N studies.)

Quantitative method: A research method involving variables rather than cases, and attempting to explain political phenomena using statistics.

The most basic form of quantitative research is counting populations, which provides an underrated beginning. As John (2010) says, asking the plain question 'How many of them are there?' is worthwhile. For instance: how many federations are there, how many states are democratic, and how many authoritarian regimes from 1980 are democratic today? Just as straightforward case studies can contribute more to comparative politics than elaborate attempts at theory testing, so descriptive counts can sometimes provide more useful results than sophisticated statistical analyses. Once we go beyond the basics, though, we enter the more analytical world of dependent and independent variables.

To illustrate the statistical approach, consider the example in Figure 6.3, which is a scatterplot showing the relationship between the number of members in a national legislature (the dependent variable) and a country's population (the independent variable). The simple question being asked is whether population impacts the size of the legislature, and the graph reveals a modest positive **correlation**: the larger the population, the larger the assembly. If there was a negative correlation, the **regression line** would slope down rather than up: in that unlikely case, a larger population would be associated with a smaller legislature.

Correlation: A relationship between two or more variables or attributes.

Regression line: The line of best fit in a scatterplot, summarizing the relationship between two variables.

The content of the graph is summarized more precisely by calculating a regression line: the line giving the best fit to the data, and which is determined

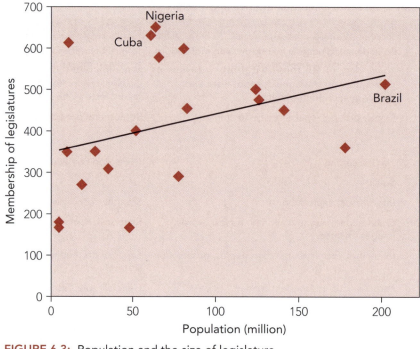

FIGURE 6.3: Population and the size of legislature

Note: Membership of legislatures refers to lower chamber only.

Sources: Membership of legislatures from Inter-Parliamentary Union (2015); population size from World Bank (2015)

by a formula linking the two variables. In this case, the equation reveals that, on average, the size of a legislature increases by one for each increment of a million in a country's population. Given such an equation, which also gives a base estimate for assembly size given a notional population of zero, we can use the population of any particular country to predict its assembly size.

One important virtue of a regression line is that it allows us to identify **outliers** or off-the-line cases. The larger the difference between the predicted and the actual assembly size, the greater the need for additional explanation, thus providing a link to deviant case analysis. In our example, the membership of Brazil's legislature is just slightly below that expected from the country's population but both the Cuban and the Nigerian legislatures are larger than predicted. Cuba's National Assembly of People's Power has 612 members in a country with just over 11 million people, or one representative for 18,000 people, giving Cuba a higher level of representation than almost any other country in the world. How is this explained? It could be that

communist states created large legislatures as a way of reducing any threat they might pose to the party's power. This, at least, is a plausible hypothesis for further investigation, giving us a case selection strategy in which the case is nested within a statistical framework (Lieberman, 2005).

Outliers: The observations furthest away from the value predicted by the regression line.

The value of quantitative comparisons is that they can provide precise summaries of large amounts of data using standard techniques whose application can be checked by other researchers. But, as always, interpretation is the difficult part, requiring attention to two main dangers. First, a strong correlation between two variables may arise simply because both depend on a third, unmeasured factor. In such cases, there is no relationship of cause and effect. For example, a correlation between proportional representation (PR) and multiparty systems might arise because both factors emerge in divided societies, not because PR itself increases the number of parties. This problem of a spurious correlation can be addressed by including all relevant variables in an analysis, but we may not know how many are relevant, and may not have data on all those we think might be relevant.

The second problem in interpreting statistical results is that, even if a relationship is genuine, the direction of causation remains to be established. Suppose we find that liberal democracies have higher rates of economic growth than authoritarian regimes; does the correlation arise because democracy encourages economic growth, or because economic growth encourages democracy? A case can be made either way, or both. A statistical correlation by itself will not provide the answer, and a correlation in itself does not show the direction of causation.

Worthwhile quantitative comparisons can be made even when the variables take the form of categories (such as yes/no) rather than numerical scores. For example, are federations less likely than unitary states to develop welfare states? Is proportional representation linked to coalition government? Are people from poor countries more likely to turn to terrorism than people from rich countries? A country is either a federation or not, a government is either a coalition or not, and so on. In these circumstances, a straightforward cross-tabulation is the qualitative equivalent of the scatterplot in Figure 6.3. Correlation-like statistics can nonetheless be calculated for such tables (Pennings et al., 2006).

The challenges of comparison

As we saw in Chapter 1, comparison pays dividends: it broadens our understanding of the political world, leads to improved classifications, and gives potential for explanation and even prediction. And as we have just seen, there are different approaches to using cases and variables in comparative study. Despite the variety of advantages and options, the very breadth of comparison brings its own difficulties, of which four in particular stand out (see Table 6.2).

Too few cases, too many variables

This is a problem for those who think of comparative politics as a version of the experimenter's laboratory, in which researchers patiently seek to isolate the impact of a single variable. As outlined by Lijphart (1971), it arises when a researcher wants to control for many variables at the same time and quickly runs out of cases. In other words, the number of variables exceeds the number of cases. Even with nearly 200 sovereign states, we do not have enough cases to allow political comparisons to be as precise as laboratory experiments. To make the same point from another angle, we will never be able to test all possible explanations of a political difference between states.

For example, why was New Zealand particularly sympathetic to introducing the private sector into the running of its public services during the 1990s? Perhaps it was a reflection of the pro-market thinking of the country's political and business elite (Boston et al., 1995), or perhaps it was because the public sector in New Zealand, unlike many democracies in continental Europe, was not protected by the constitution and civil law codes (Hood, 1996). So we have two potential explanations, one based on ideology and the other on law, and both are broadly consistent with the facts, but we have no way of isolating which factor is decisive. Ideally, we would want to see if the public sector had been reformed in a state identical to New Zealand except that only one of these two factors applied. But there is no such state; we have run out of cases.

TABLE 6.2: Some challenges of comparison

Too few cases, too many variables	The problem of having more explanatory factors for a given outcome than there are cases available to study.
Selection bias	The cases selected for study are often an unrepresentative sample, limiting the significance of the findings. The selection may be influenced in particular by survivorship, value, or confirmation bias.
Understanding meaning	The 'same' phenomenon can mean different things in different countries, creating difficulties in comparing like with like.
Globalization	States cannot be regarded as entirely independent of each other, thus reducing the effective number of cases available for testing theories.

There are several potential solutions to the problem. We could increase the number of cases in a study by turning to history and comparing cases over an extended period of time. We could also use most similar system designs to achieve a more focused study of a few cases, or a most different system design to reduce the number of variables. Finally, we could resort to asking hypothetical 'What if …?' questions by using **counterfactuals**. What would the outcome have been in New Zealand had its reforming elite confronted an unsympathetic legal framework? Would public sector reform still have proceeded? What would our world be like if Britain had won the US War of Independence, if Hitler had died in a car crash in 1932, or if the attacks of 9/11 had never happened? Tetlock and Belkin (1996) have developed useful guidelines for judging the plausibility of counterfactuals, but the outcome of such thought experiments can – by definition – never be tested against reality.

> **Counterfactual:** A thought experiment speculating on possible outcomes if a particular factor had been absent from a process, or an absent factor had been present.

Selection bias

A second handicap to comparison is raised by **selection bias**, which is at issue whenever the units of analysis (such as states, cities, interest groups, or electoral systems) are chosen intentionally rather than randomly. In these circumstances, the danger is that these units are unrepresentative of the wider population and, in consequence, results cannot be generalized to the broader category from which the cases are drawn. For example, studies of English-speaking democracies are unrepresentative of all democracies, and studies of political parties in sub-Saharan Africa are untypical of those in Europe or Latin America. Given the rarity of random sampling in qualitative comparisons, the point is not so much to eliminate such bias as to be aware of its presence.

> **Selection bias:** Arises when selected cases and variables are unrepresentative of the wider class from which they are drawn.

This danger often emerges as an unintended result of haphazard selection. For example, we might choose to study those countries which speak our language, or which we feel are safe to visit. As a result, large and powerful states might be studied more intensively than small and less powerful ones, even though large states are untypical. By contrast, countries in which it is difficult to conduct research receive insufficient attention. For example, Goode (2010) suggests that authoritarian regimes such as Russia are under-studied because of the political sensitivity of conducting research in such domains. The result of such selection biases is that published work is unrepresentative of all states. So while most university libraries will contain many books on American, British, or German politics, they will contain fewer studies of Haiti, Somalia, or Chad.

One virtue of large-N statistical designs is that they reduce the risk of selection bias. Indeed, when a study covers every existing state, selection bias should disappear altogether. But the problem may just resurface in another form, through an unrepresentative selection of variables, rather than countries. For example, much statistical research in comparative politics relies on data collected by governments, think-tanks, and international bodies whose priorities are often economic rather than political (this book, for example, draws on data gathered by the World Bank). So the availability of data means that financial and economic variables receive more attention and politics runs the risk of being treated as a branch of economics.

A particularly troubling form of selection bias comes from examining only positive cases, thus eliminating all variation in the phenomenon we seek to explain. King et al. (1994: 129) explain the problem as follows:

> The literature is full of work that makes the mistake of failing to let the dependent variable vary; for example, research that tries to explain the outbreak of wars with studies only of wars, the onset of revolutions with studies only of revolutions, or patterns of voter turnout with interviews only of non-voters.

When only positive cases are studied, several potential conclusions about the causes and consequences of the phenomenon are ruled out. Contrast is needed to give variation, so that we can then consider what factors distinguish times of war from times of peace, periods of revolution from periods of stability, and abstainers from voters.

Even without variation in the dependent variable, we can still identify common characteristics of the cases. For example, we may find that revolutions are always preceded by war, or that all non-voters are cynical about politics. However, we have no contrast to explore and explain. We do not know how often war occurs without triggering a revolution, or whether the political cynicism we find among abstainers is equally prevalent among those who turn out on election day (Geddes, 2003). Put differently, war may be a necessary condition of revolution (no revolution in the absence of war) without being a sufficient condition (whenever there is a war, revolution follows).

Three particular forms of selection bias raise their own unique problems. First, **survivorship bias** arises when non-survivors of a temporal process are excluded, leading to biased results. Studying the few surviving communist states or military governments as representative of the entire class of such regimes (past and present) is an error because the few that have survived may differ systematically from those that have disappeared. Similarly, if we want to study federations, we should appreciate that some have failed and should ask not only whether current federations are successful, but also what proportion of all federations, past and present, have survived and prospered. And just because every example from history of a confederation has failed or morphed into a federation, does that mean that future examples are also doomed to fail? In designing our research, we should look through both ends of the telescope – at starters as well as finishers, at casualties as well as survivors.

> **Survivorship bias:** A form of selection bias that crops up when we study only surviving examples of political types, overlooking past examples.

Second, **value bias** arises when researchers allow themselves to be guided by values or ideology. As we read reports, journal articles, and books (even this one), we have to allow that the authors will have political preferences, and in the case of sponsored research we have to consider who paid for the research, whether conditions were imposed on the researchers by the sponsors, or whether there is an underlying political agenda at work. Value bias is a particular problem in comparative studies, because other than the country or countries in which researchers have spent most or all of their lives, they will initially know little directly about the objects of their study, and they face the

danger of seeing others through the lenses of their own experiences, values, and learning. Without even trying, they will be biased by politics, culture, race, gender, religion, age, economic situation, and a host of other factors.

> **Value bias:** Allowing assessments, the choice of facts, and conclusions to be impacted by the values of the researcher.

> **Confirmation bias:** The tendency to seek out or interpret information that confirms pre-existing beliefs and attitudes, and to ignore information that does not.

Finally, **confirmation bias** arises when researchers have a view in mind before they undertake their research, and pay attention only to the facts and analyses that support that view, ignoring or downplaying any contrary evidence. Those who sponsor research are likely to seek out and support researchers who seek out data that support their interests. Whether it is conscious or unconscious, confirmation bias has the same effect of producing skewed results and conclusions. In regard to climate change, for example, both advocates and deniers sometimes seize on any study which supports their beliefs, while ignoring or rejecting findings which run against their entrenched positions. In principle, we can counter confirmation bias by asking how new findings should lead us to amend our current understanding of the world but this level of objectivity is not easy to sustain.

Understanding meaning

Because the meaning of a political action depends on the conventions of the state concerned, comparing like with like is not always as straightforward as it seems. Take the question of styles of political representation, which vary across states. Where Nigerian politicians might seek to impress by acts of flamboyant extravagance, Swedish politicians are more likely to set out to affirm their very ordinariness. The same goal of impressing constituents is achieved by culturally specific means, such that what works in Lagos would be disastrous in Stockholm, and what succeeds in Stockholm would be met with apathy in Abuja.

Similarly, when members of a legislature vote against their party's line, the consequences can range by state from complete indifference to expulsion from the party. What appears to be the same act carries varying significance, and thus meaning depends on context.

So, before we begin any cross-national comparison we should ensure that we understand the relevant cultural codes of the states we are studying. Failure here results in cultural imperialism, in which the meaning of an action in our home state is incorrectly projected onto other societies.

Globalization

The final handicap to comparison comes from globalization (Teune, 2010). Although 193 'independent' states belonged to the United Nations in 2015, in reality these states were interdependent, or even dependent. Countries learn from, copy, compete trade with, influence and even invade each other in a constant process of interaction. The result can be homogenization, where politics and government in different countries become increasingly similar (though specialization, where each country focuses on its distinctive strengths in the global order, is another possible outcome). The KOF Globalization Index maintained by the Swiss Economic Institute offers some insight into this problem by ranking the countries of the world in terms of the extent to which they are globally connected in economic, political and social terms (see Table 6.3). Among other things, this table reveals that it is the smaller democracies with

advanced economies such as Belgium and the Netherlands that have achieved the highest levels of global connectivity. Larger countries such as India and even the United States remain somewhat less well integrated. And indeed, both India and the United States have been able to carve out distinctive political paths in a manner that would be impractical for small countries. But overall, considerable levels of interdependence are the norm, limiting the extent to which we can treat states as separate cases.

Opinion is divided on the implications of globalization. In his book *Jihad vs. McWorld*, Benjamin Barber (1995) suggests that the forces of globalization/globalism and tradition/tribalism are at odds with one another. Where Jihad (literally, the obligation of Muslims to propagate the faith) delivers such qualities as a vibrant local identity, a sense of community, and solidarity among kinsmen, neighbours, and countrymen, McWorld delivers peace, prosperity, and relative unity, albeit at the cost of independence, community, and identity. He concludes that globalization will eventually win out. But the struggle has already been won, according to the sociologist George Ritzer (2011), who writes of the McDonaldization of society. This suggests that culture has come to be dominated by the goals of efficiency, predictability and standardization; related arguments could be made about politics and political expectations.

TABLE 6.3: The KOF Globalization Index

	Ranking	Score		Ranking	Score
Ireland	1	92	South Africa	58	65
Belgium	2	92	Japan	59	65
Netherlands	3	91	Mexico	70	61
Sweden	7	87	China	72	60
Canada	12	86	Brazil	76	60
UK	17	84	Egypt	85	57
France	21	83	Nigeria	90	56
Germany	26	79	India	112	50
United States	32	75	Afghanistan	184	30
Russia	56	65	Somalia	191	24

Note: Numbers indicate scores out of 100, with 100 representing the most globalized and 0 indicating the least globalized. Numbers are rounded out to nearest whole figure.

Source: Swiss Economic Institute (2015) at www.kof.ethz.ch

The major transitions of world history – industrialization, colonialism, decolonization, democratization – unfolded on a world stage. States themselves did not develop independently, but the idea of statehood instead diffused outwards from its proving ground in Europe. In that sense we inhabit one global system, rather than a world of independent states. Green (2002: 5) puts the point well when he says the world is arranged 'as if national polities are in fact cells of a larger entity with a life all its own'. The implication is that we should study this larger organism, rather than comparing its component parts as if they were unconnected.

Specific institutional forms also reflect diffusion. The presidential systems of Latin America were imported from the United States; prime ministers and parliaments grew out of the specific circumstances of British political history; and the ombudsman (see Chapter 10) was a device copied from Sweden. The development of international organizations, from the United Nations to the European Union, also creates a newer layer of governance to which all member states must react.

These links do not invalidate comparative analysis; indeed, they allow studies comparing the impact of an international factor on different states, thus bridging the study of international and comparative politics. But interdependence creates technical difficulties for statistical analysis. Treating states as independent entities artificially inflates the effective sample size in statistical research, resulting in exaggerated confidence in the significance of the results obtained (Tilly, 1997). To put the point more intuitively, treating states as separate can lead to false inferences if in reality they are all subject to a common external influence, such as globalization.

Historical method

Most studies in politics – and in comparative politics, especially – focus on the present and leave history to the historians. But this division of labour is both arbitrary and artificial, because today's present is tomorrow's past. Political science can, and perhaps should, make more use of the past as a treasure trove of additional cases, whether of rare events such as genocide and revolution or of particular episodes that exemplify, challenge, or refine existing theories. The **historical method** can enlarge our database, enabling us in particular to employ

the most different system design to examine the robustness of findings across distinct time periods.

> **Historical method:** A research method based on studying cases from the past, often with a focus on their development through time.

The question that arises for political scientists is how to make the transition from taking snapshots of the present – the traditional focus of most political research – to developing moving pictures of change over time. Part of the answer lies in using an **analytic narrative** that seeks to combine history and political science. It examines how a particular sequence of moves, made by calculating actors aware of the options available to them, produces a particular result (Bates *et al.*, 1998). In contrast to a case study, an analytic narrative is concerned with sequence, the goal being to identify the key factors driving towards the outcome.

> **Analytic narrative:** An attempt to integrate historical and political science research methods in seeking to explain a specific outcome.

The European Union offers a good example. We can study its institutions, the dynamics of its decision-making processes, and the policies it pursues, but we will never fully understand it without appreciating why it was created in the first place (the desire to achieve peace among European states was first and foremost) or how it has evolved, or how the particular steps in its evolution resulted in both its current structure and its current membership. It has been built piece by piece, and the order in which the pieces were added, for example how membership expanded, and the particular order in which new members joined the EU will reveal much about the changing perspective and priorities of European integration.

Iran offers another example. At first glance, it can appear over-concerned with criticizing the West – particularly the United States – and the instinctive reaction of Western political leaders is to reward Iran's petulance with criticism, mistrust, and an unwillingness to engage. And yet although Iran was never a colony, its perspective is still coloured by the long history of Western interference in its politics and economics. It remains critical of foreign involvement in the problems of Iran's neighbours, such as Yemen. It is only through an analytic narrative of this kind that the present can be understood in terms of the past.

Process tracing reconnects political science with history by identifying and describing the historical sequence linking a cause to an effect. For example, what were the steps leading from Hitler's anti-Semitism to the Holocaust? Through what mechanisms does defeat in war lead to a change of regime? Often, however, the outcome is far from predetermined. It is here that the concepts of critical junctures, sequences, and slow-moving causes provide tools for thinking about how the political past influences the political present.

> **Process tracing:** The study of the sequence of events linking a cause to an effect.

Although analytic narratives provide a way of examining politics over time, broader approaches are still needed. Pierson (2004) brings together some concepts for thinking about politics in the context of time, helping tease out our often submerged thoughts about political change. First among these concepts is **path dependence**, which describes a political process whose outcome depends on earlier decisions; that is, the destination depends on the route. The idea was borrowed from physics by economists seeking to explain how changes in technology impacted the evolution of business practices, and it has since spread throughout the social sciences. It might be used, for example, to argue that the return of authoritarianism in Putin's Russia can be traced back to decisions made or steps taken during the reform era following the collapse of the USSR in 1991.

> **Path dependence:** The idea that the outcome of a process depends on earlier decisions that lead down a particular path.

Path dependence implies an emphasis on history generally and branching points specifically. By contrast, path independence means that the same destination will be reached, regardless of the route; all roads lead to Rome. Path independence implies an emphasis on underlying structures and resources rather than historical sequences. For example, the result of a football game is path dependent if the first score is vital, and path independent if the better team is sure to win in the end, no matter who scores first. To take a more political illustration, the outcome of a war is path dependent if a particular battle proves decisive, and path independent if

the stronger side is sure to win eventually, whatever the result of a specific confrontation.

Path dependence can be initiated by **critical junctures**, key moments that clear a new path that continues to be followed long after the juncture itself has passed. During the critical phase (often, a moment of crisis), all options really are on the table and history is written. Revolutions are one example; constitutional conventions another. Once the new order has consolidated, however, politics settles down and the choices realistically available to decision-makers shrink. The revolutionary generation gives way to pragmatic operators of the new regime. As ideas are displaced by institutions, so the constitution as choice is supplanted by the constitution as constraint.

> **Critical juncture:** A turning point which establishes interests, structures, or institutions persisting through time.

By dividing history into critical and normal eras, we arrive at a plausible perspective on the old debate about whether people make their own history. The answer is perhaps that they do, but only occasionally. In other words, critical junctures are rare choice points in which human agency really can be decisive for the long term.

Ideas, in particular, rise to prominence during critical junctures. In normal times, much political discussion is what Schmidt (2002: 252) calls 'cheap talk', expressing negotiating positions which defend established interests. But, sometimes, the existing stock of ideas becomes incapable of responding to a shift in circumstances, creating pressures for established procedures to be revised or completely rethought. A country may experience economic decline; a party may lose voter support; a trade union may experience a collapse in membership. Suddenly, ideas that had previously received scant consideration find themselves at the centre of the table. When disintegration threatens, new thoughts are urgently needed.

Sequencing, the order in which events unfold, can help to account for path dependence. For example, communist regimes which introduced economic reform before political liberalization (such as China) were more likely to survive than those beginning the reform process with political change (such as the USSR). In European countries where trade unions developed before socialism became a full-blooded ideology (such as Britain), the labour movement took on a moderate reformist character. But where Marxist thought was already

| FOCUS 6.2 | Path dependence, critical junctures, and the Greek financial crisis |

The financial crisis that emerged in Greece over the past decade is an example both of path dependence at work, and of critical junctures at which decisions were taken leading to new paths.

The immediate beginnings of the crisis date to 2002, when Greece became one of 12 European Union states to adopt the new EU single currency, the euro. Even then, there were doubts about its readiness to take this step, because it had not met all the criteria needed to join the euro, including limits on its budget deficit. It was allowed to join regardless. One of the effects of membership of the euro was that poorer states such as Greece, Portugal, and Spain had access to lower interest rates on their loans; as a result, Greece went on a spending spree fuelled by cheaper borrowing, built a budget deficit that, at nearly 13 per cent, was far above the three per cent limit set for eurozone membership, manipulated its official statistics to exaggerate its levels of economic growth, and accumulated a national debt that was ultimately bigger than its national economy.

Greece might have struggled on indefinitely in this weakened condition but for the onset in 2007 of a financial crisis in the United States that quickly spread to Europe. European states felt the effects of the crisis, but those in a weaker condition suffered the most. In 2009, the Greek government finally admitted the size of its budget deficit, sparking a broader crisis within the eurozone. Greece was offered a financial bailout, but only on condition that it cut public spending and increased its tax revenues. The terms of the deal sparked riots in the streets of Athens and encouraged little improvement in investor confidence.

The European Union revised its policies on the management of the euro, making sure that a closer watch would be kept in future on the size of national budget deficits, but the crisis in Greece rumbled on. Questions were asked not only about how long it could remain within the eurozone, but also about the future of the euro and of Greece's membership of the European Union itself.

The entire history is path dependent in that each effort to resolve the issue failed, leading only to further plans for reform. And what about the critical juncture: the decisive moment when Greece finally addressed its core economic problems and the eurozone carved out a more secure future for itself, with or without Greece? That moment has yet to arrive and may or may not ever do so. Talking up their story, journalists identify too many historical turning points; political scientists are right to be more cautious.

established, as in France, communist unions developed a more radical political agenda. So, whether trade unions emerged before or after the onset of Marxism helps to explain whether particular European countries developed a reformist or radical labour movement. The outcome was not predetermined but, rather, depended on the sequence of events.

Sequencing: The idea that the order of events, not merely their occurrence, affects the outcome.

In a similar way, the order in which government departments are created influences their contemporary status. Those created earliest (such as the finance and justice ministries) typically constitute the core of government, with later departments (such as environment and transport) occupying a more peripheral position. Thus, the functioning of the central government is likely to be incompletely understood if this historical sequence is ignored and all departments are treated as equal in status.

One form of 'sequence' is a conjuncture in which separate events occur at the same time, enlarging their political impact. The collision of the First World War with the emergence of working-class socialism, or of the Vietnam War with the student movement, generated political effects which were greater than would have been the case had these events unfolded separately. These confluences are typically made by history, and are another contributor to path dependence.

Slow-moving causes, finally, are processes that unfold over a long period. Examples include modernization and technological advance, the spread of education, and the growth of the mass media. Such processes often need to reach a threshold or a tipping point beyond which a variable begins to exert a visible, dramatic effect. For example, there has been a resurgence of right-wing anti-immigrant political parties in Europe that dates back at least to the early 1990s, reflecting long-term concerns about immigration, law and order, unemployment and, more recently, the 'Islamization' of Europe. At least in some countries, for example Austria and France, a threshold seems to have been passed, with the far right in Austria even enjoying a spell in government. When thresholds are involved, long-term but otherwise slow-moving causes need to be understood historically. Contemporary explosions have long fuses and political scientists need to search into the past to uncover them.

> **Slow-moving cause:** An influence which changes slowly but, over a long period, dramatically.

DISCUSSION QUESTIONS

- What does it take for the study of politics to be scientific, and where is it most likely to fail?

- In what way (or ways) could your country serve as a representative or deviant case study?

- What are the advantages and disadvantages of quantitative and qualitative approaches to comparative political research?

- How can comparative political research best be protected from value bias?

- What challenges does globalization pose for comparative politics?

- How does the study of politics differ from the study of history?

KEY CONCEPTS

Analytic narrative
Case study method
Comparative method
Confirmation bias
Correlation
Counterfactual
Critical juncture
Dependent variable
Historical method
Hypothesis
Independent variable
Level of analysis
Methodology
Most different system

Most similar system
Outliers
Path dependence
Process tracing
Qualitative method
Quantitative method
Regression line
Selection bias
Sequencing
Slow-moving cause
Survivorship bias
Unit of analysis
Value bias
Variable

FURTHER READING

George, Alexander L. and Andrew Bennett (2004) *Case Studies and Theory Development in the Social Sciences*. Examines the role of case studies in social science research, including politics.

Halperin, Sandra and Oliver Heath (2012) *Political Research: Methods and Practical Skills*. An introduction to qualitative and quantitative research methods in politics.

Landman, Todd (2008) *Issues and Methods in Comparative Politics*, 3rd edn. A concise survey of the methods and approaches to comparison, including chapters on particular themes in comparative politics.

Pennings, Paul, Hans Keman, and Jan Kleinnijenhuis (2006) *Doing Research in Political Science: An Introduction to Comparative Methods and Statistics*, 2nd edn. Introduces statistical methods in the context of comparative politics.

Pierson, Paul (2004) *Politics in Time: History, Institutions and Social Analysis*. A thoughtful discussion of the relationship between history and political analysis.

Yin, Robert K. (2013) *Case Study Research: Design and Methods*, 5th edn. A standard source on conducting case studies, using examples from a range of disciplines.

7 Constitutions and courts

PREVIEW

So far we have looked mainly at broad concepts and ideas in comparative politics, including theoretical approaches and research methods. We now focus on
institutions, opening in this chapter with a review of constitutions and the
courts that support them. Constitutions tell us much about the goals and purposes of government, as well as the rights of citizens, while courts strive to make
sure that these rules are respected and equally applied. Just as humans are imperfect, so are the political institutions they create and manage; there are significant
gaps, in other words, between constitutional ideals and practice.

　　The chapter begins with an assessment of constitutions: what they are, the
purposes they serve, their character and durability, how their performance can
be measured, and how they are changed. There is no fixed template for constitutions, they vary enormously in terms of their length and efficacy, and the gap
between aspiration and achievement differs from one constitution to another.

　　The chapter goes on to look at the role of courts and their relationship
with constitutions, examining the differences between supreme courts and
constitutional courts, and the incidence of judicial activism. It then addresses
the manner in which judges are recruited, the terms of their tenure, and how
such differences impact judicial independence. It then briefly reviews the three
major legal systems found in the world – common law, civil law, and religious
law – before assessing the often modest place of constitutions and courts in
authoritarian regimes.

CONTENTS

- Constitutions and courts:
  an overview

- The character of
  constitutions

- The durability of
  constitutions

- The role of courts

- Judicial activism

- Judicial independence
  and recruitment

- Systems of law

- Constitutions and courts
  in authoritarian states

KEY ARGUMENTS

- Constitutions are critical to achieving an understanding of government, providing – as they do – a power map
  containing key political principles and rules.

- Understanding governments requires an appreciation of the content of constitutions, as well as their durability and
  how they are amended.

- Awareness of the structure and role of courts is also critical, as is the distinction between supreme courts and
  constitutional courts.

- Judicial activism has become an increasingly important concept, as judges have become more willing to enter
  political arenas. In turn, the rules on judicial recruitment – and their impact on judicial independence – must be
  taken into consideration.

- In comparing constitutions and courts, the distinction between common and civil law has long been important, and
  more attention needs to be paid to the political significance of religious law.

- In authoritarian regimes, constitutions and courts are weak, with governments either using them as a facade or
  entirely bypassing them.

Constitutions and courts: an overview

A **constitution** is a power map containing a set of principles and rules outlining the structure and powers of a system of government, describing its institutions and the manner in which they work and relate to one another, and typically describing both the limits on governmental power and the rights of citizens. A system of government without a constitution is not a system at all, but rather an unorganized collection of habits that can be changed at the whim of the leaders or the people. In the case of democracies, the authority provided by a constitution helps provide predictability and security. In the case of authoritarian regimes, the constitution is more often a fig leaf behind which elites hide, the terms of the constitution being interpreted to suit their needs, or ignored altogether. As well as providing the rules of government, constitutions also offer benchmarks against which the performance of government can be measured.

> **Constitution:** A document or a set of documents that outlines the powers, institutions, and structure of government, as well as expressing the rights of citizens and the limits on government.

Recent decades have seen a growth of interest in the study of constitutions, for four main reasons:

- We have seen an explosion of constitution-making, with 99 countries adopting new constitutions between 1990 and 2012 (Comparative Constitutions Project, 2015).
- Judges and courts in many liberal democracies have become more willing to step into the political arena, not least in investigating corrupt politicians.
- The growing interest in human rights lends itself to judicial engagement.
- The expanding body of international law increasingly impinges on domestic politics, with judges called on to arbitrate the conflicting claims of national and supranational law.

A key link between constitutions, law and government is found in the idea of the **rule of law**. In the words of the nineteenth-century English jurist, A. V. Dicey (1885: 27), the purpose of the rule of law is to substitute 'a government of laws' for a 'government of men'. When rule is by law, political leaders cannot exercise arbitrary power and the powerful are (in theory, at least) subject to the same laws as everyone else. More specifically, the rule of law implies that laws are general, public, prospective, clear, consistent, practical, and stable (Fuller, 1969).

> **Rule of law:** The idea that societies are best governed using laws to which all the residents of a society are equally subject regardless of their status or background.

The implementation of the rule of law and due process (respect for an individual's legal rights) is perhaps the most important distinction between liberal democracies and authoritarian regimes. In the case of the latter, the adoption and application of laws is more arbitrary, and based less on tried and tested principles than on the political goals and objectives of top leaders. No country provides completely equal application of the law, but democracies fare much better than authoritarian regimes, many of whose political weaknesses stem back to constitutional weaknesses.

The character of constitutions

Most constitutions are structured similarly in the sense that they include four elements (see Figure 7.1). They often start out with a set of broad aspirations, declaring in vague but often inspiring terms the ideals of the state, most often including support for democracy and equality. The core of the document then goes into detail on the institutional structure of government: how the different offices are elected or appointed, and what they are allowed and not allowed to do. There will usually be a bill of rights or its equivalent, outlining the rights of citizens relative to government. Finally, there will be a description of the rules on amending the constitution.

Much is made of the distinction between written and unwritten constitutions, and yet no constitution is wholly unwritten; even the 'unwritten' British and New Zealand constitutions contain much relevant statute and common law. A contrast between **codified** and **uncodified** systems is more helpful. Most constitutions are codified; that is, they are set out in detail

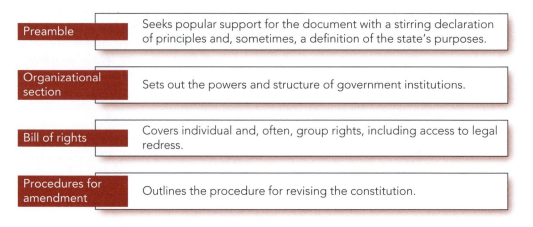

Preamble	Seeks popular support for the document with a stirring declaration of principles and, sometimes, a definition of the state's purposes.
Organizational section	Sets out the powers and structure of government institutions.
Bill of rights	Covers individual and, often, group rights, including access to legal redress.
Procedures for amendment	Outlines the procedure for revising the constitution.

FIGURE 7.1: The elements of constitutions

within a single document. By contrast, the uncodified constitutions of Britain and New Zealand are spread out among several sources; in the British case, these include statute and common law, European law, commentaries written by constitutional experts, and customs and traditions. Establishing the age of uncodified constitutions is far from easy. Britain, for example, does not have (a) a single document that was (b) drawn up at a particular point in time and (c) went into force on a given date (three features of most of the world's codified constitutions). But the distinction between codified and uncodified is not always neat and tidy. Sweden falls somewhere in between, because its constitution comprises four separate acts passed between 1810 and 1991.

> **Codified constitution:** One that is set out in a single document.

> **Uncodified constitution:** One that is spread among a range of documents and is influenced by tradition and practice.

We can look at constitutions in two ways. First, they have a historic role as a regulator of a state's power over its citizens. For the Austrian philosopher Friedrich Hayek (1899–1992), a constitution was nothing but a device for limiting the power of government, whether unelected or elected. In similar vein, the German-American political theorist Carl Friedrich (1901–84) defined a constitution as 'a system of effective,

regularized restraints upon government action' (1937: 104). From this perspective, the key feature of a constitution is its statement of individual rights and its expression of the rule of law. In this sense, constitutions express the overarching principles within which non-constitutional law – and the legal system, generally – operates.

A bill of rights now forms part of nearly all written constitutions. Although the US Bill of Rights (1791) confines itself to such traditional liberties as freedom of religion, speech, and assembly, recent constitutions are more ambitious, often imposing duties on rulers such as fulfilling the social rights of citizens to employment and medical care. Several post-communist constitutions have extended rights even further, to include childcare and a healthy environment. As a result, the documents are expanding: the average length (including amendments) is now 29,000 words (Lutz, 2007).

The second, more political and more fundamental role of constitutions is to outline a power map, defining the structure of government, identifying the pathways of power, and specifying the procedures for law-making. As Sartori (1994: 198) observes, the key feature of a constitution lies in this provision of a frame of government. A constitution without a declaration of rights is still a constitution, whereas a document without a power map is no constitution at all. A constitution is therefore a form of political engineering – to be judged, like any other construction, by how well it survives the test of time.

In the main, constitutions are a deliberate creation, designed and built by politicians and typically forming part of a fresh start after a period of disruption. Such circumstances include:

- Regime change, as in the wake of break-up in the 1990s of the Soviet Union, Yugoslavia, and Czechoslovakia, and of Sudan in 2011.
- Efforts to bring about wholesale political change or confirm agreements made between competing political groups, as in the cases of Bolivia (2009), Kenya (2010), Zimbabwe (2013), and Tunisia (2014).
- Reconstruction after defeat in war, as in the case of Japan after 1945 or Iraq after 2005.
- Achieving independence, as in the case of much of Africa in the 1950s and 1960s, or the 15 republics created by the break-up of the Soviet Union.

New constitutions are typically written by conventions of politicians, usually working in closed session. The voice of 'the people' is directly heard only if a state holds a referendum to ratify the new constitution. Many countries, including the United States, have never held such a vote. Interestingly, Iceland recently tried an exceptionally open process in constitution-crafting. It engaged a group of citizens to list priorities for a new constitution, and appointed a different set of citizens to undertake the drafting. Social media were then used to elicit comments on a draft, which was approved in a non-binding 2012 referendum but failed to win legislative support in 2013.

Constitutions often experience a difficult birth, particularly when they are compromises between political actors who have substituted distrust for conflict. In Horowitz's terms (2002), constitutions are built from the bottom up, rather than designed from the top down. For instance, South Africa's post-apartheid settlement of 1996 achieved a practical accommodation between leaders of the white and black communities against a backdrop of near slavery and continuing racial hostility. Acceptability was everything; elegance was nothing – see Spotlight.

As vehicles of compromise, most constitutions are vague, contradictory, and ambiguous. They are fudges and truces, wrapped in fine words (Weaver and Rockman, 1993). As a rule, drafters are more concerned with a short-term political fix than with establishing a resilient structure for the long run. In principle, everyone agrees with Alexander Hamilton (1788a: 439), that

constitutions should 'seek merely to regulate the general political interests of the nation'; in practice, they are often lengthy documents reflecting an incomplete settlement between suspicious partners. The US constitution, though shorter than most, is no exception, being – in the words of Finer (1997: 1495) – 'a thing of wrangles and compromises. In its completed state, it was a set of incongruous proposals cobbled together. And furthermore, that is what many of its framers thought.'

The main danger of a fresh constitution is that it fails to endow the new rulers with sufficient authority. Too often, political distrust means that the new government is hemmed in with restrictions, limiting its effectiveness. The Italian constitution of 1948 illustrates this problem with its hallmark of *garantismo*, meaning that all political forces are guaranteed a stake in the political system. It established a strong bicameral legislature and provided for regional autonomy, while trying to prevent a recurrence of fascist dictatorship and to accommodate the radical aspirations of the political left. The result was ineffective governance.

The durability of constitutions

In assessing the practical worth of constitutions, it is tempting to look at their age. The most impressive such documents, it might seem, are those that have lasted the longest. Conversely, a state that keeps changing its constitution is clearly experiencing difficulty in securing a stable framework of governance. In this sense, the United States – which adopted its constitution in 1789 – stands in contrast to Haiti, which drew up its first constitution shortly after independence in 1804, and adopted its 23rd and latest constitution in 1987. More important than age, however, is the question of quality. All constitutions contain a degree of idealism, and make claims that either cannot objectively be measured, or else are not reflected in reality. But how can we measure the quality of a constitution? At least in part, the answer lies in determining the size of the gap between what it says and what happens in practice.

The Mexican constitution, for example, was both radical and progressive from the time it was adopted in 1917: it contains principles that prohibit discrimination of any kind, provide for free education, establish the equality of men and women, limit the working day to eight hours, and prohibit vigilante justice. But many Mexicans argue that too many of its goals have

Oldest still in use	United States (1789), Netherlands and Norway (1814), Belgium (1831). Britain and San Marino have older uncodified constitutions.
Newest	Fiji and Zimbabwe (2013), Egypt and Tunisia (2014).
Average age in 2015	17 years.
Shortest	Jordan, Libya, Iceland (each 2,000–4,000 words).
Longest	India (146,000 words), Nigeria (66,000 words).
Least amended	United States (27 in 226 years).
Most amended	Mexico (more than 500 changes in just under 100 years), India (98 in just under 70 years), for example.
States with the fewest constitutions to date	Australia, Belgium, Canada, India, Netherlands, Norway, United States (1 each), among others.
States with the most constitutions to date	Dominican Republic (32), Venezuela (26), Haiti (23), Ecuador (20).
States with uncodified constitutions	Britain, Israel, New Zealand, Saudi Arabia.

FIGURE 7.2: Ten facts about constitutions

Source: Based on information in Comparative Constitutions Project (2015)

not been met in practice, and thus they consider the constitution to be a work in progress. Matters are complicated by the ease with which it can be amended, requiring the support of only two-thirds of members of Congress and a majority of state legislatures. The result is that Mexican leaders will propose constitutional amendments even for minor matters: a package of electoral reforms in August 1996 alone involved 18 amendments. The constitution of India offers another example of the gap between goals and practice; its 448 articles guide the world's largest democracy, and yet India suffers massive poverty, widespread corruption, human rights abuses (particularly in regard to women),

unequal access to education, and an extraordinarily slow-moving legal process.

Recent developments in the United States offer additional insights into the problem. The US constitution did not change after the terrorist attacks of 11 September 2001, but the detention of alleged terrorist in Guantanamo Bay and revelations about the use of torture and the increased monitoring by government agencies of phone and electronic communications raised troubling questions about the health of individual rights in the United States. It is often said that truth is the first casualty of war; in a similar vein, it is often the case with countries facing external threats

FOCUS 7.1 | Constitutional amendments

Times, needs, and expectations change, and constitutions should change with them, up to a point. So while there should always be allowances for amendments, the procedures involved have critical implications: too many amendments can result in instability, while too few can result in stagnation. Here we meet the matter of **entrenchment**, a term referring to procedures which set a higher level and wider spread of support for amendments than is the case for ordinary legislative bills.

In the case of **rigid constitutions**, change is more difficult, usually demanding super- or concurrent majorities (see Figure 7.3). In the case of a **flexible constitution**, changes can be made more easily. Rigidity offers the general benefit of a stable political framework, and benefits rulers by limiting the damage should political opponents obtain power, because they would face the same barriers to change. On the other hand, non-entrenchment (which is rare) offers the advantage of ready adaptability. In New Zealand, this flexibility allowed changes to the electoral system and government administration in the 1980s and 1990s, while in the United Kingdom it allowed the devolution of significant powers to Scotland and Wales in 1999 without much constitutional fuss.

The most extreme form of entrenchment is a clause that cannot be amended at all. For example, the French and Turkish constitutions guarantee the republican character of their regimes. These statements set out to enforce a break with the old regime, but they also provide ammunition to those who see constitutions as the dictatorship of the dead over the living. In new conditions, past solutions sometimes have a way of turning into current problems.

A key element of the amendment procedure concerns the role of the legislature. On the one hand, some constitutions can be amended simply through special majorities within the legislature, thereby reducing the relative status of the constitution. This approach is found in European states with a strong commitment to parliamentary supremacy, such as Germany: amendments there (where permitted at all) require only a two-thirds majority in both houses. On the other hand, where modifications cannot be approved by the legislature alone, the constitution stands supreme over the legislature. In Australia, for example, amendments must be endorsed not only by the national parliament, but also by a referendum achieving a concurrent majority in most states and in the country as a whole.

Changes can also be initiated by other means than a formal amendment. The most important of these devices are judicial interpretation (the rulings of constitutional courts), and the passage of new laws that modify some aspect of the rules of government. And even when constitutions are codified, simple customs and traditions should not be forgotten; there is often much about the structure of government that is not written down, but has simply become a tradition. Political parties play a critical role in government all over the world, for example, but there may not always be much said about them in constitutions.

➡

that the rule of law takes second place to national security, and needs to be rebuilt subsequently through the courts.

The role of courts

Constitutions are neither self-made nor self-implementing, and they need the support of institutions that can enforce their provisions by striking down offending laws and practices. This role has fallen to the

Entrenchment: The existence of special legal procedures for amending a constitution.

Rigid constitution: One that is entrenched, requiring more demanding amendment procedures.

Flexible constitution: One that can be amended more easily, often in the same way that ordinary legislation is passed.

FOCUS 7.1   Constitutional amendments (Continued)

Amendments require the approval of …

Australia	Both houses of the legislature, then a referendum achieving a concurrent majority both overall and in a majority of states.
Canada	Both houses of the legislature and two-thirds of the provinces containing at least half the country's population.
Germany	A two-thirds majority in both houses of the legislature.
Nigeria	A two-thirds majority in both houses of the legislature and approval by two-thirds of state legislatures.
India	A two-thirds majority in both houses of the legislature and a majority of the total membership of each house.
Ireland	A majority in both houses of the legislature and majority approval in a national referendum.
Sweden	Majority vote by two successive sessions of the legislature with an intervening election.
United States	A two-thirds majority in both houses of the legislature and approval by three-quarters of the states.

FIGURE 7.3: Comparing constitutional amendments

Notes:
Germany: The federal, social, and democratic character of the German state, and the rights of individuals within it, cannot be amended.
India: Selected amendments, such as those changing the representation of states in parliament, must also be approved by at least half the states.
Sweden: Has four fundamental laws which comprise its 'constitution'. These include its Instrument of Government and Freedom of the Press Act.
United States: An alternative method, based on a special convention called by the states and by Congress, has not been used.

judiciary; with their power of **judicial review** (allowing them to override decisions and the laws produced by governments), judges occupy a unique position in and above politics. They constrain the power of elected rulers, thereby both stabilizing and limiting democracy. Hirschl (2008: 119) has gone so far as to refer to the rise of juristocracy, or government by judges:

> Armed with judicial review procedures, national high courts worldwide have been frequently asked to resolve

a range of issues, varying from the scope of expression and religious liberties, equality rights, privacy, and reproductive freedoms, to public policies pertaining to criminal justice, property, trade, and commerce, education, immigration, labor, and environmental protection.

Judicial review: The power of courts to nullify any laws or actions by government officials that contravene the constitution.

The function of judicial review can be allocated in one of two ways. The first and more traditional method – used in the United States and much of Latin America – is for the highest or supreme court in the ordinary judicial system to take on the task of constitutional protection. A supreme court rules on constitutional matters, just as it has the final say on other questions of common and statute law. A second and more recent method – favoured in Europe – is to create a special constitutional court, standing apart from the ordinary judicial system.

Supreme courts

As the name implies, a supreme court is the highest court within a jurisdiction, whose decisions are not subject to review by any other court. They are usually the final court of appeal, listening – if they choose – to cases appealed from a lower level. They also mainly use **concrete review**, meaning that they ask whether, given the facts of the particular case, the decision reached at lower level was compatible with the constitution. By contrast, constitutional courts mainly practise **abstract review**, judging the intrinsic constitutional validity of a law without limiting themselves to the particular case. In addition, constitutional courts can issue advisory judgments on a bill at the request of the government or assembly, often without the stimulus of a specific case at all. These latter judgments are often short and are usually unsigned, lacking the legal argument used by supreme courts. So concrete review provides decisions on cases with constitutional implications, while abstract review is a more general assessment of the constitutional validity of a law or bill. (Some courts, such as those in Ireland and Germany, use both concrete and abstract review.)

> **Concrete review:** Judgments made on the constitutional validity of law in the context of a specific case.

> **Abstract review:** An advisory but binding opinion on a proposed law, based on a suspicion of inconsistency with a constitution.

Confusingly, the name of a given court does not always follow its function. Hence the supreme courts of Australia and Hong Kong go under the title of High Court, those of France and Belgium under the title Cour de Cassation (Court of Appeal), and that of the European Union is the European Court of Justice, while a number of European countries – including Spain – have supreme courts whose decisions (some or all) can be appealed to constitutional courts.

The United States is the prototypical case of concrete review. The US constitution vests judicial power 'in one Supreme Court, and in such inferior Courts as the Congress may from time to time ordain'. Although the Court possesses **original jurisdiction** over cases to which a US state or a representative of another country is a party, its main role is **appellate**. That is, constitutional issues can be raised at any point in the ordinary judicial system and the Supreme Court selects only those cases that it believes raise significant constitutional questions; the vast majority of petitions for the Court to review a case are turned down.

> **Original jurisdiction:** This entitles a court to try a case at its first instance.

> **Appellate:** The power of a court to review decisions reached by lower courts.

Constitutional courts

This approach was born with the Austrian constitution of 1920, and became established in continental Europe after the Second World War. The success of

TABLE 7.1: Comparing supreme courts and constitutional courts

	Supreme court	Constitutional court
Form of review	Primarily concrete	Primarily abstract
Relationship to other courts	Highest court of appeal	A separate body dealing with constitutional issues only
Recruitment	Legal expertise plus political approval	Political criteria more important
Normal tenure	Until retirement	Typically one non-renewable term (6–9 years)
Examples	Australia, Canada, United States	Austria, Germany, Russia

SPOTLIGHT

SOUTH AFRICA

Brief Profile: South Africa languished for many decades under a system of institutionalized racial separation known as *apartheid*. This ensured privileges and opportunities for white South Africans at the expense of black, mixed race, and Asian South Africans. In the face of growing resistance, and ostracism from much of the outside world, an agreement was reached that paved the way for the first democratic elections in 1994. Much was originally expected from a country with a wealth of natural resources and the African National Congress has since won majorities at every election. Yet corruption is a growing problem, unemployment remains stubbornly high, many still live in poverty, and South Africa faces major public security challenges: it has one of the highest per capita homicide and violent assault rates in the world. Despite being the second largest economy in Africa (after Nigeria), it has only partly realized its potential as a major regional power.

Population (52.5 million)

Gross National Income ($351 billion)

Per capita GNI ($7,190)

Democracy Index rating

| Not Rated | Hybrid Regime | Full Democracy |
| | Authoritarian | Flawed Democracy |

Freedom House rating

| Not Free | Partly free | Free |

Human Development Index rating

| Not Rated | Medium | Very High |
| | Low | High |

Form of government ⇨ Unitary parliamentary republic. State formed 1910, and most recent constitution adopted 1997.

Legislature ⇨ Bicameral Parliament: lower National Assembly (400 members) elected for renewable five-year terms, and upper National Council of Provinces with 90 members, ten appointed from each of the nine provinces.

Executive ⇨ Presidential. A president heads both the state and the government, ruling with a cabinet. The National Assembly elects the president after each general election. Presidents limited to two five-year terms.

Judiciary ⇨ The legal system mixes common and civil law. The Constitutional Court decides constitutional matters and can strike down legislation. It has 11 members appointed by the president for terms of 12 years.

Electoral system ⇨ The National Assembly is elected by proportional representation using closed party lists; half are elected from a national list and half from provincial lists.

Parties ⇨ Dominant party. The African National Congress (ANC) has dominated since the first full democratic and multi-racial election in 1994. The more liberal Democratic Alliance, now the leading party in the Western Cape, forms the official opposition.

Germany's Federal Constitutional Court encouraged non-European countries to follow suit, such that nearly half the world's states had such a court by 2005 (Horowitz, 2006). As with the constitutions they nurture, these courts represented a general attempt to prevent a revival of dictatorship; in the case of new democracies, constitutional courts have been created separately from the ordinary judicial system to help overcome the inefficiency, corruption, and opposition of judges from the old order.

Where a supreme court is a judicial body making the final ruling on all appeals (not all of which involve the constitution), a constitutional court is more akin to an additional legislative chamber. Hans Kelsen

The constitution and courts in South Africa

South Africa's transformation from a militarized state based on apartheid (institutionalized racial segregation) to a more constitutional order based on democracy was one of the most remarkable political transitions of the late twentieth century. What was the nature of the political order established by the new constitution?

In 1996, after two years of hard bargaining between the African National Congress (ANC) and the white National Party (NP), agreement was reached on a new 109-page constitution to take full effect in 1997. The NP expressed general support despite reservations that led to its withdrawal from government.

In a phrase reminiscent of the US constitution, South Africa's constitution declares that 'the Executive power of the Republic vests in the President'. As in the United States, the president is also head of state. Unlike the United States, though, presidents are elected by the National Assembly after each general election. They can be removed through a vote of no confidence in the assembly (though this event would trigger a general election), and by impeachment. The president governs in conjunction with a large cabinet.

Each of the country's nine provinces elects its own legislature and forms its own executive headed by a premier. But far more than in the United States, authority and funds flow from the top down. In any case, the ANC provides the glue linking not only executive and legislature, but also national, provincial, and municipal levels of government. So far, at least, the ruling party has dominated the governing institutions, whereas in the United States, the institutions have dominated the parties.

South Africa's rainbow nation faces some difficulties in reconciling constitutional liberal democracy with the political dominance of the ANC. The modest reduction in the size of the ANC's parliamentary majority in the 2009 elections exerted a moderating effect, reducing the ANC's desire and capacity to amend the constitution in its favour. But the country's politics, more than most, should be judged by what preceded it. By that test the achievements of the new South Africa are remarkable indeed.

(1881–1973), the Austrian inventor of constitutional courts, argued that such courts should function as a negative legislator, striking down unconstitutional bills but leaving positive legislation to parliament. In this system, ordinary courts are not empowered to engage in judicial review, with appeals to the supreme court; instead, the review function is exclusive to a separate constitutional authority. This approach is more political, flexible, and less legal than is the case with supreme courts.

Germany has become the exemplar of the constitutional court approach. Its Federal Constitutional Court (FCC) has the following powers: judicial review, adjudication of disputes between state and federal political institutions, protection of individual rights, and protection of the constitutional and democratic order against groups and individuals seeking to overthrow it (Conradt, 2008: 253). The 'eternity clause' in the Basic Law means that the FCC's judgments in key areas of democracy, federalism and human rights are absolutely the final word. (The term *basic law*, used in Germany in place of *constitution*, implies a temporary quality that makes it different from an entrenched constitution. In spite of this, the two are functional equivalents. Other countries using the term *basic law* include Hong Kong, Israel, and Saudi Arabia.)

The FCC consists of 16 members appointed by the legislature for a non-renewable term of 12 years. The Court is divided into two specialized chambers, of which one focuses on the core liberties enshrined in the Basic Law. The Court's public reputation has been enhanced by the provision of constitutional complaint, an innovative device allowing citizens to petition the Court directly once other judicial remedies are exhausted.

The Court actively pursued its duty of maintaining the new order against groups seeking its overthrow; for instance, by banning both communist and neo-Nazi parties in the 1950s. For this reason, Kommers (2006) describes the Court as 'the guardian of German democracy'. It has continued in this role by casting a careful eye on whether European Union laws and policies detract from the autonomy of the country's legislature. The Court has also been active on policy topics as varied as abortion, election procedures, immigration, party funding, religion in schools, and university reform.

Judicial activism

Perhaps with the exception of Scandinavia, judicial intervention in public policy has grown throughout the liberal democratic world since 1945, marking a transition from **judicial restraint** to **judicial activism**. For Hirschl (2008: 119), this is one of the most significant phenomena of government in the late twentieth and early twenty-first centuries. Judges have become more willing to enter political arenas that would have once been left to elected politicians and national parliaments; for instance:

- India's Supreme Court has 'appointed itself as the guardian of vulnerable social groups and neglected areas of public life, such as the environment' (Mitra, 2014: 587).

- Israel's Supreme Court addressed such controversial issues as the West Bank barrier, the use of torture in investigations by the security service, and the assassination of suspected terrorists (Hirschl, 2008).

- The US Supreme Court decided the outcome of the 2000 presidential election by voting along party lines that George W. Bush had won the election in the state of Florida, and thus the presidential election. One commentator controversially described the vote as 'the single most corrupt decision in Supreme Court history' and 'a violation of the judicial oath' because the majority decided on the basis of 'the personal identity and political affiliation of the litigants' (Dershowitz, 2001: 174 and 198).

> **Judicial restraint:** The view that judges should apply the letter of the law, leaving politics to elected bodies.

> **Judicial activism:** The willingness of judges to venture beyond narrow legal reasoning so as to influence public policy.

There are four key reasons for the drift from restraint to activism:

- The decline of the political left has enlarged the scope of the judiciary. Socialists were once suspicious of judges, believing them to be unelected defenders of the status quo, and of property specifically. The left has since discovered in opposition that the courtroom can be a venue for harassing governments of the right.

- The increasing reliance on regulation as a mode of governance encourages court intervention. A government decision to deny gay partners the same rights as married couples is open to judicial challenge in a way that a decision to go to war or raise taxes is not.

- International conventions give judges an extra lever to move outside the limits of national law. Documents such as the United Nations Universal Declaration of Human Rights and the European Convention on Human Rights provide a base on which judges can construct what would once have been viewed as excessively political statements. The emergence of international courts such as the International Criminal Court (founded in 2002) has also encouraged national courts to become more assertive.

- The continuing prestige of the judiciary encouraged some transfer of authority to its domain. The judicial process in most liberal democracies has retained at least some reputation for integrity and impartiality, whereas the standing of many other institutions – notably political parties – has declined.

Whatever the factors lying behind the expansion of judicial authority, the process seems to reinforce itself. Stone Sweet (2000: 55) makes the point that 'as constitutional law expands to more and more policy areas, and as it becomes "thicker" in each domain, so do the grounds for judicialized debate. The process tends to reinforce itself.' Sensing the growing confidence of judges in addressing broader political issues, interest groups, rights-conscious citizens, and even political parties have become more willing to continue their struggles in the judicial arena.

Of course, judicial activism has gone further in some democracies than in others, few states having taken it further than the United States. The US is founded on a constitutional contract and an army of lawyers forever quibbles over the terms. Armed with a written constitution, federalism, judicial independence, no system of separate administrative courts, a legal system based on judge-made case law, and high esteem for judges, the US has moved ever further into a culture of judicial activism. The influence of the US Supreme Court on American public policy has led one critic of 'government by judges' to dismiss it as 'a nine-man, black-robed junta' (Waldron, 2007: 309).

Fewer conditions of judicial autonomy are met in Britain, where parliamentary sovereignty long reigned supreme. Lacking the authority to annul legislation, judicial review in the British context normally refers to the capacity of judges to review executive decisions against the template provided by administrative law. Even so, judicial activism has grown in Britain, reflecting European influence. British judges were willing accomplices of the European Court of Justice as it established a legal order applying to all member states. Judicial assertiveness was further encouraged by the country's belated adoption of the European Convention on Human Rights in 1998, the decay of the royal prerogative which once allowed the state to stand above the law, and the establishment of a British Supreme Court in 2009.

Formal statements of rights have also encouraged judicial expansion in other English-speaking countries. In Canada, a Charter of Rights and Freedoms was appended to the constitution in 1982, giving judges a more prominent role in defending individual rights. Similarly, New Zealand introduced a bill of rights in 1990, protecting 'the life and security of the person' and also confirming traditional, but previously uncodified, democratic and civil rights.

Judicial independence and recruitment

Given the growing political authority of the judiciary, the question of maintaining its independence gains in importance. Liberal democracies accept judicial autonomy as fundamental to the rule of law, but how is this independence achieved in practice? Security of tenure is important, which is why it is hard to remove them during their terms in office. But judicial autonomy also depends on how they are recruited. Were the selection of judges on the highest court to be controlled by politicians, the judiciary would simply reinforce partisan authority, providing an integration (rather than a separation) of powers. This danger is particularly acute when judicial tenure is short, limiting the period in which judges can develop their own perspective on the cases before them.

As a result, governments have developed multiple solutions to the issue of judicial selection, ranging from democratic election to co-option by judges already in post (see Figure 7.4). The former is democratic but political, while the latter offers the surest guarantee of independence but can lead to a self-perpetuating elite because it runs the danger that the existing judges will seek out new recruits with an outlook resembling their own. In between these extremes come the more conventional methods: appointment by the legislature, by the executive, and by independent panels. Many countries combine these orthodox methods, with the government choosing from a pool of candidates prepared by a professional body. Alternatively, and more traditionally, some judges on the senior court can be selected by one method, while others are chosen by a different method.

The British government recently ceded power of appointment to an independent commission, a decision justified by the relevant minister in the following way:

> In a modern democratic society it is no longer acceptable for judicial appointments to be entirely in the hands of a Government Minister. For example the judiciary is often involved in adjudicating on the lawfulness of actions of the Executive. And so the appointments system must be, and must be seen to be, independent of Government. It must be transparent. It must be accountable. And it must inspire public confidence. (Falconer, 2003: 3–4)

For most courts charged with judicial review, selection still involves a clear political dimension. For example, the stature of the US Supreme Court combines with the unusual rule of lifetime appointments to make sure that nominations are key decisions. In these contests, the judicial experience and legal ability of the nominee may matter less than ideology, partisanship, and a clean personal history. Even so, Walter Dellinger, former acting US Solicitor General, argues that 'the political appointment of judges is an appropriate "democratic moment" before the independence of life tenure sets in' (Peretti, 2001).

A political dimension is also apparent in selection to constitutional courts. Typically, members are selected by the legislature in a procedure that can involve party horse-trading. For instance, 8 out of the 12 members

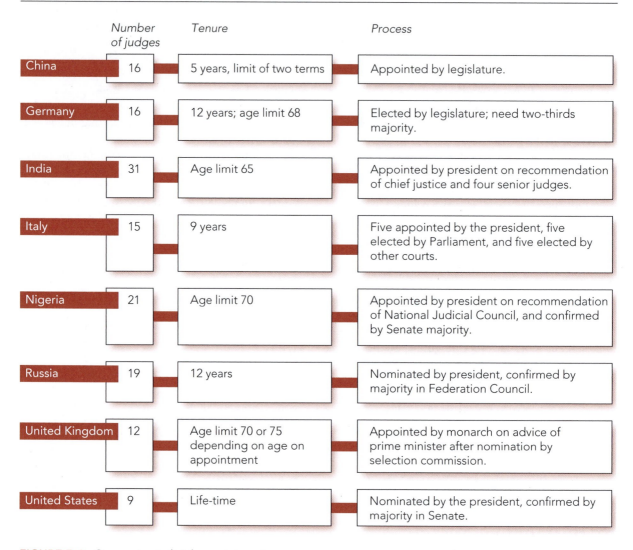

	Number of judges	Tenure	Process
China	16	5 years, limit of two terms	Appointed by legislature.
Germany	16	12 years; age limit 68	Elected by legislature; need two-thirds majority.
India	31	Age limit 65	Appointed by president on recommendation of chief justice and four senior judges.
Italy	15	9 years	Five appointed by the president, five elected by Parliament, and five elected by other courts.
Nigeria	21	Age limit 70	Appointed by president on recommendation of National Judicial Council, and confirmed by Senate majority.
Russia	19	12 years	Nominated by president, confirmed by majority in Federation Council.
United Kingdom	12	Age limit 70 or 75 depending on age on appointment	Appointed by monarch on advice of prime minister after nomination by selection commission.
United States	9	Life-time	Nominated by the president, confirmed by majority in Senate.

FIGURE 7.4: Comparing judicial appointments

of Spain's Constitutional Court are appointed by the party-dominated parliament.

Below the level of the highest court, judicial autonomy raises the issue of **internal independence**. The judiciary is more than the highest court of the land; it is an elaborate, multi-tiered structure encompassing ordinary courts, appeal courts, and special bodies such as tax and military courts. Whether justices at lower levels are inhibited or empowered shapes the effectiveness of the judicial system as a whole in resolving conflicts in a fair, effective and predictable fashion.

Internal independence: Refers to the autonomy of junior judges from their senior colleagues, who often determine career advancement. Where this autonomy is limited, judicial initiative may be stifled.

Guarnieri (2003: 225) emphasizes the importance of internal independence. Noting that 'judicial organizations in continental Europe traditionally operate within a pyramid-like organizational structure', he argues that 'the role played by organizational hierarchies is crucial in order to highlight the actual dynamics of the judicial corps'. This issue arose in acute form in some

FOCUS 7.2 | Models of judicial decision-making

Because senior judges are such key actors in shaping government, it is important to ask how they go about reaching their decisions. Three explanatory models have been developed:

- **Legal**: This is the most traditional, and assumes that judges are driven in their decisions by an understanding of the law. Of course, the fact that an issue has reached the highest court means that it is legally uncertain, so the law itself is not wholly determining. Even so, judges are likely to bear in mind precedent, legal principles, and the implications of their judgment for the future development of the law. They can hardly reach a particular decision unless they can wrap it in at least some legal covering.

- **Attitudinal**: This assumes that judges are driven by politics and ideology. The US Supreme Court is a primary example, because its verdicts are given in the form of unanimous or majority opinions, with dissenting opinions often also produced, and it is known how each of the justices voted. These open procedures allow researchers to assess whether, across a series of cases, a particular justice can be classified as consistently liberal or conservative, and to relate their ideological profile to such factors as the justice's social background. The answer is usually quite clear, which is why appointments to the US court generate so much public interest, and the likely outcome of votes can be anticipated well in advance.

- **Strategic**: This regards judges as sensitive to the likely reactions of other political actors and institutions to their pronouncements. As with any other institution, the highest courts (and often lower ones, too) act to maintain their standing, autonomy, and impact. Accordingly, judges will think hard before courting controversy or making decisions that will be ignored, or even reversed through constitutional amendment. This strategic model invites us to think of judges on the highest court as full players in the game of elite politics, who must abide by the rule of anticipated reactions. Germany's constitutional court is an example, concerned as it is to sustain democracy by defending the autonomy of its country's legislature.

continental European countries after 1945, when judges appointed under right-wing regimes continued in post, discouraging initiatives by new recruits lower in the pyramid. Guarnieri concludes that promotion and salary progression within the judiciary should depend solely on seniority, noting that such reforms were needed in Italy before younger 'assault judges' became willing to launch investigations into government corruption. This blanket solution may be extreme but it is important to recognize that the decisions of judges lower in the hierarchy will be influenced by anticipated effects on their career prospects.

Systems of law

As well as understanding constitutions and courts, it is also important to understand systems of law. The two most important of these are common law and civil law, whose contrasting principles are essential to an appreciation of the differences in the political role of judiciaries everywhere outside the Middle East. The third is sharia law, found in most Muslim countries, and even coexisting with common or civil law in countries with large Muslim populations, such as Nigeria, or in countries with a colonial history, such as Egypt.

Common law

The key feature of **common law** systems is that the decisions made by judges on specific cases form an overall legal framework which remains distinct from the authority of the state. It is found mainly in Britain and in countries that were once British colonies, such as Australia, Canada (except Quebec), India, Kenya, Nigeria, Pakistan, and the United States (except Louisiana). Originally based on custom and tradition, such decisions were first published as a way of standardizing legal judgments across the territory of a state. Because judges abided by the principle of *stare decisis* (stand on decided cases), their verdicts created precedents and established a predictable legal framework, contributing thereby to economic exchange and nation-building.

Where common law is judge-made law, **statute law** is passed by the legislature in specific areas but these statutes usually build on case law (the past decisions of courts) and are themselves refined through judicial interpretation. The political significance of common law systems is that judges constitute an independent source of authority. They form part of the governance, but not the government, of society. In this way, common law systems contribute to political pluralism.

> **Common law:** Judicial rulings on matters not explicitly treated in legislation, based on precedents created by decisions in specific cases.
>
> **Statute law:** Laws enacted by a legislature.
>
> **Civil law:** Judicial rulings founded on written legal codes which seek to provide a single overarching framework for the conduct of public affairs.

Civil law

Civil law springs from written legal codes rather than cases, the goal being to provide a single framework for the conduct of public affairs, including public administration and business contracts. The original codes were developed under Justinian, Roman emperor between 527 and 565. This system of Roman law has evolved into distinct civil codes, which are then elaborated through laws passed by the national legislatures. Civil law is found throughout Latin America, in all of continental Europe, in China and Russia, and in most African countries that were once colonies of continental European powers.

In civil law, judges (rather than juries) identify the facts of the case, and often even direct the investigation. They then apply the relevant section of the code to the matter at hand. The political importance of this point is that judges are viewed as impartial officers of state, engaged in an administrative task; they are merely *la bouche de la loi* (the mouth of the law). The courtroom is a government space, rather than a sphere of independent authority; judge-made law would be viewed as a threat to legislative supremacy.

The underlying codes in civil law systems often emphasize social stability as much as individual rights. The philosophy is one of state-led integration, rather than pluralism. Indeed, the codes traditionally functioned as a kind of extensive constitution, systematically setting out obligations as well as freedoms. However, the more recent introduction of distinct constitutions (which have established a strong position in relation to the codes) has strengthened the liberal theme in many civil law countries. In addition, judges have inevitably found themselves filling gaps in the codes, providing decisions which function as case law, even though they are not acknowledged as such. These developments dilute, without denying, the contrast between civil law and common law (Stone Sweet, 2000).

Religious law

In reviewing different legal systems, it is important not to overlook those that are related to religion: Islam, Judaism, Hinduism, Buddhism, and the Catholic Church all have their own distinctive bodies of law, some of which remain important in regulating the societies in which they are found. Some states, such as Bangladesh, also have polycentric legal systems that include separate provisions for different religions. Of all such religious legal systems, the one that has attracted the most international attention – and the one that is most widely misunderstood – is the **sharia law** of Muslim states.

> **Sharia law:** The system of Islamic law – based on the Quran and on the teachings and actions of Muhammad – which functions alongside Western law in most Islamic states.

In the West, Islamic law tends to come to attention only when someone has been sentenced to be stoned to death for adultery, or in the context of the unequal treatment of women in many Muslim societies. The result is a misleading conception of how it works, and an unfortunate failure to understand that Islamic law is deep and sophisticated, with its own courts, legal experts, and judges and its own tradition of jurisprudence (see Hallaq, 2007 for a survey). At the same time, however, while the use of Islamic law is one of the ideals of an Islamic republic, sharia law is not universally applied in any. It is widely used in Iran, Jordan, Libya, Mauritania, Oman, and Saudi Arabia, but most Islamic states use a mix of common or civil law and Islamic religious law, turning to the former for serious crime and to the latter for family issues.

Unlike Western law, where lawbreakers must account only to the legal system, the Islamic tradition holds that lawbreakers must account to Allah and all other Muslims. Also unlike Western law, the sharia outlines not only what is forbidden for Muslims but also what is discouraged, recommended, and obligatory. So, for example, Muslims should *not* drink alcohol, gamble, steal, commit adultery, or commit suicide, but they *should* pray every day, give to charity, be polite to others, dress inoffensively, and – when they die – be buried in anonymous graves. When Muslims have doubts about whether something they are considering doing is acceptable, they are encouraged to speak to a Muslim judge, called a *mufti*, who will issue a legal judgment known as a *fatwa*.

Constitutions and courts in authoritarian states

The nature of authoritarian regimes is such that restraints on rule go unacknowledged, and power, not law, is the political currency. Constitutions are weak, and the formal status of the judiciary is similarly reduced. In fact, it is often only in the transition to democracy that the old elite empowers the courts, seeking guarantees for its own diminished future (Solomon, 2007). In instances where courts do have power, it tends to be only because authoritarian leaders use them to further their control.

Non-democratic rulers follow two broad strategies in limiting judicial authority. One is to retain a framework of law and a facade of judicial independence, but to influence the judges indirectly through recruitment, training, evaluation, promotion, and disciplinary procedures. In the more determined cases, they can simply be dismissed. Egypt's President Nasser adopted this strategy with vigour in 1969 when he fired 200 in one fell swoop in the 'massacre of the judges'. Uganda's notorious military dictator Idi Amin adopted the ultimate form of control in 1971 when he had his chief justice shot dead.

A second more subtle strategy is to bypass the judicial process. For instance, many non-democratic regimes use Declarations of Emergency as a cover to make decisions which are exempt from judicial scrutiny. In effect, a law is passed saying there is no law. Once introduced, such 'temporary' emergencies can drag on for decades. Alternatively, rulers can make use of special courts that do the regime's bidding without much pretence of judicial independence; Egypt's State Security Courts were an example, hearing matters involving 'threats' to

'security' (a concept that was interpreted broadly) until they were closed down in 2008. Military rulers have frequently extended the scope of secret military courts to include civilian troublemakers. Ordinary courts can thus continue to deal with non-political cases, offering a thin image of legal integrity to the world.

Under the circumstances, it is little surprise that authoritarian regimes have a poor record on human rights. Comparative data in this area lack the established record of the indices we have reviewed for democracy and corruption. One index that has generated data since 1981, but has not been published since 2011, is the CIRI Human Rights Data Project, which used information from the US State Department on human rights in countries around the world, including their records on free speech, freedom of movement, execution, torture, disappearances, and political imprisonment. The project gave scores ranging downward from 30; in 2010, the world average was 18, Denmark and Iceland scored 30 and the United States ranked fifth equal with 26. The ten countries with the lowest scores are shown in Table 7.2.

As Table 7.2 suggests, one state with an extended history of human rights abuses is Zimbabwe, which has languished under the government of Robert Mugabe since independence in 1980. Following a period of growing political conflict and economic decline, a new constitution was adopted in 2013, offering hope that life for Zimbabweans might become more secure. But the governing party ZANU-PF – which won nearly three-quarters of the seats in the legislature in deeply flawed 2013 elections – dragged its feet in implementing the provisions of the constitution and in amending existing laws restricting freedom of expression and assembly. Media and academic freedom remain limited,

TABLE 7.2: The ten countries with the lowest scores on human rights

	Score out of 30		
Burma	2	Yemen	3
Eritrea	2	Zimbabwe	3
Iran	2	Saudi Arabia	4
China	3	Congo (Dem Rep)	5
North Korea	3	Nigeria	5

Source: CIRI Human Rights Dataset 2011, at www. humanrightsdata.com

opponents of the regime are still routinely harassed, property rights are ignored, the military is used to support the regime, and the courts are manipulated to suit Mugabe's purposes. For example, the courts ruled the 2013 elections to be free and fair in spite of clear evidence to the contrary.

In states with a ruling party, courts are viewed not as a constraint upon political authority but as an aid to the party in its policy goals. China is currently on its fourth and most recent constitution (dating from 1982), and even though it begins by affirming the country's socialist status, and warning against 'sabotage of the socialist system' it is the least radical of the four. It seeks to establish a more predictable environment for economic development and to limit the communist party's historic emphasis on class conflict, national self-reliance, and revolutionary struggle. The leading role of the party is now mentioned only in the preamble, with the main text even declaring that 'all political parties must abide by the Constitution'. Amendments in 2004 gave further support to private property and human rights. In the context of communist states, such liberal statements are remarkable, even if they remain a poor guide to reality.

In addition to moderating the content of its constitution, today's China also gives greater emphasis to law in general. There were very few laws at all in the early decades of the People's Republic, reflecting a national tradition of unregulated power, and leaving the judiciary as, essentially, a branch of the police. However, laws did become more numerous, precise, and significant after the hiatus of the Cultural Revolution (1966–76). In 1979, the country passed its first criminal laws; later revisions abolished the vague crime of counter-revolution and established the right of defendants to seek counsel. Law could prevail to the benefit of economic development. For law-abiding citizens, life became more predictable.

Despite such changes, Chinese politics remains authoritarian. 'Rule by law' still means exerting political control through law, rather than limiting the exercise of power. The courts are regarded as just one bureaucratic agency among others, legal judgments are not tested against the constitution, and many decisions are simply ignored. Rulings are unpublished and difficult cases are often left undecided. In comparison with liberal democracies, legal institutions remain less specialized, and legal personnel less sophisticated. Trial procedures, while improving, still offer only limited

protection for the innocent. The death penalty remains in use, the police remain largely unaccountable, political opponents are still imprisoned without trial, and party officials continue to occupy a protected position above the law. Because the party still rules, power continues to trump the constitution and human rights.

Iran offers a further case of a legal system operating in the context of an authoritarian regime. To be sure, the country exhibits all the trappings of a constitution supported by a court system. The constitutional document makes noble statements about an Islamic Republic 'endorsed by the people of Iran on the basis of their long-standing belief in the sovereignty of truth and Quranic justice', and about the 'exalted dignity and value of man' and the independence of the judiciary. But Iran has one of the weaker records on human rights in the world. Many activists languish in jail on political charges, Iran has a rate of execution that is probably second only to that of China (there are many capital offences in Iran, include apostasy (abandonment of Islam) and *moharebeh* ('enmity against God')), and women and minorities face discrimination of many kinds. In contrast to Western states, the constitution expresses Islamic more than liberal values and the court system is a channel rather than a limitation on power.

In hybrid or competitive authoritarian regimes, too, constitutions and the law are subsidiary to political authority. The leader may be elected within a constitutional framework, but that environment has been shaped by the leader, and the exercise of power is rarely constrained by an independent judiciary. Presidents occupy the highest ground, defining the national interest under the broad authority granted to them by the voters. In other words, presidential accountability is vertical (to the voters) rather than horizontal (to the judiciary). In contrast to a liberal democracy, where the main parties have concluded that being ruled by law is preferable to being ruled by opponents, under competitive authoritarianism the commanding figure still sees the constitution, the law, and the courts as a source of political advantage. Legal processes operate more extensively than in pure authoritarian regimes but remain subject to political manipulation.

The Russian experience shows that law can gain ground – if only slowly and with difficulty – in at least some authoritarian regimes. Russia's post-communist constitution of 1993 set out an array of individual rights (including that of owning property); proclaimed that 'the individual and his rights and freedoms are the supreme value'; and established a tripartite system of general, commercial, and constitutional courts. The Constitutional Court, in particular, represented a major innovation in Russian legal thinking.

Since 1993, the government has established detailed and lengthy (if not always well-drafted) codes appropriate for a civil law system. From 1998, criminal defendants who have exhausted all domestic remedies have even been able to appeal to the European Court of Human Rights (Sharlet, 2005: 147). More prosaically, tax law and business law have been modernized.

But in Russia, as in other authoritarian regimes (and even some liberal democracies), 'there has been and remains a considerable gap between individual rights on paper and their realization in practice' (Sharlet, 2005: 134). For instance:

- The conviction rate in criminal cases remains suspiciously high.
- Expertise and pay within the legal system are low, sustaining a culture of corruption.

- Violence by the police is common.
- Politics overwhelms the law on sensitive cases (such as the imprisonment in 2005 of business oligarch, Mikhail Khodorkovsky).
- Legal judgments, especially against the state, can be difficult to enforce.
- The public still shows little faith in the legal system (Smith, 2010: 150).

So, Russia has made more progress towards achieving the rule of law than has China, but assuming that law in Russia will eventually acquire the status it possesses in liberal democracies still involves drawing a cheque against the future. Smith (2010: 135) concedes that much progress has been made in establishing 'a workable and independent judiciary and legal system', with new laws enacted and legal reforms undertaken, but notes that 'the enforcement of laws has been uneven and at times politicised, which erodes public support and belief in the courts'.

DISCUSSION QUESTIONS

- Which is best: a constitution that is short and ambiguous, leaving room for interpretation, or one that is long and detailed, leaving less room for misunderstanding?

- What are the advantages and disadvantages of codified and uncodified constitutions?

- What are the advantages and disadvantages of supreme courts against constitutional courts?

- Judicial restraint or judicial activism – which is best for the constitutional well-being of a state?

- What is the best way of recruiting judges, and what are the most desirable limits on their terms in office, if any?

- Can religious and secular law coexist?

KEY CONCEPTS

Abstract review	Judicial activism
Appellate	Judicial restraint
Civil law	Judicial review
Codified constitution	Original jurisdiction
Common law	Rigid constitution
Concrete review	Rule of law
Constitution	Sharia law
Entrenchment	Statute law
Flexible constitution	Uncodified constitution
Internal independence	

FURTHER READING

Guarnieri, Carlo and Patrizia Pederzoli (2002) *The Power of Judges: A Comparative Study of Courts and Democracy*. A cross-national study of the judiciary.

Harding, Andrew and Peter Leyland (eds) (2009) *Constitutional Courts: A Comparative Study*. A comparative study of constitutional courts, with cases from Europe, Russia, the Middle East, Latin America, and Asia.

Issacharoff, Samuel (2015) *Fragile Democracies: Contested Power in the Era of Constitutional Courts*. Argues that strong constitutional courts are a powerful antidote to authoritarianism, because they help protect against external threats and the domestic consolidation of power.

Lee, H. P. (2011) *Judiciaries in Comparative Perspective*. An edited collection of studies of judiciaries in Australia, Britain, Canada, New Zealand, South Africa, and the United States.

Sunstein, Cass (2001) *Designing Democracy: What Constitutions Do*. A provocative assessment of how constitutions can be used to constructively channel political divisions.

Toobin, Jeffrey (2009) *The Nine: Inside the Secret World of the Supreme Court*. A journalist looks at the workings of the US Supreme Court.

8 Legislatures

PREVIEW

Legislatures are the institutions of government that are closest to the citizens, since they are typically directly elected and are often responsible for representing local districts, rather than – as is the case with executives – the entire country. They are thus a key part of representative democracy. But how representation should be ensured or understood is an important question. And the tasks of legislatures go beyond representation, including also deliberation, the approval of legislation, the authorization of expenditure, the making of governments, and oversight of the executive.

This chapter begins with a review of these multiple roles, opinion on the dynamics of which is often divided. In terms of representation, for example, should members of legislatures be focused on their districts, the people who voted for them, their parties, or the broad national interest? And how good a job do they actually do at representation?

The chapter goes on to look at the structure of legislatures, and in particular at the differences between those with one chamber and those with two chambers. It then reviews the work of committees, whose influence depends on the strength of the legislature in the political system. It then considers the members of legislatures, with a particular focus on the rise of the career politician, and the pros and cons of imposing term limits on legislators. Finally, it looks at the shadow role of legislatures in authoritarian states. While they may appear weak, however, they do possess a number of uses for leaders and ruling elites.

CONTENTS

- Legislatures: an overview
- Functions
- Structure
- Members
- Legislatures in authoritarian states

KEY ARGUMENTS

- Legislatures link society and state, making them an essential device in a representative democracy.
- Legislatures are not governing bodies, do not take major decisions, and do not even normally initiate proposals for laws; but they provide the foundations of liberal democracy.
- The issue of whether legislatures should have one chamber or two exposes contrasting perspectives on how democracy should be conceived.
- Oversight is an increasingly important function of nearly all legislatures in liberal democracies. Understanding this role means looking carefully at the work of legislative committees.
- Legislatures are increasingly home to career politicians, who collectively constitute a political class with a background and interests removed from the people it represents.
- Legislatures are found in most authoritarian regimes, but they mainly provide only a fig leaf of legitimacy, or 'controlled institutional channels' through which demands and concessions can be made.

Legislatures: an overview

Legislatures are symbols of popular representation in politics, and understanding the way they work is central to institutional theory. They are not governing bodies, they do not take major decisions and they do not even normally initiate proposals for laws. Yet, they remain a foundation of both liberal and democratic politics. The words used to denote these bodies reflect their original purpose: assemblies gather, congresses congregate, diets meet, dumas deliberate, legislatures pass laws, and parliaments talk. Their significance arises from their representative role; for Olson (1994: 1), they 'join society to the legal structure of authority in the state. Legislatures are representative bodies: they reflect the sentiments and opinions of the citizens.' As the English political theorist John Locke observed:

> It is in their legislative, that the members of a commonwealth are united, and combined together into one coherent living body. This is the soul that gives form, life, and unity, to the commonwealth: from hence the several members have their mutual influence, sympathy, and connexion: and, therefore, when the legislative is broken, or dissolved, dissolution and death follows. (Locke, 1690: sec. 212)

Legislature: A multi-member representative body which considers public issues and either accepts, amends or rejects proposals for new laws and policies.

The earliest popular assemblies in the Western tradition were the Ecclesia of Athens, open to all male citizens with two years of military service. Later, in the ancient royal courts of Europe, monarchs would judge important legal cases and meet with nobles of the realm. Gradually these assemblies became more settled, coming to represent the various estates – the clergy, the nobility, and the towns – into which society was then divided. In the thirteenth and fourteenth centuries, kings began to consult estate leaders more consistently on issues of war, administration, commerce, and taxation. These early European assemblies were viewed as possessing a right to be consulted long before they became modern legislatures with the sovereign authority to pass laws.

Where European parliaments accumulated powers gradually and with difficulty, most modern constitutions emphasize the importance of the legislature.

In the debates surrounding the US constitution, for instance, James Madison declared that 'in republican government, the legislative power necessarily predominates' (Hamilton, 1788b: 265). A leading role for the assembly was judged to be an essential defence against executive tyranny; in consequence, the list of powers awarded to Congress was longer and more detailed than that given to the president. The principle of expressing the popular will through an assembly is today a fundamental tenet of liberal democracy. Modern democratic legislatures contribute to detailed governance as well as to broad expressions of the popular will: they can improve the quality of legislation, oversee the actions of the executive, and hold influential hearings on matters of public concern. And as representative bodies, they are closer to the citizens than the more distant political executive. In authoritarian states, by contrast, they may be useful in providing a fig leaf of legitimacy, in incorporating moderate opponents, in helping integrate centre and periphery, in recruiting for the elite, and in containing demands for change.

Functions

Democratic legislatures have six major functions, ranging from representation to oversight (see Figure 8.1), the balance varying from one legislature to another. Hence while they all 'represent' in one form or another, for example, they will have different roles in the budgetary process, and parliamentary legislatures are more critical to the making of governments than those in presidential executives.

Representation

While this is undoubtedly the essence of the work of legislatures, it is not always easy to judge whether, and how well, that function is fulfilled. The meaning of *representation* should be obvious, and yet political science has been unable to develop a definition with which everyone can agree. Pitkin (1967) set the terms of the debate by outlining four different ways of understanding representation:

- *Formalistic*: Concerned with the rules and arrangements for representation, asking how representatives come to office, how they enforce their decisions, how they respond to their constituents, and how they are held accountable by voters.

FIGURE 8.1: The functions of legislatures

- *Symbolic*: Concerned with how representatives are perceived by their constituents. For example, are they seen to be competent and concerned with the broad interests of their district, or are they regarded as too partisan, captured by special interests, or unapproachable?

- *Descriptive*: Suggests that a legislature should be society in miniature, literally 're-presenting' society and not simply acting on its behalf (Phillips, 1995). Thus its members would have the same balance of men and women, rich and poor, black and white, straight and gay, educated and uneducated, as the general population. But how many different segments of society should, or realistically could, be represented? With the good, we would have to accept the bad, the incompetent, the corrupt, and the ignorant.

- *Substantive*: Concerned with how representatives respond to the needs of their voters. While this may be the most important and obvious kind of representation, it raises the question of the extent to which voters have well-developed political needs, or understand all the options available to them. In most cases, levels of political interest and knowledge are low, making it difficult for representatives

to be fully responsive. A given district will also contain a variety of interests, concerns, and values among its population, requiring its representative to somehow achieve a balance among competing demands.

A fifth option to add to Pitkin's list is *collective representation*, which suggests that members of a legislature should collectively represent the interests of all voters, not just those in the districts they represent. The Irish-born politician Edmund Burke offered the classic account of this position after being elected Member of Parliament for the English constituency of Bristol in 1774. He admitted in his victory speech that he knew nothing about his constituency and had played little part in the campaign, but, he continued:

> Parliament is not a congress of ambassadors from different and hostile interests [but is instead] a deliberative assembly of one nation, with one interest, that of the whole; where, not local purposes, not local prejudices, ought to guide, but the general good, resulting from the general reason of the whole. You choose a member indeed; but when you have chosen him, he is not a member for Bristol, but he is a member of Parliament. (Burke, 1774)

In spite of these competing analyses, representation in practice operates in a somewhat prosaic way: through political parties. Victorious candidates owe their election largely to their party and they vote in the legislature largely according to the commands and expectations of the party. This is particularly true of parliamentary systems, where representatives are expected to toe the party line; in India, members of Parliament can even lose their seat if they vote against their party, the theory being that they are deceiving the voters if they switch parties after their election. Representatives are also assessed by voters in terms of party affiliation; a voter will look on a representative as more approachable, responsive, and trustworthy if they are both from the same party, and less so if they are not.

Deliberation

Many legislatures serve as a deliberative body, considering public matters of national importance. The main contrast here is between a **debating legislature** and a **committee-based legislature**. In the former, deliberation takes the form of general discussion in the chamber, in what is sometimes known as a **plenary session**, or a meeting of the whole. In the British House of Commons, for example, key issues eventually make their way to the floor of the House of Commons where they are discussed with passion, partisanship, and sometimes flair. Floor debate becomes the arena for national political discussion, forming part of a continuous election campaign. The mood of the House, as revealed in debate, is often more significant than the vote which follows.

> **Debating legislature:** One where floor debate is the central activity, through which major issues are addressed and parties gain or lose ground.
>
> **Committee-based legislature:** One where most work takes place in committees, where members transform bills into laws, conducting hearings, and scrutinizing the executive.
>
> **Plenary session:** A meeting of the entire legislature, as distinct from committee meetings.

Appropriately, it was the nineteenth-century English political philosopher John Stuart Mill who made the case for a debating assembly:

> I know not how a representative assembly can more usefully employ itself than in talk, when the subject of talk is the great public interests of the country, and every sentence of it represents the opinion either of some important body of persons in the nation, or of an individual in whom such bodies have reposed their confidence. (Mill, 1861: 353)

In committee-based legislatures, by contrast (such as the US Congress and the Scandinavian parliaments) deliberation is less theatrical, taking the form of policy discussion in committees. The practical task is to assess the government's proposals, while also providing measured scrutiny of its actions. This deliberative style is less dramatic than a set-piece debate but often more constructive.

Legislation

Legislatures are often alone in having the right to make laws, the painstaking process for passing bills into law underlining the importance attached to government by rules, rather than by individuals. The procedure is explicitly deliberative, involving several readings (debates) as the bill moves from the floor to committee and back again (Figure 8.2). In bicameral legislatures, differences in the versions of the bill passed by each chamber must be reconciled.

But legislation is rarely the function in which 'legislatures' exert the greatest influence, because effective control over legislation in most liberal democracies rests with the government; bills pass through the assembly without being designed, or even transformed, there. In Britain, the governing party has historically dominated law-making. As Moran (2011: 157) points out:

> The House of Commons is misunderstood if viewed as a legislator. Virtually all legislative proposals originate from, and are shaped by, the executive. Nor are the Commons' extensive debates on legislative proposals of great significance in shaping the law: secure government majorities (which up to now have been the usual state of affairs) mean that legislative proposals are hardly ever overturned wholesale, and detailed amendments are usually the result of concessions by ministers.

In party-dominated Australia, the government treats the legislative function with virtual contempt. On a single night in 1991 it tried to put 26 bills through the Senate in three hours. Before New Zealand adopted

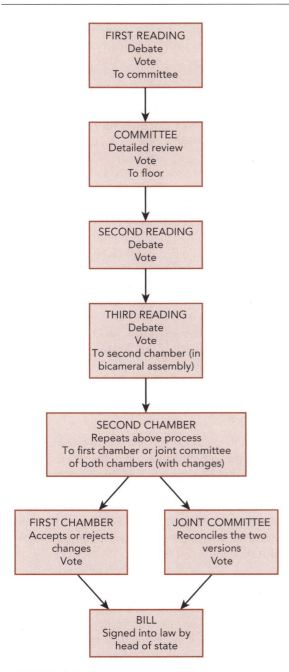

FIGURE 8.2: Stages in the making of a law
Source: Adapted from Mahler (2007: table 4.9)

is reactive in the sense that it is reduced to quality control: patching up errors in bills prepared in haste by ministers and bureaucrats. By contrast, committee-based legislatures in continental Europe play a more positive role in law-making, with a combination of coalition governments, influential committees, and an elite commitment to delivering laws acceptable to all sides.

In presidential systems such as the United States, Brazil, and Mexico, assemblies have the most autonomy in law-making. Only members of Congress can formally introduce bills, although executives can work around this by finding a friendly representative to initiate a bill on its behalf. The separation of powers and personnel inherent in a presidential regime limits executive influence over the legislature, an institutional separation that is often reinforced by divided government (the president may come from a different party than the one that dominates one or both chambers of the legislature), further reducing the legislature's willingness to convert the administration's proposals into laws.

Bicameral legislatures face an additional hurdle in making law, which arises when one chamber amends a bill passed by the other. In some countries, such as Britain and Spain, the lower house is more powerful and can decide whether to accept or reject amendments from the upper house. In others, including Australia, Brazil and India, there will be a joint vote of both chambers, the larger lower chamber having the most numerical weight. In yet others, including France, Germany, and the United States, a special conference committee, made up of an equal number of members from each chamber, will meet to work out an agreed bill. Italy takes a different approach, allowing amended versions of bills to shuttle indefinitely between chambers until agreement is reached (if ever). The effect is illustrated by a bill on rape that was introduced in 1977 and did not become law in Italy until 1995.

Authorizing expenditure

This is one of the oldest functions of legislatures, and of the lower house in particular. Its origins stem from the original purpose of European assemblies, which was to review requests for funds from monarchs. But it has since – in many parliamentary democracies – become nominal. What usually happens is that the executive

proportional representation in 1996, one prime minister boasted that if an idea came to him while shaving, he could have it on the statute book by the evening.

In the party-dominated parliaments of Britain and some of its ex-colonies, the legislative function prepares the budget, which is then reported to the legislature but rarely modified there.

For the legislature to possess the power of the purse, suggests Wehner (2006), it must have the ability to amend the budget (as opposed to simply being authorized to make cuts), an effective committee system, enough time to consider the budget in detail, and access to background information underlying the budget. Few countries meet all these conditions, and parliamentary approval is generally given after the fact, serving to confirm compromises worked out between government departments. In many democracies, the budget is a done deal once it reaches the assembly. If parliament began to unpick any part of a complicated package, it would fall apart.

The United States is the clearest exception to the thesis of executive control of the purse. Congress remains central to budget-making, since all money spent by executive departments must be allocated under specific expenditure headings approved by Congress. As Flammang *et al.* (1990: 422) wrote, 'without the agreement of members of Congress, no money can be doled out for foreign aid, salaries for army generals or paper clips for bureaucrats'. The result is that the annual federal budget debate has become an elaborate game of chicken: the president and Congress each hopes that the other side will accede to its own proposals before the money runs out.

Making governments

Legislatures are a key part of government, in the sense not just that they take care of government business but also that the abilities of executives to govern depend in large part on the political make-up of legislatures. In presidential systems such as Brazil, Mexico, or the United States, the president – being separately elected – does not rely on sympathetic party members in the legislature to stay in office. But those members play a critical role in determining the capacity of the executive to lead; a supportive or sympathetic legislature provides a clearer path to effective leadership, while one dominated by opposition parties will provide obstacles and road blocks.

In parliamentary systems, by contrast, the government is entirely dependent upon the party make-up of the legislature; a party can neither take office, nor continue in power, without a supporting majority (or, at least, a workable minority) in the legislature. Furthermore, the strength of the ruling party or coalition in the legislature influences the government's stability. A government based on a single party with a legislative majority is likely to prove more stable than a minority government. For Laver (2006), the most important role of a legislature in a parliamentary system is not legislating, but 'making and breaking governments'.

One of the more extreme illustrations of this role can be found in Italy, which has long suffered from an excess of parties in its legislature. In part because of a desire to avoid the kind of centralization of power that allowed the dictatorship of Benito Mussolini, and in part because of the ongoing regional and economic divisions within Italy, building stable coalitions is difficult, governments regularly fall, and prime ministers routinely serve only short terms in office. Between 1946 and 2015 there were 63 governments, lasting an average of less than a year. Only one – the government of Silvio Berlusconi between 2001 and 2006 – saw out its full parliamentary term, but even he had to resign four years into his administration and form a new government. Amintore Fanfani, meanwhile, had the shortest term in office – just 21 days in January–February 1954 (although he had five more terms in office between then and 1987).

Oversight

The final function of legislatures is oversight (or scrutiny) of the executive. In many countries, the oversight role has been growing in significance and value in recent decades, helping compensate for the downgrading of the legislative and expenditure functions of assemblies, and providing a new direction to their work. Parliamentary systems offer several instruments with which to monitor the executive:

- *Questions* can be posed to leaders and ministers, whether oral or written. In Britain, for example, members of the House of Commons ask over 500 questions per day, keeping many bureaucrats busy as they prepare answers for their ministerial masters (House of Commons Procedure Committee, 2009). Prime Minister's Question Time, a weekly event, remains a theatrical joust between the prime minister and the leader of the opposition. In other legislatures, however, questions are accorded lower status, with French ministers often failing to answer them at all.

- *Interpellations* are an alternative form of interrogation in some European assemblies, including Finland, France, and Germany. A form of confidence motion, an interpellation is a substantial question demanding a prompt response which is followed by a short debate and usually a vote on whether the government's answer is considered acceptable.

- *Emergency debates* are a higher-profile means of calling executives to account. Typically, a minimum number of members, together with the presiding officer (Speaker), must approve a proposal for an emergency debate. The discussion usually ends with a government win; the significance lies in the debate itself and the fact of its having been called. An emergency debate creates publicity and demands a considered response from the government's spokesperson.

Without question, though, the most important means by which legislatures can hold executives accountable is through a **vote of confidence** or a censure motion. The former is a vote that – if it goes against the government – leads to compulsory resignation, while the latter indicates disapproval of a specific minister for a stated reason. Confidence votes are not so much a form of detailed oversight as a decision on whether the government can continue at all. Even though such votes are rare, they can determine the fate of the executive, with the potential to lead to a change of leadership and even new elections. In the British Parliament, a government can be brought down by losing a vote of confidence or by losing a vote on a matter of policy that has been described as a 'matter of confidence'. In France and Sweden, a majority of all members (not only those voting) is required to confirm a legislature's loss of confidence. In other countries, a confidence motion is not specifically designated but is simply any vote on which the government would feel obliged to resign if defeated. Defeat on a motion to approve the budget would be a typical example. In some countries, again including Sweden, votes of confidence can be directed against individual ministers as well as the government as a whole.

> **Vote of confidence:** A vote in a legislature on the question of its confidence in the government to lead. If lost, it normally requires the resignation of the government.

Structure

While the functions of legislatures (and the dynamics of those functions) vary from one to another, on matters of structure the options are more limited. First, almost every legislature has either one or two chambers, the number being determined by a combination of history and political need. Second, most legislatures operate through specialist committees where much of the work of law-making is actually done, with plenary sessions playing only a formal role in the legislative process.

Chambers

For most countries, a single-chambered (or **unicameral**) legislature is enough to represent the interests of the population and to manage its responsibilities; hence about 60 per cent of the world's legislatures have just one chamber (Inter-Parliamentary Union, 2015). Their number increased in the second half of the twentieth century as several smaller democracies – including Sweden (1971) and Iceland (1991) – abolished their second chamber, and many smaller post-colonial and post-communist states also opted for a single chamber. For reasons of history, politics, or practical need, the rest have **bicameral** (double-chambered) legislatures. South Africa even went so far between 1984 and 1994 as to have a tricameral legislature, with each chamber representing a different race.

> **Unicameral and bicameral:** Terms referring to the number of chambers in a legislature.

In the case of bicameral legislatures, one is usually known as the first (or lower) chamber and the other as the second (or upper) chamber. Perhaps counterintuitively, the lower chamber is usually the bigger and the more powerful; while some upper chambers have near-equal powers with their lower partners, most are both smaller and weaker. The lower chamber is almost always the originator of new proposals for legislation (bills), with the second chamber playing the role of taking a second look, and the lower chamber often has sole or dominating control over budgetary matters. The origins of the lower/upper designation are unclear, but they probably trace back to the manner in which the British Parliament was divided between aristocrats and commoners, with the 'Lords Spiritual and Temporal' comprising the more historic and exclusive 'upper' chamber.

The choice between one and two chambers reflects contrasting visions of democracy. Unicameral legislatures are justified by a majoritarian reading of popular

Chamber of Deputies	Argentina, Brazil, Chile, Czech Republic, Haiti, Italy, Mexico, Romania, Rwanda.
National Assembly	Afghanistan*, Angola, Bulgaria, Cuba, France, Greece, Hungary, Kuwait, Nigeria*, Pakistan, South Africa, Thailand*, Turkey, South Korea.
House of Representatives	Australia, Egypt, Japan, Netherlands, New Zealand, Nigeria, United States.
House of Commons	Canada, United Kingdom.

* Both chambers. All others refer to lower or sole chambers only.

FIGURE 8.3: A selection of lower chambers

control, the idea being that an assembly based on direct popular election reflects the popular will and should not be obstructed. The radical French cleric Abbé Sieyès (1748–1836) put the point well: 'if a second chamber dissents from the first, it is mischievous; and if it agrees, it is superfluous' (Lively, 1991). Also, a single chamber is more accountable, economical, and decisive; it lacks the petty point-scoring which becomes possible with two houses representing distinct interests.

But the defenders of bicameral legislatures reject both the majoritarian logic of the Abbé and the penny-pinching of accountants. Bicameralists stress the liberal element of democracy, arguing that the upper chamber offers checks and balances, provides more considered debate because its members usually have longer terms in office, it can be more collegial because it is usually smaller, and it can defend individual and group interests against a potentially oppressive majority in the lower house. Bicameral legislatures are most often found in larger countries and in democracies, and they are universal in federations, where the second chamber typically represents the component states.

The second chamber can also share the workload of the lower chamber, and serve as a house of review, revising bills, examining constitutional amendments, and eliminating intemperate legislation. In short, it can be a second chamber for second thoughts. James Madison, one of America's founding fathers, suggested that an upper house afforded protection against 'an excess of law-making' (Hamilton, 1788c). As such, it can offer a modern approximation to the traditional idea of a council of elders, often debating in a less partisan style than the lower house. Or to adopt the terms used by Edmund Burke (quoted earlier in this chapter), the upper house can be a 'deliberative assembly of one nation', rather than a mere 'congress of ambassadors'.

Where legislatures consist of two chambers, the question arises of the relationship between them. Usually, the lower chamber dominates in an arrangement known as **weak bicameralism**. In this system, which is typical of parliamentary governments in unitary systems, the government's survival depends on maintaining the assembly's support, and for clarity one chamber must (or should) become the focus of such accountability. The task of sustaining or voting down the government falls naturally to the lower house, with its popular mandate.

Weak bicameralism: This arises when the lower chamber dominates the upper, providing the primary focus for government accountability.

Strong bicameralism: This occurs when the two chambers are more balanced, as in federations with presidential executives.

The dominance of the lower chamber can also be seen in other ways:

- It is usually the larger house, averaging 254 members compared with 95 in the upper house (IPU, 2015).

FOCUS 8.1 | Does the size of legislatures matter?

It makes intuitive sense that the size of a legislature should reflect the size of a country's population. Thus China, the world's most populous country, has a National People's Congress with almost 3,000 members, while the assembly in the South Pacific island state of Micronesia (with a population of 104,000) contains just 14 representatives.

However, size is a poor measure of strength. Giant assemblies may seem powerful, but they are rendered impotent by their inability to act cohesively, and are in constant danger of being taken over by more coherent actors, such as political parties, or even their own committees. Ruling communist parties, as in China, prefer a large legislature precisely because it is easier to control. By contrast, a small chamber – numbering, say, under 100 – offers more opportunities for all deputies to have their say in a collegial environment.

A more telling statistic is the number of representatives per head of population (see Figure 8.4). The Chinese legislature may be large, but once its members are divided up among China's population, we find that each delegate represents about 460,000 people. By contrast, the Swedish Riksdag is much smaller, but its 349 members each represent only 27,500 people, and thus Swedes have more intensive representation at the national level than do the Chinese.

At first glance, Indians may seem to have the worst level of political representation, with more than 2.3 million people per member of Parliament. But India is a federal system, so Indians are also represented in state and local legislatures. The same point applies to other countries with relatively high numbers of people per representative, such as the United States and Nigeria. Conversely, Britain and Sweden appear to have the most generous levels of representation, but they have weaker local units of government than is the case with federations.

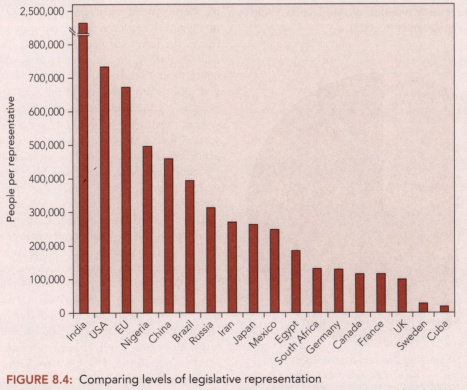

FIGURE 8.4: Comparing levels of legislative representation

Notes: Calculated based on data in Inter-Parliamentary Union (2015) (assembly size) and in World Bank (2015) (population). For bicameral assemblies, the size of the lower chamber only is used.

- It often has special responsibility for the budget.
- It is the forum where major proposals are introduced.
- It is entitled to override vetoes or amendments proffered by the second chamber.

In presidential systems, where presidents are directly elected and their continuation in office does not depend on the confidence of the legislature, there is no need for the executive's accountability to focus on a single chamber. **Strong bicameralism** can emerge in these conditions, especially when combined with federalism. The US Congress is the best illustration of this more balanced arrangement. With its constitutional position as representative of the states, the Senate plays a full part in the country's governance.

Selection of the upper chamber

There is not much point in a bicameral legislature unless the two chambers represent public interests differently; if they are the same size, are elected in the same way, and have the same powers, they will simply replicate one another. One means of avoiding this duplication is to select the chambers in different ways, to which end there are three main options: direct election, indirect election, or appointment (Fig 8.5).

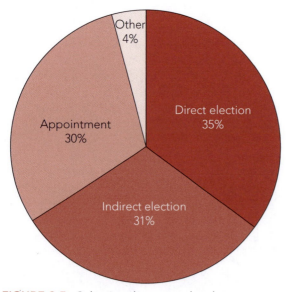

FIGURE 8.5: Selecting the upper chamber

Note: Based on total number of seats, not number of upper chambers. For comparison, 95 per cent of members of the first (lower) chamber are directly elected.

Source: Inter-Parliamentary Union (2015)

An example of indirect election can be found in France, where members of the Senate are elected by members of electoral colleges in each of France's *départements* (counties). These colleges are made up of regional councillors, mayors, city councillors, and members of the National Assembly from the area, with a weighting towards rural areas that has helped keep the Senate politically conservative, and prevented the socialists from winning a majority until 2011. An example of appointment can be found in Canada, where all 105 members of the Senate are appointed by the governor-general (representative of the British monarch) on the recommendation of the prime minister. This might make the Senate seem as undemocratic as the Federation Council of Russia (see later in this chapter), where appointments are controlled by the president. However, Canadian prime ministers are sensitive to regional considerations and will appoint independents and members of the opposition in addition to members of their own party. In any case, the Senate rarely goes against the will of the lower House of Commons, and has a tradition of being less partisan than the House.

Even when upper chambers are directly elected, a contrast with the lower house is still normally achieved by offering members of the upper house a longer tenure: typically five or six years compared with four or five in the lower chamber (Table 8.1). To sharpen the contrast further, the election cycle is often staggered; hence federal senators in the United States serve six-year terms, with one-third of the seats up for election every two years, while senators in France serve three-year terms with half the seats up for election every three years. A federal structure also produces a natural divergence between chambers. This contrast arises because elections to federal upper chambers are arranged by state, with smaller states deliberately over-represented. For instance, the US Senate contains two members for each of 50 states, meaning that California (population 39 million) has the same representation as Wyoming (580,000). The same is true of the Brazilian Senate, which has three members for each state, meaning that São Paulo in the south (population 44 million) has the same representation as Amapá in the north (population 750,000). Meanwhile, electoral districts for the US House of Representatives and the Brazilian Chamber of Deputies (the lower chambers) are designed to be equal in population. The US fares better than Brazil, where the number of citizens per deputy runs from a low of 53,000 to a high of 570,000, greatly distorting the equality of representation.

TABLE 8.1: Comparing upper chambers

	Name	Members	Term (years)	Method of selection
Australia	Senate	76	6	Direct election by single transferable vote in each state.
Germany	Bundesrat (Federal Council)	69	—	Appointed by state governments.
Ireland	Senate	60	5	Appointed by the prime minister (11), elected from vocational panels (43), and from two universities (6).
India	Rajya Sabha (Council of States)	245	6	Indirectly elected through state assemblies (233), or appointed by the president (12).
Mexico	Senate	128	6	Direct election. Biggest party in each state wins two seats from the state, second-placed party wins one seat, and 32 senators elected at-large for the country.
Russia	Federation Council	166	6	Appointed by president with 'approval' of local legislatures.
United States	Senate	100	6	Direct election by plurality voting in each state.

Source: Inter-Parliamentary Union (2015)

Committees

Committees are the workhorses of effective legislatures, offering detailed examination of matters of national interest, including executive and legislative proposals. A legislative committee is a small working group of legislators, created to cope with the volume and detail of legislative business, particularly in larger and busier lower chambers. Committees come in three different forms:

- *Standing committees* are permanent, and grouped by policy specialties; so there will usually be separate committees dealing with foreign affairs, economic affairs, budgets, health, education, the environment, and so on. They offer line-by-line examination of bills in their particular areas of policy responsibility.
- *Select committees* monitor the main executive departments or are set up temporarily to hold hearings on matters of public concern.
- *Conference committees* reconcile differences in bicameral legislatures in the wording of bills.

Whatever the committee type, members are usually allocated in proportion to overall party strength. In operation, however, partisanship is often held in check, yielding a more cooperative outlook than on the floor.

> **Committee:** A group of legislators assigned to examine new bills, monitor executive departments or hold hearings on matters of public concern.

The US Congress is the classic example of a committee-based legislature. Although not mentioned in the constitution, committees rapidly became vital to the work of Congress. 'Congress in session is Congress on public exhibition, whilst Congress in its committee rooms is Congress at work', wrote Woodrow Wilson (1885: 79). In the 114th Congress (2015–17), there were 21 standing committees in the House, 18 in the Senate, and multiple subcommittees in both chambers. Their most important role is in deciding the shape and fate of bills. Committee hearings allow interest groups to express their views, while committee members take care not only of the interests of their constituents, but also of those groups offering support, including campaign contributions, to the legislator. But party leaders are important, and we should not overestimate committee autonomy.

Committees are generally less influential in the more party-dominated legislatures found in most parliamentary systems. In Britain's House of Commons, for instance, government bills are examined by standing committees which largely replicate party combat on the floor of the chamber. These committees do not challenge executive dominance in framing legislation, and they tend to be unpopular, unspecialized, and under-resourced. However, like many other legislatures, the Commons has expanded its system of select committees; these shadow all the main government departments, probing government policy and

SPOTLIGHT

UNITED KINGDOM

Brief Profile: One of the world's oldest states, and birthplace of the parliamentary system, the United Kingdom of Great Britain and Northern Ireland and its four constituent parts (England, Scotland, Wales, and Northern Ireland) has undergone many changes since 1945 that have left troubling questions hanging over its future. The creation and now the decay of a welfare state, the end of empire, and the country's declining economic and military weight have forced a redefinition of the role of government, and of Britain's place in the world. Membership of the European Union has proved controversial, as has the definition of what it means to be British – a failed independence referendum in Scotland in 2014 has not ended the debate over the future of the union. What is clear is that many of the old assumptions about British politics have ceased to apply; in a more complicated and fragmented polity, replacement clichés are harder to find.

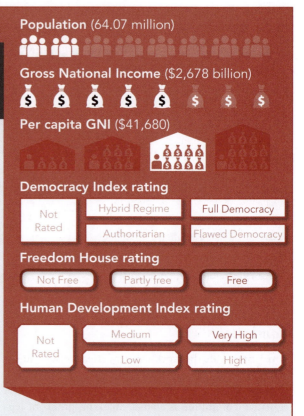

Population (64.07 million)

Gross National Income ($2,678 billion)

Per capita GNI ($41,680)

Democracy Index rating

| Not Rated | Hybrid Regime | Full Democracy |
| | Authoritarian | Flawed Democracy |

Freedom House rating

| Not Free | Partly free | Free |

Human Development Index rating

| Not Rated | Medium | Very High |
| | Low | High |

Form of government ⇨ Unitary parliamentary constitutional monarchy. Date of state formation arguably 1066; no codified constitution.

Legislature ⇨ Bicameral Parliament: lower House of Commons (650 members) elected for renewable five-year terms, and upper House of Lords (about 790 members) consisting of a mix of hereditary and life peers, and senior members of the Church of England.

Executive ⇨ Parliamentary. The head of government is the prime minister, who is head of the largest party or coalition, and governs in conjunction with a cabinet. The head of state is the monarch.

Judiciary ⇨. Based on the common law tradition. The creation in 2009 of a 12-member Supreme Court, albeit without the authority to veto legislation, strengthened the autonomy of the judiciary. Judges appointed for life, with mandatory retirement at 70 or 75, depending on date of appointment.

Electoral system ⇨ The House of Commons is elected using single-member plurality. A range of systems is used for elections to other bodies such as regional assemblies in Scotland, Wales, and Northern Ireland.

Parties ⇨ Multi-party, although traditionally dominated by Conservatives on the right and Labour on the left. Smaller parties and regional parties also significant.

➡

monitoring its implementation. Their reports contribute to governance and sometimes attract wider interest. In 2011, for example, a committee interrogation of the media magnate Rupert Murdoch in the wake of a phone-hacking scandal attracted international attention.

Scandinavia provides cases of influential committees operating in the context of both strong parties and parliamentary government. Scandinavia's main governing style, sometimes known as 'committee parliamentarianism', is one in which influential standing committees negotiate the policies and bills on which the whole

→

The British Parliament

The British Parliament is often known as the 'Mother of Parliaments', being the model upon which legislatures in parliamentary systems are modelled. Traditionally, it mixed omnipotence and impotence in a seemingly impossible combination; it was considered omnipotent because parliamentary sovereignty, allied to an uncodified constitution, meant there was no higher authority in the land, but it was considered impotent because the governing party exercised tight control over its Members of Parliament (MPs), turning Parliament into an instrument, rather than a wielder, of power.

In the twenty-first century, Parliament's position has become less certain. The tired rituals of adversary politics in the House of Commons have become less convincing, not least for its newest members. The notion that Parliament possesses sovereignty still carries weight but it risks being left behind as European law becomes more important and powers are devolved to regional assemblies, by competition from the media as an arena of debate, and by the indifference of prime ministers who choose to spend less time in the House.

But MPs themselves have become more committed, and the era of the amateur legislator is over. They are predominantly drawn from professional, business, and political backgrounds, they devote more time to an increasing volume of constituency casework, and the number of late sittings has been cut. Select committees have established themselves in the debate over policy and contribute to scrutinizing the executive. The prime minister now appears twice a year before a select committee for a more detailed discussion than is possible during weekly Question Time. Kelso (2011: 69) notes that there has been a clear shift away from 'a chamber-based institution towards a committee-based institution, illustrated by the growing emphasis given to new public bill committees, select committees and committee-based scrutiny of the prime minister'.

The upper House of Lords occupies an uncertain position. Its 790 members consist mainly of appointed life peers but reform, when finally agreed, is likely to involve a substantial measure of election. Such a development may well make the Lords more assertive in challenging the executive. Yet, even as Britain's Parliament updates its skills, it will continue to do what it has always done best: acting as an arena for debating issues of significance to the nation, its government, and its leaders.

---

parliament later votes. In Sweden, for instance, committees modify about one in three government proposals and have the right to put their own proposals (including bills) to the assembly as a whole. Parliamentary committees are partners in a remarkably deliberative law-making process.

Members

It is important to understand legislatures as institutions, but also important to understand their members and how they go about their work. The most important development in liberal democracies has been the rise of the career politician: the degree-educated legislator with limited experience outside politics who expects politics to provide a full-time, fulfilling profession. The amateurs of yesteryear have given way to political professionals who know no other job, and for whom specialization is necessary for success. Even when politicians have experience of other careers such as law, the earlier occupation is often chosen as a pathway to politics.

In many democracies, the rise of the professional politician has led to speculation about the growth of a **political class** with a background and interests removed from the broad electorate, and quite often captured by particular interests (Borchert and Zeiss, 2003). While professionals might offer advantages in expertise and even commitment over amateurs, the rise of a professional class could also be interpreted as a threat to representative democracy, particularly if that class does not reflect the backgrounds and attitudes of the general population. In a sense, it threatens democracy with oligarchy (rule by a few). Reports of corruption in a number of assemblies support this notion of a horizontal 'class' division between legislators and electors which supplements the traditional vertical distinction between parties. An example here is the damaging expenses scandal which engulfed Britain's House of Commons in 2009. Members of all parties, it turned out, had been claiming 'expenses' for all kinds of spurious costs such as cleaning moats and tuning pianos. Several members resigned, were de-selected by their parties, or announced that they would not run again, while the Speaker of the House of Commons stood down from his job and criminal proceedings were begun against the worst offenders. Faith in politicians, already low, sank even lower.

> **Political class:** A group of professional politicians that possesses, and can act on, its shared interests (Mosca, 1896).

More importantly, incumbent members from all parties typically seek re-election. To achieve this goal, they arm themselves with campaign resources (e.g. free mail) unavailable to their challengers, thus creating a powerful cartel against newcomers. Viewing politics as a clash between parties often leads to inadequate emphasis on this distinction within parties between incumbents and challengers. As in any other established class, politicians in post are reluctant to upset the apple cart that has served them so well. Indeed, the greater the proportion of professional politicians in an assembly, the more likely it is that incumbent candidates will be re-elected (Berry et al., 2000).

Politics as a profession implies a distinct view not only of representation, but also of politics. It rejects the notion that governance is a task which Athenian-style citizen-legislators can undertake. It implies dissatisfaction with the idea that an assembly should draw together a representative sample of citizens 'different in nature, different in interests, different in looks, different in language' (Bagehot, 1867: 155). Rather, politics as a profession implies an emphasis on elitism, training, knowledge, experience, and skill. Politics becomes a job, in the same way as law, medicine, and teaching.

There is a contrast here between the kinds of political entrepreneurs found in the United States and the more party-based careerists found in the legislatures of other liberal democracies. In the US Congress, candidates must compete against opponents from their own party in a primary; in office, they must build a personal profile and record of achievement which protects them from challenge, and they must raise money for their campaign – which, for members of the House of Representatives, takes place every two years. In short, members of Congress must nurture their personal brand. In most other liberal democracies, strong parties at both parliamentary and electoral level leave less room for independent action, resulting in loyal legislators rather than political entrepreneurs. Even when partisanship is important, however, younger and better educated members seek to express their professionalism by making a difference. Although the French National Assembly remains a weak institution, Kerrouche (2006: 352) reports that even here 'deputies want to criticize, to attract media attention and to put forward alternative policies'. These aspirations are reflected in a substantial number of private members' bills and legislative amendments.

Just as we sometimes find people following the same career paths as their parents, so one of the outcomes of the rise of the career politician has been the emergence of political dynasties. In Asia, political families often reflect the value of the political brand established by their founder, with children inheriting the founder's electoral district. In India, for example, the Nehru-Gandhi dynasty goes back to the nineteenth century, but has been particularly important since independence in 1947: it produced Jawarhalal Nehru (prime minister 1947–64), his daughter Indira Gandhi (prime minister 1966–77 and 1980–4), her son Rajiv Gandhi (prime minister 1984–9), his widow Sonia (leader of the Congress Party from 1998), and their son Rahul (member of Parliament since 2004). In Japan, meanwhile, more than one-third of the members of the Japanese Diet before the 2009 election were second-generation lawmakers, often inheriting the same seat as their family predecessor (Martin and Steel, 2008). Similar family dynasties are evident in Bangladesh, Pakistan, and the Philippines.

The phenomenon of second-generation legislators may also reflect socialization: children growing up in a family where politics is viewed as an achievable career are more likely to enter the profession themselves. This effect helps to explain why as many as one-quarter of the candidates standing in the Australian election of 2001 had a close family member who had also stood for elected office (McAllister, 2003). In the United States, meanwhile, the Kennedy family is less prominent than it once was, but the Bushes and the Clintons have developed some of the trappings of political dynasties.

From one perspective, political families may be no more disturbing than family lines of physicians. Yet, just as the notion of the professional politician gave rise to the concept of a political class, so too does the idea of

FOCUS 8.2 | The pros and cons of term limits

As we will see in Chapter 9, presidents in democracies are often limited by law in the number of terms they can serve in office. Even in parliamentary systems, where no such limits apply, it is rare that governments stay in office for more than about 8–10 years.

But the story is quite different in legislatures. Unless representatives are also faced with a **term limit**, they will often seek to stay in office as long as their energy and the tolerance of voters will last. Generally, re-election is the norm in liberal democracies, and most sitting legislators return for a new term. Defining the ideal level of turnover is not easy. On the one hand, the return rate should be high enough to sustain professionalism, allowing the development of experience and expertise. On the other hand, it should not be so high as to sustain corruption or create the 'three As' which Jackson (1994) associated with a surfeit of incumbency: arrogance, apathy, and atrophy.

Turnover is greater in countries using party list proportional representation, which allows party leaders to ensure at least a trickle of fresh blood. In countries using plurality elections, turnover is mainly lower, the extreme case being the United States, where – between 1982 and 2014 – re-election rates never fell below 85 per cent in the House and 75 per cent in the Senate (Bardes *et al.*, 2014: table 12.4). In contrast, Mexico does not allow members of Congress to serve more than one term at a time, so deputies must step down after three years and senators after six years, returning only at the next election (assuming they win).

Arguments in favour	Arguments against
Prevents the development of career politicians and a political class, and reduces the likelihood of corruption.	Term limits can prevent the best legislators from staying on and working in the national interest.
The longer legislators stay in office, the greater the chances of their losing touch with the needs of voters.	Makes it more difficult for legislators to develop long-term relationships with their districts and constituents.
Brings new perspectives and generations to bear, which can be more important than keeping experienced legislators in office.	Prevents voters from benefiting from the accumulated experience of longer-term legislators.
Term limits provide a check on the accumulation of power by individual legislators.	Creates lame duck legislators, who cannot plan beyond the date of the next election.
	Turnover can be encouraged by levelling the playing field between incumbents and challengers, not by banning experienced players.

Term limits: Rules that restrict elected politicians to a maximum number of periods in office, or ban re-election without a break.

the political family encourage us to think in terms of a political caste. Both ideas imply a measure of closure in political recruitment; they rest uneasily alongside the traditional interpretation of democracy as government by the people.

Legislatures in authoritarian states

Since assemblies are symbols of popular political representation, their significance in authoritarian regimes has long been regarded as inherently limited. Such legislatures have generally functioned only as shadow institutions: sessions are often short and members are occasionally appointed by the government. Legislators concentrate on raising grievances, pressing constituency interests, and sometimes lining their own pockets. The rulers regard these activities as non-threatening because the real issues of national politics are left untouched.

Yet, legislatures are difficult to extinguish, and the braver members of assemblies in authoritarian states can sometimes emerge as the only substantial voices of opposition. Schuler and Malesky (2014) note that there has been a recent tendency among scholars to see authoritarian regimes relying less on repression and more on using legislatures to either co-opt, empower, or weaken the opposition: 'assemblies are seen as constraints willingly constructed by dictators in order to maximize the benefits of continued rule or increase regime stability' (p. 676). Except for a few traditional and dictatorial systems, most authoritarian regimes continue to possess an assembly of some description, their value being fivefold:

- A legislature provides a fig leaf of legitimacy, both domestic and international, for the regime. Rulers can try and detract criticism from other governments and donor agencies by pointing to their national legislature as evidence of a national political debate.

- The legislature can be used to incorporate moderate opponents into the political system, providing a forum for negotiating matters that do not threaten the key interests of rulers.

- Raising the grievances of constituents and lobbying for local interests provide a measure of integration between centre and periphery, and between state and society. Such activity oils the political wheels without threatening those who control the machine.

- Assemblies provide a convenient pool of potential recruits to the elite. Behaviour in the legislature provides a useful initial test of reliability.

- For dictators, argues Gandhi (2008: 181), legislatures serve as 'controlled institutional channels' through which outside groups can make their demands and leaders can 'make concessions without appearing to cave in to popular protest'.

At the heart of the role of legislatures in authoritarian regimes is the idea of co-option: authoritarian leaders may not have to worry about public opinion, but they always face the prospect of challenges from within the elite, or at least of demands for a share of the spoils of control. Svolik (2012: 12–13) contrasts the roles of legislatures in democracies, where they serve to represent the diversity of political interests, with those in

authoritarian states, where their role 'is to enhance the stability of authoritarian power-sharing by alleviating commitment and monitoring problems among authoritarian elites'.

In hybrid regimes, legislatures are an essential part of the political furniture. Their position can be significant in areas that do not threaten the realities of presidential leadership: in representing local districts, for example, and in passing routine legislation. However, such assemblies still operate in the shadow of executive authority. A nose for power will lead us away from the legislature and towards the presidential office. There, we may discover an incumbent who governs by decree as well as by law and who may, *in extremis*, simply dissolve a recalcitrant legislature in search of more congenial arrangements.

The political environment of hybrid regimes is particularly hostile to the idea that assemblies can hold the government to account through detailed oversight. On the contrary, national leaders consider themselves responsible to the whole nation, not to what they see as corrupt, partisan, and parochial representatives in the assembly. In addition, many hybrid systems are either new regimes, or located in relatively poor countries; both factors militate against the development of a professional legislature with a stable membership, extensive research support, and a well-developed committee system.

The case of the Egyptian legislature illustrates some of the problems found in hybrid regimes. Egypt has had a legislature since 1923, but first the king and then – following the revolution of 1952 – the president have always had the capacity to override its votes or to manipulate elections to ensure a majority of friendly legislators. The legislature was renamed the People's Assembly in 1971, and was granted several constitutional powers that seemed to limit those of the president: it could reject laws proposed by the government, propose laws of its own, had close control over the national budget, and could debate government policy. But the latter meant little in real terms, and its debates were described by Waterbury (1983, p 16) as follows: 'The normal pattern … has been to tear a given policy to pieces in committee … to give ample newspaper … coverage to the findings, and then to have the Assembly as a whole approve the policy with marginal modifications.'

A new House of Representatives was created in 2014, but the tradition of strong executives and relatively weak legislatures seemed destined to continue, but for different reasons. Where the old People's Assembly had been dominated by the governing National Democratic Party, which was in turn manipulated by the president, the new legislature is likely to suffer from too many parties, creating divisions that will make it ineffective either as a support for government or as a site of opposition.

In wholesale authoritarian regimes, by contrast, the manner in which ruling parties or presidents exploit the legislature is more obvious, as the cases of China and Russia illustrate. China exemplifies the trend in one-party states for assemblies to acquire modest significance as such regimes become a little more pluralistic. A growing emphasis on the rule of law raised the status of the National People's Congress (NPC), which has also more often expressed popular hostility to corruption. Many votes are no longer unanimous, proceedings are less easily choreographed, committees are growing in authority, some professional support is available, and the Communist Party must anticipate the NPC's reaction to its proposals.

However, the NPC, still the world's largest legislature with members indirectly elected through subnational governments and the military, remains strongly hierarchical. It meets only once a year for a session lasting about two weeks. Even more than in committee-based assemblies in democracies, the NPC's influence operates through smaller sub-groups. The most important of these is the Standing Committee, a group of about 150 members which meets regularly throughout the year; most also belong to the party, giving the leadership an additional mechanism of control.

Of course, party domination of legislative proceedings is also found in parliamentary systems in liberal democracies, but there the party in command changes with the election results. Although the NPC and its sub-groups have become part of the Chinese power network, the party's supremacy is such that these bodies still cannot be understood through Western notions of the separation of powers and parliamentary sovereignty.

In Russia, the Federal Assembly occupies a secondary position to the executive. Russia's constitution makes allowance for a bicameral legislature whose powers helped make sure that laws take precedence over presidential decrees. But the ambitions of Vladimir Putin have combined with the Russian preference for strong government to tilt the balance of power towards the presidency. The constitution states that Russia's president is not only 'guarantor of the constitution', but is also required to 'ensure the coordinated functioning and collaboration of bodies of state power'. So far, presidents have performed this role with no great regard for the legislature.

During the 1990s, the Duma (lower house) became a site of resistance to Boris Yeltsin's reforms, producing vigorous debate. President Putin himself once claimed to find value in legislative institutions: 'today, we can justifiably call this period a time of strengthening the country's parliamentary and legal culture. One can speak about a modern State Duma as a working instrument of power' (quoted in Donaldson, 2004: 249). But much has changed since then, and Putin's United Russia Party today dominates the Duma, reducing it to subservient status.

The most blatant instance of Putin's manipulation of the legislature can be found in the upper house, the Federation Council. Given the sheer size and diversity of Russia, and its federal structure, the Council might logically function as a Russian Senate, providing a form of representation that could complement that provided by the Duma. In reality, it has been openly exploited by Putin to extend his power, encouraged by the lack of detail in the Russian constitution about how its members must be chosen. It initially consisted of two representatives elected from each of the 83 regions and republics of Russia, who were replaced in 1995 by the chief executives and heads of the legislatures in the regions, holding their Council positions ex officio.

In 2000, in an attempt to limit the powers of the regional leaders, Putin steered a new law through the State Duma that replaced them with full-time representatives appointed by local legislatures and their executives. Another change came in 2012, so that regional assemblies each elected one of their members and regional governors chose representatives from the regional executives. In practice, though, Putin's advisers have the final say over the selection of members (Remington, 2014: 53). Since the Council must approve presidential nominees to the Russian high courts, and must approve the declaration of martial law or emergencies by the president, Putin – by extension – controls these decisions.

DISCUSSION QUESTIONS

- We have suggested that 'effective control over legislation in most liberal democracies rests with the government'. Is this state of affairs satisfactory?

- Could a legislature made up entirely of heterosexual white middle-class men effectively represent a country? If not, why not?

- Should members of an upper chamber be appointed for their experience and wisdom, or elected for their popular appeal?

- Other than in federal systems, do bicameral legislatures serve any real purpose?

- Is there anything particularly wrong with the rise of career politicians and a political class?

- Should legislators be subject to term limits?

KEY CONCEPTS

Bicameral	Political class
Committee	Strong bicameralism
Committee-based legislature	Term limits
Debating legislature	Unicameral
Legislature	Vote of confidence
Plenary session	Weak bicameralism

FURTHER READING

Arter, David (ed.) (2013) *Comparing and Classifying Legislatures*. A survey of the state of knowledge about legislatures, with chapters on European, Latin American, and African cases.

Cotta, Maurizio and Heinrich Best (eds) (2007) *Democratic Representation in Europe: Diversity, Change and Convergence*. A comparative treatment of long-term changes in parliamentary careers.

Dodd, Lawrence C. and Bruce I. Oppenheimer (eds) (2012) *Congress Reconsidered*, 10th edn. A collection of articles on the world's most intensively studied legislature: the US Congress.

Fish, M. Stephen and Matthew Kroenig (2009) *The Handbook of National Legislatures: A Global Survey*. An extensive reference work assessing the powers of national legislatures by their autonomy, capacity, influence, and powers.

Martin, Shane, Thomas Saalfeld, and Kaare W. Strøm (eds) (2014) *The Oxford Handbook of Legislative Studies*. A comprehensive edited collection of essays on legislatures.

Norton, Philip (2013) *Parliament in British Politics*, 2nd edn. A case study of the Mother of Parliaments, including its relations with voters, the government, courts, and the European Union.

9 Executives

PREVIEW

The focus of this chapter is the most visible tier in any system of government: the top level of leadership. Whether we are talking about presidents, prime ministers, chancellors, dictators, or despots, those who sit at the peak of the pyramid of governmental power typically excite the most public interest, whether opinions are positive or negative. To be sure, executives – in democracies, at least – consist not just of individual leaders but of large networks of people and institutions, including the ministers and secretaries who form the cabinet or the council of ministers. But a single figure usually becomes the best-known face of government, representing its successes and failures and acting as a focus of popular attention.

The chapter begins by looking in turn at the three major forms of executive: presidential, parliamentary, and semi-presidential. It compares and contrasts their roles and powers, focusing in particular depth on the various sub-types of parliamentary executive and the experience they have had with legislative coalitions. The contrasting roles of head of state and head of government are also reviewed; they are combined in presidential systems and divided in others, with important and contrasting consequences. The chapter then looks at executives in authoritarian systems, and at the particular qualities and effects of personal rule. Authoritarian leaders may enjoy more power than their democratic peers, but they also enjoy fewer formal protections on their person or their tenure in office. This inevitably affects the way they approach their positions.

CONTENTS

- Executives: an overview
- Presidential executives
- Parliamentary executives
- Semi-presidential executives
- Executives in authoritarian states

KEY ARGUMENTS

- The political executive is the top tier of government, responsible for setting priorities, mobilizing support, resolving crises, making decisions and overseeing their implementation.
- Executives take three main institutional forms: presidential, parliamentary, and semi-presidential.
- Studies of presidential executives routinely refer back to the somewhat atypical case of the United States. There is ongoing debate about the strengths and weaknesses of the presidential model.
- Parliamentary government is often studied through the British example, even if it is more accurately represented through the multi-party coalitions of continental Europe. The smaller countries, in particular, provide opportunities to address the origins, stability, and effectiveness of different types of coalition.
- Semi-presidential systems combine elements of the presidential and parliamentary formats (for example, there is both a president and a prime minister). They are less common, and less thoroughly studied.
- Executives in authoritarian states are particularly intriguing because they face fewer constraints than those in liberal democracies, as well as fewer guarantees regarding their tenure.

SPOTLIGHT

BRAZIL

Brief Profile: The recent rise of Brazil exemplifies the phenomenon of the emerging economy, and earned it inclusion in the informal cluster of BRIC states (Brazil, Russia, India, and China). As the world's fifth biggest country by land and population, Brazil is one of the world's largest democracies. It is the most important state in South America and has expanded its influence to the developing world more broadly. However, in common with the other BRIC states, Brazil still faces many domestic problems. There is a wide gap between rich and poor, much of the arable land is owned by a few wealthy families, social conditions in its major cities are poor, the deforestation of the Amazon basin has global ecological implications, and corruption is rife at all levels of government. Recent economic developments have sent mixed signals, with oil discoveries pointing to energy self-sufficiency, but an economic downturn and a return to politics as usual casts clouds over Brazil's continued progress.

Population (202 million)

Gross National Income ($2,246 billion)

Per capita GNI ($11,690)

Democracy Index rating

Not Yet Rated | Hybrid Regime | Full Democracy
Authoritarian | Flawed Democracy

Freedom House rating

Not Free | Partly free | Free

Human Development Index rating

Not Rated | Medium | Very High
Low | High

Form of government ⇨ Federal presidential republic consisting of 26 states and a Federal District. State formed 1822, and most recent constitution adopted 1988.

Legislature ⇨ Bicameral National Congress: lower Chamber of Deputies (513 members) elected for renewable four-year terms, and upper Senate (81 members) elected from the states (three members each) for renewable eight-year terms.

Executive ⇨ Presidential. A president directly elected for no more than two consecutive four-year terms.

Judiciary ⇨ A dual system of state and federal courts, with justices of superior courts nominated for life by the president and confirmed by the Senate. Supreme Federal Court serves as constitutional court: 11 members, nominated by president and confirmed by Senate for life, but must retire at 70.

Electoral system ⇨ A two-round majority system is used for elections to the presidency and the Senate, while elections to the Chamber of Deputies use proportional representation.

Parties ⇨ Multi-party, with more than a dozen parties organized within Congress into four main coalitions and a cluster of non-attached parties.

Executives: an overview

The political executive is the core of government, consisting as it does of the political leaders who form the top level of the administration: presidents, prime ministers, ministers, and cabinets. The institutional approach to comparison focuses on the role of the executive as a government's energizing force, setting priorities, mobilizing support, reacting to problems, resolving crises, making decisions, and overseeing their execution. Governing without an assembly or judiciary is feasible, but ruling without an executive is arguably impossible. And in authoritarian systems, the executive is often the only institution that wields true power.

The political executive in Brazil

The American model of the presidential executive is used in most Latin American countries, but often with local variations. Brazil is a case in point. On the one hand, its president would seem to be more powerful than the US equivalent, being able to issue decrees in specified areas, to declare bills to be urgent (forcing Congress to make a prompt decision), to initiate bills in Congress, and to propose a budget which goes into effect, month by month, if Congress does not itself pass a budget.

But Brazilian presidents must work with two features of government (proportional representation and a multi-party system) that are absent in the United States, and that make it more difficult to bend Congress to their will. First, they are faced by a much more complex party landscape. For example, the October 2014 legislative elections resulted in 28 parties winning seats in the Brazilian Chamber of Deputies: no party won more than 70 seats, 13 parties each won less than ten seats, and the parties formed themselves into four groupings, with the pro-government coalition holding 59 per cent of the seats.

To further complicate matters for the president, party discipline is exceptionally weak. Deputies often switch party in mid-term, and are more concerned with winning resources for their districts than with showing loyalty to their party (a reality also, but to a lesser extent, in the United States). In response, Brazil's presidents build informal coalitions by appointing ministers from a range of parties in an attempt to extract loyalty from them.

The Brazilian case shows that the executive in presidential government does not need to be drawn from a single party. However, the coalitions they form are more informal, pragmatic, and unstable than the carefully crafted inter-party coalitions which characterize parliamentary government in Europe. In presidential systems, after all, the collapse of a coalition does not mean the fall of a government, reducing the incentive to sustain a coalition. So, although Latin American constitutions appear to give the chief executive a more important political role, appearances are deceptive. The Latin American experience confirms that presidents operating in a democratic setting confront inherent difficulties in securing their programme.

It is important to distinguish the political executive (which makes policy) from the bureaucracy (which puts policy into effect). Unlike appointed officials, the members of the executive – in democracies, at least – are chosen by political means, most often by election, and can be removed by the same method. The executive is accountable for the activities of government; it is where the buck stops.

It is also important to distinguish between two different roles carried out by executives: the **head of state** (the figurehead representative of the state and all its citizens) and the **head of government** (the political leader of a government). In presidential executives such as the United States, Mexico, and Nigeria, the two jobs are combined in one office. In parliamentary systems, the prime minister or chancellor is the head of government, while monarchs or non-executive presidents carry out the role of head of state. In semi-presidential systems, the division of roles – as we will see – is more complicated.

Head of state: The figurehead leader of a state, who may be elected or appointed, or – in the case of monarchs – may inherit the position. The role is non-political and has many functions but few substantive powers.

Head of government: The elected leader of a government, who comes to office because of the support of voters who identify with their party and platform.

In liberal democracies, understanding the executive begins with the study of institutional arrangements. Liberal democracies have succeeded in the delicate and difficult task of subjecting executive power to constitutional constraint. The government is not only elected, but remains subject to rules which limit its power; it must also face regular re-election.

In authoritarian regimes, by contrast, constitutional and electoral controls are absent or ineffective. The scope of the executive is limited not so much by the constitution as by political realities, and the executive tends to be more fluid, patterned by informal relationships rather than formal rules.

The executives of liberal democracies fall into three main groups: presidential, parliamentary, and semi-presidential. In all three types, power is diffused, and they can each be understood as contrasting methods for dividing and controlling executive authority. These arrangements can be tested against their contributions to political stability and effective governance. In presidential and semi-presidential regimes, the constitution sets up a system of checks and balances between distinct executive, legislative and judicial institutions. In parliamentary systems, the government is constrained in different ways, its survival depending on retaining the confidence of the assembly. Typically, its freedom of action is limited by the need to sustain a coalition between parties that have agreed to share the task of governing.

Presidential executives

The world contains many presidents but fewer examples of **presidential government.** This is in part because many parliamentary systems possess a president who serves only as ceremonial head of state, and in part because any dictator can style themselves 'president', and many do so. For these reasons, the existence of a president is an insufficient sign of a presidential system.

> **Presidential government:** An arrangement in which power is divided between a president and a legislature. This distinction is achieved by separate elections and also by separate survival; the president cannot dissolve the legislature and the legislature can only remove the president through impeachment.

In essence, a presidential executive is a form of constitutional rule in which a single chief executive governs using the authority derived from popular election, alongside an independent legislature. The election normally takes the form of a direct vote of the people, with a limit on the number of terms a president can serve. The president directs the government and, unlike most prime ministers in parliamentary government, also serves as the ceremonial head of state. The president makes appointments to other key government institutions, such as the heads of government departments, although some may be subject to confirmation by the legislature. Because both president and legislature are elected for a fixed term, neither can bring down the other, giving each institution some autonomy.

Presidential executives have both strengths and weaknesses. Among the strengths:

- The president's fixed term provides continuity in the executive, avoiding the collapse of governing coalitions to which parliamentary governments are prone.
- Winning a presidential election requires candidates to develop broad support across the country.
- Elected by the country at large, the president rises above the squabbles between local interests represented in the legislature.
- A president provides a natural symbol of national unity, offering a familiar face for domestic and international audiences alike.
- Since a presidential system necessarily involves a separation of powers, it should also encourage limited government and thereby protect liberty.

But presidential government also carries risks. Only one party can win the presidency; everyone else loses. All-or-nothing politics can lead to political instability, especially in new regimes. Fixed terms of office are inflexible, and the American experience shows that deadlock can arise when executive and legislature disagree, leaving the political system unable to

TABLE 9.1: Presidential executives

- Elected president steers the government and makes senior appointments.
- Fixed terms of offices for the president and the legislature, neither of which can ordinarily bring down the other.
- Presidents are usually limited to a specified number of terms in office; usually two.
- Little overlap in membership between the executive and the legislature.
- President serves as head of government as well as head of state.
- Examples: Afghanistan, Argentina, Brazil, Egypt, Indonesia, Nigeria, United States.

> ◆ **FOCUS 9.1** │ **The separation of powers**
>
> The **separation of powers** is the hallmark of the presidential system: executives have the power to lead and to execute, legislatures have the power to make law, and courts have the power to adjudicate. While there is certainly an overlap in practice, the focus of responsibilities is generally clear, and is typically reinforced by a separation of personnel. Neither the president nor members of the cabinet can sit in the legislature, creating further distance between the two institutions. Similarly, legislators must resign their seats if they wish to serve in the government, meaning the president's ability to buy members' votes with the promise of a job is self-limiting.
>
> Contrasting methods of election create a natural difference of interests. Legislators depend only on the support of voters in their home district, while the president (and the president only) is elected by a broader constituency – typically, the entire country. This divergence generates the political dynamic whereby the president pursues a national agenda as distinct from the special and local interests of the legislature. So, despite the focus on a single office, presidential government divides power. The system creates a requirement for the executive to negotiate with the legislature, and vice versa, and thereby ensures the triumph of deliberation over dictatorship.
>
> There is a practical separation of powers in parliamentary systems as well, in the sense that executive and legislative functions are distinct. But members of the executive also sit in the legislature, and rather than legislators having to resign in order to serve in government, occupying a seat in the legislature is all but a prerequisite to being appointed to a top government job, such as the head of a government department. Above all, the very survival of the executive in a parliamentary system depends on it retaining the legislature's confidence.

Separation of powers: An arrangement in which executive and legislature are given distinct but complementary sets of powers, such that neither can govern alone and that both should, ideally, govern together.

address pressing problems. Presidential systems also lack the natural rallying-point for opposition provided by the leaders of non-ruling parties in some parliamentary systems. In particular, there is no natural equivalent to Britain's notion of the Leader of Her Majesty's Opposition.

Under these circumstances, there is a danger that presidents will grow too big for their boots. In the past, Latin American and African presidents have frequently amended the constitution so as to continue in office beyond their one- or two-term limits. Even worse, a frustrated or ambitious president can turn into a dictator; presidential democracies are more likely than parliamentary democracies to disintegrate (Cheibub, 2002).

Presidential government predominates in the Americas, and is also found in many African countries, such as Nigeria. The United States is the representative case, and as such provides important insights into how the presidential executive works. The framers of the US constitution wanted to create an office that could both make decisions and be prevented from accumulating too much power. They also wanted to insulate the office from influence by the 'excitable masses', so they created an Electoral College within which each state had a specific number of votes, all of which – in most cases – go to the candidate who wins the most votes in each state. Controversially, it is possible for a presidential candidate to win the popular vote but lose in the College, as Al Gore discovered in his defeat by George W. Bush in 2000.

In addition to a general obligation to oversee the execution of laws, the president is given explicit duties (such as commander-in-chief) that have been interpreted over time as giving presidents further implied powers. For instance, presidents can claim executive privilege: the right to withhold information from Congress and the courts which, if released, would damage the president's capacity to execute the laws. Presidents can also issue executive orders, statements, and proclamations. At the same time, they also often find their hands tied, because they share important powers with Congress:

- The president is commander-in-chief but only Congress can declare war.
- The president can make government appointments and sign treaties, but only with the consent of the Senate.
- The president can veto legislation, but Congress can override the veto.
- Congress, not the president, controls the purse strings.

Describing the relationship between the president and Congress as a separation of powers is misleading, because there is in reality a separation of institutions: the two share authority, each seeking to influence the other but neither being in a position to dictate. In parliamentary systems, prime ministers can normally rely on strong support in the legislature from their party or coalition; this is rarely the case in presidential executives.

The paradox of the American presidency – a weak governing position amid the trappings of omnipotence – is reflected in the president's support network. To meet presidential needs for information and advice, a conglomeration of supporting bodies has evolved, including the White House Office, the National Security Council, and the Office of Management and Budget. Collectively, they provide far more direct support than is available to the prime minister in a parliamentary system, forming what is sometimes known as the 'institutional presidency' (Burke, 2010).

Relative to parliamentary systems, the US presidential system lacks a strong **cabinet**. There is a federal cabinet, but it is not mentioned in the constitution, its meetings are usually little more than a presidential photo opportunity, and cabinet members often find it hard to gain access to the president through the thicket of advisers. As we will see later, presidential government is never cabinet government as it formally is in parliamentary executives.

> **Cabinet:** A body consisting of the heads of the major government departments. Sometimes known as a Council of Ministers. More important in parliamentary than in presidential systems.

The norm in a presidential system is for the president to be elected separately from the legislature.

Presidential survival (if not success) is thus independent of party numbers in the legislature, and the president is tied to a national constituency while members of the legislature are elected from local districts. This is not how matters are organized in South Africa, however, which offers an interesting variation on the theme of a presidential executive. It has a president, but the officeholder is elected by members of the legislature rather than in a direct national vote. This makes the South African president more like a prime minister in a parliamentary system, particularly since the president is usually head of the largest party in the legislature. However, the South African president is both head of state and head of government, is limited to two five-year terms in office, and while required to be a member of the legislature in order to qualify to be president, must resign from the legislature upon election as president. Only two other countries – Burma and Botswana – use this system. Determining the political impact of this rare format has been complicated by the dominance in post-apartheid South Africa of a single party, the African National Congress. Were legislative elections to produce no clear majority party, it would be interesting to see how the election of the president would be affected.

Parliamentary executives

Unlike presidential systems, in which the chief executive is separate from the legislature and independently elected, the executive in a **parliamentary government** is organically linked to the assembly. The leader (the prime minister, or – in Germany and Austria – the chancellor) is normally the head of the largest party in parliament (or head of one of the parties in the governing coalition), continues to hold a seat in parliament while also running the country, works in conjunction with a separate head of state who has little substantive power, and is subject neither to a separate election nor to term limits. Most government ministers are also members of parliament (although, in some countries – such as Sweden – this dual mandate is not allowed). Like presidents, prime ministers make appointments to other key government institutions, but these are rarely subject to confirmation by the legislature. And in two other key contrasts with the presidential executive, a prime minister can be removed from office as the result of a vote of no confidence, and can usually call new elections before the full term of a legislature has run its course.

TABLE 9.2: Parliamentary executives

- Prime minister (or chancellor, premier) is normally head of the biggest political party in the legislature.
- Governments emerge from the legislature and the prime minister can be dismissed from office by losing a legislative majority or a vote of confidence.
- Executives can serve an unlimited number of terms in office.
- The executive is collegial, taking the form of a cabinet (or council of ministers) in which the prime minister is traditionally first among equals. The cabinet typically contains around two dozen members.
- Prime minister is head of government, working with a separate ceremonial head of state.
- Examples: most European countries, Australia, Canada, India, Japan, New Zealand.

Parliamentary government: An arrangement in which the executive emerges from the legislature (most often in the form of a coalition), remains accountable to it, and must resign if it loses a legislative vote of no confidence.

Parliamentary government lacks the clear focus of the presidential system on a single chief executive, and instead involves a subtle and variable relationship between prime minister, cabinet, and government ministers. Figure 9.1 distinguishes between cabinet, prime ministerial, and ministerial governments; examining the balance between these nodes in the governing network, and how they are changing over time, helps us better appreciate the realities of parliamentary government.

For advocates of the parliamentary system, *cabinet government* has the advantage of encouraging more deliberation and collective leadership than occurs in a presidential system. When Olsen (1980: 203) wrote that 'a Norwegian prime minister is unlikely to achieve a position as superstar', many advocates of parliamentary

government would have regarded his comment as praise. Finland provides a clear case of cabinet government at work: by law, the Finnish State Council (the cabinet) is granted extensive decision-making authority, prime ministers are mainly chairs of Council meetings, and it is at these meetings that decisions are reached and compromises made. Meanwhile, both the prime minister and individual ministers are subject to constraints arising from Finland's complex multi-party coalitions. But the system works best in smaller countries; in many larger countries, the number and complexity of decisions means they cannot all be settled around the cabinet table.

As regards *prime ministerial government*, the guiding principle is hierarchy rather than collegiality. Germany has an arrangement known as a 'chancellor democracy' in which the Bundestag (Germany's lower house) appoints the chancellor, and accountability to the Bundestag is mainly through the chancellor's office. The chancellor answers to parliament, while ministers answer to the chancellor. The strong position of Germany's chief executive derives from the Basic Law (the

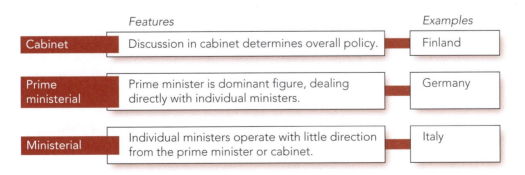

FIGURE 9.1: Types of parliamentary government

Note: None of these features is institutionalized or constitutionalized. Instead, each is a matter of politics and tradition.

German constitution) which says that the 'chancellor shall determine, and be responsible for, the general policy guidelines'.

Several commentators suggest that parliamentary executives are moving in the direction of prime ministerial government; prime ministers have ceased to be *primus inter pares* (first among equals) and have instead become president-ministers. Writing of Canada, Savoie (1999) suggests that in setting the government's agenda and taking major decisions, there is no longer any *inter* or *pares*, only *primus*. Similarly, Fiers and Krouwel (2005: 128) argue that since the 1990s prime ministers in Belgium and the Netherlands have acquired more prominent and powerful positions, transforming these democracies into a kind of 'presidentialized' parliamentary system. King (1994) identified three factors at work: increasing media focus on the prime minister, the growing international role of the chief executive, and the emerging need for policy coordination as governance becomes more complex. A substantial prime minister's office reflects these distinctive responsibilities and reinforces prime ministerial authority.

The third type is *ministerial government*, which arises when ministers operate without extensive direction from either prime minister or cabinet. This decentralized pattern can emerge either from respect for expertise, or from the realities of a coalition. Looking again at Germany, the chancellor sets the overall guidelines but the constitution goes on to say that 'each Federal Minister shall conduct the affairs of his department autonomously and on his own responsibility'. Ministers are appointed for their knowledge of the field and are expected to use their professional experience to shape their ministry's policy under the chancellor's guidance. So, Germany mixes two models, operating ministerial government within the framework of chancellor democracy.

In many coalitions, parties appoint their own leading figures to head particular ministries, again giving rise to ministerial government. In the Netherlands, for instance, the prime minister does not appoint, dismiss, or reshuffle ministers. Cabinet members serve with, but certainly not under, the government's formal leader. In these conditions, the prime minister's status is diminished, with ministers owing more loyalty to their party than to either the prime minister or the cabinet. The chief executive is neither a chief nor an executive but, rather, a skilled conciliator. In India's multi-party coalitions, too, open defiance of the prime minister is far from unknown (Mitra, 2014: 583).

In Japan, too, ministers must often operate without strong guidance from the prime minister. The prime minister is more like the keeper of the helm than captain of the ship and few officeholders leave a lasting personal stamp on government. Turnover has been rapid: while the United States had four presidents and Britain had four prime ministers between 1990 and 2015, Japan had 14 prime ministers serving 21 terms among them, some of those terms lasting only a matter of months. The comparison is with Italy (see Chapter 8) rather than the United States or Britain. In Japan, limits are placed on prime ministerial power by the powerful bureaucracy and upper legislative chamber, factions within political parties, other party leaders, and the consensus style of Japanese politics. In particular, prime ministers from the leading Liberal Democratic Party are limited by the requirement to secure regular re-election as party leader. Japanese prime ministers are far from powerless, because they can – for example – hire and fire members of the cabinet and all other senior members of the government. And reflecting the wider international trend towards a focus on the prime minister, Shinzō Abe (prime minister, 2006–7, 2012–) has achieved a higher domestic and international profile than most of his predecessors. Even so, the contrast with, say, Germany's chancellor democracy remains acute.

If the paradox of the presidential executive is weakness amid the appearance of strength, the puzzle of parliamentary government is to explain why effective government can still emerge from the mutual vulnerability of legislature and executive. The solution is clear: the party provides the necessary unifying device, bridging government and legislature in a manner that presidential systems are designed to prevent. Where a single party has a parliamentary majority, government can be stable and decisive, perhaps excessively so. But majority governments are increasingly rare, with the result that the typical parliamentary executive is a coalition government or a minority administration. Looking in more depth at different kinds of coalitions provides more insight into how parliamentary executives work.

Majority, coalition, and minority governments

In presidential and semi-presidential systems of government, executives and legislatures are elected separately and have distinct powers. The reach and authority of presidents is impacted by party numbers in the legislature, but there is much that the president can do regardless. In parliamentary systems, by contrast, the executive and the legislature are fused, and the power of the executive depends greatly upon the party balance in the legislature. A prime minister whose party has a clear majority will be in a much stronger situation than one governing a coalition or running a minority government. For this reason, no review of parliamentary executives can be complete without taking each of these variations into account.

Majority government. Britain is the classic example of parliamentary government based on a single ruling party with a secure majority. The plurality (or winner-take-all) method of election (see Chapter 16) usually delivers a working majority in the House of Commons to a single party, the leader of that party normally becomes prime minister (PM), and the cabinet is made up of 20 or so parliamentary colleagues from the same party. The cabinet is still the formal lynchpin of the system: it is the focus of accountability to Parliament, formally ratifies important government decisions, and coordinates the work of government departments. Its political support is essential to even the strongest PM.

The key to the system's stability is the party discipline that turns the cabinet into the master of the Commons, rather than its servant. The governing party spans the cabinet and the legislature, ensuring domination of the parliamentary agenda. The cabinet is officially the top committee of state but it is also an unofficial meeting of the party's leaders. As long as senior party figures remain sensitive to the views of other Members of Parliament (MPs) (and, often, even if they do not), they can control the Commons. The government may emerge from the parliamentary womb but it dominates its parent from the moment of its birth.

How does the ruling party achieve this level of control? Each party has a Whip's Office to ensure that MPs vote as its leaders require. Even without the attention of the whips, MPs will generally toe the party line if they want to become ministers themselves. In a strong party system such as Britain's, a member who shows too much independence is unlikely to win promotion. In extreme cases, MPs are thrown out of their party for dissent and are then unlikely to be re-elected by constituents for whom a party label is still key. Whatever their personal views, it is in the interests of MPs to show public loyalty to their party.

Coalition and minority governments. It is quite usual in parliamentary systems (particularly those using proportional representation, discussed in Chapter 16) for no single party to win a majority after an election. In this situation, the tight link between the election result and government formation weakens, and government takes one of three main forms:

- A majority **coalition government** in which two or more parties with a majority of seats join together. This is the most common form of rule in continental Europe.

- A minority coalition or alliance in which parties, even working together, still lack a parliamentary majority. Minority coalitions have predominated in Denmark since the 1980s.

- A single-party minority government formed by the largest party. These are common in Norway and Sweden.

> **Coalition government:** An arrangement in which the government is formed through an agreement involving two or more parties which divide government posts between them.

Figure 9.2 shows the party composition of West European governments in the second half of the twentieth century, revealing that majority coalitions were the most frequent, followed by single-party minority governments, minority coalitions, and single-party majority governments. So unusual are single-party majority governments that many national constitutions explicitly specify the hurdles a new government must clear before taking office. Some demand that the legislature shows majority support for a new government through a formal vote of investiture, a requirement that encourages the formation of a majority coalition with an agreed programme.

Others, however, do not require a majority vote for a new administration. In Sweden, for example, the proposed prime minister can form a government as long as no more than half the members of the Riksdag object (Bergman, 2000). This requirement is to avoid majority opposition rather than to achieve majority assent. Where constitutions say nothing on the procedure for approving a new government, as in Denmark, the new administration takes office – and continues in power – until and unless it is voted down by the legislature. These less demanding conventions facilitate the formation and survival of minority governments.

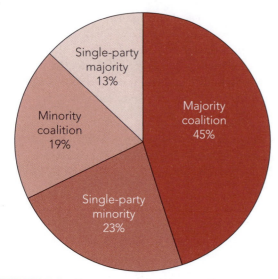

FIGURE 9.2: Governments in Western Europe, 1945–99

Note: Based on 424 governments from 17 countries. Non-party administrations (3 per cent) excluded.

Source: Adapted from Strøm and Nyblade (2007: table 32.1)

In regard to timing, some coalitions are promised or arranged before an election is held, helping voters to make a more informed judgement about the likely consequences of their voting choices. Most often, though, the coalitions are arranged after the election, with the outgoing government remaining as caretaker while negotiations are under way. Agreements can be reached in a matter of days, but the more complex negotiations take longer: it took 208 days for agreement on a new Dutch government in 1977, and a record 541 days (18 months) for a new Belgian government in 2010–11.

It would be logical to suggest that coalitions will form between the largest parties in the legislature, but this is rarely the case, and coalitions come in several different types. Most contain the smallest number of parties needed to make a viable government, which is typically, two to four. Party interests favour these 'minimum winning coalitions' (MWCs) because including additional parties in a coalition which already has a majority would simply dilute the number of posts and the amount of policy influence available to each participant.

In addition, coalitions are usually based on parties with adjacent positions on the ideological spectrum. These 'connected coalitions' particularly benefit

centre parties, which can jump either way. In Germany, for instance, the small liberal Free Democrat Party has been a part of most coalitions, sometimes with the left-wing Social Democrats and, between 2009 and 2013, with the more conservative Christian Democrats. Either coalition could be presented as ideologically coherent. Germany, however, also has some experience of *grand coalitions* between the two major parties, marginalizing the Free Democrats. When the Free Democrats failed to win any seats at the 2013 election, Chancellor Angela Merkel's Christian Democrats took the decision to form a grand coalition with the Social Democrats.

Occasionally, 'oversized coalitions' emerge, containing more parties than are needed for a majority. These arrangements typically emerge when the partners are uncertain about the stability of their pact, or there is need to address policy problems of a kind where it makes strategic sense to win the support of as many parties as possible. For example, when Hungary was in the throes of its post-communist reforms, the 1994 election gave the social democrats an absolute majority of 209 out of 386 seats. Even so, they invited the liberals (with 70 seats) to join them in an oversized coalition, and then launched an austerity programme that included unpopular cuts in public sector wages and employee numbers. Because the government had a broad-based coalition, its ability to impose unpopular policies in the interests of promoting the market economy was strengthened (Wittenberg, 1999).

> **Semi-presidential government:** An arrangement in which an elected president coexists with a separately elected prime minister and legislature.

Semi-presidential executives

The third major form of executive is a combination of the presidential and the parliamentary, mixing both models to produce a distinct system with its own characteristics, advantages, and disadvantages. In **semi-presidential government** (otherwise known as a 'dual executive') we find both an elected president *and* a prime minister and cabinet accountable to the legislature. The president is separately elected, and shares power with a prime minister who heads a cabinet accountable to the legislature. The prime minister is usually appointed by the president, but must

| FOCUS 9.2 | Heads of state in parliamentary systems |

No analysis of parliamentary executives is complete without saying something about the distinction between the head of state and the head of government. The classic analysis was offered by the Victorian British commentator Walter Bagehot (a one-time editor of *The Economist*). In his book *The English Constitution*, he wrote of the two key elements of constitutions (boldface added):

> first, those which excite and preserve the reverence of the population – the ***dignified*** parts, if I may so call them; and next the ***efficient*** parts – those by which it, in fact, works and rules ... every constitution must first *gain* authority and then *use* authority; it must first win the loyalty and confidence of mankind, and then employ that homage in the work of government. (Bagehot, 1867: 6)

Unlike presidential systems, which combine the offices of head of state and head of government, parliamentary systems separate the two positions. Dignified or ceremonial leadership lies with the head of state, while efficient leadership is based on the prime minister. Heads of state possess few significant political powers, and their job is primarily non-political, and to act as a unifying influence. Prime ministers, meanwhile, are the elected political leaders with executive power. This separation of roles creates more time for prime ministers to concentrate on running the country, and also helps to separate government and state in the public mind. Heads of state are not entirely non-political, however, and sometimes play a role in the formation of governments. In India, for example, the president had to oversee the formation of a caretaker government in 1979 that governed until new elections in 1980; stepped in on three occasions between 1996–7 to identify the party leader best placed to form a new government following indecisive elections; and was involved in 2004 in naming Manmohan Singh as prime minister after Congress Party leader Sonia Gandhi turned down the job.

Heads of state are typically either monarchs who inherit their position, or presidents who are appointed or elected (see Table 9.3). Eight European countries – Belgium, Denmark, Luxembourg (a duchy), the Netherlands, Norway, Spain, Sweden, and the United Kingdom – have a **constitutional monarchy**, while Malaysia's supreme head of state provides a rare contemporary example of an elected monarch. Some former British colonies, such as Australia and Canada, have a governor-general who stands in for the monarch. Most monarchs are reluctant to enter the political arena in democratic times, but royal influence can occasionally be significant, especially in eras of crisis and transition. King Juan Carlos helped to steer Spain's transition to democracy in the 1970s, for example, while the King of Belgium played a conciliatory role in his country's long march to federal status between 1970 and 1993.

Elsewhere, heads of state in parliamentary systems are presidents, and are elected either through a popular vote (e.g. Ireland), by parliament (e.g. Israel), or by a special electoral college, often comprising the national legislature plus representatives from regional or local government (e.g. Germany).

➡

Constitutional monarchy: A state headed by a monarch, but where the monarch's political powers are severely limited by constitutional rules. Stands in contrast with an absolute monarch (see Chapter 4).

have the support of a majority in the legislature. The president is head of state, and shares the duties of being head of government with the prime minister; the president has an oversight role and responsibility for foreign affairs, and can usually take emergency powers, while the prime minister is responsible for day-to-day domestic government. The president has more opportunity to play the role of head of state than is the case with a presidential executive, but must also deal with a division of authority within the executive that creates the potential for a struggle between president and prime minister.

FOCUS 9.2   Heads of state in parliamentary systems (Continued)

TABLE 9.3: Selecting the head of state in parliamentary democracies

	Head of state	Method of selection	Tenure
Australia, Canada, Jamaica	Governor-General	Nominated by prime minister or government and confirmed by British monarch	At monarch's pleasure
Austria	President	Direct popular election by a two-round system	6 years
Germany	President	Election by a joint Bundestag and *Land* convention	5 years
India	President	Election by a college of federal and state assemblies	5 years
Italy	President	Election by a joint session of parliament and regional representatives	7 years
Japan	Emperor	Heredity (eldest male)	Life
Malaysia	Supreme head of state	Elected (by rulers of the nine Malay states)	5 years
Spain	Monarch	Heredity (eldest male)	Life
Sweden	Monarch	Heredity (eldest child)	Life
UK	Monarch	Heredity (eldest child)	Life

The French political scientist Maurice Duverger (1980: 166) provided an influential definition of a semi-presidential system:

> A political regime is considered semi-presidential if the constitution which established it combines three elements: (1) the president of the republic is elected by universal suffrage; (2) he possesses quite considerable powers; (3) he has opposite him, however, a prime minister and ministers who possess executive and governmental power and can stay in office only if the parliament does not show its opposition to them.

The 'quite considerable powers' of the president typically include special responsibility for foreign affairs, appointing the prime minister and cabinet, issuing decrees and initiating referendums, initiating and veto-ing legislation, and dissolving the assembly. In theory, the president can offer leadership on foreign affairs, while the prime minister addresses the needs of domestic politics through parliament.

In cases where the president's party has a majority in the legislature, the power advantage lies with the president; the prime minister and the cabinet both follow the president's lead, and the prime minister promotes the president's programme in the legislature. But when voters give an opposition party a majority in the legislature, the president has no choice but to work with a prime minister and cabinet from that party in an arrangement known as 'cohabitation'. In such circumstances,

TABLE 9.4: Semi-presidential executives

- Combines an elected president and an appointed prime minister.
- President usually appoints the prime minister and can dissolve the legislature.
- President usually serves a limited number of fixed-length terms.
- Prime minister and cabinet are accountable to both the president and the legislature.
- President serves as head of state and shares the responsibilities of being head of government with the prime minister.
- Examples: France, Mongolia, Russia, Sri Lanka, Ukraine, several former French colonies in Africa.

the prime minister must cooperate with the president in the national interest, but also becomes the leader of the opposition in what is, in effect, a grand coalition. An ambitious prime minister can also use the position to build the foundations for later contesting the presidency.

Shugart and Carey (1992) distinguish between two kinds of semi-presidential government: president-parliamentary and premier-presidential. In the former (found in Peru and Russia), the prime minister and the cabinet are collectively responsible to both the president and the legislature, meaning that they can be dismissed by one or the other. In the latter (found in France, Portugal, Romania, and Ukraine since 2005), the prime minister and cabinet are collectively responsible only to the legislature, meaning that while the president can appoint the prime minister and the cabinet, they can only be removed from office through a vote of no confidence in the legislature. As a result, the position of the president is weakened.

If the United States exemplifies the presidential system, France provides the archetype of the semi-presidential executive. In an effort to move away from the unstable Fourth Republic, which had seen 23 prime ministers in its short 12-year life, the 1958 constitution of the Fifth Republic created a presidency fit for the

dominating presence of its first occupant, Charles de Gaulle (president, 1959–69). De Gaulle saw himself as a national saviour, arguing that 'power emanates directly from the people, which implies that the head of state, elected by the nation, is the source and holder of that power' (Knapp and Wright, 2006: 53). The president has been directly elected since 1962, with recent modifications introducing slight limitations. In 2000, the presidential term was reduced from seven to five years, with a two-term limit following in 2008.

The French president is guarantor of national independence and the constitution, heads the armed forces, negotiates treaties, calls referendums, presides over the Council of Ministers, dissolves the National Assembly (but cannot veto legislation), appoints (but cannot dismiss) the prime minister, and appoints other ministers on the recommendation of the prime minister and dismisses them.

The main concern of French prime ministers is with domestic affairs, casually dismissed by de Gaulle as including such mundane matters as 'the price of milk'. Appointed by the president but accountable to parliament, the prime minister formally appoints ministers and coordinates their day-to-day work, operating within the president's style and tone. The ability of the assembly

TABLE 9.5: Comparing executives

	Presidential	Parliamentary	Semi-presidential
Method of election	Direct, whole country.	Indirect via legislature.	President: direct, whole country. Prime minister: indirect.
Separate head of state	No.	Yes.	Yes.
Does executive serve in legislature?	No.	Yes.	Prime minister only, not president.
Separation of powers	Yes.	No.	To some extent.
Fixed terms in office	Yes.	No.	President only.
Means for dismissal from office	End of term, loss of presidential election, impeachment, resignation.	Loss of legislative election, loss of vote of confidence, loss of party leadership, resignation.	President: end of term, loss of presidential election, impeachment, resignation.
Role of cabinet	More marginal and individualistic.	More central and collective.	More marginal and individualistic.
Can executive work with legislature controlled by another party?	Yes, but weakened.	Only in case of minority government.	Yes, but weakened.
Where found?	United States, most of Latin America, Burma, Indonesia, Nigeria, Philippines.	Most of Europe and Caribbean, Australia, Canada, Iraq, New Zealand, Pakistan, India.	France, Russia, Kazakhstan, Ukraine, Romania, Zimbabwe.

to force the prime minister and the Council of Ministers to resign after a vote of censure provides the parliamentary component of the semi-presidential executive.

Presidents and prime ministers need to work in harmony, a task made easier when the same party controls both branches of government. This is usually the case, but occasionally France has gone through a period of cohabitation. Between 1986 and 1988, for example, the socialist president François Mitterrand had to share power with the conservative prime minister Jacques Chirac. The latter won the presidency in 1995, and was obliged in turn to share power with socialist prime minister Lionel Jospin between 1997 and 2002. This arrangement intensifies competition between the two principals, and places the president in the awkward position of leading both the country and the opposition.

Beneath the president and prime minister, the government's day-to-day political work is carried out by 20 senior ministers, but the Council of Ministers is less significant than the cabinet in parliamentary systems. Most modern French governments have been multiparty coalitions, the Council of Ministers involves more ritual than discussion, ministers are more autonomous because they often come to their job with a background in their given policy area, and interventions by the prime minister and the president are often to resolve disputes, rather than to impose an overall agenda.

Executives in authoritarian states

So far we have looked at executives in democratic settings, and at the many nuances bearing on what are complex institutions. Constitutional rules and political realities help define what a democratic executive can or cannot do, and they both shape and protect the structures of government. By contrast, understanding executives in authoritarian states is more about political realities; there are constitutions and rules, to be sure, but there is less constraint on their capacity to execute policy, and there are fewer formal protections on the officeholder. As Svolik (2012: 39) points out, dictators lack the support of independent political authorities that would help them enforce agreements, as well as the rules that govern the work of formal government institutions. As a result, the violent resolution of conflicts is an everpresent possibility. In short, authoritarian leaders can wield more power and yet they also often face greater personal risks than their democratic counterparts.

The characteristic form of the executive in hybrid and authoritarian regimes is presidential, but as we saw in Chapter 4 the term *president* takes on a quite different meaning from what we find in democracies. Presidential government in authoritarian settings provides a natural platform for leaders who seek to set themselves apart from – and above – all others. In such systems, the president operates without the same constitutional restraints faced by the chief executive of a liberal democracy. Instead, presidents use what they define as their direct mandate from the people to cast a shadow over competing institutions such as the courts and the legislature. Excepting the simplest systems, though, they do not usually go so far as to reduce these bodies to completely token status.

Authoritarian leaders seek to concentrate power on themselves and their supporters, not to distribute it among institutions; it is this lack of institutionalization that is the central feature of the authoritarian executive. Although developed in the context of African politics, the idea of **personal rule** developed by Jackson and Rosberg (1982) travels widely through the authoritarian world. Politics takes precedence over government, and personalities matter more than institutions: there is, in other words, a feast of presidents but a famine of presidencies.

> **Personal rule:** A form of rule in which authority is based less on office as such than on personal and often corrupt links between rulers and patrons, associates, clients and supporters. Personal rule can be stable but remains vulnerable because of its dependence upon persons rather than institutions.

The result of personal rule is often a struggle over succession, insufficient emphasis on policy, and poor governance. In particular, the lack of a succession procedure (excepting hereditary monarchies) can create a conflict among potential successors not only after the leader's exit, but also in the run-up to it. Authoritarian leaders keep their job for as long as they can ward off their rivals. They must monitor threats and be prepared to neuter those who are becoming too strong. Politics comes before policy.

The price of defeat, furthermore, is high; politics in authoritarian systems can be a matter of life and death. When the leaders of Western democracies leave office, they can often give well-paid lectures, write and sell their memoirs for large sums, be appointed to well-paid consultancies, or set up foundations to do good works. Ousted dictators risk a harsher fate, assuming they even live long enough to have a 'retirement'. Some might live in wealthy exile, a few languish in prison, and the least fortunate are murdered. It is hardly surprising, then, that the governing style of authoritarian rulers inclines to the ruthless.

Particularly in its most authoritarian phase before the 1990s, post-colonial Africa illustrated the importance of personal leadership in non-democratic settings. Leaders were adept at using the coercive and financial resources of the regime to reward their friends and punish their enemies. As an example, Sandbrook (1985) wrote this of the administration of Mobutu Sese Seko during his dictatorial tenure as president of Zaire (1965–97):

> No potential challenger is permitted to gain a power base. Mobutu's officials know that their jobs depend solely on the president's discretion. Frequently, Mobutu fires cabinet ministers, often without explanation. Everyone is kept off balance. Everyone must vie for his patronage.

However, in post-colonial Africa, as in other authoritarian settings, personal rule has been far from absolute. Inadequately accountable in a constitutional sense, many personal rulers have found themselves constrained by other political actors, including the military, leaders of ethnic groups, landowners, the business class, the bureaucracy, multinational companies, and even factions in the leader's own court.

To survive, leaders have to distribute the perks of office so as to maintain a viable coalition of support. Enemies can be bought off by allowing them a share of the pie, but their slice must not become so large as to threaten the big man himself. Mobutu's own ground rules illustrate the dilemma: 'if you want to steal, steal a little in a nice way. But if you steal too much to become rich overnight, you'll be caught' (Gould, 1980: 485).

In the Middle East, personal rule remains central to those authoritarian regimes that survived the Arab Spring of 2011. The absolute monarchs discussed in Chapter 4 continue to rule oil-rich kingdoms in traditional patriarchal style. 'Ruling' rather than 'governing' is the appropriate term. In Saudi Arabia, for instance, advancement within the ruling family depends less on merit than on proximity to the family's network of advisers, friends, and guards. Public and private are interwoven, each forming part of the ruler's sphere. Government posts are occupied on the basis of good behaviour, as demonstrated by unswerving loyalty to the ruler's personal interests.

Such systems of personal rule have survived for centuries, limiting the development of strong institutions. The Arab Spring revealed their weaknesses, as frustrated populations in several Arab states protested against the absence of opportunity in corrupt, conservative regimes headed by ageing autocrats. But the challenges of switching from autocracy to democracy were also revealed. In the case of Egypt, Hosni Mubarak was ousted from office in 2011 in the wake of demonstrations against his 30-year regime, and in 2012 the country's first ever truly competitive elections resulted in the victory of Mohamed Morsi. But because he came from the Islamist Muslim Brotherhood, nervousness grew abroad, particularly in the United States. And when Morsi started showing signs of authoritarianism, he was removed in a July 2013 military coup. Military leader Abdel Fattah el-Sisi then reinvented himself as a civilian, won elections held in May 2014, and quickly showed an unwillingness to tolerate opposition. After a brief and hopeful flirtation with democracy, Egypt was soon back to its old ways. This was not what most Egyptians wanted, and opposition to the el-Sisi regime began to grow; the point, though, is that Egypt's other political institutions were too weak to resist a return to personal rule.

The theme of the president operating without the constitutional restraints found in democracies is illustrated by Vladimir Putin's Russia. Formally, Russia is a semi-presidential system arranged along French lines, with a directly elected president coexisting with a chairman of the government (i.e. prime minister) who is nominated by the president and approved by the Duma (the lower chamber of the legislature).

In some minor respects, the Russian president's position is only slightly stronger than that of a US president. Both are limited to two terms in office, but the Russian leader can stand again after a term out. Both are subject to impeachment but the threshold is more demanding in Russia: the US requires only a majority of members in favour in the House of Representatives, while Russia requires a two-thirds majority in both parliamentary chambers plus confirmation by the courts.

In reality, though, Russian presidents can grasp the levers of power more easily than either their American or French equivalents. Under the 1993 constitution, the president acts as head of state, commander-in-chief, and guarantor of the constitution. In the latter capacity, presidents can suspend the decisions of other state bodies. They can also issue decrees, though these can be overridden by legislation. In contrast to most semi-presidential systems, the president can remove ministers without the consent of the Duma, and does so.

Russia's president is also charged with 'defining the basic directions of the domestic and foreign policy of the state', and with 'ensuring the coordinated functioning and collaboration of bodies of state power'. These broad duties affirm Russia's long tradition of executive power, a norm which both predates and was reinforced by the communist era. Strong government is regarded as a necessary source of effective leadership for a large and sometimes lawless country.

Putin had no choice but to step down as president upon the completion of his two terms in 2008, but he continued to hold on to power through the cynical means of becoming prime minister to the weak new president, Dmitry Medvedev. As president, Medvedev's influence seemed to be marginal compared with his predecessor, and he was little more than a place-holder awaiting Putin's return in 2012. And with the term of a president increased from four years to six, Putin could reasonably look forward to running Russia (his health allowing) until 2024. So, even in Russia, with its powerful state institutions centred on the Kremlin, a substantial measure of personal rule is superimposed on the institutions of state.

China is the most important example of the supremacy of politics over government in an authoritarian setting. It combines some formal features of a semi-presidential system with political dominance by the Chinese Communist Party (CCP). In understanding this system, two points are key. First, in spite of China's intricate governmental structure (which includes a cabinet, a legislature, and a network of supporting agencies), these bodies do little more than legitimize the decisions already taken by the party leadership (Saich, 2015: ch. 4). Second, identifying who holds power is less a question of formal titles and offices than of understanding links across institutions, personal networks, and the standing of key figures in the system. For instance, Deng Xiaoping was 'paramount leader' of China from 1978 until his death in 1997, yet the most senior posts he ever held were those of party vice chairman and chairman of the party's Military Commission; by 1993, the only position of any kind that he held was the presidency of China's bridge association. So even in China,

with its enormous population, we see strong elements of personal rule.

As China's politics has stabilized, so recent changes have given a government that looks more like some of its democratic counterparts. At the apex is the president, who is nominated by the leadership of the Chinese legislature, the National People's Congress (NPC), and then elected (or confirmed) by the NPC for a maximum of two five-year terms. The presidency is mainly a ceremonial head of state, but has many conventional executive powers, such as the ability to appoint (with NPC approval) all members of the State Council (the functional equivalent of a cabinet). The officeholder is also conventionally head of the CCP and of the Central Military Commission, posts that provide enormous political power. The president must also work with a premier, who is the *de facto* head of government, is always a senior member of the party, and is nominated by the president and confirmed by the NPC. The CCP continues to drive the governmental machine.

Military leaders are perhaps the ultimate form of the authoritarian executive, combining as they do control over civilian and military institutions. But while great power in democracies is said to come with great responsibilities, in military dictatorships it also comes with great risks. Executives in democratic states must always worry about their standing in the opinion polls, their capacity to work with legislatures, and threats to their leadership from others seeking power; for their part, military leaders face threats that are both closer to home (from within the ruling elite) and more unpredictable and violent. When Winston Churchill said that 'dictators ride to and fro on tigers from which they dare not dismount', he was speaking in the context of the rise of Hitler and Mussolini, but the adage also applies to military leaders who must be constantly on the lookout for threats from numerous quarters.

The story of Nigeria's leaders is illustrative. Since independence in 1960, it has had 15 leaders: six civilian presidents (although two of these six were former military leaders who came back to office as civilians) and nine military leaders. Of the 15, three were removed from office through military coups in which the leaders were killed, and four were removed from office but survived. All have had to keep a careful eye on critics within the military, who have always been ready to organize opposition and, if necessary, a coup to remove the incumbent.

DISCUSSION QUESTIONS

- What are the advantages and disadvantages of dividing the roles of head of state and head of government?

- Separation of powers: a good idea or not?

- Is presidential or parliamentary government the most appropriate system for (a) new democracies, (b) divided societies?

- Have prime ministers become presidential and, if so, why?

- 'Uneasy lies the head that wears a crown' (Shakespeare, *Henry IV Part II*). Discuss in the context of democracies and of authoritarian states.

KEY CONCEPTS

Cabinet	Parliamentary government
Coalition government	Personal rule
Constitutional monarchy	Presidential government
Head of government	Semi-presidential government
Head of state	Separation of powers

FURTHER READING

Elgie, Robert (2011) *Semi-Presidentialism: Sub-Types and Democratic Performance*. Examines how different forms of semi-presidentialism affect the quality and durability of democracy.

Han, Lori Cox (ed.) (2011) *New Directions in the American Presidency*. Explores current themes in the study of the presidential system in the United States.

Helms, Ludger (2005) *Presidents, Prime Ministers and Chancellors: Executive Leadership in Western Democracies*. A comparison of the political executive in Britain, Germany, and the United States.

Lijphart, Arend (ed.) (1992) *Parliamentary versus Presidential Government*. A classic collection of essays on parliamentary and presidential government.

Poguntke, Thomas and Paul Webb (eds) (2005) *The Presidentialization of Politics: A Comparative Study of Modern Democracies*. An investigation of whether the operation of the executive has become more presidential in a range of liberal democracies.

Strøm, Kaare, Wolfgang C. Müller, and Torbjörn Bergman (eds) (2008) *Cabinets and Coalition Bargaining: The Democratic Life Cycle in Western Europe*. A comparative examination of cabinet formation.

10 Bureaucracies

PREVIEW

Bureaucracies are the institutions responsible for implementing public policy, and are thus a key part of the structure of government. Bureaucrats are also the only employees of the government with which most of us have much direct contact, whether we are applying for a driving licence or a passport, paying our taxes, or buying property. Just as executives and legislatures come in different forms, and are subject to complex pressures, the same applies to bureaucracies.

Rarely formally studied in the West until Max Weber turned his attention to them in the early twentieth century, the stereotype of bureaucracies is that they are hierarchical, driven by procedure, and unresponsive to customer needs. But they are an essential part of government, and in order to understand their dynamics we need to understand how they are structured, the political and professional pressures that come to bear on the work of bureaucrats, and how bureaucracies are changing.

This chapter begins with a review of how bureaucracies evolved and how they are organized, ranging from the largest government departments down through the divisions within each department to the non-departmental public bodies that are increasingly used to deliver public services. It then looks at how bureaucrats are recruited and kept accountable, before briefly assessing the new public management approach that caused some excitement in the late twentieth century, and the rise of e-government that many wealthier countries are witnessing today. The chapter ends with a review of the contrasting role that bureaucracies play in authoritarian regimes.

CONTENTS

- Bureaucracies: an overview
- Evolution
- Organization
- Recruitment
- New public management
- E-government
- Bureaucracies in authoritarian states

KEY ARGUMENTS

- Max Weber's traditional model of bureaucracy remains the starting point for understanding the modern bureaucracy.

- In liberal democracies, the public sector is a complex network encompassing departments (ministries), divisions, and non-departmental public bodies such as regulatory agencies. Increasingly, outsourcing to private companies is a factor in understanding public service provision.

- Two questions running through our understanding of bureaucracies concern how best to recruit public employees and how to keep them accountable. The issue of recruitment has recently focused on the challenges of promoting diversity in the public sector.

- New public management emerged in the 1980s as an attempt to apply business-like practices in the public sector. It is now past its peak but still offers an interesting contrast to Weber's traditional model.

- The newest aspect of bureaucracy is e-government. This offers numerous opportunities for comparative research and lesson-drawing, while also raising concerns about surveillance, privacy, and data protection.

- Bureaucracies are one of the exceptions to the rule of marginal political institutions in authoritarian regimes. Dictators cannot dictate without officials to give effect to their will.

Bureaucracies: an overview

The study of the **bureaucracy** (also known as the 'civil service') focuses on the networks of central departments and public agencies that underpin the political executive. These networks have two main functions: they give advice to politicians before policy is made, and they help to implement decisions once reached. The head of department offering advice to the government minister or secretary, the inspector checking tax returns, the health officer implementing a national anti-obesity strategy – all are part of the complex operation that is the public bureaucracy. The notion of 'bureaucracy' can be extended further: the administrative staff of any large organization – such as a university, a political party, or a corporation – can be considered a bureaucracy, and the nature of the organizations of which they are a part gives them many of the same incentives, limitations, and motives as we find in the public bureaucracy.

> **Bureaucracy:** Literally, rule by officials. Used more precisely to describe the organizations employing appointed public officials and forming the public administration.

Traditionally, studies of the bureaucracy focused on the permanent salaried officials employed in central government departments. These elite officials, and the departments they occupy, remain of obvious importance, and the term *bureaucracy* is sometimes confined to them. However, attention increasingly focuses on the wider governance beyond: in semi-independent agencies, local governments, and even the non-governmental organizations and the private corporations to which the delivery of public programmes is increasingly outsourced. We refer here to all public networks as comprising the bureaucracy; others employ such terms as *public administration* or *public management* to denote the study of the public sector in this wider sense. Whatever the labels, understanding the modern state, and following a career within it, requires a mental map of what are remarkably complex networks.

In understanding bureaucracies, we need to review how they are structured, how their staff are recruited and held accountable, how best to achieve coordination across departments, and how to ensure that services are delivered efficiently in the absence of a normal market. Seeking out the best recruits and then giving employees of public agencies – particularly those at the less skilled and lower paid end of the spectrum – a sense of mission

and a desire to serve is not easy. Professionals providing a key public service – such as doctors and nurses in a public health system – will have the highest sense of mission, but the stereotypical view of bureaucrats pushing paper (literally or metaphorically) and tying services in **red tape** still often holds true.

> **Red tape:** The classic image of bureaucracies tied up in procedure and rules, deriving from the habit in some sixteenth-century European countries of binding administrative documents in red tape. Reducing red tape is a common election promise.

Bureaucracies have undergone substantial changes in recent decades, however, pressed by efforts to reform the delivery of public services, and caught up in the transition to e-government. Two major themes in understanding the modern bureaucracy (in wealthier democracies at least) are the outsourcing that has led to many services being transferred to private contractors, and the switch to a reliance on the provision of information and services through the internet.

Evolution

To appreciate today's bureaucracy, we must first consider what preceded it. Ancient kingdoms and empires had some form of bureaucracy, perhaps the most famous being that of China. Based on principles set down by Confucius in the sixth century BC, China established the first **meritocracy**, with bureaucrats earning their positions through formal examination and being used by emperors to run the country (a relationship that generally worked well in good times, but collapsed occasionally in the bad times, such as in the wake of war). In Europe, meanwhile, clerical servants were originally agents of the royal household, serving under the personal direction of the monarch. Many features of modern bureaucracies – regular salaries, pensions, open recruitment – arose from a successful attempt to overcome this idea of public employment as personal service to the monarch.

> **Meritocracy:** A system in which career advancement and leadership are based upon talent, qualifications and achievement.

The evolution of European royal households into twentieth-century bureaucracies was a massive transformation, intimately linked to the rise of the modern state. Today, the institutional approach to comparison takes the features of bureaucratic organization for granted, and even reacts against them, but in the late nineteenth and early twentieth century the form was strikingly new: a phenomenon to be both admired and feared.

Karl Marx (1818–83) was one of the first to theorize about the bureaucracy, arguing that its development was a natural counterpart to the development of the private corporation, and that the two were mutually reliant. But the first systematic study of the bureaucracy was undertaken by the German sociologist Max Weber (1864–1920), and many of his arguments continue to underpin our understanding of Western bureaucracy. Weber's model was based on the traditional view of public administration as a disciplined hierarchy in which salaried officials who are recruited and promoted on merit reach rational decisions by applying explicit rules to the facts before them (Figure 10.1).

Weber's model imagines public service as professional and legalistic, rather than managerial and business-like. His central claim was that bureaucracy made administration more efficient, providing the means by which the techniques of modern industry and military organization could be brought to bear on civil affairs:

> The fully developed bureaucratic apparatus compares with other organizations exactly as does the machine with non-mechanical modes of production.

Precision, speed, clarity, knowledge of files, continuity, discretion, unity, strict subordination, reduction of friction and of material and personal costs – these are raised to the optimum point in the strictly bureaucratic administration. (quoted in Kahlberg, 2005: 199)

While Weber's ideas were highly influential in continental Europe, they were less so in the New World. There, civil services developed in more pragmatic fashion. Lacking the European monarchical and state tradition, public management was at first considered to be a routine application of political directives. In the United States, for example, the original philosophy was one of governance by the common person; almost every citizen, it was assumed, qualified for almost every public job. The notion of a professional civil service was considered somewhat elitist and undemocratic.

This populist theory of bureaucracy conveniently underpinned the **spoils system,** a term deriving from the phrase 'to the victor, the spoils'. In the United States, the spoils system ensured that the election of a new president led to a virtually complete turnover of employees in what was then a small federal government. It continued at least until 1883, when the Pendleton Act created a Civil Service Commission to recruit and regulate federal employees. In Canada, the merit principle was introduced in 1908 and adopted fully in the Civil Service Act, 1918. So, where a meritocracy emerged in Europe in reaction to monarchy, in North America it supplanted spoils.

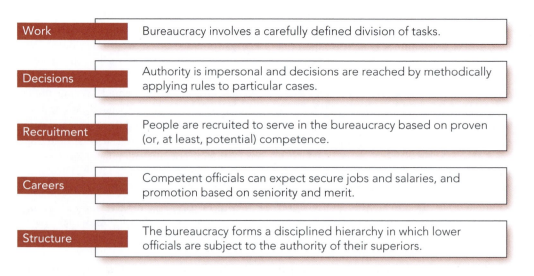

Work	Bureaucracy involves a carefully defined division of tasks.
Decisions	Authority is impersonal and decisions are reached by methodically applying rules to particular cases.
Recruitment	People are recruited to serve in the bureaucracy based on proven (or, at least, potential) competence.
Careers	Competent officials can expect secure jobs and salaries, and promotion based on seniority and merit.
Structure	The bureaucracy forms a disciplined hierarchy in which lower officials are subject to the authority of their superiors.

FIGURE 10.1: Weber's model of bureaucracy

Western bureaucracies reached their zenith in the twentieth century. The depression and two world wars vastly increased government intervention in society. The welfare state, completed in Western and especially Northern European countries in the decades following the Second World War, required a massive bureaucratic apparatus to distribute grants, allowances, and pensions. By 1980, public employment accounted for almost one-third of the total workforce in Britain and Scandinavia, though much of this expansion had taken place at local level.

But then the closing decades of the twentieth century witnessed declining faith in bureaucratic solutions. Where Weber had lauded the efficiency of the administrative machine, critics now judged civil servants to be engaged in unproductive games to increase the budgets and staff of their particular sections (Niskanen, 1971). More generally, the policy-forming community in many liberal democracies widened, and there has been a trend towards outsourcing government services (see later in this chapter), diminishing any monopoly which

central government civil servants once exerted over policy advice. Instead, officials are today encouraged to focus more on delivery, and specifically on the three Es: economy, efficiency, and effectiveness (which can be summarized as spending less and spending wisely). The rapid rise of e-government (the use of the internet to provide public services) promises to bring further important changes.

Two factors to take into account when looking comparatively at bureaucracies are the numbers of civil servants, and the balance between those employed by central and by local government. The overall numbers are an indicator of the size of government, and of the extent to which different governments choose to deliver services such as education and health care through public programmes. International Labour Organization data indicate that the Scandinavian countries have the biggest public sectors when measured by share of employment (see Figure 10.2) and that the size of bureaucracies has grown in recent decades. The balance of employment, meanwhile, is an indicator of centralization. Generally speaking, most democracies employ most of their civil servants at the sub-national rather than at the national level, the proportion working at the sub-national level being larger in federal systems such as Canada, Germany,

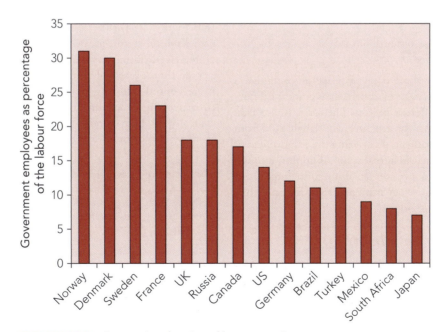

FIGURE 10.2: Comparing the size of bureaucracies

Source: Adapted from International Labour Organization, quoted in OECD (2013: 103). Figures are for 2011.

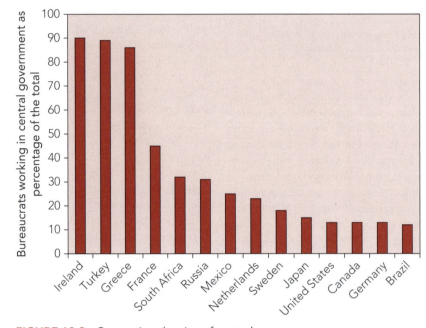

FIGURE 10.3: Comparing the size of central government

Source: Adapted from International Labour Organization, quoted in OECD (2013: 105). Figures are for 2011.

and the United States (see Figure 10.3). Unitary Sweden also devolves most policy implementation to the local level.

Organization

We have seen that while every state has an executive, a legislature, and a system of courts, they come in different forms with different powers. The same is also true of bureaucracies, whose structures and labels vary from one country to another, emphasizing the importance of taking structural factors into account. Running through the differences, though, we can distinguish three main kinds of organization: departments, divisions, and non-departmental public bodies.

Departments (or ministries)

The centrepiece of modern bureaucracies is formed by what is known in some countries as **departments**, and in others as ministries. In nearly all cases, these departments form the core of central government. The total number varies but is typically between 12 and 24: there are almost always departments dealing with foreign affairs, the economy, justice, health care,

and the environment, with others added depending on the list of policy areas considered important to a country and the responsibility of central government (see Figure 10.4). These core departments also have cabinet-level status, meaning that they are headed by secretaries or ministers who are members of the cabinet or the council of ministers, which gives them a more central role in government. There is also a distinct pecking order: the most important departments typically include foreign affairs, the economy, the treasury, and justice.

> **Department** (or ministry): An administrative unit over which a secretary or minister exercises direct management control. Usually structured as a formal hierarchy, often established by statute, and usually having cabinet-level status.

Both the range of public activities and their organization in government varies across countries. While most countries have a single department of energy, for example, Nigeria has separate departments of energy, petroleum resources, and power. Some countries have a department of culture but many do not, the United States is almost unique in having a Department of

Policy area	United States	Britain	Japan	Mexico	Nigeria
Foreign					
Treasury/finance					
Defence					
Health					
Internal affairs					
Agriculture					
Education					
Justice					
Trade					
Environment					
Business					
Local government					
Culture					
Regional affairs					
Labour					
Urban					
Transport					
Energy					
TOTAL	15	24	11	17	27

FIGURE 10.4: Government departments in selected countries

Note: Arrangements as of mid-2015. Names, number, and distribution of departments change over time.

Veterans Affairs, and countries vary in how they allocate responsibility for economic policy, finance, investment, and monetary affairs. Finally, departments will periodically be renamed, split, or combined, producing a changing departmental landscape.

Most countries have followed a similar sequence in creating departments, a pattern that reflects the expansion of the state. The oldest are typically those performing essential state functions such as finance, law and order, defence, and foreign affairs. In the United States, for instance, the Department of State and the Treasury date from 1789. But other countries have much older treasuries, that of Britain dating back at least to the Norman invasion of 1066, while the French Ministry of Foreign Affairs can be traced back at least to the sixteenth century. Subsequently, countries added extra departments to deal with new functions, including agriculture, trade, and labour. Later in the twentieth century came welfare departments dealing with social security, education, health, and housing. Among the more important recent additions have been departments of the environment, founded in nearly every country since the late 1960s. Several countries – including Afghanistan, Cambodia,

India, New Zealand, South Africa, and Sri Lanka – have departments dealing with women's affairs.

Reflecting Weber's principles, the internal structure of departments is usually hierarchical (see Figure 10.5). At the top there are secretaries or ministers who are

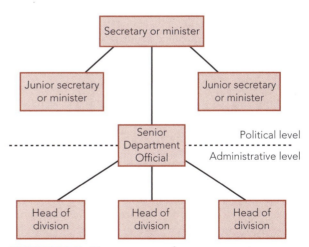

FIGURE 10.5: The structure of a government department

political appointees, and who will come and go as they are reshuffled or as governments change. Below them sits the permanent career civil service, headed by a senior department head responsible both for administration and for providing the crucial bridge between political and bureaucratic levels. In theory, secretaries direct and public servants execute, but the behavioural approach to comparison reveals that the reality is more complex and perhaps even disturbing. After all, permanent officials have the advantage over transient political secretaries of longer service, deeper experience, greater information, and denser networks of peers in other departments. In these circumstances, providing the department with effective political leadership requires skills for which secretaries are usually inadequately prepared.

Two factors can facilitate political control of a department. First, the greater the number of appointments made by a secretary within a department, the easier it is to impose a specific direction. Recognizing that senior bureaucrats themselves require political craft, many liberal democracies now tend to staff important departments with politically loyal and sympathetic bureaucrats. This practice, long familiar in Germany and Finland, has spread to other Western democracies (Peters and Pierre, 2004). Deepening the political tier gives the secretary more friends in the department.

Second, direction can also be helped by providing secretaries with political advisory staff. Because such advisers do not form part of the department's permanent staff, they too can act as their secretary's eyes and ears, reporting back on issues which might otherwise be lost in the official hierarchy. In New Zealand, every minister's office featured a political adviser by 2006 (Eichbaum and Shaw, 2007). Alternatively, as in France, ministers are helped by a personal cabinet of about 15 to 20 people who form an advisory staff working directly under the control of the secretary. This model is reflected in the European Commission, the main bureaucratic and executive body of the European Union, where the commissioners each have a cabinet of advisers, with rules designed to ensure a good mix from several EU countries. Where bureaucrats know that they can outlast a particularly difficult secretary, personal advisers realize that their position depends on providing effective support to the current occupant (see also Focus 10.2 on keeping bureaucrats accountable).

Divisions

Government departments are typically arranged into **divisions** or sections, each responsible for a particular aspect of the department's work. Thus, an education department might include separate divisions for primary, secondary, and higher education. Divisions are the operating units of departments, the sections within which the work gets done. They are the workhorses of government, the store of its experience and, in practice, the site where many important decisions are reached.

> **Division:** An operating unit of a department, responsible to the secretary but often with considerable independence. Also known as *sections* or *bureaus*, or (confusingly) as *departments* in countries where the larger unit is a ministry.

In some democracies, divisions acquire added importance because they are partially autonomous from their parent department. The extreme case is the United States, whose bureaucracy is the great exception to Weber's principle of hierarchy in departments. Even in their formal structure, US federal government departments are more like multinational corporations, containing many divisions (or agencies) jostling within a single shell. The departments are the wrapping around a collection of disparate divisions and it is these bureaus which form the main operating units of the federal government. For example, the Department of Health and Human Services includes 11 operating divisions (see Table 10.1). The autonomy of bureaus within US departments derives from their direct funding by Congress, and is a major and underestimated reason why US presidents experience such difficulty in imposing their will on the federal administrative process.

Even in governments with more hierarchical departments, it would be wrong to suppose that working practices correspond exactly to organizational charts. Rarely does information move smoothly up and down the administrative pyramid. For instance, the many divisions in Germany's 14 federal ministries possess a concentration of expertise that enables them to block, or at least circumvent, reforms proposed from on high. A monopoly of knowledge creates the potential to neutralize change. In most liberal democracies, divisions within departments also possess their own ethos derived from long experience with their subject area.

TABLE 10.1: Divisions within the US Department of Health and Human Services

Administration for Children and Families

Administration for Community Living

Agency for Healthcare Research and Quality

Agency for Toxic Substances and Disease Registry

Centers for Disease Control and Prevention

Centers for Medicare and Medicaid Services

Food and Drug Administration

Health Resources and Services Administration

Indian Health Service

National Institutes of Health

Substance Abuse and Mental Health Services

Source: Department of Health and Human Services website (2015)

This entrenched in-house view breeds a natural cynicism towards the latest political initiative, and helps to account for the frustration many newly appointed secretaries feel in steering their department in new directions. The dynamic of relations within departments and divisions has changed of late, however, as a result of a growing tendency in many countries to outsource government work to private contractors, a practice that comes with both advantages and disadvantages (see Focus 10.1).

Non-departmental public bodies

Departments and their internal divisions are what we usually associate with bureaucracies, but there is another type of public organization that is growing in importance: the **non-departmental public body**. These are entities that operate at one remove from government departments, with a formal relationship of at least semi-independence. Throughout the democratic world, these non-departmental bodies are growing in number, complicating not only the academic task of mapping government, but also the practical job of ensuring that the government as a whole acts coherently.

Non-departmental public body: Operates at one or more removes from the government, thereby providing management flexibility and political independence.

These bodies include state-owned entities (such as postal services or health care services), agencies contracted to deliver government services, agencies providing advice to government, and agencies charged with regulating an aspect of social life in which the public interest is at stake. They occupy an ambivalent position, created and funded by the government, but – unlike divisions within a department – free from day-to-day secretarial control. Once appointed by the government, their leaders and staff operate with considerable autonomy.

There are several reasons behind their creation and continued existence:

- To operate with more flexibility (and at lower cost) than would be acceptable for a department.
- To acknowledge the professional status and autonomy of their staff.
- As a response to short-term pressures to do something about a problem.
- To allow departments to focus on policy-making.
- To provide protection from political interference in day-to-day operations.

The most important type of the species is a **regulatory agency**. These are bodies set up to oversee the implementation of government regulations, in areas that include natural monopolies (such as water or energy supply), communications, elections, food standards, and environmental quality standards. Regulatory agencies are increasing in number in nearly all liberal democracies, partly to balance risks which cannot be well judged by the private sector. For example, weighing the benefits of introducing a new drug against the danger of side-effects is a task for public-minded experts, rather than for self-interested drug companies. Britain has embraced regulatory agencies with particular enthusiasm; over 140 agencies, from the Food Standards Agency to Ofcom (the regulator of the communications industries) now provide a central device through which the state seeks to oversee society.

Regulatory agency: An independent government body created to set and impose standards in a focused area of activity.

The United States offers the most established system of independent regulatory agencies. The first such body created there was the Interstate Commerce

> ### FOCUS 10.1 | The pros and cons of outsourcing government work
>
> Many governments have long relied on outside contractors to provide them with goods and supporting services, but since the 1980s there has been a growing trend in this direction. **Outsourcing** is one reason, for example, why the number of federal government employees in the United States fell from 4.3 per cent of the workforce in 1966 to 2 per cent in 2013, and why the number of people working through contracts was double that employed directly by the federal government.
>
> There have been many start-up problems as governments and contractors work through the process and learn what is possible (or not), but the trends suggest that outsourcing is here to stay; a growing number of jobs and services are shifting out of government to the private sector, boosted in part by the internet, but primarily by a desire on the part of governments to save money. Examples of outsourcing include the collection of garbage, water and wastewater treatment, security services, equipment servicing, technology support, the management of public schools and hospitals, and even private prisons (home to almost one-fifth of prisoners in Australia). One variation on the theme is co-sourcing, where work is shared between public and private agencies.
>
> | Arguments in favour | Arguments against |
> |---|---|
> | Competition among contractors helps bring down costs and makes it easier to terminate under-performing workers. | Without careful choices and monitoring, outsourcing can result in a reduction in the quality of services. |
> | Knowing they are competing for work, employees in private agencies will be more concerned with customer satisfaction. | Government departments often have a larger store of knowledge and experience than private companies entering a field for the first time. |
> | To increase profits, private contractors have incentives to manage their tasks more efficiently, where government departments are less sensitive to productivity issues. | There is less direct and political accountability with private contractors. |
> | Private contractors may be less subject to political manipulation and control. | Not all government services lend themselves to provision by private contractors (e.g. policing). |
> | Outsourcing lets government departments pay only for the services they need, and when they need them. | There may be substantial start-up costs in transferring work to a new private body. |
> | | Outsourcing raises new concerns about security and fraud. |
> | | Outsourcing to a single contractor just replaces a public monopoly with a private one. |

Outsourcing: The practice of contracting private contractors to provide services previously under the control of the public bureaucracy.

Commission (1887–1995). The list has since grown to include the Federal Communications Commission, the Environmental Protection Agency, the Federal Trade Commission, the Securities and Exchange Commission, and a host of others. The idea behind these bodies is that they should operate in a technical and non-political fashion. Despite their power to make, implement, and settle disputes about regulations in their sector, commissioners do not report to the president and can only be dismissed by the president for specific reasons set out in the law creating the agency.

The European Union has also been active on the regulatory front; indeed, regulation is its primary mode of governance. Its laws include regulations that are applicable in all the 28 member states and that typically set a technical standard or objective that member states are required to implement by a set target date. Along the way, it has created an expanding body of regulatory agencies that are charged with overseeing policy implementation in areas ranging from drugs and drug addiction to health and safety at work, new medicinal products, trademarks, maritime and aviation safety, food safety, disease prevention, and electronic communication (see McCormick, 2015: ch. 14). In many cases – such as the registration of new chemicals – the EU has gone on to establish global standards and to compel regulatory change in its major trading partners.

In general terms, charting non-departmental public bodies in any liberal democracy confirms the complexity of governance. The rise of regulatory agencies, in particular, gives the lie to any claims of a declining role for the state. It also relates to the broader issue, discussed in Chapter 3, of whether professional influence on public policy is increasing as the decision-making scope of government secretaries is increasingly circumscribed by non-departmental bodies.

Recruitment

Recruitment is a key theme in the debate about bureaucracies; the means by which bureaucrats are selected, and the kinds of people employed, are studied more carefully than is the case with the private sector. Here the main difference is between **unified** and **departmental** recruitment; the former is based on recruitment to the bureaucracy as a whole, and the latter on recruitment to specific departments based on technical skills. Britain exemplifies the unified approach, pushing the cult of the amateur to extremes. Administration is seen as the art of judgement, born of intelligence and matured by experience. Specialist knowledge should be sought by bureaucrats but then treated with scepticism; experts should be on tap but not on top. A good administrator is expected to serve in a variety of departments and is considered more rounded for having done so. Given this philosophy, it is natural for recruits to be sought for the civil service as a whole, not for a particular department.

> **Unified recruitment:** An approach based on recruitment to the civil service as a whole, not to a specific job within it, and in which administrative work is conceived as requiring intelligence and education, rather than technical knowledge.

> **Departmental recruitment:** An approach based on recruiting people with technical backgrounds to a specific department or job.

An alternative method of pursuing the unified approach is to recruit to a *corps* (body) of civil servants, rather than to a specific job in a ministry. France is an example of this approach. It recruits civil servants through competitive examinations to such bodies as the Diplomatic Corps and the Finance Inspectorate. Although recruitment is to a specific *corps* with a specialized title, it is as much an enrolment into an elite encompassing both public and private realms. Even within the civil service, more than one-third of *corps* members are working away from their home *corps* at any one time. At its highest levels, the French bureaucracy is clearly generalist, albeit within a *corps* framework that recognizes specialized training.

Some unified bureaucracies stress one particular form of technical expertise: law. In many European countries with a codified law tradition, legal training is common among higher bureaucrats. Germany is a leading case (and one which provided the context for Weber's thinking); there, most top bureaucrats are lawyers.

In the departmental recruitment model, recruiters look for specialist experts for individual departments; so the finance department will employ economists and the health department will employ staff with medical training. Recruitment is to particular posts, not to an elite civil service or a *corps*. When staff leave, they often move to similar jobs in the private sector rather than to different departments in government.

This emphasis on specific jobs and specialist expertise is common in countries with a weak state in which the administration lacks the status produced by centuries of service to pre-democratic rulers. The Netherlands, New Zealand, and the United States are examples. In the Netherlands, for instance, each department sets its own recruitment standards, usually requiring prior training and expertise in its own area. Once appointed, worker mobility is limited: staff who remain in public service typically stay in the same department for their entire career (Andeweg and Irwin, 2009: 176). The notion of recruiting talented young graduates to an elite, unified civil service, or even to a *corps*, is weak or non-existent.

One exception to the general rule of selection on merit is **affirmative action**, found in countries that have worked to address the dominating position in the higher levels of the bureaucracy of men from the major ethnic group and from middle- or upper-class families with a background in public affairs (Aberbach *et al.*, 1981: 80).

SPOTLIGHT

JAPAN

Brief Profile: Japan is a leading example of a state where Western ideas of liberal democracy have been grafted onto a society with its own distinctive traditions. Notable for its long history of isolation (helped by its physical isolation from the Asian continent), and for its reinvention following defeat in the Second World War, Japan is modern but not Western, its experience proving that it is possible for a society to advance economically and technologically without losing sight of its identity. The most obvious signs of its modernity can be found in its economic and technological development; it is the third largest economy in the world, and a major source of global capital and credit, as well as home to many of the world's major corporations. Its political system has, however, been compromised by traditional Japanese ideas about faction, obligation, and group identity, and by the long-time dominance of a single political party, the Liberal Democrats.

Population (126 million)

Gross National Income ($4,920 billion)

Per capita GNI ($46,330)

Democracy Index rating

| Not Rated | Hybrid Regime | Full Democracy |
| | Authoritarian | Flawed Democracy |

Freedom House rating

Not Free   Partly free   Free

Human Development Index rating

| Not Rated | Medium | Very High |
| | Low | High |

Form of government ⇨ Unitary parliamentary democracy with a ceremonial emperor. Date of state formation debatable, and most recent constitution adopted 1947.

Legislature ⇨ Bicameral Diet: lower House of Representatives (480 members) elected for renewable four-year terms, and upper House of Councillors (242 members), which is less significant.

Executive ⇨ Parliamentary. The head of government is the prime minister, who is head of the largest party or coalition, and governs in conjunction with a cabinet. The head of state is the emperor.

Judiciary ⇨ The 15-member Supreme Court possesses the power of judicial review but has proved unassertive. Unusually, the Court's justices are directly appointed by the cabinet, and subject to voter confirmation at the first general election that follows, and every ten years thereafter, with mandatory retirement at age 70.

Electoral system ⇨ Mixed member majoritarian system: 300 members of the lower house are elected using single-member plurality, and 180 through party list proportional representation (PR). In the upper house, 146 elected using single non-transferable vote, and 96 through PR.

Parties ⇨ Multi-party. Long dominated by the conservative Liberal Democratic party (LDP). The Democratic Party is more socially liberal, the Innovation Party is nationalist, and Japan still has an active Communist Party.

The goal here has been to make the bureaucracy more representative of the wider population, by gender, race, education, and economic background. In a logic related to the idea of descriptive representation in legislatures (see Chapter 8), there are various arguments in favour:

- Bureaucrats whose work involves direct contact with a specific group will perform better at the job if they themselves belong to that group.

- A public sector drawn from a range of religions and regions will encourage stability in divided societies.

The bureaucracy in Japan

The Japanese bureaucracy is probably more touted than any other bureaucracy in the world, write Rosenbluth and Thies (2014: 321). It is accorded an important place in the country's remarkably rapid post-war economic growth, a role it played while remaining relatively small, but having the advantage of enjoying a high status and the capacity to motivate its recruits with the thought of good post-retirement jobs in the private sector and local government. It is also remarkably selective: in 2009, for example, only 600 people of the 22,000 who took the entrance exam for the higher civil service were hired.

The philosophy of the Japanese bureaucracy is unified, rather than departmental, but movement between departments is rare. Each group of recruits forms a cohort within a ministry, progressing through the hierarchy but with a smaller proportion achieving promotion to the next level; the convention is that staff should not expect to serve under anyone recruited later than they were.

The bureaucracy undoubtedly played a substantial role in post-war reconstruction, and was closely intertwined with the governing Liberal Democratic Party as well as big business. In the post-war decades of high growth, Japan provided the pre-eminent example of how a small, merit-based bureaucracy, operating largely on the basis of persuasion, could guide rapid economic development within a mainly market framework. But this changed in the 1990s, against a background of state-led deflation and the involvement of bureaucrats in bribery cases, scandals which made some large companies more wary of hiring retired bureaucrats. More fundamentally, civil servants could no longer offer the same strategic direction to industry in a global economy, given that the largest companies now operated on a world scale and some overseas corporations had become established in Japan.

Reflecting these developments, as well as a desire to improve coordination, the central bureaucracy was reorganized in 2001, with the number of departments reduced from 22 to 12. The Japan Fair Trade Commission acquired a more extensive role in enforcing competition, signalling greater emphasis on the interests of consumers, rather than those of the large, export-oriented manufacturers which had emerged during Japan's high-growth phase.

- A diverse and representative bureaucracy, involving participation by all major social groups, will enhance the acceptability of decisions among the public at large.
- Employment of minorities in the public sector will ripple through the labour market, including private companies.

Affirmative action: Policies designed to overcome the legacy of past discrimination by emphasizing the recruitment of women, ethnic minorities, and other groups under-represented in the bureaucracy.

In the 1960s and 1970s, considerable efforts were made in the United States to ensure that staff profiles matched those of the wider population. The stimulus here was an order by President Johnson, in 1965, that all government agencies must introduce affirmative action policies. Something similar happened in Canada, where governments were concerned to improve recruitment from French speakers. However, such schemes never achieved the same popularity in Europe, perhaps because they would have involved accepting the inadequacy of the constitutional requirement of neutrality imposed on some civil services. The Weberian philosophy of recruitment on merit was preserved.

At least in democracies, women today make up a larger percentage of the workforce in government than in the general labour force (see Figure 10.6). This has been the result not just of affirmative action but also of efforts by government to offer more flexible working conditions, paid parental leave, subsidised childcare, and other benefits that make it easier for women to work. Unfortunately, women in most bureaucracies are still over-represented in secretarial, part-time, and social care positions, and under-represented at the higher managerial and policy-influencing levels (OECD, 2013: 122).

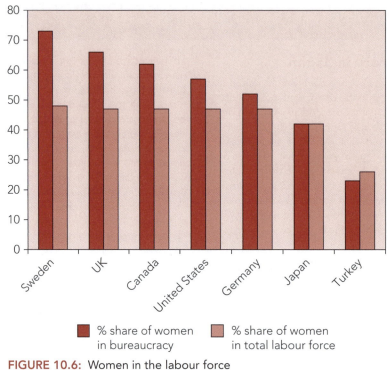

FIGURE 10.6: Women in the labour force

Source: Adapted from International Labour Organization, quoted in OECD (2013: 121). Figures are for 2011.

New public management

'Government is not the solution to the problem', Ronald Reagan once famously declared; 'government is the problem.' This sentiment was one of the inspirations behind a revised and market-oriented approach to bureaucracy that came to be known as **new public management** (NPM), a creed which swept through the Anglo-American world of public management in the final decade of the twentieth century.

> **New public management:** A new approach to bureaucracy that emerged in the 1980s, and was based on the idea that a market-oriented approach would make it more efficient.

Although now past its peak, NPM remains interesting as a critique of Weber's ideas about bureaucracy. It attracted even those who did not share Reagan's conservative perspective, and was spoken of warmly by international bodies such as the Organisation for Economic Co-operation and Development (OECD). It led to radical change in the public sectors of Australia, Britain, Canada, and New Zealand, and it provides the

backdrop against which the less fervent reforms of the twenty-first century have developed.

It is summarized neatly by Osborne and Gaebler's best-selling 1992 book *Reinventing Government*, which came with the subtitle *How the Entrepreneurial Spirit Is Transforming the Public Sector*. Where Weber's model of bureaucracy was based on ideas of efficiency drawn from the Prussian army, Osborne and Gaebler were inspired by the more freewheeling world of American business, and they outlined ten principles that government agencies were advised to adopt in order to enhance their effectiveness. These included promoting competition between service providers, measuring performance through outcomes rather than inputs, redefining clients as customers, and decentralizing authority.

The underlying theme was the gains achievable by giving public servants the flexibility to manage by results. The significance of this empowerment, in turn, was the break it represented with Weber's view that the job of a bureaucrat was simply to apply fixed rules to cases. The role model for NPM was the entrepreneur rather than the judge. For its supporters, NPM was public management for a new century; Weber's model was

FOCUS 10.2 | Keeping bureaucrats accountable

Max Weber warned of the difficulties of keeping bureaucrats accountable, and of preventing them from obstructing the goals of elected governments. Commentators continue to recognize that the bureaucracy's expertise, permanence, scale, and control of implementation mean that it is bound to be more than a mere conduit for political directives. Increasingly, the philosophy pursued by democratic governments is to encourage bureaucrats to defend their behaviour after the fact, rather than to seek pre-emptive control over the actions themselves. In this way, accountability both acknowledges and potentially defuses Weber's fear of bureaucratic power – a neat move all round.

Senior officials are accountable not only to ministers in their own departments, but also to the prime minister, the finance ministry, and to the obligations inherent in agreements with other national, and even international, organizations. For the highest officials, accountability extends beyond the private world of government to external bodies. Because they control the purse strings, legislatures can exert control over bureaucrats, who are increasingly willing to report back to select committees on their work. The judiciary is another external arena in which the bureaucracy can be called to account. Finally, outsourcing has helped changed the channels of accountability, because issuing and renewing contracts is tied directly to performance.

A distinctively European tool that has much unmet potential is the **ombudsman**. A public watchdog that investigates claims of maladministration, the first ombudsman was created in Sweden in 1809, but the idea was not emulated elsewhere until much later: 1919 in Finland, after 1945 in other liberal democracies, and 1995 in the European Union. They are now found in about 90 countries, but most work at the local or sectional level; states with a national ombudsman include Argentina, Australia, Botswana, Gambia, Indonesia, New Zealand, Nigeria, Peru, and most European countries. A single advocate may cover the entire public sector or, at the risk of reducing visibility and overlapping jurisdictions, separate commissioners may be appointed for specific areas. So far, ombudsmen outside Scandinavia have neither been given strong powers of investigation nor is the public widely aware of their existence (Ansell and Gingrich, 2003). In the search for bureaucratic accountability, this gap is unfortunate.

Ombudsman: A public official appointed by a legislature to investigate allegations of maladministration in the public sector.

dismissed as history. Public administration, it was alleged, had been displaced by public management.

In the history of NPM, New Zealand stands out as the pioneer. In the 1980s and 1990s, it undertook what was probably 'the most comprehensive and radical set of reforms of any Western democracy' (Pollitt and Bouckaert, 2011: 302). A coalition of business leaders, government economists, and senior politicians from both major parties came together to force through unpopular but far from inconsequential reforms. One particular feature of the new model was its massive use of contracts, going far beyond the standard fare of using private firms to supply local services, such as refuse collection. Instead, private suppliers were contracted to

address even such sensitive areas as debt collection. By such means, the number of bureaucrats in New Zealand was reduced from 88,000 in 1988 to 37,000 in 1994 (even if some were simply reallocated to other segments of the public sector). In addition, contracts were introduced within New Zealand's public sector to govern the relationships between purchasers (e.g. the Transport Department) and providers (e.g. Transit New Zealand, responsible for roads).

What lessons can be learned from the New Zealand experience? Mulgan (1997: 146) concluded that it led to 'greater clarity of government functions and to increased efficiencies in the provision of certain services to the public', but also that it was expensive in the amount of resources consumed by the reform process and in the added problems of coordination caused by the increased number of public agencies. But the wide-ranging and sometimes diffuse nature of NPM reforms makes precise evaluation difficult: effects have varied by country, reform, and sector. Overall, its biggest contribution was probably a change in thinking, and promotion of 'visions of privatization, marketization, participation, deregulation, and flexibility' (Pollitt and Bouckaert, 2011: 156).

E-government

New public management has been replaced by a new flavour of bureaucratic potential in the shape of **e-government**, or the use of the internet to provide public services. The idea is that the internet has created new channels for communication among and between governments, government departments, and citizens. Some caution is needed: the overselling of NPM suggests that we need to be careful about making too many claims about the possibilities of e-government, and that we need to recognize that anticipated efficiency gains often disappear as new channels supplement old ones without replacing them. We also need to be aware that while e-government can ease citizen access to government departments and to public information, as well as reducing government costs and providing a boost to the digital services industry, it also carries the increased risk of cyberattacks on governments, and can make it easier for governments to keep an eye on citizens. But a combination of outsourcing and e-government could mean that we are in the middle of a revolution in the operation of bureaucracy, the full consequences of which might only become clear decades from now.

> **E-government (or digital era governance):** The use of information and communication technology to provide public services.

It is clear that e-government is most advanced in wealthier countries with the best telecommunications infrastructure. Table 10.2 shows the top ten countries ranked for e-government readiness in a periodic survey compiled by the UN Public Administration Network. The other side of the coin is e-participation, or the extent to which citizens use online services. E-government is no longer new, but it is constantly evolving, and its implications are not yet fully understood. What *is* clear, however, is that there is a digital divide not only between rich countries and poor, but also between the connected and the unconnected within countries.

Australia provides an example. While it has one of the most digitally connected governments in the world,

TABLE 10.2: The world's top ten countries for e-government

1	South Korea	6	Japan
2	Australia	7	United States
3	Singapore	8	Britain
4	France	9	New Zealand
5	Netherlands	10	Finland

Source: UN Public Administration Network (2015). Ranking is for 2014, and based on the availability of online services, the quality of telecommunications infrastructure, and overall education levels.

with policies to expand e-government dating back to the mid-1990s, it has also found exclusion based not just on technological capacity but also on a host of social and economic barriers such as poverty. Australia is also a large country with a few large concentrations of population, and small and widely dispersed rural populations that are not easy to reach. The irony in Australia, as in many other countries, is that those most likely to benefit from access to e-government are also those least likely to have such access (Baum, 2014).

At least for citizen-facing departments, there is something in the proposition that the government department has become its website. Technology has created unprecedented opportunities for states to store, integrate, and analyse information about their populations. As with other political resources, these facilities can be used for purposes benign, malevolent, or both.

Four stages have been identified in the development of e-government (Baum and Di Maio, 2000; Montargil, 2010). The first is the provision of information, perhaps with a website outlining the details of a public service. This is useful, not least for people looking for basic information on the work of a department or agency. The second stage involves interaction, perhaps by downloading a form or sending an email, while the third stage involves a transaction, such as paying a bill online or submitting an application.

The final stage is integration, the most demanding and significant for the bureaucracy. Integration means that, in principle, all government services – from applying for a driving licence to registering a business – can be accessed from one site, with a single registration and digital signature. But such portals, or electronic one-stop shops, are difficult to implement, requiring the integration of databases from multiple departments. It is worth noting here that the highly detailed and coordinated nature of such work is far removed from the entrepreneurial activity expected of the new public manager.

Integration creates opportunities for public services to be more proactive. If your year of birth and address are available across government, then, as you move through life, the transport department can send you information about applying for a driving licence, the interior ministry can supply a voter registration form, and the health service can send home testing kits for age-related illnesses. Similarly, linking school records to a national database of children could help to locate children who have moved elsewhere. In such ways, e-government can give effect to joined-up government.

The biggest concerns with e-government relate to the loss of privacy, the new opportunities for political misuse such as the unauthorized transfer of data to third parties (including private companies and foreign states), and the heightened danger posed by hacking and the new targets offered to terrorists to interfere with government services. Public suspicion of e-government is heightened by awareness that private electronic records – such as text messages, phone calls, and internet use – can also be accessed by government in response to security threats. Privacy and data protection codes, such as the European Union's comprehensive Directive on Data Protection (1998), offer only limited reassurance. Access to one's own personal records allows accuracy to be checked but does not prevent misuse.

In practice, the success of integrated e-government is likely to depend on the extent to which citizens trust their present and future governments, and the extent to which hacking can be controlled. Cynical citizens may prefer personal information to be kept in departmental paper files, or even not to be recorded at all.

Bureaucracies in authoritarian states

We saw in Chapters 8 and 9 that most of the institutions that form the basis of power and government in democracies are weaker or more marginalized in authoritarian systems. There are two key exceptions to this general rule: the military and the bureaucracy. By definition, institutions of representation – elections, competitive parties, and freely organized interest groups – are weak in authoritarian systems, because control is top-down rather than bottom-up; but while

dictators can manipulate or even dispense with elections or legislatures, they cannot rule without officials to give effect to their will.

The case of Nigeria under military rule offers an example. Early military administrations (1966–79) governed through two bodies: a Supreme Military Council (SMC) made up of selected senior officers and which functioned as the principal policy-making forum, and a Federal Executive Council made up of senior federal bureaucrats which was responsible for implementing the decisions of the SMC. Much the same happened during the second military era (1983–99), with the difference that the SMC was renamed the Armed Forces Ruling Council. A military coup does not itself overcome a recurring feature of Nigerian politics, namely the relatively small pool of qualified and experienced individuals from which the bureaucracy can draw.

The bureaucracy can be more than a dictator's service agency; often in conjunction with the military, it can itself become a leading political force, claiming that its technical expertise and ability to resist popular pressure is the only route to long-term economic development. This assertion may have superficial merit but many bureaucracies in authoritarian regimes eventually become bloated, over-politicized, and inefficient, acting as a drag on further progress. In the long run, bureaucratic regimes, as with military governments, become part of the problem rather than the solution.

Certainly, the bureaucracy has played a positive role in most authoritarian regimes experiencing rapid economic growth. In the 1950s and 1960s, it helped to foster economic modernization in several regimes in the Middle East and North Africa. The term **bureaucratic authoritarianism** was even coined (O'Donnell, 1973) to describe the phenomenon by which the bureaucracy in Latin American countries such as Argentina and Brazil ruthlessly pursued economic reform, with cover provided by repressive military leadership. The high-performing economies of East Asia, such as Indonesia and Malaysia, offer more recent examples of the contribution that the bureaucracy can make to development in largely authoritarian settings.

> **Bureaucratic authoritarianism:** Regimes in which technocrats in the bureaucracy impose economic stability within a capitalist framework under the protection of a military government.

The concept overlaps with that of the **developmental state**, which describes a state in which government intervenes heavily in the economy through regulation and planning, relying on an efficient bureaucracy. First used to describe Japan (Johnson, 1982), and situations in which a country that was late to industrialize was pushed by active government intervention, the term has since been used more broadly to describe countries where economic policy is guided and overseen by powerful bureaucratic elites; examples include China, Indonesia, Malaysia, the Philippines, Thailand, and Vietnam. Following the Japanese and South Korean model, most of these developmental states have seen rapid economic progress as well as democratization, and hence this list includes a mix of democratic and authoritarian systems. The contrast here is with so-called predatory states, which extract resources and provide little of value in return to their people (Evans, 1995). The broader point is that, with an eye to the long term, a government can use what might seem to be quasi-authoritarian means to push a country to a new level of economic development, generating growth that might then induce pressures to democratize.

> **Developmental state:** One in which the state makes active and deliberate efforts to modernize and industrialize a society.

But these instances of the bureaucracy instigating successful modernization are the exception. More often, the bureaucracy has inhibited, rather than encouraged, growth. The twentieth-century experience of sub-Saharan Africa provides a more sobering example: authoritarian leaders often used their control over public appointments as a political reward, denying the delicate distinction between politics and administration. This cavalier approach to public appointments even extended to absorbing excess labour, especially among new graduates, into the administration. Public sector expansion was used as a method of buying support, or at least preventing the emergence of opposition.

The outcome was uncontrolled growth of the bureaucracy. By the early 1990s, public employment accounted for most non-agricultural employment in much of Africa (Smith, 2009: 221). Once appointed, public employees found that ties of kinship meant that they were duty-bound to use their privileged positions to reward their families and ethnic group, producing further employment growth.

The bloated bureaucracy that resulted proved incapable of acting as an effective instrument for development. Rather, the administrative class extracted resources from society for its own benefit – in that sense, continuing rather than replacing the colonial model. With the main source of national wealth (e.g. commodity exports) under state control, public employment became the highway to riches, creating a bureaucratic bourgeoisie. Only relatively recently, under pressure from international agencies, have attempts made to rein in the public sector through an emphasis on building **administrative capacity** (Turner and Hulme, 1997: 90).

> **Administrative capacity:** The ability of a bureaucracy to address social problems through effective management and implementation of public policy.

Even where bureaucracy-led development has succeeded, the formula has often outlasted its usefulness. Several East Asian states discovered at the end of the twentieth century that public administrators were more effective at building industrial capacity than at managing a mature, open economy with an expanding number of small service companies. In Indonesia, for example, the Asian financial crisis of the late 1990s exposed the extent to which investment patterns had been distorted by **crony capitalism**, with access to capital depending more on official contacts than on rates of return.

> **Crony capitalism:** A phenomenon in which economic development is based on a close relationship between government officials and business leaders, reflected in special tax breaks and favouritism in issuing contracts, permits, or grants.

The position of the bureaucracy in communist systems in some ways echoed its role in authoritarian regimes more generally. However, one key difference was the sheer scale of the bureaucracy under communist rule. To achieve its theoretical mission of building a new society, the ruling party had to control all aspects of development, both economic and social, through the state. Most obviously, the private sector disappeared and the economy became an aspect of state administration. In these circumstances, the party tried to pacify the bureaucracy in the same way that it controlled the armed forces: by controlling all major appointments.

In discussion of authoritarian regimes, the bureaucracy receives less attention than it deserves. The reason is understandable: such regimes are typically founded on a personal relationship between president and people. This implicit contract works against the strengthening of rule-governed institutions, including a bureaucracy. Authoritarian regimes are political in nature, rather than bureaucratic.

Further, authoritarian rulers often present themselves in opposition to institutions such as the civil service. In Latin America, particularly, administrators frequently imitated the haughty remoteness of their long-gone colonial predecessors, producing a corrupt and unresponsive bureaucracy which provided a convenient target for populist politicians. Such rulers need enemies, and an inflexible civil service provides one. When the political leader of a authoritarian regime can secure the financial benefits from natural resources such as oil, he can spend these resources on maintaining a viable political coalition through informal patronage, thus further weakening the civil service. (See discussion of the resource curse in Chapter 18.)

In Venezuela, for instance, Hugo Chávez introduced a new constitution in 1999 which defined the country's political system as 'democratic, participatory, elective, decentralized, responsible to the people, pluralist, based on term limits for elected officials and revocable mandates' (Alvarez, 2004: 152). The pretensions and inherent uncertainties of this new constitution contributed nothing to building an effective bureaucracy, instead concentrating attention on the political realm and on Chávez himself. His own local committees could distribute resources to his base in the shanty towns, securing a greater political gain than if the same resources were made available through a rule-based bureaucracy.

Russia's authoritarian regime also shows an ambivalent relationship to the official bureaucracy. Certainly, Russia's presidents have drawn on – rather than defined themselves in opposition to – the country's long tradition of state power. But in the post-communist era,

securing control over these bureaucratic agencies has not been easy. In contrast to most liberal democracies, Russia never developed an integrated public bureaucracy with standard rules and merit-based appointments. Under communism, party and state became so intertwined that the collapse of the former came close to bringing down the latter. In the chaotic early years of post-communism, provision of public services inevitably devolved to the local level, fragmenting the administration of a large, diverse country.

The Civil Service Act (1995) did introduce more uniform provisions across the public sector, including for example a rigid grading structure, but the operation of Russia's bureaucracy still falls short of Weber's standards. Even today, the legacy of inefficiency and corruption renders most of Russia's bureaucracy far less professional and responsive than its liberal democratic equivalent.

In an attempt to resolve these problems, Russia's post-communist presidents have developed a massive constellation of supervisory agencies, based in or reporting to the Kremlin. By 2009, the president's Executive Office contained 15 separate units, staffed mainly by loyal, competent, and reliable supporters. These offices include the Presidential Control Directorate which 'oversees and checks that federal laws, decrees, orders and other presidential decisions are enforced by the federal executive bodies of power, the regional authorities, and organizations' (President of Russia, 2009). Frequent reorganization of the Executive Office suggests that its success remains incomplete.

To some extent, however, such efforts are undermined by the very nature of elite politics in Russia's authoritarian system. Clans of influential oligarchs operating in and around the presidency seek favourable business judgements in a manner which pays little heed to the requirements of bureaucratic, rule-based governance.

DISCUSSION QUESTIONS

- What images most immediately come to mind when you think of bureaucrats, and to what extent do you think those images reflect reality?

- Outsourcing: good idea or bad? Are there some services that cannot or should not be carried out by private contractors? If so, which ones and why?

- What is the best strategy for reducing the under-representation of women and minorities in the bureaucratic workforce?

- To what extent are outsourcing and e-government revolutionizing the idea of bureaucracy? Are the changes good or bad?

- Think of some examples of regulatory agencies in your country. Are they, and should they be, politically accountable?

- Have you personally experienced e-government, and how has it altered your view of bureaucracy?

KEY TERMS

Administrative capacity	Meritocracy
Affirmative action	New public management
Bureaucracy	Non-departmental public body
Bureaucratic authoritarianism	Ombudsman
Crony capitalism	Outsourcing
Department	Red tape
Departmental recruitment	Regulatory agency
Developmental state	Spoils system
Division	Unified recruitment
E-government	

FURTHER READING

Hummel, Ralph P. (2014) *The Bureaucratic Experience: The Post-Modern Challenge*, 5th edn. Argues that despite talk of bureaucratic reform, its organizational structure continues to remain mainly unchanged.

Mulgan, Richard (2003) *Holding Power to Account: Accountability in Modern Democracies*. A thoughtful discussion of the concept of accountability.

Nixon, Paul G., Vassiliki N. Koutrakou, and Rajash Rawal (eds) (2010) *Understanding E-Government in Europe: Issues and Challenges*. The mainly thematic chapters in this book examine the impact of information and communication technology on governance in Europe.

Peters, B. Guy (2016) *The Politics of Bureaucracy: An Introduction to Comparative Public Administration*, 7th edn. A widely used comparative introduction to bureaucracy.

Peters, B. Guy and Jon Pierre (eds) (2004) *The Politicization of the Civil Service in Comparative Perspective*. Country-based chapters address issues such as compensation, external appointments and partisanship in the bureaucracies of liberal democracies.

Pollitt, Christopher and Geert Bouckaert (2011) *Public Management Reform – A Comparative Analysis: New Public Management, Governance, and the Neo-Weberian State*, 3rd edn. A detailed analysis of changes in public management in Australasia, Europe, and North America.

11 Sub-national government

PREVIEW

The comparison of political systems focuses mostly on activities at the national level, but it can just as easily focus on more localized activities, and involve comparison of regional, city, and local governments. The functional equivalents of national executives, legislatures, and courts can all be found at the regional level, at least in federal systems, and no understanding of politics and government in a given state can be complete without looking at the full picture. Unfortunately, sub-national politics tends to attract less interest among voters, who – for example – tend to turn out at regional and local elections in much smaller numbers than at national elections. This is ironic, given that many of the services that most immediately impact their lives come from sub-national government, and local officials are usually more accessible than their national counterparts.

This chapter begins with a review of the concept of multilevel governance, which describes the many horizontal and vertical interactions that often exist among different tiers of government. It then looks at the two most common models for the functioning of systems of national government: unitary and federal. Unitary systems are found in most countries, but many people live under federal governments because most of the world's largest countries are federations. The chapter then compares and contrasts unitary and federal systems before looking at the structures and functions of local government. It ends with a review of the dynamics of sub-national government in authoritarian regimes, where – more often than not – the periphery is marginal to the centre.

CONTENTS

KEY ARGUMENTS

- Multilevel governance is a framework for examining the relationships among different levels of administration (supranational, national, regional, and local).

- Most countries in the world use a unitary form of government, in which regional and local units are subsidiary to national government.

- Other countries are federal, made up of two or more levels of government with independent powers. But there is no uniform template for a federal system, and federations come in many different forms.

- Although the constitutional contrasts between unitary and federal systems are clear, unitary states are just as tiered as federal states – and often more so. The strengthening of regional government is a significant trend within unitary states.

- Local government is still the place where the citizen most often meets the state. Regrettably understudied, its organization and functioning raise some interesting questions, including the enabling authority of elected mayors.

- Sub-national government in authoritarian states has less formal power and independence than its democratic equivalent, but authoritarian rulers often depend on local leaders to sustain their grip on power.

Sub-national government: an overview

Sub-national government and politics describe the institutions and processes found below the level of the state. While national or central government (the terms are interchangeable) concerns itself with the interests of the entire state, and with the relationships that exist among sovereign states, sub-national government focuses almost entirely on domestic matters. It involves different kinds of mid-level government (states, provinces, or regions within a country), as well as local government units of the kinds found in towns, cities, and other localities, and coming under a variety of names, including counties, communes, prefectures, districts, boroughs, and municipalities.

Every country orders sub-national government in one of two ways: as a **unitary system** or as a **federal system**. In the former, national government has sole sovereignty, meaning that mid-level and local government exists at the pleasure of national government, with only as much power as is granted to it by the centre. In the latter, the national and regional governments possess independent existence and powers; neither level can abolish the other. There are many nuances in the manner in which unitary and federal systems are arranged; both types come in different varieties, a picture that is further complicated by federal systems that function more like unitary systems (such as Russia), and unitary systems that function more like federal systems (such as Britain and Spain).

> **Unitary system:** One in which sovereignty rests with the national government, and regional or local units have no independent powers.

> **Federal system:** One in which sovereignty is shared between two or more levels of government, each with independent powers and responsibilities.

About two dozen countries are constitutionally established as federations, but because they include almost all the largest countries (the most obvious exception being China), they contain a substantial share of the world's population: about 37 per cent to be exact. Nearly 90 per cent of the member states of the United Nations are unitary, but because many of them are so small, they are home to only 63 per cent of the world's population (or only 43 per cent if we exclude China).

The internal relationships within unitary states differ from those in federal states, as does the way in which citizens view government. In unitary systems, politics tends to be focused at the national level. Lower tiers still matter, but the most substantial political issues are national in scope, and there is more of a sense among citizens that they are part of the state political community. In federal systems, by contrast, the various local units have more independence, their agendas can achieve more prominence, and they matter more in the political calculations of citizens. Furthermore, because they have independent powers, states within federations have more leverage relative to national government than is the case in unitary systems.

Some of the states within federal systems are substantial political and economic units in their own rights. California, for example, has a bigger economy than India, Canada, Mexico, or Saudi Arabia. Meanwhile, the Indian state of Uttar Pradesh, with a population just short of 200 million, is the same size as Brazil and bigger than Japan or Russia. In short, sub-national government is an important part of comparative studies, it merits close consideration.

Multilevel governance

Multilevel governance (MLG) is a term used to describe how policy-makers and interest groups in liberal democracies, whether unitary or federal, find themselves discussing, persuading, and negotiating across multiple tiers in their efforts to deliver coherent policy in specific functional areas such as transport and education. The underlying argument is that no one level of government acting alone can resolve most policy problems, and thus that multiple levels must cooperate. MLG is defined by Schmitter (2004: 49) as follows:

> an arrangement for making binding decisions that engages a multiplicity of politically independent but otherwise interdependent actors – private and public – at different levels of territorial aggregation in more-or-less continuous negotiation/deliberation/implementation, and that does not assign exclusive policy competence or assert a stable hierarchy of political authority to any of these levels.

> **Multilevel governance:** An administrative system in which power is distributed and shared horizontally and vertically among different levels of government, from the supranational to the local, with considerable interaction among the parts.

Communication is not confined to officials working at the same or adjacent levels. Rather, international, national, regional, and local officials in a given sector will form their own policy networks, with interaction through all tiers (see Figure 11.1 for an illustration of MLG in the European Union). The use of the term 'governance' instead of 'government' directs our attention to these relationships between institutions, rather than simply the organizations themselves.

The idea of multilevel governance carries a further implication. As with pluralism, it recognizes that actors from a range of sectors – public, private, and voluntary – help to regulate society. In the field of education, for example, the central department will want to improve educational attainment in schools; but, to achieve its target, it will need to work not only with lower tiers within the public sector (such as education boards), but also with wider interests such as parents' associations, teachers' unions, private sector suppliers, and educational researchers.

In common with pluralism, MLG can be portrayed in a positive or negative light. On the plus side, it implies a pragmatic concern with finding solutions to shared problems through give-and-take among affected interests. On the negative side, it points to a complicated, slow-moving form of regulation by insider groups,

resisting both democratic control and penetration by less mainstream groups and thinking. Multilevel governance may be a fashionable term but its popularity should not lead us to assume that the form of rule it describes is optimal.

Understanding MLG requires an appreciation of the resources all tiers bring to the table. Typically, the national level has political visibility, large budgets and strategic objectives, but officials from lower levels will possess their own power cards: detailed knowledge of the problem and the ability to judge the efficacy of the remedies proposed. If lower tiers are both resourced and enthused, they can make a difference; if not, they may lose interest, limiting the ability of the centre to achieve its policy goals.

It would be wrong to infer that power in multilevel governance is merely the ability to persuade. Communication still operates in a constitutional framework that provides both limits and opportunities for representatives from each tier. If the constitution allocates responsibility for education to central government, local authorities are unlikely to build new schools unless the department of education signs the cheque. Thus, the formal allocation of responsibilities remains the rock on which multilevel governance is built; it develops from, without replacing, multilevel government.

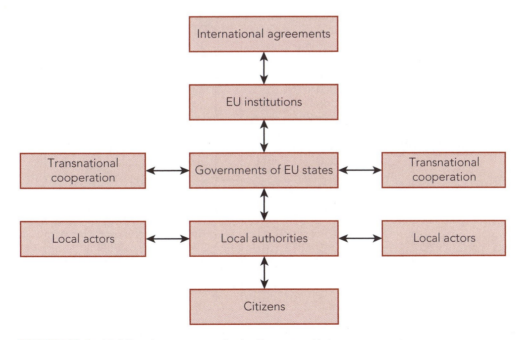

FIGURE 11.1: Multilevel governance in the European Union

Unitary systems

Most states in the world have a unitary form of government, meaning that while they have regional and local political institutions, sovereignty lies exclusively with the national government. Sub-national administrations, whether regional or local, can make and implement policy, but they do so by leave of the centre. And while sub-national government can adopt local laws and regulations, it can only do so on topics that are not the preserve of national government. Reflecting this central supremacy, the national legislature in most unitary states has only one chamber, since there is no need for a second house to represent entrenched provinces.

Unitary systems have emerged naturally in societies with a history of rule by sovereign monarchs and emperors, such as Britain, France, and Japan. In such circumstances, authority radiates from a historic core. Unitary structures are also the norm in smaller democracies, particularly those without strong ethnic divisions. In Latin America, nearly all the smaller countries (but neither of the two giants, Argentina and Brazil) are unitary. The countries of Eastern Europe have also chosen a unitary structure for their post-communist constitutions, viewing federalism as a spurious device through

which Russia tried to obscure its dominance of the Soviet Union.

In contrast to the complexities of federalism (discussed later in this chapter), a unitary structure may seem straightforward and efficient: there is one central government that holds all the cards that matter, other levels doing only what they are allowed to do by the centre. However, the location of sovereignty is rarely an adequate guide to political realities, because unitary government is often decentralized. Indeed, there has been an effort in recent decades in many unitary states to push responsibility for more functions to lower levels.

There are three ways in which this can happen (see Figure 11.2). The first is *deconcentration*, through which central government tasks are relocated from the capital to other parts of the country. Deconcentration spreads the work around, can help bring jobs and new income to poorer parts of the country, reduces costs by allowing activities to move to cheaper areas, and frees central departments to focus on policy-making rather than execution. So, for example, routine tasks such as issuing passports can be deconcentrated to an area with higher unemployment and lower costs. Deconcentration is made easier by the internet, because so much government work can be done online that geographical location has become less important.

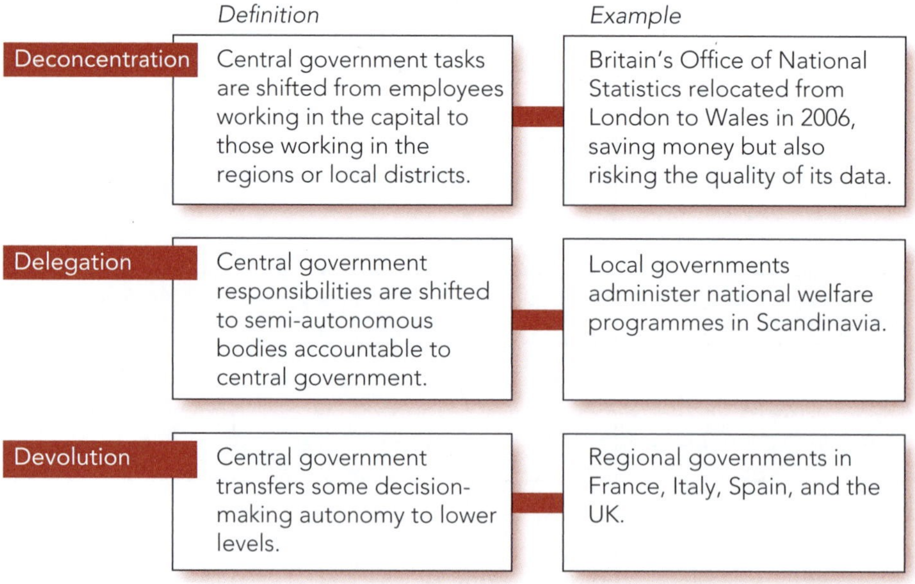

	Definition	*Example*
Deconcentration	Central government tasks are shifted from employees working in the capital to those working in the regions or local districts.	Britain's Office of National Statistics relocated from London to Wales in 2006, saving money but also risking the quality of its data.
Delegation	Central government responsibilities are shifted to semi-autonomous bodies accountable to central government.	Local governments administer national welfare programmes in Scandinavia.
Devolution	Central government transfers some decision-making autonomy to lower levels.	Regional governments in France, Italy, Spain, and the UK.

FIGURE 11.2: Dispersing power in unitary systems

Note: Deconcentration and decentralization occur in federal as well as unitary states.

The second and politically more significant way of dispersing power is through *delegation*. This involves transferring or delegating powers from central government to sub-national bodies, such as local authorities, and has been very much in favour in recent decades. Treisman (2007: 1) notes that, along with democracy, competitive markets, and the rule of law, this form of decentralized government 'has come to be seen as a cure for a remarkable range of political and social ills'. Sceptics raise doubts, however, noting that many policy problems – such as economic management – are better dealt with in a unified fashion at the national level.

Scandinavia is the classic example of delegation, where local governments put into effect many welfare programmes agreed at national level. Sweden in particular has seen an exceptional array of implementation tasks delegated by the national parliament (the Riksdag) to regional and local authorities. County councils focus in particular on health care and aspects of transport and tourism, while lower-level municipalities administer a wide range of responsibilities, including education, city planning, rescue services, water and sewage, waste collection and disposal, and civil defence. Together with transparency, accountability and autonomy for civil servants, such extensive delegation forms part of what has been described as the 'Swedish model' (Levin, 2009).

The third and most radical form of power dispersal is *devolution.* This occurs when the centre grants decision-making autonomy (including some legislative powers) to lower levels. Spain is an example here. Where once it was tightly controlled from the centre, its regions were strengthened in the transition to democracy following the death of Francisco Franco in 1975, and devolution has continued apace ever since. The Basque region in the north of the country possesses substantial self-government, and Catalonia in the east was recognized as a distinct nationality in 2006. Although Spain is often treated as a *de facto* federation, in theory its framework is unitary but devolved.

In the UK, too, the contrast with federations remains even after devolution. Britain is formally a unitary state, because although devolved assemblies were introduced in Northern Ireland in 1998 and in Scotland and Wales in 1999, they could theoretically be abolished by the national government in London through normal legislation. Because of problems stemming from the institution of the Northern Irish peace agreement, for example, the Northern Ireland Assembly was suspended between 2002 and 2007, and elections were postponed. This could not normally happen in a federal system. But the position of Scotland within the UK remains difficult and continues to pose a threat to the survival of the entire kingdom, whether federal or unitary. Although a referendum in Scotland on independence for the country was narrowly defeated in 2014, the pro-independence Scottish National Party swept the board in Scotland at the 2015 British general election, winning 56 of the 59 parliamentary seats there. The future of the 'United' Kingdom remains firmly on the agenda.

Regional government

The creation and expansion of the middle tier of government – the regional level – has been an important trend in many unitary states. In a study of 42 mainly high-income countries between 1950 and 2006, Hooghe *et al.* (2010: 54) found that 29 saw an increase in regional authority compared with only two showing a decline. The larger the country, the more powerful this middle tier tended to be. As a result of these developments, unitary states such as France, Italy, and Poland now have three levels of sub-national government: **regional**, provincial, and local (Table 11.1). By contrast, China has gone further, with five levels ranging from provinces to villages. The result is an intricate multilevel system of government.

TABLE 11.1: Sub-national government in unitary states

	France	Italy	UK	Poland	Sweden	China
Highest tier	26	20	3	16	—	33
Middle tier	100	103	35	314	20	2,862
Lowest tier	36,683	8,101	434	2,478	290	41,636

Source: European data from Loughlin *et al.* (2011: appendix)

In origin, many regions were merely spatial units created by the centre to present figures on inequalities within a country and to spark policies to reduce them. But in most large unitary states, specific regional organizations were soon established, and became an administrative vehicle through which the centre could decentralize planning. Regional bodies took responsibility for economic development and related public infrastructure; notably, transport. These bodies were not always directly elected, and were typically created by a push from the centre, rather than a pull from the regions. Regions now provide a valuable middle-level perspective below that of the country as a whole but above that of local areas. Amalgamation of local governments can achieve some of the same effect but often at greater political cost, given the importance of traditional communities to many inhabitants.

A key factor influencing the development of regional institutions is whether or not they are directly elected. Election enhances visibility but, for better or worse, political and partisan factors come to intrude more directly into their operations. France is an example of this transition. The 22 regional councils established there in 1972 at first possessed extremely limited executive powers. However, their status was enhanced by a decentralization law passed in 1982 providing for direct election. The first round of these elections took place in 1986. Even though French regional bodies continue to operate with small budgets, they have won greater visibility and authority.

The case for direct election is perhaps strongest where regions are already important cultural entities, providing a focus for citizens' identities. In the United Kingdom, for example, the national government succeeded in establishing regional assemblies in Scotland, Wales, and Northern Ireland, where national loyalties were well established, but failed to generate much enthusiasm for its efforts to create elected regional assemblies in England.

The European Union has encouraged the development of a regional level within its member states. The European Regional Development Fund, established in 1975, distributes aid directly to regions, rather than through central governments. The EU went further in 1988 by introducing a Committee of the Regions composed of sub-national authorities. But this proved to be merely consultative, and national executives remain more central to the policy process than the more committed proponents of regional governance in the EU had envisaged.

Federal systems

In contrast to unitary systems of government, where power rests at the national level, sovereignty and power in federal systems are shared among different levels of government within a single state. By definition there must be at least two such levels, but there are typically three: national, regional, and local. (The terminology can be confusing: the national or central government is usually known as the federal government, and the regional governments are known variously as states, provinces, or in Germany and Austria as *Länder* – see Table 11.2.) Federalism usually works best either in large or deeply divided countries, and about two dozen countries meet the definition of a **federation**, including Brazil, India, Russia, and the United States. Despite its size and diversity, China remains unitary because this allows for tighter control by the Communist Party.

The key point about a federal partnership is that neither the national nor the regional tier can abolish the other, and it is this protected position of the regional governments – not the extent of their powers – that distinguishes federations from unitary states. Federations allocate specific functions to each tier, so that the centre usually takes charge of external relations (defence, foreign affairs, and immigration) as well as key domestic functions, such as the national currency. The states, meanwhile, are usually left in charge of education, law enforcement, and local government, and residual powers often lie with the states, not the centre (see Table 11.3). In nearly all federations, the states have a guaranteed voice in national policy-making through an upper chamber of the national legislature, in which each state normally receives equal or nearly equal representation.

There are two routes to a federation: the first – and most common – involves creating a new central authority for previously separate political units ('coming together'),

TABLE 11.2: The world's federations

	Year established as a federation	Population (world ranking)	Area (world ranking)	Number of units in federation
India	1947	2	7	29 states and 7 union territories
United States	1789	3	4	50 states and 1 capital district
Brazil	1891	5	5	26 states and 1 Federal District
Nigeria	1960	7	31	36 states and one Federal Capital Territory
Russia	1991	9	1	85 'subjects', including oblasts, republics, and 3 federal cities
Mexico	1810	11	13	31 states and 1 Federal District
Germany	1949	16	62	16 *Länder* (states)
Canada	1867	37	2	10 provinces and 3 territories
Australia	1901	52	6	6 states and 2 territories
Belgium	1993	76	137	3 regions
Switzerland	1848	98	132	26 cantons

Other federations

Austria	Micronesia	St Kitts and Nevis
Bosnia and Herzegovina	Pakistan	United Arab Emirates
Ethiopia	Palau	

Transitional or quasi-federations

Argentina	Iraq	Spain
Comoros	Malaysia	Sudan
Democratic Republic of Congo	South Africa	Venezuela

Source: Based on list in Watts (2008)

and the second involves transferring sovereignty from an existing national government to lower levels ('holding together'). Australia, Canada, Nigeria, Switzerland, and the United States are examples of the first kind, while Belgium is the main example of the second. First established in 1830, Belgium has been beset by divisions between its French- and Dutch-speaking regions. After constitutional revisions in 1970 and 1980, which devolved more power to these separate groups, the country finally became a federation in 1993, with three regions:

- Predominantly French-speaking Wallonia in the south, including a small German-speaking community.
- Dutch-speaking Flanders in the north.
- The Brussels region, centred on the bilingual but mainly French-speaking capital (see Map 11.1).

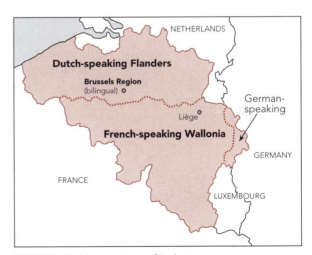

MAP 11.1: The regions of Belgium

TABLE 11.3: Comparing Canadian, German and Indian federations

	Canada	Germany	India
Exclusive jurisdiction – federal	29 functions, including criminal law, monetary policy, defence.	Includes defence, citizenship and immigration.	100 items, including defence, foreign affairs, trade, citizenship, and banking.
Exclusive jurisdiction – state/provincial	Control of 'all matters of a merely local or private nature'.	Few specific powers are explicitly granted to the *Länder*, which nonetheless implement federal laws 'in their own right'.	61 items, including policing, law and order, transport, and health care.
Shared jurisdiction	Both levels can pass laws dealing with agriculture and immigration.	Include criminal law and employment. The constitution also lists joint tasks, including agriculture.	47 items, including education, contracts, and transfer of property.
Residual – responsible level not specifically allocated by constitution	Federal parliament can make laws for the 'peace, order and good government of Canada'.	Any task not otherwise allocated remains with the *Länder*.	Any matter not listed as under shared or state responsibility remains with Parliament.

Variations on the theme of federalism

Just as there is no fixed template for a unitary system of government, so federations differ in terms of their internal dynamics. The baseline would be a symmetrical arrangement in which all the states within a union were similar in size, wealth, and influence, but this never happens. The reality is an **asymmetric federalism** which arises when some states are more powerful than others (because they are bigger or wealthier) or are given more autonomy than others, typically in response to cultural differences. In India, for example, Uttar Pradesh in India is 182 times bigger in terms of population than the state of Mizoram, while the Brazilian state of São Paulo is 88 times bigger than the state of Roraima. As an example of cultural asymmetry, Quebec nationalists in Canada have long argued for special recognition for their French-speaking province, viewing Canada as a compact between two 'equal' communities (English- and French-speaking, the former outnumbering the latter by 4:1) rather than as a contract between ten equal provinces.

Asymmetric federalism: The phenomenon of states within a federation having unequal levels of power and influence due to size, wealth, and other factors.

It was usual in most federations during the twentieth century for national governments to steadily gain power, helped by three main factors:

- The flow of money was more favourable to the centre as tax revenues grew with the expansion of economies and workforces. For independent revenue, states must depend on smaller and less dynamic sales and property taxes.
- National government benefited from the emergence of national economies demanding overall coordination.
- Wars and depressions empowered some national governments, while the post-1945 expansion of the welfare state enhanced European governments still further.

Since the 1980s, however, the trends have become less clear-cut. On the one hand, big projects run by the centre have gone out of fashion, partly because national governments have found themselves financially stretched in eras of lower taxation and financial crisis. On the other hand, the centre has still sought to provide overall direction.

Dual federalism: National and local levels of government function independently from one another, with separate responsibilities.

Cooperative federalism: The layers are intermingled and it is difficult always to see who has ultimate responsibility.

Where **dual federalism** provided the original inspiration for the US, Europe (and especially Germany and Austria) has found more appeal in the contrasting notion of **cooperative federalism**. Where the US

FOCUS 11.1 | The motives behind creating federations

The motives behind the creation of federations tend to be more often negative than positive; fear of the consequences of remaining separate must overcome the natural desire to preserve independence. Rubin and Feeley (2008: 188) suggest that federalism becomes a solution when, in an emerging state, 'the strong are not strong enough to vanquish the weak and the weak are not strong enough to go their separate ways'.

Historically, the main incentive for coming together has been to exploit the economic and military bonus of size, especially in response to strong competitors. Riker (1996) emphasized the military factor, arguing that federations emerge in response to an external threat. The 13 original American states, for instance, joined together partly because they felt vulnerable in a predatory world. However, US and Australian federalists also believed that a common market would promote economic development.

A more recent motivation has been ethnic federalism, as with the Belgian case. Further south, Switzerland integrates 26 cantons, four languages (German, French, Italian, and Romansh), and two religions (Catholic and Protestant) into a stable federal framework. But the danger with federalizing a divided society is that it can reinforce the divisions it was designed to accommodate. The risk is particularly acute when only two communities are involved, because the gains of one group are the losses of another. Federations are more effective when they cut across (rather than entrench) ethnic divisions, and when they marginalize (rather than reinforce) social divisions.

The challenges faced by Nigeria are illustrative. It became independent in 1960 with three regions, added a fourth in 1963, replaced them with 12 states in 1967, and has since cut the national cake into ever smaller pieces in an effort to prevent the development of powerful states based around particular ethnic groups. There are now 36 states and a Federal Capital Territory, and yet regionalism and ethnic divisions continue to handicap efforts to build a sense of Nigerian unity.

federation was based on a contract in which the states joined together to form a national government with limited functions, the European form rests on the idea of cooperation between levels, with a shared commitment to a united nation binding the participants together. The moral norm is solidarity and the operating principle is **subsidiarity**: the idea that decisions should be taken at the lowest feasible level. The national government offers overall leadership but implementation is the duty of lower levels: a division, rather than a separation, of tasks.

Subsidiarity: The principle that no task should be performed by a larger and more complex organization if it can be executed as well by a smaller, simpler body.

Since its inception in 1949, the Federal Republic of Germany has been based on interdependence, not independence. All the *Länder* (states) are expected to contribute to the success of the whole, and in return are entitled to respect from the centre. The federal government makes policy but the *Länder* implement it, a division of administrative labour expressed in the constitutional requirement that 'the *Länder* shall execute federal laws as

matters of their own concern'. But this cooperative ethos has come under increasing pressure from a growing perception that decision-making has become cumbersome and opaque. Constitutional reforms finalized in 2006 sought to establish clearer lines of responsibility between Berlin and the *Länder*, giving the states – for example – more autonomy in education and environmental protection. Although this package represents a move away from cooperative federalism towards greater subsidiarity, consultation remains embedded in German political practice.

The waters of federalism have been muddied by developments in several countries that have never legally declared themselves to be federations, but where the transfer of powers to regional units of government has resulted in a process of federalization. In Britain, for example, the creation in the 1990s of regional assemblies in Scotland, Wales, and Northern Ireland made all three more like states within a federal United Kingdom; all that is missing is an equivalent English regional assembly. In Argentina, Spain, and South Africa, too, powers have devolved to provinces and local communities without the formal creation of a federation, creating *de facto* federations or **quasi-federations**.

Quasi-federation: A system of administration that is formally unitary but has some of the features of a federation.

South Africa is an interesting case of a quasi-federation. When the Union of South Africa was created in 1910, it brought together four British colonies that had different and distinctive histories, and that might have followed the Australian and Canadian lead and formed a federation. Today the country has nine provinces, several of which have close historical and cultural links with important minorities: Afrikaners (white Africans with Dutch heritage) are associated with the Free State, Zulus (who still have their own king) with Kwazulu-Natal, and white South Africans with British heritage with the Eastern Cape and the Western Cape. The provinces have their own premiers and cabinets, and have powers over health, education, public housing, and transport, making them similar in many ways to states within a federation.

The final variation on the theme of federalism is a looser form of political cooperation known as a **confederation**. Where a federation is a unified state, within which power is divided between national and sub-national levels of government, and where there is a direct link between government and citizens (the national government exercises authority over citizens, and is answerable directly to the citizens), a confederation is a group of sovereign states with a central authority deriving its authority from those states, and citizens linked to the central authority through the states in which they live. The central authority remains the junior partner and acts merely as an agent of the component states, which retain their own sovereignty.

Confederation: A looser form of a federation, consisting of a union of states with more powers left in the hands of the constituent members.

While the number of federations worldwide has grown, there have been few examples in history of confederations, and none have lasted; they include the United States from 1781 to 1789, Switzerland from 1815 to 1848, and Germany from 1815 to 1866. The only political association that might today be described as a confederation is the European Union (see Lister, 1996). It is not a federal United States of Europe, but neither has it formally declared itself to be a confederation, leaving it literally nameless as a political form. Many commentators avoid giving it a label at all, simply describing it as sui generis, or unique. The extent

TABLE 11.4: Comparing the United States and the European Union

	United States	European Union
Founding document	A constitution	Treaties
Single federal government	Yes	No
Elected legislature	Yes	Yes
Single market (free movement of people, money, goods, services)	Yes	Incomplete
Single currency	Yes	In 18 of 28 states
Single legal citizenship	Yes	No
Federal tax	Yes	No
Common trade policy	Yes	Yes
Common foreign and defence policies	Yes	Much collaboration, but no common policies as such
Combined armed forces	Yes	No
Single seat at meetings of international organizations	Yes	Some, but not in United Nations, for example
Shared identity	Yes	Yes, but most Europeans identify primarily with their home state

to which it has or has not federalized is best illustrated through comparison; Table 11.4 contrasts the EU with the United States, showing some areas of similarity but others of marked contrast.

Comparing unitary and federal systems

As is almost always the case in comparative exercises, a review of unitary and federal systems reveals that both have their strengths and weaknesses, their advantages and disadvantages, and their particular idiosyncrasies. The case for unitary government is that it normally provides enough government and regulation for smaller societies, encourages a sense of national unity where citizens feel that they are all involved in the key public issues of the day, and makes sure that there are common standards and regulations. The case for federalism is that it offers a natural and practical arrangement for organizing large or divided states, providing checks and balances on a territorial basis, keeping some government functions closer to the people, and allowing for the representation of cultural, economic, and ethnic differences.

Federalism also reduces overload in the national executive, while the existence of multiple states or provinces produces healthy competition and opportunities for experiment. States can also move ahead even when the federal level languishes; hence while the federal government in the United States has been slow to respond to demands for action on same-sex marriage, climate change, gun control, and the legalization of marijuana, individual states have often gone ahead with their own responses. Citizens and businesses also have the luxury of choice inside a federal system: if they dislike governance in one state, or feel that it offers them only limited personal or employment opportunities, they can easily move to another.

But a case can also be mounted against federalism. Compared with unitary government, decision-making in a federation is complicated, slow-moving, and hesitant. When a gunman ran amok in the Australian state of Tasmania in 1996, killing 35 people, federal Australia experienced some political problems before it succeeded in tightening gun control uniformly across the country. An even worse outrage in 2012 in Newtown, Connecticut, which resulted in the deaths of 20 children and six staff, generated almost no significant change in policies outside the state of Connecticut. By contrast, unitary Britain acted speedily in banning guns when a comparable incident occurred in 1996 at a primary school in Dunblane, Scotland, resulting in the deaths of 16 children and one teacher.

Federalism can also place the political interests of rival governments above the resolution of shared problems. Fiscal discipline becomes harder to enforce, which is why several Latin American federations have struggled to control their free-spending (and free-riding) provinces. Extravagant spending by provinces – aware that they will be bailed out, if necessary, by the centre – can dent the fiscal strength of the federal state as a whole (Braun *et al.*, 2003).

TABLE 11.5: The strengths and weaknesses of federalism

Strength	Weakness
A practical arrangement for large or divided countries.	May be less effective in responding to security threats.
Provides stronger checks and balances.	Decision-making is slower and more complicated.
Allows for the recognition of diversity.	Can entrench internal divisions.
Reduces overload at the centre.	The centre finds it more difficult to launch national initiatives.
Encourages competition between states or provinces and allows citizens to move between them.	How citizens are treated depends on where they live.
Offers opportunities for policy experiments.	Complicates accountability: who is responsible?
Allows small units to cooperate in achieving the economic and military advantages of size.	May permit majorities within a province to exploit a minority.
Brings government closer to the people.	Basing representation in the upper chamber on states violates the principle of one person, one vote.

Any final judgement on federalism must consider the proper balance between the concentration and diffusion of political power. Should it rest with one body in order to allow decisive action, as it does in unitary systems? From this perspective, federalism is likely to be seen as an obstacle and impediment, and even as an anti-democratic device. Alternatively, should power be dispersed so as to reduce the danger of majority dictatorship? Through this lens, federalism appears as an indispensable aid to liberty.

Local government

Local government is universal, found in unitary and federal states alike. It may be the lowest level of elected territorial organization, but it is 'where the day-to-day activity of politics and government gets done' (Teune, 1995: 16). The terrorist attacks in the United States in 2001, in Spain in 2004, in Britain in 2005, and in India in 2008, were events of national and global significance, but it was local officials in New York, Madrid, London, and Mumbai who faced the immediate task of providing emergency services. Given its role in service delivery, local government should not be what it tends to be: the forgotten tier. And we should not forget the quip of the American politician Tip O'Neill that 'all politics is local', implying as it does that the success of politicians is closely tied to their ability to meet the demands of local voters.

At its best, local government expresses the virtues of limited scale. It can represent natural communities, remain accessible to its citizens, reinforce local identities, offer a practical education in politics, provide a recruiting ground to higher posts, serve as a first port of call for citizens, and distribute the kinds of resources that matter most immediately to people. Yet, local governments also have weaknesses: they are often too small to deliver services efficiently, lack sufficient fundraising powers to set their own priorities, and are easily dominated by traditional elites.

The balance struck between intimacy and efficiency varies over time. In the second half of the twentieth century, local governments were encouraged to become more efficient, leading to larger units. For example, the number of Swedish municipalities fell from 2,500 in 1951 to 274 in 1974 (Rose, 2005: 168), and today stands at 290. In Britain, where efficiency concerns have been a high priority, the average

population served by local authorities had reached more than 142,000 by 2007, the highest in Europe (Loughlin *et al.*, 2011: appendix 1).

Towards the end of the twentieth century, signs emerged of a rebirth of interest in citizen involvement, stimulated by the need to respond to declining turnout at local elections. In New Zealand, successful managerial reforms introduced in 1989 were followed by the Local Government Act (2002), which outlined a more expansive, participatory vision for local authorities.

Similarly, where Dutch local government had once been preoccupied with a concern for effectiveness and efficiency, the emphasis during the 1990s switched to public responsiveness (Denters and Klok, 2005: 65). In 1995, Norway resolved that 'no further amalgamations should be imposed against the wishes of a majority of residents in the municipalities concerned' (Rose, 2005: 168). This cycling between efficiency and participation concerns suggests not only a real trade-off between the two, but also the difficulty of arriving at a stable balance between them.

Functions and structure

The broad tasks of local governments are twofold. First, they provide an extensive and often significant range of local public services, including public libraries, local planning, primary education, provision for the elderly, refuse collection, and water supply. Second, they implement national welfare policies.

This static description of functions fails to reveal how the role of local government has evolved since the 1980s, particularly in those countries where large local governments perform significant functions. One important trend, especially prominent in the English-speaking world and Scandinavia (see Chapter 10), has been for municipal authorities to reduce their direct provision of services by outsourcing to non-governmental organizations, both profit-making and voluntary. In theory, most local government services – from libraries to street-cleaning – can be outsourced, with potential gains in

Global city: A city that holds a key place within the global economic system via its financial, trade, communications, or manufacturing status. Examples include Dubai, London, Moscow, New York, Paris, Shanghai, and Tokyo.

FOCUS 11.2 | The government of cities

With most of the world's people now living in urban areas, the question of how cities are best governed has become more pressing, as has the question of how best to treat the interdependence of cities and suburbs. The argument that they should be treated as single metropolitan areas – as city regions – has proved difficult to address given traditional boundaries. To complicate matters, cities confront distinctive issues arising from their social diversity. Within a concentrated area, they embrace rich and poor, natives and immigrants, black and white, gay and straight, believers and atheists, in a kaleidoscopic combination.

Not all countries have made a success of metropolitan governance, as the case of Australia shows (Gleeson and Steele, 2012). It is a nation of cities, with the five largest state capitals – Adelaide, Brisbane, Melbourne, Perth, and Sydney – being home to nearly two-thirds of the country's people (see Map 11.2). These urban areas are inadequately governed in the existing three-tier (national, state, local) federation. National involvement in running cities is limited by the constitution; state administrations must also confront other pressures (including those from rural areas); and local government itself is subordinate and fragmented, with 34 local authorities operating in Sydney alone. A federal structure does not mesh well with a population concentrated in a few large cities.

In the governance of cities, the national capital occupies a special place. As an important component of the national brand, the capital's leaders merit regular communication with the central government. But the capital's international connections (and even those of major non-capital cities such as Frankfurt, New York, Hong Kong, Mumbai, and São Paulo) mean it can become semi-detached from its national moorings, as implied by the notion of a **global city**. Even though they are located in the same country, the interests of the centre and the capital can diverge. Inevitably, the capital is treated differently from other cities, providing further complexity to the idea of multilevel governance.

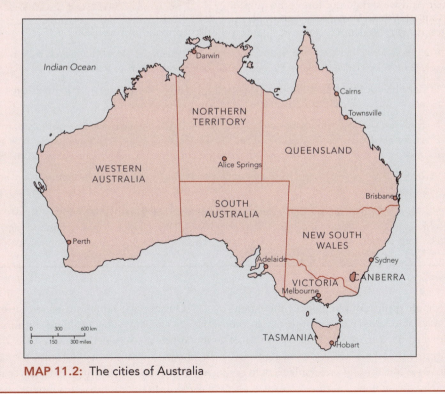

MAP 11.2: The cities of Australia

SPOTLIGHT

FRANCE

Population (66.2 million)

Gross National Income ($2,806 billion)

Per capita GNI ($43,460)

Brief Profile: France is an important European state facing the challenge of adapting its unique traditions to a more competitive world. The country has a reputation for exceptionalism based on the long-term impact of the French Revolution of 1789, which created a distinctive ethos within France. As with other states built on revolution – such as the United States – France can be considered an ideal as well as a country. However, where American ideals led to pluralism, the French state is still expected to take the lead in implementing the revolution's ideals of liberty, equality, and fraternity. As the country became more modern, urban, and industrial after 1945, however, so French uniqueness declined: retreat from empire left France, as Britain, as a middle-ranking power with a new base in the European Union, its society made more complex by immigration from North Africa, and its economy and governing elites challenged by globalization.

Democracy Index rating

| Not Yet Rated | Hybrid Regime | Full Democracy |
| | Authoritarian | Flawed Democracy |

Freedom House rating

| Not Free | Partly free | Free |

Human Development Index rating

| Not Rated | Medium | Very High |
| | Low | High |

Form of government ⇨ Unitary semi-presidential republic. State formed 1789, and most recent constitution (the Fifth Republic) adopted 1958.

Legislature ⇨ Bicameral Parliament: lower National Assembly (577 members) elected for renewable five-year terms, and upper Senate (348 members) indirectly elected through local governments for six-year terms.

Executive ⇨ Semi-presidential. A president directly elected for no more than two five-year terms, governing with a prime minister who leads a Council of Ministers accountable to the National Assembly. There is no vice president.

Judiciary ⇨ French law is based on the Napoleonic Codes (1804–11). The Constitutional Council has grown in significance and has had the power of judicial review since 2008. It has 12 members serving single nine-year terms. Three are former presidents of France, and three each are appointed by the incumbent president, the National Assembly, and the Senate.

Electoral system ⇨ A two-round system is used for both presidential and legislative elections, with a majority vote needed for victory on the first round.

Parties ⇨ Multi-party, with the Socialists dominating on the left, backed by greens, leftists and radicals, while the Union for a Popular Movement dominates on the right. The far-right National Front has been making gains, moving France more towards a three-party system.

efficiency and service quality. But in practice these benefits are not always achieved, creating some risk in the transfer, and leaving us with the broader question of whether direct provision of services by a local government to the citizen is intrinsically preferable to delivery by a contractor to a consumer.

Outsourcing represents an evolution from providing to enabling. The enabling authority does not so much provide services as ensure that they are supplied. In theory, the authority becomes a smaller, coordinating body, more concerned with governance than government. In addition to outsourcing, a greater number

Unitary government in France

France has three levels of local government: regions (22), *départements* (96), and municipalities (nearly 37,000). Adding to the complexity of the picture, it also has six overseas regions or counties (including French Guiana and French Polynesia), and 'intercommunalities', which bring together *départements* and municipalities.

The network of *départements* was created by Napoleon early in the nineteenth century, and each is run by its own prefect and elected assembly. Napoleon called prefects 'emperors with small feet' but, in practice, the prefect must cooperate with local and regional councils, rather than simply oversee them. The prefect has ceased to be the local emperor and is instead an agent of the *département*, representing interests upwards as much as transmitting commands downwards. Many other countries have adopted this model, including all France's ex-colonies and several post-communist states.

In 1972, the *départements* were grouped into 22 regions, each with their own elected councils, as well as regional economic and social committees that have an advisory role. Meanwhile, the basic unit of government is the commune, governed by a council and a mayor. Communes vary in size from a few dozen people to several tens of thousands, although most have populations of less than 1,500; a recent trend has been for the smallest commune to amalgamate with their neighbours. More pressures have been exerted on local government in recent years by the efforts of the French government to cut spending in order to control the national budget deficit. In spite of this, every commune has a mayor and a council based in the local city hall, and each has the same powers regardless of size.

In France, national politicians often become or remain mayor of their home town. This simultaneous occupancy of posts at different tiers is known in France as the *cumul des mandats* (accumulation of offices). Even after the rules were tightened in 1985 and 2000, the most popular *cumul* – combining the office of local mayor with membership of the National Assembly – is still allowed. It is an entrenched tradition reflecting the fused character of French public authority even in an era of decentralization.

---

of organizations can become involved in local policy-making, many of them functional (e.g. school boards), rather than territorial (e.g. county governments). This more coordinating and strategic approach is often linked to a growing concern among local governments with economic development, especially in attracting inward investment.

There are two broad ways of organizing local government (see Table 11.6). The first and most traditional method is the *council system*. This arrangement concentrates authority in a college of elected councillors which is formally responsible for overseeing the organization's work. The council often operates through powerful committees covering the main local services. The mayor is appointed by the council itself, or by central government, and has relatively few powers. Whatever virtues this format may have, its collegiate character presents an opaque picture to residents and the wider world.

One example of the council system is the historic network of *panchayat* (literally, 'assemblies of five') found in India and the neighbouring countries of

---

TABLE 11.6: The structures of local government

	Description	Examples
Council system	Elected councillors form a council which operates through a smaller subgroup or functional committees. The unelected mayor is appointed by the council, or by central government.	Belgium, Netherlands, Sweden, England, Ireland, South Africa, Australia, Egypt, India.
Mayor-council system	An elected mayor serves as chief executive. Councillors elected from local wards form a council with legislative and financial authority.	Brazil, Japan, Poland, and about half the cities in the United States, including Chicago and New York.

Bangladesh, Nepal, and Pakistan. Traditionally consisting of groups of respected elders chosen by the village to settle disputes, India's *panchayat* have grown in significance (and acquired a more structured character) as more administrative functions have been moved to the local level, and as the bigger *gram panchayats* have been elected, each with a *sarpanch* (elected leader). There are now three levels of *panchayat*: those based in individual villages (of which there are nearly 600,000 in India), those bringing together clusters of villages, and those covering districts within India's 29 states. Although their financial resources remain limited, *panchayats* are protected by the constitution and remain embedded in India's cultural attachment to the ideal of village self-governance.

The second method of organization is the *mayor-council system*. More presidential than parliamentary, it is based on a separation of powers between an elected mayor and an elected council. The mayor is chief executive; the council possesses legislative and budget-approving powers. Used in Brazil, Japan, and many large American cities (such as New York and Chicago), this highly political format allows a range of urban interests to be represented within an elaborate framework. The mayor is usually elected at large (from the entire area), while councillors represent specific neighbourhoods.

The powers given to the mayor and council vary considerably. In the 'strong mayor' version (such as New York City), the mayor is the focus of authority and accountability, with the power to appoint and dismiss department heads without council approval. In the 'weak mayor' format (such as London), the council retains both legislative and executive authority, keeping the mayor on a closer leash. Whether strong or weak, an elected mayor does at least offer a public face for the area.

In an era of falling voter turnout (which tends to be worst at local elections because of their second-order qualities; see Chapter 16), new efforts have been made in recent years to make local decision-making more visible to voters. One means for doing this – tried, for example, in Britain, Italy, and the Netherlands – has been to repackage mayors as public figureheads of the districts they represent, and to introduce direct mayoral elections. A high profile mayor, such as Boris Johnson in London, can enhance the district's visibility not only within the area but also, and equally importantly, among potential visitors and investors.

Sub-national government in authoritarian states

Studying the relationship between centre and periphery in authoritarian states confirms the relative insignificance of institutions in non-democracies. Sub-national government is weak, authority flows down from the top, and bottom-up institutions of representation are subordinate. When national power is exercised by the military or a ruling party, these bodies typically establish a parallel presence in the regions, where their authority overrides that of formal state officials. For a humble mayor in such a situation, the main skill required is to lie low and avoid offending the real power-holders. Little of the pluralistic policy-making suggested by the notion of multilevel governance takes place and the more general description 'central–local relations' is preferable.

But it would be wrong to dismiss local government altogether. In truth, central rulers – just like medieval monarchs – often depend on established provincial leaders to sustain their own, sometimes tenuous, grip on power. Central–local relations therefore tend to be more personal and less structured than in a liberal democracy. Particularly in smaller countries, the hold on power of regional leaders is not embedded in local institutions; instead, such rulers command their fiefdoms in a personal fashion, replicating the authoritarian pattern found at national level. Central and local rulers are integrated by patronage: the national ruler effectively buys the support of local bigwigs who, in turn, maintain their position by selectively distributing state resources to their own supporters. Patronage, not institutions, is the rope that binds.

The weakness of modern institutions of sub-national government in many authoritarian regimes is reflected in, and perhaps even balanced by, the continued significance of traditional rulers. Nigeria offers an example. There, as in many of its colonies, Britain had strengthened the position of local rulers by governing indirectly through them, and these traditional elites remain influential. Nowhere is this clearer than in the Sokoto, a Nigerian state created in 1976 but with origins in an Islamic Sokoto caliphate of the early nineteenth century. Sokoto state is led by a governor, typically a military officer, but the position of sultan, who once ruled the caliphate, continues to exist. Indeed, the sultan remains the spiritual leader of Nigeria's Muslims. In this way, traditional Islamic leadership coexists alongside conventional sub-national government.

Traditional political units in Nigeria retain the advantages over modern, post-colonial units of longevity, legitimacy, and deep roots in local culture (Graf, 1988: 186). By contrast, elected legislatures and competing political parties are alien and experience difficulty in establishing firm foundations. Nigerian federal governments face a dilemma: should the special place of traditional leaders in the community be exploited to extend the reach of federal government and to support programmes of modernization and democratization (which might then weaken the authority of traditional leaders), or should traditional leaders be bypassed and their powers reduced, thereby risking the anger of local Islamic communities and reducing the credibility of the federal government?

In some of the least stable states, the institutions of sub-national government are supplanted by opportunistic and/or informal control in the form of **warlords**. While much has been made of warlords' recent role in Afghanistan and Somalia, they are far from a new phenomenon, and in some ways are perhaps the oldest form of political domination. Basing their control on military power, they are found sprinkled through the history of China, Japan, and Mongolia, and have been a more recent phenomenon in several parts of Africa and Asia.

> **Warlords:** Informal leaders who use military force and patronage to control territory within weak states with unstable central governments.

Field research on warlords is, by definition, dangerous, but our understanding of their motives and methods has improved thanks to their new prominence in several parts of the world. In a study of their role in Liberia, Sierra Leone, and the Democratic Republic of the Congo, Reno (1997) made the link between warlords and weak states with rich resources such as diamonds, cobalt and timber. For Marten (2012), warlords are not state-builders, like some of their feudal Asian and European predecessors, but instead rely on private militias to extract resources, enforce support and threaten state officials. They thrive on their capacity to provide brutal political control in situations where the formal institutions of state have failed to develop or simply failed.

In larger authoritarian states, such as China and Russia, sub-national government is more developed. Personal links remain important but institutional arrangements cannot be dismissed. Rather, sub-national government is actively exploited to ensure the continued power of the centre. China, for example, is a massive unitary state whose regions, with exceptions such as Hong Kong and Tibet, are ruled in imperial fashion from Beijing. Sub-national government takes the form of 22 provinces, 6 of which (Guangdong, Shandong, Henan, Sichuan, Jiangsu, and Hebei) each contain more than 70 million people, making them bigger than most countries. There are further subdivisions into either counties and townships, or cities and districts.

The Communist Party itself provides a method of integrating centre and periphery. In particular, the circulation of party leaders between national and provincial posts helps to connect the two tiers, providing China's equivalent to the European *cumul des mandats*. Several provincial leaders serve on the party's central politburo, and most members of this key body have worked in top provincial posts at some point in their career. It is these party linkages that provide the key channel through which Beijing maintains a measure of control over the country.

However, recent research suggests that the balance between the centre and the parts has changed. Zhong (2015) shows that after more than a decade of administrative and economic reform, central government has become increasingly remote and less important for many localities, and that the centre's mobilization capacity has weakened. Increasingly, central government policies are ignored and local officials are often more interested in local or even personal projects than in centrally directed economic plans. This effective decentralization allows provinces to become laboratories for new policies but simultaneously accentuates inequalities between them, leading to occasional expressions of concern about the possibility of the country disintegrating.

By contrast to unitary China, Russia is a federation, but one in which the parts have less independence from the centre than is found in most federations. Although Russia saw a remarkable decentralization of power under Boris Yeltsin (president, 1991–9), Vladimir Putin has since overseen a recentralization of power, providing a contrast to the decline of central control in China. Putin's success is based on four main developments:

- Establishing a uniform system designed to eliminate special deals established by Yeltsin with many regions.
- Acquiring the power of appointment and dismissal over regional governors.

- Creating seven extra-constitutional federal *okrugs* (districts) to oversee lower-level units. Each *okrug* is responsible for between 6 and 15 regions. These over-lords ensure that branches of the federal government in the regions remain loyal to Moscow.
- Reducing the powers of the Federation Council, the upper chamber of the national legislature, but giving the president the authority to appoint its members.

Through these devices, Putin has increased the capacity of the central state to govern the Russian people, so much so that Ross (2010: 170) concludes that 'Russia is now a unitary state masquerading as a federation.' Certainly, Putin's reforms contributed to his project of creating what he termed a 'sovereign democracy' in Russia. In Putin's eyes, a sovereign democracy is not built on the uncertain pluralistic foundations of multilevel governance. Rather, it gives priority to the interests of Russia, which include an effective central state capable of controlling its population. On that foundation, the Russian state seeks to strengthen its position in what it still sees as a hostile international environment.

DISCUSSION QUESTIONS

- In what circumstances is a unitary system a more appropriate form of government, and in what circumstances is a federal system more appropriate?

- Why is there is no exact template for a unitary or a federal system, and does it matter?

- Should local governments replicate national governments and be headed by elected legislatures and executive mayors?

- How many global cities does your country have? If it has none, does this matter to national or local politics?

- Why is local government studied so much less than national government?

- Are sub-national government and politics more important in authoritarian states than in democracies?

KEY CONCEPTS

Asymmetric federalism
Confederation
Cooperative federalism
Dual federalism
Federal system
Federation
Global city

Multilevel governance
Regional government
Subsidiarity
Quasi-federation
Unitary system
Warlord

FURTHER READING

Bache, Ian and Matthew Flinders (eds) (2004) *Multilevel Governance*. Examines multilevel governance and applies the notion to specific policy sectors.

Burgess, Michael (2006) *Comparative Federalism: Theory and Practice*. A survey of the meaning of federalism, and approaches to comparing how it works in different societies.

Lazin, Fred, Matt Evans, Vincent Hoffmann-Martinot, and Hellmust Wollmann (eds) (2008) *Local Government Reforms in Countries in Transition: A Global Perspective*. A study of developments in local government in transitional states such as China, Colombia, Egypt, Poland, Russia, and South Africa.

Loughlin, John, Frank Hendriks, and Anders Lidström (eds) (2011) *The Oxford Handbook of Local and Regional Democracy in Europe*. Surveys sub-national democracy in 29 countries and assesses the Anglo, French, German, and Scandinavian state traditions.

Pierre, Jon (2011) *The Politics of Urban Governance*. Assesses four models of governance against the challenges facing cities.

Watts, Ronald J. (2008) *Comparing Federal Systems*, 3rd edn. Considers the design and operation of a wide range of federations.

12 Political culture

PREVIEW

Political culture is essential to an understanding of government and politics in its many varieties. The preceding chapters looked at the structure, rules, and personalities of institutions, but in order to compare effectively, we need also to understand the 'personalities' of different political systems, as reflected in the beliefs, values, attitudes, and norms that characterize those systems. What do people expect of government, how much do they trust it, how do values vary in space and time, and how do attitudes compare in democratic and authoritarian systems? These are all critical questions that need to be answered.

Offering a key point of reference, this chapter begins with a discussion of the idea of civic culture, a particular form of political culture based on an acceptance of the authority of the state and a belief in civic participation; in other words, probably the ideal when it comes to understanding how democracies should work. It goes on to discuss the decline in political trust in democracies and the implications for stocks of social capital. It then reviews the debate over post-materialism as an explanation for changes in Western political culture, followed by an examination of the controversial arguments made by Samuel Huntington in his book *The Clash of Civilizations*, and what this analysis might tell us about political culture at the global level. Finally, the chapter looks at the particular challenges of understanding political culture in authoritarian regimes, where there have been fewer substantive studies.

CONTENTS

- Political culture: an overview

- The civic culture

- Political trust and social capital

- Elite political culture

- Post-materialism

- Huntington's *Clash of Civilizations*

- Political culture in authoritarian states

KEY ARGUMENTS

- The concept of political culture is attractive, but can be misused: cultures do not always coincide with states, and we should avoid the pitfalls of stereotypes about 'national cultures'.

- The classic concern of research in political culture has been to identify the political attitudes most supportive of stable liberal democracy. Ideas such as the civic culture, political trust, social capital, and post-materialism have all been used, and in some cases developed, with this goal in mind.

- While most studies concentrate on mass culture, elite values possess direct political significance. Elites can exploit culture to further their political goals.

- Although political culture is sometimes criticized for its static quality, the drift to post-materialism – values that emphasize self-expression and the quality of life over materialist values such as economic growth and physical security – is an interesting attempt to understand how political cultures change.

- The idea of conflict between transnational civilizations is a controversial attempt to apply cultural analysis to a post-ideological world. Within this strand, one interesting focus is provided by studies investigating the alleged contrasts between Western and Islamic cultures.

- Much of the evidence suggests that, in authoritarian regimes, there is more support for strong leaders than for freedom and self-expression.

Political culture: an overview

Culture is defined by UNESCO (2002) as 'the set of distinctive spiritual … intellectual and emotional features of society or a social group. It encompasses, in addition to art and literature, lifestyles, ways of living together, value systems, traditions and beliefs.' In other words, culture is the central human characteristic, expressing our essence as aware social beings. Unlike nature (with which it is often contrasted), culture involves values, symbols, meanings, and expectations. It tells us who we are, what is important to us, and how we should behave.

The concept of **political culture** flows from this broader account of culture. It describes the overall pattern in society of beliefs, attitudes and values towards the political system, or 'the sum of the fundamental values, sentiments and knowledge that give form and substance to political processes' (Pye, 1995: 965). It is not the same as public opinion; it is concerned, instead, with what is normal and acceptable, as well as abnormal and unacceptable. We can usefully contrast political culture with political ideology. Where an ideology refers to an explicit system of ideas, political culture comes closer to Linz's notion (1975: 162) of mentalities: 'ways of thinking and feeling, more emotional than rational, that provide non-codified ways of reacting to different situations'. So, political culture is the broader, more diffuse but also more widely applicable notion. With the decay of ideology, political culture is a major highway into understanding the role of beliefs and attitudes in politics.

> **Political culture:** The sum of individual values and norms regarding politics and the political system, or the culture of a group which gives shared meaning to political action.

While we can usually identify major themes in a national political culture, we must also recognize some potential dangers. First, almost every country – except perhaps the very smallest – will contain multiple culturally distinctive social groups. The result may be either a national political culture with one or more subcultures, or even, as for example in Brazil and India, a multicultural society. Second, we should remember that cultures do not always coincide exactly with countries; most religions, ethnic groups, and civilizations span national borders. Third, we must acknowledge that political culture can change over time; it is far from a static concept, and can both influence and be influenced by broader changes in the way societies approach government and politics. Fourth, there is a danger of invoking cultural factors when we can think of nothing else: 'it's just part of their culture'. Above all, we should always beware of reducing political culture to a stereotyped 'national character'.

In comparative politics, political culture is most often studied from a behavioural perspective, using surveys of the attitudes of individuals. This approach is defensible if perhaps rather narrow. It downplays the notion of political culture as shared symbols and stories expressed in the public realm, in arenas such as advertising, art, campaigns, ceremonies, literature, museums, and mass media (Ross, 2009). Given that politics is a collective activity, there is certainly a case for studying political culture in its public manifestations. But public statements may not be matched by private opinion, in spite of how many times we hear the leader of country X telling us that 'the people of X have spoken', or 'this is what the people of X want'. What they are usually really saying is 'this is what my group of supporters or my section of the electorate is saying'. For all these reasons, political culture can be a helpful way of comparing political systems, but we must also beware of its shortcomings.

The civic culture

Political culture has a natural appeal for comparativists. Studying, and especially visiting, another country for the first time, we are naturally drawn to the differences with our home culture. Yet, it is dangerously easy to use cultural contrasts as an explanation for political differences. For one thing, culture can influence how the political game is played – the rituals, the moves, and the language do not necessarily affect the content of politics. For instance, the earthy nature of Australian political debate does not necessarily indicate the presence of sharper underlying conflict than might be found in a country with a more restrained political style, such as Sweden; rather, debate by insult is simply found more often in the national political conversation. (A leading exponent of the style was Paul Keating, prime minister from 1991 to 1996, who once described the debating skills of an opposition party leader as 'like being flogged with a warm lettuce', and described another prime minister – John Howard – as like 'a dead carcass, swinging in the breeze'.)

An additional danger in cultural analysis is that we mistake a dominant culture for a national culture. The dominant culture – as expressed in the national media to which the visitor is usually exposed – may reflect only the values of the political elite or the national capital. The powerful usually seek to validate inequalities of power; the wealthy, to legitimize the economic system from which they benefit. Underlying this dominant discourse, but less visible to the superficial observer, we often find layers of cynicism and opposition. On closer inspection, shared understandings may turn out not to be shared at all – see Focus 12.1.

We can illustrate these points about political cultural differences by considering *The Civic Culture*, the classic 1963 study by Gabriel Almond and Sidney Verba. Their investigation was the first systematic study of political culture, and – in seeking to identify the culture within which a liberal democracy is most likely to develop and consolidate – became a political science equivalent of Weber's attempt (1905) to discover the cultural source of modern capitalism. Where Weber located the spirit of capitalism in protestant values, Almond and Verba found the source of stable democracy in what they called a **civic culture**. This is a particular form of

---

FOCUS 12.1 | Elazar's three types of political culture

The difficulties of identifying a national political culture are illustrated in the arguments made by the political scientist Daniel Elazar (1934–99), a pioneer in the study of political culture. While his work focused on the United States, his ideas have wider applicability. He identified three subcultures that were founded in history and could be identified with different parts of the United States: the individualistic, the moralistic, and the traditionalistic (Elazar, 1966).

Individualistic culture sees politics as a marketplace of competing interests that use the political system to further their own causes, and prefer to limit community involvement. Leaders and citizens are less interested in furthering the common good than in their private concerns. People see government as an adversary and believe that its intervention in public life should be limited. For its part, government only acts if there is a public demand for services, at which point politicians will promote new policies in the hope of achieving electoral success. Patronage drives politics, which is considered a cut-throat business that is best left to the professionals.

Moralistic culture views government as a public service, and believes that its role is to improve living conditions and to create a just society. Political participation is high because it is seen as a public duty, and government is expected to advance the public good, intervening in private affairs if this advances the general interest. Politics is a high calling, political activities revolve around the community interest rather than the individual interest, and political leaders will launch new solutions to problems even if there is no prospect of an immediate electoral return. Issues are important, as opposed to the interests that dominate the individualistic view.

Traditionalistic culture is primarily interested in preserving the status quo, defined as one where elites have the power. A hierarchy exists, with wealthy business and landed interests tied by social connections and having their own definitions of the public good. Only members of these interests are expected to be politically active, and the participation of citizens is not expected, particularly if it might undermine the position of the politically powerful.

It is questionable how Elazar's analysis still applies to understanding subculture in the United States. The broader point, though, is that while we might be tempted to ask what is American political culture, or Swedish political culture, or Brazilian political culture, we would be better advised to look at the differences that exist within societies. They help explain why different groups have different definitions of political behaviour, of the most pressing policy issues, and of the best responses to those issues. They also help explain why different countries often have quite different responses to shared or common policy problems.

allegiant political culture in which most citizens accept the authority of the state and believe in civic participation, and includes such features as an expectation of fair treatment by government authorities, the ability to talk freely about politics, tolerance towards opposition, and civic cooperation and trust.

> **Civic culture:** A moderate political culture in which most people accept the obligation to participate in politics while still acknowledging the authority of the state and its right to take decisions.

In thinking about liberal democracy, we would instinctively begin by imagining that a healthy political system is one whose citizens believe they can contribute to, and are affected by, government decisions. But the interest of Almond and Verba's study rested in its rejection of such a proposition. The authors proposed, instead, that liberal democracy will prove most stable in societies blending different cultures in a particular mix they term the 'civic culture'. The ideal conditions for democracy, they suggested, emerge when an essentially participant culture is balanced by attitudes leading to low levels of participation. A measure of passivity provides ballast for the political system, enabling it to survive periods of stress.

In this way, a civic culture resolves the tension within democracy between popular control and effective governance: it allows for citizen influence while retaining flexibility for the government. As Almond and Verba (1963: 347) summarized their perspective:

> A citizen within the civic culture has ... a reserve of influence. He is not constantly involved in politics, he does not actively oversee the behaviour of political decision makers. But he does have the potential to act if there is need ... He is not the active citizen: he is the potentially active citizen.

Armed with this theory, Almond and Verba set out to discover which countries came closest to having a civic culture. Based on sample surveys in Britain, Italy, Mexico, the United States, and West Germany, they found that Britain, and to a lesser extent the United States, came closest to the civic ideal. In both countries, citizens felt they could influence the government but often chose not to do so, thus conferring on the government its required agility. By contrast, the political cultures of Italy, Mexico, and West Germany all deviated in various ways from the authors' prescription.

Like most original research, Almond and Verba's study attracted considerable scrutiny. Two criticisms highlighted limitations in the concept of political culture itself. First, critics alleged that the whole notion of a national political culture was inherently vague; they suggested that the authors should have focused more on subcultures of race and class. Had they done so, suggested Macpherson (1977: 88), they would have discovered that the most active participants are the educated middle class, while those least engaged with formal politics are the poorly educated working class.

Second, critics pointed out that Almond and Verba failed to offer a detailed account of the origins and evolution of political culture. It was instead largely presented as a given, raising the suspicion that the concept is little more than a sophisticated restatement of simplistic assumptions about national character. In addition, the authors initially had little to say about the evolution of political culture over time. Critics suggested that a country's political culture should not be seen as fixed and stable but should instead be regarded as a dynamic entity which is at least partly shaped by the operation of politics itself. Later research confirmed this position.

Political trust and social capital

In the half century following Almond and Verba's study, many liberal democracies hit turbulent waters. Student activism, oil crises, and financial crises were interspersed with phases of growth and unparalleled prosperity. Inevitably, Western political cultures responded to these events, demonstrating the danger of drawing general conclusions about a country's political culture from a single survey. Much of the recent research has examined the evolution of one particular theme examined by Almond and Verba: **political trust**. This term refers to the belief that the system and institutions of government generate competent decisions which reflect the concern of leaders for those they govern (Hardin, 2006). Political trust indicates diffuse support for the regime, facilitating sound governance, while distrust can lead to a lack of compliance with government in such areas as tax collection.

> **Political trust:** The belief that rulers are generally well intentioned and effective in serving the interests of the governed.

Particularly in the 1990s and 2000s, the conventional wisdom was that political trust was decaying in many Western democracies, indicating trouble ahead. However, the fall in trust was by no means consistent across countries, and it focused more on public confidence in the performance of democratic institutions than on the principle of democracy itself. In a 1999 comparative study, Norris (1999: 20) showed that overall public confidence in such institutions as legislatures, bureaucracies, and the military fell between 1981 and 1991 in each of the 17 countries she examined. However, updating her analysis to include the first decade of the twenty-first century led to a more qualified interpretation (Norris, 2011: 82). She now challenged 'the over-simple views of an inevitable downward spiral of public disenchantment', and instead found that fluctuations over time were more common than linear or downward trends.

If there is a predominant pattern here, it appears to be that a decline in trust in the second half of the twentieth century gave way in the twenty-first century to event-driven fluctuations around a newly established lower level. This is illustrated by the case of the United States (Figure 12.1). In 1964, around three-quarters of Americans professed trust in the federal government; by 1994, only about one-fifth did so. Trust then improved somewhat, with Americans rallying around the flag in the fallout from the attacks of September 2001. With the intelligence failings exposed by 9/11 a, mixed opinions about the wisdom of invading Iraq in 2003, and the financial crisis that broke in 2007, trust fell back to new lows.

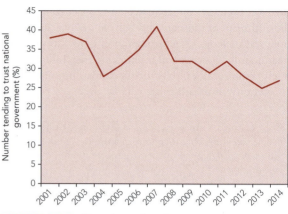

FIGURE 12.2: Trust in national government: European Union

Source: Eurobarometer surveys 55 (spring 2001), 57 (spring 2002), 59 (spring 2003), 61 (spring 2004), and 81 (spring 2014). Data for 2001–3 include 15 countries, rising to 25 in 2004, 27 in 2007, and 28 in 2013. Spring cycles only.

A more short-term picture of the member states of the European Union finds that trust in national government has been low since at least 2001, and has only gone lower (Figure 12.2). Levels of trust by country in 2014 were highest in Finland, Sweden, the Netherlands, and Germany (48–56 per cent), close to average for the EU in Hungary, Austria, and Britain (25–37 per cent), and lowest in Italy, France, Greece and Spain (10–17 per cent) (Eurobarometer 81, spring 2014: 63). Numbers remained fairly steady even as the membership of the EU expanded to Eastern Europe in 2004–7, and even after the onset of the eurozone crisis in 2009. In the UK, meanwhile, the proportion of people saying they would 'trust a British government of any party to place the needs of this country above the interests of their own political party' more than halved from 40 per cent in 1986 to a low point of 16 per cent in 2000, before a modest recovery to 20 per cent in 2010 (British Social Attitudes, 2012). But it is important to note that – at least in the American and British cases – 'civic' cultures have seen a shift towards more sceptical attitudes without threatening the survival of liberal democracy itself.

An important concept related to political trust is **social capital**, which refers to the social networks of which people are members (consciously or unconsciously) and the inclinations that they have as members of these networks to contribute and also to draw from others. The more contacts people possess, the greater the knowledge, advice, and funding on which they can

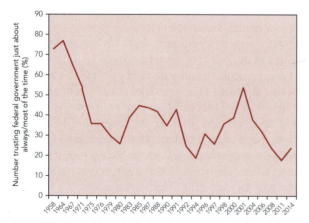

FIGURE 12.1: Trust in federal government: United States

Source: Various, compiled by Pew Research Center (2015)

draw, and the more engaged people become (Lin and Erickson, 2008). Social capital can be seen at work when neighbours keep an eye on each other's homes, or when parents contribute towards the functioning of the school attended by their children, or when a petition circulates among like-minded people calling on the government to act or refrain from acting in a particular way.

> Social capital: The collective value of social networks, derived from communication, help and support among the members of these networks.

Just as trust in others builds social capital, so trust in government creates political capital. Where the bond between citizens and government is strong, the government will be granted the flexibility needed to respond effectively to shared problems, a phenomenon illustrated by its absence in Italy. In their original work, Almond and Verba had portrayed Italy as a country whose political culture was distinctly uncivic, lacking positive and supportive attitudes among the majority. Much later, Robert Putnam took another look, paying more attention to diversity within the country. In the influential study that resulted (Putnam, 1993), he showed how cultural variations within Italy influenced the effectiveness of the twenty new regional governments created in the 1970s; while similar in structure and formal powers, they varied greatly in performance. Some (such as Emilia-Romagna in the north) proved stable and effective, capable of making and implementing innovative policies. Others (such as Calabria in the south) achieved little.

The explanation for the difference, Putnam concluded, lay in political culture. The most successful regions, he argued, had a positive political culture: a tradition of trust and cooperation which resulted in high levels of social capital. By contrast, the least effective governments were found in regions lacking a tradition of collaboration and equality. In such circumstances, supplies of social capital ran low and governments could achieve little. Putnam attributed the uneven distribution of social capital in Italy to events deep within each area's history. The more effective governments in the north draw on a tradition of communal self-government dating from the twelfth century. The least successful administrations in the south are burdened with a long history of feudal, foreign, bureaucratic, and authoritarian rule. Putnam's analysis not only illustrated the importance of political trust and social capital, and of taking regional variations into

account, but it also showed how political culture can be a device through which the past influences the present.

Elite political culture

Political culture is a concept applicable not only to the mass population, but also to political elites. Even where mass attitudes to politics are well developed, it is still the views of the elite which exert the most direct effect on political decisions. Thus we need to look in particular detail at **elite political culture**, or the beliefs, attitudes, and ideas about politics held by those who are closest to the centres of political power. The values of elites are more explicit, systematic and consequential than are those of the population at large (Verba, 1987: 7).

> Elite political culture: The values and norms regarding politics and the political system held by those closest to the centres of political power, including elected officials, bureaucrats, and business leaders.

In a liberal democracy, parties offer contrasting and competing values and policies. But underlying these contrasts, we often find tacit agreements and shared understandings, creating an elite culture that can be more than a representative fragment of the values of the wider society. Looking to history for an example, an important factor in the consolidation of democracy in the unpromising conditions of post-colonial India was the pro-democratic values of its political elite, as channelled through the dominant Congress Party. The party's leaders, many legally trained, had absorbed the British traditions of parliamentary government, an independent judiciary, and the rule of law.

Consider, also, the post-war construction of a united Europe from the ashes of a shattered continent. A generation of leaders designed and built the foundations of the elaborate supranational and intergovernmental institutions which form the European Union today. Without their sustained commitment to what was an explicit European project, this achievement would have been impossible. It was a triumph not only of interests, but also of the will. (Today, however, critics of the EU often charge it with being not only a construction of elites, but also a club run by – and which promotes the interests of – elites.)

Education is a key factor: in most democracies, politics has become virtually a graduate profession. The experience of higher education nurtures an optimistic view of human nature, strengthens humanitarian values, and encourages a confident belief in the ability of politicians to solve social problems (Farnen and Meloen, 2000). Elite confidence also has important bearings on political stability: a political order is more likely to survive if the ruling group genuinely believes in its own right to govern, and inter-group hostility can be contained by a willingness to compromise among the leaders representing different groups in divided societies.

The importance of elite confidence (or, rather, its absence) can be illustrated with examples from authoritarian regimes. The revolutions of 1989 in Eastern Europe dramatically illustrated how a collapse of confidence among the rulers helped to precipitate major political change. As Schöpflin (1990) points out:

> an authoritarian elite sustains itself in power not just through force and the threat of force but, more importantly, because it has some vision of the future by which it can justify itself to itself. No regime can survive long without some concept of purpose.

In the initial phase of industrialization, communist rulers in the Soviet Union and Eastern Europe had good reason to believe their new planned economies were producing results. By the late 1980s, however, progress had given way to decline. As any remaining support from intellectuals faded, so party officials began to doubt their own legitimacy. Communist rulers were aware that they had become a barrier to, rather than a source of, progress. Elite values had ceased to underpin the system of government.

By comparison, economic growth in China has continued apace, at least until recently, sustaining the elite's confidence in its own authority. If communist rule in China does come under threat, it could well be because a segment of the elite concludes that the party's dominance is holding back further national and economic progress, creating an opening for mass protests which would not otherwise have occurred. In China, as elsewhere, the fragmentation of elite values will be the catalyst of any regime change that takes place.

One country where political culture offers support to established elites, even if it is not always driven by them, is Japan. Political power has long been based on notions of group identity, as reflected in loyalty, obligation, and hierarchy, with a web of social and financial ties binding a small political elite together and promoting nepotism and factionalism. This distinctive culture is expressed in the way workers tend to stay with one company all their lives, in the persistence of factions within political parties, and in the frequency of influence peddling in politics. The emphasis on status and rank means that all people are made aware of their position in the group, that a premium is placed on allegiance to the group, and that criticism from below is discouraged as a threat to group harmony (McCargo, 2012: 70–3). But these values have received increasing criticism for acting as a brake on Japan's political modernization, for interfering with the free exchange of ideas, and for contributing to complacency and conservatism in the management of the country's largest corporations.

Post-materialism

One factor which has been measured over a long period, and which illustrates how the concept of political generations introduced in Focus 12.2 can be applied, is **post-materialism**. This is a term developed by the American social scientist Ronald Inglehart in the early 1970s to distinguish the new focus on quality of life issues – such as environmental protection, nuclear disarmament, gender equality, and freedom of expression – from so-called materialist interest in economic growth and security. The idea was that Westerners born after the Second World War had grown up during a time of unprecedented prosperity and relative international peace, with an expanded welfare state offering security to many against the demands of illness, unemployment, and old age. Freed from the kinds of precarious security concerns about survival that had influenced earlier generations, post-war generations were more inclined to focus on the quality of life. These post-material values gave the educated young different priorities from the generation of their parents and grandparents.

> **Post-materialism:** A set of values emphasizing self-expression and the quality of life over materialist values such as economic growth and physical security. They include a commitment to self-expression, human diversity, individual liberty, and autonomy.

According to Inglehart (1971), this unique combination of affluence, peace, and security led to a 'silent revolution' in Western political cultures. He later suggested that the priority accorded to economic achievement made way for increased emphasis on the quality of life: 'in a major part of the world, the disciplined, self-denying and achievement-oriented norms of industrial

FOCUS 12.2 | Political generations

Some of the earliest applications of political culture were criticized for being too static, leading later researchers to look instead at changes in political culture. The concept of **political generations** proved useful, suggesting as it does that each generation has the potential to develop a perspective on politics which distinguishes it both from the one before and the one after. Typically, this distinctive outlook reflects the formative experience of the cohort as it matures. For example, growing up in an environment of war or depression colours political attitudes in a manner that persists throughout life. Values can also shift across generations in a more gradual fashion. Thus, each new cohort might be slightly more sympathetic to causes such as same-sex marriage or environmental protection. Through generational turnover, a political culture can be slowly transformed. There is an important technical point here. In studying political generations, life-cycle or ageing effects must be incorporated. As a generation ages, its values will inevitably adjust (becoming more conservative, for instance), so any differences between generations can only be identified by comparing two or more generations at the same life stage. The fact that the young are more left-wing than the old at a particular time is not enough to demonstrate a generational divide. Such a contrast may reflect a life-cycle effect; it is entirely possible that a cohort of elderly conservatives might, in its youth, have been even more left-wing than the new radicals coming up behind. Figure 12.3 has two downward slopes that show a life-cycle effect, the difference between them showing a generational effect. The lesson is that capturing a generational divide requires long-term data enabling like to be compared with like.

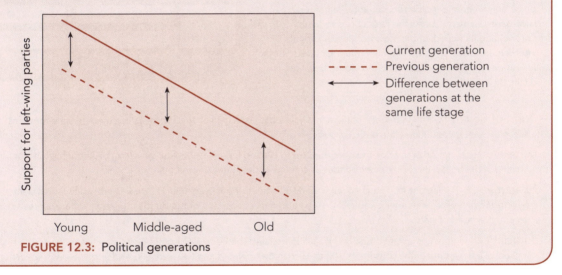

FIGURE 12.3: Political generations

Political generation: An age cohort sharing distinctive experiences and values which shape its perspective through its life course. Generational turnover can gradually transform a political culture without individuals changing their views.

society are giving way to the choices over lifestyle which characterize post-industrial economies' (Inglehart, 1997: 28).

Based on extensive survey evidence, Inglehart showed that the more affluent a democracy, the higher the proportion of post-materialists within its borders. Within Europe, for example, post-materialism came first to, and made deepest inroads in, the wealthiest democracies such as Denmark, the Netherlands, and West Germany. Norway apart, the other affluent Scandinavian countries were also receptive to these values. Post-materialism was less common in poorer European democracies with lower levels of education, such as Greece (Knutsen, 1996).

Assuming a generational effect, post-material values will continue to become more prominent. When

SPOTLIGHT

GERMANY

Brief Profile: Germany provides a fascinating case study for comparative politics. Created in 1871, it went on to play a key role in two world wars, was then divided into separate democratic and communist countries, was reunited in 1990, and has played a key role as a leader and paymaster of European integration. Because Germany naturally views European developments through the lens of its own system of government, the country's political institutions are of continental significance. Within a parliamentary framework, Germany offers a distinctive form: a chancellor democracy in which the nation's leader determines government policy, appoints cabinet ministers, heads a large staff, and can be removed from office only when the legislature can agree a named successor. Germany boasts the largest economy in Europe, and its skilled employees, working in capital-intensive factories, produce premium manufactured goods for export. Its military influence in the world, however, is distinctly limited.

Population (81 million)

Gross National Income ($3.73 trillion)

Per capita GNI ($47,270)

Democracy Index rating

| Not Rated | Hybrid Regime | Full Democracy |
| | Authoritarian | Flawed Democracy |

Freedom House rating

Not Free | Partly free | Free

Human Development Index rating

| Not Rated | Medium | Very High |
| | Low | High |

Form of government ⇨ Federal parliamentary republic consisting of 16 *Länder* (states). Modern state formed 1949, and most recent constitution (the Basic Law) adopted 1949.

Legislature ⇨ Unicameral: a 631-member Bundestag elected for renewable four-year terms. Although it functions like an elected upper house, the 69-member Bundesrat consists of delegates drawn from the *Länder*.

Executive ⇨ Parliamentary. The chancellor leads a cabinet of between 16 and 22 ministers, while a president (elected to five-year terms – renewable once – by a special convention of the Bundestag and *Länder*) serves as ceremonial head of state.

Judiciary ⇨ Germany is a state based on law (a *Rechtsstaat*). The Federal Constitutional Court has proved to be highly influential as an arbiter of the constitution. It has 16 members divided into two 'senates', and appointed for 12-year terms with mandatory retirement at age 68.

Electoral system ⇨ The Bundestag is elected through mixed member proportional representation, with half elected using single-member plurality and half using *Länder* party list proportional representation. Members of the Bundesrat are nominated by the *Länder*.

Parties ⇨ Multi-party. The leading parties are the Christian Democratic Union (CDU), with its Bavarian partner the Christian Social Union (CSU), and the Social Democratic Party (SPD). Other significant players are the Left Party and the Green Party.

➡

Political culture in Germany

Political culture is often taken as a given but is itself shaped by a country's history. Here, the post-war division of Germany provides a rare natural experiment, allowing us to gauge how these developments affected popular thinking.

Two main processes can be observed. The first is the positive impact of post-war economic recovery on political culture in western Germany. Between 1959 and 1988, the proportion of West Germans expressing pride in their political institutions increased from 7 to 51 per cent. Over a similar period, support for a multi-party system grew from 53 to 92 per cent. This experience shows that economic growth can deliver political legitimacy, and offers hope to other transitional countries seeking to build a democratic culture on an authoritarian history.

The second process is the impact of reunification. At the time of German reunification in 1990, people in the east were significantly less trusting of the legislature, the legal system and each other than were people in the west. The experience of living under a communist regime, particularly one which engaged in such close surveillance of its population, had left its mark (Rainer and Siedler, 2009).

There has since been evidence of declining contrasts between east and west, but considerable differences remain: disposable income and the percentage of younger people are both higher in the west, while unemployment and support for the right-wing National Democratic Party are higher in the east. Easterners tend to perceive westerners as bourgeois, patronizing, materialistic, and individualistic, while many westerners seem to look down on easterners, and certainly are perceived to do so by easterners themselves. Ironically, a 2014 poll found that 75 per cent of easterners considered reunification to have been a success, but only 50 per cent of westerners felt the same way (Noack, 2014).

It is reasonable to suppose that cultural contrasts will continue to weaken if (and this is a big if) living standards in the east converge on those in the west. In such circumstances, the more political culture in the east is likely to acquire the post-material tinge long found in the west. For now, though, unification without unity remains a common theme in discussions of German political culture.

Inglehart began his studies in the early 1970s, materialists outnumbered post-materialists by about four to one in many Western countries. By 2000, the two groups were more even in size, a change that represented a major transformation in political culture. Globalization plays a key role in spreading post-materialist values even more widely, as does the never-ending expansion of education. In fact, experience of higher education (especially in the arts and social sciences) is the best single predictor of a post-material outlook. Liberal values acquired or reinforced at college are then sustained through careers in expanding professions where knowledge, rather than wealth or management authority, is the key to success. In France, surveys conducted between 2005 and 2008 showed that 56 per cent of those with at least some university education were post-materialists, compared with only 25 per cent among those with lower educational achievement (Dalton, 2013: 101).

Although post-materialism is normally interpreted as a generational value shift among the general public, its most important political effect may operate through political elites. As post-materialists moved into positions of power, so they secured a platform from which their values could directly affect government decisions. For instance, the 1960s generation retained touches of radicalism even as it secured the seductive trappings of office. Thus, Bill Clinton (born 1946, the first US president to be born after the war) offered a more liberal agenda to the American people than did his predecessor, George H. W. Bush (born 1924). And Tony Blair (born 1953) represented a similar transition from his predecessor but one, Margaret Thatcher (born 1925). These two pairs of leaders were from different generations as well as different parties.

However, post-materialism did not carry all before it. Culture may influence the agenda but it certainly does not drive it. Not only have many conservative parties continued to prosper in the post-material age, but also extreme right-wing parties have emerged in several European democracies, partly as a reaction against self-expression values. More broadly, the distinctive challenges of the twenty-first century include issues such as terrorism, energy supply, climate change, youth unemployment, and social security. These problems invite a renewed focus on the value of security, rather than self-expression. Such issues force themselves onto the political agenda with an energy that can, in the short run, overwhelm cultural change emerging gradually through the march of the generations.

Huntington's *Clash of Civilizations*

Political culture is not only a national or a local phenomenon, but can also be understood at the global level. A key example of global-scale analysis is offered by the best-selling (and controversial) study by the American political scientist Samuel Huntington entitled *The Clash of Civilizations* (Huntington, 1996). It was particularly influential in introducing the issue of religion into the discussion about political culture.

Writing before the September 2001 terrorist attacks, Huntington suggested that cultures, rather than countries, would become the leading source of political conflict in the twenty-first century. The conclusion of the Cold War did not mean the end of cultural divisions, he said. Instead, the focus would shift from a battle of ideologies to a clash of civilizations. Since such groupings are supranational, Huntington claimed that political culture had escaped its national moorings to embrace wider identities: civilizations were the broadest cultural entities in the world, he argued, or 'cultures writ large'.

Huntington saw seven or eight of them in all: Western, Japanese, Islamic, Hindu, Slavic–Orthodox, Latin American, Chinese, and (possibly) African. Between the contradictory worldviews of these civilizations, he argued, there is little room for compromise. Economic conflicts can be bargained away but cultural differences carry no easy solutions. He suggested that, as globalization proceeded, friction and conflict would intensify, reversing the standard 'McWorld' thesis (Barber, 1995) of a world converging on American norms that we saw in Chapter 6.

Huntington noted, for example, how cultural kinship influenced the choice of sides in the wars of the 1990s: in the conflicts in Yugoslavia, 'Russia provided diplomatic support to the Serbs, not for reasons of ideology or power politics or economic interest but because of cultural kinship' (1996: 28). Later, in

2006, the Russian defence minister warned the West to steer clear of Belarus, citing cultural affinities: 'Belarusians and Russians are one people' (Shepherd, 2006: 19). Cultural kinship was the excuse for takeover of the Crimean peninsula by Russia's Vladimir Putin in 2014 and his subsequent efforts to destabilize eastern Ukraine, a country long torn between Europe and Russia. Other former Soviet states with significant Russian minorities (such as the Baltic countries) now had clear cause to be concerned about Russian intervention.

How do states relate to Huntington's civilizations? He provided an intriguing classification, though countries can fall into more than one category – see Table 7.1. A core state leads a civilization; a member state is identified with a single civilization; a lone state either forms its own civilization or stands in a league of its own. Huntington also discussed mixed or torn states whose leaders attempt the difficult assignment of moving their country from one civilization to another, an effort about which Huntington was sceptical. Australia had failed to reinvent itself as an Asian country, he said, simply because – in cultural terms – it was not Asian. In a similar way, Turkey's application to join the European Union may stall because of a 'cultural chasm' (Scherpereel, 2010). In the long debate about Turkey's European aspirations, which date back to the early 1960s, there has always been a question of whether the country is primarily European or Asian, and of how an Islamic state (even if it is mainly a secular one) can integrate with Christian states (even ones where church attendance has declined). Russia, positioned between Western and Slavic–Orthodox civilizations, provides another example of perpetual ambivalence.

Huntington's thesis has drawn considerable criticism, with many scholars either rejecting the idea of distinct civilizations, or at least questioning the evidence of clashes between them (see, for example, Said, 2001; Berman, 2003). The thesis has been particularly criticized for its assessment of the relationship between Islam and the West, which Huntington had portrayed (p. 217) as a permanent conflict of civilizations:

> The underlying problem of the West is Islam, a different civilization whose people are convinced of the superiority of their culture and are obsessed with the inferiority of their power. The problem for Islam is the West, a different civilization whose people are convinced of the universality of their culture and who believe that their superior, if declining, power

TABLE 12.1: Huntington's structure of states and civilizations

	Qualities	Example
Core state	The most powerful and culturally central state in a civilization.	India (Hindu)
Member state	A state fully identified with a particular civilization.	UK (Western)
Lone state	A state lacking cultural commonality with other societies.	Japan (Japanese)

Source: Huntington (1996: 135–54)

imposes on them the obligation to extend that culture throughout the world.

Many critics reject Huntington's focus on the inherent characteristics of Islam. Stepan (2001: 234), for instance, interprets Islam as multi-vocal, capable of varying its voice across place and time. In similar fashion, Gregorian (2004) describes Islam as 'a mosaic, not a monolith'. Consider the contrasts offered by Turkey and Saudi Arabia: both are Muslim countries, but Turkey's state is secular and partially democratic, while Saudi Arabia's authoritarian regime leads a society guided by a severe form of Islam. The reaction to 9/11 confirms Islam's multi-vocal character: the hijackers undoubtedly drew on one anti-Western dialect within Islam but most Muslims, as most Christians, regarded the attacks as morally unjustified (Saikal, 2003: 17).

Furthermore, the idea of a monolithic Islam is invalidated by the tensions that have long existed between Sunni and Shia Muslims, and by the increasingly overt expression of this divide within Middle Eastern societies following the Arab Spring of 2011. (Sunnis make up about 80 per cent of all Muslims, and found their practices on the actions of Muhammad, while accepting some separation of political and religious authority, while Shia Muslims advocate a more direct political role for religious leaders, and form a majority in Iran and Iraq.) The monolithic nature of Christianity is also a myth; for centuries, the major cause of war in Europe was religious differences, and even today there are tensions between Protestants, Catholics, and the myriad other doctrines to be found within the broad label of Christianity.

It is also important not to forget the political source of tensions between Islam and the West. Western states – beginning with Britain and France, and moving more recently to the United States – have a history of interference in the internal affairs of Middle Eastern states that dates back more than a century, and is driven by a combination of strategic concerns and the need to control and assure supplies of oil. In their efforts to champion their political priorities, Western states have caused considerable offence, not least in their failure to push Israel and the Palestinians into a peace agreement, and in their stationing of troops in the Muslim holy land of Saudi Arabia.

In spite of the criticisms, Huntington's thesis of a divide succeeded in stimulating badly needed research into the cultural differences between Muslim and Western countries, which has mainly revealed only limited differences in political attitudes between the two worlds. From their study of more than fifty countries between 1995 and 2001, for example, Norris and Inglehart (2011: 146) concluded that there were 'no significant differences between the publics living in the West and in Muslim religious cultures in approval of how democracy works in practice, in support for democratic ideals, and in approval of strong leadership'. But the study did find Muslim publics supporting a stronger social role for religious authorities, although this difference proved to be a case of the West versus the rest, rather than the West versus Islam. In this respect, the secular character of Western civilization (excluding the United States) proved to be the odd man out. It is instructive for the West, accustomed to imagining the Islamic world as an alien other, to see its own secular civilization as the exception.

There are bigger differences when it comes to sexual and gender issues, with Norris and Inglehart (p. 149) drawing the following conclusion:

> All the Western nations, led by Sweden, Germany, and Norway, strongly favor equality for women and also prove tolerant of homosexuality … In contrast the Muslim cultures, including Egypt, Bangladesh, Jordan, Iran, and Azerbaijan, all display the most traditional social attitudes, with only Albania proving slightly more liberal.

Other scholars reach similar conclusions. Thus, Steven Fish (2011: 257), using the same data source as Norris and Inglehart, concludes that some of his most noteworthy findings are about 'how different

Muslims are not'. In fact, he finds that 'Muslims partake of a global consensus on keeping those who convey God's word and ways away from the realm of political decision-making.' But he, too, finds that 'being a Muslim is generally associated with stronger opposition to homosexuality, abortion, and divorce'.

The overall conclusion is that neither cultural differences nor the historical record justify the thesis of an inherent clash of civilizations between the Islamic world and the West. Political culture (and equivalent terms such as *civilization*) can only take us so far. As Roy (1994: viii) observes, 'culture is never directly explanatory and in fact conceals all that is rupture and history: the importation of new types of states, the birth of new social classes and the advent of contemporary ideologies'. Over time, political debate itself shapes political culture as leaders selectively exploit its themes in pursuit of their own goals. By themselves, concepts such as *political culture* and *civilization* are blanket terms, offering a seductively easy frame of comparison, but also obscuring many crucial details.

Political culture in authoritarian states

Just as Almond and Verba argued that stable liberal democracies are underpinned by a pluralist civic culture emphasizing self-expression, so Welzel and Inglehart (2005, 2009) suggest that many authoritarian regimes are sustained by a cultural emphasis among their populations on security. From this perspective, it is wrong to see non-democratic rule as secured only by repression of a disaffected citizenry. Rather, authoritarian regimes can be as legitimate as democracies; it is only the basis of their authority that differs. So, we have here a cultural theory of political stability in authoritarian settings.

Specifically, Welzel and Inglehart (2009: 131) suggest that people in low-income countries 'give priority to authority and strong leadership over freedom and expression'. What is more, if a democracy does emerge in such unsympathetic cultures, it may be unstable: 'democracy is fragile when it is a "democracy without democrats"'. Even if people reject the current leaders of an authoritarian government, they may simply want to replace them with another set of non-democratic rulers. In other words, Western analysts who interpret all dissent in dictatorships as a plea for democracy may simply be seeing what they wish for. Furthermore, people

living under non-democratic governments who favour democracy may interpret the term as referring not so much to self-rule as to social order, national autonomy, and a strong economy.

A good example of an authoritarian culture centred on security and order is Russia. Many in the West wanted to believe that they were witnessing a transition to liberal democracy in Russia throughout the 1990s, and were then surprised to see a 'return' to authoritarianism during the Putin years. But Russian political culture includes only limited support for democratic principles. Thus, Gitelman (2005: 248) writes that:

> the authoritarian traditions of Russia mean that people are not used to democratic behaviours and values, such as welcoming pluralism in thinking and behaving, tolerating dissent and supporting seemingly less efficient methods of democratic decision-making. They do not easily see the advantages of debate, discussion and non-conformity, and not deferring to a class of 'superiors'.

Inglehart (2000) also early argued that Russian culture was exceptionally stony ground on which to nurture a liberal democracy. Drawing on a survey conducted in 1999 and 2000, he found that Russians were less trusting, tolerant, and happy than people in most other countries – cultural features reinforced, but not created, by communist rule. His conclusion was that the prospects for a transition from a competitive authoritarian regime to a liberal democracy were, at that stage, somewhat limited.

It is revealing that in spite of the criticism that has been directed at Putin from abroad since Russia intervened in Georgian affairs in 2008 (ostensibly to protect Russian interests in the breakaway region of South Ossetia), and that moved into even higher gear as Russia injected itself into Ukrainian affairs in 2014, Putin has enjoyed remarkably high approval ratings in Russia (Taylor, 2014). Polls from both state-run and independent sources found that he had the approval of 72 per cent of Russians in March 2014, a three-year high. (President Obama meanwhile had 43 per cent approval and President Hollande of France less than 20 per cent approval.) Putin's approval had peaked at 88 per cent in September 2008, just after the intervention in Georgia, and was now high again during the intervention in Ukraine. Some of his popularity could be credited to his strong response to what his government had portrayed as threats to Russian security and the support of Russian minorities in both countries. But clearly

Russians admire strong and decisive leadership, even – seemingly – if it involves breaking international law.

Elsewhere, many non-democratic Islamic countries are led by authoritarian rulers who seek to draw from the well of Islamic culture in a way that supports their hold on power. They present democracy as an alien Western concept which in practice leads to licence rather than freedom, to an emphasis on material rather than spiritual values, and to the pursuit of individual self-interest rather than social harmony. For example, Mahathir bin Mohamad, prime minister of Malaysia (1981–2003), condemned Western democracies in which 'political leaders are afraid to do what is right, where the people and their leaders live in fear of the free media which they so loudly proclaim as inviolable'. Through such statements, authoritarian rule can be presented as expressing an indigenous cultural tradition inherently opposed to Western liberalism.

One objection to the position that non-democratic regimes are supported by political culture is that the relationship is really the other way round. As we have already suggested, culture can reflect rather than sustain the nature of a regime. Consider Russia: the lack of political trust there may well reflect the country's non-democratic history and the corrupt nature of its contemporary governance. But were a secure liberal democracy to take root in Russia, by whatever means, the nation's political culture would probably also shift in a democratic direction. In other words, over the longer term political culture reflects the nature of the regime, rather than vice versa.

Interestingly, Welzel and Inglehart (2009: 136) reject this rebuttal. They insist, as did Gabriel Almond a generation earlier, that political culture is an independent force. In rejecting the view that it is merely a mirror of the current political system, they suggest that 'high levels of intrinsic support for democracy emerged in many authoritarian societies *before* they made the transition to democracy', citing such examples as South Korea and Taiwan. Their view is that, as societies modernize, so too do its better educated segments give more emphasis to self-expression and post-material values. This cultural shift then leads to pressure to democratize.

But how should we explain the recent story of Egypt? First we see its people standing at the forefront of the Arab Spring, with massive public demonstrations in early 2011 that led to the toppling in February of the Mubarak regime, in office for nearly 30 years. Egyptians then embraced democracy, taking part in competitive

elections in 2011–12, and electing the government of Mohamed Morsi, who was notable not just for heading the first Islamist government in Egypt's history, but also for being the only civilian among the five leaders that Egypt has had since the overthrow of the monarchy in 1952. When Morsi began to show signs of authoritarianism, he was removed by the military in July 2013, and eventually replaced by the then little-known head of the Egyptian military, Abdel Fattah el-Sisi.

For Maghraoui (2014), the dynamics behind Sisi's rise are 'a mystery when abstracted from the general context of Egypt's authoritarian past. He is a man with no charisma, no political experience, no warrior's aura, no distinct ideology, and no clear plan of how to tackle Egypt's chronic social and economic problems.' It seems that in spite of the support that Egyptians gave to democratic change in 2011, many still hold on to the idea of strong leadership, suggesting that there is still a core streak of authoritarianism within Egyptian political culture, at least among older Egyptians if not the mainly younger protestors who were at the forefront of the protests against Mubarak and Morsi. Sisi made the 'war on terror' a cornerstone of his government, an idea that appealed to many Egyptians and that helped strengthen his base of support. In the view of Cambanis (2015), Sisi needed 'just enough power to stay in charge, and enough international support to ignore the outrage of Egyptians who want civil rights, political freedom, and genuine economic development'. How long he can make this last, however, remains to be seen.

A critical complication in trying to understand political culture in post-colonial societies rests in distinguishing indigenous political values from those created by the colonial experience. In the case of Nigeria, one of the major barriers to the success of democracy lies in the multi-ethnic nature of the Nigerian state. So persistent have Nigeria's ethnic divisions become that they once led a frustrated Wole Soyinka – the Nigerian novelist and 1986 Nobel laureate for literature – to dismiss the idea of a Nigerian nation as a 'farcical illusion'.

The problems can be contrasted with pre-colonial times, when ethnic groups had worked out a balance among themselves that protected them from too much external interference. But the creation of Nigeria by British colonialism forced these groups to live and work together and to build shared systems of government and administration, setting them on a path of mutual hostility as they competed for power and resources and struggled to preserve their identity. Lacking a state tradition,

Nigerians continue to find it hard to trust government officials, so they look instead to their communities for stability, and they believe that loyalty to the community is the paramount virtue.

One of the consequences is a tradition of systemic corruption, which has become so normal that many locals call it 'the Nigerian factor'. As well as reflecting all the obvious and standard features discussed in Chapter 4, the Nigerian brand has gone international via the multiple emails sent from Nigeria to Western recipients offering millions of dollars to help settle the affairs of people who have allegedly died and left no successors. Named '419 scams' after the section of the Nigerian penal code dealing with fraud, they have been so successful that they have become Nigeria's second biggest source of foreign revenues after oil (Smith, 2007).

How much of the Nigerian experience with political culture is truly Nigerian, and how much is a consequence of Nigeria's difficulties in building a sense of national unity? Can modernization make a difference in such circumstances? Does Nigeria even have discernible political cultural trends that have roots in Nigerian society and that are subject to the same kinds of pressures and influences as the trends we find in more democratic Western states with a longer history of relatively stable national identity? Or is the best that we can say about political culture in authoritarian systems is that it exists, but that it is fundamentally negative in nature?

DISCUSSION QUESTIONS

- What are the major features of political culture in your country?

- How healthy is the civic culture in today's democracies?

- What can be done to reverse the decline in political trust?

- Does post-materialism still make sense as a way of understanding political culture in the West?

- Is there a clash of civilizations between the Muslim and Western worlds?

- Is there such a thing as a Western political culture, and – if so – what are its features?

KEY CONCEPTS

Civic culture
Elite political culture
Political culture
Political generation

Political trust
Post-materialism
Social capital

FURTHER READING

Calvert, Peter and Susan Calvert (2007) *Politics and Society in the Developing World*, 3rd edn. Little has been written about political culture in developing or authoritarian states, leaving studies such as this to offer tangential but still helpful insights.

Chabal, Patrick and Jean-Pascal Daloz (2006) *Culture Troubles: Politics and the Interpretation of Meaning*. An interpretative perspective on political culture which suggests that political analysis should be grounded in what makes sense to the actors involved.

Huntington, Samuel (1996) *The Clash of Civilizations and the Making of World Order*. An original and controversial book arguing not only that civilizational clashes are a threat to world peace, but also that a world order based on civilizations is the best safeguard against war.

Inglehart, Ronald and Christian Welzel (2005) *Modernization, Cultural Change and Democracy: The Human Development Sequence*. Presents a broad intellectual framework in which modernization is seen as initiating cultural change and cultural change is seen as a driver of democracy.

Norris, Pippa (2011) *Democratic Deficit: Critical Citizens Revisited*. Based on extensive survey analysis, this book challenges the claim that liberal democracies have experienced a continuously rising tide of public disaffection since the early 1970s.

Putnam, Robert D. (ed.) (2002) *Democracies in Flux: The Evolution of Social Capital in Contemporary Society*. A group of scholars examine the state of social capital in eight liberal democracies.

Political participation

PREVIEW

For any democrat, the quality of governance must depend – in large part – on the extent to which citizens participate (or are allowed to participate) in the process of governing. In this chapter we review the many channels through which people can participate in government, ranging from the conventional to the unconventional. Two points will soon become clear. First, the quantity and the quality of participation vary not only between regime types but also within individual countries over time and between its social groups. Even in democracies, participation is far from equal. Second, opinion polls reveal that large numbers of people are either poorly informed about the issues at stake, or choose not to express themselves. And in authoritarian systems, of course, their views and opinions are not usually entertained to begin with.

This chapter begins with an assessment of who participates and why, looking in particular at the problem of political exclusion, and reviewing the distinctions between conventional, unconventional and illegal forms of participation. It then ties participation to public opinion, explaining how opinion is measured, and discusses the implications of variable levels of knowledge about political affairs. The chapter then considers the particular place of women in politics, looking at handicaps to their participation and asking why government is still often dominated by men. The chapter ends with a discussion of how participation is managed and limited in authoritarian states, pointing out that levels of participation are often higher than might be expected.

CONTENTS

KEY ARGUMENTS

- Participation might seem to be wholly beneficial for democracy, but heavy participation can indicate strain on a political system.

- Approaches to participation vary, ranging the civic duty school of thought to the idea that people are not naturally political animals.

- Studies of participation in liberal democracies focus on who takes part, to what extent and through what channels. The resulting bias is towards privileged social groups, reflecting inequalities of resources and interest.

- Participation is intimately tied to levels of public knowledge about government and politics, with one driving the other. Some authors suggest that public opinion has become the central mechanism of representation in liberal democracy.

- While female participation has increased substantially, especially in democracies, gender inequalities in participation continue to pose troubling questions.

- It is often argued that political participation in authoritarian regimes is an empty concept, and yet mobilized participation and clientelism are important phenomena, social movements have occasionally been a significant feature, and gauging public opinion is more important than it might at first seem.

Political participation: an overview

Political participation describes any of the ways in which people seek to influence the composition or policies of government. **Conventional** forms of participation include citizens contacting their representative and activists campaigning for their favoured candidate. But participation can also take **unconventional** forms – such as signing a petition, or taking part in a demonstration – and may even involve breaking the law or turning to violence, as in the case of terrorist acts against the state.

> **Political participation:** Activity by individuals formally intended to influence who governs or the decisions taken by those who do.
>
> **Conventional participation:** Takes place within formal politics and the law.
>
> **Unconventional participation:** Takes place outside formal politics or even the law.

In a liberal democracy, people can choose whether to be involved in politics, to what extent, and through what channels. Participation of a sort is also found in authoritarian regimes, even if it is only to create a facade of engagement, manipulated so as to support, rather than threaten, the existing rulers. The forms and the costs of participation are somewhat different.

What expectations should be brought to the study of participation? One perspective, dating back to the ancient Greeks, is that involvement in collective decision-making is both an obligation owed to the community and an exercise in personal development, broadening individual horizons and providing political education. From this standpoint, participation benefits both the political system and the individual, and non-participants are free-riders who gain from the efforts of others. This approach finds echoes in recent writing on the duties (as opposed merely to the rights) of the citizen (Bellamy, 2008).

A second perspective, rooted in practical realities more than high ideals, sets a lower bar. This suggests that people are not naturally political animals, and that we should interpret extensive participation as a sign of unresolved tensions within a political system. Demonstrations, protests, and even high voter turnout may be indicative of a system that is overheating, rather than one that is in

good health. In normal times, limited participation may indicate the system's success in meeting popular demands, freeing citizens to pursue more fulfilling activities.

In the second account, all that matters in a liberal democracy is that citizens monitor political events, and become involved as necessary; that the channels are open, not that they are in constant use. Schudson (1998: 311) suggests that, even when citizens appear inactive, they remain poised for action, like parents watching their children play in a swimming pool. Especially in an age when some conventional forms of participation have declined, such surveillance can even be seen as a central mechanism of democracy: 'To be watchful, alert, and on guard are essential attributes of citizenship', suggests Rosanvallon (2008: 33), who argues that monitoring should be understood as a form of participation, and vigilance as 'a mode of action'.

A third perspective argues that many of those who fail to participate do so because they feel marginalized or alienated, or think that their involvement will make no difference, or see government as a set of institutions dominated by elites. Humans may not be political animals, but they routinely make cost–benefit calculations, and some make the rational calculation that participating is not worth the time or the trouble. Or, more worryingly, they believe that the only way to make themselves heard is through extremism and violence.

Who participates, and why?

Although the debate about how much participation is desirable raises issues of judgement rather than fact, the numbers are nonetheless relevant. If we discover, for instance, that non-participants are clustered in lower social strata, then we might well conclude that lack of engagement reflects political cynicism or alienation, rather than satisfaction. The positive functions of apathy, as seen from a professor's office, may be less apparent in the ghetto.

The most striking result of studies of participation in democracies is how little most people involve themselves other than through voting. In an influential comparative analysis of participation in the United States that drew an analogy from ancient Rome, Milbrath and Goel (1977: 11) divided the population into a small group of active gladiators, a large group of spectators, and a mid-sized group of disengaged apathetics (see Figure 13.1). This classification has since been applied to other liberal democracies.

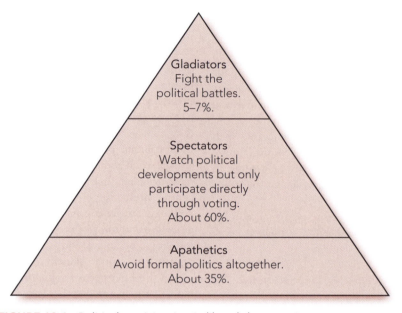

FIGURE 13.1: Political participation in liberal democracies

In another influential study, Verba *et al.* (1978) found that there was a tendency for people to specialize, such that participation is, to some degree, a matter of 'how' as well as of 'how much'. In other words, those who engage do so in different ways. This study identified four types of participant:

- Voters, who participate in local as well as national elections.
- Campaigners, such as those who engage in canvassing.
- Communal activists, such as those who participate in organizations concerned with a particular issue.
- Contactors, or those who communicate with officials about an individual problem.

The small proportion of gladiators in the study by Milbrath and Goel probably comes as no surprise, and yet while these people are likely to exert political influence, they are far from a cross-section of society. In most democracies, participation is greatest among well-educated, upper-income, white men. In addition, for all but protest behaviour (found disproportionately among the young), participation peaks among the middle-aged. Furthermore, the highest layers of political involvement show the greatest skew. As Putnam (1976: 33) put it:

> The 'law of increasing disproportion' seems to apply to nearly every political system; no matter how we

measure political and social status, the higher the level of political authority, the greater the representation for high-status social groups.

This bias in participation towards upper social groups is significant because it suggests that apathy may not, after all, be a sign of satisfaction with the existing order. In that case, we would expect the well-heeled to be less involved in politics because they have relatively little to complain about – exactly the opposite of the observed pattern.

So, why does participation increase as we move up the social scale? According to Verba *et al.* (1995), two factors are influential. First, resources are important. People in high-status groups are equipped with such assets as education, money, status, and communication skills. Education gives access to information and strengthens the ability to interpret it. Money buys the luxury of time for political activity. High status provides the opportunity to obtain a respectful hearing. And communication skills help in presenting one's views persuasively. Added together, these resources provide a useful tool kit for effective political intervention; their unequal distribution helps to account for under-participation by less privileged social groups.

Second, political interest is important. High-status individuals are more likely to be engaged with formal politics, having the motive as well as the means to become involved. No longer preoccupied with the daily struggle, they can take satisfaction from engagement in collective activity (Inglehart and Welzel, 2010). The wealthy are also more likely to be able to see how politics can impact their wealth and prospects. So, higher social groups possess an interest in politics and can afford to put their concerns into practice. Conversely, those in lower social strata are more likely to come from a family and community where the main focus is the challenges of daily life, rather than the remote goings-on of national politics.

As for the spectators in the study by Milbrath and Goel, their characteristics are harder to pin down, but their role has changed with the increased availability of information. The internet and the rise of social media have made it possible to gather political information at a level of detail that was impossible 40 years ago. If watching without necessarily speaking is a form of participation, then the channels through which we can spectate have grown enormously, such that political spectating may now be a leading and highly influential form of participation. In an age of spectatorship, suggests Green (2010a), the disciplinary gaze of the people – their eyes, rather than their voice – has become the source of their power.

While the emphasis of research on political participation is on explaining what distinguishes the gladiators from the spectators, we should not ignore the apathetics, the people who do not participate at all. This group raises the problem of **political exclusion**. As Verba *et al.* (1995) write, the apathetics effectively exclude themselves – or, sometimes, are deliberately excluded – from the normal means by which citizens collectively shape their society. The archetypal non-participant might be an unemployed young person with no qualifications, inhabiting a high-crime, inner-city neighbourhood, often from a minority culture and perhaps not even speaking the dominant language. Such a profile may encourage radical activity among a few but, in general, a preoccupation with everyday life limits or eliminates formal participation in conventional political processes.

> **Political exclusion:** The phenomenon by which some are discouraged from taking part in collective decision-making because of their marginal position in society. Examples of excluded groups include the poor and the unemployed.

Because participation in most liberal democracies is an option rather than a requirement (however, see discussion about mandatory voting in Chapter 16), it is unlikely ever to be equal; and, because inequalities in participation are deeply rooted in social differences in resources and interest, so the active minority is sure to remain sociologically unrepresentative of the passive majority. But our understanding of participation will always be incomplete without an understanding of the motives behind political apathy. The aims of universal participation and political equality coexist alongside the facts of limited and unequal involvement.

Having asked who participates in politics, it is also worth briefly asking why they take part. The obvious answer is a desire to play a part in shaping government policies, but there are different elements to this calculation:

- *Idealism.* People believe in ideas and wish to bring about change.
- *Responsibility.* At least some citizens feel that it is their civic responsibility, and might think about the amount of blood that has been shed over the centuries to win the right to vote and to freely express opinions.
- *Concern.* Some will participate because they are concerned about the problems facing society, and wish to be counted as part of the potential solution, and/or wish to promote parties and politicians that they believe are willing and able to address these problems.
- *Self-interest.* Some will participate because they seek to promote issues and causes that bring personal profit and benefits.
- *Enjoyment.* Others will participate because they find it enjoyable, whether for social reasons, engagement with the community, or the thrill of the competition.

In addition to voting, the conventional forms of participation include anything involving contacts with – or support for – elected officials, political parties, or interest groups (see Table 13.1). But recent evidence suggests a decline not just in voting (see Chapter 17) but also in other forms of conventional participation, a trend that is indicative of growing disillusionment with government and 'politics as usual'. This is particularly true with younger citizens, who are not so much apathetic as rejecting the conventional channels and leading the move towards a diversification of participation. They are building wider networks using social media, and many are engaging in consumer politics – see Focus 13.1. For the most marginalized or distrustful, meanwhile, the

TABLE 13.1: Forms of political participation

Conventional	Voting in elections Joining or donating to political parties Joining, supporting or donating to interest groups Contacting elected representatives Volunteering in political campaigns or running elections Organizing community campaigns Attending political rallies or meetings
Less conventional/unconventional	Taking part in peaceful demonstrations or protests Mobilizing or expressing opinions through social media Posting comments on online news stories Signing petitions Organizing or taking part in consumer boycotts Writing letters to media outlets
Illegal	Civil disobedience Occupation of buildings or public spaces Sabotaging the efforts of parties, candidates, or elected officials Politically motivated crime Political violence, including terrorism and assassination

switch has been away from convention and towards support for anti-establishment political parties, extremism, and even political violence.

We can always hope that politics remains peaceful, but it often spills over into confrontation and violence. This has been a reality throughout history, of course, with examples found in many different societies at many different times, but at no time in history have so many people been potentially a target as is the case today: the means used have expanded, the targets have

Consumer politics: Buying or boycotting goods or services for political or ethical reasons.

FOCUS 13.1 | The consumer as political participant

One form of political participation that rarely appears on most lists of options, in spite of being a device with which many people engage, is **consumer politics**. This involves a decision to buy or boycott goods or services for political reasons. It is nothing new, and can be an enormously effective way of making a point or achieving a goal at little cost to the person making that point. These boycotts have long been used to express opinions about everything from human rights to consumer safety, animal rights, health concerns, and environmental concerns.

One of the most famous examples of consumer politics at work was the start of the US war of independence, which was sparked by protests in the American colonies about trade policies pursued by England. Two other examples were the Don't Buy Jewish campaign that emerged in parts of Europe at the end of the nineteenth century, and the boycott of Jewish-owned businesses imposed by the Nazis in Germany.

More recent examples include the efforts made by consumers to reduce their own energy consumption, or that of targeted companies, so as to limit their carbon footprints; seeking out fair trade products that offer a higher or guaranteed price to the original producers; and boycotts of retail chains that exploit sweat-shop labour.

On the other hand, consumers have also been known to organize anti-boycotts, or 'buycotts', where a deliberate effort is made to make purchases in the face of efforts to express political protest through boycotts. For example, when a campaign was launched in the Middle East to use a boycott to protest the publication in Denmark in 2005 of cartoons depicting the prophet Muhammad, a counter-protest was organized in the form of the Buy Danish campaign, aimed at offsetting the effects of the boycott.

broadened, and the channels available to spread the underlying message have grown. While there may not always be a deliberate effort to cause injury or death in such instances, this cannot be said in the case with two other forms of political expression: assassination and terrorism.

Assassination has long been part of the political landscape. The original 'Assassins' (the *Hashshashin* or hashish-eaters) were a twelfth-century Muslim sect whose members believed their duty was to hunt down Christians. Political killing remains potentially one of the most influential of all forms of political participation; a single shot or thrust of the knife by an individual can bring about a change of government or spark a war and so change the course of history. It is hard to measure its impact or understand its causes, in part because it is an underground activity, in part because it can be opportunistic as opposed to carefully planned, and in part because so many attempts to kill political leaders have failed. In the nationalist twentieth century, many political killings seemed to originate in extreme nationalist ideology, but in other cases the assassins were simply mentally unstable, or the motive was unknown (see Table 13.2). Even so, we cannot ignore assassination as a form of political participation.

> **Assassination:** The murder of a prominent public figure for political reasons.

Terrorism is a form of participation of a different order, since it typically targets civilians and is specifically aimed at changing policy by striking fear into large populations. It too is one of the oldest forms of political participation, but has taken on new significance in recent decades as it has gone global. Where terror was once aimed mainly at changing domestic policy – as in the case of Irish republicanism in Britain, independence in the Basque region of Spain, or protests against capitalism in Germany and Italy – the advanced sophistication of terrorist techniques has combined with the instant availability of information on a global basis to allow terrorists to reach a worldwide audience. In an environment of heightened security concerns, terrorists do not even need to act; the credible threat of action can itself be enough to instil fear and change policy.

> **Terrorism:** The use of violence against civilian targets in order to instil fear with the goal of achieving political change.

Public opinion

Participation, we have suggested, can take the form of monitoring political events, even if that surveillance does not lead to participatory behaviour. Given that broad approach, we can view **public opinion** as an arena of political participation. When people discuss the issues of the day in a way that shapes public opinion, they are taking part not simply in politics, but also in democratic politics.

> **Public opinion:** The range of views held on an issue of public concern by the members of an affected community.

Public opinion matters, especially, but not only, in democracies. Opinion pollsters measure public opinion through survey research, internet research companies monitor Twitter trends, and the political class engages

TABLE 13.2: Some (in)famous assassinations

	Victim	Primary cause
1914	Franz Ferdinand, archduke of Austria	Bosnian nationalism
1948	Mahatma Gandhi, Indian nationalist leader	Hindu nationalism
1963	John F. Kennedy, US president	Unknown
1966	Hendrik Verwoerd, South African prime minister	Assassin judged insane
1981	Anwar Sadat, Egyptian president	Islamic terrorists objecting to accord with Israel
1984	Indira Gandhi, Indian prime minister	Sikh extremism
1995	Yitzhak Rabin, Israeli prime minister	Israeli ultranationalism
2007	Benazir Bhutto, former Pakistani prime minister	Unclear

in a continuous debate on what 'the public' thinks about particular issues. They do this because they know that politicians take note. A case can even be made that public opinion is a more powerful influence on political decisions than elections, given that public opinion is measured continuously and on specific issues. What applied during the French Revolution still speaks to us today:

> Public opinion was a power that manifested itself always and everywhere without being represented or instituted in any particular place. Hence it became the essential manifestation of the people as an active and permanent presence. (Rosanvallon, 2008: 31)

Although we can define public opinion as whatever the population thinks about a given issue, and assume that it can be measured using polls, this simple definition fails to capture what most politicians understand by 'public opinion'. Their thinking is sensitive to structured and organized opinion as expressed through the media, or by opinion leaders. This more political perspective links the idea of a 'public' to an informed community sharing basic political principles.

In terms of how public opinion is measured, there are several options available (in liberal democracies, at least). Prime among these are **opinion polls** and **sample surveys**, the most accurate methods of identifying what people profess to believe. Although the public itself remains resolutely sceptical of sample surveys, their accuracy is now well attested, at least in predicting election outcomes in countries where pollsters know how to interpret the numbers. In modern presidential elections in the United States, for example, the difference between the number of votes projected for the eventual winner and the final result has rarely been more than 3 per cent. One pollster – Nate Silver of the *New York Times* – was even able to correctly predict the winner in 49 out of 50 states in 2008, and all 50 states in 2012.

Opinion poll: A series of questions asked in a standard way of a systematic sample of the population in order to gauge public opinion.

Sample survey: Similar to an opinion poll but involving a more detailed questionnaire. Such surveys are often commissioned by governments or academic researchers.

But in an era of declining turnout at elections and a falling response rates to surveys, pollsters do face increasing technical challenges. In the 2015 British general election, for example, they significantly under-estimated the number of seats that the Conservatives would win. One factor here seems to have been the tendency for Labour supporters in particular to exaggerate their likelihood of voting. A broader interpretation distinguishes between values and choices. Voters might not like the values of a particular political party (such as the Conservatives), but still vote for it because they judge that it will govern more effectively than the alternatives, not least on the economy (Booth, 2015).

Counter-intuitive though it may be, a group of 1,000 people carefully selected for an opinion poll can accurately represent the whole population. The key phrase here is 'carefully selected'. The procedure must be systematic, and the sample must be compared with known figures for the population, with adjustments (known as 'weighting') for any discrepancies. Weighting is particularly important when the sample is self-selected, as with people who agree to take part in polls conducted through the internet. Weighting or not, some self-selected samples, such as the small minority of constituents who contact their representative about their pet topic, should not be regarded as a valid basis for estimating public opinion at all – at least not when public opinion is equated with the whole adult population.

Even when a sample is chosen systematically, it would be wrong to overstate the reliability of opinion polls in measuring the opinions of individual respondents. Polls are usually commissioned by political parties or mass media, not by the ordinary people who answer the questions. As a result, people may never have thought about a topic before they are invited to answer questions on it (Althaus, 2003). They may give an opinion when they have none, or they may agree to a statement because it is the easiest thing to do ('yea-saying') or because it is socially acceptable. Certainly, one danger of opinion polls is that they help to construct the public opinion they claim they are simply measuring.

A **focus group** overcomes some of these difficulties by allowing researchers to gather small groups of people – typically eight to ten – with a common characteristic: they may be non-voters, for example, or donors to a particular party. The idea is to explore, in open-ended style, the perspectives through which participants view the issue. Unlike an opinion poll, the agenda can be at least partly driven by those taking part. A focus group is a qualitative technique, smaller in scale than an opinion poll and often self-selected, but aiming at a deeper understanding than is possible with the pre-coded answers used in most quantitative surveys.

Because opinion polls do not give respondents a chance to discuss the issue before expressing their views, their results are criticized by those who favour more ambitious interpretations of the public's role. Building on a richer view of the public's capacity, scholars have developed the idea of a **deliberative opinion poll** or **citizens' jury** (Fishkin, 2011). This technique involves exposing a small sample of voters to a range of viewpoints on a selected topic, perhaps through presentations by experts and politicians. With the background to the problem established, the group proceeds to a discussion and a judgement. Opinion is only measured when the issues have been thoroughly aired. As Fishkin (1991: 1)

explains, an opinion poll 'models what the public thinks, given how little it knows', while a deliberative opinion poll 'models what the public would think, if it had a more adequate chance to think about the questions at issue'.

> **Focus group:** A moderated discussion among a small group of respondents on a particular topic, used to explore the thinking and emotions behind people's attitudes.

> **Deliberative opinion poll** or **citizens' jury:** An arrangement by which people are briefed by, and can question, experts and politicians on a given topic before their own opinions are measured.

Deliberative polling can therefore be used to anticipate how opinion might develop on new issues. It is also helpful on issues with a large technical content; for example, global warming or genetic testing. In such areas, expert explanation can usefully precede an

---

FOCUS 13.2 | The problem of the uninformed citizen

The quality and quantity of political participation are driven in part by the knowledge of citizens. Those who keep up with public affairs and have opinions about public matters are more likely to participate than those who do not. But there is no guarantee even that those who participate really know much about the issues at stake. In reality, most people are poorly or selectively informed on most public issues most of the time. This raises the troubling question of the uninformed citizen, and how low levels of knowledge impact government and politics.

This is far from a new problem. In *The Republic*, Plato argued that government was best conducted by knowledgeable experts, free from the influence of the uninformed majority. In *Leviathan*, Hobbes suggested that the role of the public should not extend much further than the formation of government. Alexander Hamilton spoke of 'the imprudence of democracy' and of the 'turbulent and changing' nature of the people, who could 'seldom judge or determine right' (Morris, 1966: 154). Others – including Machiavelli, Hume and Hegel – conceded that while the involvement of citizens in government was important, it was no more than a necessary evil. John Stuart Mill (1861: 268) regarded public opinion as representing the views of a 'collective mediocrity', and favoured a weighted system that gave more votes to university graduates on the grounds that they were more politically competent.

However, many political scientists favour a more nuanced approach. They argue that voters can use effective shortcuts such as party labels, expert endorsements, and campaign cues to help them make intelligent choices (Somin, 2004). Downs (1957) suggested that voters can infer the policy stance of candidates in an election from their party affiliations, while Popkin (1994) argues that most of the information voters learn about politics is picked up as a by-product of activities pursued as a part of daily life; the media help, he argues, by explaining the actions of political leaders and parties, and the relevance of those actions for voters, while campaigns do help to clarify the issues. For Lupia (1994), the use of shortcuts can in certain cases allow badly informed voters to emulate the behaviuor of relatively well-informed voters. Uninformed voters, it seems, are far from unintelligent.

expression of public opinion. Though not widely used, citizens' juries are an ingenious attempt to overcome the problem of ill-informed replies which bedevils conventional opinion polls.

In terms of the impact of public opinion, in some ways it pervades all policy-making. It forms the environment within which politicians work, sitting in on many government meetings even though it is never minuted as a member. In such discussions, public opinion usually performs one of two roles: acting either as a prompt or as a veto. 'Public opinion demands we do something about traffic congestion' is an example of the former; 'public opinion would never accept restrictions on car use' illustrates the latter. So, as Qualter (1991: 511) suggests, 'while public opinion does not govern, it may set limits on what governments do'.

Yet, public opinion is never all-powerful, even in liberal democracies. It informs agendas, rather than policy, and four limits are worth noting:

- Public opinion offers few detailed policy prescriptions. A few important objectives preoccupy the public but most policies are routine and uncontroversial. In detailed policy-making, expert and organized opinion matters more than public opinion.
- The public as a whole is often ill-informed, especially, but not only, on foreign policy (see Focus 13.2). Asked before the invasion of Iraq in 2003, 'To the best of your knowledge, how many of the September 11 hijackers were Iraqi citizens?', only 7 per cent of Americans gave the correct answer (which was zero) (Pryor, 2003).
- Public opinion can evade trade-offs but governments cannot, though they sometimes try. The public may want lower taxes, more government spending, and a lower budget deficit but leaders must choose between these incompatible objectives. Further, the risks associated with a policy are superficially assessed by the public but require close attention from decision-makers (Weissberg, 2002).
- Politicians' perceptions of public opinion are often inaccurate, because they are influenced by personal contacts and by their natural tendency to project their own views onto the wider electorate (Herbst, 1998).

Public opinion is most influential when it is seen to change. Only foolhardy politicians ignore developments in the overall climate of opinion, and many politicians are sensitive to changes in the national mood (Stimson, 2004). So same-sex marriage can be an irrelevance one year and the topic everyone is talking about the next; a skilled politician can spot and respond to such agenda shifts. What this tells us is that changes in public opinion matter as much as the levels of opinion. But just how far political leaders should follow the public mood, and how far they should actually lead, is another matter, as we saw in Chapter 8.

Women and political participation

Participation by women is an interesting sub-field within the broader field of political engagement. It is an area where significant trends are apparent within liberal democracies, reinforced in some countries by policies aimed at increasing the proportion of women legislators. Yet, women remain under-represented at the top tiers of government – often severely so – raising the question of whether a glass ceiling still limits women's progress, even in an era when open prejudice has waned.

In many liberal democracies, women are now at least equally as likely to vote as men, and often more so. In the 1920s and 1930s, after women had won the right to vote, studies in Western Europe and North America found that men were more likely to vote than women (Norris, 2009: 728). The balance has since been reversed in most democracies: among those registered to vote in the United States, for example, a higher proportion of women than men turned out at every presidential election between 1980 and 2012. In 2012, this gender gap was nearly four points (Center for American Women and Politics, 2014). In other democracies, too (including France, Germany, and the Scandinavian countries), women voters outnumber men (Stevens, 2007: 49). Male turnout still remains higher among the elderly, but that will likely change as generational replacement proceeds.

But in most forms of formal political participation beyond voting, men still hold the lead; they tend to dominate political party activities, making direct contact with politicians and bureaucrats, and protest activities (Adman, 2009: 315). And at least in the United States and the UK, men remain more interested in and knowledgeable about politics (Norris, 2009: 728; Hansard Society, 2012: 66). When it comes to holding political office, women are found disproportionately at the local rather than the national level (Stokes, 2005: pt V), and the higher the political office, the more likely it will be that a man will hold the post. The number of women

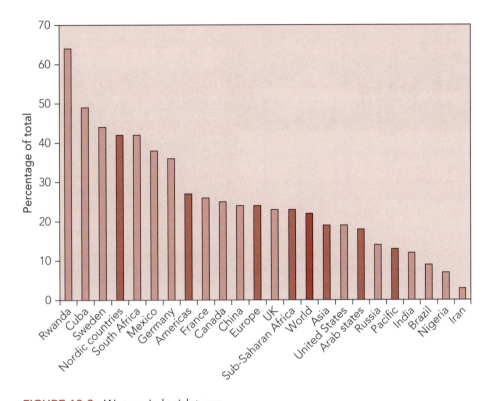

FIGURE 13.2: Women in legislatures

Source: Inter-Parliamentary Union (2015). Data for lower chambers of legislatures only. Europe bar for members of OSCE, excluding Nordic countries (Scandinavia and Iceland).

elected as legislative representatives is growing, to be sure (see Figure 13.2), but high-level politics continues to be dominated by men. There are several possible explanations for this:

- Women are less likely than men to be found in occupations that serve as a springboard to political careers, notably law (Darcy et al., 1994).

- Confidence may still be an issue. Even among those with similar levels of experience and achievement, argues Thomas (2005: 12), many women still tend to perceive themselves as less qualified than men.

- Legislatures remain, or at least are seen by many women, as **gendered institutions** – meaning that they still advantage men over women by, for example, having working hours that are unwelcoming to women with more than their fair share of family responsibilities (Kittilson and Schwindt-Bayer, 2012). The effect is that even when women are elected to office, they remain outsiders (Duerst-Lahti, 2002: 22).

> **Gendered institution:** A body that operates with formal rules and informal conventions which, often unintentionally, advantage men over women.

Many countries have adopted formal means to increase the number of women in legislatures, but this is a relatively recent development, with the 1995 UN-sponsored Beijing Platform for Action providing new momentum. Three main methods are used:

- **Reserved seats.** This is the oldest but rarest method, by which a party selects women members for special seats granted in proportion to its share of the vote; the more seats a party wins in the general election, the more reserved seats it is allocated. In Pakistan, where this format is well established, 60 special seats in the national assembly are reserved for women. The method is also used in Rwanda, which has the world's highest proportion of female legislators. There, 24 of 80 seats in the lower house are reserved for women; other female candidates are elected directly.

RUSSIA

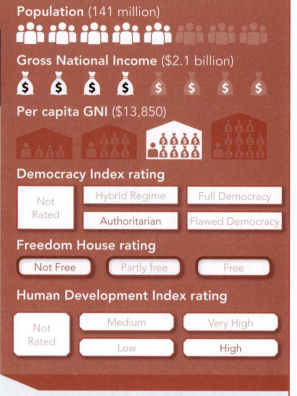

Population (141 million)

Gross National Income ($2.1 billion)

Per capita GNI ($13,850)

Democracy Index rating

| Not Rated | Hybrid Regime | Full Democracy |
| | Authoritarian | Flawed Democracy |

Freedom House rating

| Not Free | Partly free | Free |

Human Development Index rating

| Not Rated | Medium | Very High |
| | Low | High |

Brief Profile: Russia has undergone dramatic changes in recent decades. For nearly 70 years, Russia was the dominant partner in the Union of Soviet Socialist Republics (USSR), a state that most Westerners feared, distrusted, and misunderstood. The USSR collapsed in 1991, but its state socialist political and economic system still casts a shadow over modern Russia. The challenge has been to build a multi-party democracy in a culture unfamiliar with and unsympathetic to democracy. Its leaders have never lost sight of the national tradition of strong executive authority, and understanding Russia today is as much a question of assessing the actions and motives of President Vladimir Putin, and the clique around him, as of comprehending the country's governing institutions. Putin served two terms in office between 2000 and 2008, then stepped down as required by the constitution, winning re-election in 2012. Despite a static economy and population, Putin seeks to reassert what he sees as Russia's rightful position as a leading international power.

Form of government ⇨ Federal semi-presidential republic consisting of 83 'subjects', including republics, provinces, and territories. Modern state formed 1991, and most recent constitution adopted 1993.

Legislature ⇨ Bicameral Federal Assembly: a 450-member State Duma elected for five-year terms, and a relatively weak 166-member Federation Council with two members appointed by the president from each federal unit.

Executive ⇨ Semi-presidential. The president is directly elected, and limited to two consecutive six-year terms. The prime minister, appointed by the President and confirmed by the Duma, heads the Council of Ministers, and succeeds the president if needed (no vice president).

Judiciary ⇨ Based on civil law and the constitution of 1993. Headed by a 19-member Constitutional Court (members nominated for 12-year terms by the president and confirmed by the Federation Council) and, for civil and administrative cases, a Supreme Court.

Electoral system ⇨ Direct elections for the president, with the possibility of two rounds if no one wins a majority in the first ballot. Party list proportional representation is used for the State Duma.

Parties ⇨ Multi-party, but parties are weak and unstable – reflecting, rather than shaping, power. The leading party, United Russia, provides a foundation for the authoritarian rule of Vladimir Putin.

● **Party quota**. By far the most common method, introduced and prevalent in Europe, this typically occurs when one party adopts a quota (typically 25–50 per cent) for women candidates (or, more neutrally, for candidates from each gender) and others follow in order to avoid being seen as falling behind. To forestall a token effort, additional stipulations may require some women to be placed high on a party's

Participation in Russia

Russia presents a clear case of the limits of political participation in an authoritarian regime. On the one hand, Russia is an intensely political society with an educated people fully aware of national developments, which they follow using television in particular. On the other hand, political participation is shallow, held back by pervasive cynicism about the capacity of ordinary people to make a difference. The authoritarianism of the past and the present pervades political attitudes, creating a country with a passive majority. According to a 2012 survey, 57 per cent of Russians felt that a strong leader was more important than democracy (while 32 per cent opted for democracy), and 75 per cent felt that a strong economy was more important than a good democracy (while 21 per cent opted for democracy) (Pew Research Center, 2012).

Suspicion of organizations is endemic, with more people distrusting than trusting even the highest-rated institutions (the army and the Church), and placing most of their trust in personal networks of friends and family. Political parties languish near the bottom of the trust list, being mainly the creatures of politicians and the

president, and proving themselves to be unstable, with an insecure social base.

Few people belong to any voluntary public organizations, membership of trade unions is low, and regular church attendance is uncommon. Few social organizations have lasted long or built large memberships, while others have been incorporated into the regime, and any with foreign links are charged by the Putin administration with being engaged in espionage. With few organizations standing between citizen and state, mass political participation is concentrated on national elections, and Russia remains a distinctly uncivil society. The Russian people are subjects first and participants second.

Public protest in Russia against Putin's manipulation of parliamentary elections in 2011, and of the presidential contest of 2012, represented an important development. Younger, better educated people in the largest cities, notably Moscow, showed their dissatisfaction with their country's highly managed politics. At least in the short term, however, the most concrete outcome was a new law restricting (but not banning) such protests.

list (in list systems), or to be selected for winnable districts (in plurality systems) (see Chapter 16).

• **Legislative quota**. This is the most recent method. It is particularly common in Latin America and operates in a similar way to the party quota except that it is mandated by law and applies to all parties. The rules may be vague, allowing wiggle room for unenthusiastic parties, but they enable the government to parade its commitment to gender equality.

Quotas are no cure-all, not least because they can be seen as a remedy that fails to address the underlying causes of unequal representation. Also, they do not always work, a problem reflected in the fact that the percentage of women in legislatures in most countries remains lower than the numbers set in party, or even legislative, quotas. France passed an ambitious parity law in 2000, for example, but by 2012, the proportion of women in the National Assembly had only increased to 26 per cent. One reason for such discrepancies is implementation failure: not all parties deliver on the quota to

which they have subscribed. For Hughes (2011: 604), quota policies 'rarely challenge men's majority dominance of national legislatures'. Even so, they are a widely used device for influencing patterns of participation and have rapidly become a global standard (Dahlerup, 2006; Krook, 2009).

In spite of the problem of the glass ceiling, the number of women being elected to the highest executive offices has grown, such that when a woman is elected as a president or prime minister it is much less noteworthy than it once was. Indeed, one argument for legislative quotas is that the number of women in legislatures seems to influence the number in executive office. Since Sirimavo Bandaranaike became prime minister of Ceylon (now Sri Lanka) in July 1960, more than four dozen countries have elected women as presidents or prime ministers – see Table 13.3 for some examples.

Globally, the number of women holding cabinet positions has also grown, with several countries – including Finland, France, Iceland, Norway, Spain, South Africa, Sweden, and Switzerland – having achieved, or

TABLE 13.3: Women executives (selected)

	Country	In office
Sirimavo Bandaranaike[1]	Sri Lanka	1960–65, 1970–77, 1994–2000
Indira Gandhi[2]	India	1966–77, 1980–84
Golda Meir	Israel	1969–74
Margaret Thatcher	Britain	1979–90
Eugenia Charles	Dominica	1980–95
Gro Harlem Brundtland	Norway	1981, 1986–89, 1990–96
Corazon Aquino	Philippines	1986–92
Benazir Bhutto	Pakistan	1988–90, 1993–96
Jenny Clark	New Zealand	1999–2008
Megawati Sukarnoputri	Indonesia	2001–04
Luisa Diogo	Mozambique	2004–10
Angela Merkel	Germany	2005–
Ellen Johnson Sirleaf	Liberia	2006–
Jóhanna Sigurðardóttir[3]	Iceland	2009–13
Julia Gillard	Australia	2010–13
Dilma Rousseff	Brazil	2011–

Notes:
[1] First female head of government of modern era.
[2] Assassinated.
[3] World's first openly lesbian head of government.

coming close to achieving, an equal number of women as men in cabinet. While many women ministers are still found in the 'soft' areas of education and social policy, they have also moved into more powerful fields such as defence, finance, and foreign policy (Bauer and Tremblay, 2011). Despite this progress, it is as well to remember that the glass of participation remains well over half empty. In a large majority of countries, most ministers and legislators – as most top business executives – are still men.

Participation in authoritarian states

The argument is sometimes made that political participation, at least as understood in liberal democracies, is an empty concept in non-democratic settings. After all, the nature of authoritarian regimes is that they must seek to control popular activity in order to ensure their own survival and retention of power.

Yet the evidence suggests that there is substantial participation in many countries beyond the liberal democratic world (see Figure 13.3), even if its character is often distinctive. Writing before the Arab uprisings, for example, Albrecht (2008: 16) suggested that 'the concept of participation is not only applicable in the authoritarian states of the Middle East and North Africa, but also critical to a comprehensive understanding of state–society relationships in this region'. What we often find, for example, is **mobilized participation**. In contrast to the autonomous participation found in liberal democracies, where citizens make their own choices as it suits them, mobilized participation is managed and obligatory: people may be encouraged to take part in political rallies in return for rewards such as food and entertainment, or may be induced to do so by threats. Participation typically operates through informal sectors such as ethnic groups, rather than formal channels such as political parties, and is not without benefit: 'Citizens can sometimes learn by doing, gradually adopting new

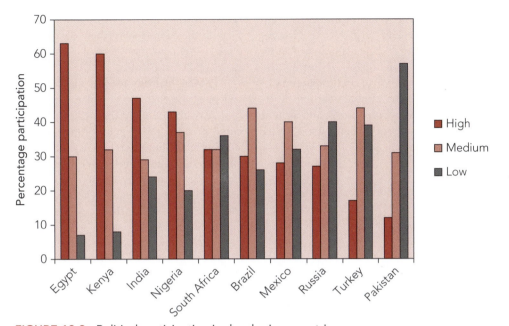

FIGURE 13.3: Political participation in developing countries

Source: Pew Research Center (2014). Participation is measured by frequency of voting, participation in protests, signing petitions, and other forms of engagement.

attitudes as the upshot of practical experience', suggest Bratton *et al.* (2005: 310).

> **Mobilized participation:** Elite–controlled involvement in politics designed to express popular support for the regime.

In authoritarian regimes, the limits and nature of participation are often subject to an implicit dialogue as activists test the boundaries of the acceptable. Authoritarian rulers may allow free space in those areas such as local politics which do not directly threaten the central leadership. They may permit the expression of opinion on the internet even as they censor television broadcasts. Further, as societies grow more complex, rulers often come to realize that responding to popular pressure on non-sensitive issues can limit dissent and enhance political stability.

In communist regimes, participation is both more extensive and more regimented than in liberal democracies: ordinary people sit on comradely courts, administer elections, join para–police organizations, and serve on people's committees covering local matters. But the quality of participation does not match its quantity. To ensure that mass engagement always strengthens the party, communist party members guide all the avenues of political expression. Communication flows only from top to bottom. So, people behave as they are treated: as passive, rather than active. Because no real channels exist for airing grievances, people are left with two choices: to shut up and continue with life, or to air their complaints outside the system.

Against the background of a long history of authoritarianism, the Chinese Communist Party has opened some social space in which sponsored groups can operate with relative freedom. For example, more than 150,000 civic associations were registered in 2007, providing an opportunity for citizen-to-citizen communication under the party's watchful eye in such areas as education and the environment (Guo, 2007). But explicit opposition to the party remains forbidden. The topic may go unmentioned but memories remain of the Tiananmen Square massacre of 1989, when the army's tanks turned on pro-democracy demonstrators in Beijing. At the local level, sometimes violent protests continue against corruption, unemployment, pollution, illegal levies, or non-payment of wages or pensions. Demonstrations by ethnic minorities aside, these local protests do not threaten the party's dominance but are directed at local failures to implement national policies.

Elsewhere, a common technique for channelling, but also controlling, participation in authoritarian states is **clientelism**, or patron–client relationships. These are traditional, informal hierarchies fuelled by exchanges between a high-status patron and clients of lower status. The colloquial phrase 'big man/small boy' conveys the nature of the interaction: patrons are landlords, employers, party leaders, government ministers, ethnic leaders, or anyone with control over resources, and around whom clients – lacking resources of their own – gather for protection and security.

> **Clientelism:** Politics substantially based on patron–client relationships. A powerful figure (the patron) provides protection to a number of lower-status clients who, in exchange, offer their unqualified allegiance and support.

Although patron–client relationships are found to some extent in all political systems, including liberal democracies, they are of greatest political significance in authoritarian regimes. Particularly in low-income countries, and unequal societies with weak governing institutions, personal networks of patrons and clients can be the main instrument for bringing ordinary people into contact with formal politics, and are often the central organizing structure of politics itself (Figure 13.4). Despite their informality, these networks underpin, and often overwhelm, more formal channels of participation such as political parties.

Political patrons control the votes of their clients and persuade them to attend meetings, join organizations, or simply follow their patron around in a deferential manner. These public (on stage) affirmations of support are politically relevant, even though they often fail to reflect clients' private (off stage) opinion (Scott, 1985). Participation by clients is controlled and mobilized, but the patron–client relationship is based on personal exchange rather than a political party or a shared political outlook.

The patron's power, and its inhibiting effect on democracy, is illustrated in this comment by Egypt's President Abdul Nasser, interviewed in 1957 when he was still a reforming leader (Owen, 1993):

> We were supposed to have a democratic system between 1923 and 1953. But what good was this democracy to our people? You have seen the landowners driving the peasants to the polling booths. There they would vote according to the instructions of their masters. I want the peasants to be able to say

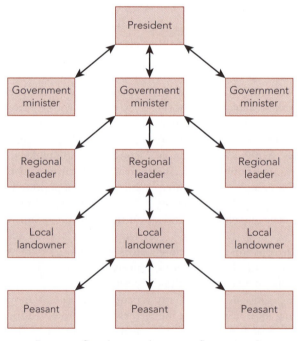

Resources flow downwards, support flows upwards.

FIGURE 13.4: A patronage network linking centre and periphery

'yes' and 'no' without this in any way affecting their livelihood and daily bread. This in my view is the basis for freedom and democracy.

Participation through patronage appeals in authoritarian settings because it links elite and mass, centre and periphery, in a context of inequality. Although inequality provides the soil in which patronage networks flourish, these relationships still act as political glue, binding the highest of the high with the lowest of the low.

By linking people across social levels, patron–client relationships limit the expression of solidarity among people of the same class, such as peasants. For the elite, they are a useful tactic of divide and rule. The decay of such hierarchical networks of dependence can be an indication of a transition to a more modern society in which people have acquired sufficient resources to be able to participate in an autonomous fashion. Put bluntly, security means people no longer need to trade their vote. Poverty and authoritarian rule provide a setting in which patron–client relationships flourish; affluence and democracy generate a climate in which they decay.

Although social movements face stronger opposition and run greater risks for the lives and well-being of their participants, they have occasionally been a significant feature in many authoritarian regimes. They tend to mobilize the poor and the marginalized, as people facing acute problems of daily life collaborate to improve their living conditions in a hostile political environment. The urban poor organizing soup kitchens, the inhabitants of shanty towns lobbying for land reform, groups of mothers pressing for information on their sons who had 'disappeared' under military rule – all were examples of this blossoming of popular political activity. Such movements were a response to political exclusion.

A problem with understanding participation in the many authoritarian regimes in developing societies stems from the difficulties of measuring public opinion in such states:

- In poorer countries where most people are focused on daily survival, and both education and communication are limited, there may be no such thing as public opinion on anything beyond local matters.

- Sample surveys are hard to run when it is unclear how to define a representative sample.

- Since urban elites are the easiest to reach, they will be the people most often surveyed, but their interests (and levels of participation or engagement) will differ from those of the rural poor.

- People may be unfamiliar and uncomfortable with the formal interviewing techniques used in liberal democracies. More appropriate formats may be less systematic. In authoritarian states, people will be naturally suspicious of pollsters, and unwilling to express their true feelings.

- Polling may not be allowed, or may be heavily controlled. In Mexico, for example, the governing Institutional Revolutionary Party did not allow the first independent polls until the late 1980s (Romero, 2004: 485).

It might be natural to suppose that authoritarian leaders are not much interested in what their citizens think, but this is not necessarily the case. In fact, suggests Romero (2004: 487), while democratic leaders want to bring together large groups of citizens in order to win elections or succeed with policy goals, authoritarian leaders will want information on those groups in order to monitor threats to their own survival in office.

DISCUSSION QUESTIONS

- Is participation in the political process a civic obligation?

- Which groups under-participate in politics in your country and what can be done to engage those who belong to them?

- What do you think of the argument that people can use information short cuts to help them make intelligent decisions?

- Have social media made any difference to the way you or those you know engage with politics?

- Given human nature, is clientelism avoidable?

KEY TERMS

Assassination
Clientelism
Consumer politics
Conventional participation
Deliberative opinion poll
Focus group
Gendered institution
Mobilized participation

Opinion poll
Political exclusion
Political participation
Public opinion
Sample survey
Terrorism
Unconventional participation

FURTHER READING

Bishop, George F. (2005) *The Illusion of Public Opinion: Fact and Artefact in American Public Opinion Polls.* A critique of polling, addressing the problems arising from public ignorance and poorly informed opinion.

Dalton, Russell J. (2013) *Citizen Politics: Public Opinion and Political Parties in Advanced Industrial Democracies*, 5th edn. This comparative text provides a wide-ranging review of political attitudes and behaviour in liberal democracies.

Kittilson, Mike and Leslie Schwindt-Bayer (2012) *The Gendered Effects of Electoral Institutions: Political Engagement and Participation.*

Krook, Mona Lena (2009) *Quotas for Women in Politics: Gender and Candidate Selection Reform Worldwide.* One of the first global analyses of gender quotas for legislative office.

Lust-Okar, Ellen and Saloua Zerhouni (eds) (2008) *Political Participation in the Middle East.* Predating the Arab Spring, this book offers one of the rare studies of participation outside the liberal democratic world, with studies of seven Middle Eastern states.

Norris, Pippa (2002) *Democratic Phoenix: Reinventing Political Activism.* A widely cited study suggesting that new forms of political participation have emerged to supplement traditional modes.

14 Political communication

PREVIEW

Mass communication lies at the heart of political discourse. It informs governments and citizens, it defines the limits of expression (fewer in democracies than in authoritarian states), and it provides us with 'mental maps' of the political world outside our direct experience. The technology of mass political communication has changed dramatically over the past century, taking us from a time when newspapers dominated to the era of broadcasting (first radio and then television), and bringing us to the age of the internet, with instant information in unparalleled quantities from numerous sources, at least for the half of the world's households that currently have access. As technology has changed, so have the dynamics of political communication; conveying and receiving news is increasingly interactive, with consumers playing a critical role in defining what constitutes 'the news'.

This chapter begins with a brief survey of the evolution of the mass media and political communication, progressing to an assessment of the as-yet not entirely understood implications of social media. It then looks at how the political influence of mass media is felt, reviewing the key mechanisms of influence: reinforcement, agenda-setting, framing, and priming. After reviewing recent trends in political communication (commercialization, fragmentation, globalization, and interaction), the chapter compares different media outlets, and ends with an assessment of political communication in authoritarian states. There, the marketplace of ideas is more closely controlled, though the internet in general, and social media in particular, have created more space for free communication among some citizens.

CONTENTS

- Political communication: an overview
- Media development
- Media influence
- Recent trends in political communication
- Comparing media outlets
- Political communication in authoritarian states

KEY ARGUMENTS

- Communication is a core political activity and its study forms an important part of political analysis. In particular, a free flow of communication provides one test for distinguishing between liberal democracies and authoritarian regimes.

- The technology of mass media has undergone rapid change over the last century, most importantly with the rise of the internet. But the political impact of the internet remains a matter of much speculation, particularly given that levels of access vary, and that half the households in the world are still unconnected.

- Researchers identify four classes of media effects: reinforcement, agenda-setting, framing, and priming. But much of our understanding of these effects is based on single-country studies, and comparative data on political media effects are scarce.

- Too often, mass media coverage is assumed to be influential without there being any evidence cited in support. A broader perspective suggests that the media provide a structure for our worldview, rather than simply an influence on it.

- Current trends – including the shift to more commercial, fragmented, global, and interactive media – are reshaping the environment of political communication. These developments impact politicians, voters, and the relationship between them (e.g. election campaigns).

- In authoritarian regimes, leaders have varied and often subtle means for limiting independent journalism, though in the internet age censorship is rarely complete.

Political communication: an overview

Society – and, with it, government and politics – is created, sustained, and modified through mass communication. Without a continuous exchange of information, attitudes, and values, society would be impossible, as would meaningful political participation. Efficient and responsive government depends on such an exchange, without which leaders would not know what citizens needed, and citizens would not know what government was doing (or not doing). Mass communication is also a technique of control: 'Give me a balcony and I will be president', said José Maria Velasco, five times president of Ecuador. It is, in short, a core political activity, allowing meaning to be constructed, needs transmitted, and authority exercised.

Assessments of the quality of **political communication** are key to the process classifying political systems. Democracies are characterized by a free flow of information through open and multiple channels. Dahl (1998: 37) argues that a liberal democracy must provide opportunities for what he calls enlightened understanding: 'within reasonable limits as to time, each member [of a political association] must have equal and effective opportunities for learning about relevant alternative policies and their likely consequences'. In a hybrid regime, by contrast, dominance of major media outlets is a tool through which leaders maintain their ascendancy over potential challengers. For their part, authoritarian regimes typically allow no explicit dissent at all. Media channels are limited and manipulated, and citizens – as a result – must often rely more on unofficial channels, including the internet, for their political news.

> **Political communication:** The means by which political information is produced and disseminated, and the effects of this information flow on the political process.

Even though much recent research in political communication focuses on the message itself and the meanings embedded within it, the transmission model is – as we will see – a helpful way of understanding the broad process of communication via mass media. This takes into consideration the sender of the message, the nature of the message itself, the channel used, the user, and the impact of the message. The danger of focusing solely on content is that we learn nothing about the receivers and even less about the political effect of the message. Blaming media bias for why others fail to see the world as we do can be tempting, but is usually superficial and unenlightening.

Jones (2005: 17) has few doubts about the importance of the media to politics in democracies. He judges that media consumption should now be seen as a vital form of political participation:

> Media are our primary point of access to politics – the space in which politics now chiefly happens for most people, and the place for political encounters that precede, shape and at times determine further bodily participation (if it is to happen at all) … Such encounters do much more than provide 'information' about politics. They constitute our mental maps of the political world outside our direct experience. They provide a reservoir of images and voices, heroes and villains, sayings and slogans, facts and ideas that we draw on in making sense of politics.

Politics and government is only partly about creating efficient institutions and developing effective policies; it is also about persuasion and information, whether this takes place in the free market of ideas or whether it is manipulated for political ends.

Media development

The political significance of the media is famously encapsulated in the quip attributed (depending on the source used) either to Edmund Burke or to Thomas Macaulay, both British politicians (see Spilchal, 2002: 44). Noting the existence of three existing political 'estates' (the monarchy, the peerage, and the House of Commons), Burke or Macaulay referred to the reporters sitting in the gallery of the House of Commons as the **fourth estate**, a term that has since been used to denote the political significance of journalists.

> **Fourth estate:** A term used to describe the political role of journalists.

Although we take access to a variety of **mass media** for granted, their rise has been a relatively recent development, dating back no more than two centuries (see Figure 14.1). The first printed book dates from China in 686, the Gutenberg press started printing with moveable type in 1453, and the first newspaper appeared in 1605. But most of what we now consider mass media came with the development

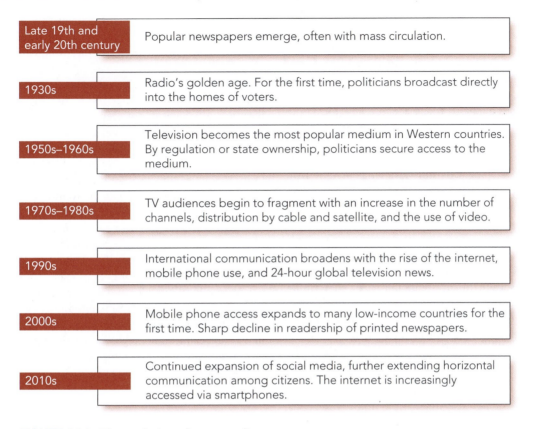

FIGURE 14.1: The evolution of mass media

of new technology in the nineteenth and twentieth centuries, allowing true mass communication. This, in turn, facilitated the emergence of a common national identity and the growth of the state. For the first time, political communication meant a shared experience for dispersed populations, providing a glue to connect the citizens of large political units.

> **Mass media:** Channels of communication that reach a large number of people. Television, radio, and websites are examples. Until the advent of social media, mass media were one-to-many and non-interactive.

Newspapers

Widespread literacy in a shared language permitted the emergence of popular newspapers in Western states, the key development in political communication during the nineteenth and early twentieth centuries (Dooley and Baron, 2001). Advances in printing and distribution opened up the prospect of transforming party journals with a small circulation into populist and profitable papers funded by advertising. By growing away from their party roots, newspapers became not only more popular but also, paradoxically, more important to politics.

In compact countries with national distribution, such as Britain and Japan, newspapers built enormous circulations, and owners became powerful political figures. In inter-war Britain, for example, four newspaper barons – Lords Beaverbrook, Rothermere, Camrose, and Kemsley – owned papers with a combined circulation of over 13 million, amounting to one in every two daily papers sold. Stanley Baldwin, a prime minister of the time, famously described such proprietors as 'aiming at power without responsibility – the prerogative of the harlot throughout the ages' (Curran and Seaton, 2009: 64).

Broadcasting

Although newspapers remained significant channels of political communication, their primacy was supplanted in the twentieth century by broadcasting. Cinema newsreels, radio, and then television enabled communication with the mass public to take place in a new form: spoken rather than written, personal rather than abstract, and – increasingly – live rather than reported. Communication also went international, beginning in the 1920s with the development of shortwave radio, used by Britain and the Netherlands to broadcast to their empires. Nazi Germany, the United States, the Soviet Union, and other major Western states then followed. Shortwave radio continued to provide an inexpensive and easy link with the outside world for many countries through to the Cold War and beyond.

Domestically, broadcasting's impact in Western liberal democracies was relatively benign. A small number of national television channels initially dominated the airwaves in most countries after the Second World War, providing a shared experience of national events and popular entertainment. By offering some common ground to societies which were, in these early postwar decades, still strongly divided by class and religion, these new media initially served as agents of national integration.

Even more dramatic was the impact of broadcasting on politicians themselves. A public speech to a live audience encouraged expansive words and dramatic gestures but a quieter tone was needed for transmission from the broadcasting studio direct to the living room. The task was to converse with the unseen listener and viewer, rather than to deliver a speech to a visible audience gathered together in one place. The art was to talk to the millions as though they were individuals.

President Franklin Roosevelt's fireside chats, broadcast live by radio to the American population in the 1930s, exemplified this new approach. The impact of Roosevelt's somewhat folksy idiom was undeniable. He talked not so much to the citizens but as a citizen and was rewarded with his country's trust. In this way, broadcasting – and the medium of radio, specifically – transformed not only the reach, but also the style, of political communication (Barber, 1992).

Broadcasting has also made a substantial contribution to political communication in most low-income countries, albeit for different reasons. In the developing world, broadcasting (whether radio or television) has two major advantages over print media. First, it does not require physical distribution to each user; second, it is accessible to the one in five of the world's population who cannot read.

These factors initially encouraged the spread of radio. Villagers could gather round the shared set to hear the latest news, not least on the price of local crops. Today, satellite television and mobile phones are also accessible to many of the world's poor, expanding opportunities not only for downward communication from the elite, but also for horizontal communication between ordinary people. In Kenya, for example, internet access was expensive and slow until just a few years ago, when the government opened up the mobile phone market. This sparked a fierce war for market share among carriers, leading to a simultaneous reduction in prices and a broadening of options. Safaricom became a successful local provider, and many Kenyans now have access to M-Pesa, a mobile banking platform that allows bills to be paid and funds moved online. How this dramatic communications revolution will impact politics in Kenya, and other developing countries that follow in Kenya's wake, remains to be seen.

Just as some lower-income countries have moved directly to mobile phones, eliminating the need for an expensive fixed-wire infrastructure, so also have they developed broadcasting networks without passing through the stage of mass circulation newspapers. The capacity of ruling politicians to reach out to poor, rural populations through these radio and television networks remains an important component of governance in hybrid and authoritarian regimes.

Social media

The rise of the internet and the growing use of **social media** (see Table 14.1) has brought perhaps the fastest and most widespread changes ever seen in mass communication. The internet has made copious new amounts of information available (albeit of variable quality), while social media have fundamentally changed the ways in which governments and citizens communicate, and in which citizens communicate with one another.

> **Social media:** Interactive online platforms with designated recipients, which facilitate collective or individual communication for the exchange of user-generated content. Social media bridge mass and personal communication.

TABLE 14.1: Forms of social media

	Features	Examples
Social networking	Allow people to connect with one another and to share information and ideas.	Facebook (created in 2004) is the best known, but others include LinkedIn, MySpace, Academic, and Google+.
Media sharing	Otherwise known as content communities. Allows users to upload pictures, videos and other media.	YouTube (created 2005), Reddit, and Pinterest.
Collaborative sites	Allow users to post content.	Wikipedia is the best known, created in 2001.
Blogs and microblogs	Allow users to share ideas and hold online conversations on matters of shared interest.	Twitter (created 2006) is the best-known microblog, although several social networking sites include microblogging options.

The internet connects people who would not otherwise be able to communicate with one another, potentially encouraging political communication and debate across a wide variety of sectors. Political leaders and parties can communicate more often and more directly with citizens via social media, although the most active users are already politically active, and many of the posts provided are partisan. Studies find that while most people agree that the internet offers access to a wider range of views than is the case with traditional media, it has also increased the influence of more extreme views, and poses new challenges to users in separating truth from fiction (Pew Research Center, 2011).

It is also important to note that access to the internet is far from equal. Many people have no access at all (because they have no access to electricity and/or computers and/or smartphones and/or broadband services), authoritarian regimes such as China and Iran continue to censor the internet, even in wealthy countries there are still many older citizens who decline to go online, and there are many people who do not use the internet for news, or use it only in a selective manner. And access to the internet does not mean that it will necessarily be used for political ends, as shown by the case of Singapore (listed as a flawed democracy in the Democracy Index). While this affluent island state has one of the highest rates of internet penetration in the world, many of its people remain uncomfortable about using the internet to exchange political information because of the tight controls and regulations imposed by the government (Lee and Willnat, 2009). The regime also discourages research into political communication; the

technology is advanced but understanding of its impact lags substantially.

As of 2015, just over half the households in the world still did not have internet access, with rates of connection ranging from 82 per cent in Europe to 60 per cent in the Americas, 39 per cent in Asia and the Pacific, and 11 per cent in Africa (see Figure 14.2). It might also be suggested that the historic Western dominance of platforms such as social media and search engines created a new form of information imperialism, even if that pre-eminence is now being countered by their Chinese equivalents (Jin, 2015). The sheer variety of opinions that are now available online might also militate against the idea of homogenization, and might actually exert the opposite effect.

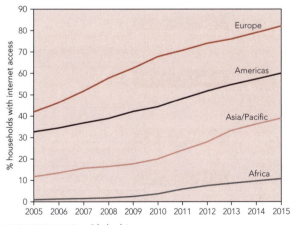

FIGURE 14.2: Global internet access
Source: International Telecommunication Union (2015)

Media influence

In seeking to understand the political influence of the mass media, we can use the **transmission model** as a guide. This distinguishes five components in any act of political communication: who says what to whom, through which medium and with what effects (see Figure 14.3). Working our way through these components, it soon becomes clear that the media are a structure within which many people live their political lives. In turn, there are four potential mechanisms of influence: reinforcement, agenda-setting, framing, and priming (Figure 14.4). Each of these has contributed to academic thinking about how we should address media impact, and together they provide a helpful repertoire in analysing the more tangible effects of the media.

> **Transmission model:** A model that intreprets any communication as consisting of a *sender* sending a *message* through one or more *channels* to a *receiver* with potential *effects*.

In the 1950s, before television became pre-eminent, the **reinforcement** thesis – also known as the 'minimal effects model' – held sway (Klapper, 1960). The argument then was that party loyalties initially transmitted through the family acted as a political sunscreen protecting people from media effects. People saw what they wanted to see and remembered what they wanted to recall.

In Britain, for instance, where national newspapers were strongly partisan, many working-class people brought up in Labour households continued to read Labour papers as adults. The correlation between the partisanship of newspapers and their readers reflected **self-selection** by readers, rather than the propaganda impact of the press. Given strong self-selection, the most the press could do was to reinforce readers' existing dispositions, encouraging them to stay loyal to the cause and to turn out on election day. Those effects may have been significant but they hardly justified the more extreme statements about the power of the media.

> **Self-selection:** The biased choice of media sources made by an individual. For example, people who are already racist may choose to visit racist websites, complicating the task of estimating the impact of those sites.

The reinforcement theory is still relevant. Consider, for example, the polarized environment in some segments of the American media. The typical viewer of Fox News or reader of the *Wall Street Journal* is more likely to be a conservative drawn to these outlets than to be an ex-liberal converted to the right as a result of stumbling upon their news coverage. To some extent, at least, Fox News and the *Wall Street Journal* preach to the converted.

Alternatively, consider the internet. The web allows voters to seek out, and be reinforced by, any shade of opinion with which they already sympathize, experiencing the kind of confirmation bias discussed in Chapter 6. In the main, opponents will choose not to go there, except if they are one of the few who wish to

Component	Quality	Example
Sender	Who?	A local political party organization
Message	What?	Encouraging voting at a forthcoming election
Channel	How?	Email or leaflet
Receiver	To whom?	Party supporters
Impact	Effect?	Voter turnout goes up

FIGURE 14.3: The transmission model of political communication

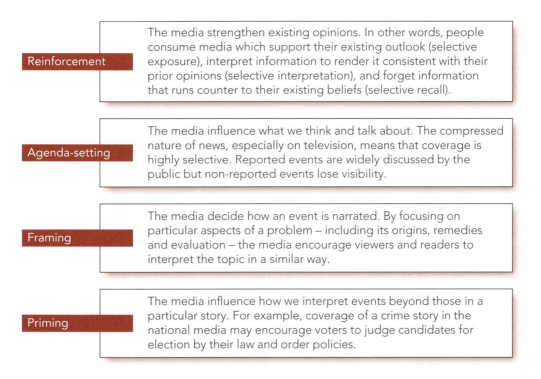

Reinforcement	The media strengthen existing opinions. In other words, people consume media which support their existing outlook (selective exposure), interpret information to render it consistent with their prior opinions (selective interpretation), and forget information that runs counter to their existing beliefs (selective recall).
Agenda-setting	The media influence what we think and talk about. The compressed nature of news, especially on television, means that coverage is highly selective. Reported events are widely discussed by the public but non-reported events lose visibility.
Framing	The media decide how an event is narrated. By focusing on particular aspects of a problem – including its origins, remedies and evaluation – the media encourage viewers and readers to interpret the topic in a similar way.
Priming	The media influence how we interpret events beyond those in a particular story. For example, coverage of a crime story in the national media may encourage voters to judge candidates for election by their law and order policies.

FIGURE 14.4: Mechanisms of media impact

know their enemy. Here, too, the effect of self-selection is to facilitate reinforcement but limit conversion.

Even so, the reinforcement account is past its best as a primary perspective on media effects. In the era of the internet, we can no longer imagine the typical voter as living wholly in an information silo dominated by one political outlook. This was understood as long ago as the 1970s and 1980s, when the agenda-setting role of the media won more attention. This perspective contends that the media (and television in particular) influence what we think about, though not necessarily what we think. The media write certain items onto the agenda and, by implication, keep other issues away from the public's gaze. Thus the influence of the media stems not only from what is said but also from what is not said (Lazarsfeld and Merton, 1948).

In an election campaign, for example, television directs our attention to major candidates and to the race for victory; by contrast, fringe candidates and the issues are often treated as secondary. Walter Lippman's widely quoted view (1922) of the press articulated the agenda-setting perspective: 'it is like a beam of a searchlight that moves restlessly about, bringing one episode and then another out of the darkness and into vision'. In deciding how to reduce a day's worth of world events into the span of a 30-minute evening broadcast (including commercials), programme editors set the agenda and exert their impact, asking questions such as these:

- Will the story have a strong impact on the audience?
- Does the story involve violence? ('If it bleeds, it leads.')
- Is the story current and novel?
- Does the story involve well-known people?

Because news programmes often focus on the exceptional, their content is invariably an unrepresentative record of events. Policy fiascos receive more attention than policy successes; corruption is a story but integrity is a bore; a fresh story gathers more coverage than a new development of a tired theme. As a result, agenda-setting creates a warped image of the world.

But we should recognize two limitations to the agenda-setting perspective. First, editors do not select stories on a whim, but are instead highly sensitive to the potential impact of different items on audience size and appreciation, and are paid to demonstrate their news sense; if they consistently fail to do so, they lose their jobs. Hence it is naive to attribute broad agenda-setting power to editors simply because they make specific judgements about what is to appear on screen or on the front page. They too reflect the agenda.

A more nuanced view, that the media circulate rather than create opinions, is implicit in Newton's assessment of the relationship between journalists and society (2006: 215):

> Implicit in many statements about media effects on society is the idea that somehow the media are quite separate from society, firing their poison arrows from a distance. In fact, the media are part of society; journalists and editors do not arrive on Earth from Mars and Venus, they are part of society like the rest of us.

Second, the explosion of channels in the electronic era means that agenda control is no longer as strict as in the heyday of broadcast television. Even if people still search for reinforcement, they can, if they wish, follow even the most specialized political interests through some media outlet somewhere. As the media become more pluralistic, so consumers acquire the capacity to follow their noses and shape their own agendas.

The framing of a story – the way in which reports construct a narrative about an event – is a more recent attempt to understand media impact. This is a prime example of the interpretive approach to understanding politics, and reflects Plato's observation that 'those who tell the stories also rule society'. The journalist's words, and the camera's images, help to frame the story, providing a narrative which encourages a particular reaction from the viewer.

For example, are immigrants presented as a stimulus to the economy, or as a threat to society? Do media in particular European countries portray membership of the European Union critically or positively? Is a criminal who has been sentenced to be executed receiving their just deserts, or a cruel and unusual punishment? As the concept of a 'story' suggests, the journalist must translate the event covered into an organized narrative which connects with the receiver: the shorter the report, the greater the reliance on the shared, if sometimes simplistic, presuppositions which Jamieson and Waldman (2003) term 'consensus frames'.

Finally, the media may exert a priming effect, encouraging people to apply the criteria implicit in one story to new information and topics. For example, the more the media focuses its coverage on foreign policy, the more likely it is that voters will be primed to judge parties and candidates according to their policies in this area, and perhaps even to vote accordingly. Similarly, it is possible that coverage of racist attacks may prompt some individuals to engage in similar acts themselves, should the opportunity arise in their neighbourhood.

Recent trends in political communication

Four broad changes in political communication have been underway in higher-income countries, the combined effect of which has changed the nature of news and the choices available to consumers. Where the mass media once performed a nation-building function, their emerging impact today is to splinter the traditional national audience, as media become more commercial, fragmented, global, and interactive.

Commercialization

The commercialization of the mass media has meant the decline of public broadcasting and the rise of for-profit media treating users as consumers rather than citizens. It also allows media moguls such as Rupert Murdoch to build transnational broadcasting networks, achieving on a global scale the prominence which the newspaper barons of the nineteenth century acquired at national level.

Such developments have threatened the previously cosy links between national political parties and national broadcasters. Parties no longer called the shots and politics has had to justify its share of screen time. In an increasingly commercial environment, Tracey (1998) claims that public service broadcasting has become nothing more than 'a corpse on leave from its grave'. In a similar way, McChesney (1999) argues that commercialization has shrunk the public space in which political issues are discussed. Channels in search of profit devote little time to serious politics, and instead concentrate on soft news, or 'news you can use'. Certainly, profit-seeking media have no incentive to supply public goods such as an informed citizenry and high voter turnout, which were traditional concerns of public media.

Against this, commercial broadcasters reply that it is preferable to reach a mass audience with limited but stimulating political coverage than it is to offer extensive but dull political programming which, in reality, only ever reached a minority with a prior interest in public affairs (Norris, 2000). Specialist political programmes continue for political junkies but such broadcasts can no longer be foisted on unwilling audiences.

Fragmentation

With more channels and an enhanced ability to download and consume programmes on demand, consumers are increasingly able to watch, hear, and read what they want, when they want, and how they want. Long gone are the days when TV viewers were restricted to a few major stations or networks, and in many countries young people are now more likely to be found watching via the internet than through the traditional TV set (Murrie, 2006). Distribution by cable, satellite, the internet, and mobile devices allows viewers to receive a greater range of content, and through the use of DVRs and on-demand services, viewers can record and create programming to suit their personal tastes and schedules.

In the US, these changes are reflected in the falling audience shares for nightly news on the three major television networks (ABC, CBS, and NBC), which fell from 42 per cent of the adult population in 1980 to just 16 per cent in 2012 (Pew Research Center, 2013). Printed newspaper circulations are also plummeting throughout the developed world: by 23 per cent for dailies in the United States and by 16 per cent in Western Europe between 2006 and 2015 (World Association of Newspapers, 2015). Local and evening newspapers are closing (though some are reinventing themselves online), with some shift of printed material to generally less political free papers.

The political implications of this transition from broadcasting to 'narrowcasting' are substantial. Governments, parties, and commercial advertisers have more difficulty reaching a mass audience when viewers can simply choose another channel online or via their remote control. Where earlier generations would passively watch whatever appeared on their television screen, the internet is inherently user-driven, and TV is rapidly following suit; people decide for themselves where to go.

Overall exposure to politics falls as voters become harder to reach. In response, political parties are forced to adopt a greater range and sophistication of marketing strategies, including the use of personalized but expensive contact techniques such as direct mail, email, social networks, and telephone – as skilfully exploited by Barack Obama in securing donations and volunteers for his successful election campaigns in 2008 and 2012 (Kreiss, 2012).

In this more fragmented media environment, politicians continue their migration from television news to higher-rated talk shows, blurring the distinction between the politician and the celebrity in the expanding Pollywood zone where Politics meets Hollywood (Street, 2011: ch. 9). They compete for followers on Facebook and Twitter against sports personalities, movie stars and the latest reality show. The sound bite, never unimportant, becomes even more vital as politicians learn to articulate their agenda in a short interview, or an even briefer commercial.

Just as the balance within the media industry has moved from public service to private profit, so fragmentation has shifted the emphasis in political communication from parties to voters. Politicians rode the emergence of broadcasting with considerable success in the twentieth century, but they are experiencing a rougher ride in the new millennium of fragmented media. As Mazzoleni (1987) pointed out, the balance of power between parties and the media has switched from a 'party logic' to a 'media logic'.

Globalization

In 1776, the English reaction to the American Declaration of Independence took 50 days to filter back to the United States. By 2003, global viewers were watching broadcasts of the invasion of Iraq in real time. We now take for granted the almost immediate transmission of newsworthy events around the world, and even authoritarian governments find it harder than ever to isolate their populations from international developments. Even before the internet, communist states found it difficult to jam foreign radio broadcasts aimed at their people. Discussing the collapse of communist states, Eberle (1990: 194–5) claimed that 'the changes in Eastern Europe and the Soviet Union were as much the triumph of communication as the failure of communism'. Today, China's iron curtain of censorship can easily be circumvented by those of its people who take the trouble to access the range of overseas blogs and sites documenting the latest developments within their country.

SPOTLIGHT

VENEZUELA

Brief Profile: Venezuela should by all rights be a Latin American success story, but a combination of political and economic difficulties has left it languishing as a hybrid regime in the Democracy Index. It is rich in oil (as well as coal, iron ore, bauxite, and other minerals) but most of its people live in poverty. The wealth of the rich, displayed through European cars, manicured suburbs, and gated communities, coexists with public squalor. Much of the failure can be attributed to Hugo Chávez, elected president in 1998 on a populist left-wing platform. His supporters, known as *chavistas*, claim that his policies of economic nationalization and expanded social programmes helped the poor, but his critics charge that they contributed to inflation and unemployment. He died in 2013, but his successor Nicolas Maduro has built on the Chávez legacy, continuing to distort the economy, demonize opponents and over-politicize the country's culture.

Population (30.8 million)

Gross National Income ($510 billion)

Per capita GNI ($12,820)

Democracy Index rating

Not Rated | Hybrid Regime | Full Democracy
Authoritarian | Flawed Democracy

Freedom House rating

Not Free | Partly free | Free

Human Development Index rating

Not Rated | Medium | Very High
Low | High

Form of government ⇨ Federal presidential republic consisting of 23 states and a Capital District. State formed 1811, and most recent constitution adopted 1999.

Legislature ⇨ Unicameral National Assembly of 165 members elected for fixed and renewable five-year terms.

Executive ⇨ Presidential. A president elected for an unlimited number of six-year terms, supported by a vice president and cabinet of ministers.

Judiciary ⇨ Supreme Tribunal of Justice, with 32 members elected by the National Assembly to 12-year terms.

Electoral system ⇨ President elected in national contest using a plurality system. National Assembly elected using mixed member proportional representation, with 60 per cent elected by single-member plurality and the balance by proportional representation.

Parties ⇨ Multi-party, with a changing roster of parties currently dominated by the United Socialist Party of Venezuela.

Recent technological developments also facilitate underground opposition to authoritarian regimes. A small group with internet access now has the potential to draw the world's attention to political abuses, providing source material for alert journalists. The governments of Iran and Saudi Arabia have each suffered from overseas groups in this way, though both regimes remain in place. The internet can also be used by small groups to convey less edifying messages. Both al-Qaeda and the so-called Islamic State (ISIS) have been adept at releasing online images that can be seen by anyone with access to the internet, containing propaganda, warnings, and scenes of violence intended both to encourage supporters and to scare enemies.

➡

Political communication in Venezuela

One of the sources of Venezuela's low ranking in indices of democracy is its poor record on media freedom. As elsewhere in Latin America, the media establishment is privately owned, but this status does not prevent chronic intervention by government. In its *Freedom of the Press* report, Freedom House ranks Venezuela as Not Free, and the annual reports published by Reporters Without Borders (a French-based group that promotes press freedom) charge the government with imposing pressure on independent media. The means used include a travel ban on editors and media executives, the biased adjudication of court cases involving journalists, a reduction in access to newsprint, and even death threats against journalists.

The 1999 Venezuelan constitution guarantees freedom of expression, but a 2004 law includes wording that limits expression; for example, news that could 'incite or promote hatred' or foment the 'anxiety' of Venezuelan citizens can be banned, as can media coverage considered to 'disrespect authorities'. Regulations also allow the president to interrupt regular television programming to deliver what are known as *cadenas*, or live official broadcasts that can include attacks on the opposition.

The constitution also guarantees the rights of citizens to access public information, but journalists find it hard to implement these rights. The government actively bars access to information that would reflect poorly on its policies. For example, when reports broke of the possible outbreak of a mosquito-borne disease in a coastal province of Venezuela, President Maduro accused journalists who wanted to issue public warnings of practising 'terrorism', and issued orders for their prosecution.

The political style of former president Hugo Chávez provides a good example of a populist leader using broadcast media to influence the poorer voters who are his natural support base. Many callers to his lengthy Sunday morning broadcast show, *Aló, Presidente*, petitioned the president for help in securing a job or social security benefit, usually citing in the process the callousness of the preceding regime. The president created a special office to handle these requests. In Chávez's governing style, we see how the leader of a hybrid regime can strengthen his authority through dominance of the broadcast media even against the opposition of many media professionals themselves.

Further evidence of globalization can be seen in the rise of global 24-hour news stations. These trace their roots to national all-news stations such as CNN, which began broadcasting in the United States in 1980. It was followed by CNN International in 1985, and then by BBC World (1991), Deutsche Welle from Germany (1992), Al-Jazeera from Qatar (1996), NHK World from Japan (1998), RT from Russia (2005), and France 24 (2006). These stations have not always proved profitable, and they reach only those audiences that have access to the necessary cable or satellite providers, but access to global television broadens the options for sources of political information.

Interaction

Undoubtedly the most important development in political communication has been its increased interactivity. Radio phone-ins allow ordinary people to listen to their peers discussing current issues, without mediation by a politician; blogs perform the same function in cyberspace. Messaging systems and social media are inherently interactive, allowing peer-to-peer interchanges which tend to crowd out top-down communication from politicians to voters.

The growth of interactive platforms sits uneasily alongside the reactive role expected of most voters in a representative democracy. Implicitly, a new generation schooled on interactive media is raising an important question to which politicians have yet to find an adequate answer: why should we listen to you when we have the option to interact electronically with friends of our own age who share our interests?

Interaction is a key theme in speculation about the future of political communication, with a series of scenarios developed by the Dutch Journalism Fund (Kasem *et al.*, 2015) offering alternatives that range from dominance of the political, economic and social agenda by a handful of internet giants to a world dominated by start-ups and cooperative relationships, with government restricted to a facilitating role. The conclusion of René van Zanten, general director of the Netherlands Press Fund, is particularly interesting:

> The most important thing to emerge seems to be the new and very important role that users play in the process … News is no longer the news that journalists and editors think is important. People have opinions about that. They show you the way to their world by clicking and scrolling. Media had better take that seriously and prepare not only for new ways of publishing, but also new ways of defining news.

Comparing media outlets

One danger in discussing the mass media lies in treating its various channels as uniform – as though books, films, newspapers, radio, television, and websites were identical in their partisanship and effects. True, the same content can increasingly be accessed in a variety of media – newspapers and television news can both be accessed on the internet, for example – so we should not overstate the importance of the platform. 'Yet the medium is the message', was the famous claim by Marshal McLuhan, who argued that the medium used influenced how the message was received (McLuhan, 1964). Even in an era of social media, there remains value in contrasting the impact of the two key channels of the mass media age: broadcast television and newspapers.

Even in its heyday, broadcast television was far from all-powerful. By the 1980s, it had certainly become the pre-eminent mass medium in all democracies, and even today remains a visual, credible, and easily digested format which reaches almost every household. Consider election campaigns. Here, the broadcasting studio has become the main site of battle. The party gladiators participate through appearing on interviews, debates, talk shows, and commercials; merely appearing on television confirms some status and recognition on candidates. Ordinary voters consume the election, if at all, through watching images, whether on television, computer screens, or smartphones.

But to say that the studio is the site of battle is one thing; to say that it determines the outcome is quite another. In fact, it is difficult to demonstrate a strong connection between television coverage of campaigns and voter responses. For instance, one frequent observation about the electoral impact of television is that it has primed voters to base their decision more on

personalities, especially those of the party leaders. But compared to when? Even the claim that the broadcasting media as a whole have led voters to decide on personality neglects the importance of personalized press coverage of the parties in earlier times.

To be sure, some studies have shown a modest increase in recent decades in the focus of media coverage of election campaigns on party leaders (Mughan, 2000). However, it is far from proven that votes are increasingly cast on the basis of the personalities of leaders and even less clear that any such increase is attributable to broadcasting. Certainly, research does not support the proposition that television has rendered the images of the leaders the key influence on electoral choice.

Where television may initially have made a broader but larger contribution is in partisan dealignment: the weakening of party loyalties among voters (see Chapter 17). Because of the limited number of channels available in television's early decades, governments required balanced and neutral treatment of politics. The result was an inoffensive style that contrasted with the more partisan coverage offered in many national newspapers. In the Netherlands, for instance, television helped to break down the separate pillars comprising Dutch society in the 1950s, providing a new common ground for citizens exposed to a single national channel: 'Catholics discovered that Socialists were not the dangerous atheists they had been warned about, Liberals had to conclude that orthodox Protestants were not the bigots they were supposed to be' (Wigbold, 1979: 201).

Despite the primacy of television, it would be wrong to discount the political impact of newspapers. Falling circulation notwithstanding, quality newspapers possess an authority springing from their longevity. In nearly all democracies, newspapers are freer with comment than is television. In an age when broadcasters still lead the provision of instant news, the more relaxed daily schedule of the press allows print columnists to offer interpretation and evaluation.

While television tells us what happened, newspapers place events in a broader context. The press helps to frame the political narrative in a way that television finds difficulty in matching. Broadcast news can only cover one story at a time whereas newspapers (in print or online) can be scanned for items of interest and can be read at the user's convenience. Newspapers offer a luxury which television can rarely afford: space for reflection. For such reasons, quality newspapers remain the trade press of politics, read avidly by politicians

FOCUS 14.1 | Comparing media structures

The way in which the mass media have developed, and been integrated into national politics, varies significantly across societies, yielding distinctive **media structures**. One ground-breaking study of these structures in liberal democracies (Hallin and Mancini (2004) distinguished between three different types:

Anglo-American: In this model, market mechanisms predominate and the mainly private media respond to commercial considerations. Reflecting the early achievement of mass literacy, newspaper circulation still remains relatively high. The notion of journalism as a news-gathering profession is entrenched, while the media and political worlds inhabit distinct spheres, with the former acting as a self-appointed watchdog over the latter. There are contrasts within the model, though: for example, public broadcasting and partisan national daily newspapers remain more significant in the UK than in the United States, where commerce dominates and newspapers are primarily local.

Northern European: Here, the media are seen as responsible social actors with their own contribution to make to society in general, and to political stability in particular. Newspapers and even television networks represent particular groups (e.g. religions, trade unions, political parties) but do so in an environment shaped by an interventionist state. Public broadcasting is significant and the government subsidizes private media in support of both their information and representation functions. Regulations governing media coverage, such as the right to privacy and to reply, are more extensive than in the Anglo-American structure. Journalistic professionalism is fully supported, but is tempered by an awareness of the media's role as an actor in, and not merely an observer of, politics and society.

Southern European: In Greece, Portugal, and Spain, authoritarian regimes initially acted as a brake on the development of universal literacy, mass circulation newspapers, and a vibrant civil society. Even following the democratic transitions of the 1970s, governing parties still strongly influenced public broadcasting, while newspapers and other television stations were subject to party political influence. Television became a potent vehicle of popular entertainment but newspaper circulation remained low, with journalists seeing themselves as providing ideologically loaded commentary, rather than hard news. In these party-dominated Southern European countries, the political position of the media remains even more subdued today than in the Northern European format. Elements of this format can also be found in many non-Western countries (Hallin and Mancini, 2012).

There are several telling contrasts among the three models, for example in regard to the task of the journalist. In the Anglo-American world, journalists are news-gathering professionals who speak truth to power and engage in a combative relationship with government. In Northern Europe, journalists are less adversarial: they are expected to add greater sensitivity to the national interest, political stability, their newspaper's outlook and the social group it serves. In Southern Europe, journalism focuses less on information and more on commentary from an ideological perspective.

The value of Hallin and Mancini's scheme is being eroded by the contemporary media trends discussed earlier in the chapter. Within Western liberal democracies, the tendency is to a more Anglo-American approach, especially in conceptions of the journalist's task. Still, the authors provide insight into where the media in the Western world are coming from – if less so on where they are going.

➡

Media structure: Refers to historically stable patterns of media use and, in particular, to the relationships between media, the state, and the economy. Components include the extent of newspaper circulation, the scope of public broadcasting, the partisanship of the press, and internet access.

themselves. In countries with a lively press tradition, newspapers retain a political significance greatly in excess of their circulation.

Newspapers also influence television's agenda: a story appearing on evening TV news often begins life in the

FOCUS 14.1   Comparing media structures (Continued)

	Anglo-American	Northern European	Southern European
Newspaper circulation	High	High	Low
Professionalism of journalism	High	High	Low
Links between media and politics	Low	High	High
State intervention	Low	High	High
Examples	Britain, Canada, Ireland, US	Denmark, Finland, Norway, Sweden	Greece, Portugal, Spain

FIGURE 14.5: Media structures in liberal democracies

Source: Adapted from Hallin and Mancini (2004), who also refer to the Anglo-American structure as 'liberal'; to the Northern European structure as 'democratic corporatist'; and to the Southern European structure as 'polarized pluralist'.

morning paper. This agenda-influencing role, it is worth noting, does not depend on a newspaper's circulation. But when a voter sees a story covered both on television and in the press, the combined impact is likely to exceed that of either medium considered alone (Miller, 1991).

Given the rise of online newspaper readership, the dramatic decline in the circulation of printed copies is an incomplete guide to the continuing significance of newspapers. Indeed, migration to the internet has allowed the leading newspaper groups to engage a new international audience, albeit usually with little commercial benefit.

Still, the drop in both newspaper readership and viewing of television news does pose a significant threat to the quality of political communication and, hence, to the political process itself. Quality newspapers (local as well as national) and major broadcasting networks traditionally provided the means by which society gathered news about itself and the wider world. But as the advertising revenues of traditional media decline, so it becomes more difficult to maintain expensive networks of professional journalists to gather, report, and interpret the news. The danger is that the profession of journalism becomes populated with amateurs, as low-cost media look for no-cost content from readers and others.

We may live in an information-rich age, but more does not always mean better. In fact, the hard news-gathering performed by many traditional media groups, whether directly or through contracts with news agencies, compares favourably with the 'comment-rich,

fact-poor and analysis-thin' character of blogs, many of which just react to stories generated offline (McCargo, 2012). There is some truth in the comment of Brian Williams (former anchor of NBC Nightly News) that 'these days he's up against a guy called Vinny who hasn't left his apartment in two years' (quoted in Fox and Ramos, 2012: 10). Fox and Ramos go on to make the general point:

> As traditional journalistic outlets shrink and blogs and other internet outlets ascend to greater levels of prominence, citizens experience increasingly unfiltered news and information. Many blogs lack a traditional journalistic hierarchy in which an editor, who has the power to withhold publication, can demand writer accountability and accuracy.

If it is to be sustained, professional news-gathering and interpretation (whether by print or broadcast journalists) may need to be reinterpreted as a public good and provided with a public subsidy. In any event, the decline of broadcast television and newspapers in the internet age poses a major challenge to the quality of political communication.

Political communication in authoritarian states

Just as democracy thrives on a flow of information, so authoritarian rulers limit free expression; this leads to media coverage of politics which is subdued and, usually, subservient. It has also led to relatively little research on the dynamics of political communication in authoritarian systems. Far from acting as the fourth estate, casting a searchlight into the darker corners of government, journalists in authoritarian states defer to political authority. Lack of resources within the media sector limits professionalism and increases vulnerability to pressure. Official television stations and subsidized newspapers reproduce the regime's line, while critical journalists are harassed and the entire media sector develops an instinct for self-preservation through self-censorship.

The consequence is an inadequate information flow to the top, expanding the gap between state and society, and leading ultimately to incorrect decisions. A thoughtful dictator responds to this problem by encouraging the media to expose malfeasance at the local level, thus providing a check on governance away from the centre. But there is no escape from the paradox of authoritarianism. By controlling information, rulers may secure their power in the short run, but they also reduce the quality of governance – potentially threatening their own survival over the longer term. The more developed the country, the more severe is the damage inflicted by an information deficit at the top.

How exactly do authoritarian rulers limit independent journalism? The constraints are varied and sometimes subtle. An understanding of these limitations contributes to an appreciation of authoritarian rule. In her study of sub-Saharan Africa before the wave of liberalization in the 1990s, Bourgault (1995: 180) identified a typical list of means for limiting media development and coverage:

• Declaring lengthy states of emergency which formally limit media freedom.
• Passing broad libel laws that can be selectively applied.
• Threatening the withdrawal of government advertising.
• Selectively restricting access to newsprint.
• Requiring publications and journalists to be licensed.
• Taxing printing equipment at a high rate.
• Requiring a bond to be deposited with the government before new publications can launch.

As we saw in Chapter 4, authoritarian states are also most often low-income states, and limited resources undoubtedly hold back the development of the media. Restricted means stifle journalistic initiative and increase vulnerability to pressure. Sometimes impoverished journalists are reduced to publishing favourable

stories (or withdrawing the threat to write critical ones) in exchange for money. The established media in authoritarian states become channels for **propaganda** rather than for hard political news.

> **Propaganda:** Information used to promote a particular political cause or ideology with a view to changing public opinion.

In much of post-communist central Asia, large parts of the media remain in state hands, giving the authorities direct leverage. The state also typically retains ownership of a leading television channel. The outcome is subservience:

> From Kazakhstan to Kyrgyzstan and Tajikistan to Belarus and Ukraine, the story is a dismal one: tax laws are used for financial harassment; a body of laws forbids insults of those in high places; compulsory registration of the media is common. In Azerbaijan, as in Belarus, one-man rule leaves little room for press freedom. (Foley, 1999: 45)

The justification for these restrictions is typically an overriding national requirement for social stability, nation-building, and economic development. The subtext is that we cannot afford Western freedoms until we have caught up, and perhaps not even then. Before the Arab Spring, for instance, the Egyptian government expected that 'the press should uphold the security of the country, promote economic development, and support approved social norms' (Lesch, 2004: 610). A free press is presented as a recipe for squabbling and disharmony.

Even though many of these justifications are simply excuses for authoritarian government, we should not assume that the Western idea of a free press garners universal appeal. Islamic states, in particular, stress the media's role in affirming religious values and social norms. A free press is seen as an excuse for licence. The question is posed: why should we import Western ideas of freedom if the practical result is the availability of pornography? When society is viewed as the expression of an overarching moral code, whether Islamic or otherwise, the Western tradition of free speech appears alien – and even unethical.

The remaining states with a nominal communist allegiance also keep close control over the means of mass communication. In China, access to information has traditionally been provided on a need-to-know basis. The country's rulers remain keen to limit dissenting voices,

> ## FOCUS 14.2 | Online interaction and the Arab Spring
>
> The use of online platforms for interaction among citizens has weakened political control in some authoritarian regimes, the case of the Arab Spring offering a revealing illustration. As Table 14.2 shows, internet access grew dramatically in the first decade of the new millennium in the Middle East and North Africa, allowing peer-to-peer communication among alienated urban youth, as in Iran's *Blogistan* (Sreberny and Khiabany, 2010). This growth was not confined to those countries experiencing regime change in 2011 but became a significant factor in some overthrows, notably in Egypt and Tunisia.
>
> Online facilities not only permitted rapid circulation of news about the latest protest venues, but also created a rare free space for social interaction – for example, between people of the opposite sex (Bayat, 2010). The word on the tweet proved harder to censor than the word on the street. In this way, social media created a model of a free and exciting democratic society against which authoritarian political systems in the Arab world seemed ever more ossified. Facebook became the freedom forum, leading Lynch (2011: 301) to claim boldly that 'the long term evolution of a new kind of public sphere may matter more than immediate political outcomes'. Wheeler and Mintz (2012: 260–1) argue along similar lines when they suggest that 'The ground for significant political change in authoritarian contexts can be readied by people using new media tools to discover and generate new spaces within which they can voice their dissent and assert their presence in pursuit of bettering their lives.'
>
> **TABLE 14.2:** The internet and the Arab Spring
>
> | | Internet users | | Population using the internet (%) 2009 | Regime overthrown in 2011? |
> |---|---|---|---|---|
> | | 2000 | 2009 | | |
> | Iran | 250,000 | 32.2 million | 48 | No |
> | Morocco | 100,000 | 10.3 million | 33 | No |
> | Saudi Arabia | 200,000 | 7.7 million | 27 | No |
> | Tunisia | 100,000 | 2.8 million | 27 | Yes |
> | Egypt | 450,000 | 12.6 million | 16 | Yes |
> | Algeria | 50,000 | 4.1 million | 12 | No |
> | Libya | 10,000 | 323,000 | 5 | Yes |
> | Yemen | 15,000 | 370,000 | 2 | Yes |
>
> *Source*: Adapted from Wheeler and Mintz (2012: table 10.1)

even though they do now permit 'newspapers, magazines, television stations and news web sites to compete fiercely for audiences and advertising revenue' (Shirk, 2011: 2). In 2011, the Communist Party even cancelled *Super Girl*, a television talent show with a peak audience of 400 million, fearing the subversive effect of allowing the audience to vote for their favourite act.

Although the Chinese government is keen to promote e-commerce, internet users who search for 'inappropriate' topics such as democracy or Tibetan independence will find their searches blocked and their access to search engines withdrawn. The government even pays selected citizens to post pro-government messages online (Fox and Ramos, 2012: 8). Of course, sophisticated users find a way round the regime's electronic censorship, producing a parallel communications system which may eventually prove to be politically transformative, but for now the Great Firewall of China holds.

He (2009) describes political communication in China as taking place in two separate 'discourse universes'. The first is the official universe, which occupies the public space, while the second is the private universe, which consists mainly of oral and person-to-person communication. He argues that applying Western theories of political communication to the Chinese context is difficult, because these models assume free and democratic elections. Since most political communication in China is controlled by the Communist Party, and takes the form of propaganda, a specialized field of political communication studies has less meaning there than it does in the West.

In hybrid regimes, control over the media is less extensive than in authoritarian states. The press and the internet are often left substantially alone, offering a forum for debate which perhaps offers some value, as well as danger, to the rulers. Yet the leading political force also dominates broadcast coverage, even where explicit or implicit censorship is absent. To some extent, such an emphasis reflects political reality: a viewer is naturally most interested in those who exert the greatest influence over their life.

Latin America provides a good example. In many countries on the continent, a tradition of personal and populist rule lends itself well to expression through broadcasting media which reach many poor and illiterate people seeking salvation through 'their' leader. Foweraker et al. (2003: 105) describe the origins of this tradition in the twentieth century, when 'populist leaders in Latin America made popular appeals to the people through mass media in newspapers and especially radio'. These authors comment that contemporary populism continues in the same vein, albeit now operating through television.

In Russia, pressures on the media – from powerful business people, as well as politicians – remain intense, an influence deriving from the centrality of television to political communication. As in Latin America, broadcasting is the main way of reaching a dispersed population for whom free television has greater appeal than papers for which they must pay. In a 2008 survey, 82 per cent of Russians said they watched television routinely, compared with just 22 per cent who said they were regular readers of national newspapers (Oates, 2014: 134). The television audience in Russia for nightly news programmes is substantial. In the size and interest of its audience, Russia's television news is the equivalent of soap operas elsewhere. Particularly during elections, television showcases the achievements of the administration and its favoured candidates; opposition figures receive less, and distinctly less flattering, attention.

With over 100 laws governing media conduct in Russia, and the occasional journalist still found murdered by unknown assailants, self-censorship – the voice in the editor's head which asks 'Am I taking a risk in publishing this story?' – remains rife. Because editors know on which side their bread is buttered, there is no need for politicians to take the political risk involved in explicit instruction. The internal censor allows the president to maintain deniability. 'Censorship? What censorship?' he can ask, with a smile.

By comparison with television, the internet and the press are less explicitly controlled in Russia, an important change to the all-embracing censorship of the communist era. Internet access, in particular, has allowed younger people in urban areas to express and organize opposition to the authoritarian style of President Vladimir Putin. As befits a competitive authoritarian regime, dominance of the major media does not imply complete censorship.

DISCUSSION QUESTIONS

- How does the medium impact the political message?

- Which exerts more influence on people's political values: (a) the internet, (b) broadcast television, or (c) friends and family?

- To what extent do social media add to or detract from the idea of opinion reinforcement?

- Do the media shape or reflect public opinion?

- What are the likely implications of the decline of newspapers and broadcast television, and the growth of the internet, as a source of political news?

- Is the problem of propaganda notably worse in authoritarian than in democratic systems, or are the attempts to influence public thinking simply couched differently?

KEY CONCEPTS

Fourth estate

Mass media

Media structure

Political communication

Propaganda

Self-selection

Social media

Transmission model

FURTHER READING

Ekström, Mats and Andrew Tolson (eds) (2013) *Media Talk and Political Elections in Europe and America*. An analysis of the links between media and elections, including chapters on the political interview, political debates, and uses of the internet to engage with voters.

Hallin, Daniel C. and Paolo Mancini (2004) *Comparing Media Systems: Three Models of Media and Politics*. This influential book presents an original classification of media systems.

Hallin, Daniel C. and Paolo Mancini (eds) (2012) *Comparing Media Systems Beyond the Western World*. This collection applies the classification in *Comparing Media Systems: Three Models of Media and Politics* to a wider range of countries.

Reinemann, Carsten (ed.) (2014) *Political Communication*. An edited collection of the current state of understanding about political communication, including chapters on its role in various facets of politics. Robertson, Alexa (2015) *Media and Politics in a Globalization World*. An assessment of the impact of globalization and technology on the relationship between media and politics.

Semetko, Holli A. and Margaret Scammell (eds) (2012) *The Sage Handbook of Political Communication*. An edited collection that helps bring together themes in a fragmented and multidisciplinary field.

Street, John (2011) *Mass Media, Politics and Democracy*, 2nd edn. A survey of the evolving relationship between mass media and politics, including chapters on media bias, media control, and the politics of journalism.

15 > Political parties

PREVIEW

For most residents of democracies, political parties are the channel through which they most often relate to government and politics. Parties offer them competing sets of policies, encourage them to take part in the political process, and are the key determinant of who governs. It is all the more ironic, then, that while parties are so central to politics, they are often not well regarded by citizens. They are increasingly seen less as a means for engaging citizens and more as self-serving channels for the promotion of the interests of politicians; as a result, support for parties is declining as people move towards other channels for political expression. In authoritarian regimes the story is even less palatable: parties have routinely been the means through which elites manipulate public opinion, and have been both the shields and the instruments of power.

This chapter begins with a brief survey of the origins and changing roles of parties, before looking at the variety of party systems around the world, ranging from states where parties are not allowed through single-party, dominant party and two-party systems to the multi-party systems found in the majority of democracies. It reviews the quite different dynamic of parties in these different systems. It then looks at the manner in which parties are organized, and at how leaders and candidates are recruited. After reviewing the changing significance of party membership, it looks at how parties are financed, and concludes with an examination of the different roles parties play in authoritarian systems.

CONTENTS

- Political parties: an overview
- Origins and roles
- Party systems
- Party organization
- Party membership
- Party finance
- Political parties in authoritarian states

KEY ARGUMENTS

- The key dilemma facing parties is that they are poorly rated by the public yet they remain an essential device of liberal democracy.
- Major political parties began as agents of society (representing a particular group or class) and have since become agents of the state (so much so that the public funding of parties is quite normal). The implications of this change are important.
- Understanding the role of parties involves looking at party systems, not simply individual parties. The major theme here is the decline of dominant party and two-party systems, and the rise of multi-party systems.
- The selection process for party leaders and candidates has been changing, but its causes, and the effects on candidate quality, are less clear.
- The combination of falling party membership and growing public funding has changed the base of parties.
- Parties in authoritarian regimes play a different role from their democratic counterparts. Rather than providing a foundation for the creation of governments, they are a means for controlling citizens, disguising the power of elites, and distributing patronage.

Political parties: an overview

It would be hard to imagine political systems functioning without **political parties**, and yet their history is far shorter than most people might imagine. The nineteenth-century Russian-born political thinker Moisei Ostrogorski was one of the first to recognize their growing importance in modern politics. His study of parties in Britain and the United States was less interested, as he said, in political forms than in political forces; 'wherever this life of parties is developed', he argued, 'it focuses the political feelings and the active wills of its citizens' (1902: 7). His conclusions were fully justified: in Western Europe, mass parties were founded to battle for the votes of enlarged electorates; in communist and fascist states, ruling parties monopolized power in an attempt to reconstruct society; in the developing world, nationalist parties became the vehicle for driving colonial rulers back to their imperial homeland.

> **Political party:** A group identified by name and ideology that fields candidates at elections in order to win public office and control government.

Parties were a key mobilizing device of the twentieth century, drawing millions of people into the national political process for the first time. They jettisoned their original image as private factions engaged in capturing, and even perverting, the public interest. Instead, they became accepted as the central representative device of liberal democracy. Reflecting this new status, they began to receive explicit mention in new constitutions, some countries even banning non-party candidates from standing for the legislature, or preventing members from switching parties once elected (Reilly, 2007). Such restrictions were judged necessary for implementing party-based elections. By the century's end, most liberal democracies offered some public funding to support party work. Parties had become part of the system, providing functions ranging from being the very foundations of government, to aggregating interests, mobilizing voters, and recruiting candidates for office.

Therein rests the problem. No longer do parties seem to be energetic agents of society, seeking to bend the state towards their supporters' interests. Instead, they appear to be at risk of capture by the state itself. They also often seem to be less concerned with offering voters alternatives than with promoting their own interests, and competing for power for its own sake. No longer do parties provide the only home for the politically engaged; instead, people are moving towards social movements, interest groups, and social media. Western publics still endorse the principle of democracy, but they seem to be increasingly disillusioned with achieving it through competing political parties. With many parties now seen as self-serving and corrupt, Mair (2008: 230) could speculate, in contrast to Ostrogorski, that parties are in danger of ceasing to be a political driving force.

In authoritarian states, parties tend to be either non-existent (in a few cases) or else one official party dominates. The notion of competitive parties does not fit with the notion of centralized control, and parties are not so much the representatives of groups or interests as tools by which authoritarian leaders can exert power. Excepting the enormous power of ruling communist parties, they tend to be weak, lacking autonomy from the national leader, and reinforcing elite control of society. In countries that are poor and ethnically divided, parties typically lack the ideological contrasts that provided a base of party systems in most liberal democracies.

Origins and roles

Political parties are neither as old nor as central to government as we might suppose. They seem to be the lifeblood of democratic politics, and yet governments and states have long been wary of their potentially harmful impact on national unity, which is one reason why parties – unlike the formal institutions of government – went unmentioned in early constitutions. In examining party origins, we can distinguish between two types: cadre parties that had their origins in legislatures, and mass parties that were created to win legislative representation for a particular social group, such as the working class.

Cadre (or elite) parties were formed by members within a legislature joining together around common concerns and fighting campaigns in an enlarged electorate. The earliest nineteenth-century parties were of this type; they include the conservative parties of Britain, Canada, and Scandinavia, and the first American parties (the Federalists and the Jeffersonians). Cadre parties are sometimes known as 'caucus' parties, the caucus denoting a closed meeting of the members of a party in a legislature. Such parties remain heavily committed to their leader's authority, with ordinary members playing a supporting role.

By contrast, mass parties – which emerged later – originated outside legislatures, in social groups seeking representation as a way of achieving their policy objectives. The working-class socialist parties that spread across Western Europe around the turn of the twentieth century epitomized these externally created parties. Mass socialist parties exerted tremendous influence on European party systems in the twentieth century, stimulating many cadre parties to copy their extra-parliamentary organization. Mass parties acquired an enormous membership organized in local branches, and – unlike cadre parties – tried to keep their representatives on a tight rein. They played an important role in education and political socialization, funding education, organizing workshops, and running party newspapers, all designed to tie their members closer to their party.

As cadre and mass parties matured, so they tended to evolve into catch-all parties (Kirchheimer, 1966). These respond to a mobilized political system in which electoral communication takes place through mass media, bypassing the membership. Such parties seek to govern in the national interest, rather than as representatives of a social group, the reality being that 'a party large enough to get a majority has to be so catch-all that it cannot have a unique ideological program' (Kirchheimer, quoted in Krouwel, 2003: 29). Catch-all parties seek electoral support wherever they can find it, their purpose being to govern rather than to represent.

The broadening of Christian democratic parties in Europe from religious defence organizations to broader parties of the centre-right is the classic case of the transition to catch-all status. The subsequent transformation of several mass socialist parties into leader-dominated social democratic parties, as in Spain and the United Kingdom, is another example. While most major parties are now of the catch-all type, their origins inside or beyond legislatures continue to influence party style, the autonomy of their leaders, and the standing of ordinary members.

Modern democratic parties fulfil several functions that are critical to the formation of governments and the engagement of voters. Prime among these is the formation of governments. They also (at least ideally) offer voters guidance by helping them make choices among different sets of policies, help voters make themselves heard by pulling together like-minded segments of the electorate, encourage voters to participate in politics, and feed government by recruiting candidates for public office (see Figure 15.1).

Party systems

Just as the international system is more than the states that comprise it, so a **party system** is more than its individual parties. The term describes the overall pattern formed by the component parties, the interactions between them, and the rules governing their conduct. Parties copy, learn from, and compete with each other, with innovations in organization, fundraising, and campaigning diffusing across the system. By focusing on the relationships between parties, a party system means more than just the parties themselves, and helps us understand

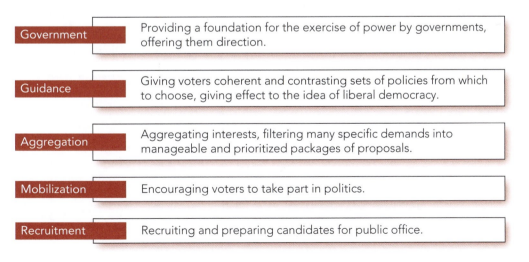

Government	Providing a foundation for the exercise of power by governments, offering them direction.
Guidance	Giving voters coherent and contrasting sets of policies from which to choose, giving effect to the idea of liberal democracy.
Aggregation	Aggregating interests, filtering many specific demands into manageable and prioritized packages of proposals.
Mobilization	Encouraging voters to take part in politics.
Recruitment	Recruiting and preparing candidates for public office.

FIGURE 15.1: Five roles of political parties

how they interact with one another, and the impact of that interaction on the countries they govern.

> **Party system:** The overall configuration of political parties, based on their number, their relative importance, the interactions among them, and the laws that regulate them.

There are also close links between the structure of elections and the party systems that result, if we accept the findings of the political scientist Maurice Duverger. As a result of research undertaken during the 1940s, he developed two principles published in his 1951 book *Political Parties*: first, that single-member plurality elections tend to produce two-party systems, and second that two-round and proportional representation elections tend to produce multi-party systems (Duverger, 1951). Others noticed the same effects, which eventually came to be known – respectively – as **Duverger's law** and Duverger's proposition (Benoit, 2006).

> **Duverger's law:** More of a hypothesis than a universal law, this holds that 'The simple-majority single-ballot system favours the two-party system' (Duverger, 1951).

Party systems fall into one of five types: no-party, single-party, dominant party, two-party, and multi-party (see Figure 15.2). In democracies, both dominant and two-party systems are in decline, meaning that multi-party systems have become the most common configuration in the democratic world.

No-party systems

There are a small number of authoritarian states – mainly in the Middle East – that either do not allow political parties to form and operate, or where no parties have been formed. In the cases of Oman and Saudi Arabia, there is no legislature and the formation of parties is banned, although there are several movements

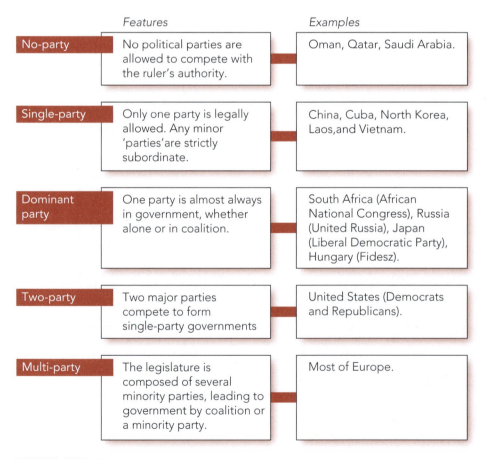

	Features	*Examples*
No-party	No political parties are allowed to compete with the ruler's authority.	Oman, Qatar, Saudi Arabia.
Single-party	Only one party is legally allowed. Any minor 'parties'are strictly subordinate.	China, Cuba, North Korea, Laos,and Vietnam.
Dominant party	One party is almost always in government, whether alone or in coalition.	South Africa (African National Congress), Russia (United Russia), Japan (Liberal Democratic Party), Hungary (Fidesz).
Two-party	Two major parties compete to form single-party governments	United States (Democrats and Republicans).
Multi-party	The legislature is composed of several minority parties, leading to government by coalition or a minority party.	Most of Europe.

FIGURE 15.2: Comparing party systems

in place that would evolve into parties if allowed, and Saudi Islamists made a largely symbolic request to the king in 2011 that they be allowed to form a party. There is no formal legal framework for parties in Bahrain, but there are active 'political associations' that compete in elections and are the functional equivalent of parties.

Single-party systems

These were once common, being found throughout the communist world as well as in most African and Arab countries. The argument made by most communist parties is that communism is the answer to all needs, alternative ideologies are moot, and democracy exists within communist parties in a phenomenon dubbed 'democratic centralism' by Lenin. The idea is that in a hierarchical system, each level is elected by the one below, to which it must in turn account (the *democratic* part) but decisions reached by higher levels are to be accepted and implemented by lower levels (the *centralism* part). In truth, the party is anything but democratic, and is instead highly elitist, based on alleged democracy *within* a party rather than *among* competing parties. In addition, membership is restricted, and offers a gateway to political influence and economic privileges, with non-party members being marginalized and, as a result, often resentful.

In China, the Chinese Communist Party (CCP) is the source of all meaningful political power, controls all other political organizations, plays a key role in deciding the outcome of elections, and dominates both state and government. Policy changes come not through a change of party at an election or a substantial public debate, but rather through changes in the balance of power within the leadership of the party.

From a base of 3.5 million primary party organizations – found in villages, factories, military units, and other local communities – the party works its way up through an elaborate hierarchy to the National Party Congress, which meets infrequently and delegates authority to a 370-member Central Committee, to a 25-member Politburo, and finally to the seven people who make up the Standing Committee of the Politburo, from which they exert enormous influence over the most populous country on earth – in itself, an astonishing political achievement.

Dominant party systems

In a dominant party system, one party outdistances all the others and becomes the natural party of government, even if it sometimes governs in coalition with junior partners. Dominant parties may fall victim to their own success, their very strength meaning that factions tend to develop internally, leading to an inward-looking perspective, a lack of concern with policy, excessive careerism, and increasing corruption. This is not to suggest that a dominant party system is inherently corrupt and undemocratic, though, and there are several examples of parties that once dominated but which have had to learn to share power; these include the Institutional Revolutionary Party in Mexico, Japan's Liberal Democrats, Sweden's Social Democrats (which since 1932 has been in government for all but 16 years), and Italy's Christian Democrats.

The Japanese Liberal Democratic Party (LDP) has governed the country since 1955, except for breaks in 1993–6 and 2009–12. Although supposedly a united political party, the LDP is made up of several factions, each with its own leader, and these factions provide a form of intra-party competition. During times of LDP rule, the prime minister is not necessarily the leader of the LDP, nor even the leader of the biggest faction, nor even the leader of *any* faction, but rather the person who wins enough support among the competing factions to form a government. The LDP has kept power for many reasons, including its association with Japan's post-war economic renaissance, an impressive network of grassroots supporter groups, the distribution of patronage to its own electoral districts, and the inability of opposition parties to mount an effective challenge.

A classic example of diminished dominance is offered by the Indian National Congress, most often known simply as Congress. Under Mahatma Gandhi it provided the focus of resistance to British colonial rule, and rose to leadership with India's independence in 1947. To maintain its position, the party relied on a patronage pyramid of class and caste alliances to sustain a national organization in a fragmented and religiously divided country. Lacking access to the perks of office, no other party could challenge its hegemony. But authoritarian rule during the state of emergency declared by Prime Minister Indira Gandhi (1975–7) cost Congress dear, and the party suffered its first defeat at a national election in 1977. It regrouped briefly but has been unable to fend off rising support for the Hindu nationalist Bharatiya Janata Party, and in 2014 suffered its biggest defeat ever with just 19 per cent of the vote.

An example of a party which retains its dominant position is South Africa's African National Congress (ANC). This party has multiple advantages, stemming not only from cultural memories of its opposition to apartheid and from its strong position among the black majority, but also from its use of office to reward its own supporters. Since the end of the apartheid regime in 1994, there have been five sets of elections in South Africa and the ANC has never won less than 62 per cent of the vote, a remarkable achievement. However, factions and corruption are growing problems, and they may eventually threaten the ANC's supremacy.

Two-party systems

In a two-party system, two major parties of comparable size compete for electoral support, providing the framework for political competition while the other parties exert little, if any, influence on the formation and policies of governments. The two major parties alternate in power, with one or the other always enjoying a majority. Having said that, though, the two-party format – like dominant parties – is rare and becoming rarer.

The United States is one of the last hold-outs, dominated since 1860 by the Democrats and the Republicans. These two parties have been able to hold their positions in part because of the arithmetic of plurality electoral systems (see Chapter 16), and in part because – in most US states – the parties decide the borders of electoral districts and can design them to maximize their chances of winning seats. In particular, winning a US presidential election is a political mountain which can only be climbed by major parties capable of assembling a broad national coalition and of raising the astronomical funding needed to launch a bid. The two major parties have also proved adept at moving to the left or the right in order to absorb the policies and the voters of any third party that might seem to be on the rise. In the temple of free-market economics, the two leading parties form a powerful duopoly.

Australia is another example of a two-party system, again reinforced by a non-proportional electoral system. Liberals and Labor have consistently been the two biggest parties since the Second World War, winning 80–90 per cent of the seats in Parliament between them. They have only been stopped from forming a US-style duopoly by the much smaller National Party, whose base lies in the rural areas. Government in Australia has alternated between Labor governing alone and the Liberals governing in coalition with the Nationals.

Elsewhere, Britain was long presented as an emblem of the two-party pattern, but it has recently struggled to pass the test. The Conservative and Labour parties regularly alternated in office, with plurality elections meaning that their share of seats exceeded their share of votes, but third parties have gained ground. In 2010, the centre Liberal Democrats won 57 seats in a Parliament of 650 members, forming a coalition with the Conservatives after no party won an overall majority. However, the Conservatives were able to win with a small majority in 2015 when the Liberal Democrats imploded and the Labour Party failed to offer a credible challenge.

Multi-party systems

In multi-party systems, several parties – typically, at least five or six – each win a significant bloc of seats in the legislature, becoming serious contenders for a place in a governing coalition. The underlying philosophy is that political parties represent specific social groups (or opinion constituencies such as environmentalists) in divided societies. The legislature then serves as an arena of conciliation, with coalitions forming and falling in response to often minor changes in the political balance. Europe exemplifies the phenomenon, most countries in the region having parties drawn from some, but not all, of nine major party families (see Table 15.1).

A good example is offered by Denmark, where no party has held a majority in the unicameral Folketing since 1909. The country's complex party system has been managed through careful consensus-seeking but this practice has come under some pressure from the rise of new parties. In an explosive election in 1973, three new parties achieved representation and, since then, a minimum of seven parties have won seats in the legislature. The centre-right 'Blue' coalition that followed the 2015 election comprised five of these, controlling 90 seats, or just five more than the opposition 'Red' coalition.

Brazil has developed a particularly colourful multi-party system since its return to civilian government in 1985. No less than 28 parties won seats in the 2014 elections to the Chamber of Deputies, representing a wide range of opinions and interests that coalesced into

TABLE 15.1: Europe's major party families

	Examples
Far left	Left Front (France), Left Party (Sweden).
Green	Alliance '90/The Greens (Germany), Green League (Finland), Greens (Sweden).
Social democrat	Social Democrats (Denmark, Finland, Sweden), Democratic Party (Italy), Labour (UK).
Christian democrat	Christian Democratic Union (Germany), Fine Gael (Ireland), People's Party (Spain).
Conservative	Conservative Party (UK, Norway).
Centre	Centre Party (Finland, Norway, Sweden).
Liberal	People's Party (Netherlands), Venstre (Denmark), Liberal Democrats (UK).
Far right	New Flemish Alliance (Belgium), National Front (France), Party for Freedom (Netherlands), Sweden Democrats.
Regional	Scottish National Party, Christian Social Union (Bavaria), New Flemish Alliance (Belgium).

a pro-government coalition, two opposition coalitions, and a cluster of stand-alone parties. Twelve parties each had fewer than ten members, and the pro-government coalition contained nine parties that together controlled 59 per cent of the seats. The picture in Brazil is complicated by a widespread aversion to right-wing parties (stemming from the heritage of the military years), weak discipline within many of the smaller parties, and the powerful role played by other actors, such as state governors. The result is a system that has been labelled 'coalition presidentialism', describing presidents who must rely on large and unstable coalitions to pass legislation (Gómez Bruera, 2013: 94–5).

An important element of multi-party systems in several countries is parties that operate only at the regional level (or at the state level in federations). Britain, for example, has parties that represent the interests of Scotland, Wales, and Northern Ireland, while the German Christian Democratic Union is in a sustained coalition with the Christian Social Union, which operates only in the state of Bavaria. Few countries offer a more varied array of regional parties than India, where such parties now play an expanded role in national politics. For example, the Congress-led United Progressive Alliance relied heavily after the 2009 elections on regional parties in the states of West Bengal, Tamil Nadu, and Maharashtra. The 2014 election resulted in an 11-seat majority for the Bharatiya Janata Party, but it continued to be part of a coalition originally formed in 1998, in which it worked with nearly 30 regional parties with nearly 60 seats in the Lok Sabha, the lower chamber of the Indian Parliament.

Party organization

Large political parties are multilevel organizations, with their various strata united by a common identity and, sometimes, shared objectives. A major party's organization will include staff or volunteers operating at national, regional, and local levels, and even at a wider level in the case of those national parties in Europe that have formed pan-European federations. This complexity means that any large party is decentralized. While references to 'the party' as a single entity are unavoidable, they simplify a highly fragmented reality. As Bolleyer (2012: 316) says, 'parties are not monolithic structures'.

Party 'organization' is sometimes too grand a term. Below the centre, and especially in areas where the party is electorally weak, the party's organization may be little more than an empty shell. And coordination between levels is often weak. Some authors even draw a comparison between parties and franchise organizations such as McDonald's (Carty, 2004). In a franchise structure, the centre manages the brand, runs marketing campaigns, and supports the operating units, leaving local units to act with considerable autonomy. Party leaders set policy priorities, develop their organization's image, and provide material for election campaigns. But local agents are left to get on with key tasks: selecting candidates, for example, or implementing election strategy at local level.

Opinion has been changing as regards the question of where authority lies in parties. Thinking was long dominated by the arguments posed by the German scholar Robert Michels (1875–1936). In *Political Parties*

> ### FOCUS 15.1 | The rise of niche parties
>
> A recent phenomenon in many European countries has been the rise of **niche parties** that appeal to a narrow part of the electorate. These include far right, nationalist, regional, and green parties, which – unlike mainstream parties – rarely prosper by moderating their position, instead achieving most success from exploiting their natural support group (Meguid, 2008). Several of these parties – including the German Greens, Austria's Freedom Party, and Switzerland's People's Party (Ignazi, 2006) – have participated in coalitions, while others (such as the Scottish National Party) have succeeded in influencing the agenda of mainstream parties.
>
> Niche parties of the far right deserve particular attention. They are an exception to the thesis that parties emerge to represent well-defined social interests. Evidence suggests that they draw heavily on the often transient support of uneducated and unemployed young men. Disillusioned with orthodox democracy and by the move of established conservative parties to the centre, this constituency is attracted to parties that blame immigrants, asylum seekers, and other minorities not only for crime in general, but also for its own insecurity (cultural, as well as economic) in a changing world (Kitschelt, 2007).
>
> It is tempting to identify a new cleavage here: between the winners and losers from contemporary labour markets. In the winner's enclosure stand well-educated, affluent professionals, proudly displaying their tolerant post-material liberalism. But in the shadows we find those without qualifications, without jobs, and without prospects in economies where full-time unskilled jobs have been exported to lower-cost producers. In this context, the perceived economic success of immigrants, especially those of a different colour, is easily regarded with resentment.
>
> Such analysis is plausible, but we should note that the division between labour market winners and losers is not a social cleavage in the classic sense. The traditional industrial working class was supported by an organizational infrastructure of labour unions and socialist parties. But far right parties are supported by alienated individuals, rather than by social and political institutions. So, in considering the far right it may be preferable to speak not of a new cleavage but, rather, of post-cleavage analysis – of what Betz (1994: 169) called 'political conflict in the age of social fragmentation'.
>
> We should not be carried away. Many right-wing movements have proved to be short-lived flash parties whose prospects are held back by inexperienced leaders with a dubious background who have proved to be inept participants in coalition governments (Akkerman, 2012). Many protest voters might cease to vote for niche parties if they became leading parties, thus creating a natural ceiling to their support. Even joining a coalition dilutes the party's outsider image. So, in this sense, niche parties may lack the potential of those based on a more secure and traditional cleavage (McDonnell and Newell, 2011).

> **Niche party:** A political party that appeals to a narrow section of the electorate. They are positioned away from the established centre and highlight one particular issue.

(1911), Michels argued that even organizations with democratic pretensions become dominated by a ruling clique of leaders and supporting officials. Using Germany's Social Democrats as a critical case, he suggested that leaders develop organizational skills, expert knowledge, and an interest in their own continuation in power. The ordinary members, aware of their inferior knowledge and amateur status, accept their own subordination as natural. Michels's pessimism about the possibility of democracy within organizations such as political parties was expressed in his famous **iron law of oligarchy**: 'to say organization is to say a tendency to oligarchy' (often reproduced as 'who says organization, says oligarchy').

> **Iron law of oligarchy:** As developed by Robert Michels, this states that the organization of political parties – even those formally committed to democracy – becomes dominated by a ruling elite.

Elite recruitment continues to be a vital and continuing function of parties: even as parties decline in other ways, they continue to dominate elections to the national legislatures from which, in democracies, most political leaders are drawn. Given that candidates nominated for **safe districts**, or appearing near the top of their party's list, are virtually guaranteed a place in the legislature, it is the **selectorate**, not the electorate, which makes 'the choice before the choice'. The nominators open and close the door to the house of power (Rahat, 2007). At the same time, there is evidence of a growing role for ordinary party members in the selection of leaders and candidates, a finding which suggests that Michels's iron law is corroding as parties seek to retain members by giving them a greater if still limited voice in party affairs (Cross and Katz, 2013). If parties are becoming more democratic, the democracy is of a representative rather than direct kind.

Safe district: An electoral district in which a political party has such strong support that its candidate/s are all but assured of victory.

Selectorate: The people who nominate a party's candidates for an election.

Party leaders

The method of selecting the party leader deserves more attention that it usually receives (Pilet and Cross, 2014), for the obvious reason that party leaders in most parliamentary systems stand a good chance of becoming prime minister. In some countries, to be sure, including many in continental Europe, the chair of the party is not allowed to be the party's nominee for the top post in government (Cross and Blais, 2012a: 5). In Germany, for instance, the party's candidate for chancellor is appointed separately from the party leader and need

not be the same person. In the United States, the presidential candidate and chair of the party's national committee are different people; indeed, the former usually chooses the latter. Nonetheless, it is important to review the mechanics and implications of the selection of the party's leader.

In the same way that many parties afford their ordinary members a greater voice in candidate selection, so too has the procedure for selecting the party leader become more inclusive. As Mair (1994) notes, 'more and more parties now seem willing to allow the ordinary members a voice in the selection of party leaders'. One factor here is the desire to compensate members for their declining role in what have become media-driven election campaigns; after all, party volunteers, unlike paid employees, can just walk away if they are given nothing interesting to do. The catalyst for reform is often an electoral setback or a desire to be seen as inclusive (Cross and Blais, 2012b).

The traditional method for choosing party leaders is election by members of the party in the legislature, a device that is still used in several parliamentary systems, including Australia, Denmark, and New Zealand. Interestingly, several parties give a voice both to members of parliament and ordinary members, either through a special congress or a two-stage ballot. For instance, the British Conservatives offer ordinary members a choice between two candidates chosen by the parliamentary party. Although this would appear to be a more democratic option, it can lead to problems when the rank-and-file membership is out of step with the national party, resulting in the triumph of local over national interests.

A vote of the party's members of the legislature alone is, of course, a narrow constituency. And the ability of potential leaders to instil confidence in their parliamentary peers may say little about their capacity to win a general election fought through television and

TABLE 15.2: Selecting party leaders in liberal democracies

	Countries	Number of parties using this method
Party congress or convention	Finland, Norway, Sweden	37
Rank-and-file members	Belgium	19
Members of the parliamentary party	Netherlands, New Zealand	17
Party committee	Italy	8

Note: Analysis based on 16 democracies.
Source: Adapted from Hazan (2002: 124)

social media. Even so, colleagues in the assembly will have a close knowledge of a candidate's abilities; they provide an expert constituency for judging the capacity to lead not only the party, but also – more importantly – the country. Members of a legislature appear to be more influenced by experience than are ordinary party members. It is perhaps for this reason that many parties still permit the parliamentary party to remove the leader, even if the initial selection now extends to other groups (Cross and Blais, 2012a).

A ballot of party members is an alternative and increasingly popular method of selecting leaders. Such elections, often described as OMOV (one member, one vote) contests, provide an incentive for people to join the party, and can also be used to limit the power of entrenched factions within it. In Belgium, for example, all the major parties have adopted this approach to choosing their party president. In Canada, too, all major parties (except the Liberals) have adopted OMOV.

Candidates

There are several options available for selecting legislative candidates, ranging from the exclusive (selection by the party leader) to the inclusive (an open vote of the entire electorate) (Figure 15.3). Reflecting the complexity of party organization, the nomination process is generally decentralized; a few parties give control to the national leadership, but even here the leaders usually select from a list generated at lower levels. More often, local parties are the active force, either acting autonomously or putting forward nominations to be ratified at national level. Smaller and more extreme parties tend to be the most decentralized in their selection procedures.

The nomination task is constrained by three wider features of the political system:

- *The electoral system*: Choosing candidates for individual constituencies in a plurality system is a more decentralized task than preparing a single national list in a party list system (see Chapter 16).
- *Incumbents*: Sitting members of a legislature have an advantage almost everywhere, usually achieving reselection without much fuss. Often, candidates for office are only truly 'chosen' when the incumbent stands down.
- *Rules*: Nearly all countries impose conditions such as citizenship on members of the legislature while many parties have also adopted gender quotas for candidates.

Consider how the electoral system affects the nomination process. Under the list form of proportional representation, parties must develop a ranked list of candidates to present to the electorate. This obliges central coordination, even if candidates are suggested locally. In the Netherlands, for example, each party needs to present a single list of candidates for the whole country. The major parties use a nominating committee to examine applications received either from local branches, or directly from individuals. A senior party board then produces the final ordering.

In the few countries still using the single-member plurality method, the nomination procedure is typically more decentralized. Candidates must win selection by a local party in a specific district, though often they must pre-qualify by gaining inclusion on a central master list of approved candidates. The result of this can be to put the interests of the local party and individual districts above the interests of the national party and voters at large.

The United States has gone furthest in opening up the selection process. There, **primary elections** enable a party's supporters to choose their candidates for a particular office, ranging as high as the presidency. In the absence of a tradition of direct party membership, a 'supporter' is generously defined in most states as anyone who declares, in advance, an affiliation to that party,

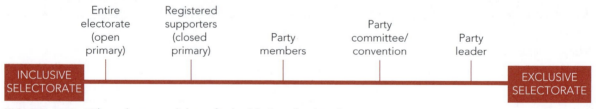

FIGURE 15.3: Who selects candidates for legislative elections?

Source: Adapted from Hazan and Rahat (2010: figure 3.1)

and can thereby take part in a closed primary. The holding of an open primary extends the choice still further: to any registered elector.

> **Primary election:** A contest in which a party's supporters select its candidate for a subsequent election (a direct primary), or choose delegates to the presidential nominating convention (a presidential primary). A closed primary is limited to a party's registered supporters.

An increasing number of countries operate a mixed electoral system, in which voters make choices for both a party list and a district candidate. These circumstances complicate the party's task of selecting candidates, requiring a national or regional list, plus local constituency nominees. In this situation, individual politicians also face a choice: should they seek election by means of the party list, or through a constituency? Many senior figures ensure they appear on both ballots, using a high position on the party's list as insurance against restlessness in their home district.

Party membership

Party membership was once an important channel for participation in politics, but this is no longer the case: most major European countries saw a dramatic fall in party membership between the 1960s and the 1990s (see Table 15.3), for instance in Denmark where membership collapsed from one in every five people to one in every 20. The drop continued into the 2000s, with membership of Sweden's Social Democrats falling by nearly 70 per cent between 1999 and 2005 alone (Möller, 2007: 36). Writing about the Netherlands, Voerman and

van Schurr (2011) concluded that 'the era of the mass party [was] over'. Across the democratic world, millions of party foot soldiers have simply given up.

Furthermore, many new members do not engage with their party beyond paying an annual subscription; these credit card supporters tend also to be fair-weather supporters, resulting in increased turnover. Their commitment to the party is often no greater than to other voluntary groups to which they donate. Lacking a steady flow of young members, the average age of members has gone up; belonging to a party is increasingly a pastime for the middle-aged and elderly (Scarrow and Gezgor, 2011).

However, we should place this recent decline in a longer perspective. If statistics were available for the entire twentieth century, they would probably show a rise in membership over the first two-thirds of the century, followed by a fall in the final third. The recent decline is from a peak that was only reached, in many countries, in the 1970s. In other words, it is arguably the bulge in membership after the Second World War, rather than the later decline, which requires explanation.

The recent reduction in membership has occurred in tandem with dealignment among voters (see Chapter 17) and reflects similar causes. These include:

- The weakening of traditional social divisions such as class and religion.
- The loosening of the bond linking labour unions and socialist parties.
- The decay of local electioneering in an era of media-based campaigns.
- The greater appeal of social movements and social media.

TABLE 15.3: Europe's declining party membership

	Party membership as a percentage of the electorate			
	Beginning of 1960s	Beginning of 1980s	End of 1990s	Change +/–
Denmark	21	8	5	–16
Finland	19	13	10	–9
Norway	16	14	7	–9
Italy	13	10	4	–9
Austria	26	22	18	–8
UK	9	3	2	–7
Netherlands	9	3	3	–6

Sources: Adapted from Mair (1994: table 1.1); Mair and van Biezen (2001: table 1); Sundberg (2002: table 7.10); Miller (2005: table 1.1)

- The declining standing of parties, often linked to cases of corruption.
- The perception of parties as forming a single structure of established authority with the state (Whiteley, 2011).

As we saw in discussing political participation generally (Chapter 13), it should not automatically be assumed that less is worse. The fall may indicate an evolution in the nature of parties, rather than a weakening of their significance in government. Crotty (2006: 499) notes how 'the demands of society change, and parties change to meet them'. Scarrow and Gezgor (2010) also argue that while membership has been falling, some parties in Europe have seen a growth in the power of their members to select candidates, leaders, and party policies. This suggests, they conclude, that 'today's smaller but more powerful memberships still have the potential to help link their parties to a wider electoral base'. Social and political change has meant that it is unrealistic to expect the rebirth of mass membership parties with their millions of members and their supporting pillars of labour unions and churches. Instead we find the modern format of parties found in new democracies: lean and flexible, with communication from leaders through television and social media. Rather than relying on a permanent army of members, such parties mobilize volunteers for specific, short-term tasks – notably, election campaigns.

Party finance

Falling membership means reduced income for parties in an era when expenses (not least for election campaigns) continue to rise. The problem of funding political parties has therefore become highly significant. Should members, donors, or the state pay for the party's work? Should private donations be encouraged (to increase funds and encourage participation) or restricted (to maintain fairness and reduce scandals)? Do limits on contributions and spending interfere with free speech? Whichever is the case, some method of funding parties must be found while also minimizing the ever-present danger of corruption.

In the main, the battle for public funding has been won. State support for national parties is now all but universal in liberal democracies. On a global level, research by the Swedish-based International Institute for Democracy and Electoral Assistance (IDEA) has found that more than two-thirds of 180 countries studied made provision for public funding of parties by 2011; a similar proportion offer free or subsidized access to the media (IDEA, 2014). As Fisher and Eisenstadt (2004: 621) had earlier commented, 'public subsidies have replaced private sponsorship as the norm in political finance'. State subsidies have also developed quickly in the new democracies of Eastern Europe, where party memberships are far smaller than in the West.

Typically, support is provided for legislative groups, election campaigns, or both. Campaign support, in turn, may be offered to parties, candidates, or both. In an effort to limit state dependence, public funding may be restricted to matching the funds raised by the party from other means, including its members. In any case, most funding regimes only reimburse a specified amount of party spending.

As with many political issues, there are costs and benefits involved in the question of state funding of parties (see Focus 15.2). One of the biggest points of concern is the advantage that large established parties have over small news ones in access to public funding. Some authors have developed this point by suggesting that the transition to public funding has led to a convergence of the state and major parties on a single system of rule. Governing parties, in effect, authorize subsidies for themselves, a process captured by Katz and Mair's idea (1995) of **cartel parties**: 'colluding parties become agents of the state and employ its resources to ensure their own survival'. The danger of cartel parties is that they become part of the political establishment, weakening their historic role as agents of particular social groups and inhibiting the growth of new parties in the political market.

> **Cartel party:** Leading parties that exploit their combined dominance of the political market to establish rules of the game, such as public funding, which reinforces its own strong position.

On a worldwide basis, and including authoritarian regimes in which parties are permitted, nearly all countries now regulate donations in some way. The vast majority ban political donations by government and its agencies to parties and candidates (other than through regulated public funding); most also disallow donations from overseas parties and candidates. However, only a few countries currently place limits on the size of donations, and only one-fifth ban corporate donations. As

> ### FOCUS 15.2 | The pros and cons of public funding for political parties
>
> Because they started out by representing the interests of groups, political parties were once supported mainly by these groups, whether through membership fees or donations. But as membership has fallen, parties have had to look for other sources of financial support, and they have focused increasingly on public funding; that is, taxpayer support. The rising use of public funding has both advantages and disadvantages.
>
> | Arguments in favour | Arguments against |
> |---|---|
> | Parties perform a public function by supplying leaders, candidates, and policies. | Public financing reduces a party's incentive to attract members. |
> | Parties should be funded to a professional level and not appear cheap. Marketing should match private sector standards. | Public funding reinforces the status quo, because it favours large established parties over new ones. |
> | Public funding creates a level playing field between parties. | Public funding is a form of creeping nationalization, creating parties that serve the state, not society. |
> | Without public support, pro-business parties gain access to greater funding. | Public funding favours established and large parties, encouraging a cartel. |
> | Relying on public funding decreases the opportunities for corruption. | To maintain a level playing field, spending should be capped, rather than subsidized. |
> | | Why should taxpayers fund parties against their wishes? A tax credit for voluntary donations is a preferable compromise. |
> | | Corruption can be reduced by banning anonymous donations, rather than adopting public funding. |

IDEA (2012: 51) points out, even these limits can be ineffective, either because financial reports are inadequately monitored, or because restrictions on donations to parties are circumvented by helping candidates directly, or because the limits are ignored.

The main outlier in the discussion about political funding is the United States, where campaigns are uniquely expensive and few limits have been imposed on the sources of funding. According to the Center for Responsive Politics (2015), a Washington DC-based watchdog body, spending on American elections grew from $3 billion in the 2000 cycle to nearly $6.3 billion in the 2012 cycle. Such massive figures are beyond compare, and detailed regulation of contributions has proved ineffective; there is no cap on spending (except for presidential candidates unwise enough to accept public funding), campaign costs continue to escalate, and the US Supreme Court has determined that limits on contributions are unconstitutional on the grounds of

free speech. Campaign advertising by groups which are independent of candidates is also unrestricted.

Political parties in authoritarian states

'Yes, we have lots of parties here', says President Nazarbaev of Kazakhstan. 'I created them all' (quoted in Cummings, 2005: 104). This quote reflects the secondary character of parties in most authoritarian regimes. The party is a means of governing, and neither a source of power in itself nor a channel through which elections are contested, won and lost. As Lawson (2001: 673) says of parties under dictatorships, 'the party is a shield and instrument of power. Its function is to carry out the work of government as directed by other agents with greater power (the military or the demagogue and his entourage).' In doing this, it often presents itself as

SPOTLIGHT

MEXICO

Brief Profile: Although Brazil is widely regarded as the major rising power of Latin America, further north there have been critical developments in Mexico. A programme of democratization since the 1990s has been so successful that the Institutional Revolutionary Party – in power without a break since 1929 – lost the presidency in 2000. Almost equally significant have been Mexico's economic reforms, which have brought greater freedom to a large market and have broadened the economic base of one of the world's biggest oil producers. But the intertwined problems of drugs, violence and corruption remain, and political scientists are divided about how best to describe Mexico; analyses are peppered with terms such as *bureaucratic*, *elitist*, and *patrimonial*. And while the economy is one of the world's 15 largest, many of its people remain poor and under-employed. It is common to hear talk of two Mexicos: one wealthy, urban, modern and well educated and the other poor, rural, traditional and under-educated.

Population (124 million)

Gross National Income ($1.26 trillion)

Per capita GNI ($9,940)

Democracy Index rating

| Not Rated | Hybrid Regime | Full Democracy |
| Authoritarian | Flawed Democracy |

Freedom House rating

| Not Free | Partly free | Free |

Human Development Index rating

| Not Rated | Medium | Very High |
| Low | High |

Form of government ⇨ Federal presidential republic consisting of 31 states and the Federal District of Mexico City. State formed in 1821, and most recent constitution adopted 1917.

Legislature ⇨ Bicameral National Congress: lower Chamber of Deputies (500 members) elected for three-year terms, and upper Senate (128 members) elected for six-year terms. Members may not serve consecutive terms.

Executive ⇨ Presidential. A president is elected for a single six-year term, and there is no vice president.

Judiciary ⇨ A Supreme Court of 11 members nominated for single 15-year terms by the president and confirmed by the Senate.

Electoral system ⇨ A straight plurality vote determines the presidency, while mixed member majoritarian is used for the Chamber of Deputies and the Senate: 300 single-member plurality (SMP) seats and 200 proportional representation seats in the Chamber, and a combination of SMP, first minority and at-large seats in the Senate.

Parties ⇨ Multi-party. Mexico was long a one-party system, but democratic reforms since the 1990s have broadened the field such that three major parties now compete at the national and state level, with a cluster of smaller parties.

pursuing a national agenda based on a key theme such as anti–imperialism, national unity, or economic development, but such messages are often a means of legitimizing power rather than a substantive commitment.

Geddes (2005) argues that in spite of the risks potentially posed to authoritarian regimes by allowing

parties and elections, there are several roles they can fulfil that dictators find useful:

• Helping solve intra–regime conflicts – or enforcing elite bargains – that might otherwise end or destabilize the rule of the dictator.

Political parties in Mexico

Mexico has seen a remarkable transformation in recent decades from a one-party dominant system to a truly competitive multi-party system, with three major national parties capable of winning the highest offices: a greater selection than is offered by the country's northern neighbour, the United States.

Between 1929 and 2000, power was all but monopolized by the Institutional Revolutionary Party (PRI), which won every presidential election, held large majorities in both chambers of Congress, and won almost all state and local elections as well. It kept its grip on power by multiple means, including being a source of patronage, incorporating the major social and economic sectors in Mexico, co-opting rival elites, mobilizing voters during elections, and overseeing the electoral process. It had no obvious ideology, but instead shifted with the political breeze and with the changing priorities of its leaders.

When economic problems began to grip Mexico in the 1970s, and again in the 1990s, PRI could not blame the opposition. Mexicans were also becoming better educated and more affluent, with increasing demand for more choice in their political system. PRI began to change the rules in order to allow opposition parties to win more seats, hoping that this would defuse demands for change. Instead, it lost its first national legislative elections in 1997, and lost the presidency for the first time in 2000, to the more conservative National Action Party (PAN). In 1997, the leftist Party of the Democratic Revolution (PRD), won the second most powerful executive post in the country: the office of mayor of Mexico City.

Questions continue to be asked about the fairness of elections, but today Mexican voters have a wide array of political parties from which to choose, ranging across the political spectrum: PAN sits on the right, PRI straddles the centre, and PRD sits on the left, with a cluster of smaller parties including greens and the left-wing Labor Party. PRI regained the presidency in 2012 with the victory of Enrique Peña Nieto, and PRI and PAN are developing a track record as the two largest parties in the Mexican Congress, with PRD and smaller parties holding the balance.

* A ruling party provides a counter-balance to other potential threats, notably the military.
* Elections help to identify and purge potential rivals for power.
* A dominant party can oversee elections, distribute bribes to voters and provide a channel for rewarding loyal members.
* A leading party and election campaigns provide a useful channel of information from government to the people and, on routine matters, from people to the government.
* A national party must organize supporter networks throughout the country, thereby extending the government's reach into outlying districts.
* A governing party educates and socializes members to support the regime's ideology and economic strategy. Elections campaigns attempt the same for ordinary citizens.

The longer-term result is that, rather than threatening authoritarian regimes, what Geddes describes as 'support parties' can prolong the political life not just of individual leaders but also of the regimes themselves. Of course, many of these functions are also performed by parties in democracies but parties in democracies provide additional value. They were often founded as a result of social cleavages, and continue today to appeal to groups of voters based on competing views about economic and social issues. In many poorer authoritarian states, politics is driven more by differences of identity and interest rather than policy. Ethnic, racial, religious and local identities matter more than policy preferences.

Nigeria illustrates these points. It has a long history of political party activity, predating its independence from Britain in 1960. Its first party – National Council of Nigeria and the Cameroons – was founded in 1944 on a platform of Nigerian nationalism, but was quickly joined (in 1948 and 1949 respectively) by the Action Group and the Northern People's Congress, based respectively in western and northern Nigeria. It was the breakdown of parties along ethnic lines that led to the collapse of two civilian governments in 1966 and 1983, and a futile effort was made by the military government in 1987 to invent two political parties named the Social

Democratic Party and the National Republican Convention. Concerns remain that in a strongly regional country, parties will continue to drift towards identification with the different ethnic groups. However, a peaceful election in 2015 did witness the first-ever defeat for an incumbent president standing for re-election, suggesting a maturing of the country's party system and a transition to a more democratic order.

Political parties in Africa are a puzzle, in the sense that many seemingly similar countries have had very different records. Following independence in the 1950s and 1960s, the heroes of the nationalist struggle routinely put a stop to party competition, and one-party systems were established; the official party was often justified in terms of the need to build national unity, even if it only served as the leader's personal vehicle. The tradition of the benevolent chief was skilfully exploited by dictators such as President Mobutu of Zaire (now the Democratic Republic of the Congo):

> In our African tradition, there are never two chiefs; there is sometimes a natural heir to the chief, but can anyone tell me that he has known a village that has two chiefs? That is why we Congolese, in the desire to conform to the traditions of our continent, have resolved to group all the energies of the citizens of our country under the banner of a single national party. (quoted in Meredith, 2006: 295)

But these single parties proved to be weak, they lacked autonomy from the national leader, and rather than building unity they merely entrenched the control of the elites. As with government itself, they had an urban bias, lacked presence in the rural areas, and showed little concern with policy. True, the party was one of the few national organizations and proved useful in recruiting supporters to public office but these functions could not disguise a lack of cohesion, direction, and organization. Indeed, when the founder-leader eventually departed, his party would sometimes disappear at the same time. This was what happened, for example, with the United National Independence Party (UNIP) in Zambia. Founded in 1959, it formed the first government of an independent Zambia in 1964, and stayed in power – as did Zambian President Kenneth Kaunda – until 1990. Following riots and a coup attempt that year, free elections were held in 1991 at which Kaunda was defeated. He retired from politics and UNIP sank into obscurity.

Despite recent economic growth, many African states still experience poverty, cultural heterogeneity,

and centralized political systems that would seem to pose severe handicaps to democracy. Even so, Reidl (2014) finds that nearly two dozen have achieved a measure of democratic competition since the early 1990s; these include South Africa, Botswana, Ghana, Tanzania, and Mozambique. She suggests that the nature of the democratic transition shapes its success (see Chapter 3). In a counter-intuitive conclusion, she argues that where authoritarian incumbents are strong, they tightly control the democratic transition, leading to a stronger party system subsequently. Where the ruling party is weak, it loses control of the transition, allowing others to enter the process, resulting in a weaker party system.

An interesting – albeit rare – sub-variety of parties in authoritarian systems is one where the political party, rather than a dominant individual, is truly the real source of power. Singapore is one such case. The People's Action Party (PAP) maintains a close grip despite permitting a modest, and perhaps increasing, level of opposition. Lee Kuan Yew, the island's prime minister from 1959 to 1990, acknowledged that his party post, rather than his executive office, was the real source of his authority: 'all I have to do is to stay Secretary-General of the PAP. I don't have to be president' (Tremewan, 1994: 184). Tremewan (p. 186) went on to refer to the 'PAP-state', in which the party uses its control of public resources to ensure citizen quiescence:

> It is the party-state with its secretive, unaccountable party core under a dominating, often threatening personality which administers Singaporeans' housing, property values, pensions, breeding, health, media, schooling and also the electoral process itself.

More typical of the story in authoritarian regimes is the case of Russia. At first glance it appears to have a wide range of political parties from which its voters can choose, but few of these have been able to develop either permanence or real influence. In fact, so many new parties were formed in the early years of democracy in the 1990s that they were often disparagingly described as 'taxi-cab parties' (driving around in circles, and stopping occasionally to let old members off and new ones on), or even 'divan parties' (they were so small that all their members could fit on a single piece of furniture). Clearly, when parties cease to exist from one election to the next, it is impossible for them to be held to account. Not surprisingly, they are the least trusted public organizations in a suspicious society (White, 2007: 27).

Far more than in the United States, voters in Russia's presidential elections are choosing between candidates, not parties. The party is vehicle rather than driver. The biggest party in Russia today is United Russia, but Vladimir Putin was only informally allied with the party (and its predecessor Unity party) in the 2000 and 2004 elections. As prime minister in 2008–12 he became leader of the party, and was its candidate in the 2012 election, after which leadership moved to Prime Minister Dmitry Medvedev. United Russia is what Russians term a 'party of power', meaning that the Kremlin uses threats and bribes to ensure it is supported by powerful ministers, regional governors and large companies.

Given the weak position of Russia's parties, it is not surprising that they are poorly organized, with a small membership and minimal capacity to integrate a large and diverse country. In a manner typical of competitive authoritarian regimes, the rules concerning the registration of parties, the nomination of candidates, and the receipt of state funding are skewed in favour of larger parties. Minor parties are trapped: they cannot grow until they become more significant but their importance cannot increase until they are larger (Kulik, 2007: 201).

Party weakness of another kind is found in Haiti, also ranked as an authoritarian regime in the Democracy Index. A country that suffers at least as much from natural disasters as from political problems, Haiti is currently working off its 23rd constitution since becoming independent in 1804. Such volatility is both a cause and an effect of Haiti's political difficulties, and its political parties demonstrate even less ability than its formal political institutions. It has elections, but they are rarely fair or efficient. It has a long history of political party activity, but has never developed durable parties with deep social roots. Party activity is at its greatest during presidential election seasons, when new parties emerge around the campaigns of the leading candidates. These have represented a wide range of issues, from Haitian nationalism to the interests of rural peasants, Haitian youth, communism, workers' rights, and opposition to the incumbent government. However, they rarely survive much longer than the terms in office of the leaders with whom they are associated, and so parties play only a peripheral role in Haitian politics.

DISCUSSION QUESTIONS

- Do we need political parties? If so, what are the most valuable functions they perform?

- Which is best: a multi-party system, or a two-party system?

- Which type of party system exists in your country? Does it reflect social divisions, voter preferences, the structure of government, or something else?

- Is it more democratic and effective for parties to choose leaders and candidates themselves, or for the choice to be put in the hands of voters?

- What is the fairest and most democratic means of financing political parties and election campaigns?

- Are political parties dead, dying, or simply reforming?

KEY CONCEPTS

Cartel party
Duverger's law
Iron law of oligarchy
Niche party
Party system

Political party
Primary election
Safe district
Selectorate

FURTHER READING

Brooker, Paul (2013) *Non-Democratic Regimes: Theory, Government and Politics*, 3rd edn. This wide-ranging examination of authoritarian rule includes a chapter on one-party rule.

Cross, William P. and Richard S. Katz (eds) (2013) *The Challenges of IntraParty Democracy*. This book considers the principal issues that parties and the state must address in introducing greater democracy within parties.

Gallagher, Michael, Michael Laver, and Peter Mair (2011) *Representative Government in Modern Europe*, 5th edn. An informative source on European politics, including extensive material on political parties.

Hazan, Reuven Y. and Gideon Rahat (2010) *Democracy within Parties: Candidate Selection Methods and Their Political Consequences*. A comparative analysis of candidate selection methods.

Riedl, Rachel Beatty (2014) *Authoritarian Origins of Democratic Party Systems in Africa*. A study of parties in Africa, looking at the challenging transitions from authoritarianism to competitive party systems.

Scarrow, Susan E. (ed.) (2002) *Perspectives on Political Parties: Classic Readings*. An interesting and unusual collection of primary documents, from various countries, revealing changing understandings of party politics in the nineteenth century.

16 Elections

PREVIEW

Elections lie at the heart of representative democracy. They are the primary means by which most voters connect with government, and they provide the brief moment during which politicians and parties are supplicants rather than supervisors. As liberal democracies have grown in number, so elections have become more widespread and the number of votes cast around the world has grown.

The key function of elections is to serve as a competition for office and a means of holding the government to account. But election campaigns also permit a dialogue between voters and parties, and so between society and state: 'no part of the education of a politician is more indispensable than the fighting of elections', claimed Winston Churchill. Competitive elections endow office-holders with authority (contributing to the effectiveness with which leaders can perform their duties), and facilitate choice, accountability, dialogue, and legitimacy.

In arranging elections, governments have many different options for converting votes into seats. These systems reflect contrasting ideas of representation and of democracy itself, not least because the results differ according to the methods used. This chapter begins with an assessment of those options, ranging from plurality to majority and proportional systems, and looking in turn at legislative and presidential elections. It then looks at the dynamics of campaigns, and at the particular effects of referendums, initiatives, and recalls. It ends with a discussion of the role of elections in authoritarian regimes, where despite active manipulation of outcomes, elections still perform some political functions.

CONTENTS

- Elections: an overview
- Electing legislatures
- Electing presidents
- Election campaigns
- Referendums, initiatives, and recalls
- Elections in authoritarian states

KEY ARGUMENTS

- Elections lie at the heart of the democratic process, and understanding the wide range of electoral systems used to translate votes into seats helps in appreciating contrasting ideas of representation.
- Although the issue of who can vote is usually regarded as settled, some interesting questions remain. Sixteen and seventeen year olds? Non-citizen residents? Prisoners?
- Legislative and executive elections differ in both their mechanics and their implications; voting for a multi-member legislature requires different rules than electing a one-person chief executive.
- For all the fuss devoted to election campaigns, they make less difference to the result than we might think, because party efforts often cancel out and even today many voters have made up their minds before campaigns enter their final phase. Campaigns are less important for the result they produce than for their role as learning opportunities for voters, candidates, and parties.
- The political impact of an election depends on the narrative established about it after the results are in, with exaggeration often being the order of the day.
- Numerous controls are imposed on elections in authoritarian regimes, but the effect is usually to constrain rather than to formally eliminate political choice.

Elections: an overview

Elections are fundamental to the idea of representative democracy. The quality of representation is directly related to the quality, regularity, and arithmetic of elections, and one of the key distinctions between democracies and authoritarian systems is that elections in the former are generally free and fair, while in the latter they are not.

The democratic purpose of elections is to ensure that the wishes and preferences of voters are reflected in the make-up of legislatures and governments. An electoral system cannot be expected by itself to resolve underlying social conflicts, but it can be considered to be performing its function if it is both widely acceptable and stable over time, if the winners do not seek to modify the system to their own advantage, and if the losers do not blame the election rules for their own defeat.

In terms of the mechanics of elections, the manner in which votes are turned into seats in a legislature varies: the major alternatives are plurality, majority, proportional and mixed systems. Whatever the system, voter preferences are rarely exactly reflected in the make-up of legislatures, but the extent of this bias varies greatly and is far from the only test we can use to judge electoral systems.

Elections also vary in their significance and effects; where **first-order elections** include national elections that involve the prospect of a change of leader or government, **second-order elections** include less significant mid-term and local elections. In European countries, for example, general elections draw much more attention, and attract a much higher turnout, than do local elections or elections to the European Parliament. Because there is a change of national government at stake, general elections are clearly first-order elections. Meanwhile, local elections – usually held at a different time from general elections – attract less voter interest and turnout, and voters use them to comment on national government. These are clearly second-order elections.

The outcomes of second-order elections tend to reflect the popularity of national parties, even though they do not result in a change of national government. They weaken the link between the representative's performance and the voters' response, such that a competent local administration might find itself dismissed for no other reason than the unpopularity of its party at the national level.

In understanding elections, we also need to consider their scope: while American government includes more than 500,000 elected posts (a figure reflecting a strong tradition of local self-government), European voters have traditionally been limited to voting for their national assemblies and local government, with regional and European elections added more recently. To illustrate the contrast, Dalton and Gray (2003: 38) calculated that between 1995 and 2000 a resident of Oxford in England could have voted just four times, while a resident of Irvine, California, could have cast more than 50 votes in 2000 alone.

There are dangers in too many elections, not least of which is voter fatigue, leading to a fall in interest, turnout, and quality of choice. Estimates from the United States suggest that five additional trips to the polls over a five-year period are likely to depress turnout by around 4 per cent (Dalton and Gray, 2003: 39).

Electing legislatures

At the heart of any discussion about **electoral systems** is the question of how best to convert votes into seats. In this section, we examine the rules for translating votes into seats in legislative elections (Table 16.1), and we follow this with a discussion of presidential elections in the next section. The key characteristic of an **electoral formula** is whether the legislative seats obtained by a party are directly proportional to the votes it receives. In proportional representation (PR) systems, a mechanism to achieve this goal is built into the allocation of seats. In non-proportional systems, by contrast, parties are not rewarded in proportion to the share of the vote they obtain, which usually results in skewed representation.

First-order elections: Elections at which the stakes are highest, usually involving the prospect of a change of national leadership or government.

Second-order elections: Elections at which the stakes are lower, such as local or mid-term elections, and which are used by many voters to express a judgement on the national government.

Electoral system: A general term for the rules governing an election, including the structure of the ballot (e.g. how many candidates are listed per party), the **electoral formula** (how votes are converted to seats), and districting (the division of the territory into separate constituencies).

TABLE 16.1: Comparing legislative electoral systems

	Procedure	Examples
PLURALITY		
Single-member plurality (SMP)	The candidate winning most votes (not necessarily a majority) is elected on the first and only ballot within each single-member district.	Bangladesh, Canada, India, Malaysia, Nigeria, UK, USA
MAJORITY		
Two-round system	If no candidate wins a majority on the first ballot, the leading candidates (usually the top two) face a second, runoff election. Used more often for presidential elections.	Belarus, France, Haiti, Iran, Vietnam
Alternative vote (AV) or instant runoff	A complex system of ranking candidates and – if needed – reassigning votes until one person has won a majority.	Australia, Papua New Guinea
PROPORTIONAL		
List system	Votes are cast for a party's list of candidates, and the seats in a district divided up among parties in proportion to their respective shares of the votes.	Most of Europe and Latin America, Russia, South Africa
Single transferable vote (STV)	Similar to AV but based on achieving proportionality rather than a majority winner.	Ireland, India (upper house), Malta
MIXED		
Parallel, or mixed member majoritarian (MMM)	Some seats are determined by PR and others by SMP or two-round elections. Effectively two separate elections.	Egypt, Japan, Philippines, South Korea, Ukraine
Mixed member proportional (MMP)	Much like MMM except that PR seats are used to determine the total share of seats.	Germany, Hungary, Mexico, New Zealand, Romania

For a full list of electoral systems and the countries that use them, see International Institute for Democracy and Electoral Assistance (IDEA) at www.idea.int

Plurality system

In the **single-member plurality** (SMP) format (also called 'first-past-the-post' or 'winner-take-all'), territories are divided into districts (or constituencies) that are each represented by a single member of the legislature. Each district is contested by multiple candidates, and the winner is the one receiving the greatest number of votes, whether this is a plurality (more than anyone else) or a majority (more than 50 per cent). Despite its antiquity, the plurality system is becoming less common, surviving mainly in Britain and British-influenced states. However, because several are so populous (such as India, the United States, and Nigeria), more people living in democracies vote using this method than any other.

> **Single-member plurality:** An electoral system based on districts that each have one representative, and in which the winner is the candidate with the most votes, but not necessarily a majority of those votes.

SMP is a simple system that can deliver a of unbalanced results. Consider an extreme example in which just two parties, the Reds and the Blues, compete in every constituency, and the Reds win by one vote in each district. There could hardly be a closer contest, and yet the Reds would win every district and the Blues would be left with nothing. Consider, also, the following practical examples:

- In 17 of the 19 general elections held in Britain between 1945 and 2015, a single party won a majority in the House of Commons, even though no party ever won a majority of votes.
- A similar pattern holds for some, but not all, federal elections in Canada. In 2011, for instance, the Conservatives won a majority of seats with less than 40 per cent of votes, while the other parties combined won nearly 60 per cent of votes but only 45 per cent of seats (Figure 16.1).

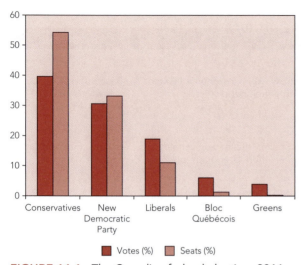

FIGURE 16.1: The Canadian federal election, 2011

- Much the same happened in India in 2014, when the Bharatiya Janata Party won only 31 per cent of votes but nearly 52 per cent of seats in the national Parliament.

The system favours dominant parties with widespread support throughout the country, but tends to work against weaker parties with geographically even support. These smaller parties may pile up votes without topping the poll in many, or any, districts. Meanwhile, in SMP systems that have seen a decline of two-party systems and the retreat of major parties into regional strongholds, leading parties have not benefited as much. In short, the plurality system is less likely to deliver a single-party majority, a point rarely recognized by the system's defenders.

Majority systems

As the name implies, majority electoral systems require the winning candidate to obtain a majority of votes, the democratic argument being that no candidates should be elected without proving themselves acceptable to most voters. There are two usual ways of doing this: through a two-round election (also known as a 'runoff election'), or – more uncommonly – using a complicated alternative vote arrangement.

In the case of the former, all candidates run against each other in a district, and if someone wins more than 50 per cent of the vote they are declared the winner. But if no one passes the 50 per cent mark, the top two candidates from the first round compete in a second round held soon afterwards, thereby ensuring that one wins a majority. (In France, any candidate winning more than 12.5 per cent of the vote in the first round can run in the second, although deals are often brokered in order to clear the way for the leading candidates to compete in the second and decisive round.) Many Western European countries used two-round majority voting before switching to proportional representation early in the twentieth century. For legislative elections, it now remains significant only in France and its ex-colonies, and is used in a small number of elections in the United States, including selected primaries and the Louisiana Senate election. It is used for presidential elections in several countries, and so is covered in more detail later in this chapter.

The alternative vote (AV) or instant-runoff arrangement takes matters to a higher level of complexity and demands more thought from voters. All candidates must be ranked by voters, and if one wins a majority of first preferences, that candidate is elected. But if no one wins a majority, the last-placed candidate is eliminated and their votes reassigned, a process which continues until one candidate has a majority. Only Australia and Papua New Guinea use this system for national legislative elections, but it is also used in some local elections in Britain, New Zealand, and the United States. An effort to introduce AV for British general elections was heavily defeated in a 2011 national referendum.

Proportional representation

The most common electoral system found in Europe and Latin America is **proportional representation** (PR), in which seats are assigned in the legislature in proportion to the number of votes that each of them wins, and voters make their choices more on the basis of parties than of individual candidates. Because a single party rarely wins a majority of seats, the usual result is a coalition government. And because PR usually leads to post-election negotiations about which parties will form the next government, it is best interpreted as a means of electing legislatures rather than governments.

> **Proportional representation:** An electoral system in which the number of seats won by each of the competing parties is proportional to the number of votes they each win.

> ## FOCUS 16.1 | Who should be allowed to vote?
>
> The question of the franchise (who can vote) is given surprisingly little attention in discussions about elections. Voting restrictions have been lifted steadily over the past century or so, the most recent change in most democracies being a reduction of the voting age to 18 in the 1960s and 1970s. But questions remain. Should the age be reduced to 16, as in Austria and Brazil? Should prisoners be allowed to vote? Should non-citizen legal residents be allowed to vote?
>
> In a few countries, many convicted criminals are still denied the vote; the United States is the prime exhibit. The number of disenfranchised felons and ex-felons there exceeds five million; about one in seven black men cannot vote for this reason. Britain also takes a tough line, resisting rulings from the European Court of Human Rights to grant the vote to prisoners. Prime Minister David Cameron even once claimed that the prospect of inmates voting made him 'physically sick'.
>
> Although Weale (2007: 157) suggests that 'there are probably as many arguments against depriving prisoners of the right to vote as there are in favour', not everyone accepts that being locked up should also mean being locked out. Canada's highest court has ruled that prisoner disenfranchisement 'has no place in a democracy built upon the principles of inclusiveness, equality and citizen participation'. Israel's Supreme Court even restored the right to vote to the assassin of Prime Minister Yitzhak Rabin, declaring that 'we must separate contempt for his act from respect for his right' (Manza and Uggen, 2008: 232).
>
> There also remains the question of non-citizen residents; should they be granted the vote in the country where they live, work, and pay taxes alongside citizens? If so, should they also retain the vote in their home country? The slow trend here is to greater inclusiveness, with about 40 countries having now approved some form of non-citizen voting rights (Immigrant Voting Project, 2012). Within the European Union, all EU citizens living legally in a country of which they are not a national can vote and can stand as a candidate at local and European elections. This policy is a tangible step towards maintaining voting rights in an age of mobility.

In a perfectly proportional system, every party would receive the same share of seats as of votes: hence 40 per cent of the votes would mean 40 per cent of the seats. In practice, though, most PR systems fall short, because they usually offer some bonus to the largest party (though less than most non-proportional methods) and they cut out the smallest parties. So, it is a mistake to assume that any system labelled 'proportional' is completely so.

There are two variations on the theme of PR: the party list system and the single transferable vote. The list system is the most common, and itself comes in several varieties. Constituencies are represented by multiple members (in contrast to the single members that we find in plurality systems), each of the parties contesting an election puts forward a list of candidates (typically the same number of names as there are representatives from the district), and voters choose among the parties offering those lists. The number of votes won by a party determines how many candidates are elected from each party list, while the order in which candidates appear on the list (predetermined by the party itself) usually determines who is elected.

Many countries – such as Belgium, South Africa, and Spain – use closed party lists that allow voters only a straight choice among parties. In this format, party officials exert enormous control over the writing of each list, including the ability to include women and minorities near the top. However, most list systems in Europe are open lists that give voters at least some choice between candidates. This option, known as 'preference voting', allows voters to select one or more candidates from the party list. The total of votes cast for a given list still determines the party's overall representation, but a candidate's preference votes influence (to varying degrees) which candidates on each list are elected.

SPOTLIGHT

UNITED STATES

Brief Profile: As the world's most important economic and military power, the United States has both driven and been deeply affected by the global changes of the last few decades. During the Cold War, it led the Western alliance against the Soviet Union and its clients, and was seen as the political, economic and military leader of the 'free world'. Today it must use its continuing strengths to confront a more complex set of international challenges: it is caught up in the struggle against global terrorism and faces economic competition on an unprecedented level. Domestically, it suffers the effects of deficit spending and a record national debt, and must respond to challenges ranging from deep racial tensions to decaying infrastructure, an expanding gap between rich and poor, concerns over immigration and declining faith in government.

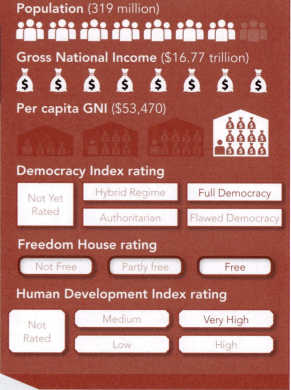

Population (319 million)

Gross National Income ($16.77 trillion)

Per capita GNI ($53,470)

Democracy Index rating

| Not Yet Rated | Hybrid Regime | Full Democracy |
| | Authoritarian | Flawed Democracy |

Freedom House rating

| Not Free | Partly free | Free |

Human Development Index rating

| Not Rated | Medium | Very High |
| | Low | High |

Form of government ⇨ Federal presidential republic consisting of 50 states and the District of Columbia. State formed 1776, and most recent constitution adopted 1787.

Legislature ⇨ Bicameral Congress: lower House of Representatives (435 members) elected for renewable two-year terms, and upper Senate (100 members) containing two senators from each state, elected for renewable six-year terms.

Executive ⇨ Presidential. A president elected for a maximum of two four-year terms, supported by a vice president, an Executive Office of the President, a White House Office, and a federal cabinet.

Judiciary ⇨ A dual system of federal and state courts headed by the federal Supreme Court with nine members appointed by the president (and confirmed by the Senate) for lifetime terms.

Electoral system ⇨ One of the few large countries still employing the single-member plurality method. Formally, the president is elected indirectly through an electoral college.

Parties ⇨ Multi-party, but dominated by the moderately conservative Republican Party and the moderately liberal Democratic Party.

The second and less common variety of proportional representation is the single transferable vote (STV) system, which is easy neither to describe nor for voters to understand. It requires voters to rank the candidates running in their district, and when one of the candidates reaches a preset quota of first preferences, they are declared elected and their surplus first preferences distributed to other candidates according to second preferences. Candidates with the fewest votes are eliminated. This process continues until all the seats available have been filled. Unlike the party list system, it allows votes to be cast for individual candidates, and minimizes the

Elections in the United States

Elections in the United States are unusual (or even unique) in at least four three ways: in the sheer number of elected offices, in the astonishing amounts of money that are spent on campaigns, and in notably low turnout for many contests.

At the federal level, Americans can vote for the president and vice president, two senators per state, and their member of the House of Representatives. At the state and local level, the variety is even greater, ranging from governors and members of state legislatures to auditors, judges, school boards, sheriffs, and treasurers.

The large number of elected posts reflects not only the practical requirements of governing a large and one-time frontier society, but also a culture that emphasizes equality, competence, and a belief that administration is a practical matter. In addition, the distinctly American institution of primary elections opens up the selection of a party's candidates to the general population (although turnout at primaries is often low).

While the large amounts spent on campaigning are no guarantee of electoral success, it is all but impossible to make a mark on the electorate without having access to large advertising budgets. The 2000 election (all offices) topped $3 billion for the first time in history, but was rapidly eclipsed by more than $5 billion spent in 2008 and nearly $7 billion spent in 2012. In the name of free speech, a 2010 Supreme Court ruling overturned some previous limits on campaign financing and allowed all but unlimited spending, often by groups protected by anonymity.

The 2000 presidential election raised troubling questions about American democracy, because the winner of the popular vote (Al Gore) lost the Electoral College vote to George W. Bush, against a background of deeply flawed vote recording and rules on access to voting booths. The 2008 presidential election had a different outcome: Barack Obama won 68 per cent of the votes in the Electoral College, despite winning just 53 per cent of the popular vote.

'wasting' of votes. At the national level it is used only in Ireland and Malta, but is also used for upper house elections in India and Pakistan, and for selected state or local elections in Australia, Britain, New Zealand, and the US.

Most PR systems include a minimum threshold, so that if a party's share of the vote falls below a given level it wins no seats. The threshold varies, with a range of 3–5 per cent in most countries, and a high of 10 per cent in Turkey. Explicit thresholds help to protect the legislature from fragmentation and extreme parties, or the problem of the tail wagging the dog. The effect of a threshold that is too low is most clearly on show in Israel, where the 2013 election – based on a 2 per cent threshold – saw 12 parties winning seats in the 120-member Knesset. Six of these parties each won less than 5 per cent of the vote, but among them they controlled 25 seats, while the biggest party, Likud, controlled only 31. The threshold was raised in 2014 to 3.25 per cent, but it only reduced the number of parties to ten after the 2015 elections.

Mixed systems

The fourth kind of electoral system involves a hybrid of plurality and PR systems, designed to maximize their respective advantages and minimize their disadvantages. The simplest of the variations is parallel voting, or mixed member majority (MMM), which uses unlinked SMP and party list votes, amounting to what is effectively two separate campaigns; voters choose among competing candidates to represent their local district, and among party lists to represent larger regions. In Japan's House of Representatives, for example, 300 members are elected by SMP and 180 by PR. Voters cast two ballots (one for a candidate and one for a party), and because parties can assign candidates to both the single-member districts and the PR lists, candidates who lose in the former still have a chance of winning in the latter. MMM contains no mechanism to secure a proportional result.

However, another version of a mixed system, mixed member proportional (MMP) (sometimes called 'compensatory PR'), is proportional in character. This format also uses a hybrid of SMP and PR, but links the two tiers by using the PR list vote to 'top up' seats so as to deliver a proportional outcome overall. Germany is the inspiration for this system. Voters in Germany's 299 electoral districts cast a 'personal' ballot to elect representatives from their local districts on the basis of SMP, while also filling an additional 299 seats by casting a 'party' ballot to choose among parties running in Germany's 16 *Länder* (states) on the basis of PR. It is this second, party ballot that determines a party's total representation in the legislature. A party that wins a larger share of the party ballot than of the district contests will have its representatives 'topped up' from the party list, and from additional 'balance' seats, to achieve a more proportional outcome overall. The result is not an exact correlation between votes cast and seats won (see Table 16.2), but it allows for adjustments to be made. The PR element particularly helped the Left Party and the Greens, who won 127 seats in the legislature between them despite winning just five district seats. The German system is widely accepted within the country itself and has attracted outside interest because of its success in combining district representation with a proportional outcome.

Electing presidents

While the electoral systems used for legislatures are varied and often complex, those used for presidents are relatively straightforward, since a one-person presidency cannot be shared between parties. This eliminates PR as an option, leaving the main choice between plurality and majority systems.

While plurality systems tend to be the simplest, they can also fail to produce a convincing mandate: the more candidates contesting the election, the more this is likely to happen. Presidents who win office without a majority will have less credibility and less ability to pursue their policy agendas. This problem is particularly acute when the victorious candidate secures only a small plurality of the total vote. For example, Fidel Ramos became president of the Philippines in 1992 with just 24 per cent of the vote – hardly a resounding endorsement with which to send the winner to the highest executive office in the land. Benigno Aquino won in 2010 with 42 per cent of the votes; better, but still not a majority. In Mexico, following electoral reforms in the 1990s, no winning candidate has garnered more than 42 per cent of the vote. In 2006, Felipe Calderón's winning share was just 36 per cent.

For this reason, most presidential electoral systems force a majority by using a two-round system. In the first round, all eligible candidates compete, and if one wins more than half the vote, that candidates is declared the winner. If no one wins more than half the vote, then a second round is held between the two top-placed candidates, usually within two or three weeks of the first contest. As well as ensuring that the winner attracts the support of the majority of voters, the two-round system also encourages the two runoff candidates to reach out to unsuccessful candidates from the first round, which may be helpful in promoting more broadly based politics. Two-round elections extend the campaign season

TABLE 16.2: The German federal election, 2013

	Party list vote (%)	Number of district seats won	Number of seats in lower house	Share of seats in lower house (%)
Christian Democrats/Christian Social Union	45.3	236	311	49.3
Social Democrats	29.4	58	193	30.6
Left Party	8.2	4	64	10.1
Green Party	7.3	1	63	10.0
Others	9.8	0	0	10.0
Total	100	299	631	100

and its associated costs, run the danger that turnout may fall in the second round, and open the door to tactical voting in the first round.

France is an influential case; French voters, it is said, vote with their hearts in the first round and with their heads in the second, which creates the possibility of unexpected surprises, as in the 2002 presidential election (see Table 16.3). The incumbent, Jacques Chirac, was running for a second term, but had lost popularity and the election was held against a background of concerns about law and order. It was expected that the two major contenders would be Chirac and his socialist opponent, Lionel Jospin, but many voters expressed their displeasure with Chirac by voting for minor candidates at the first round. While Chirac came out top, it was by only a small margin, and Jospin was knocked into third place by the right-wing National Front candidate Jean-Marie Le Pen. Shocked by this result, most voters determined to block Le Pen at the second round, turnout grew to nearly 80 per cent, and Chirac won more than 82 per cent of the vote, the biggest winning margin for a leader in the history of democratic France.

As an interesting side-note, three countries – Indonesia, Kenya, and Nigeria – go beyond a simple run-off by requiring winning candidates to meet additional **distribution requirements** proving the breadth as well as the depth of their support. In the case of Nigeria, which experiences substantial ethnic, regional, and religious divisions, a victorious president must demonstrate regional as well as national support. In the first round, the winning target is a majority of all votes cast and at least 25 per cent of the vote in at least two-thirds of

Nigeria's 36 states. If no candidate crosses this barrier, a second round is held with the same requirements. If the barrier is still not crossed, a third round is held between the two top finishers, a simple majority sufficing.

> **Distribution requirements:** Rules specifying how a winning candidate's votes must be arranged across different regions or social groups.

Indirect election is still employed in a number of countries to elect the president. Examples include several parliamentary systems where the president possesses few meaningful executive powers, such as Germany and India. The United States is now highly unusual in using an Electoral College to elect an executive president. The College was originally designed to filter the voice of the people through an assembly of 'wise men'; votes were cast for members of the College, rather than directly for presidential candidates. Today, the College survives only as a procedural relic mandated by the constitution. Complicating matters, some states use a winner-take-all formula where the candidate with the biggest popular vote in the state wins all the College votes from that state, while others split them by proportion, and yet others still allow 'faithless electors' in the College to opt for the candidates of their choice, regardless of the winner. One quirk of the College is that, as G. W. Bush demonstrated in 2000, it is possible (albeit highly unusual) to lose the popular vote while winning in the Electoral College and so becoming president. Even the possibility of such an outcome demonstrates the weakness of indirect election in a democratic era.

TABLE 16.3: The French presidential election, 2002

	Party	First round (%)	Second round (%)
Jacques Chirac	Rally for the Republic	19.8	82.2
Jean-Marie Le Pen	National Front	16.8	17.7
Lionel Jospin	Socialist	16.1	—
François Bayrou	Union for French Democracy	6.8	—
Arlette Laguiller	Workers' Struggle	5.7	—
11 other candidates		34.5	—
Votes cast		28.5 million	31.0 million
Turnout (%)		71.6	79.7

Three other features of presidential elections, whether direct or indirect, are worth noting. First, presidential terms are sometimes longer, but rarely shorter, than those for legislators. The longer the term, the easier it is for presidents to adopt a broad perspective free from the immediate burden of re-election. With terms of just four years, first-term presidents in Argentina, Brazil and the United States are likely to find themselves acquiring experience during their first year and campaigning during their fourth year, leaving only the middle phase for real accomplishments.

Second, presidents are more likely than legislators to be subject to term limits; it is usual to restrict an incumbent to just one or two terms in office, or to require a cap of no more than two consecutive terms (see Table 16.4). The fear is that without such constraints presidents will be able to exploit their unique position to secure endless re-election. But term limits can have unintended consequences: a president who cannot be re-elected is no longer directly accountable to the voters, a reality which constitutes a limitation on democracy. Also, such presidents often lose political clout as their term nears its end. At the same time, term limits prevent popular and effective presidents from continuing to bring their experience to bear. One of the more stringent sets of limits is found in Mexico, where neither presidents nor state governors can serve more than one term, and legislators are barred from serving consecutive terms.

Third, the timing of presidential elections matters. When they occur at the same time as elections to the legislature, the successful candidate is more likely to be drawn from the largest party in the legislature. Without threatening the separation of powers, concurrent elections limit fragmentation, increasing the likelihood that the president and the legislature will be of similar mind. Such thinking lay behind the decision in 2000 to reduce the French president's term from seven years to five years, the same tenure as that of the National Assembly.

Election campaigns

Election campaigns are hard to ignore. In the more extreme cases, it can sometimes seem as though democracies are in a state of permanent campaigning: media experts constantly speculate about possible outcomes, and the campaign itself often takes on the trappings of a horse race, with polls pinning down the changing state of the parties and the leading candidates. At the same time, campaigns are often notable for what they do not achieve: they rarely bring about decisive changes in party support or widespread conversions among voters from one major party to another, and political advertising – for all the attention it is given, and no matter how negative its tone – rarely makes a great difference. One reason for this is that many voters have already decided how to vote before the **short campaign** begins. This should come as no surprise, because elections are, in part, referendums on government performance, and this record (though not its interpretation) is fixed by the start of the short campaign.

TABLE 16.4: Comparing presidential elections

	Method	Term (years)	Limits
Argentina	Two round	4	No more than two consecutive terms
Brazil, Colombia, Egypt, Iran	Two round	4	Two terms
Chile	Two round	4	No consecutive terms allowed
United States	Electoral college	4	Two terms
South Africa	Elected by legislature	5	Two terms
France	Two round	5	Two terms
Russia	Two round	5	No more than two consecutive terms
Peru	Two round	5	No consecutive terms allowed
Mexico, Philippines	Plurality	6	One term
Finland	Plurality	6	No consecutive terms allowed

Short campaign: A term used in countries with variable election dates to describe the period between the announcement of an election and election day.

We should also bear in mind the difference between gross and net effects: voters who change their preference from Party X to Y may be cancelled out by those moving from Y to X, limiting the net impact. And finally, many campaign effects have only a short life. Some – often including leader debates, for example – produce a temporary bounce in a party's support, but even though the media often portray them as having long-term consequences, the effects usually decay before the election arrives. Events with longer-term effects are less common (Wlezien, 2010: 111), and most would agree with Butler (1989: 116) that 'the function of elections is to record the decisions of individuals rather than to create them'.

In seeking to separate campaign myths and realities, it is worth observing that switches between supporters of the major parties from one election to the next are often only a minor source of the gross or net change that occurs. Reflecting this reality, party strategies often

Mandate: A commission to act on another's behalf in a specific area. An election mandate is an authorization from the people for the government to follow a particular course.

FOCUS 16.2 | Electoral messages and mandates

An election does not end when the results are declared. Far from it. After the declaration comes the interpretation, which plays a large part in shaping the impact of an election on the politics that follow. Was it a mandate for change? A repudiation of the government? A referendum on the economy? Have 'the people' indeed spoken? What have they said? Here we can see the relevance of an interpretive approach to politics (see Chapter 5); the election narrative can influence later politics, even if vote shares or the party composition of the government remain unchanged.

The primary focus is usually on the victor, or on a small party that has done surprisingly well; losers tend to be quickly forgotten unless the scale of the loss is dramatic. The larger and more unexpected the winner's margin, the greater the demand for a narrative giving positive reasons for the victor's triumph. Claiming that Party X won because of Party Y's unpopularity, or that Candidate A won because Candidate B performed poorly, rarely fits the bill. One benign effect of this search for the winning party's merits is to add to its authority as it begins to govern.

Interpretations of election results focus on the distinctly opaque notion of a **mandate**. Winners routinely claim that their victory is a repudiation of the former government and confirmation of the changes they propose to make, and the media can often be persuaded to agree. Only individual voters, not the electorate as a whole, have reasons for their decisions. Even so, editorials and blogs can be found after every campaign explaining what the electorate intended by its collective judgement.

The case of the 2015 British general election offers an example. For five years, the Conservative Party of David Cameron had been governing in a troubled coalition with the much smaller Liberal Democrats, and had been influenced by three major issues: the economy, a Scottish independence movement, and a debate over the continued membership of the UK in the European Union. The polls had the Conservatives and Labour parties neck and neck in votes but in fact the Conservatives won a majority of seats, enabling them to form a single-party government. The result was greeted with terms such as *surprising*, *stunning*, and *astonishing*, and was interpreted both as a mandate for the Conservatives to continue with their pro-market policies and as a rejection of Labour's more radical approach. But the Conservative majority was just 12 seats on just 37 per cent of the vote (a modest 0.7 per cent increase over 2010), and Labour's defeat probably reflected doubts about its governing capacity more than its left-wing policies. Still, the story has been written, the message has been transmitted and the mandate has been secured. And all (or mainly) because the polls underestimated Conservative support.

focus more on mobilizing existing supporters and new voters than on attempting to convert the supporters of other parties. Target groups typically include first-time voters, previous abstainers, previous defectors, supporters of minor parties, and, of course, the undecided. Collectively, such niche groups are significant but they still – in most countries – comprise a minority of the electorate.

There is, finally, reason to doubt the impact of paid advertising, a form of campaign communication allowed in most liberal democracies (de Vreese, 2010). Certainly, advertising can provide information about candidates and their positions, at least in sub-national contests receiving little news coverage. Attack advertisements and those making emotional appeals appear to be particularly memorable (Corrigan and Brader, 2011). But, as with campaigns, when advertising resources are roughly equal, any effects tend to cancel each other out.

None of these points should be interpreted to mean that campaigns are irrelevant. One of their positive functions is to provide an intense political seminar for the country as a whole, enlightening voters about parties, candidates, and policies. They also educate politicians about the electorate, either through public opinion research, or through direct encounters on the campaign trail (Schmitt-Beck and Farrell, 2002). At a minimum, they provide a final test which candidates and parties must pass if they wish to win elected office: in that sense, campaigns always have the potential to be decisive. And in a close contest, the campaign, as any other influential factor, can be crucial.

Above all, perhaps, election campaigns advance political debate within the elite. For a short period, politicians, journalists, and experts engage in an intense, public and competitive scrutiny of the political agenda. Of course, parties seek to focus on the issues on which they possess a natural advantage, but complete agenda control is rarely possible. In the course of the debate, political reputations are made and lost and, more importantly, policy proposals are floated, dissected, amended, and sometimes discarded. In public, parties may appear to talk past each other but, in private, every move is closely monitored and lessons are drawn. At the end of the campaign, the debate about what government should do, and how it should do it, has often moved forward. In some respects, election campaigns are politics speeded up.

Referendums, initiatives, and recalls

Elections may be instruments of representative democracy, but the role of the people is only to decide who will decide. By contrast, the referendum and the initiative make voters into decision makers, allowing them to shape specific policy issues, while the recall permits voters to dismiss elected officials during their term of office. But while these mechanisms are good examples of direct democracy, are they necessarily good for democracy?

Referendums

The **referendum** is the most important form of direct democracy. The term implies a reference from another body – typically the government, or legislature – to the people. Referendums may be mandatory (meaning that they must be called on specified topics, such as constitutional amendments), optional, or even constitutionally forbidden on a few reserved subjects such as taxation and public spending. Their outcome may be binding – as with constitutional amendments requiring popular approval, or merely consultative – as with Sweden's vote in 1994 on membership of the European Union (which came down in favour).

> **Referendum:** A vote of the electorate on a limited issue of public policy such as a constitutional amendment.

Referendums are growing in frequency (Figure 16.2). Switzerland heads the list, holding nearly 400 referendums between 1940 and 2006 on a range of issues including nuclear power, same-sex partnerships, and immigration. Australia, too, makes use of state and national referendums, but only in relation to changes to the constitution: more than 40 have been held since the creation of the federation of Australia in 1901. They have dealt mainly with economic and legislative issues, but less than a quarter have resulted in a Yes vote. One of the more notable was the 1999 referendum on whether or not Australia should cut its last links with the British crown and become a republic; nearly 55 per cent of voters said No, but the issue has not gone away. Few other countries have made more than occasional use of the device, although they have become more common in EU member states, where they have been used for

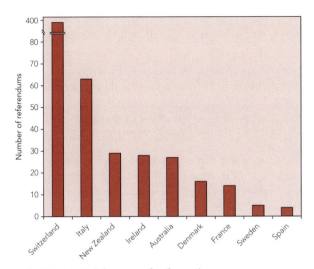

FIGURE 16.2: The use of referendums

Source: Adapted from Morel (2007: table 1). Data are for the period 1940–2007.

decisions on joining the EU or the euro, and for adopting new EU treaties.

Referendums offer several advantages. First, they provide a channel by which governments can hear directly from voters rather than via elected officials, parties, or interest groups. Second, there is evidence that they help improve voter understanding of the issue at stake, and increase voters' confidence in their own political abilities and their faith in government responsiveness (Bowler and Donovan, 2002). Third, they can inform politicians. For instance, the rejection of the proposed European Union constitutional treaty by French and Dutch voters in 2005 taught the European elite that national electorates had grown weary of grand European projects. Finally, they can provide a safety valve, allowing governments, particularly coalitions, to put an issue to the people when it is incapable of reaching a decision itself.

But there are also several reasons for caution:

- Referendums can be expensive to organize and to hold.
- The issues at stake may be too complex for a straight Yes/No choice.
- They can polarize the electorate by creating controversy and division.
- In order to be fully effective, voters must do their research.
- The timing of the vote can be critical.

- Too many referendums can tire the voters, depressing turnout.
- There is no mechanism for ensuring consistency in referendum decisions; neither is it always clear for how long the results should be considered decisive.
- Voter judgements are often informed by wider considerations than the specific proposition on the ballot.

Many referendums have the additional complication of being ad hoc in character, with the government picking and choosing topics on which it feels a ballot would be to its political benefit. More crudely, rulers can simply ignore the result of a referendum. In 1955, Swedes voted decisively to continue driving on the left; eight years later, the legislature passed a law introducing driving on the right.

In addition to all these difficulties, referendums can easily be compromised by confusion about the precise wording of the question to be put to the voters. Examples from Britain confirm this point. When a referendum was proposed in 2013–14 on the UK's continued membership of the European Union, it was suggested that the referendum should ask 'Do you think that the United Kingdom should be a member of the European Union?' The UK Electoral Commission pointed out that there were enough people in Britain who did not know that their country was *already* a member of the EU as to create confusion.

In the case of the referendum about Scottish independence held in 2014, the Scottish National Party initially proposed the question, 'Do you agree that Scotland should be an independent country?' Again, the Electoral Commission intervened, arguing successfully that 'Should Scotland be an independent country?' was more neutral. Later, though, there were concerns that the wording made the pro-independence campaign into a positive Yes campaign, and the anti-independence campaign into a negative No campaign. Such intricacies of wording and tone do not arise with conventional elections.

Initiatives

As its name suggests, an **initiative** allows the people to take the lead in calling for a referendum on – or requiring the legislature to discuss – a particular topic. By giving the power of initiative to the people, this device is more interesting for students of direct democracy than referendums sponsored by the government.

There are two kinds of initiative. The first is a *referendum initiative*, which allows a given number of citizens to initiate a popular vote on a given proposal. Nearly 40 countries, most of them in Europe and Latin America, allow this option. In Switzerland, for example, 100,000 electors can propose a new law at canton level, or an amendment to the constitution at federal level. The government offers advice, usually to reject, before the ballot. Elsewhere, referendum initiatives can be employed more broadly, for ballots on proposed or existing policies. Referendum initiatives are commonly included in post-authoritarian constitutions in an attempt to prevent a return to dictatorship, and they have also been adopted by many western states in the United States, notably California.

The second type is an *agenda initiative*, which functions as a petition to the legislature, requiring it to discuss a particular topic if the required number of voter signatures is reached. One advantage of this technique is that it allows minorities to place their concerns on the table. This mechanism was introduced to the constitutions of several European countries (e.g. Austria and Spain) after the First World War and has been extended to a number of other states (e.g. Poland and Thailand) since 1989 (IDEA, 2008). Agenda initiatives are particularly well established in Austria (Giese, 2012). In 2006, for example, over 250,000 signatories requested a national referendum in the event that Turkey be proposed for European Union membership by the EU, a demand accepted by Austria's prime minister. In Britain, a petition obtaining at least 100,000 signatures must now be considered by the House of Commons for debate, provided at least one member speaks in support of a debate.

Recalls

The **recall** is a ballot on whether an elected official should be removed from office during normal tenure. A vote is initiated by a petition signed by a minimum proportion (typically, around 25 per cent) of the votes cast for that office at the previous election (so, the recall is a form of popular initiative). Unlike impeachment, the recall is a political rather than legal device, a modern

equivalent of the old device of denunciation (Rosanvallon, 2008: 207). Where an election is a vote of confidence, the recall is a vote of no confidence. It seeks to improve governance by removing incompetent or corrupt incumbents before their normal term is up.

One of the few countries to employ recalls at the national level is Venezuela. There, a recall vote can be held on any elected official, including the president, on the initiative of 20 per cent of the relevant electorate. Fifteen US states also make provision for recall elections for all state officials, with even more allowing the recall of local officials. However, the device has rarely been used, although it did make international headlines when Arnold Schwarzenegger became governor of California following the successful recall of incumbent Gray Davis in 2003.

Elections in authoritarian states

Most non-democratic rulers recognize that elections can be a useful political device. Internationally, they please donors who are often content even if it is only the facade that is democratic. Domestically, they create friends for the ruling elite by establishing a pool of successful candidates who can be given access to resources to distribute to their own supporters in their home districts (Blaydes, 2011). But the outcome is usually predetermined. We begin this section by looking at elections in communist states before turning to their functions in other authoritarian regimes.

Elections in communist states made little pretence of offering choice. There was no possibility that the ruling party could be defeated, or even opposed, through elections. In the Soviet Union, for instance, the official candidate was simply presented to the electorate for ritual endorsement. The voter's task was simply to turn up at the polls and confirm the party's choice. Some communist states in Eastern Europe eventually introduced a measure of choice to their elections by allowing a choice of candidates from within the ruling party. Central rulers found these candidate-choice elections useful in testing whether local party officials retained the confidence of their communities.

This local monitoring is one reason for the gradual introduction of such elections to many of China's one million or so villages since 1987 and, more recently and tentatively, to some townships. The aim of these elected committees is to limit corruption in the villages and to reduce what are often violent conflicts between leaders and peasants. However, even in today's China no explicit opposition to the policy platform of the Chinese Communist Party is allowed. In many villages, real authority still resides with the local party official, who may also serve as chair of the village committee. In fact, a revision to the election law in 1997 explicitly affirmed the party's supervisory role.

Neither in the countryside nor in the towns are there many signs of elections threatening the party's control. The remarkable free election in 2012 in the southern Chinese village of Wukan, agreed by the Communist Party after extensive local protests against corrupt land sales, is an exception. In general, tight limits on what elections can achieve dashed expectations raised by the original reform, thereby increasing popular frustration. In that respect, manipulated elections are worse than no elections at all.

In the case of elections in non-communist authoritarian regimes, competition is usually constrained rather than eliminated. Some opposition victories may be permitted, but too few to affect the overall result. Independent candidates find themselves operating in a threatening environment. The secret police follow them around, breaking up some of their meetings. Using arbitrary registration rules, independent politicians may be banned from standing. Control over the media, the electoral system, and the government is exploited to favour the ruling party. Through its conduct of campaigns, the regime projects both the illusion of choice (not least for outsiders) and the reality of power (for the domestic population). It usually secures its victory without needing to falsify the count – though this option remains, if all else fails.

Until the Arab uprisings, Egypt provided an example of such manipulated elections. From 1976, numerous parties competed for seats in the People's Assembly, offering the appearance of a vigorous multiparty system. But President Hosni Mubarak's National Democratic Party held its dominant position throughout. According to official figures, turnout at legislative elections was 80 per cent or more, but the figures were almost certainly inflated by the government. In 1990, with most of the opposition parties boycotting the election in protest at government controls over the process, only 15 per cent of eligible voters turned out, and only one opposition party won enough votes to be represented in the People's Assembly. At the 1995 elections, turnout was back up to 48 per cent, but only 13 opposition deputies were elected. In more than half the districts, opposition candidates challenged the results in court. These 'contests' contributed to public cynicism and, eventually, to the overthrow of the regime in 2011.

A similar case of manipulation hiding behind free choice is offered by Iran. It has an incomplete system of political representation in the sense that while it holds regular elections for its president and legislature, the Supreme Leader of the country is exempt, political parties are controlled so closely as to be all but non-existent, and elections are manipulated by the Supreme Leader, the Guardian Council and Iran's religious elite to reduce the prospects of regime opponents. The Supreme Leader uses his powers to undermine any candidates who might threaten the conservative Islamic agenda that has dominated Iranian politics since 1979, and the Guardian Council (a group of 12 clerics and jurists) checks the credentials of all candidates to ensure that they support the ideals of the revolution. All candidates are required to proclaim their loyalty both to the rule of the Leader and to the proposition that religious clerics hold ultimate political power. In this way, a large number of potentially troublesome candidates are excluded. The Guardian Council has also interpreted the constitutional requirement that candidates should be 'religious or political personalities' to ban women from standing for president.

In hybrid regimes, elections play a more important part in confirming the authority of the ruler; indeed, they are central to its democratic pretensions. The election outcome is more than just a routine acceptance by the people of the realities of power. Explicit vote rigging is avoided, some candidates from non-governing parties gain election, and the possibility of a low turnout, and even defeat, cannot be entirely dismissed.

But elections do not operate on as free and fair a playing field as in a liberal democracy. In particular, the leading figure dominates media coverage, using television to trumpet what are often real achievements in office. In contrast to authoritarian regimes, the emphasis is as much on the carrot (providing reasons for voting for the dominant figure) as on the stick (threatening opposition supporters).

Incumbents in hybrid regimes can exploit unique resources. They are well known to voters, draw on the state's coffers for their campaign, implement a favourable electoral system, lead extensive patronage networks, give hand-outs to their election districts, and call in political credits carefully acquired while in office. Anticipating the president's re-election, underlings currying favour will seek to help the campaign. Credible opponents will be deterred from embarking on a hopeless fight: why annoy the candidate who is sure to win? Bratton (1998: 65) summarizes the position in many African countries: 'in a "big man" political culture, it is unclear whether the re-election of an incumbent constitutes the extension of a leader's legitimacy or the resignation of the electorate to his inevitable dominance'.

President Vladimir Putin has proved to be a skilled exponent of election management in an authoritarian regime. Indeed, Russians employ a special term for these dark arts: political technology. McFaul (2005) describes how Putin moved early in the 2004 election season to neutralize potential threats in the media, the regions, and business. In each sector, a few opponents were removed from office, yielding the desired servility among the remainder. McFaul's summary of Putin's electoral strategy is as follows:

> The effect of these reforms occurred well before the votes were actually cast. The absence of independence within media, regional elite and oligarchic ranks

reduced the freedom of manoeuvre for opposition political parties and candidates. At the same time, the state's larger role gave incumbents enormous advantages, be it national television coverage, massive administrative support from regional executives or enormous financial resources from companies like Gazprom. (McFaul, 2005: 77)

Such techniques presuppose weaknesses in the rule of law, the market economy, and civil society in general. These deficits are not easy to measure, making the task of effective election monitoring extremely difficult. If the political technologists have done their job, the election is over by election day.

But by 2012, when Putin secured his return to the presidency after a term out of office, such deficits had become more visible. In the context of an increasingly sophisticated urban citizenry, and a decline in Putin's own popularity and aura of invincibility, blatant manipulation of the count attracted considerable protest. The result stood but the climate changed. Even in Russia's authoritarian regime, the presidential election (as with legislative elections the previous year) had sent a message. So elections in hybrid or even fully authoritarian settings always possess the potential to serve as catalysts of change once the existing regime is already weakened.

DISCUSSION QUESTIONS

- Considering the number of elected offices at various levels of government, can there be such a thing as too much democracy?
- What is the best electoral system for choosing (a) a legislature, and (b) a president, and why?
- Which, if any, of these groups should be entitled to vote in national elections: (a) non-citizen legal residents, (b) prisoners, (c) 16–17-year-olds?
- What functions do election campaigns perform?
- Referendums – good idea or bad?
- Why do authoritarian regimes hold elections?

KEY CONCEPTS

Distribution requirements
Electoral formula
Electoral system
First-order elections
Initiative
Mandate

Proportional representation
Recall
Referendum
Second-order elections
Short campaign
Single-member plurality

FURTHER READING

Farrell, David M. (2011) *Electoral Systems: A Comparative Introduction*, 2nd edn. Provides a helpful and accessible guide to electoral systems.

Gallagher, Michael and Paul Mitchell (eds) (2005) *The Politics of Electoral Systems*. Through four general chapters and 22 country essays, this volume seeks to apply themes in the study of electoral systems to particular liberal democracies.

LeDuc, Lawrence, Richard G. Niemi, and Pippa Norris (eds) (2014) *Comparing Democracies 4: Elections and Voting in a Changing World*. A comparative review of elections and voting that includes chapters on electoral systems, parties, campaigns, the media, participation, the economy, and women in elections.

Lindberg, Staffan I. (2006) *Democracy and Elections in Africa*. Argues that democratizing countries can learn to become democratic through repeated democratic behaviour, even if their elections are often flawed.

Geissel, Brigitte and Kenneth Newton (eds) (2012) *Evaluating Democratic Innovations: Curing the Democratic Malaise?* This comparative volume analyses and evaluates devices of direct and deliberative democracy.

Setälä, Maija and Theo Schiller (eds) (2009) *Referendums and Representative Democracy*. A study of the role of referendums in democracies, and their political effects.

17 Voters

PREVIEW

Given that voters in democracies have a choice, how do they decide which party to support? This is the most intensively studied question in political science, and yet there is no agreed answer. Media coverage of election results tends to focus on often small and short-term shifts in party support, while academic studies are focused on broader and longer-term sociological and psychological questions such as social and economic change, electoral stability, and on how voters decide.

This chapter begins with a discussion of the long-term forces shaping electoral choice; specifically, party identification and trends suggesting that the ties between parties and voters are eroding. It then goes on to look at the impact on voter behaviour of social class and religion. As these older long-term pillars of electoral stability weaken, there is more room for new influences to affect voting choices. The chapter addresses three of these: political issues, the economy, and the personality of leaders.

The chapter also looks at rational choice analysis of voters and parties, a topic which gives us a case study of one of the theoretical approaches we reviewed in Chapter 5. It then discusses the more specific question of voter turnout: the declines witnessed in recent decades in many democracies, the impact of turnout on the quality of democracy, and the implications of compulsory voting. The chapter closes with a review of voters and voting in

CONTENTS

KEY ARGUMENTS

- Party identification lies at the heart of approaches to understanding voters, but there are questions about how much it applies outside its birthplace of the United States. And while partisan dealignment is an important trend, it is not always clear when it began or to what extent it is still active.

- The social bases of voting have weakened since the 1960s, although religion continues to play an important role in several countries.

- The rational choice approach offers a different way of looking at voters and parties. It raises intriguing theoretical puzzles, such as the apparent irrationality of turning out to vote.

- The evidence for more short-term explanations regarding voter choice – such as issue voting, the economy, and the personality of leaders – is variable.

- The decline in voter turnout has been important but this trend may now be weakening. Political science has generated clear findings about the features of both the individual voter and the electoral system that encourage turnout.

- Voting in authoritarian states is less a matter of free choice (and thus of understanding voter motives) than a matter of the manipulation of choice (and thus of understanding the motives of ruling regimes).

authoritarian states, and of the different ways in which they limit, manipulate, and coerce their voting publics.

Voters: an overview

If elections lie at the heart of representative democracy, as we saw in the previous chapter, then voters are the lifeblood of those elections. Although the primary role of voters in a representative democracy is to decide between the choices offered by parties, the values, preferences, agendas, instincts, and understandings of voters all combine to influence what options parties place on the campaign table. The challenge is to understand how voters make up their minds, in which regard there are several different options.

Explanations can be broadly categorized into the sociological and the psychological. The former include a focus on the social and economic background of voters, such that parties of the left might have an advantage among poorer voters, the less educated, ethnic minorities, and residents of cities, while those of the right might tend to attract the support of wealthier and older voters, the better educated, and residents of the suburbs and rural areas. By contrast, psychological explanations focus on what goes on in the mind of voters, and what they think about parties, candidates, and issues. The argument here is that choices increasingly depend on dynamic factors such as changing public agendas and less on static factors such as social class.

Identification with a party has long been a key element linking these two approaches. Voters develop a long-term commitment to 'their' party, which in turn shapes their values, opinions, and voting choice. This psychological attachment will in turned be shaped and reinforced by the social position of voters: their family background, their peer group, and their workmates. There has been a weakening of the bonds between voters and parties, however, as social divisions weaken, education becomes more available, people have become more mobile, parties change in order to widen their appeal, and some voters become more disillusioned with politics as usual.

Increasingly, shorter-term influences have supplemented long-term influences in explaining voter behaviour: not just which party to support, but also whether to vote at all. As the impact of social class and religion declines, so voters are more likely to be influenced by the particular issues they care about most,

the state of the economy, and the personalities of party leaders and candidates. Voter choice is increasingly responsive, rather than based on 'push' factors such as social class or religion. When it comes to the economy, for example, most voters choose less on the basis of their grasp of complex economic issues than on the basis of factors that make intuitive sense: the number of people out of work, the number of new jobs being created, changes in the cost of living, and the state of the national economy.

Voter behaviour in authoritarian regimes, meanwhile, is subject to quite different influences, driven primarily by the desire of leaders and elites to retain their hold on power using means which would not be acceptable in a democracy. In a democratic setting, voting is an autonomous endeavour; voters will have their opinions formed by multiple influences, but it is still ultimately up to them how to vote. In authoritarian regimes, voters are more likely to be influenced by having their choices restricted, whether through a limit on the number of parties running, or through manipulation and coercion, or through the use of illegal means to shape election outcomes. Even in democracies, it is important to note, ruling politicians use their privileged position to tilt the playing field in their favour; they have more access to more funds, exploit their name recognition, offer what amounts to bribes to their constituents, and structure the electoral system in their favour. That said, democratic leaders have fewer such techniques available than their authoritarian counterparts.

Party identification

The starting point for any discussion of voting in liberal democracies is *The American Voter* (Campbell *et al.*, 1960). This classic book established a way of studying voters, and of thinking about how voters decide, which remains influential. Its authors obtained national sample surveys of individual voters and assessed the attitudes expressed in these polls. The task was judged to be one of objective investigation into subjective states – the behavioural approach at work. Other traditions, notably those placing the individual voter in the social and spatial context provided by family, friends, neighbours, workmates, electoral districts, and regions, lost ground.

The central concept in *The American Voter* was **party identification**, meaning a commitment to a particular party which helps voters decide which party to vote for as well as providing them with a road map through the remote world of politics. As with many other identities, party allegiance emerges in childhood and early adolescence, influenced by parents and peer groups, and then deepens as a person moves through adulthood, reinforced by commitment to the social groups to which that person belongs. Party identification is the engine of the voter's political belief system; the best leaders are seen to come from the voter's favoured party, and the best policies must be those the party supports. The more often voters choose the party with which they identify, the stronger their allegiance becomes.

> **Party identification:** Long-term attachment to a particular political party, which provides a filter for understanding political events.

Party identification means not so much enthusiastic support for party as an underlying disposition to support that party. Just as regularly buying a particular brand of car short-circuits the need to make a full-scale assessment of automobile engineering with every purchase, so voting for a given party becomes a standing commitment which precludes the need to go for a political test drive at each election. For many, voting for a given party is a pragmatic, long-term brand choice. Occasionally, special circumstances might lead a Toyota buyer to choose a Ford, and a liberal to vote for a conservative party, but the homing tendency will do its job and normality will be restored next time.

The distinctive features of American politics – including an entrenched two-party system, closed party primaries, and the ability to vote a party ticket for the large number of elected offices – combine to mean that the notion of party identification does not necessarily travel well. In Europe, for example, voters historically identified with class and religion, and the labour unions and churches which expressed these affiliations. Parties formed part of such networks, rather than free-standing entities. In addition, the concepts of left and right provide alternative reference points, notably in countries such as France and Italy where parties are, or have become, weak. Also, there are few signs of strong party loyalties emerging in the more fluid party systems found in the newer democracies of Eastern Europe and beyond. Finally, Europeans have a greater range of parties from which

to choose, meaning more opportunity to move from one to another.

Still, the political market – as with most others – remains generally stable in most liberal democracies, with the result that a party's share at a previous election is usually a good predictor of its support at an upcoming election, except in the event of major political or economic events; economic downturns in most European states in 2008–12, for example, led to a notable switch to parties of the right, and particularly to anti-establishment parties of the far right. And at the individual level, too, stability of electoral choice remains substantial. Before we can explain electoral change, we must understand this continuity. Party identification, the habit of voting for the same party, ideological labels, and group loyalties all fit the bill, even if the balance between them varies across countries and over time. At the same time, we also need to track changes in support for parties, which is where partisan dealignment enters the equation.

Partisan dealignment

The weakening of bonds between voters and their parties – otherwise known as **partisan dealignment** – is a clear and widespread trend in democracies. It may also be true of some emerging states, but survey research is often less sophisticated in these cases, making it difficult to find meaningful comparative data (see discussion about polling in India in Kumar and Rai, 2013). Also, parties in emerging democracies do not have as long a history as those in democracies, and the ties that bind voters to parties, as well as the explanations for how voters choose, are somewhat different.

> **Partisan dealignment:** The weakening bonds between voters and parties, reflected both in a fall in the proportion of voters identifying with any party and a decline in the strength of allegiance among those retaining a party loyalty.

In one recent study of 19 advanced industrial democracies for which there are long-term survey data, 17 were found to have seen a decrease in the percentage of partisans, as well as a decrease in the strength of partisanship (Dalton, 2013: 183). Britain is a striking example. Between 1964–6 and 2010, the proportion of voters identifying with a party fell from 90 to 82 per cent. This may not seem very much, but over the same period the proportion of respondents with a 'very strong' allegiance to any party collapsed from 40 to 11 per cent. The result,

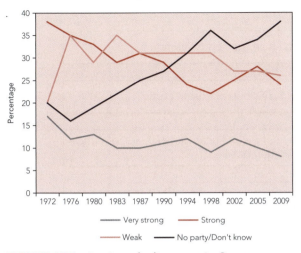

FIGURE 17.1: Partisan dealignment in Germany
Source: Dalton (2014). Data are for western Germany only.

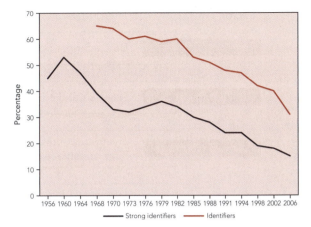

FIGURE 17.2: Partisan dealignment in Sweden
Source: Oscarsson and Hölmberg (2010: 9)

say Denver *et al.* (2012: 71), is that strong Conservative and Labour identifiers are 'now something of an endangered species'.

Comparable changes can be seen in Germany, with the rise of a class of independent voters who – argues Dalton (2014) – 'are more sophisticated apartisans who are politically engaged even though they lack party ties'. As shown in Figure 17.1, the proportion of western Germans with very strong or strong party identification fell between 1972 and 2009 from 55 per cent to 32 per cent, while the proportion with weak or no party identification rose from 40 per cent to 64 per cent. There has been an even more precipitous decline in Sweden, where the proportion of people identifying with a party halved between 1968 and 2006 (see Figure 17.2).

What has caused this dealignment? Although commentators within a country often concentrate on national influences, comparison across borders points to a common set of political and sociological factors (see Figure 17.3). Politically, the role of parties changed dramatically in the final third of the twentieth century, as we saw in Chapter 15. Their funding increasingly comes from the state rather than their own members; scandals and corruption tied to parties have reduced voter trust; election campaigning increasingly involves the media (the air war) as well as, or in place of, local parties (the ground war); party members have drifted towards single-issue groups; and major parties have become increasingly indistinct in their programmes and their social base. Now viewed as part of the system, rather than as

expressions of social interests, parties in many countries face the same loss of trust as other state institutions.

Sociologically, the weakening of historic social divisions and the expansion of education contributed to a thinning of political identities. Dalton (2013: 187–9) suggests that what he calls 'cognitive mobilization' is an increasingly common way in which citizens connect themselves to politics. By this, he means that educated and politically interested voters can orient themselves to politics on their own, using the media for information and their own understanding to interpret it. The effects of dealignment have been substantial: issue voting has increased, electoral volatility has grown, turnout and active participation in campaigns has fallen, more voters wait until the last minute to decide which party to support, and new parties such as the Greens and parties on the far right have gained ground (in Europe, at least).

How voters choose

In trying to explain how voters make their choices, there are several options available. Longer-term influences include social class and religion, the first of which has been weakening as an indicator, while the second remains a factor in a surprising number of supposedly secular liberal democracies. Shorter-term influences – which tend to draw most media attention during election campaigns – include issue voting, the state of the economy and the personality of political leaders.

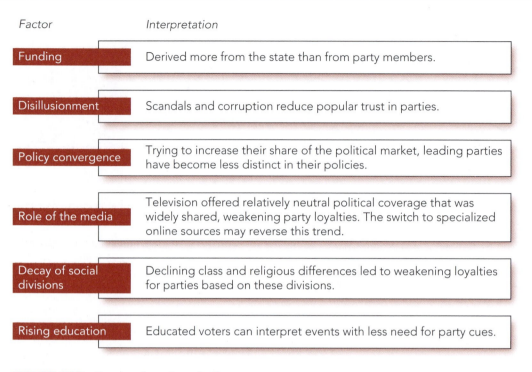

Factor   *Interpretation*

Funding — Derived more from the state than from party members.

Disillusionment — Scandals and corruption reduce popular trust in parties.

Policy convergence — Trying to increase their share of the political market, leading parties have become less distinct in their policies.

Role of the media — Television offered relatively neutral political coverage that was widely shared, weakening party loyalties. The switch to specialized online sources may reverse this trend.

Decay of social divisions — Declining class and religious differences led to weakening loyalties for parties based on these divisions.

Rising education — Educated voters can interpret events with less need for party cues.

FIGURE 17.3: Causes of partisan dealignment

Social class

Since the industrial revolution, social class has influenced electoral choice in all liberal democracies: the working class has been inclined to support parties of the left, while the middle class has leaned towards parties of the right. To some extent, then, party activists campaigning in a neighbourhood can usually sense from its economic character whether it will be for or against them even before they start knocking on doors. But the evidence in recent decades points to a decline in class voting, with some (such as Knutsen, 2006) finding a particular decline of class voting in several Western European countries, such as Denmark, the Netherlands, and Britain. In general, class voting has declined the most where it was previously highest, notably in the Nordic countries.

The explanation for this change lies in a combination of political and sociological factors. At a political level, the collapse of socialism initiated a move to the centre by many left-wing parties, where traditional class themes were played down; thus Knutsen (2006) finds in a comparative analysis that 'the political strategies of the major leftist parties showed a consistent pattern where a decisive move towards the centre was accompanied by a decline in class voting'.

But familiar sociological processes are also at work. As the service sector displaces manufacturing in advanced economies, so large unionized factories have been replaced by smaller service companies offering more diverse work to qualified staff. These skilled employees derive their power in the labour market from their individual qualifications, experience, and ability; unlike manual employees performing uniform tasks, they are not drawn to labour unions promoting collective solidarity. In this way, the foundations on which class parties were based have eroded. Comparative evidence suggests that the smaller the size of the working class in a country, and the lower the proportion of its workforce employed in industry, the greater the decline in class voting (Knutsen, 2006).

Growing income inequality in some liberal democracies, notably the United States and Britain, may represent an offsetting trend. Resentment grew against what were seen as excessive earnings by the best-paid workers in the financial sector in the wake of the financial crisis of 2008–9 (Hacker and Pierson, 2010). But individual income is not a dominant influence on how people vote, and this theme of resentment against the highest earners lacked the same resonance in other liberal democracies, such as the Nordic countries, where inequality remained less pronounced.

Religion

'Want to know how Americans will vote next Election Day?' asked a 2003 news story. 'Watch what they do the weekend before … If they attend religious services regularly, they probably will vote Republican by a 2–1 margin. If they never go, they likely will vote Democratic by a 2–1 margin' (quoted in Green, 2010b: 433). Leaving the exact figures to one side, what became known in the United States as the 'God Gap' illustrates the continuing relevance of religion (as indicated here by church attendance) to voting behaviour. Religion's electoral influence remains widespread in liberal democracies, offering a contrast to the fall in class voting. Religion is not a single variable, however, and can be studied from three main angles:

- We can distinguish broadly between religious and secular voters, the former tending to vote for the right and the latter for the left.
- We can separate voters by religiosity (the importance of religion to the individual). Typically, the distinction between the religiously committed and the rest produces the largest contrasts in voting choice and

also in electoral participation, with churchgoers more likely to turn out.

- We can examine the impact of specific denominations. Catholics, for example, might be inclined to vote for the right and Jewish voters for the left. Such studies can be extended to examine the electoral impact of other religions and denominations, including Islam and evangelical movements.

Comparative research has long recognized the electoral importance of religion. From a study of 16 Western democracies, Rose and Urwin (1969: 12) concluded that 'religious divisions, not class, are the main social bases of parties in the Western world today'. Later, in examining voters rather than parties, Lijphart (1979) concluded from a study of countries where both class and religion played a political role that 'religion tends to have a larger influence on party choice'. More recently, Esmer and Petterson (2007: 409) found that 'religiosity still significantly shapes electoral choice in most European countries' – noting, in particular, that 'the devout and the pious are more likely to vote for the political right and the Christian Democrats'. The exceptions to religiosity's continuing impact on voting are all in Northern Europe, including the United Kingdom.

Head to head, religion matters more than class, and – in a sense – class matters most when religion is weak. Thus, traditionally high levels of class voting in Scandinavia can be seen as reflecting the absence of

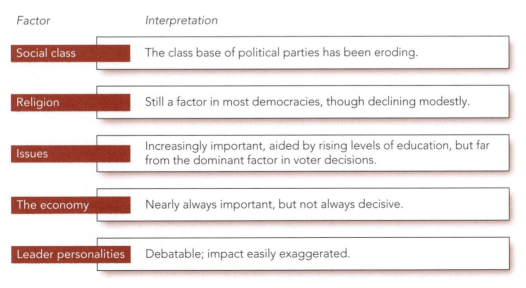

Factor	Interpretation
Social class	The class base of political parties has been eroding.
Religion	Still a factor in most democracies, though declining modestly.
Issues	Increasingly important, aided by rising levels of education, but far from the dominant factor in voter decisions.
The economy	Nearly always important, but not always decisive.
Leader personalities	Debatable; impact easily exaggerated.

FIGURE 17.4: Key factors explaining voter choice

religious conflict there once national Lutheran churches were established in the Reformation. Just as industrial change has contributed to the decline of class voting, so **secularization** might be expected to lead to a fall in religious voting; as societies modernize, so they naturally become more secular. And certainly, church attendance and religious belief continues to decline in many liberal democracies, not least in Europe (and increasingly among young Americans) (Esmer and Pettersson, 2007: table 25.2). Yet it is difficult to find evidence that religious voting has declined to the same extent as class voting. Some reduction is apparent but, overall, the religious base of electoral behaviour has considerable staying power.

> **Secularization:** The declining space occupied by religion in political, social, and personal life.

Issue voting

Election campaigns will routinely bring up topics such as crime, defence, the environment, foreign affairs, education, public spending, and taxation. These are the 'issues' that are routinely discussed by parties, the media, and politicians, the implication being that they are a key element of voter choice. To what extent is this true? In reality, there are several rivers to cross before someone can be described as an issue voter. They must (1) be aware of the issue, (2) have an opinion on the issue, (3) believe that parties differ on the issue, and (4) vote for the party closest to their position.

These are considerable barriers. Studies conducted during the era of party alignment concluded that only a minority of voters passed them all. Writing of Britain, and using the metaphor of a famous English steeplechase, Denver *et al.* (2012: 96) conclude that 'when aligned voting was the norm, relatively few voters fulfilled the conditions for **issue voting**. As in the Grand National, large numbers fell at every fence.' *The American Voter* was equally sceptical, classifying no more than one-third of the electorate as passing the first three of the four necessary conditions on each of a long list of issues.

> **Issue voting:** The phenomenon of voters making choices at elections based on the policies that most interest them, rather than solely on the basis of sociological or demographic factors.

Having said this, more recent studies show that voting on the basis of specific policies (and also broader ideologies) has increased. As early as 1992, Franklin concluded from a study in 17 liberal democracies that the rise of issue voting matched more or less precisely a decline in voting on the basis of social position. Lewis-Beck *et al.* (2008: 425) reach a similar conclusion for the United States, where comparable information is available for the longest period:

> The level of education within the American electorate has increased sharply since the 1950s, and this is reflected in more frequent issue voting, greater overall clarity in the structure of mass issue attitudes, and enhanced salience of ideological themes within the public's political thinking.

But Lewis-Beck *et al.* go on to warn against falling too easily into the tempting narrative of issue voting supplanting party identification, and warn that the peripheral nature of politics to most Americans continues to create a ceiling to policy voting. And the nature of the political times is an understated factor: a return to the quiescence of the 1950s, when the initial studies were conducted, might lead to a reduction in issue voting, even as education levels continue to rise. Policy issues are far from irrelevant but they remain only a partial explanation for why people vote as they do.

The economy

Linking government popularity to economic performance is hardly a new idea, but it was most famously expressed by James Carville, lead strategist for Bill Clinton's 1992 presidential campaign, when he posted a list of key themes for the election at campaign headquarters, heading it with 'The economy, stupid'.

With data on economic performance and political popularity available for most liberal democracies, this is a topic well suited to comparative analysis. The evidence suggests that the economy does matter; it affects not only government popularity, as recorded in opinion polls, but also how people behave in the polling booth. At the same time, there is a case for paraphrasing Winston Churchill's view of democracy, and arguing that the economy is the worst explanation of election results – except for all the others (Hellwig, 2010: 200).

How exactly does the economy exert its influence? Just as it is unwise to discuss media effects without

FOCUS 17.1 | Are voters rational?

The behavioural account offers one means for understanding voters. Another is offered by the rational choice approach, which assumes that voters are rational participants in the political market, and seek to maximize their utility. The most influential study by far along these lines is Anthony Downs's *An Economic Theory of Democracy*, published in 1957. Downs was concerned not only with voters but also with parties, and even more with the relationship between the two.

He asks us to imagine that parties act as if they are motivated by power alone, and that voters want only a government which reflects their self-interest, as represented in their policy preferences. He also assumes that voter policy preferences can be shown on a simple left–right scale, with the left end representing full government control of the economy and the right end a completely free market. Given these assumptions, he asks, what policies should parties adopt to maximize their vote?

The crucial result, now known as the 'median voter theorem', is that vote-maximizing parties in a two-party system will converge at the midpoint of the distribution, and that the position of the median voter is critical. A party may start at one extreme but it will move towards the centre because there are more votes to be won there. In moving to the centre, the party remains closer to voters at its own extreme, but it also attracts middle-of-the-road voters who were previously closer to the competitor. Once parties have converged at the position of the median voter, they reach a position of equilibrium and have no incentive to change their position.

But what should we make of Downs's assumption that voters behave rationally by voting for the party closest to their policy preferences on a single left–right scale? There are at least three objections (Ansolabehere, 2006):

- Why would self-interested voters turn out to vote at all, given the small possibility of a single ballot determining the outcome?
- Since no single ballot is likely to be decisive, why should voters go to the trouble of acquiring the information needed to cast a rational vote?
- We can question the assumption that elections are best understood as debates over policies on which voters adopt different positions. For example, voters may be more focused on a party's competence than its policies.

Overall, Downs's theory leads us to some interesting paradoxes. His notions of self-interest and rationality, while standard for rational choice thinking, appear to result in ignorant voters who fail to vote and in parties that adopt virtually indistinguishable policy positions. Still, the very process of comparing predictions with reality does generate puzzles whose resolution creates insight.

---

specifying a particular medium, so too should we avoid discussing economic effects without specifying a particular component. Three variables often emerging as significant are trends in real disposable personal income (i.e. after taxes and inflation), unemployment, and inflation.

Personal income appears to be particularly important, as the case of the United States suggests. In the second half of the twentieth century, the growth of personal income over an electoral cycle predicted the vote share of American presidents with remarkable accuracy. One analysis suggested that 'each percentage point increase in per capita real income [averaged across a presidential term] yielded a four per cent increase of the incumbent party's vote share from a constant of 46 per cent' (Hibbs, Jr, 2006: 576–7). In other words, incumbent presidents who achieve an annual average of 1 per cent growth in personal income over their first term in office should score 50 per cent of the vote; 2 per cent growth is rewarded with 54 per cent of the vote; and so on.

Studies of the impact of an incumbent government's actual economic record dominated early research into economic voting. In recent decades, attention has shifted to how these effects operate. In particular, researchers have investigated how electoral choice varies with voters' own assessments of how the economy has performed. After all, voters will differ in how they judge the economic record; some will see inflation where others see stable prices. Such opinions provide a channel through which the objective economy affects votes.

Studies strongly confirm the presence of an economic vote. For example, Hellwig (2010) combined the results from surveys conducted in 28 countries between 1996 and 2002 to examine the electoral effect of respondent perceptions of whether the state of the economy over the previous 12 months had improved, stayed about the same, or worsened. As Table 17.1 shows, the results were striking: voters who believed the economy had improved were twice as likely to vote for the party of the incumbent president or prime minister as voters who thought the state of the economy had worsened. Of course, those who already support the governing party are inclined to view the economy through rose-tinted glasses, exaggerating the real economic vote. Partisanship is at work here, as everywhere. Even so, the observed relationship between economic assessments and electoral choice appears to reflect more than simply the projections of the partisans (Lewis-Beck *et al.*, 2008: table 13.8).

The actions of poor voters – whether they live in wealthy or poor countries – sets up an interesting paradox. Many studies have shown that a significant number often vote for parties that do not appear to stand for their material interests, and that instead seem to represent the interests of the wealthy. Huber and Stanig (2009) point out, for example, that large numbers of voters in wealthy democracies support parties that are opposed to the kinds of higher taxes and redistributive policies from which such voters would benefit.

Turning to voting in poorer democracies, which have been much less studied than in their wealthier counterparts, the evidence gathered to date points to a somewhat different economic incentive: the link between voting and the promise of tangible vote-specific material rewards. For example, Thachil (2014) looks at India, and specifically at the curious success of the Bharatiya Janata Party (BJP) (a party usually identified with India's privileged upper castes) among poorer Indians. The explanation, he suggests, lies in the way the BJP has won over disadvantaged voters by privately providing them with basic social services via grassroots affiliates. This 'outsourcing' allows the party to continue to represent the policy interests of its privileged base, while also drawing in many votes from the poor.

This example illustrates the widespread phenomenon of **vote buying**, whereby rewards are offered to individual voters in return for their support at elections. It has made something of a comeback in recent decades as a consequence of democratization; in parts of the world where party labels and electoral platforms may not mean much, argues Schaffer (2007), parties and candidates try to win votes by offering tangible rewards. These may take the form of cash, of commodities (Schaffer lists everything from cigarettes to watches, coffins, haircuts, bags of rice, birthday cakes, and TV sets), or of services. If impoverished voters can achieve a little more security for their family by trading their vote in this way, who is to blame them for doing so? However, the phenomenon is far from limited to poorer states or communities. Governments legally and routinely 'buy' the votes of other governments in meetings of international organizations (Lockwood, 2013), and almost any instance where elected representatives can point to a new factory, school or military facility that was brought to their district through their efforts might be defined as

TABLE 17.1: The economy and voter choice

Perception of the economy over the past 12 months	Percentage voting for the party of the incumbent president or prime minister
Has got better	46
Has stayed the same	31
Has got worse	23

Source: Adapted from Hellwig (2010: table 9.1), rebased to 100 per cent. Based on 28 countries, 1996–2002.

vote buying. Is there much difference between buying a voter in, say, India and buying an electoral district in, say, the United States?

> **Vote buying:** The process whereby parties and candidates provide material benefits to voters in return for their support at elections.

Brazil provides an interesting example of vote buying operating within the political elite. A major scandal broke there in 2005, with charges that the ruling Worker's Party had paid a number of congressional deputies a monthly stipend in return for their support for legislation supported by the party. Known as the Mensalão (big monthly stipend) scandal, it threatened to bring down the government of President Lula da Silva (in office 2003–10). Lula himself won election to a second term, but 25 of the 38 defendants in the resulting court case were found guilty on a variety of charges. The trial came to exemplify the issue of corruption in Brazil, a problem reflected in more low-level instances of candidates paying cash to voters for their support. The problem, argues Yadav (2011: 124–5) has worsened with the advent of stronger political parties able to exploit the Brazilian state as a source of funds.

The personality of leaders

Political leaders are obviously important to the process of reshaping political parties and their policies, but their character and personality is also important. Just how much voters can be swayed by how much they like, or do not like, the personal traits of leaders is – however – questionable.

Perhaps the most famous example of the importance of appearance, style and likeability was the first television debate involving presidential candidates in the United States, between John F. Kennedy and Richard Nixon in 1960. Kennedy looked relaxed and used the medium well, while Nixon looked nervous and unwell. Polls found that those who watched the TV debate thought Kennedy had won, while those who listened on radio thought Nixon had won. Later, in the United Kingdom, Margaret Thatcher was encouraged by her advisers to lower the tone of her voice so as to sound more authoritative. In France and the US, polls found that François Hollande and Barack Obama won their respective presidential elections in 2012 at least in part

because they were seen as more likable than their competitors, Nicolas Sarkozy and Mitt Romney.

There are obvious weaknesses in using such examples to conclude that the traits of leaders have become electorally decisive. The discussion of leaders often reveals a selection bias, focusing on the characterful while forgetting the anonymous. And, as with other factors affecting electoral choice, the net effects of a leader's character may be limited, even if gross effects are large. For instance, as many voters may be repelled as attracted by a particular candidate's personality, resulting in no net impact.

In the first comparative study of this subject, King (2002) attempted to judge whether the personalities of leaders determined the winning party in 52 elections held between 1960 and 2001 in Canada, France, Britain, Russia, and the United States. His conclusion was 'No' in 37 cases, 'Possibly' in 6, 'Probably' in 5, and 'Yes' in just 4 (Harold Wilson, Great Britain, 1964 and February 1974; Charles de Gaulle, France, 1965; and Pierre Trudeau, Canada, 1968). King's general conclusion (p. 221) was that 'most elections remain overwhelmingly political contests, and political parties would do well to choose their leaders and candidates in light of that fact'.

Much subsequent research has confirmed King's views. Not least in parliamentary systems, the difference that leaders' characters make is typically, but not always, shown to be modest, with only limited evidence of an increase over time. For instance, a statistical study edited by Aarts *et al.* (2011) and covering nine liberal democracies confirms the unimportance of the characteristics of leaders. As part of this study, Holmberg and Oscarsson (2011: 51) conclude that the greater influence of leaders on the vote 'is simply not substantiated'. Leader traits are only a part, and often a minor part, of the factors shaping individual votes and overall election results.

Where leader traits do make a difference, which matter most? The key characteristics appear to be those directly linked to performance in office. By comparison, purely personal characteristics, such as appearance and likeability, are unimportant. Specifically, the two main factors for candidates are competence and integrity. In the United States, there is broad agreement on two core traits: 'one, ability to do the job well, based on performance in office (incumbency) or a previous record of accomplishment; and two, a reputation for honesty' (Lewis-Beck *et al.*, 2008: 55–6).

Extending the analysis to Australia, Germany, and Sweden, Ohr and Oscarsson (2011: 212) reach similar conclusions, judging that 'politically relevant and

SPOTLIGHT

IRAN

Brief Profile: Iran has long played a critical role in the Middle East, first because of the oil reserves that the British long sought, then because of the close strategic relationship between the United States and the regime of the Shah of Iran, and now because of the significance of the Islamic Republic created in the wake of the 1979 Iranian revolution. It has an elected president and legislature, but power is manipulated by an unelected Supreme Leader surrounded by competing cliques, candidates for public office are vetted, laws must be approved by an unelected clerical–juridical council, political rights are limited, and women are marginalized. It is a poor country that controls enormous oil and mineral wealth, and is socially diverse. Even if most Iranians are joined by a shared religion, they are still divided between those espousing conservative and reformist views. These differences are strongly structured by gender, generation and level of education.

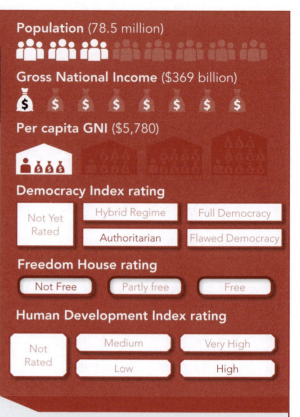

Form of government ➾ Unitary Islamic republic. Date of state formation debatable, and most recent constitution adopted 1979.

Legislature ➾ Unicameral Majlis, with 290 members elected for renewable four-year terms.

Executive ➾ Presidential. President elected for maximum of two consecutive four-year terms, but shares power with a Supreme Leader appointed for life by an Assembly of Experts (effectively an electoral college), who must be an expert in Islamic law, and acts as head of state with considerable executive powers.

Judiciary ➾ Supreme Court with members appointed for five-year terms. The Iranian legal system is based on a combination of Islamic law (sharia) and civil law.

Electoral system ➾ Single-member plurality for the legislature, simple majority for the president.

Parties ➾ No-party system. Only Islamist parties can operate legally, but organizations that look like parties operate regardless. They are not formal political parties as conventionally understood, however, and instead operate as loose coalitions representing conservative and reformist positions.

➡

performance-related leader traits are important criteria for voters' political judgements'. They conclude that 'leader evaluations and their effect on the vote in the electorate are firmly based on politically "rational" considerations – be it in a presidential or in a parliamentary system'. If personal traits matter, it is because they are judged to be relevant to government performance.

In general, leaders are higher in visibility than in impact. There is also a wider lesson here for students of electoral behaviour. As Key (1966: 7) pointed out long ago, 'voters are not fools' and little insight is gained from treating them as such. Before dismissing voters as dupes, remember that you, too, are or may well become a voter (Goren, 2012).

Voters in Iran

Iran does not fare well on comparative democratic rankings. Since the 1979 revolution that removed the Western-backed (and authoritarian) regime of the Shah of Iran, and ushered in the era of the ayatollahs (an *ayatollah* is a high-ranking Shia cleric), Iran has possessed a pariah status in the eyes of most Western governments. It has been accused of repression at home, of efforts to support terrorist organizations such as Hezbollah in Lebanon, and of covert plans to build nuclear weapons.

It is all the more ironic, then, that it seems to have an active electorate faced with a significant number of circumscribed choices at the polls. The ruling clerics and the military still wield considerable power, many in the political opposition languish in jail, and elections are contested less by political parties than by religiously based factions. This does not mean, however, that many Iranians do not hanker after democratic choice, nor that they are unwilling to voice opposition to the regime and support reform-minded candidates at elections.

The 2009 and 2013 elections, for example, provided choice among candidates opting for different solutions to the country's severe economic problems. Open campaigning included debates involving the major candidates. While there is no dependable way to measure Iranian public opinion, it was clear that many citizens – particularly younger voters suffering the most from high unemployment – were willing to express themselves. Turnout in 2013 was estimated to have exceeded 70 per cent, but charges of fraud continue to surround Iranian elections, although they are hard to verify in the absence of independent election monitoring (Addis, 2009).

With problems ranging from high population growth to unemployment, inflation, pollution, drug addiction, and poverty, Iran faces difficulties which the regime that has been in power since 1979 has intensified rather than resolved. But there is hope in the substantial desire for change among its many young, educated voters, leading Mohammadi (2006: 3) to conclude that Iran's problems are not so much external threats as 'the enemy within', in the form of unresolved conflicts among major political interests.

Voter turnout

So far, this chapter has focused on the forces shaping voter choice. Equally important for political science, perhaps, is the question of voter turnout, and – more specifically –the decline in turnout in many democracies over the second half of the twentieth century. What initiated this drop? Has turnout now begun to recover? And what can be done to strengthen any recovery that is taking place? A fall in turnout is not to be equated with declining political interest since political participation may simply be evolving rather than declining (see Chapter 13). Still, turnout is important in its own right because of its effect on the outcome of an election and the relative legitimacy of the resulting government.

Despite rising education, turnout fell in most of the democratic world in the second half of the twentieth century. In 19 liberal democracies, it declined on average by 10 per cent between the 1950s and the 1990s (Wattenberg, 2000). Figure 17.5 reflects the trends by contrasting countries with different levels of turnout, all of which show declines over this period. To an extent, the reasons vary from one country to another, but the overall decline has formed part of a wider trend in

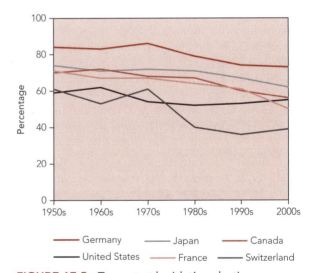

FIGURE 17.5: Turnout at legislative elections

Source: Institute for Democracy and Electoral Assistance (IDEA), Voter Turnout Database at www.idea.int/vt/viewdata.cfm (accessed June 2015)

democracies that has seen a growing distance between citizens on the one hand, and parties and government on the other. It is no coincidence that turnout has fallen as partisan dealignment has gathered pace, as party membership has fallen, and as the class and religious cleavages which once sustained party loyalties have decayed.

In an influential analysis, Franklin (2004) linked the decline of turnout to the diminishing significance of elections. He suggested that the success of many democracies in sustaining welfare states and full employment in the post–war era resolved long-standing conflicts between capital and labour. With class conflict on the decrease, citizens had fewer incentives to vote. As Franklin (2004: 174) wrote, 'elections in recent years may show lower turnout for the simple reason that these elections decide issues of lesser importance than elections did in the late 1950s'. As Downs would predict, when less is up for grabs, people are more likely to stay at home.

But declining satisfaction with the performance of democratic governments has also played its part. We saw in Chapter 12 how trust in government has fallen in Europe and the United States; even though mass support for democratic principles remains strong, rising cynicism about government performance has undoubtedly encouraged more people to stay away from the polls. But there are also some very practical reasons for deflated turnout: it tends to be higher in those countries where the costs or effort of voting are low and the perceived benefits are high, and patterns of turnout are also impacted by the distinctive demographic profile of voters (see Table 17.2).

As Figure 17.5 confirms, turnout continues to vary markedly between countries. There are some very practical reasons for this divergence. Overall, turnout tends to be higher in those countries where the costs or effort of voting are low and the perceived benefits are high. On the cost side, turnout is reduced when the citizen is required to take the initiative in registering as a voter, as in the United States. In most European countries, by contrast, registration is the responsibility of government. Turnout is also lower when citizens must vote in person and during a weekday. So, higher turnout can be encouraged by allowing voting at the weekend, by proxy, by mail, by electronic means, and at convenient locations such as supermarkets (Blais et al., 2003). The ability to vote in advance is also helpful; it is notable that over 30 million votes in the US presidential election of 2012 were cast before election day (United States Elections Project, 2012).

On the benefit side, the greater the impact of a single vote, the more willing voters are to incur the costs of voting. Thus, the closer the contest, the higher the turnout. Because each ballot affects the outcome, proportional representation also enhances turnout. The effect here is quite significant: turnout is about eight percentage points higher among countries using party list PR than in those using single-member plurality (IDEA, 2012).

Within countries, variations in turnout reflect the pattern found with other forms of political participation; the likelihood of voting is shaped by an individual's political resources and political interest (see Table 17.2, right column). Those most likely to vote are educated, affluent, married, middle-aged citizens with a job and a strong party loyalty, who belong to a church or a trade union, and are long-term residents of a neighbourhood. These are the people with both resources and an interest in formal politics. By contrast, abstention is most frequent among those with fewer

TABLE 17.2: A recipe for higher voter turnout

Features of the political system	Features of voters
Compulsory voting	Middle-aged
Automatic registration	Well educated
Voting by post and by proxy permitted	Married
Advance voting permitted	Higher income
Weekend polling	Employed
Election decides who governs	Home owner
Cohesive parties	Strong party loyalty
Proportional representation	Churchgoer
Close result anticipated	Member of a labour union
Small electorate	Has not changed residence recently
Expensive campaigns	Voted in previous elections
Elections for several posts held at the same time	

Sources: Endersby et al. (2006); Geys (2006); IDEA (2012)

resources and less reason to be committed to formal party politics; the archetypal non-voter is a young, poorly educated, single, unemployed man who belongs to no organizations, lacks party ties, and has recently moved to a new address.

Attempts to boost turnout must be sensitive to political realities: while increased participation may benefit the system as a whole, it will have an unequal impact on the parties within it. Conservative parties in particular will be cautious about schemes for encouraging turnout, because abstainers would probably vote disproportionately for parties of the left. There remains one other blunt but effective tool for promoting turnout: compulsory voting. We discuss this drastic solution in Focus 17.2.

Voters in authoritarian states

So far in this chapter the focus has been on the influences that shape voter choice in democracies: identification with parties, the drift away from parties, the impact of social class, religion, issues, and the economy, and the personalities of leaders. The general point is that voter choice is indeed *choice*: voters are faced with alternatives and bring multiple considerations to bear in deciding which party or leader to support, or even

FOCUS 17.2 | The pros and cons of compulsory voting

In encouraging voter turnout, compulsion can be considered the nuclear option. It is used in Argentina, Australia, Belgium, Brazil, Singapore, Turkey and a handful of other countries, although a distinction has to be made between countries that actually enforce the law (such as Australia and Brazil) and those that do not (such as Belgium and Turkey).

The case for compulsory voting is worth making. Most citizens acknowledge obligations such as paying taxes, serving on juries, and even fighting in war; why, then, should they oppose what Hill (2002) calls the 'light obligation and undemanding duty' of voting at national elections? Without it, abstainers take a free ride at the expense of the efforts of the conscientious.

But the arguments against are also strong. Mandatory voting undermines the liberty which is an essential part of liberal democracy: requiring people to participate smacks of authoritarianism rather than free choice. Paying taxes and fighting in battle are duties where every little helps and where numbers matter. In all democracies, elections still attract more than enough votes to form a decision. There is no evidence that high turnout increases the quality of the political choices made, so why not continue to rely on the natural division of labour between interested voters and indifferent abstainers?

Arguments in favour	Arguments against
A full turnout means the electorate is representative.	The freedom to abstain should be part of a liberal democracy.
Disengaged groups are drawn into the political process.	Compulsory voting gives influence to less informed and less engaged voters.
The authority of the government is enhanced by a fuller turnout.	Abstention may reflect contentment and is not necessarily a problem.
More voters will lead to a more informed electorate.	In practice, turnout remains well below 100 per cent even when voting is mandatory.
People who object to voting on principle can be exempted.	Voting (and deciding who to support) takes time.
Blank ballots can be permitted for those who oppose all candidates.	The better policy is to attract voters to the polls through their own volition.
Parties no longer need to devote resources to encourage their supporters to vote.	

whether to vote at all. Turning to authoritarian regimes, the dynamics of voting may at first seem much simpler: voters keep their heads down and do as they are told. But the process of voting in these states presents its own particular complexities, which are far less well studied and understood than is the case with democracies. Generally speaking, understanding the motives of rulers in authoritarian states is more important than understanding the motives of voters.

At the opposite end of the spectrum from democracies are no-party or one-party political systems where voters are not given much in the way of alternatives but may still be expected to endorse the regime's candidates by turning out to vote. In communist systems, ruling parties cannot be meaningfully opposed or defeated, and official candidates are simply presented to voters for ritual endorsement. Any opinions that voters might have about the electoral process, or about party policies or pressing public issues, are not for expression in the voting booth. Undoubtedly voters do have such opinions, for politics in authoritarian states is more central to ordinary life than in democracies, and people are adept at distinguishing between national propaganda and local reality. With a 'choice' of one party on election day, however, such opinions are effectively suppressed. This phenomenon ties in with what we saw in Chapter 13 about mobilized participation, where the actions of voters are managed and obligatory, their involvement organized by leaders and elites in order to give the impression of support for the regime.

In today's largely post-communist world, regimes denying all choice to voters are few and far between. More common, and more interesting, is the phenomenon of **electoral authoritarianism**, a term which sits on the spectrum between clear authoritarianism, on the one hand, and democracy on the other. Like so many concepts in the social sciences, its exact meaning is disputed, but Schedler (2009: 382) uses it to describe regimes that 'play the game of multiparty elections' while violating 'the liberal-democratic principles of freedom and fairness so profoundly and systematically as to render elections instruments of authoritarian rule rather than "instruments of democracy"'. In other words, there are regular elections with multiple candidates, but voting is so manipulated as to effectively remove the elements of choice and meaningful competition. The result (typically known in advance) is proclaimed by the regime as signalling support for its policies. In effect, voters are co-opted, even against their will, to 'approve' the work

of the regime. Schedler (2006) considers this to be 'the most common form of political regime in the developing world', but also 'the one we know least about'.

> **Electoral authoritarianism:** An arrangement in which a regime gives the appearance of being democratic, and offering voters choice, while maintaining its authoritarian qualities.

Algeria is an example of elections in an authoritarian setting, and offers insight into the kinds of responses prompted from voters who are often quite aware of the manipulation to which they are being subjected. In 1991, the Islamic Salvation Front seemed poised to win legislative elections, prompting the military to step in and cancel them. This intervention sparked a civil war in Algeria in which an estimated 200,000 people died. Since 1999 there have been several elections, but they are so closely managed that they have little democratic value. The 2007 election season exemplified some of the longer-term effects (Tlemcani, 2007). Superficially, voters seemed to be presented with an impressive range of choices, with two dozen parties fielding more than 12,200 candidates. But the official turnout figure was a low 35.6 per cent, a number that was cut still further by a large number of spoiled ballots, meaning that probably only about 15 per cent of Algerians cast a legitimate vote. The problem, argues Tlemcani, was not so much that Algerians were depoliticized (as the government claimed), but that they used non-participation as a last resort in expressing their opposition. There were hopes that Algeria would democratize in response to the Arab Spring, but this has not so far come to pass.

A variation on the theme of electoral authoritarianism is found in states where there is a modicum of political choice, but the meaning of that choice is undermined by the manner in which government turns a blind eye to the manipulation of voters. In the lead-up to the 2007 elections in Nigeria, for example, Human Rights Watch (2007) recalled the widespread violence, intimidation, bribery, vote rigging and corruption that had surrounded the 1999 and 2003 elections. It pointed to violent clashes between supporters of parties in the 2007 campaign that had already claimed perhaps several hundred lives. Little effort had been made by the government to investigate or prosecute the offenders, encouraging powerful politicians to recruit and arm gangs to intimidate voters. The government had also done little to ensure accurate voter registration, casting doubt on the integrity of voter lists.

This portrait of a compromised election exemplifies the problems faced by a large, divided and volatile society such as Nigeria, where voters identify above all with their ethnicity, where parties have routinely reflected ethnic divisions, and where ethnic, religious and community tensions have generated considerable violence. The International Society for Civil Liberties and the Rule of Law and Human Rights Watch estimated that between 1999 and 2010, the number of Nigerians killed in such violence ranged between 11,000 and 13,500 (quoted in Campbell, 2013: xvii). Instability from another source – the infiltration of the Boko Haram Islamist movement into north-eastern Nigeria – was the immediate reason given for the postponement by six weeks of presidential and legislative elections in Nigeria in 2015. But critics charged that the motive was politics rather than security, and was aimed at giving the incumbent president Goodluck Jonathan more time to rebuild flagging support for his campaign. In the event, he lost to his northern opponent, Muhammadu Buhari, providing the first occasion on which an incumbent president in Nigeria had lost a re-election contest.

While many countries were involved in the third wave of democratization discussed by Huntington (see Chapter 3), they varied in their historical backgrounds, ranging from former military regimes to former communist states. Few, however, had much prior experience with democracy. As a result, argues Hagopian (2007), the relationship between parties and voters in these emerging democracies is neither strong nor stable. Party identification is often weak, and **electoral volatility** (the net change in party support from one election to another) is relatively high. The original measure of such volatility was developed by Mogens Pedersen (1979), who produced an index that ranges between 0 per cent (no parties gain or lose vote share from one election to the next) and 100 per cent (no parties from the last election win any votes at the new election). As a point of reference, Pedersen's original study of parties in Western Europe between 1948 and 1977 produced an average figure of 8.1 per cent; that is, low volatility. By contrast, later research revealed much higher levels of volatility in emerging democracies, ranging as high as 45 per cent or more in Eastern Europe and Russia (see Figure 17.6).

> **Electoral volatility:** A measure of the degree of change in support for political parties from one election to another.

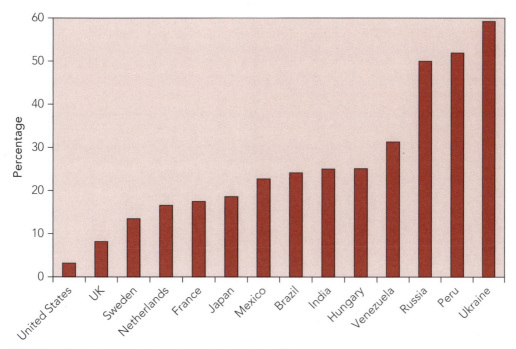

FIGURE 17.6: Comparing levels of electoral volatility
Source: Mainwaring and Torcal (2006). Figures are for elections held between 1978 and 2003.

These higher levels can be explained in part by the newness of democracy in these countries, and by the changing face of party systems: parties have not developed deep roots, must work harder to establish themselves, and face voters who are still working their way through the changing political landscape. Furthermore, as states democratize, so the factors that have most often driven party identification in democracies – such as social class and the state of the economy – change more quickly. Voters must also learn to trust and understand the new options available to them.

Measuring voter turnout in authoritarian systems is difficult, in part because of manipulated results. When dead people are listed as having voted, sometimes several times, we can be sure turnout figures are exaggerated. Generally, when official turnout figures are high, and the percentage of those votes won by the victor are high, the numbers are almost certainly fabrications. (The claim by Saddam Hussein that he won the 2002 Iraq election – actually, a referendum – with 100 per cent support on 100 per cent turnout particularly beggars belief.) Where dependable independent data are available, however,

and the numbers are more realistic, we find that turnout in authoritarian states is often comparable with that in democracies. Based on polls asking people if they had voted at the most recent election, for example, de Miguel et al. (2015) found that turnout in seven Arab countries (Algeria, Bahrain, Jordan, Morocco, Lebanon, Palestine, and Yemen) ranged between 51 and 72 per cent, with an average of 61 per cent.

It would be reasonable to ask why voters make the effort to turn out in elections in authoritarian states, given the combination of their probable cynicism about the process and their distance from the interests of the elites. In their study of elections in the Arab world, de Miguel et al. (2015) reject the standard view of elections in the region as purely patronage contests. While conceding that patronage does play a role, they argue that voters also care about policy and use elections to express their views about the regime and its performance, particularly on the economy. 'Positive evaluations of economic performance', they conclude, 'lead individuals to have more positive overall evaluations of the regime, which in turn increases the likelihood of voting.'

DISCUSSION QUESTIONS

- What role – if any – do social class and religion play in voter choices in your country?

- If identification with parties is declining, what prevents them from disappearing altogether?

- Is it irrational to vote?

- Is the role of personality underrated or overrated as an explanation for voter choices?

- Does it matter how many voters turn out at elections?

- This chapter has suggested that the motives of leaders are more important than the motives of voters in explaining voting behaviour in authoritarian states. To what extent can the same logic be applied to democracies?

KEY CONCEPTS

Electoral authoritarianism
Electoral volatility
Issue voting
Partisan dealignment

Party identification
Secularization
Vote buying

FURTHER READING

Aarts, Kees, André Blais, and Hermann Schmitt (eds) (2011) *Political Leaders and Democratic Elections*. Assesses the role of political leaders in voting decisions in nine democracies, suggesting that characteristics of leaders are less important than conventional wisdom imagines.

Caplan, Bryan (2007) *The Myth of the Rational Voter: Why Democracies Choose Bad Policies*. A study by an economist of the misconceptions and biases held by voters, and how these make them choose badly at elections.

Duch, Raymond M. and Randolph T. Stevenson (2008) *The Economic Vote: How Political and Economic Institutions Condition Election Results*.

An authoritative analysis of economic voting in liberal democracies.

Eijk, Cees van der and Mark Franklin (2009) *Elections and Voters*. A comparative textbook including chapters on voter orientations, public opinion, and voters and parties.

Franklin, Mark (2004) *Voter Turnout and the Dynamics of Electoral Competition in Established Democracies*. An influential comparative study of turnout and its decline.

Schedler, Andreas (ed.) (2006) *Electoral Authoritarianism: The Dynamics of Unfree Competition*. An edited collection on voting and elections in states that are neither wholly authoritarian nor wholly democratic.

18 Interest groups

PREVIEW

Where most institutions of government are formally outlined in the constitution, interest groups (like parties) are founded and operate largely outside these formal structures. Their goal – for those that are politically active – is to influence policy without becoming part of government. They come in several types: protective groups work in the material interests of their members, promotional groups advocate ideas and policies of a more general nature, peak associations bring together multiple like-minded groups to help them exploit their numbers, and think-tanks work to shape the policy debate through research. A vibrant interest group community is generally a sign of a healthy civil society but it can also become a barrier to the implementation of the popular will as expressed in elections.

This chapter begins with a survey of the different types of group, and the manner in which they work. It then critiques the idea of pluralism, contrasting the free marketplace of ideas with the privileged role that groups can come to play within the political process. The chapter next assesses the channels of influence used by groups before looking at the ingredients of influence and asking what gives particular groups the ability to persuade. It then looks at the distinctive qualities and effects of social movements, before assessing the place of interest groups in authoritarian regimes, where they are typically seen either as a threat to the power of the regime or as a device through which the regime can maintain its control over society.

CONTENTS

- Interest groups: an overview
- Types of interest groups
- The dynamics of interest groups
- Channels of influence
- Ingredients of influence
- Social movements
- Interest groups in authoritarian states

KEY ARGUMENTS

- Interest groups are central to the idea of a healthy civil society. Their ability to organize and lobby government is a hallmark of liberal democracy and a condition of its effective functioning.

- Interest groups exert a pervasive influence over the details of the public policies that affect them. But groups are far from omnipotent; understanding them also requires an awareness of their limits as political actors.

- Pluralism, and the debate surrounding it, is a major academic interpretation of the political role of interest groups. But there are reasons to question whether the pluralist ideal is an accurate description of how groups operate in practice.

- Interest groups use a combination of direct and indirect channels of influence. Where ties with government are particularly strong, the danger arises of the emergence of sub-governments enjoying preferred access.

- Interest groups are often complemented by wider social movements, whose activities challenge conventional channels of participation.

- Where the governments of liberal democracies may be too heavily influenced by powerful groups, the problem can be reversed in authoritarian states.

Interest groups: an overview

Interest groups – also known as 'pressure groups' – are bodies which seek to influence public policy from outside the formal structures of government. Examples include employer organizations, consumer groups, professional bodies, trade union federations, and single-issue groups. Traditionally, the term only covered bodies specifically created for lobbying purposes, and excluding businesses, churches, and sub-national or overseas governments. But since lobbying is pursued by many organizations whose primary focus is elsewhere, the restriction is too limiting (Scholzman, 2010). Even corporations can be seen as a form of interest group.

> **Interest group:** A body that works outside government to influence government policy.

Like political parties, interest groups are a crucial channel of communication between society and government, especially in liberal democracies. But they pursue specialized concerns, seeking to influence government without becoming the government. They are not election-fighting organizations; instead, they typically adopt a pragmatic, low-key approach in dealing with whatever power structure confronts them, using whatever channels are legally (and occasionally illegally) available to them.

Although many interest groups go about their work quietly, their activity is pervasive. Their staff are to be found negotiating with bureaucrats over the details of proposed regulations, pressing their case in legislative committee hearings, and taking journalists out to lunch in their efforts to influence media coverage. As Finer noted decades ago, 'their day-to-day activities pervade every sphere of domestic policy, every day, every way, at every nook and cranny of government' (1966: 18). Without question, interest groups are central to a system of functional representation, especially on detailed issues of policy. Even so, political cultures vary in how they define the relationship between interest groups and the state. Thus groups can be seen as:

- An essential component of a free society, separate from the state.
- Partners with the state in achieving a well-regulated society.
- Providers of information and watchdogs on the performance of government.

- An additional channel through which citizens can be politically engaged.
- Promoters of elitism, offering particular sectors privileged access to government.

Interest groups are a critical part of a healthy **civil society**. In a liberal democracy, the limited role of government leaves space for groups and movements of all kinds to emerge and address shared problems, often without government intervention. A rich civic tradition also provides the context in which interest groups can develop their capacity to influence government, encouraged by the expectation that government will entertain competing views about the sources and effects of social problems. But some interests can become too powerful, developing an insider status with government, and compromising the principle of equal access.

> **Civil society:** The arena that exists outside the state or the market and within which individuals take collective action on shared interests.

Types of interest group

Interest groups come in many varieties, based on their size, geographical reach, objectives, methods, and influence. Many form for practical or charitable purposes rather than for political action, but develop a political dimension as they begin working either to modify public policy or to prevent unfavourable changes. Their methods include fundraising (and spending), promoting public awareness, generating information, mobilizing their members, directly lobbying government, advising legislators, and encouraging favourable media. Their variety, in short, is so great, their methods so varied, and their overlap so considerable that it is not easy to develop a list of discrete types (Figure 18.1).

To simplify the list somewhat, it is helpful to distinguish between protective and promotional groups. **Protective groups** are perhaps the most prominent and powerful. They articulate the material interests of their members: workers, employers, professionals, retirees, military veterans, and so on. Sometimes known as 'sectional' or 'functional' groups, these protective bodies represent clear interests, and are well established, well connected and well resourced. They give priority to

Economic	Represent groups of people with material economic interests, such as business, industry, producers, trades, and workers.
Public	Promote public concerns, such as consumer, public health, human rights, and environmental interests.
Professional	Promote the interests of specific professions, such as lawyers, doctors, and university professors.
Single-issue	Concerned with distinct and narrow issues, such as animal rights or domestic violence.
Religious	Promote causes and issues tied to particular religions, often with a significant moral element.
Government	Groups that represent the interests of city, local and regional governments to the national administration.
Institutional	Other public organizations that influence government even though they are not organized as interest groups. Examples include hospitals, universities and the armed forces.

FIGURE 18.1: Types of interest group

influencing government, and can invoke sanctions to help them achieve their goals: workers can go on strike, and business organizations can withdraw their cooperation with government.

> **Protective group:** An interest group that seeks selective benefits for its members and insider status with relevant government departments.

But protective groups can also be based on local, rather than functional, interests. Geographic groups emerge when the shared interests of people living in the same location are threatened by plans for, say, a new highway, or a hostel for ex-convicts. Because of their negative stance – 'build it anywhere but here' – these kinds of bodies are known as Nimby groups: not in my back yard. Collectively, Nimby groups can generate a Banana outcome: 'build absolutely nothing anywhere near anyone'. Unlike permanent functional organizations, however, Nimby groups often come and go in

response to particular threats and changing levels of public interest.

A particular concern of protective groups is scrutinizing government activity; for example, by monitoring proposed regulations. A trade association will keep an eye on even the least newsworthy of developments within its zone of concern. A detailed regulation about product safety may be politically trivial but commercially vital for a group's members. Much activity of protective groups involves technical issues of this kind.

In contrast to the more material goals of protective bodies, **promotional groups** advocate ideas, identities, policies, and values. Also known as 'public interest', 'advocacy', 'attitude', 'campaign' or 'cause' groups, such organizations do not expect to profit directly from the causes they pursue, nor do they possess a material stake in how it is resolved. Instead, they seek broad policy changes in the issues that interest them, which include consumer safety, women's interests, the environment, or global development. These are public interests, as distinct from the narrower interests of single-issue groups.

> **Promotional group:** An 'interest' group that promotes wider issues and causes than is the case with protective groups focused on the tangible interests of their members.

In liberal democracies, promotional groups have expanded in number and significance, their growth since the 1960s constituting a major trend in interest politics. However, even more than for members of political parties, many who join promotional groups are credit card affiliates only; they send donations or sign up for membership, and perhaps follow news about the issue concerned, but otherwise remain unengaged. To be sure, a financial contribution expresses the donor's commitment, but it also delegates the pursuit of the cause to the group's leaders and staff. For this reason, the effectiveness of promotional bodies as schools for democracy can easily be overstated (Maloney, 2009).

The boundary separating protective and promotional groups is poorly defined. For example, bodies such as the women's and gay movements seek to influence public opinion and are often classified as promotional. However, their prime purpose remains to protect the interests of specific non-occupational groups. Perhaps they are best conceived as protective interests employing promotional means.

Protective interest groups representing a specific industry not only lobby government directly, but will often also join a **peak association**, or a body that consists of multiple like-minded interest groups. Their members are not individuals but other organizations such as businesses, trade associations, and labour unions. For example, industrial associations and individual corporations may join a wider body representing business interests to government, and labour unions may do the same for wider bodies representing worker interests. Examples of peaks include the National Association of Manufacturers in the United States, the Federal Organization of German Employers, and the Confederation of British Industry (CBI) in the UK. The CBI's direct business members, and indirect members through trade associations, amount to 190,000 organizations employing around one-third of the private sector workforce.

> **Peak association:** An umbrella organization representing the broad interests of business or labour to government.

Despite the widespread decline in union membership and labour militancy, many labour peak associations still speak with an influential voice. In 2011, the Confederation of German Trade Unions (DGB) comprised eight unions with a total of more than six million individual members. Britain's Trades Union Congress had 52 affiliated unions in 2015, representing a comparable number of working people. Such numbers are usually enough to earn a seat at the policy table.

In seeking to influence public policy, peak associations usually succeed, because they are attuned to national government, possess a strong research capacity and talk the language of policy. For example, the DGB (2012) defines its task thus:

> the DGB represents the German trade union movement in dealing with: the government authorities at state and national level; the political parties; the employers' organisations; and other groups within

TABLE 18:1: Comparing protective and promotional interest groups

	Protective	Promotional
Aims	Defend an interest	Promote a cause
Membership	Closed: membership is restricted	Open: anyone can join
Status	Insider: frequently consulted by government and actively seeks this role	Outsider: consulted less often by government; targets public opinion and the media
Benefits	Selective: only group members benefit	Collective: benefits go to both members and non-members
Focus	Aim to influence national government on specific issues affecting members	Also seek to influence national and global bodies on broad policy matters

society. The DGB itself is not directly involved in collective bargaining and cannot conclude pay agreements. However, it is significant for its specialist competence on broader issues of a general political nature.

Throughout the democratic world, the rise of pro-market thinking, international markets, and smaller service companies has restricted the standing of peak associations. Trade union membership has fallen (see later in this chapter), and the voice of business is now often expressed directly by leading companies. In addition, the task of influencing the government is increasingly delegated to specialist lobbying companies. In response to these trends, peak associations have tended to become policy-influencing and service-providing bodies, rather than organizations negotiating collectively with government on behalf of their members (Silvia and Schroeder, 2007).

Even so, extensive consultation – if no longer joint decision-making – continues between the peaks and government, not least in Scandinavia. And some smaller countries, including Ireland and the Netherlands, have even developed or revived wide-ranging agreements designed to combine social protection with improved economic efficiency. Such structured arrangements provide a contrast to the pluralist interpretation of interest groups which we discuss in the next section.

Another kind of group, often overlooked in discussions about interest politics, is the **think-tank**, or policy institute. These are private organizations set up to undertake research with a view to influencing both the public and the political debate. They typically publish reports, organize conferences, and host seminars, all with the goal of sustaining a debate over the issues in which they are interested, and to influence government and legislators either directly or indirectly. Most think-tanks are privately funded, but some are supported by governments, political parties, or corporations, and have a clear national, corporate, or ideological agenda. Examples include the Fabian Society in Britain, the Institute for National Strategic Studies in the US, the European Policy Centre in Belgium, the Centre for Civil Society in India, and the Stockholm International Peace Research Institute in Sweden.

Think-tank: A private organization that conducts research into a given area of policy with the goal of fostering public debate and political change.

The dynamics of interest groups

Debate on the role of interest groups has long centred on the concept of **pluralism**, or competition for influence in the political market. This is a model that regards competition between freely organized interest groups as a form of democracy. Supposedly, interest groups can represent all major sectors of society so that each sector's interests receives political expression. Groups compete for influence over government, which acts as an arbiter rather than an initiator, an umpire rather than a player. Groups compete on a level playing field, with the state showing little bias towards one over others. As new interests and identities emerge, groups form to represent them, quickly finding a place in the house of power. Overall, pluralism depicts a wholesome process of dispersed decision-making in which government's openness allows its policies to reflect developments in the economy and society.

Pluralism: A political system in which competing interest groups exert influence over a responsive government.

The reality of interest group dynamics is somewhat different from this ideal (see Focus 18.1), and many political scientists accept that the original pluralist portrayal of the relationship between groups and government was one-sided and superficial (McFarland, 2010). Criticism focuses on four areas:

- Interest groups do not compete on a level playing field. Some interests, such as business, are inherently powerful, while others are less powerful, and even marginal. The result is that groups form a hierarchy of influence, with their ranking reflecting their value to government.

- Pluralism overlooks the bias of the political culture and political system in favour of some interests but against others. Groups advocating modest reforms within the established order are usually heard more sympathetically than those seeking radical change (Walker, 1991). Some interests are inherently different.

- The state is far more than a neutral umpire. In addition to deciding which groups to heed, it may regulate their operation and even encourage their formation in areas it considers important, thus shaping the interest group landscape itself.

> ## FOCUS 18.1 | Pluralism undermined: the cases of the United States and Japan
>
> The weaknesses in pluralist thinking are illustrated by the contrasting cases of the United States and Japan, where group access to government is unbalanced, but for different reasons. The United States is often considered as an exemplar of the pluralist model, home as it is to numerous visible, organized, competitive, well-resourced, and successful interest groups. One directory listed more than 27,000 organizations politically active in Washington DC between 1981 and 2006 (Schlozman, 2010: 431), working to influence policy at the federal, state, and local levels on a wide range of interests. The separation of powers gives interest groups several points of leverage, including congressional committees, executive agencies, and the courts.
>
> But – charge the critics – government entrenches the interests of those who are already wealthy and powerful, including financial institutions deemed too big to fail. In 2006, more than half the groups registered in Washington DC were business interests (Schlozman, 2010: 434). The general interest often drowns in a sea of special pleading, certainly avoiding majority dictatorship, but substituting the risk of tyranny by minorities.
>
> Japan, too, is a society that places an emphasis on group politics, and so would seem to be a natural habitat for pluralism. Many groups are indeed active, using standard tactics such as lobbying and generating public awareness. But economic groups also try to influence the political system from inside, for example by trying to secure election of their members to public office, thus blurring the line between an interest group and a political party. There has been a particularly close relationship between business and government, and more specifically between large corporations and the dominant Liberal Democratic Party. This relationship helped Japanese companies to borrow and invest, and protected emerging industries as they sought to become internationally competitive. Public policy in Japan emerges less from electoral competition and public debate than from 'Japan Inc.': bargaining within a form of **iron triangle** involving the higher levels of the governing political party (or coalition), the bureaucracy, and big business. Organized labour, meanwhile, has relatively little influence over government. The outcome of this distinctly non-pluralist pattern, it used to be said, was a rich country with poor people.
>
> Both countries experience the problem of iron triangles though in the US, congressional committees are more important players (see Figure 18.2). In policy sectors where resources are available for distribution, legislative committees in Congress appropriate funds which are spent by government departments for the benefit of members of interest groups, which in turn offer electoral support and campaign funds for members of the committee. Perhaps most (in)famous among these triangles is the military-industrial complex of which President Eisenhower warned in his farewell address. Eisenhower described the close relationship between the US Department of Defense, the armed services committees in Congress, and the enormous defence contractors that provide most of the country's weapons. In many sectors, these relationships have loosened, but they remain exceptions to the pluralist model of competitive policy-making.

Iron triangle: A policy-influencing relationship involving (in the United States) interest groups, the bureaucracy, and legislative committees, and a three-way trading of information, favours, and support.

• Pluralist conflict diverts attention away from the interests shared by leaders of mainstream groups, such as their common membership of the same class and ethnic group. There is still some truth, it is argued, in the conclusion drawn in 1956 by C. Wright Mills, who famously argued in his book *The Power Elite* that American leaders of industry, the military, and government formed an interlocking power elite, rather than separate power centres.

One famous analysis with critical implications for pluralist theory was offered in 1965 by the political scientist Mancur Olson in his book *The Logic of Collective Action*. Until then, it had often been assumed

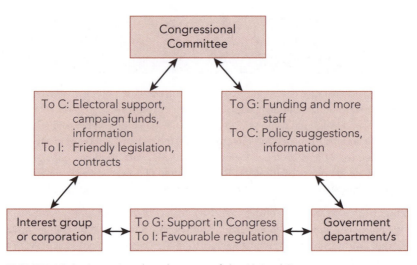

FIGURE 18.2: Iron triangles: the case of the United States

that all interests could achieve an approximately equal place at the bargaining table. But, Olson argued, it is difficult for people with diffuse interests to find each other, to come together, to organize themselves, and to compete against narrower and better organized interests. Each individual consumer, patient or student had less incentive to organize than is the case for the much smaller number of corporations, hospital and universities. This helped explain why it was so hard, for example, for ordinary citizens to compete against large corporations, which had funds, resources, contacts, and much else that could be used to influence policy-makers. Olson's analysis overlapped with rational choice arguments that citizens did not have sufficient incentives to become informed about politics and to engage with other citizens. Certainly, the assumption of a balanced market for influence began to look unrealistic.

Not everyone agrees with this analysis, however. Since Olson's day, organizations representing consumers and many other dispersed groups have emerged, grown and acquired a sometimes significant voice, not least in Washington DC. Trumbull (2012) argues that it is a misreading of history to believe that diffuse interests are impossible to organize or too weak to influence policy. Indeed, he suggests that weak interests often do prevail. His proposition is that organization is less important than legitimation: in other words, alliances forged among activists and regulators can form 'legitimacy coalitions' linking their agendas to the broader public interest. Hence, for example, such

coalitions have limited the influence not only of the agricultural and pharmaceutical sectors in Europe, but also of some multinational companies in some developing countries.

If iron triangles are an American exception to pluralism, **corporatism** is the equivalent in continental Europe. (On iron triangles, see Focus 18.1 and 18.2.) Where classic iron triangles operated within particular sectors, corporatism engages the peak associations representing business and labour in wider social and economic planning. The groups become 'social partners' with government, engaging in tripartite discussions to settle important political questions such as wage increases, tax rates and social security benefits. Once a 'social pact' or 'social contract' is agreed for the year, the peak associations are expected to ensure the compliance of their members, thus avoiding labour unrest.

> **Corporatism:** The theory and practice by which peak associations representing capital and labour negotiate with the government to achieve wide-ranging economic and social planning.

'Social corporatism', as this formula is called, worked best in smaller, highly organized countries where central agreements could be delivered by powerful peak associations with extensive membership. In the post-war decades, Austria was the clearest example but elements of the corporate model could also be found in Scandinavia and the Netherlands. Like iron triangles, corporatism has decayed. Peak associations have weakened, union membership has collapsed, smaller service companies have replaced large manufacturing industries and the ideological climate has shifted in favour of the market. Yet even today, corporatist thinking and practice provides a further challenge to the pluralist model.

Just as social corporatism has declined, so too have iron triangles. Factors involved include closer media scrutiny, new public interest groups that protest loudly when they spot the public being taken for a ride, and legislators who are more willing to speak out against closed and even corrupt policy-making. As policy issues has become more complex, so more groups have been drawn into the policy process, making it harder to stitch together insider deals. Reflecting more open government, the talk now is of **issue networks**. These refer to relationships between the familiar set of organizations involved in policy-making: government departments, interest groups, and legislative committees, with the addition of expert outsiders. However, issue networks are more open than iron triangles or corporate structures. A wider range of interests take part in decisions, the bias towards protective groups is reduced, new groups can enter the debate, and a sound argument carries greater weight.

> **Issue network:** A loose and flexible set of interest groups, government departments, legislative committees, and experts that work on policy proposals of mutual interest.

As we saw in earlier chapters, the internet promises to shake things up in ways that are not yet fully understood. Where Olson argued that interests were handicapped by the difficulties that people had in finding each other and organizing, the rise of social media largely removed this problem from the equation. Anyone with access to the internet can now create advocacy sites dealing with everything from local to international interests, and invite users to Like them, post information, debate the issues, and network with like-minded users and engage the opposition. Online communities are both significant and challenging for interest groups. Opening a site by clicking a button takes little effort, and engagement may not go much beyond posting a comment or a link, but these online conversations can create small informal communities that add up to larger movements influencing public opinion.

Channels of influence

Interest groups have a nose for where policy is made, and are adept at following the debate to the arenas where it is resolved. Generally, there are three key channels through which groups do most of their work: the direct channel that takes them to policy-makers, and the indirect channels through which they seek to influence political parties and public opinion.

Direct influence with policy-makers

Those who shape and apply policy are the ultimate target of most groups. Direct conversations with government ministers are the ideal, and talking with ministers before specific policies have crystallized is particularly valuable because it enables a group to enter the policy process at a formative stage. But such privileges are usually confined to a few well-connected individuals, and most interest group activity focuses in practice on the bureaucracy, the legislature and the courts. Of these, the bureaucracy is the main pressure point: interest groups follow power and it is in the offices of bureaucrats that detailed decisions are often formed.

For instance, ministers may decree a policy of subsidizing consumers who use renewable energy, a strategy that most groups must accept as given. However, the precise details of these incentives, as worked out in consultation with officials, will impinge directly on the profitability of energy suppliers. Even if access to top ministers is difficult, most democracies follow a convention of discussion over detail with organized opinion through consultative councils and committees. Often, the law requires such deliberation. In any case, the real expertise frequently lies in the interest group rather than the bureaucracy, giving the government an incentive to seek out this knowledge. Besides, from the government's viewpoint, a policy which can be shown to be acceptable to all organized interests is politically safe.

While the bureaucracy is invariably a crucial arena for groups, the significance of the legislature depends on its political weight. Comparing the United States and Canada illustrates the differences:

- The US Congress (and, especially, its committees) forms a vital cog in the policy machinery. Members of Congress realize they are under constant public scrutiny, not least in the House of Representatives,

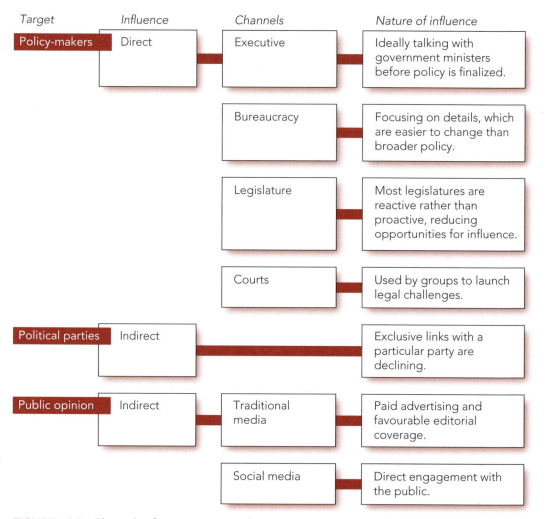

FIGURE 18.3: Channels of interest group influence

where a two-year election cycle means that politicians must be constantly aware of their ratings by interest groups. The ability of groups to endorse particular candidates – and, indirectly, to support their re-election campaigns – keeps legislators sensitive to group demands (Cigler and Loomis, 2015), especially those which resonate in their home districts.

- In Canada, as in most democracies, Parliament is more reactive than proactive; as a result, interest groups treat its members as opinion-formers rather than policy-makers. Party voting is entrenched in the House of Commons, extending beyond floor votes to committees and, in any case, 'committees seldom modify in more than marginal ways what is placed

before them and virtually never derail any bill that the government has introduced' (Brooks, 2012: 257). Such a disciplined environment offers few opportunities for influence.

Lobbying is a core activity of most interest groups and is usually conducted directly by group leaders. Increasingly, however, such efforts can take the form of hiring a specialist lobbying firm to represent the group to key decision-makers (see Focus 18.2). This development raises some troubling questions. Is it now possible for wealthy interest groups and corporations simply to pay a fee to a lobbying firm to ensure that a bill is defeated or a regulation deferred? Is lobbying just a fancy word for bribery? On the whole,

FOCUS 18.2 | Lobbying

In the British Parliament, between the chambers of the House of Commons and the House of Lords, is an open lobby where citizens could once approach their Members of Parliament in order to plead their case or request help. From this habit derived the terms *lobbying* and *lobbyist*. The essential meaning of these terms remains the same but has evolved into the more specific idea of organized efforts by paid intermediaries to influence government. Lobbyists are professionals, often working for corporations or even for lobbying firms consisting of hired guns in the business of interest group communication. Such services are offered not only by specialist government relations companies, but also by divisions within law firms and management consultancies. These operations are growing in number in liberal democracies, with some companies even operating internationally.

Lobbying is growing for three main reasons:

- Government regulation continues to grow. A specialist lobbying firm working for a number of interest groups can often monitor proposed regulations more efficiently than would be the case if each interest group undertook the task separately.
- Public relations campaigns are becoming increasingly sophisticated, often seeking to influence interest group members, public opinion and the government in one integrated project. Professional agencies come into their own in planning and delivering multifaceted campaigns, which can be too complex for an interest group client to manage directly.
- Many firms now approach government directly, rather than working through their trade association. Companies, both large and small, find that using a lobbying company to help them contact a government agency or a sympathetic legislator can yield results more quickly than working through an industry body.

The central feature of the lobbying business is its intensely personal character. A legislator is most likely to return a call from a lobbyist if the caller is a former colleague. Lobbying is about who you know. For this reason, lobbying firms are always on the look-out for former legislators or bureaucrats with a warm contact book, although the rules on registration and financial disclosure have tightened recently in some democracies.

the answer is 'no'. Professional lobbyists are inclined to exaggerate their own impact for commercial reasons but, except in countries where there are particularly strong links between government and key interests (such as Japan), most can achieve little more than access to relevant politicians and, perhaps, bureaucrats. Often, the lobbying firm's role is merely to hold the client's hand, helping an inexperienced company find its way around the corridors of power when it comes to town.'

> **Lobbying:** Efforts made on behalf of individuals, groups or organizations to influence the decisions made by elected officials or bureaucrats.

Rather than viewing professional lobbying in a negative light, we should recognize its contribution to effective political communication. It can focus the client's message on relevant decision-makers, ensuring that the client's voice is heard by those who need to hear it. Furthermore, lobbyists spend most time with sympathetic legislators, contributing to their promotion of a cause in which they already believe. Long-time Brussels-based commercial lobbyist Stanley Crossick (quoted in Thomas and Hrebenar, 2009: 138) said that 'successful lobbying involves getting the right message over to the right people in the right form at the right time on the right issue'. In that respect, at least, it enhances the efficiency of governance.

Of course, not everything in the lobby is rosy. Even if a company achieves no more for its fee than access to a decision-maker (and even if that meeting would have been possible with a direct approach), perhaps such exchanges in themselves compromise the principle of equality which underpins democracy.

Because buying access and buying influence are rarely distinguished in the public's mind, meetings arranged through lobbyists damage the legitimacy of the political process and generate a need, only now being met, for effective regulation. But as long as petitioning the government is a right rather than a requirement, it is difficult to see how inequalities in interest representation can be avoided.

Indirect influence through political parties

In the past, many interest groups sought to use a favoured political party as a channel of influence, with group and party often bound together as members of the same family. For instance, socialist parties in Europe have long seen themselves engaged with trade unions in a single drive to promote broad working-class interests. In a similar way, the environmental movement spawned both promotional interest groups dealing with specific problems (such as pollution, waste, and threats to wildlife) and green political parties.

Such intimate relationships between interest groups and political parties have become exceptional. Roles have become more specialized as interest groups concentrate on the specific concerns of their members, while parties have broader agendas. For instance, the religious and class parties of Europe have broadened their appeal, seeking to be viewed as custodians of the country as a whole, while green parties have long since moved far beyond their environmental roots into a wide range of policy interests. The distinction between parties seeking power and interest groups seeking influence has sharpened as marriages of the heart have given way to alliances of convenience. As a result, most interest groups now seek to hedge their bets, rather than to develop close links with a specific political party. Loose, pragmatic links between interests and parties are the norm, and protective interests tend to follow power, not parties.

Indirect influence through public opinion

Public opinion is a critical target for promotional interest groups, the twin goals being to shape public perceptions and also to mobilize public concern so as to bring pressure on government for policy change. This wider audience can be addressed by focusing on paid advertising (advocacy advertising), by promoting favourable coverage in conventional media (public relations), and by using social media to promote ideas and bring together like-minded constituencies.

Since many promotional groups lack both substantial resources and access to decision-makers, public opinion becomes a venue of necessity. Traditionally, though, the media are less important to protective groups with their more specialized and secretive demands. What food manufacturer would go public with a campaign opposing nutritional labels on foods? The confidentiality of a government office is a more appropriate arena for fighting rear-guard actions of this kind. Keen to protect their reputation in government, protective groups steer away from disruption; they want to be seen as reliable partners by the public servants on the other side of the table.

But even protective groups are now seeking to influence the climate of public opinion, especially in political systems where legislatures help to shape policy. Especially when groups sense that public opinion is already onside, they increasingly follow a dual strategy, appealing to the public and to the legislature. The risk lies in upsetting established relationships with bureaucrats; however, this danger has declined compared with the era of iron triangles. In Denmark, for instance, 'decision makers seem to accept that groups seek attention from the media and the general public without excluding them from access to making their standpoint heard in decision-making' (Binderkrantz, 2005: 703). Slowly and cautiously, even protective groups are emerging from the bureaucratic undergrowth into the glare of media publicity.

Ingredients of influence

There is no doubt that some interest groups exert more influence over government than others. So, what is it that gives particular groups the ability to persuade? Much of the answer is to be found in four attributes ranging from the general to the specific: legitimacy, sanctions, membership, and resources.

First, the degree of legitimacy achieved by a particular group is clearly important. Interests enjoying high prestige are most likely to prevail on particular issues. Professional groups whose members stand for social respectability can be as militant on occasion, and as restrictive in their practices, as trade unions once were. But lawyers and doctors escape the public hostility that unions continue to attract. Similarly, the intrinsic importance of business to economic performance means that its representatives can usually obtain a hearing in government.

Second, a group's influence depends on its membership. This is a matter of **density** and commitment, as well as sheer numbers. Labour unions have seen their influence decline as the proportion of workers belonging to unions fell in nearly all liberal democracies between 1980 and 2012, especially in the private sector (see Figure 18.4). Except for Scandinavia, union members are now a minority of the workforce. This has weakened labour's bargaining power with government and employers alike. Influence is further reduced when membership is spread among several interest groups operating in the same sector.

> **Density:** The proportion of all those eligible to join a group who actually do so. The higher the density, the stronger a group's authority and bargaining position with government.

The commitment of the membership is also important. For instance, the several million members of the US National Rifle Association (NRA) – described by the *New York Times* as 'the most fearsome lobbying organization in America' (Draper, 2013) – include many who are prepared to contact their congressional representatives in pursuit of the group's goal of 'preserving the right of all law-abiding individuals to purchase, possess and use firearms for legitimate purposes'. Their well-schooled activism led George Stephanopoulos, spokesman for President Clinton, to this assessment: 'let me make one small vote for the NRA. They're good citizens. They call their Congressmen. They write. They vote. They contribute. And they get what they want over time' (NRA, 2012).

Third, the financial resources available to an interest group affect influence. In the European Union, for example, as more decisions have been made at the EU level, so more interest groups have opened offices in Brussels, the seat of the major EU institutions. Prime

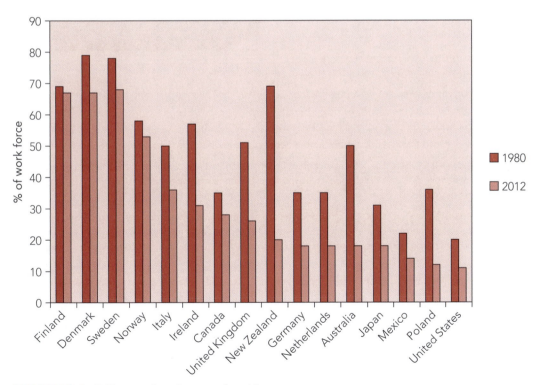

FIGURE 18.4: Falling trade union membership
Note: Earlier figure for Poland is from 1990, and for Mexico from 1992.
Source: Organisation for Economic Co-operation and Development (2015)

SPOTLIGHT

EGYPT

Brief Profile: Egypt has long been a major player in Middle East politics, thanks not only to its pioneering role in the promotion of Arab nationalism but also to its strategic significance in the Cold War and in the Arab–Israeli conflict. It was also at the heart of the Arab Spring, with pro-democracy demonstrations leading to the fall from power of Hosni Mubarak in 2011. Democratic elections brought Mohamed Morsi to power in 2012, but he was removed in a military coup the following year. Egyptians now face new uncertainties, led as they are by a military officer – Abdel Fattah el-Sisi – who has reinvented himself as a civilian leader. Egypt possesses the second biggest economy in the Arab world, after Saudi Arabia, but is resource-poor. It relies heavily on tourism, agriculture, and remittances from Egyptian workers abroad and struggles to meet the needs of its rapidly growing population.

Population (83.4 million)

Gross National Income ($272 billion)

Per capita GNI ($3,140)

Democracy Index rating

| Not Yet Rated | Hybrid Regime | Full Democracy |
| | Authoritarian | Flawed Democracy |

Freedom House rating

| Not Free | Partly free | Free |

Human Development Index rating

| Not Rated | Medium | Very High |
| | Low | High |

Form of government ⇨ Unitary semi-presidential republic. Modern state formed 1952, and most recent constitution adopted 2014.

Legislature ⇨ Unicameral People's Assembly (Majlis el-Shaab) with 567 members, of whom 540 are elected for renewable four-year terms and 27 can be appointed by the president.

Executive ⇨ Semi-presidential. A president directly elected for no more than two four-year terms, governing with a prime minister who leads a Cabinet accountable to the People's Assembly. There is no vice president.

Judiciary ⇨ Egyptian law is based on a combination of British, Italian and Napoleonic codes. The Supreme Constitutional Court has been close to recent political changes in Egypt; it has 21 members appointed for life by the president, with mandatory retirement at age 70.

Electoral system ⇨ A two-round system is used for presidential elections, with a majority vote needed for victory in the first round, while a mixed member majoritarian system is used for People's Assembly elections; two-thirds of members are elected using party list proportional representation, and one-third in an unusual multi-member plurality system in two large districts.

Parties ⇨ Multi-party, but unsettled because of recent instability. Parties represent a wide range of positions and ideologies.

➡

among those groups have been business interests: individual corporations are represented either directly or through lobbying firms, and several cross-sectoral and multi-state federations have been created to represent wider economic interests. The latter include Business Europe (with national business federations as members), the European Consumers' Organization, the European Trade Union Confederation, and the European Roundtable of Industrialists, an informal forum of chief executives from nearly 50 major European corporations.

Interest groups in Egypt

We saw in Chapter 4 how, in authoritarian political systems based on personal rule, access to policy-makers depends on patronage, clients, and contacts – proof of the adage that who you know is more important than what you know. Egypt is a case in point. It would seem to have a healthy and varied interest group community, representing business, agriculture, the professions, and religious groups, but government has long controlled access through the kind of corporatism discussed later in this chapter. At the same time, though, some interest groups have developed sufficient power and authority as to exert the influence usually associated with interest groups in liberal democracies.

The number and reach of groups in Egypt grew sharply during the administration of Hosni Mubarak (1981–2011). Groups such as the Chamber of Commerce and the Federation of Industries lobbied for economic liberalization, including the abolition of fixed prices. The leaders of professional groups such as the Journalists Syndicate, the Lawyers Syndicate, and the Engineers Syndicate used their personal contacts in government to win concessions for their members. Interest groups became so numerous that the Mubarak government felt the need to monitor them more closely, requiring that they be officially registered, and taking the controversial step in 1999 of passing a law that gave the government considerable powers to interfere in the work of groups. It could hire and fire board members, cancel board decisions, and even dissolve a group by court order. Groups were also barred from taking part in political activity, and their members were subject to imprisonment for a variety of vague and general crimes, including 'undermining national unity'. Groups affiliated with religious organizations and those working on human rights issues were particularly affected by this reassertion of traditional state authority.

The administration of Abdel Fattah el-Sisi that came to power in a military coup in 2013 remains influenced by the military, and concerned about promoting economic development and controlling Islamic militancy. For the foreseeable future, the value of interest groups is likely to be defined in Egypt by the extent to which they are consistent with these goals.

Fourth, the ability of a group to invoke sanctions is clearly important. A labour union can go on strike, a multinational corporation can take its investments elsewhere, a peak association can withdraw its cooperation in forming policy. As a rule, promotional groups (such as those with environmental interests) have fewer sanctions available to use as a bargaining chip; their influence suffers accordingly.

Social movements

Interest groups are part of conventional politics, operating through orthodox channels such as the bureaucracy. Like the political systems of which they form part, they are increasingly treated with distrust by the wider public. It is perhaps no surprise, then, that traditional interest groups have been supplemented by **social movements** – a less conventional form of participation through which people come together to seek a common objective by means of an unorthodox challenge to the existing political order. These movements do not necessarily consist of pre-existing interest groups, but groups are often at their heart; thus the environmental movement that emerged in most industrialized countries in the 1960s was driven by interest groups, which continue to carry the banner of the environmental movement today. Social movements espouse a political style which distances them from established channels, thereby questioning the legitimacy, as well as the decisions, of the government. Their members adopt a wide range of protest acts, including demonstrations, sit-ins, boycotts, and political strikes. Some such acts may cross the border into illegality but the motives of the actors are political, rather than criminal.

> **Social movement:** A movement emerging from society to pursue non-establishment goals through unorthodox means. Its objectives are broad rather than sectional and its style involves a challenge by traditional outsiders to existing elites.

Consider the example of the protestors who occupied Zuccotti Park in New York City's financial district in 2011 to express their disapproval of growing

TABLE 18.2: Comparing social movements, parties, and interest groups

	Social movements	Political parties	Interest groups
Seek to influence government?	Usually	Yes	Yes
Seek to become government?	No	Yes	No
Focus on a single issue?	Sometimes	Rarely	Usually
Formally organized?	Not usually	Yes	Yes
Tactics used?	Unconventional	Conventional	Mixture
Main levels of operation?	Global, national, local	National, regional	Global, national, local

income inequality, especially in the financial sector. Using the slogan 'We are the 99 per cent', Occupy Wall Street rapidly became not only a national, but also an international phenomenon, with tented encampments emerging in many countries, including Australia, Brazil, Canada, France, Germany, Mexico, New Zealand, Nigeria, South Africa, and Turkey. Without putting up candidates for election or engaging in conventional lobbying, the Occupy protests succeeded in focusing public attention on income disparities and unchecked corporate power.

To appreciate the character of social movements, we can usefully compare them with parties and interest groups (see Table 18.2). Movements are more loosely organized, typically lacking the precise membership, subscriptions, and leadership of parties. As with those parties whose origins lie outside the legislature, movements emerge from society to challenge the political establishment. However, movements do not seek to craft distinct interests into an overall package; rather, they claim the moral high ground in one specific area.

Like interest groups, social movements can sometimes have focused concerns, such as protests against a war or in support of nuclear disarmament, but their concerns are usually broader, as with the cases of the feminist, environmental, and civil rights movements. As with interest groups, social movements do not seek state power, aiming rather to influence the political agenda, usually by claiming that their voice has previously gone unheard. Whereas interest groups have targeted goals, social movements are more diffuse, seeking cultural as much as legislative change. For example, the gay movement might measure its success by how many gay people come out, not just by the passage of anti-discrimination legislation. Similarly, women's movements may emphasize consciousness-raising among women.

Tilly (2004: 33) regards the British anti-slavery movement of the late eighteenth and early nineteenth

TABLE 18.3: Examples of social movements

	Time and place	Focus
Gay rights	Most active 1960s–present, in developed non-Islamic countries	Equal rights for gay, lesbian, bisexual and transgender (LGBT) people
Chipko movement	1960s–1980s, India	Village- and rural-based protests against deforestation
Anti-apartheid movement	Mid-1960s–1994, mainly Britain	To end apartheid in South Africa through sporting, political, and academic boycotts
Landless workers	Mid-1980s–present, Brazil	Land reform and access to land for the poor
Anti-globalization	Late 1980s–present, many countries	Critical of the power of global corporate capitalism
Fair trade	1960s–present, originally in Europe	Higher prices and sustainable techniques for producers of commodities exporting from the developing to the developed world

centuries as the earliest example of a social move-ment as now understood. The techniques adopted in this campaign, including petitions and boycotts, estab-lished a palette of protest activities soon emulated by other reforming groups. Then came the suffragette movements of the early nineteenth and early twen-tieth centuries on both sides of the Atlantic, which were instrumental in winning the right to vote for women. Since then, the number, concerns, and sig-nificance of social movements have all expanded (see Table 18.3).

In the 1950s, 'mass movements', as they were then called, were perceived as a threat to the stability of lib-eral democracy. They were taken as a sign of a poorly functioning mass society 'containing large numbers of people who are not integrated into any broad social groupings, including classes' (Kornhauser, 1959: 14). Movements were judged to be supported by marginal, disconnected groups, such as unemployed intellectuals, isolated workers, and the peripheral middle class. Good-win and Jasper (2003a: 5) claim that until the 1960s, 'most scholars who studied social movements were frightened of them'.

The 1960s and 1970s saw a radical rethink. The civil rights movement in the United States mobilized blacks from multiple economic and social backgrounds, while Vietnam and the draft propelled parts of the edu-cated American middle class into anti-war movements. As intellectuals became more critical of government, so their treatment of social movements became more positive. By the end of the twentieth century, della Porta and Diani (2006: 10) were able to conclude that it was 'no longer possible to define movements in a prejudi-cial sense as phenomena which are marginal and anti-institutional. A more fruitful interpretation towards the political interpretation of contemporary movements has been established.'

The supporters of social movements do not always need much in the way of resources to make an impres-sion; sheer numbers may be enough, provided that the goals are clear. This means that social movements lend themselves well to political participation in poorer soci-eties, where movements also benefit from the direct and immediate interest of many participants in encourag-ing policy change. A good example is the Green Belt Movement that has been active since 1977 in Kenya. It mobilizes rural women to plant trees in an effort to stop deforestation and soil erosion, and to provide wood fuel and income. In 2004, its founder – Wangari

Maathai – became the first African woman to win the Nobel Peace Prize.

Developments in communications have lowered the barriers to entry for new movements, facilitat-ing their rapid emergence when ordinary politics has been deemed to fail. For example, farmers in France have long been renowned for taking their protests against agricultural policy (including falling prices, cheaper imports, and environmental regulation) onto the streets. They block traffic by driving their trac-tors slowly along highways, dump tons of vegetables or manure onto city squares, and set fire to hay out-side public buildings. In a digital age, such protests are easier than ever to co-ordinate, even in the absence of formal organization.

Mass communication also facilitates simultaneous global protest with virtually no central leadership at all; people in one country simply hear what is planned elsewhere and decide to join in. A remarkable example is provided by the international protests on the week-end of 15–16 February 2003 against the invasion of Iraq, which attracted an estimated six million people in about 600 cities (Figure 18.5). Bennett (2005: 207) reckons this protest, which provided a shared label for people from different backgrounds as well as coun-tries, was 'the largest simultaneous multinational dem-onstration in recorded history'. He concludes (p. 205) that 'such applications of communication technology favour loosely linked distributed networks that are minimally dependent on central coordination, leaders or ideological commitment'.

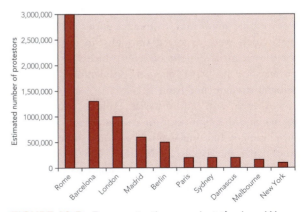

FIGURE 18.5: Demonstrations against the Iraq War, 2003
Source: Estimates reported in the *Financial Times*, 17 February 2003

Interest groups in authoritarian states

In authoritarian states, the relationship between government and interest groups is very different from the democratic model. In liberal democracies, as we have seen, powerful groups can capture elements of the government but in authoritarian states those groups that do exist are generally subordinate to the regime. Authoritarian rulers see freely organized groups as a potential threat to their own power; hence, they seek either to repress such groups, or to incorporate them within their power structure. The groups are prisoner rather than master.

In the second half of the twentieth century, many authoritarian rulers had to confront the challenge posed by new groups unleashed by economic development, including labour unions, peasant leagues, and educated radicals. One of their responses was to suppress such groups completely. Where civil liberties were weak and groups were new, this approach was feasible. In military regimes, leaders often had their own fingers in the economic pie, sometimes in collaboration with overseas corporations; the goal of rulers was to maintain a workforce that was both compliant and poorly paid. Troublemakers seeking to establish labour unions were quickly removed.

Long-term military rule in Burma offered an example of this forced exploitation. The military rulers that governed the country from 1962 to 2011 outlawed independent trade unions, collective bargaining, and strikes; imprisoned labour activists; and maintained strict control of the media. This repressive environment enabled the regime to use forced labour, particularly from ethnic minorities, to extract goods such as timber, which were exported through the black market for the financial benefit of army officers. Fortunately, governance in Burma softened considerably as political reforms strengthened from 2011.

Alternatively, authoritarian rulers could work to manage the expression of new interests created by development. In other words, they could allow interests to organize, but seek to control them: a policy of incorporation rather than exclusion. By enlisting part of the population, particularly its more modern sectors, into officially sponsored associations, rulers hoped to accelerate the push towards modernization. This is a conceptual cousin of the social corporatism discussed earlier in the chapter, the difference being that it is a form of top-down political manipulation. It was common in Latin America, where the state licensed, funded, and granted a monopoly of representation to favoured groups, reflecting a Catholic tradition inherited from colonial times (Wiarda, 2004).

Before the democratic and economic reforms of the 1980s and 1990s, Mexico offered an example of this format. Its governing system was founded on a strong ruling organization: the Institutional Revolutionary Party (PRI). This party was itself a coalition of labour, agrarian, and 'popular' sectors (the latter consisting mainly of public employees). Favoured unions and peasant associations within these sectors gained access to the PRI. Party leaders provided state resources, such as subsidies and control over jobs, in exchange for the political support (not least in ensuring PRI's re-election) of incorporated groups. The system was a giant patron–client network. For the many people left out of the organized structure, however, life was extremely hard.

But Mexican corporatism declined. The state was overregulated, giving so much power to government and PRI-affiliated sectors as to deter business investment, especially from overseas. As the market sector expanded, so the patronage available to PRI diminished. In 1997, an independent National Workers Union emerged to claim that the old mechanisms of state control were exhausted, a point which was confirmed by PRI's defeat in a presidential election three years later. (PRI regained the presidency in 2012, but its victorious candidate claimed there would be no return to the past.)

The position of interest groups in communist states was even more marginal than in other non-democratic regimes, providing a stark contrast to pluralism. For most of the communist era, there were no independent interest groups. Interest articulation by freely organized groups was inconceivable. Communist rulers sought to harness all organizations into so-called 'transmission belts' for party policy. Trade unions, the media, youth groups, and professional associations were little more than branches of the party, serving the cause of communist construction.

Elements of this tradition can still be found in contemporary China (see Table 18.4). The ruling Communist Party continues to provide the framework for most formal political activity, with a cluster of 'mass organizations' that are led by party officials and continue to transmit policy downwards, rather than popular concerns upwards. However, a new breed of non-governmental organization emerged in China in the 1980s, strengthening the link between state and society. Examples include the China Family Planning Association, Friends of Nature, the Private Enterprises Association, and the Federation of Industry and Commerce. Typically, only one body is officially recognized in each sector, confirming the state's continuing control. The limited status of these new entities is reflected in their title: government-organized non-governmental organizations (GONGOs). What we are seeing in China, then, is what Frolic (1997) calls a 'state-led civil society', with civil society serving as an adjunct, rather than an alternative, to state power.

In hybrid regimes, the position of interest groups lies somewhere between their comparative autonomy in liberal democracies and their marginal status in authoritarian states. The borders between the public and private sectors are poorly policed, allowing presidents and their allies to intervene in the economy so as to reward friends and punish enemies. But this involvement is selective, rather than comprehensive, occasionally overriding normal business practices but not seeking to replace them.

At least in the more developed hybrid regimes, the result can be a dual system of representation, combining a role for interest groups on routine matters, with more personal relationships (nurtured by patronage) on matters that are of key importance to the president and the ruling elite. In the most sensitive economic areas (control over energy resources, for example), employer is set against employer in a competition for political influence, leaving little room for the development of influential business associations. The general point is that, even though hybrid regimes allow some interests to be expressed, interest groups are far less significant than in a liberal democracy.

Russia is an interesting case. The separation between public and private sectors, so central to the organization of interests in the West, has not fully emerged. Particularly in the early post-communist years, ruthless business executives, corrupt public officials, and jumped-up gangsters made deals in a virtually unregulated free-for-all. Individual financiers pulled the strings of their puppets in government but the politics was personal, rather than institutional. In such an environment, interests were everywhere but interest groups were nowhere.

As Russian politics stabilized and its economy recovered, so some business associations of a Western persuasion emerged, even if they have not yet won extensive political influence. As early as 2001, Peregudov (2001: 268) claimed that 'in Russia a network of business organizations has been created and is up and running'. He suggested that this network was capable of adequately representing business interests to the state. However, this network has received limited attention from Vladimir Putin during his tenure as president. At a strategic level, he continues to reward his business friends and, on occasion, to imprison his enemies. Top-level relationships are still between groups of powerful individuals, not institutions.

TABLE 18.4: Social organizations in China

	Type	Features
All-China Federation of Trade Unions	Mass organization	Traditional transmission belt for the Communist Party.
All-China Women's Federation	Mass organization	Traditionally a party-led body, this federation has created some space for autonomous action.
China Family Planning Association	Non-governmental organization	Sponsored by the State Family Planning Commission, this association operates at international and local level.
Friends of Nature	Non-governmental organization	Operates with some autonomy in the field of environmental education.

Source: Adapted from Saich (2015: Chapter 7)

We must be wary of assuming that Russia will eventually develop a liberal democratic system of interest representation. Certainly, pluralism is not currently on the agenda. Evans (2005: 112) even suggests that Putin has 'sought to decrease the degree of pluralism in the Russian political system; it has become increasingly apparent that he wants civil society to be an adjunct to a strong state that will be dedicated to his version of the Russian national ideal'. In a manner resembling China's GONGOs, the state works to collaborate with favoured groups, while condemning others to irrelevance.

The Russian government's strong nationalist tone has led to particular criticism of those groups (such as women's associations) which have depended on overseas support to survive in an unsympathetic domestic environment. Few promotional groups in Russia possess a significant mass membership; most groups operate solely at grassroots level, working on local projects such as education or the environment. As in China, these groups operate under state supervision. So Russia's combination of an assertive state and a weak civil society continues to inhibit interest group development.

DISCUSSION QUESTIONS

- Are interest groups a part of, or a threat to, democracy?

- To what extent do special interests limit the functioning of the market of political ideas?

- True or false: rather than viewing professional lobbying in a negative light, we should recognize its contribution to effective political communication.

- How is the rise of social media likely to impact the organization and political role of interest groups?

- Identify any significant social movements, past or present, in your country. Do they pose a challenge to establishment politics?

- How does corporatism differ in democratic and authoritarian settings?

KEY CONCEPTS

Civil society
Corporatism
Density
Interest group
Iron triangle
Issue network
Lobbying

Peak association
Pluralism
Promotional group
Protective group
Social movement
Think-tank

FURTHER READING

Beyers, Jan, Rainer Eising, and William A. Maloney (eds) (2012) *Interest Group Politics in Europe: Lessons from EU Studies and Comparative Politics.* A collection analysing interest group politics in the European Union.

Olson, Mancur (1965) *The Logic of Collective Action: Public Goods and the Theory of Groups.* A classic study of interest group formation, and still interesting for what it says about pluralism, even if some of the core arguments have been challenged.

Tarrow, Sidney G. (2011) *Power in Movement: Social Movements and Contentious Politics,* 3rd edn. Focuses on the rise and fall of social movements as the outcome of political opportuni-

ties, state strategy, the mass media, and international diffusion.

Wilson, Graham K. (2003) *Business and Politics: A Comparative Introduction,* 3rd edn. Offers a clear comparative assessment of an important, but still understudied, topic.

Yadav, Vineeta (2011) *Political Parties, Business Groups, and Corruption in Developing Countries.* A study of the relationship between business lobbying and corruption in developing countries.

Zetter, Lionel (2014) *Lobbying: The Art of Political Persuasion,* 3rd edn. A global view of the dynamics of lobbying, including chapters on Europe, the United States, Asia and the Middle East.

19 Public policy

PREVIEW

Public policy is an appropriate topic with which to close this book, since it concerns the outcomes of the political process. The core purpose of government is to manage and address the needs of society. The approaches that governments adopt and the actions they take (or avoid) to address those needs collectively constitute their policies, and are the product of the political processes examined throughout the preceding chapters. Where political science examines the organization and structure of the political factory, policy analysis looks at how policy is formed, at the influences on policy, and at the results of different policy options.

This chapter begins with a review of three models of the policy process: the rational, the incremental, and the garbage-can model. The first provides an idealistic baseline, while the second and third are more reflective of reality, but it is debatable in which proportions. The chapter then goes on to look at the policy cycle, an artificial means for imposing some order on what is, in reality, a complex and often confusing process. The problems experienced at each step in the process – initiation, formulation, implementation, evaluation, and review – give us insight into why so many public policies fall short of their goals. The chapter then looks at the related phenomena of policy diffusion and policy convergence, before ending with a review of the dynamics of policy making in authoritarian systems, where – with greater focus on power politics – the policy process has its own distinctive dynamic.

CONTENTS

- Public policy: an overview

- Models of the policy process

- The policy cycle

- Policy diffusion and convergence

- Public policy in authoritarian states

KEY ARGUMENTS

- Studying public policy offers a distinctive perspective within the study of politics. It involves looking at what governments do, rather than the institutional framework within which they do it.

- Underlying much policy analysis is a concern with the quality and effectiveness of what government does. Policy analysis asks 'How well?', rather than just 'How?' or 'Why?'

- There is always a danger of imagining policy-making as a rational process with precise goals. The incremental and garbage-can models offer a hearty dose of realism. Policy, it is always worth remembering, is embedded in politics; a statement of policy can be a cover for inaction.

- Breaking the policy process into its component stages, from initiation to evaluation, helps in analysing and comparing policies. The later stages, implementation and evaluation, provide a different focus which is integral to policy analysis.

- Policy diffusion and convergence studies help explain how policies evolve in similar directions in multiple countries.

- Policy in authoritarian regimes plays a secondary role to politics, where the overriding requirement for survival in office often leads to corruption, uncertainty, and stagnation.

Public policy: an overview

Public policy is a collective term for the objectives and actions of government. It is more than a decision or even a set of decisions, but instead describes the approaches that elected officials adopt in dealing with the demands of their office, and the actions they take (or avoid taking) to address public problems and needs. The choices they make are driven by a variety of influences, including the priorities they face, their political ideology, the economic and political climate, and the budgets they have available. Policies consist both of aims (say, to reverse climate change) and of means (switching to renewable sources of energy in order to cut carbon dioxide emissions).

> **Public policy:** The positions adopted and the actions taken (or avoided) by governments as they address the needs of society.

When parties or candidates run for office, they will have a shopping list of issues they wish to address, and the positions they take will be their policies. When they are elected or appointed to office, they will usually continue to pursue these policies, which will be expressed in the form of public statements, government programmes, laws, and actions. If policy was limited to these published objectives, then it might be relatively easy to understand and measure. However, government and governance are also influenced by informal activities, opportunism, the ebb and flow of political and public interest, and simply responding to needs and problems as they present themselves.

Once elected to office, political leaders will often find that their priorities and preferred responses will change because of circumstances. They may be diverted by other more urgent problems, or find that their proposals lack adequate political support or funding, or discover that implementation is more difficult then they anticipated. In understanding the policy process, it is important to avoid imposing rationality on a process that is often driven by political considerations: policies can be contradictory, they can be nothing more than window-dressing (an attempt to be seen to be doing something, but without any realistic expectation that the objective will be achieved), and policy statements may be a cover for acting in the opposite way to the one stated.

But whatever the course taken and the eventual outcome, the actions of government (combined with their inaction) are understood as their policies. These policies become the defining qualities of governments and their leaders, and the records of these policies in addressing and alleviating problems will become the reference points by which governments and leaders are assessed, and a key factor in determining whether or not they will be returned to another term in office.

The particular task of **policy analysis** is to understand what governments do, how they do it, and what difference it makes (Dye, 2012). So, the focus is on the content, instruments, impact, and evaluation of public policy, more than on the influences that come to bear on the policy process. The emphasis is downstream (on implementation and results) as much as upstream (on the institutional sources of policy). Because analysts are concerned with improving the quality and efficacy of public policy, the subject exudes a practical air. Policy analysts want to know whether and why a policy is working, and how else its objectives might be pursued.

> **Policy analysis:** The systematic study of the content and impact of public policy.

Models of the policy process

In analysing the manner in which policy is made, scholars have developed three distinct models: the rational model associated with Herbert Simon (1983), the incremental model developed by Charles Lindblom (1959, 1979), and the garbage-can model, so named by Michael Cohen *et al.* (1972). In evaluating these different perspectives, and in looking at policy analysis generally, we must distinguish between accounts of how policy should be made and descriptions of how it actually is made. Moving through each of these models in order (Table 19.1) is, in part, a transition from the former to the latter:

- The rational model seeks to elaborate what would be involved in rational policy-making without assuming that its conclusions are reflected in what actually happens.
- The incremental model views policy as a compromise between actors with ill-defined or even contradictory goals, and can be seen either as an account of how politics ought to proceed (namely, peacefully reconciling different interests), or as a description of how policy is made.
- The garbage-can model is concerned with highlighting the many limitations of the policy-making process within many organizations, looking only at what is, not what ought to be.

TABLE 19.1: Three models of policy-making

	Goals and means	Optimum policy outcome	Analysis	Guidance
Rational	Goals are set before means.	Policies will achieve explicit goals.	Comprehensive; all effects of all options are addressed.	Theory.
Incremental	Goals and means are considered together.	Policies will be agreed by all the main actors.	Selective; the goal is acceptable policy, not the best policy.	Comparison with similar problems.
Garbage-can	Goals are discovered through actions taken by the organization and are not specified separately.	Some problems are partly addressed some of the time.	Little; the organization acts rather than decides.	Trial and error, plus some memory of recent experiences.

The lesson is that we should recognize the different functions these models perform, rather than presenting them as wholly competitive.

The rational model

Suppose you are the secretary of education and your key policy goal is an improvement in student performance. If you opt for the **rational model**, then you would first ensure that you had a complete and accurate set of data on performance levels, then set your goals (for example, a 10 per cent increase in the number of students going to university within five years), and then you would list and consider the most efficient means of achieving those goals. You might choose to improve secondary teaching, expand the size or the number of universities, deepen support for students from disadvantaged backgrounds, increase the number of university staff, improve facilities, or some combination of these approaches. Your approach focuses on efficiency, and demands that policy-makers rank all their values, develop specific options, check all the results of choosing each option against each value, and select the option that achieves the most values.

> **Rational model:** An approach to understanding policy that assumes the methodical identification of the most efficient means of achieving specific goals.
>
> **Cost–benefit analysis:** An effort to make decisions on the basis of a systematic review of the relative costs and benefits of available options.

This is, of course, an unrealistic counsel of perfection, because it requires policy-makers to foresee the

unforeseeable and measure the unmeasurable. So, the rational model offers a theoretical yardstick, rather than a practical guide. Even so, techniques such as **cost–benefit analysis** (CBA) have been developed in an attempt to implement aspects of the rational model, and the results of such analyses can at least discourage policy-making driven solely by political appeal (Boardman *et al.*, 2010).

Seeking to analyse the costs and benefits associated with each possible decision does have strengths, particularly when a choice must be made from a small set of options. Specifically, CBA brings submerged assumptions to the surface, benefiting those interests that would otherwise lack political clout; for example, the benefit to the national economy from a new airport runway is factored in, not ignored by politicians overreacting to vociferous local opposition. In addition, CBA discourages symbolic policy-making which addresses a concern without attempting anything more specific; it also contributes to transparent policy-making by forcing decision-makers to account for policies whose costs exceed benefits.

For such reasons, CBA has been formally applied to every regulatory proposal in the United States expected to have a substantial impact on the economy. It has also played its part in the development of risk-based regulation in the United Kingdom, under which many regulators seek to focus their efforts on the main dangers, rather than mechanically applying the same rules to all. The cost–benefit principle here is to incur expenditure where it can deliver the greatest reduction in risk (Hutter, 2005).

However, CBA, and with it the rational model of policy formulation, also has weaknesses. It underplays soft factors such as fairness and the quality of life. It calculates the net distribution of costs and benefits but ignores their distribution across social groups. It is cumbersome, expensive, and time-consuming. It does not automatically incorporate estimates of the likelihood that claimed benefits will be achieved. There is often no agreement on what constitutes a cost and what constitutes a benefit.

Take, for example, the problem of air pollution. We know it exists (particularly in and around large urban areas), we know its sources, we have a good idea of how to control and prevent it, and we have a good idea of its potential impact on human life. There is little question that it causes health problems, and can reduce overall life expectancy. However, it affects people differently, because some have a greater capacity than others to live and function in a polluted environment. The precise links between pollution and illness or death are often unclear, we cannot be sure how much health care costs are impacted by higher levels of pollution, and it is hard to place a value on a human life, or – more specifically – on extending life expectancy (Guess and Farnham, 2011: ch. 7). It is also hard to calculate the relative costs and benefits of economic development that takes pollution control into account versus such development that does not. The result of difficulties is that, in the real political world, any conclusions from CBA may be over-ridden by broader, less clear-cut but more important considerations.

The incremental model

Where the rational model starts with goals, the **incremental model** starts with interests. Taking again the example of improved educational performance, an education secretary proceeding incrementally would consult with the various stakeholders, including teachers' unions, university administrations, and educational researchers. A consensus acceptable to all interests might emerge on how extra resources should be allocated. The long-term goals might not be measured or even specified, but we would assume that a policy acceptable to all is unlikely to be disastrous. Such an approach is policy-making by evolution, not revolution; an increment is literally a small increase in an existing sequence. It ties in to the idea of path dependence discussed in Chapter 6 (the outcome of a process depends on earlier decisions that lead policy down a particular path).

> **Incremental model:** An approach to policy-making that sees policy evolution as taking the form of small changes following negotiation with affected interests.

The incremental model was developed by Lindblom (1979) as part of a reaction against the rational model. Rather than viewing policy-making as a systematic trawl through all the options, and a focus on a single comprehensive plan, Lindblom argued that policy is continually remade in a series of minor adjustments to the existing direction, in a process that he described as 'the science of muddling through'. What matters here is that those involved should agree on policies, not objectives. Agreement can be reached on the desirability of following a particular course, even when objectives differ. Hence, policy emerges from, rather than precedes, negotiation with interested groups.

This approach may not lead to achieving grand objectives but, by taking one step at a time, it at least avoids making huge mistakes. Yet, the model also reveals its limits in situations that can only be remedied by strategic action. As Lindblom (1979, 1990) himself came to recognize, incremental policy-making deals with existing problems, rather than with avoiding future difficulties. It is politically safe, but unadventurous; remedial, rather than innovative. But the threat of ecological disaster, for instance, has arisen precisely from our failure to consider our long-term, cumulative impact on the environment. For the same reasons, incrementalism is better suited to stable high-income liberal democracies than to low-income countries seeking to transform themselves through development. It is pluralistic policy-making for normal times.

The garbage-can model

To understand the title of this model, we return to our example. How would the **garbage-can model** interpret policy-making to improve educational performance? The answer is that it would doubt the significance of such clear objectives. It would suggest that, within the government's education department, separate divisions and individuals engage in their own routine work, interacting through assorted committees whose composition varies over time. Static enrolments may be a concern of university administrators and solutions may be available elsewhere in the organization, perhaps in the form of people committed to online learning, or an expansion of financial aid. But whether participants with a solution encounter those with a problem, and in a way that generates a successful resolution, is hit and miss – as unpredictable and fluctuating as the arrangement of different types of garbage in a rubbish bin (Cohen *et al.*, 1972).

> **Garbage-can model:** An approach to understanding policy-making that emphasizes its partial, fluid, and disorganized qualities.

So, the garbage-can model presents an unsettling image of decision-making. Where both the rational and incremental models offer some prescription, the garbage-can expresses the perspective of a jaundiced realist. As described by Cohen *et al.*, it is 'a collection of choices looking for problems, issues and feelings looking for decision situations in which they might be aired, solutions looking for issues to which they might be the answer, and decision makers looking for work'. Policy-making is seen as partial, fluid, chaotic, anarchic, and incomplete. Organizations are conceived as loose collections of ideas, rather than as holders of clear preferences; they take actions which reveal rather than reflect their preferences. To the extent that problems are addressed at all, they have to wait their turn and join the queue. Actions, when taken, typically reflect the requirement for an immediate response in a specific area, rather than the pursuit of a definite policy goal. At best, some problems are partly addressed some of the time. The organization as a whole displays limited overall rationality – and little good will come until we recognize this fact (Bendor *et al.*, 2001).

This model can be difficult to grasp, a fact that shows how deeply our minds try to impose rationality on the policy process. Large, decentralized, public organizations such as universities perhaps provide the best illustrations. On most university campuses, decisions emerge from committees which operate largely independently. The energy-saving group may not know what instruments can achieve its goals, while the engineering faculty, fully informed about appropriate devices, may not know that the green committee exists. The committee on standards may want to raise overall admissions qualifications, while the equal opportunity group may be more interested in encouraging applications from minorities. Even within a single group, the position adopted may depend on which people happen to attend a meeting.

Government is of course a classic example of an entity that is both large and decentralized. It is not a single entity but, rather, an array of departments and agencies. Several government departments may deal with different aspects of a problem, with none having an overall perspective. Or one department may be charged with reducing pollution while another works to attract investments in new polluting factories. By considering the garbage-can model, we can see why we should be sceptical about statements beginning 'the government's policy is …'.

Clearly, the garbage-can model suggests that real policy-making is far removed from the rigours of rationality. Even on key issues, strong, sustained leadership is needed to impose a coherent response by government as a whole. Many presidents and prime ministers advocate joined-up government but few succeed in vanquishing the garbage-can. Often, rationality is a gloss paint applied to policy after it is agreed.

The policy cycle

One way of thinking about public policy is to see it as a cyclical series of stages. This risks painting a picture of an orderly sequence that is unmatched by political reality, but it helps impose some order on a phenomenon that is often enormously complex. There are various ways of outlining the cycle, one of which is to distinguish between initiation, formulation, implementation, evaluation, and review (see Figure 19.1). Of course, these divisions are more analytical than chronological, because – in the real world – they often overlap. So we must keep a sharp eye on political realities and avoid imposing logical sequences on complex realities. Nonetheless, a review of these stages will help to elaborate the particular focus of policy analysis, including its concern with what happens after a policy is agreed.

Initiation and formulation

Policies must start from somewhere, but identifying the point of departure is not easy. What we can say is that in liberal democracies much of the agenda bubbles up from below, delivered by bureaucrats in the form of issues demanding immediate attention. These requirements include the need to fix the unforeseen impacts

FOCUS 19.1 | Policy instruments

As well as understanding how policies are made, it is also important to understand the tools that government have available. In short, how exactly do governments govern? The answer gives us insight into the complexity of governance.

It might seem as though a legislature can establish a legal entitlement to a welfare benefit, for example, and then arrange for local governments to pay out the relevant sum to those who are eligible. In reality, however, legislation and direct provision are just two of many policy instruments and by no means the most common. Consider the example of efforts to reduce tobacco consumption (Table 19.2). Policy instruments can be classified as sticks (sanctions), carrots (rewards), and sermons (information and persuasion) (Vedung, 1998). Sticks include traditional command-and-control functions, such as banning or limiting the use of tobacco. Carrots include financial incentives such as subsidising the use of nicotine replacement products. Sermons include that stalwart of agencies seeking to show their concern: the public information campaign. The list in the table is by no means comprehensive; Osborne and Gaebler (1992) have identified more than 30 different policy devices.

In addition to these traditional tools, market-based instruments (MBIs) have emerged as an interesting addition to the repertoire of policy instruments. Programmes such as tradable pollution permits and auctions are increasingly used in environmental policy, for example: limits are set on emissions, and companies or countries that fall below the limits can sell the 'right' to pollute to those that fail to meet the limits. This way, there is a financial benefit to cutting emissions, and a financial penalty to pay for exceeding the limits. In theory, MBIs resolve the conflict between regulation and markets; they aim to regulate by creating new, if in reality often imperfect, markets (Huber *et al.*, 1998).

Given a range of tools, how should policy-makers choose between them? In practice, instrument selection is strongly influenced by past practice, by national policy styles, and by political factors, such as visibility (something must be seen to be done). Policy-makers can also review questions such as effectiveness, efficiency, equity, appropriateness, and simplicity. Since most policies use a combination of tools, the overall configuration should also be addressed. Instruments should not exert opposite effects and they should form a sequence such that, for example, information campaigns come before direct regulation of behaviour (Salamon, 2002).

TABLE 19.2: Policy instruments: the example of tobacco

	Type	Content
Command and control	Legislation	Authorizing the health department to take measures to limit passive smoking.
	Regulation	Banning tobacco consumption in restaurants.
Services	Public	Funding public health clinics to provide smoking cessation sessions.
	Private	Paying private agencies to run smoking cessation sessions.
Finance	Taxation	Taxing tobacco products.
	Subsidy	Offering a rebate on purchases of nicotine replacement products.
Advocacy	Information	Launching a publicity campaign about the harmful effects of smoking.
	Persuasion	Launching a publicity campaign to encourage people to stop smoking.
	Civil society	Creating and funding anti-smoking groups.

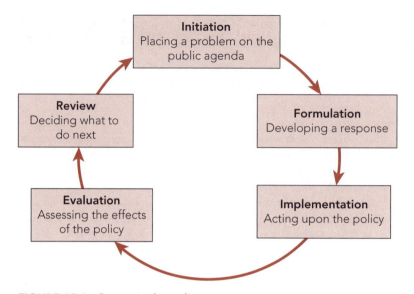

FIGURE 19.1: Stages in the policy process

of earlier decisions, leading to the notion of policy as its own cause (Wildavsky, 1979: 62). For example, once a new highway is opened, additional action will be needed to combat the spillover effects of congestion, accidents, and pollution.

Rather like the development of law, public policy naturally tends to thicken over time; the workload increases, and cases of withdrawal – such as abolishing government regulations – are uncommon. In addition, much political business, including the annual budget, occurs on a regular cycle, dictating attention at certain times. So, policy-makers find that routine business always presses; in large measure, they respond to an agenda that drives itself.

Within that broad characterization, policy initiation differs somewhat between the United States and European (and other party-led) liberal democracies. In the pluralistic world of American politics, success for a proposal depends on the opening of policy windows, such as the opportunities created by the election of a new administration. This policy window creates the possibility of innovation in a system biased against radical change. Thus, Kingdon (2010) suggests that **policy entrepreneurs** help to seize the moment. Like surfers, these initiators must ride the big wave by convincing the political elite not only of the scale of the problem, but also of the timeliness of their proposal for its resolution.

Policy entrepreneurs: Those who promote new policies or policy ideas, by raising the profile of an issue, framing how it is discussed, or demonstrating new ways of applying old ideas.

From this perspective, interest group leaders succeed by linking their own preferred policies to a wider narrative; try to save the whale and you will be seen, rightly or wrongly, as concerned about the environment generally. Develop proposals for skills training and you will be seen to be addressing the bigger question of economic competitiveness. However, policy openings soon close: the cycle of attention to a particular issue is short, as political debate and the public mood moves on. Concepts such as *policy entrepreneur* and *policy opening* carry less resonance in the more structured, party-based democracies of Europe. Here, the political agenda is under firmer, if still incomplete, control, and party manifestos and coalition agreements set out a more explicit agenda for government.

Normally, policy-formers operate within a narrow range of options, and will seek solutions which are consistent with broader currents of opinion and previous policies within the sector. Compare American attitudes to medical care with those in the rest of the industrialized world, for example. In the United States, any health care reforms (including those achieved by President Obama) must respect the American preference for private provision. Reformers have faced consistent opposition from labour unions, the medical community, the health insurance industry, and political conservatives. In every other major democracy, by contrast, public health care is entrenched, either in public provision (e.g. Britain's National Health Service) or more often through collective health insurance schemes. The general point is that policy formulation is massively constrained by earlier decisions in a path dependent fashion.

Implementation

After a policy has been agreed, it must be put into effect – an obvious point, of course, except that much traditional political science stops at the point where government reaches a decision, ignoring the numerous difficulties which arise in putting policy into practice. Probably the main achievement of policy analysis has been to direct attention to these problems of implementation. No longer can execution be dismissed by Woodrow Wilson (1887) as 'mere administration'. Policy is as policy does.

Turning a blind eye to implementation can still be politically convenient. Often, the political imperative is just to have a policy; whether it works, in some further sense, is neither here nor there. Coalition governments, in particular, are often based on elaborate agreements between parties on what is to be done. This bible must be obeyed, even if its commandments are expensive, ineffective, and outdated.

But there is a political risk in sleepwalking into implementation failure. For example, the British government's failure to prevent mad cow disease from crossing the species barrier to humans in the late 1980s was a classic instance of this error. Official committees instructed abattoirs to remove infective material from slaughtered cows but, initially, took no special steps to ensure these plans were carried out carefully. As a result of incompetence in slaughterhouses, the disease agent continued to enter the human food chain, killing over 170 people by 2012 (Ncjdrsu, 2012). The standing of the government of the day suffered accordingly.

We can distinguish two philosophies of implementation: top-down and bottom-up. The **top-down** approach represents the traditional view. Within this limited perspective, the question posed is the classical problem of bureaucracy: how to ensure political direction of unruly public servants. Ministers come and go, and find it hard to secure compliance from departments already committed to pet projects of their own. Without vigilance from on high, sound policies can be hijacked by lower-level officials committed to existing procedures, diluting the impact of new initiatives (Hogwood and Gunn, 1984).

This top-down approach focused excessively on control and compliance. As with the rational model of policy-making from which it sprang, it was unrealistic, and even counter-productive. Hence the emergence of the contrasting **bottom-up** perspective, with its starting point that policy-makers should try to engage, rather than control, those who translate policy into practice. Writers in this tradition, such as Hill and Hupe (2002), ask: what if circumstances have changed since the policy was formulated? And what if the policy itself is poorly designed? Much legislation, after all, is based on uncertain information and is highly general in content. Often, it cannot be followed to the letter because there is no letter to follow.

> **Top-down implementation:** Conceives the task of policy implementation as ensuring that policy execution delivers the outputs and outcomes specified by the policy-makers.

> **Bottom-up implementation:** Judges that those who execute policy should be encouraged to adapt to local and changing circumstances.

Many policy analysts now suggest that objectives are more likely to be met if those who execute policy are given not only encouragement and resources, but also flexibility. Setting one specific target for an organization expected to deliver multiple goals simply leads to unbalanced delivery. Only what gets measured, gets done.

Furthermore, at street level – the point where policy is delivered – policy emerges from interaction between local bureaucrats and affected groups. Here, at the sharp end, goals can often be best achieved by adapting them to local circumstances. For instance, policies on education, health care, and policing will differ between rural areas and the inner city. If a single national policy is left unmodified, its fate will be that of the mighty dragon in the Chinese proverb: no match for the neighbourhood snake.

Further, local implementers will often be the only people with full knowledge of how policies interact. They will know that, if two policies possess incompatible goals, something has to give. They will know the significant actors in the locality, including the for-profit and voluntary agencies involved in policy execution. Implementation is often a matter of building relationships between organizations operating in the field, an art which is rarely covered in central manuals. The idea of all politics being local, quoted in Chapter 11, applies with particular force to policy implementation.

So, a bottom-up approach reflects an incremental view of policy-making in which implementation is seen as policy-making by other means. This approach is also attuned to the contemporary emphasis on governance, with its stress on the many stakeholders involved in the policy process. The challenge is to ensure that local coalitions work for the policy, rather than forming a conspiracy against it.

Evaluation

Just as policy analysis has increased awareness of the importance of policy implementation, so too has it sharpened the focus on evaluation. The task of policy evaluation is to work out whether a programme has achieved its goals and if so how efficiently and effectively.

Public policies, and the organizations created to put them into practice, lack the clear yardstick of profitability used in the private sector. How do we appraise a defence department if there are no wars and, therefore, no win-loss record? Which is the most successful police force: the one that solves the greatest number of crimes, or the one that has the fewest crimes to solve?

Evaluation is complicated further because, as we have seen, goals are often modified during implementation, transforming a failing policy into a different but more successful one. This 'mushiness of goals', to use Kettl's phrase (2011: 287), means that the intent of policy-makers is often a poor benchmark for evaluation. Consider the case of the European Union's attempts to inject more rapid growth into the European economy. Much was made of the launch in 2000 of the Lisbon Strategy, whose goal was to make the EU 'the most dynamic and competitive knowledge-based economy in the world within a decade'. It soon became clear that member states were failing to make the necessary changes (such as reducing regulation

and opening markets), so the Lisbon Strategy was transformed into the Europe 2020 strategy, changing some of the specific goals and extending the target by a decade.

The question of evaluation has often been ignored by governments. Sweden is a typical case. In the postwar decades, a succession of social democratic administrations concentrated on building a universal welfare state without even conceiving of a need to evaluate the efficiency and effectiveness with which services were delivered by an expanding bureaucracy. In France and Germany, and other continental European countries where bureaucratic tasks are interpreted in legalistic fashion, the issue of policy evaluation still barely surfaces – often to the detriment of long-suffering citizens.

Yet, without some evaluation, governments are unable to learn the lessons of experience. In the United States, Jimmy Carter (president, 1977–81) did insist that at least 1 per cent of the funds allocated to any project should be devoted to evaluation; he wanted more focus on what policies achieved. In the 1990s, once more, evaluation began to return to the fore. For example, the Labour government elected in Britain in 1997 claimed a new pragmatic concern with evidence-based policy: what mattered, it claimed, was what worked. In some other democracies, too, public officials began to think, often for the first time, about how best to evaluate the programmes they administered.

> **Policy outputs:** The actions of government, which are relatively easily identified and measured.

> **Policy outcomes:** The achievements of government, which are more difficult to confirm and measure.

Evaluation studies distinguish between **policy outputs** and **policy outcomes**. Outputs are easily measured by quantitative indicators of activities: visits, trips, treatments, inspections. The danger is that outputs turn into targets; the focus becomes what was done, rather than what was achieved. So, outcomes – the actual results – should be a more important component of evaluation. The problem is that outcomes are easier to define than to measure; they are highly resistant to change and, as a result, the cost per unit of impact can be extraordinarily high, with gains often proving to be only temporary. Further, outcomes can be manipulated by agencies seeking to portray their performance in the best light. They have multiple devious devices available to them, including creaming, offloading, and reframing (see Table 19.3).

With social programmes, in particular, a creaming process often dilutes the impact. For example, an addiction treatment centre will find it easiest to reach those users who would have been most likely to overcome their drug use anyway. The agency will want to chalk up as successes cases to which it did not, in fact, make the decisive difference. Meanwhile, the hardest cases remain unreached. Just as regulated companies are usually in a position to outwit their regulator, so too do public agencies finesse measured outcomes using their unique knowledge of their policy sector.

The stickiness of social reality means that attempts to 'remedy the deficiencies in the quality of human life' can never be a complete success. Indeed, they can be, and sometimes are, a total failure (Rossi *et al.*, 2003: 6). If our expectations of a policy's outcomes were more realistic, we might be less disappointed with limited results. So, we can understand why agencies evaluating their own programmes often prefer to describe their impressive outputs, rather than their limited outcomes.

Just as policy implementation in accordance with the top-down model is unrealistic, so judging policy effectiveness against specific objectives is often an implausibly scientific approach to evaluation. A more bottom-up, incremental approach to evaluation has therefore emerged. Here, the goals are more modest: to gather the opinions of all the stakeholders affected by the policy, generating a qualitative narrative rather than a barrage of output-based statistics. As Parsons (1995: 567) describes this approach, 'evaluation has to be predicated on wide and full collaboration of all programme stakeholders including funders, implementers and beneficiaries'.

In such evaluations, the varying objectives of different interests are welcomed. They are not dismissed as a barrier to objective scrutiny of policy. Unintended effects can be written back into the script, not excluded because they are irrelevant to the achievement of stated goals. This is a more pragmatic, pluralistic, and incremental approach. The stakeholders might agree on the success of a policy even though they disagree on the standards against which it should be judged. The object of a bottom-up evaluation can simply be to learn from the project, rather than to make uncertain judgements of success.

But such evaluations can become games of framing, blaming, and claiming: politics all over again, with the most powerful stakeholder securing the most favourable write-up. To prevent the evaluation of a project from turning into an application for continued funding, evaluation studies should include external independent scrutiny.

Review

Once a policy has been evaluated, or even if it has not, three options are left: continue, revise, or terminate. Most policies – or, at least, the functions associated with them – continue with only minor revisions. Once a role for government is established, it tends to continue, even if the agencies charged with performing the function might change over time, either because a task is split between two or more agencies, or because previously separate functions are consolidated into a single organization (Bauer *et al.*, 2012). So the observation that there is nothing so permanent as a temporary government organization appears to be wide of the mark.

TABLE 19.3: Manipulating policy outcomes

	Definition	Example, using an employment service
Creaming	Give most help to the easiest clients.	Focus on those unemployed clients who are most employable.
Offloading	Keep difficult cases off the books, or remove them.	Decline to take on unemployed people with mental health difficulties, or remove them from the list.
Reframing	Relabel the category.	Where plausible, remove unemployed people from the labour market by treating them as unemployable or disabled.

Source: Adapted from Rein (2006)

SPOTLIGHT

SWEDEN

Population (9.6 million)

Gross National Income ($580 billion)

Per capita GNI ($61,760)

Democracy Index rating

Not Yet Rated	Hybrid Regime	Full Democracy
	Authoritarian	Flawed Democracy

Freedom House rating

Not Free	Partly free	Free

Human Development Index rating

Not Rated	Medium	Very High
	Low	High

Brief Profile: Sweden ranks at or near the top of international league tables focused on democracy, political stability, economic development, education, and social equality; in this sense, it can be seen as one of the most successful countries addressed in this book. The Social Democrats have held a plurality in the Swedish parliament since 1917, and Sweden traditionally lacked significant internal divisions other than class. However, a recent influx of immigrants and asylum-seekers means that one in six of the population was born in another country (notably Syria), raising integration concerns. Even so, the country combines a high standard of living with a comparatively equal distribution of income, showing – with other Scandinavian states – that mass affluence and limited inequality are compatible. Meanwhile, Sweden is neutral in international affairs, remaining outside NATO but becoming a member of the European Union in 1995.

Form of government ⇨ Unitary parliamentary constitutional monarchy. Date of state formation debatable, and oldest element of constitution dates from 1810.

Legislature ⇨ Unicameral Riksdag ('meeting of the realm') with 349 members, elected for renewable four-year terms.

Executive ⇨ Parliamentary. The head of government is the prime minister, who is head of the largest party or coalition, and governs in conjunction with a cabinet. The head of state is the monarch.

Judiciary ⇨ The constitution consists of four entrenched laws: the Instrument of Government, the Act of Succession, the Freedom of the Press Act, and the Fundamental Law on Freedom of Expression. The Supreme Court (16 members appointed until retirement at the age of 67) is traditionally restrained.

Electoral system ⇨ The Riksdag is elected by party list proportional representation, with an additional tier of seats used to enhance proportionality. The national vote threshold (the share of votes needed to be awarded any seats) is 4 per cent.

Parties ⇨ Multi-party. The Social Democrats were historically the leading party, sharing their position on the left with the Left Party and the Greens. However, a centre-right coalition (led by the conservative Moderates and including the Centre Party, the Christian Democrats, and the Liberals) has recently gained ground.

➡

Yet, even if agency termination is surprisingly common, the intriguing question remains: why is policy termination so rare? Why does government as a whole seem to prefer to adopt new functions than to drop old ones? Bardach (1976) suggests five possible explanations:

- Policies are designed to last a long time, creating expectations of future benefits.
- Policy termination brings conflicts which leave too much blood on the floor.
- No one wants to admit the policy was a bad idea.

Public policy in Sweden

Swedish policy-making was once described as 'open, rationalistic, consensual and extraordinarily deliberative' (Anton, 1969: 94). Later, Richardson *et al.* (1982) characterized Sweden's policy style as anticipatory and consensus-seeking. How do these two interpretations stand up in Sweden today?

They both remain fundamentally correct, from a comparative perspective. Even in a small unitary state with sovereignty firmly based on a unicameral legislature, Sweden has avoided the potential for centralization and has developed an elaborate negotiating democracy which is culturally and institutionally secure.

One factor sustaining this distinctive policy style is the compact size and policy focus of Sweden's 12 central government departments, which together employ less than 5,000 staff. Their core task is to 'assist the Government in supplying background material for use as a basis for decisions and in conducting inquiries into both national and international matters' (Regeringskansliet, 2015). Most technical issues, meanwhile, and the services provided by the extensive welfare state, are contracted out to more than 300 public agencies and to local government. This division of tasks requires extensive collaboration between public institutions, and is sustained by high levels of transparency and trust.

Committees of enquiry (also known as 'commissions') are key to policy making. Typically, the government appoints a committee to research a topic and present recommendations. Committees usually comprise a chair and advisers but can include opposition members of the Riksdag, or even – sometimes – just one person. The commission consults with relevant interests and political parties, its recommendations are published and discussed, the relevant ministry examines the report, a government bill is drafted if needed (and presented with a summary of comments received), and the bill is then discussed in the Riksdag, where it may be modified before reaching the statute book. This procedure is slow, but it is also highly rational (in that information is collected and analysed) and incremental (in that organized opponents of the proposal are given ample opportunity to voice their concerns).

There are downsides – extensive deliberation may contribute to bland policy, and the strong emphasis on policy formulation may be at the expense of insufficient focus on implementation – but the style is distinctively Swedish. It offers a useful yardstick against which to compare the less measured policy-making styles found in other liberal democracies.

- Policy termination may affect other programmes and interests.
- Politics rewards innovation rather than tidy housekeeping.

Policy diffusion and convergence

Once, there were no speed limits, no seat belts, no nutritional labels, no restrictions on advertising cigarettes, no gender quotas for party candidates, and no state subsidies for political parties. Now, there are. Most democracies have introduced broadly similar policies in these and many other areas – and often at a similar time. So, how did they move in tandem from then to now? The answer lies in a combination of **policy diffusion** (Dolowitz and Marsh, 1996; Rose, 2005) and **policy convergence**. The former describes the phenomenon of policy programmes spreading from one country to another, though with less emphasis on deliberate emulation than is suggested by related terms such as policy transfer, policy learning, or lesson-drawing. The latter refers to a tendency for policies to become more similar across countries, a phenomenon which can occur without explicit diffusion if different countries just respond to common problems (e.g. an ageing population) in a similar way (e.g. raising the age of retirement). Both diffusion and convergence usefully address the comparative dimension in public policy analysis.

Policy diffusion: The tendency for policy programmes to spread across countries.

Policy convergence: The tendency for policies in different countries to become more alike.

Although policy diffusion has attracted attention as an example of international influence on national policy, examples of countries clearly emulating innovations from abroad remain thin on the ground. In theory, the whole world could be a laboratory for testing policy innovation; in practice, most policy-making still runs in a national groove. How, then, do we explain why convergence occurs without explicit emulation? In other words, why do democracies adopt broadly similar policies in the same time period without the self-aware learning from abroad that policy convergence suggests?

A useful point of departure is offered by Rogers (2003), whose analysis distinguishes between a few innovators and early adopters, the majority (divided into two groups by time of adoption), and a small number of laggards, with non-adopters excluded (see Figure 19.2). Although not designed with cross-national policy diffusion in mind, this analysis allows us to interpret the spread of a particular policy and to ask why certain countries are innovators, either in a particular case, or in general. Innovation is perhaps most likely to emerge in high-income countries with (a) the most acute manifestation of a specific problem, (b) the resources to commit to a new policy, and (c) the governance capacity to authorize and deliver. A new government with fresh ideas and a desire to make its mark is an effective catalyst.

Knill and Tosun (2012: 275) identify a series of factors encouraging policy convergence (Table 19.4).

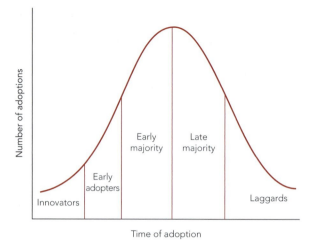

FIGURE 19.2: The diffusion of innovation
Source: Adapted from Rogers (1962)

Of these, *independent problem-solving* is one of the more significant: as countries modernize, they develop similar problems calling for a policy response. At an early stage of development, for example, issues such as urban squalor, inadequate education, and the need for social security force themselves onto the agenda. The problems of development come later: the epidemic of obesity, for example, or the rising social cost of care for the elderly. In national responses to such difficulties, we often see policy-making in parallel, rather than by diffusion. Even if the response in one country is influenced

TABLE 19.4: Mechanisms for policy convergence

	Effect	Example
Independent problem-solving	As countries develop, similar problems emerge, often resulting in similar policies.	Under-regulated industrialization leads to air and water pollution.
International agreements	National policies converge as countries seek to comply with international laws, regulations, and standards.	Membership of the World Trade Organization imposes common rules on member states.
International competition	Policies providing an economic or political advantage will be replicated elsewhere.	Privatization of state-owned enterprises has spread throughout the developed world, with New Zealand and the UK among the innovators.
Policy learning	Explicit lesson-drawing can occur even when no competitive advantage ensues.	Capital punishment is abolished because evidence from other countries indicates a limited impact on crime rates.
Coercion and conditionality	One country makes policy requirements of another, for example in return for aid.	Reforms imposed on Greece initially in 2010, in return for financial help in responding to the debt crisis.

Source: Adapted from Knill and Tosun (2012: table 11.5)

by policy innovations elsewhere, it is still the need to respond to domestic problems that drives policy.

In addition, policy convergence can result from conformity to the ever-expanding array of *international agreements*. Covering everything from the design of nuclear reactors to the protection of prisoner rights, these are agreed by national governments and monitored by intergovernmental organizations. Signing up to such agreements is voluntary, and the content may be shaped by the strongest states (the standard-makers rather than the standard-takers), but international norms remain a strong factor in encouraging policy convergence.

Moving beyond formal international regulation, *international competition* generates pressures to emulate winning policies. Here, an expanding supply of league tables produced by international bodies provides benchmarks that can have the effect of nudging governments in the direction favoured by the producer. One of those is the World Bank's Doing Business Index, which ranks countries based on criteria such as the ease of starting a business, registering a property, and securing an electricity supply. Table 19.5 lists the top ten countries in the 2014 league, along with the other cases used in this book, and – for context – last-placed Eritrea.

In the competition for foreign direct investment, for instance, what government would want to occupy a lowly position in the World Bank's table? Note, however, that there is more than one way to skin a rabbit. In seeking overseas investment, some governments emphasize workforce quality (a race to the top), while others give priority to low labour costs (a race to the bottom). Competition generates similar pressures but not identical policies; rather, it encourages countries to exploit their natural advantages, yielding divergence, rather than convergence.

The fourth mechanism behind policy convergence is direct *policy learning*, which may also be the weakest such mechanism. Governments do not select from a full slate of options but must operate in the context of national debates and their own past decisions. So, tweaking is more common than wholesale copying, and three conditions apply:

- Foreign models are only likely to be considered seriously when the domestic agenda seems to be incapable of resolving a problem. Even then, the search will not be global but will focus on similar or neighbouring countries with which the learning country has a long-standing and friendly relationship.

TABLE 19.5: The Doing Business Index

	Country
1	Singapore
2	New Zealand
3	Hong Kong*
4	Denmark
5	South Korea
6	Norway
7	United States
8	UK
9	Finland
10	Australia
14	Germany
16	Canada
29	Japan
31	France
39	Mexico
43	South Africa
62	Russia
90	China
112	Egypt
120	Brazil
130	Iran
142	India
170	Nigeria
189	Eritrea

* Hong Kong often appears in league tables of this kind, even though it is not an independent state, but a Special Administrative Region of China.

Source: Doing Business (2015). Data are for 2014.

- Policies themselves often evolve in the process of diffusion; they are translated rather than transported. Even if a government does cite foreign examples, it may be to justify a policy adopted for domestic political reasons. In general, governments find it more difficult to learn than do individuals.

- Lesson-drawing can be negative as well as positive, because models to avoid are generally more visible than those worth emulating. Germany's hyper-inflation in the 1920s and Japan's lost decades of the 1990s and 2000s continue to offer warnings that influence economic policy-makers throughout the developed world, while few countries have shown a desire to reproduce Britain's National Health Service, with its delivery of medical care through a gigantic nationalized industry.

While Knill and Tosun do not include this in their list, *coercion* and the imposing of conditions by one country on another can also be an important element in policy convergence. In extreme cases, victory in war allows the dominant power to impose its vision on vanquished states, as with the forced construction of democracy in Germany and Japan by the victorious allies after the Second World War. More commonly, economic vulnerability gives weak countries little choice but to submit to more powerful countries and to international organizations. For example, the practice of attaching strings to aid became an important theme in international politics in the 1990s, after many developing countries had become massively indebted to Western banks. Similarly, international creditors including the International Monetary Fund sought to impose challenging reforms on Greece in 2010 in an effort to reduce that country's severe financial indebtedness. The difficulty with coercion as a policy-shaping instrument is that the receiving country may lack genuine commitment to the reforms, leading to their failure over the long term.

One conclusion is that we should think in terms of the diffusion of ideas rather than policies. Even if policies remain attached to national anchors, ideas – at least for stronger states – know no boundaries. Broad agendas (where do we need policy?) and frameworks (how should we think about this area?) are often transnational in character and refined by discussions in international organizations. Ideas provide a climate within which national policies are made, whether or not national policy-makers are aware of this influence. In public policy, as in politics generally, ideas matter even if their influence is difficult to analyse on other than a case-by-case basis.

Public policy in authoritarian states

The central theme in the policy process of many non-democratic regimes is the subservience of policy to politics. Often, the key task for non-elected rulers is to play off domestic political forces against each other so as to ensure their own continuation in office. Uncertain

of their own long-term survival in office, authoritarian rulers may want to enrich themselves, their family, and their support group while they remain in control of the state's resources. These related goals of political survival and personal enrichment are hardly conducive to orderly policy development. As Hershberg (2006: 151) says:

> To be successful, policies must reflect the capabilities – encompassing expertise, resources and authority – of the institutions and individuals charged with their implementation. Those capabilities are more likely to be translated into effective performance in environments characterized by predictable, transparent and efficient procedures for reaching decisions and for adjudicating differences of interest.

But it is precisely these 'predictable, transparent and efficient procedures' that authoritarian regimes are often unable to supply. Frequently, opaque patronage is the main political currency; the age-old game of creating and benefiting from political credits works against clear procedures of any kind. The result is a conservative preference for the existing rules of the game, an indifference to policy and a lack of interest in national development. As Chazan *et al.* (1999: 171) note in discussing Africa, 'patriarchal rule has tended to be conservative: it propped up the existing order and did little to promote change. It required the exertion of a great deal of energy just to maintain control'.

In addition, rulers may simply lack the ability to make coherent policy. As a group, authoritarian rulers are less well-educated than the leaders of liberal democracies. This weakness was especially common in military regimes whose leaders frequently lacked formal education and managerial competence. The generals sometimes seized power in an honest attempt to improve public policy-making but then discovered that good governance required skills they did not possess.

Policy inertia is therefore often a standard pattern under authoritarian rule. Stagnation is reinforced when, as in many of the largest non-democracies, the rulers engage in **rent-seeking**, often using their control over natural commodities such as oil or rare minerals as their main source of revenue. For example, government officials might take bribes to provide a licence to a company, or a passport to a citizen, benefiting both buyer and seller, but imposing a hidden tax on the economy and society. In these circumstances, the government need not achieve the penetration of society required to

> ┌─ **FOCUS 19.2** │ **The resource curse**

A particular problem that skews policy in several authoritarian states is the so-called **resource curse** (Auty, 1993; Collier and Bannon, 2003). This exists when a country is particularly well-endowed in a resource that could and should be the foundation for economic development, but instead alters the economic and political balance such as to reduce economic growth below the expected level. Oil has turned out to be just such a problem for several sub-Saharan African states, such as Nigeria, Angola, Equatorial Guinea, the Republic of the Congo, Gabon, Chad, and Sudan. It is also a factor in countries rich in easily exploitable minerals such as copper or uranium, or in precious gems such as diamonds.

The policy element of the 'curse' stems from four main factors:

- Because these resources are usually relatively easy to exploit and can bring quick and often profitable returns, a state will focus its development efforts almost entirely in that sector, investing little in other sectors; this is the so-called 'Dutch disease', named for the effects of the discovery of natural gas in the North Sea off the coast of the Netherlands in the 1970s (Humphreys et al., 2007). It will thereby have an imbalanced economy and will become dependent on a product whose value may be held hostage to fluctuations in its price on the international market.

- When a government can raise adequate revenue from simply taxing a major natural resource, it lacks incentive to improve economic performance by developing the skills of its people, thus damaging growth over the long run.

- The profits that come from these commodities can encourage theft and corruption, ensuring that they find their way into the bank accounts of the rich and powerful rather than being reinvested back into the community.

- The effect of the curse is to encourage internal conflict, when poorer regions of the country find that they are not benefiting equally from the profits of resources found in other parts of the country. In the most extreme cases, it can lead to violence and civil war.

Resource curse: A phenomenon by which a state that is well-endowed in a particular natural resource, or a limited selection of resources, nonetheless experiences low economic growth. Unbalanced policy, extensive corruption and internal conflict all contribute to the resource curse.

collect taxes, expand the economy, and develop human capital. Rather, a stand-off of mutual distrust develops between rulers and ruled, creating a context which is incompatible with the more sophisticated policy initiatives found in many liberal democracies. In the absence of effective social policy at national level, problems of poverty, welfare, and medical care are addressed locally, if at all.

Rent-seeking: Seeking to make an income from selling a scarce resource without adding real value.

The absence of an extensive network of voluntary associations and interest groups in authoritarian states prevents the close coordination between state and society needed for effective policy-making and implementation. The blocking mechanism here is fear among rulers as much as the ruled. Saich (2015: 199) identifies these anxieties in the case of China's party elite:

> While it is true that public discourse is breaking free of the codes and linguistic phrases established by the party-state, it is also clear that no coherent alternative vision has emerged that would fashion a civil society. From the party's point of view, what is lurking in the shadows waiting to pounce on any opening that would allow freedom of expression is revivalism, religion, linguistic division, regional and non-Han ethnic loyalties.

As always, however, it is important to distinguish between different types of authoritarian government. At one extreme, many military and personal rulers show immense concern about their own prosperity but none at all for that of their country, leading to a policy shortage. At the other extreme, modernizing regimes whose ruling elite displays a clear sense of national goals and a secure hold on power follow long-term policies, especially for economic development. Such countries do not suffer from inertia, but instead find it easier to push through substantial policy change, because they can suppress the short-term demands that would arise in a more open political system.

China offers an example of the latter approach. It survives as an authoritarian regime partly because it pursues policies leading to rapid economic development. The capacity of the leadership of the Chinese Communist Party to form and implement coherent policy in the world's most populous country is a remarkable achievement. It owes much to political flexibility, the country's authoritarian tradition, and the legitimacy the regime has derived from economic growth. The leadership's sensitivity to public concerns, unusual in authoritarian regimes, is seen not only in the achievement of economic development but also in attempts to limit its unequal consequences. For example, the party's 2006 programme, Building a Harmonious Society, sought to reduce income inequality, improve access to medical care for rural-dwellers and urban migrants, extend social security, and contain the environmental damage from industrialization (Saich, 2015).

The story in Russia has been different. After the initially chaotic transition from communism, the country's rulers achieved considerable policy successes. A more predictable environment was created for business investment, a recentralization of power encouraged the more uniform application of a newly codified legal system, tax revenues improved, and social policy became more coherent with a controversial 2005 reform that replaced the bulk of Soviet-era privileges (such as free or subsidised housing, transportation, and medicine) with 'supposedly equivalent cash payments' (Twigg, 2005: 219).

But policy-making remains subject to the political requirements of the ruling elite. Industrialists who pose a political threat to President Putin still find that numerous rules and regulations are invoked selectively against them. The state has disposed of many enterprises but rent-seeking continues; the government has tightened its control over the oil and gas industries, political and economic power remain tightly interwoven, precluding – at the highest level – uniform policy implementation, and public control of export commodities enables the Russian elite to sustain its own position even if it neglects the development of closer connections with the Russian population. Meanwhile, social problems such as poverty, alcoholism, violent crime, and rural depopulation remain deep-rooted.

As in many poor countries, even-handed policy implementation is impossible in Russia because many public officials are so poorly paid that corruption remains an essential tool for making ends meet. It may be true that sunlight is the best disinfectant, but the improved policy process enabled by an escape from corruption and rent-seeking cannot be achieved simply by calling for more transparency. The dilemma is that transparency flows naturally from broad-based economic development, but such development itself requires a reduction in corruption.

DISCUSSION QUESTIONS

- Which of the three models of the policy process offers the most insight into the policy process, and how does their utility vary by policy issue?

- Which policy instruments are likely to be most effective in reducing (a) obesity, (b) drug addiction, (c) texting while driving, and (d) climate change?

- What additional steps, if any, would you add to the policy cycle?

- Given the uncertainties of policy-making, why do politicians keep making unrealistic promises, and why do voters keep accepting them?

- Why does policy often fail to achieve its objectives?

- Can you identify any public policies in your country which were (a) adapted from, or (b) influenced by, policies in other countries?

KEY CONCEPTS

Bottom-up implementation
Cost–benefit analysis
Garbage-can model
Incremental model
Policy analysis
Policy convergence
Policy diffusion
Policy entrepreneurs

Policy outcomes
Policy outputs
Public policy
Rational model
Rent-seeking
Resource curse
Top-down implementation

FURTHER READING

Birkland, Thomas A. (2010) *An Introduction to the Policy Process: Theories, Concepts and Models of Public Making*, 3rd edn. A thematic introduction to public policy with a particular focus on policy stages.

Dodds, Anneliese (2013) *Comparative Public Policy*. A survey of comparison in public policy, with chapters on specific issues such as economic, welfare and environmental policy.

Eliadis, Pearl, Margaret M. Hill, and Michael Howlett (eds) (2005) *Designing Government: From Instruments to Governance*. This book provides a detailed examination of policy instruments.

Knill, Christoph and Jale Tosun (2012) *Public Policy: A New Introduction*. A thematic overview of public policy, emphasizing theories and concepts.

Rose, Richard (2005) *Learning from Comparative Public Policy: A Practical Guide*. An influential examination of how countries can learn from each other about the successes and failures of policy initiatives.

Sabatier, Paul A. and Christopher M. Weible (eds) (2014) *Theories of the Policy Process,* 3rd edn. A survey and comparison of theoretical approaches to the policy process.

References

A

Aarts, Kees, André Blais, and Hermann Schmitt (eds) (2011) *Political Leaders and Democratic Elections* (Oxford: Oxford University Press).

Aberbach, Joel, Robert Putnam, and Bert Rockman (1981) *Bureaucrats and Politicians in Western Democracies* (Cambridge, MA: Harvard University Press).

Addis, Casey L. (2009) *Iran's 2009 Presidential Elections* (Washington, DC: Congressional Research Service).

Adman, Per (2009) 'The Puzzle of Gender-Equal Political Participation in Sweden: The Importance of Norms and Mobilization', in *Scandinavian Political Studies* 32:3, September, pp. 315–36.

Akkerman, Tjitske (2012) 'Comparing Radical Right Parties in Government: Immigration and Integration Policies in Nine Countries, 1966–2010', in *West European Politics* 35:3, May, pp. 511–29.

Albrecht, Holger (2008) 'The Nature of Political Participation', in Ellen Lust-Okar and Saloua Zerhouni (eds) *Political Participation in the Middle East* (Boulder, CO: Lynne Rienner), pp. 15–32.

Almond, Gabriel A. (1966) 'Political Theory and Political Science', in *American Political Science Review* 60:4, December, pp. 869–79.

Almond, Gabriel A, and Sidney Verba (1963) *The Civic Culture* (Princeton, NJ: Princeton University Press).

Althaus, Scott L. (2003) *Collective Preferences in Democratic Politics: Opinion Surveys and the Will of the People* (New York: Cambridge University Press).

Alvarez, Angel E. (2004) 'State Reform Before and After Chávez's Election', in Steve Ellner and Daniel Hellinger (eds) *Venezuelan Politics in the Chávez Era: Class, Polarization and Conflict* (Boulder, CO: Lynne Rienner), pp. 147–60.

Anderson, Benedict (1983) *Imagined Communities: Reflections on the Origins and Spread of Nationalism* (London: Verso).

Andeweg, Rudy B., and Galen A. Irwin (2009) *Governance and Politics of the Netherlands*, 3rd edn (Basingstoke: Palgrave Macmillan).

Ansell, Christopher and Jane Gingrich (2003) 'Reforming the Administrative State', in Bruce E. Cain, Russell J. Dalton and Susan E. Scarrow (eds) *Democracy Transformed? Expanding Political Opportunities in Advanced Industrial Democracies* (New York: Oxford University Press), pp. 164–91.

Ansolabehere, Stephen (2006) 'Voters, Candidates and Parties', in Barry R. Weingast and Donald A. Wittman (eds) *The Oxford Handbook of Political Economy* (Oxford: Oxford University Press), pp. 29–49.

Anton, Thomas J. (1969) 'Policy-Making and Political Culture in Sweden', in *Scandinavian Political Studies* 4:A4, January, pp. 82–102.

Apter, David E. (1965) *The Politics of Modernization* (Chicago: University of Chicago Press).

Aristotle (1962 edn) *The Politics*, trans. T. A. Sinclair (Harmondsworth: Penguin).

Armitage, David (2005) 'The Contagion of Sovereignty: Declarations of Independence since 1776', *South African Historical Journal* 52:1, pp. 1–18.

Auty, Richard M. (1993) *Sustaining Development in Mineral Economies: The Resource Curse Thesis* (London: Routledge).

B

Bachrach, Peter and Morton S. Baratz (1962) 'The Two Faces of Power', in *American Political Science Review* 56:4, December, pp. 941–52.

Bagehot, Walter (1867) [1963 edn] *The English Constitution* (London: Fontana).

Barber, Benjamin R. (1995) *Jihad vs. McWorld: Terrorism's Challenge to Democracy* (New York: Ballantine Books).

Barber, James David (1992) *The Pulse of Politics: Electing Presidents in the Media Age* (New Brunswick, NY: Transaction Books).

Bardach, Eugene (1976) 'Policy Termination as a Political Process', in *Policy Sciences* 7:2, June, pp. 123–31.

Bardes, Barbara, Mack C. Shelley, and Steffen W. Schmidt (2014) *American Government and Politics Today*, 2013–14 edn (Boston, MA: Wadsworth).

Bates, Robert H., Avner Greif, Margaret Levi, Jean-Laurent Rosenthal, and Barry R. Weingast (eds) (1998) *Analytic Narratives* (Princeton, NJ: Princeton University Press).

Bauer, Gretchen and Manon Tremblay (eds) (2011) *Women in Executive Power: A Global Overview* (Abingdon: Routledge).

Bauer, Michael W., Andrew Jordan, Christoffer Green-Pedersen, and Adrienne Héritier (eds) (2012) *Dismantling Public Policy: Preferences, Strategies, and Effects* (Oxford: Oxford University Press).

Baum, Christopher H. and Andrea Di Maio (2000) *Gartner's Four Phases of E-Government* (Stanford, CA: Gartner).

Baum, Scott (2014) 'Australia.gov.au: Development, Access, and Use of E-government', in Scott Baum and Arun Mahizhnan (eds) *E-Governance and Social Inclusion: Concepts and Cases* (Hershey, PA: IGI Global), pp. 183–98.

Bayat, Asef (2010) *Life as Politics: How Ordinary People Change the Middle East* (Stanford, CA: Stanford University Press).

BBC News (2009) *Obama Speaks of Hopes for Africa*, www.news.bbc.co.uk. 11 July. Accessed May 2015.

Beetham, David (2004) 'Freedom as the Foundation', in *Journal of Democracy* 15:4, October, pp. 61–75.

Bellamy, Richard (2008) *Citizenship: A Very Short Introduction* (Oxford: Oxford University Press).

Bendor, Jonathan, Terry M. Moe, and Kenneth W. Shotts (2001) 'Recycling the Garbage Can: An Assessment of the Research Program', in *American Political Science Review* 95:1, March, pp. 169–90.

Bennett, W. Lance (2005) 'Social Movements beyond Borders: Understanding Two Eras of Transnational Activism', in Donatella della Porta and Sidney Tarrow (eds) *Transnational Protest and Global Activism* (Lanham, MD: Rowman & Littlefield), pp. 203–26.

Benoit, Kenneth (2006) 'Duverger's Law and the Study of Electoral Systems' in *French Politics* 4:1, April, pp. 69–83.

Bergman, Torbjörn (2000) 'Sweden: When Minority Cabinets Are the Rule and Majority Coalitions the Exception', in Wolfgang C. Müller and Kaare Strøm (eds) *Coalition Governments in Western Europe* (New York: Oxford University Press), pp. 192–230.

Berman, Paul (2003) *Terror and Liberalism* (New York: Norton).

Berry, William D., Michael B. Berkman, and Stuart Schneiderman (2000) 'Legislative Professionalism and Incumbent Reelection: The Development of Institutional Boundaries', in *American Political Science Review* 94:4, December, pp. 859–74.

Betz, Hans-Georg (1994) *Radical Right-Wing Populism in Western Europe* (Basingstoke: Macmillan).

Beyme, Klaus von (2011) 'The evolution of comparative politics', in Daniele Caramani (ed.) *Comparative Politics*, 2nd edn (Oxford: Oxford University Press), pp. 23–36.

Bhagwati, Jagdish (2007) *In Defense of Globalization: With a New Afterword* (Oxford and New York: Oxford University Press).

Binderkrantz, Anne (2005) 'Interest Group Strategies: Navigating Between Privileged Access and Strategies of Pressure', in *Political Studies* 53:4, December, pp. 694–715.

Blackstone, William (1765–9) [1832 edn] *Commentaries on the Laws of England*, 4 books (New York: W. E. Dean).

Blais, André, Louis Massicotte, and Agnieszka Dobrzynska (2003) *Why Is Turnout Higher in Some Countries than in Others?* (Ottawa, Ontario: Elections Canada).

Blaydes, Lisa (2011) *Elections and Distributive Politics in Mubarak's Egypt* (New York: Cambridge University Press).

Boardman, Anthony F., David H. Greenburg, Aidan R. Vining, and David J. Weimer (2010) *Cost-Benefit Analysis: Concepts and Practice*, 4th edn (Upper Saddle River, NJ: Prentice Hall).

Boix, Carles (2003) *Democracy and Redistribution* (Cambridge: Cambridge University Press).

Boix, Carles (2011) 'Democracy, Development and the International System', in *American Political Science Review* 105:4, November, pp. 809–28.

Bolleyer, Nicole (2012) 'New Party Organization in Western Europe: Of Party Hierarchies, Stratarchies and Federations', in *Party Politics* 18:3, May, pp. 315–36.

Booth, Robert (2015) 'Why did the election pollsters get it so wrong?', in *The Guardian* at www.theguardian.com (posted 14 May).

Borchert, Jens and Jürgen Zeiss (2003) *The Political Class in Advanced Democracies: A Comparative Handbook* (Oxford: Oxford University Press).

Bourgault, Louise M. (1995) *Mass Media in Sub-Saharan Africa* (Bloomington, IN: Indiana University Press).

Boston, Jonathan, John Martin, June Pallot, and Pat Walsh (eds) (1995) *Reshaping the State: New Zealand's Bureaucratic Revolution* (Oxford: Oxford University Press).

Bratton, Michael (1998) 'Second Elections in Africa', in *Journal of Democracy* 9:3, July, pp. 51–66.

Bratton, Michael, Robert Mattes, and E. Gyimah-Boadi (2005) *Public Opinion, Democracy and Market Reform in Africa* (Cambridge: Cambridge University Press).

Braun, Dietmar, Sonja Wälti, Anne-Béatrice Bullinger, and Robert Ayrton (2003) *Fiscal Policies in Federal States* (Burlington, VT: Ashgate).

Bräutigam, Deborah, Odd-Helge Fjeldstad, and Mick Moore (2008) *Taxation and State-Building in Developing Countries: Capacity and Consent* (Cambridge: Cambridge University Press).

British Social Attitudes (2012) *Information System*, at www.britsocat.com. Accessed May 2012.

Brooker, Paul (2009) *Non-Democratic Regimes: Theory, Government and Politics*, 2nd edn (Basingstoke: Palgrave Macmillan).

Brooks, Stephen (2012) *Canadian Democracy: An Introduction*, 7th edn (Don Mills, Ontario: Oxford University Press).

Bryce, James (1921) *Modern Democracies*, Vol. 2 (New York: Macmillan).

Budge, Ian (2006) 'Identifying Dimensions and Locating Parties: Methodological and Conceptual Problems', in Richard S. Katz and William Crotty (eds) *Handbook of Party Politics* (Thousand Oaks, CA: Sage), pp. 422–34.

Burke, Edmund (1774) [1975 edn] 'Speech to the Electors of Bristol', in B. Hill (ed.) *Edmund Burke on Government, Politics and Society* (London: Fontana), pp. 156–8.

Burke, John P. (2010) 'The Institutional Presidency', in Michael Nelson (ed.) *The Presidency and the Political System*, 9th edn (Washington, DC: CQ Press), pp. 341–66.

Butler, David (1989) *British General Elections Since 1945* (Oxford: Blackwell).

C

Calhoun, Craig J. (1997) *Nationalism* (Buckingham: Open University Press).

Calhoun, John C. (1851) [2007 edn] in H. Lee Cheek (ed.) *Disquisition on Government* (South Bend, IN: St Augustine's Press).

Cambanis, Thanassis (2015) 'Egypt's Sisi Is Getting Pretty Good … at Being a Dictator', on *Foreign Policy* at http://foreignpolicy.com (posted 22 May).

Camilleri, Joseph A., and Jim Falk (1992) *The End of Sovereignty?* (Aldershot: Edward Elgar).

Campbell, Angus, Philip E. Converse, Warren E. Miller, and Donald E. Stokes (1960) *The American Voter* (New York: Wiley).

Campbell, John (2013) *Nigeria: Dancing on the Brink* (Lanham, MD: Rowman & Littlefield).

Carty, R. Kenneth (2004) 'Parties as Franchise Organizations: The Stratarchical Organizational Imperative', in *Party Politics* 10:1, January, pp. 5–24.

Case, William F. (1996) 'Can the "Halfway House" Stand? Semi-Democracy and Elite Theory in Three Southeast Asian Countries', in *Comparative Politics* 28:4, July, pp. 437–64.

Center for American Women and Politics (2014) *Gender Differences in Voter Turnout,* at www.cawp.rutgers.edu. Accessed May 2015.

Center for Responsive Politics (2015) *The Money behind the Elections,* at www.opensecrets.org/bigpicture. Accessed May 2015.

Chazan, Naomi, Peter Lewis, Robert Mortimer, Donald Rothchild, and Stephen John Stedman (1999) *Politics and Society in Contemporary Africa*, 3rd edn (Boulder, CO: Lynne Rienner).

Cheibub, José Antonio (2002) 'Minority Governments, Deadlock Situations and the Survival of Presidential Democracies', in *Comparative Political Studies* 35:3, April, pp. 284–312.

Cigler, Allan J. and Burdett A. Loomis (eds) (2012) *Interest Group Politics*, 8th edn (Washington: CQ Press).

CIRI Human Rights Dataset 2011, at www.humanrightsdata. com. Accessed July 2015.

Clayton, Cornell and Gillman, Howard (1999) 'Introduction', in Howard Gillman and Cornell Clayton (eds) *The Supreme Court in American Politics: New Institutionalist Approaches* (Lawrence, KS: University Press of Kansas), pp. 1–12.

Coase, R. H. (1960) 'The Problem of Social Cost', in *Journal of Law and Economics* 3, pp. 1–44.

Cohen, Daniel (2007) *Globalization and Its Enemies* (Cambridge, MA: MIT Press).

Cohen, Michael D., James G. March, and Johan P. Olsen (1972) 'A Garbage Can Model of Organizational Choice', in *Administrative Science Quarterly* 17:1, March, pp. 1–25.

Collier, Paul (2007) *The Bottom Billion: Why the Poorest Countries are Failing and What Can Be Done About It* (New York: Oxford University Press).

Collier, Paul, and Ian Bannon (eds) (2003) *Natural Resources and Violent Conflict: Options and Actions* (Washington, DC: World Bank).

Comparative Constitutions Project (2015), at http://comparativeconstitutionsproject.org. Accessed June 2015.

Conradt, David P. (2008) *The German Polity*, 9th edn (New York: Longman).

Corrigan, Bryce and Ted Brader (2011) 'Campaign Advertising: Reassessing the Impact of Campaign Ads on Political Behavior', in Stephen K. Medvic (ed.) *New Directions in Campaigns and Elections* (New York: Routledge), pp. 79–97.

Crawford, James (2007) *The Creation of States in International Law* (Oxford University Press).

Creveld, Martin van (1999) *The Rise and Decline of the State* (Cambridge: Cambridge University Press).

Crick, Bernard (2005) *In Defence of Politics*, 5th edn (London: Continuum).

Cross, William and André Blais (2012a) *Politics at the Centre: The Selection and Removal of Party Leaders in the Anglo Parliamentary Democracies* (Oxford: Oxford University Press).

Cross, William and André Blais (2012b) 'Who Selects the Party Leader?' in *Party Politics* 18:2, March, pp. 127–50.

Cross, William P. and Richard S. Katz (eds) (2013) *The Challenges of Intra-Party Democracy* (Oxford: Oxford University Press).

Crotty, William (2006) 'Party Transformations: The United States and Western Europe', in Richard S. Katz and William Crotty (eds) *Handbook of Party Politics* (Thousand Oaks, CA: Sage), pp. 499–514.

Cummings, Sally (2005) *Kazakhstan: Power and the Elite* (London: I. B. Tauris).

Curran, James and Jean Seaton (2009) *Power without Responsibility: The Press and Broadcasting in Britain*, 7th edn (London: Methuen).

D

Dahl, Robert A. (1961a) *Who Governs? Democracy and Power in an American City* (New Haven, CT: Yale University Press).

Dahl, Robert A. (1961b) 'The Behavioral Approach in Political Science: Epitaph for a Monument to a Successful Protest', in *American Political Science Review* 55:4, December, pp. 763–72.

Dahl, Robert A. (1998) *On Democracy* (New Haven, CT: Yale University Press).

Dahlerup, Drude (ed.) (2006) *Women, Quotas, and Politics* (New York: Routledge).

Dallmayr, Fred (ed.) (1999) *Border Crossings: Toward a Comparative Political Theory* (Lanham, MD: Lexington Books).

Dalton, Russell J. (2013) *Citizen Politics: Public Opinion and Political Parties in Advanced Industrial Democracies*, 6th edn (Washington, DC: CQ Press).

Dalton, Russell J. (2014) 'Interpreting Partisan Dealignment in Germany' in *German Politics* 23:1–2, pp. 134–44.

Dalton, Russell J. and Mark Gray (2003) 'Expanding the Electoral Marketplace', in Bruce E. Cain, Russell J. Dalton and Susan E. Scarrow (eds) *Democracy Transformed? Expanding Political Opportunities in Advanced Industrial Democracies* (New York: Oxford University Press), pp. 23–44.

Dalton, Russell J. and Hans-Dieter Klingemann (2007) 'Preface', in Russell J. Dalton and Hans-Dieter Klingemann (eds) *The Oxford Handbook of Political Behaviour,* (Oxford: Oxford University Press), pp. vii–viii.

Darcy, R., Welch, Susan, and Janet Clark (1994) *Women, Elections and Representation*, 2nd edn (Lincoln, NE: University of Nebraska Press).

Denters, Bas and Pieter-Jon Klok (2005) 'The Netherlands: In Search of Responsiveness', in Bas Denters and Lawrence Rose (eds) *Comparing Local Governance:*

Trends and Developments (Basingstoke: Palgrave Macmillan), pp. 65–82.

Denver, David, Christopher Carman, and Robert Johns (2012) *Elections and Voters in Britain*, 3rd edn (Basingstoke: Palgrave Macmillan).

Dershowitz, Alan (2001) *Supreme Injustice: How the High Court Hijacked Election 2000*, (New York: Oxford University Press).

DGB (Confederation of German Trade Unions) (2012) *Structure and Tasks*, at www.dgb.de. Accessed October 2012.

Dicey, A. V. (1885) [1959 edn] *Introduction to the Study of the Law of the Constitution*, 10th edn (London: Macmillan).

Dickson, Bruce J. (2007) 'Integrating Wealth and Power in China: The Communist Party's Embrace of the Market Sector', in *China Quarterly* 192, December, pp. 827–54.

Dogan, Mattei and Dominique Pelassy (1990) *How to Compare Nations* (Chatham, NJ: Chatham House).

Doing Business (World Bank) (2015) *Measuring Business Regulations*, at www.doingbusiness.org. Accessed May 2015.

Dolowitz, David and David Marsh (1996) 'A Review of the Policy Transfer Literature', in *Policy Studies* 44:2, June, pp. 343–57.

Donaldson, Robert H. (2004) 'Russia', in *Journal of Legislative Studies* 10:2–3, pp. 230–49.

Dooley, Brendan and Sabrina Alcorn Baron (eds) (2001) *The Politics of Information in Early Modern Europe* (New York: Longman).

Doorenspleet, Renske (2000) 'Reassessing the Three Waves of Democratization', in *World Politics* 52:3, April, pp. 384–406.

Downs, Anthony (1957) *An Economic Theory of Democracy* (New York: Harper).

Draper, Robert (2013) 'Inside the Power of the NRA', in *New York Times Magazine*, 12 December.

Duerst-Lahti, Georgia (2002) 'Knowing Congress as a Gendered Institution: Manliness and the Implications of Women in Congress', in Cindy Simon Rosenthal (ed.) *Women Transforming Congress* (Norman, OK: University of Oklahoma Press), pp. 20–49.

Duverger, Maurice (1951) [1959 English edn] *Political Parties* (London: Methuen).

Duverger, Maurice (1980) 'A New Political System Model: Semi-Presidential Government', in *European Journal of Political Research* 8:2, June, pp. 165–87.

Dye, Thomas R. (2012) *Understanding Public Policy*, 14th edn (Englewood Cliffs, NJ: Prentice-Hall).

E

Easton, David (1965) *A Systems Analysis of Political Life* (New York: Wiley).

Eberle, James (1990) 'Understanding the Revolutions in Eastern Europe', in Gwyn Prins (ed.) *Spring in Winter: The 1989 Revolutions*, (Manchester: Manchester University Press), pp. 193–209.

Eichbaum, Chris and Richard Shaw (2007) 'Ministerial Advisers, Politicization and the Retreat from Westminster: The Case of New Zealand', in *Public Administration* 85:3, September, pp. 569–87.

Elazar, Daniel J. (1966) *American Federalism: A View from the States* (New York: Thomas Y. Crowell).

Eley, Geoff and Ronald Grigor Suny (1996) 'From the Moment of Social History to the Work of Cultural Representation', in Geoff Eley and Ronald Grigor Suny (eds) *Becoming National: A Reader* (New York: Oxford University Press), pp. 3–37.

Elkit, Jorgen, Palle Svensson, and Lise Togeby (2005) 'Why is Voter Turnout in Denmark Not Declining?' Paper prepared for delivery at the *Annual Meeting of the American Political Science Association*, Washington, DC.

Endersby, James W., John R. Petrocik, and Daron R. Shaw (2006) 'Electoral Mobilization in the United States', in Richard S. Katz and William Crotty (eds) *Handbook of Party Politics* (Thousand Oaks, CA: Sage), pp. 316–36.

Esmer, Yilmaz and Thorleif Pettersson (2007) 'The Effects of Religion and Religiosity on Voting Behavior', in Russell J. Dalton and Hans-Dieter Klingemann (eds) *The Oxford Handbook of Political Behavior* (Oxford: Oxford University Press), pp. 481–503.

Eurobarometer (2001) *Eurobarometer 55*, spring.

Eurobarometer (2002) *Eurobarometer 57*, spring.

Eurobarometer (2003) *Eurobarometer 59*, spring.

Eurobarometer (2004) *Eurobarometer 61*, spring.

Eurobarometer (2014) *Eurobarometer 81*, spring.

Evans, Alfred B. (2005) 'A Russian Civil Society?', in Stephen White, Zvi Gitelman and Richard Sakwa (eds) *Developments in Russian Politics 6* (Basingstoke: Palgrave Macmillan), pp. 96–113.

Evans, Peter (1995) *Embedded Autonomy: States and Industrial Transformation* (Princeton: Princeton University Press).

F

Falconer, Lord (2003) Foreword to 'Constitutional Reform: A New Way of Appointing Judges'. Consultation paper for Department of Constitutional Affairs, UK, July.

Farnen, Russell J. and Jos D. Meloen (eds) (2000) *Democracy, Authoritarianism and Education* (Basingstoke: Macmillan).

Fiers, Stefaan and André Krouwel (2005) 'The Low Countries: From "Prime Minister" to President-Minister', in Thomas Poguntke and Paul Webb (eds) *The Presidentialization of Politics: A Comparative Study of Modern Democracies* (Oxford: Oxford University Press), pp. 128–58.

Figgis, J. N. and R. V. Laurence (eds) (1907) *Historical Essays and Studies* (London: Macmillan).

Finer, S. E. (1966) *Anonymous Empire: A Study of the Lobby in Great Britain* (London: Pall Mall).

Finer, S. E. (1997) *The History of Government from the Earliest Times*, 3 vols (Oxford: Oxford University Press).

Finnemore, Martha (1996) *National Interests in International Society* (Ithaca, NY: Cornell University Press).

Fish, M. Steven (2011) *Are Muslims Distinctive? A Look at the Evidence* (New York: Oxford University Press).

Fisher, Justin and Todd A. Eisenstadt (2004) 'Introduction: Comparative Party Finance: What Is To Be Done?', in *Party Politics* 10:6, November, pp. 619–26.

Fishkin, James F. (1991) *Democracy and Deliberation: New Directions for Democratic Reform* (New Haven, CT: Yale University Press).

Fishkin, James F. (2011) *When the People Speak: Deliberative Democracy and Public Consultation* (New York: Oxford University Press).

Flammang, Janet A., Dennis R. Gordon, Timothy J. Lukes, and K. Smorsten (1990) *American Politics in a Changing World* (Pacific Grove, CA: Brooks/Cole).

Foley, M. (1999) 'In Kiev They Fine a Journalist $1m and Cut Off All the Phones', in *The Times*, 2 April, p. 45.

Foweraker, Joe, Todd Landman, and Neil Harvey (2003) *Governing Latin America* (Cambridge: Polity).

Fox, Richard L. and Jennifer M. Ramos (2012) 'Politics in the New Media Era', in Richard L. Fox and Jennifer M. Ramos (eds) *iPolitics: Citizens, Elections and Governing in the New Media Era* (New York: Cambridge University Press), pp. 1–21.

Franklin, Mark (1992) 'The Decline of Cleavage Politics', in Mark Franklin, Thomas Mackie and Henry Valen (eds) *Electoral Change: Responses to Evolving Social and Attitudinal Structures in Western Countries* (Cambridge: Cambridge University Press), pp. 383–405.

Franklin, Mark (2004) *Voter Turnout and the Dynamics of Electoral Competition in Established Democracies* (Cambridge: Cambridge University Press).

Friedrich, Carl (1937) *Constitutional Government and Politics* (New York: Harper).

Frolic, B. Michael (1997) 'State-Led Civil Society', in Timothy Brook and B. Michael Frolic (eds) *Civil Society in China* (Armonk, NY: M. E. Sharpe), pp. 46–67.

Fukuyama, Francis (1989) 'The End of History?' in *The National Interest*, Summer.

Fuller, Lon L. (1969) *The Morality of Law* (New Haven, CT: Yale University Press).

G

Gandhi, Jennifer (2008) *Political Institutions under Dictatorship* (New York: Cambridge University Press).

Geddes, Barbara (2003) *Paradigms and Sand Castles: Theory Building and Research Design in Comparative Politics* (Ann Arbor, MI: University of Michigan Press).

Geddes, Barbara (2006) 'Why Parties and Elections in Authoritarian Regimes?' Revised version of paper prepared for presentation at the annual meeting of the American Political Science Association, Washington DC, 2005.

Geddes, Barbara (2007) 'What Causes Democratization?', in Carles Boix and Susan C. Stokes (eds) *The Oxford Handbook of Comparative Politics* (Oxford: Oxford University Press).

Geertz, Clifford (1973) [1993 edn] 'Thick Description: Toward an Interpretative Theory of Culture', in Clifford Geertz (ed.) *Interpretation of Cultures* (London: Fontana), pp. 1–33.

Gerring, John and Joshua Yesnowitz (2006) 'A Normative Turn in Political Science?', in *Polity* 38:1, January, pp. 101–13.

Gerth, Hans H. and C. Wright Mills (1948) *From Max Weber: Essays in Sociology* (London: Routledge & Kegan Paul).

Geys, Benny (2006) 'Explaining Voter Turnout: A Review of Aggregate-Level Research', in *Electoral Studies* 25:4, December, pp. 637–63.

Gheissari, Ali (ed.) (2009) *Contemporary Iran: Economy, Society, Politics* (New York: Oxford University Press).

Giese, Karim (2012) 'The Austrian Agenda Initiative: An Instrument Dominated by Political Parties', in Maija Setälä and Theo Schiller (eds) *Citizens' Initiatives in Europe: Procedures and Consequences of Agenda-Setting by Citizens* (Basingstoke: Palgrave Macmillan), pp. 175–92.

Gilens, Martin and Benjamin I. Page (2014) 'Testing Theories of American Politics: Elites, Interest Groups, and Average Citizens', in *Perspectives on Politics* 12:3, September, pp. 564–581.

Gill, Graeme (2003) *The Nature and Development of the Modern State* (Basingstoke: Palgrave Macmillan).

Gitelman, Zvi (2005) 'The Democratization of Russia in Comparative Perspective', in Stephen White, Zvi Gitelman and Richard Sakwa (eds) *Developments in Russian Politics 6* (Basingstoke: Palgrave Macmillan), pp. 241–56.

Gleeson, Brendan and Wendy Steele (2012) 'Cities', in Rodney Smith, Ariadne Vromen and Ian Cook (eds) *Contemporary Politics in Australia: Theories, Practices and Issues* (Melbourne: Cambridge University Press), pp. 320–31.

Goklany, Indur M. (2007) *The Improving State of the World: Why We're Living Longer, Healthier, More Comfortable Lives on a Cleaner Planet* (Washington, DC: Cato Institute).

Gómez Bruera, Hernán F. (2013) *Lula, the Workers' Party and the Governability Dilemma in Brazil* (New York: Routledge).

Goode, J. Paul (2010) 'Redefining Russia: Hybrid Regimes, Fieldwork, and Russian Politics', in *Perspectives on Politics* 8:4, December, pp. 1055–75.

Goodwin, Barbara (2007) 'Totalitarianism', in Barbara Goodwin, *Using Political Ideas* (Chichester: John Wiley), pp. 177–97.

Goodwin, Jeff and James M. Jasper (2003) 'Editors' Introduction', in Jeff Goodwin and James M. Jasper (eds) *The Social Movements Reader: Cases and Concepts* (Oxford: Blackwell), pp. 3–7.

Goren, Paul (2012) *On Voter Competence* (New York: Oxford University Press).

Gould, David J. (1980) 'Patrons and Clients: The Role of the Military in Zaire Politics', in Isaac James Mowoe (ed.) *The Performance of Soldiers as Governors* (Washington, DC: University Press of America), pp. 473–92.

Green, Daniel M. (ed.) (2002) *Constructivism and Comparative Politics* (Armonk, NY: M.E. Sharpe).

Green, Jeffrey Edward (2010a) *The Eyes of the People: Democracy in an Age of Spectatorship* (New York: Oxford University Press).

Green, John C. (2010b) 'Gauging the God Gap: Religion and Voting in US Presidential Elections', in Jan E. Leighley (ed.) *The Oxford Handbook of American Elections and Political Behavior* (Oxford: Oxford University Press), pp. 433–49.

Gregorian, Vartan (2004) *Islam: A Mosaic, Not a Monolith* (Washington, DC: Brookings Institution Press).

Guarnieri, Carlo (2003) 'Courts as an Instrument of Horizontal Accountability: The Case of Latin Europe', in José Maria Maravall and Adam Przeworski (eds) *Democracy and the Rule of Law* (New York: Cambridge University Press), pp. 223–41.

Guess, George M. and Paul G. Farnham (2011) *Cases in Public Policy Analysis*, 3rd edn (Washington, DC: Georgetown University Press).

Guo, Gang (2007) 'Organizational Involvement and Political Participation in China', in *Comparative Political Studies* 40:4, April, pp. 457–82.

H

Hacker, Jacob S. and Paul Pierson (2010) *Winner-Take-All Politics: How Washington Made the Rich Richer – And Turned Its Back on the Middle Class* (New York: Simon & Schuster).

Hagopian, Frances (2007) 'Parties and Voters in Emerging Democracies', in Carles Boix and Susan C. Stokes (eds) *The Oxford Handbook of Comparative Politics* (Oxford: Oxford University Press), pp. 582–603.

Hallaq, Wael B. (2007) *An Introduction to Islamic Law* (Cambridge: Cambridge University Press).

Hallin, Daniel C. and Paolo Mancini (2004) *Comparing Media Systems: Three Models of Media and Politics* (Cambridge: Cambridge University Press).

Hallin, Daniel C. and Paolo Mancini (eds) (2012) *Comparing Media Systems Beyond the Western World* (Cambridge: Cambridge University Press).

Hamilton, Alexander (1788a) [1987 edn] *The Federalist*, No. 84, ed. Isaac Kramnick (London: Penguin), pp. 436–45.

Hamilton, Alexander (1788b) [1987 edn] *The Federalist*, No. 51, ed. Isaac Kramnick (London: Penguin), pp. 263–7.

Hamilton, Alexander (1788c) [1987 edn] *The Federalist*, No. 62, ed. Isaac Kramnick (London: Penguin), pp. 314–20.

Hammerstad, Anne (2010) 'Population Movement and Its Impact on World Politics', in Mark Beeson and Nick Bisley (eds) *Issues in 21st Century World Politics* (Basingstoke: Palgrave Macmillan), pp. 238–50.

Hansard Society (2012) *Audit of Political Engagement 9: The 2012 Report*, at www.hansardsociety.org.uk. Accessed May 2012.

Hansen, Mogens Herman (1999) *The Athenian Democracy in the Age of Demosthenes* (Norman, OK: University of Oklahoma Press).

Hansen, Randall and Patrick Weil (eds) (2002) *Dual Nationality, Social Rights and Federal Citizenship in the U.S. and Europe* (New York: Berghahn).

Hardin, Russell (2006) *Trust* (Cambridge: Polity).

Hay, Colin, Michael Lister, and David Marsh (2006) 'The Transformation of the State', in Colin Hay, Michael Lister and David Marsh (eds) *The State: Theories and Issues* (Basingstoke: Palgrave Macmillan), pp. 190–208.

Hazan, Reuven Y. (2002) 'Candidate Selection', in Lawrence LeDuc, Richard G. Niemi and Pippa Norris (eds) *Comparing Democracies 3: Elections and Voting in the 21st Century* (Thousand Oaks, CA: Sage), pp. 108–26.

Hazan, Reuven Y. and Gideon Rahat, G. (2010) *Democracy within Parties: Candidate Selection Methods and Their Political Consequences* (Oxford: Oxford University Press).

He, Zhou (2009) 'Political Communication Dual Discourse Universes: The Chinese Experience', in Lars Willnat and Annette Aw (eds) *Political Communication in Asia* (New York: Routledge), pp. 43–71.

Heater, Derek (1999) *What is Citizenship?* (Cambridge: Polity).

Held, David and Anthony McGrew (2007) *Globalization/ Anti-Globalization: Beyond the Great Divide*, 2nd edn (Cambridge: Polity Press).

Hellinger, Daniel (2003) 'Political Overview: The Breakdown of *Puntofijismo* and the Rise of *Chavismo*', in Steve Ellner and Daniel Hellinger (eds) *Venezuelan Politics in the Chávez Era: Class, Polarization and Conflict* (Boulder, CO: Lynne Rienner), pp. 27–54.

Hellwig, Timothy (2010) 'Elections and the Economy', in Lawrence LeDuc, Richard G. Niemi and Pippa Norris (eds) *Comparing Democracies 3: Elections and Voting in the 21st Century* (Thousand Oaks, CA: Sage), pp. 184–201.

Herb, Michael (2005) 'Princes, Parliaments, and the Prospects for Democracy in the Gulf', in Marsha Pripstein Posusney and Michele Penner Angrist (eds) *Authoritarianism in the Middle East* (Boulder, CO: Lynne Rienner), pp. 169–92.

Herbst, Jeffrey (2001) 'Review: Political Liberalization in Africa after Ten Years', in *Comparative Politics* 33:3, April, pp. 357–75.

Herbst, Susan (1998) *Reading Public Opinion: How Political Actors View The Political Process* (Chicago: University of Chicago Press).

Hershberg, Eric (2006) 'Technocrats, Citizens and Second-Generation Reforms: Colombia's Andean Malaise', in Paul W. Drake and Eric Hershberg (eds) *State and Society in Conflict: Comparative Perspectives on the Andean Crisis* (Pittsburgh, PA: University of Pittsburgh Press), pp. 134–56.

Hibbs, Douglas A. (2006) 'Voting and the Macroeconomy', in Barry R. Weingast and Donald A. Wittman (eds) *The Oxford Handbook of Political Economy* (Oxford: Oxford University Press), pp. 565–86.

Hill, Lisa (2002) 'On the Reasonableness of Compelling Citizens to "Vote": The Australian Case', in *Political Studies* 50:1, March, pp. 80–101.

Hill, Michael and Peter Hupe (2002) *Implementing Public Policy: Governance in Theory and Practice* (Thousand Oaks, CA: Sage).

Hindmoor, Andrew (2010) 'Rational Choice', in David Marsh and Gerry Stoker (eds) *Theory and Methods in Political Science*, 3rd edn (Basingstoke: Palgrave Macmillan), pp. 42–59.

Hirschl, Ran (2008) 'The Judicalization of Politics', in Keith E. Whittington, R. Daniel Kelemen, and Gregory A. Caldeira (eds) *The Oxford Handbook of Law and Politics* (Oxford: Oxford University Press), pp. 119–41.

Hogwood, Brian W. and Lewis A. Gunn (1984) *Policy Analysis for the Real World* (Oxford: Oxford University Press).

Holmberg, Sören and Henrik Oscarsson (2011) 'Party Leader Effects on the Vote', in Kees Aarts, André Blais, and Hermann Schmitt (eds) *Political Leaders and Democratic Elections* (Oxford: Oxford University Press), pp. 35–51.

Holmes, Leslie (1997) *Post-Communism: An Introduction* (Cambridge: Polity).

Hood, Christopher (1996) 'Exploring Variations in Public Management Reform in the 1990s', in Hans A. Bekke, James L. Perry and Theo A. Toonen (eds) *Civil Service Systems in Comparative Perspective* (Bloomington, IN: Indiana University Press), pp. 268–87.

Hooghe, Liesbet, Gary Marks, and Arjan H. Schakel (2010) *The Rise of Regional Authority: A Comparative Study of 42 Democracies* (Abingdon: Routledge).

Horowitz, Donald L. (2002) 'Constitutional Design: Proposals versus Processes', in Andrew Reynolds (ed.) *The Architecture of Democracy: Constitutional Design, Conflict Management and Democracy* (New York: Oxford University Press), pp. 15–36.

Horowitz, Donald L. (2006) 'Constitutional Courts: Primer for Decision-Makers', in *Journal of Democracy* 17:4, October, pp. 125–37.

House of Commons Procedure Committee (2009) *Written Parliamentary Questions,* at www.publications.parliament.uk. Accessed December 2012.

Huber, Richard M., Jack Ruitenbeek, and Ronaldo Serôa de Motta (1998) *Market-Based Instruments for Environmental Policymaking in Latin America and the Caribbean: Lessons from Eleven Countries* (Washington, DC: World Bank).

Huber, John D. and Piero Stanig (2009) 'Individual income and voting for redistribution across democracies'. Unpublished working paper, Columbia University, New York.

Hughes, Melanie M. (2011) 'Intersectionality, Quotas, and Minority Women's Political Representation Worldwide', in *American Political Science Review* 105:3, August, pp. 604–20.

Human Rights Watch (2007) 'Election or "Selection"? Human Rights Abuses and Threats to Free and Fair Elections in Nigeria', Report 1, April.

Humphreys, Macarten, Jeffrey D. Sachs, and Joseph E. Stiglitz (2007) *Escaping the Resource Curse* (New York: Columbia University Press).

Huntington, Samuel P. (1991) *The Third Wave: Democratization in the Late Twentieth Century* (Norman, OK: University of Oklahoma Press).

Huntington, Samuel P. (1996) *The Clash of Civilizations and the Making of World Order* (New York: Simon & Schuster).

Hutter, Bridget (2005) 'Risk Management and Governance', in Pearl Eliadis, Margaret M. Hill and Michael Patrick Howlett (eds) *Designing Government: From Instruments to Governance* (Montreal: McGill-Queen's University Press), pp. 303–21.

I

Ignazi, Piero (2006) *Extreme Right Parties in Western Europe* (Oxford: Oxford University Press).

Immigrant Voting Project (2012) *Current Immigrant Voting Rights,* at www.immigrantvoting.org. Accessed July 2012.

Inglehart, Ronald (1971) 'The Silent Revolution in Europe: Intergenerational Change in Post-Industrial Societies', in *American Political Science Review* 65:4, December, pp. 991–1017.

Inglehart, Ronald (2000) 'Political Culture and Democratic Institutions', paper prepared for the *Annual Conference of the American Political Science Association,* Washington, DC.

Inglehart, Ronald and Christian Welzel (2010) 'Changing Mass Priorities: The Link between Modernization and Democracy', in *Perspectives on Politics* 8:2, June, pp. 551–67.

Inter-Parliamentary Union (2015) *Parline Database on National Parliaments,* at www.ipu.org. Accessed May 2015.

International Institute for Democracy and Electoral Assistance (IDEA) (2008) *Direct Democracy,* at www.idea.int. Accessed April 2009.

International Institute for Democracy and Electoral Assistance (2012) *Political Finance Regulations Around the World: An Overview of the International IDEA Database,* at www.idea.int. Accessed September 2012.

International Telecommunication Union (2015) *ICT Facts and Figures: The World in 2015,* at www.itu.int/en/ITU-D/statistics. Accessed June 2015.

Iyengar, Shanto, Mark D. Peters, and Donald R. Kinder (1982) 'Experimental Demonstrations of the "Not-So-Minimal" Consequences of Television News Programs', in *American Political Science Review* 76:4, December, pp. 848–58.

J

Jackson, Keith (1994) 'Stability and Renewal: Incumbency and Parliamentary Composition', in Albert Somit, Rudolf Wildenmann and Bernard Boll (eds) *The Victorious Incumbent: A Threat to Democracy?* (Aldershot: Dartmouth), pp. 251–77.

Jackson, Robert H. (1990) *Quasi-states: Sovereignty, International Relations and the Third World* (Cambridge: Cambridge University Press).

Jackson, Robert H., and Carl G. Rosberg (1982) *Personal Rule in Black Africa: Prince, Autocrat, Prophet, Tyrant* (Berkeley, CA: University of California Press).

Jamieson, Kathleen Hall, and Paul Waldman (2003) *The Press Effect: Politicians, Journalists and the Stories that Shape the Political World* (New York: Oxford University Press).

Jayal, Niraja Gopal (2007) 'Situating Indian Democracy', in Niraja Gopal Jayal (ed.) *Democracy in India* (New Delhi: Oxford University Press), pp. 1–50.

Jin, Dal Yong (2015) *Digital Platforms, Imperialism, and Political Culture* (Abingdon: Routledge).

John, Peter (2010) 'Quantitative Methods', in David Marsh and Gerry Stoker (eds) *Theory and Methods in Political Science*, 3rd edn (Basingstoke: Macmillan), pp. 267–284.

Johnson, Burke and Larry Christensen (2014) *Educational Research: Quantitative, Qualitative and Mixed Approaches*, 5th edn (Thousand Oaks, CA: Sage).

Johnson, Chalmers (1982) *MITI and the Japanese Miracle: The Growth of Industry Policy 1925–1975* (Stanford, CA: Stanford University Press).

Jones, Jeffrey P. (2005) *Entertaining Politics: New Political Television and Civic Culture* (Lanham, MD: Rowman & Littlefield).

K

Kalberg, Stephen (ed.) (2005) *Max Weber: Readings and Commentary on Modernity* (Oxford: Blackwell).

Kasem, A., M. J. F. van Waes, and K. C. M. E. Wannet, *What's New(s)? Scenarios for the Future of Journalism*, at www.journalism2025.com. Accessed July 2015.

Katz, Richard S. and Peter Mair (1995) 'Changing Models of Party Organization and Party Democracy: The Emergence of the Cartel Party', in *Party Politics* 1:1, January, pp. 5–28.

Kelso, Alexandra (2011) 'Changing Parliamentary Landscapes', in Richard Heffernan, Philip Cowley and Colin Hay (eds) *Developments in British Politics 9* (Basingstoke: Palgrave Macmillan), pp. 51–69.

Kerrouche, Eric (2006) 'The French *Assemblée Nationale*: The Case of a Weak Legislature', in *Journal of Legislative Studies* 12:3–4, September–December, pp. 336–65.

Kettl, Donald F. (2011) *The Politics of the Administrative Process*, 5th edn (Washington, DC: CQ Press).

Key, V. O. (1966) *The Responsible Electorate* (Cambridge, MA: Harvard University Press).

King, Anthony (1994) 'Ministerial Autonomy in Britain', in Michael Laver and Kenneth A. Shepsle (eds) *Cabinet Ministers and Parliamentary Government* (Cambridge: Cambridge University Press) pp. 203–25.

King, Anthony (ed.) (2002) *Leaders' Personalities and the Outcomes of Democratic Elections* (Oxford: Oxford University Press).

King, Gary, Robert O. Keohane, and Sidney Verba (1994) *Designing Social Inquiry: Scientific Inference in Qualitative Research* (Princeton, NJ: Princeton University Press).

Kingdon, John W. (2010) *Agendas, Alternatives and Public Policy*, updated 2nd edn (New York: Longman).

Kirchheimer, Otto (1966) 'The Transformation of the Western European Party Systems', in Joseph LaPalombara and Myron Weiner (eds) *Political Parties and Political Development* (Princeton, NJ: Princeton University Press), pp. 177–200.

Kitschelt, Herbert (2007) 'Growth and Persistence of the Radical Right in Post-Industrial Democracies: Advances and Challenges in Comparative Research', in *West European Politics* 30:5, November, pp. 1176–1206.

Kittilson, Miki Caul and Leslie A. Schwindt-Bayer (2012) *The Gendered Effect of Electoral Institutions: Political Engagement and Participation* (New York: Oxford University Press).

Klapper, Joseph T. (1960) *The Effects of Mass Communication* (New York: Free Press).

Knapp, Andrew and Vincent Wright (2006) *The Government and Politics of France*, 5th edn (London: Routledge).

Knill, Christopher and Jale Tosun (2012) *Public Policy: A New Introduction* (Basingstoke: Palgrave Macmillan).

Knutsen, Oddbjørn (1996) 'Value Orientations and Party Choice: A Comparative Study of the Relationship between Five Value Orientations and Voting Intention in Thirteen West European Democracies', in Oscar W. Gabriel and Jürgen W. Falter (eds) *Wahlen und Politische Einstellungen in Westlichen Demokratien* (Frankfurt: Peter Lang), pp. 247–319.

Knutsen, Oddbjørn (2006) *Class Voting in Western Europe: A Comparative Longitudinal Study* (Lanham, MD: Lexington).

Kommers, Donald P. (2006) 'The Federal Constitutional Court: Guardian of German Democracy', in *Annals of the American Academy of Political and Social Science* 603, January, pp. 111–28.

Kornhauser, William (1959) *The Politics of Mass Society* (Glencoe, IL: Free Press).

Kreiss, Daniel (2012) *Taking Our Country Back: The Crafting of Networked Politics from Howard Dean to Barack Obama* (New York: Oxford University Press).

Krook, Mona Lena (2009) *Quotas for Women in Politics: Gender and Candidate Selection Reform Worldwide* (New York: Oxford University Press).

Krouwel, A. (2003) 'Otto Kirchheimer and the Catch-All Party', in *West European Politics* 26:2, April, pp. 23–40.

Kulik, Anatoly (2007) 'Russia's Political Parties: Deep in the Shadow of the President', in Kay Lawson and Peter H. Merkl (eds) *When Parties Prosper: The Uses of Electoral Success* (Boulder, CO: Lynne Rienner), pp. 27–42.

Kumar, Sanjay and Praveen Rai (2013) *Measuring Voting Behaviour in India* (New Delhi: Sage).

L

Landman, Todd (2008) *Issues and Methods in Comparative Politics: An Introduction*, 3rd edn (London and New York: Routledge).

Langman, Lauren (2006) 'The Social Psychology of Nationalism', in Gerard Delanty and Krishan Kumar (eds) *The Sage Handbook of Nations and Nationalism* (London: Sage), pp. 71–83.

Lankov, Andrei (2013) *The Real North Korea: Life and Politics in the Failed Stalinist Utopia* (Oxford: Oxford University Press).

Lasswell, Harold D. (1936) *Politics: Who Gets What, When, How?* (New York: McGraw-Hill).

Lasswell, Harold D. (1968) 'The Future of the Comparative Method', in *Comparative Politics* 1:1, October, pp. 3–18.

Laver, Michael (1983) *Invitation to Politics* (Oxford: Martin Robertson).

Lawson, Kay (2001) 'Political Parties and Party Competition', in Joel Krieger (ed.) *The Oxford Companion to Politics of the World*, 2nd edn (New York: Oxford University Press), pp. 670–3.

Lazarsfeld, Paul F. and Robert K. Merton (1948) [2000 edn] 'Mass Communication, Popular Taste and Organized Social Action', in Paul Marris and Sue Thornham (eds) *Media Studies: A Reader,* 2nd edn (Edinburgh: Edinburgh University Press), pp. 14–24.

Le Cheminant, Wayne and John M. Parrish (eds) (2011) *Manipulating Democracy: Democratic Theory, Political Psychology and Mass Media* (New York: Routledge).

Lee, Terence and Lars Wilnat (2009) 'Media Management and Political Communication in Singapore', in Lars Willnat and Annette Aw (eds) *Political Communication in Asia* (New York: Routledge), pp. 93–111.

Lesch, Ann Mosley (2004) 'Politics in Egypt', in Gabriel A. Almond, G. Bingham Powell, Kaare Strøm and Russell J. Dalton *Comparative Politics Today: A World View,* 8th edn (New York: Longman), pp. 581–632.

Levin, Paul T. (2009) The Swedish Model of Public Administration: Separation of Powers – The Swedish Style', in *Journal of Administration & Governance* 4:1, July, pp. 38–46.

Levitsky, Steven and Lucan A. Way (2010) *Competitive Authoritarianism: Hybrid Regimes after the Cold War* (New York: Cambridge University Press).

Lewis-Beck, Michael S., Helmut Norpoth, William G. Jacoby, and Herbert F. Weisberg (2008) *The American Voter Revisited* (Ann Arbor, MI: University of Michigan Press).

Lichbach, Mark Irving and Alan S. Zuckerman (1997) *Comparative Politics: Rationality, Culture and Structure* (Cambridge: Cambridge University Press).

Lieberman, Evan S. (2005) 'Nested Analysis as Mixed-Method Strategy for Comparative Research', in *American Political Science Review* 99:3, August, pp. 435–52.

Lijphart, Arend (1971) 'Comparative Politics and the Comparative Method', in *American Political Science Review* 65:3, September, pp. 682–693.

Lijphart, Arend (1979) 'Religious vs Linguistic vs Class Voting: The Crucial Experiment of Comparing Belgium, Canada, South Africa and Switzerland', in *American Political Science Review* 73:2, June, pp. 442–58.

Lin, Nan and Bonnie Erickson (eds) (2008) *Social Capital: An International Research Program* (New York: Oxford University Press).

Lim, Timothy C. (2010) *Doing Comparative Politics: An Introduction to Approaches and Issues,* 2nd edn (Boulder, CO: Lynne Rienner).

Lindblom, Charles E. (1959) 'The Science of Muddling Through', in *Public Administration* 19:2, spring, pp. 78–88.

Lindblom, Charles E. (1979) 'Still Muddling, Not Yet Through', in *Public Administration Review* 39:6, November–December, pp. 517–26.

Linz, Juan J. (1975) [2000 edn] *Totalitarian and Authoritarian Regimes* (Boulder, CO: Lynne Rienner).

Linz, Juan J and Alfred Stepan (1996) *Problems of Democratic Transition and Consolidation: Southern Europe, South America, and Post-Communist Europe* (Baltimore, MD: Johns Hopkins University Press).

Lippman, Walter (1922) *Public Opinion* (London: Allen & Unwin).

Lipset, Seymour Martin (1959) 'Some Social Requisites of Democracy: Economic Development and Political Legitimacy', in *American Political Science Review* 53:1, March, pp. 69–105.

Lipset, Seymour Martin (1990) *Continental Divide: The Values and Institutions of the United States and Canada* (New York: Routledge).

Lister, Frederick K. (1996) *The European Union, the United Nations, and the Revival of Confederal Governance* (Westport, CT: Greenwood).

Lively, Jack (1991) 'Sièyes, Emmanuel Joseph', in David Miller (ed.) *The Blackwell Encyclopaedia of Political Thought* (Oxford: Blackwell), pp. 475–6.

Locke, John (1690) [1993 edn] in Mark Goldie (ed.) *Two Treatises of Government* (London: J M Dent).

Lockwood, Natalie J. (2013) 'International Vote Buying', in *Harvard International Law Journal* 54:1, Winter, pp. 97–157.

Loughlin, John, Frank Hendriks, and Anders Lidström (eds) (2011) *The Oxford Handbook of Local and Regional Democracy in Europe* (Oxford: Oxford University Press).

Lukes, Steven (2005) *Power: A Radical View* 2nd edn (London: Macmillan).

Lupia, Arthur (1994) 'Shortcuts versus encyclopedias: Information and voting behavior in California insurance reform elections', in *American Political Science Review* 88:1, March, pp. 63–76.

Lutz, Donald S. (2007) *Principles of Constitutional Design* (New York: Cambridge University Press).

Lynch, Marc (2011) 'After Egypt: The Limits and Promise of Online Challenges to the Authoritarian Arab State', *Perspectives on Politics* 9:2, June, pp. 301–10.

M

McAllister, Ian (2003) 'Australia: Party Politicians as a Political Class', in Jens Borchert and Jürgen Zeiss (eds) *The Political Class in Advanced Democracies* (Oxford: Oxford University Press), pp. 26–44.

McCargo, Duncan (2012) *Contemporary Japan,* 3rd edn (Basingstoke: Palgrave Macmillan).

McChesney, Robert W. (1999) *Rich Media, Poor Democracies* (Urbana, IL: University of Illinois Press).

McCormick, John (2015) *European Union Politics,* 2nd edn (London: Palgrave Macmillan).

McDonnell, Duncan and James L. Newell (2011) 'Outsider Parties in Government in Western Europe', in *Party Politics* 17:4, July, pp. 443–52.

McFarland, Andrew (2010) 'Interest Group Theory', in L. Sandy Maisel and Jeffrey M. Berry (eds) *The Oxford Handbook of American Political Parties and Interest Groups* (Oxford: Oxford University Press), pp. 37–56.

McFaul, Michael (2005) 'The Electoral System', in Stephen White, Zvi Gitelman and Richard Sakwa (eds) *Developments in Russian Politics 6* (Basingstoke: Palgrave Macmillan), pp. 61–79.

McGregor, Richard (2010) *The Party: The Secret World of China's Communist Rulers* (London: Allen Lane).

McLuhan, Marshall (1964) *Understanding Media: The Extensions of Man* (London: Routledge and Kegan).

Macpherson, C. B. (1977) *The Life and Times of Liberal Democracy* (Oxford: Oxford University Press).

Macridis, Roy (1955) *The Study of Comparative Government* (New York: Random House).

Madhukar, S. and Boppan Nagarjuna (2011) 'Inflation and Growth Rates in India and China: A Perspective of Transition Economies', in *International Proceedings of Economics Development & Research* 4, pp. 489–92.

Maghraoui, Abdeslam (2014) 'Egypt's Failed Transition to Democracy: Was Political Culture a Major Factor?' on *E-International Relations* website at www.e-ir.info (posted April 29).

Mahler, Gregory S. (2007) *Comparative Politics: An Institutional and Cross-National Approach*, 5th edn (Upper Saddle River, NJ: Pearson).

Mahoney, James (2003) 'Knowledge Accumulation in Comparative Historical Research: The Case of Democracy and Authoritarianism', in James Mahoney and Dietrich Rueschmeyer (eds) *Comparative Historical Analysis in the Social Sciences* (New York: Cambridge University Press), pp. 337–72.

Mahoney, James and Kathleen Thelen (2010) 'A Theory of Gradual Institutional Change', in James Mahoney and Kathleen Thelen (eds) *Explaining Institutional Change: Ambiguity, Agency and Power* (New York: Cambridge University Press), pp. 1–37.

Mainwaring, Scott and Mariano Torcal (2006) 'Party System Institutionalization and Party System Theory after the Third Wave of Democratization', in Richard S. Katz and William Crotty (eds) *Handbook of Party Politics* (London: Sage), pp. 204–27.

Mair, Peter (1994) 'Party Organizations: From Civil Society to the State', in Richard S. Katz and Peter Mair (eds) *How Parties Organize: Change and Adaptation in Party Organizations in Western Democracies* (Thousand Oaks, CA: Sage), pp. 1–22.

Mair, Peter (2008) 'The Challenge to Party Government', in *West European Politics* 31:1–2, January–March, pp. 211–34.

Mair, Peter (2009) 'Left-Right Orientations', in Russell J. Dalton and Hans-Dieter Klingemann (eds) *The Oxford Handbook of Political Behavior* (Oxford: Oxford University Press), pp. 206–22.

Mair, Peter and I. van Biezen (2001) 'Party Membership in Twenty European Democracies, 1980–2000', in *Party Politics* 7:1, January, pp. 5–22.

Maloney, William A. (2009) 'Interest Groups and the Revitalization of Democracy', in *Representation* 45:3, pp. 277–88.

Mandelbaum, Michael (2007) *Democracy's Good Name: The Rise and Risks of the World's Most Popular Form of Government* (New York: PublicAffairs).

Manza, Jeff and Christopher Uggen (2008) *Locked Out: Felon Disenfranchisement and American Democracy* (New York: Oxford University Press).

March, James G. and Johan P. Olsen, J. (1984) 'The New Institutionalism: Organizational Factors in Political Life', in *American Political Science Review* 78:3, September, pp. 734–49.

Marsh, David and R. A. W. Rhodes (eds) (1992) *Policy Networks in British Government* (Oxford: Oxford University Press).

Marsh, David and Gerry Stoker (2010) 'Introduction' to David Marsh and Gerry Stoker (eds) *Theory and Methods in Political Science*, 3rd edn (Basingstoke: Palgrave Macmillan), pp. 1–12.

Marshall, Monty G. and Benjamin R. Cole (2014) *Global Report 2014: Conflict, Governance and State Fragility* (Vienna, VA: Center for Systemic Peace).

Marten, Kimberly (2012) *Warlords: Strong-arm Brokers in Weak States* (Ithaca, NY: Cornell University Press).

Martin, Sherry L. and Gill Steel (eds) (2008) *Democratic Reform in Japan: Assessing the Impact* (Boulder, CO: Lynne Rienner).

Mazzoleni, Gianpietro (1987) 'Media Logic and Party Logic in Campaign Coverage: The Italian General Election of 1983', in *European Journal of Communication* 2:1, March, pp. 81–103.

Meguid, Bonnie M. (2008) *Party Competition between Unequals: Strategies and Electoral Fortunes in Western Europe* (New York: Cambridge University Press).

Melleuish, Gregory (2002) 'The State in World History: Perspectives and Problems', *Australian Journal of Politics and History* 48:3, September, 322–35.

Meredith, Martin (2006) *The Fate of Africa: From the Hopes of Freedom to the Heart of Despair* (New York: Public Affairs).

Mesquita, Bruce Bueno de and George W. Downs (2004) 'Why Gun-Barrel Democracy Doesn't Work', in *Hoover Digest* 2, spring.

Michels, Robert (1911) [1962 edn] *Political Parties* (New York: Free Press).

Miguel, Carolina de, Amaney Jamal, and Mark Tessler (2015) 'Elections in the Arab World: Why Do Citizens Turn Out?', in *Comparative Political Studies* 48:5, April, pp. 687–701.

Milbrath, Lester W. and M. L. Goel (1977) *Political Participation: How and Why Do People Get Involved in Politics*, 2nd edn (Chicago, IL: Rand McNally).

Mill, John Stuart (1859) [1982 edn] *On Liberty* (Harmondsworth: Penguin).

Mill, John Stuart (1861) [1977 edn] 'Considerations on Representative Government', in J. M. Robson (ed.) *Collected Works of John Stuart Mill*, Vol. 19 (Toronto: University of Toronto Press) pp. 371–577.

Miller, Raymond (2005) *Party Politics in New Zealand* (South Melbourne, Victoria: Oxford University Press).

Miller, William L. (1991) *Media and Voters: Audience, Content and Influence of Press and Television at the 1987 General Election* (Oxford: Clarendon Press).

Mills, C. Wright (1956) *The Power Elite* (New York: Oxford University Press).

Mitra, Subrata K. (2014) 'Politics in India', in G. Bingham Powell, Russell J. Dalton and Kaare Strøm (eds) *Comparative Politics Today*, 11th edn (New York: Pearson Longman), pp. 568–615.

Mohammadi, Ali (ed.) (2006) *Iran Encountering Globalization: Problems and Prospects* (Abingdon: Routledge).

Möller, Tommy (2007) 'Sweden: Still a Stable Party System?', in Kay Lawson and Peter H. Merkl (eds) *When Parties Prosper: The Uses of Electoral Success* (Boulder, CO: Lynne Rienner), pp. 27–42.

Monroe, Kristen Renwick (ed.) (2005) *Perestroika! The Raucous Rebellion in Political Science* (New Haven, CT: Yale University Press).

Montargil, Filipe (2010) 'E-Government and Government Transformation: Technical Interactivity, Political Influence and Citizen Return', in Paul G. Nixon, Vassiliki N. Koutrakou and Rajash Rawal (eds) *Understanding E-Government in Europe: Issues and Challenges* (Abingdon: Routledge), pp. 61–77.

Moran, Michael (2011) *Politics and Governance in the UK*, 2nd edn (Basingstoke: Palgrave Macmillan).

Morel, Laurence (2007) 'The Rise of "Politically Obligatory" Referendums: The 2005 French Referendum in Comparative Perspective', in *West European Politics* 30:5, pp. 1041–67.

Morlino, Leonardo (2012) *Changes for Democracy: Actors, Structures, Processes* (Oxford: Oxford University Press).

Morris, Richard B. (ed.) (1966) *Alexander Hamilton and the Founding of the Nation* (New York: Dial).

Mosca, Gaetano (1896) [1939 edn] *The Ruling Class* (New York: McGraw-Hill).

Mughan, Anthony (2000) *Media and the Presidentialization of Parliamentary Elections* (Basingstoke: Palgrave).

Mulgan, Richard (1997) *Politics in New Zealand*, 2nd edn (Auckland: Auckland University Press).

Munck, Gerardo L. (1994) 'Review Article: Democratic Transitions in Comparative Perspective', in *Comparative Politics* 26:3, April, pp. 355–75.

Munck, Gerardo L. (2007) 'The Past and Present of Comparative Politics', in Gerardo L. Munck and Richard Snyder, *Passion, Craft, and Method in Comparative Politics* (Baltimore, MD: Johns Hopkins University Press).

Munck, Gerardo L. and Richard Snyder (2007), 'Debating the Direction of Comparative Politics: An Analysis of Leading Journals', in *Comparative Political Studies* 40:1, January, pp. 5–31.

Munro, William Bennett (1925) *The Governments of Europe* (New York: Macmillan).

Murrie, Michael (2006) 'Broadcasters Getting Online, Staying On Air', in *Global Issues: Media Emerging*, March, pp. 11–14.

N

National Rifle Association (2012) *A Brief History of the NRA*, at www.nra.org. Accessed September 2012.

Ncjdrsu (National CJD Research and Surveillance Unit) (2012) *Creutzfeldt–Jakob Disease in the UK*, at www.cjd.ed.ac.uk. Accessed December 2012.

Newton, Kenneth (2006) 'May the Weak Force be With You: The Power of the Mass Media in Modern Politics', in *European Journal of Political Research* 45:2, March, pp. 209–34.

Nicholson, Peter P. (2004) 'Politics and the Exercise of Force', in Adrian Leftwich (ed.) *What Is Politics?* (Cambridge: Polity), pp. 41–52.

Niskanen, William A. (1971) *Bureaucracy and Representative Government* (Chicago: Aldine, Atherton).

Noack, Rick (2014) 'The Berlin Wall fell 25 years ago, but Germany is still divided', in *Washington Post*, 31 October.

Norris, Pippa (1999) 'The Growth of Critical Citizens and Its Consequences', in Pippa Norris (ed.) *Critical Citizens: Global Support for Democratic Governance* (New York: Oxford University Press), pp. 257–72.

Norris, Pippa (2000) *A Virtuous Circle: Political Communication in Postindustrial Societies* (Cambridge: Cambridge University Press).

Norris, Pippa (2009) 'New Feminist Challenges to the Study of Political Engagement', in Russell J. Dalton and Hans-Dieter Klingemann (eds) *The Oxford Handbook of Political Behavior* (Oxford: Oxford University Press), pp. 724–41.

Norris, Pippa (2011) *Democratic Deficit: Critical Citizens Revisited* (Cambridge: Cambridge University Press).

Norris, Pippa and Ronald Inglehart (2011) *Sacred and Secular: Religion and Politics Worldwide,* 2nd edn (Cambridge: Cambridge University Press).

O

Oates, Sarah (2014) 'Russia's Media and Political Communication in the Digital Age', in Stephen White, Richard Sakwa, and Henry E. Hale (eds) *Developments in Russian Politics 8* (Basingstoke: Palgrave Macmillan), pp. 130–44.

O'Donnell, Guillermo (1973) *Modernization and Bureaucratic Authoritarianism: Studies in South American Politics* (Berkeley, CA: California University Press).

O'Donnell, Guillermo (1994) 'Delegative Democracy', in *Journal of Democracy* 5:1, January, pp. 55–69.

O'Donnell, Guillermo, and Philippe C. Schmitter (1986) *Transitions from Authoritarian Rule, Vol 4: Tentative Conclusions about Uncertain Democracies* (Baltimore, MD: Johns Hopkins University Press).

O'Donnell, Guillermo, Philippe C. Schmitter, and Laurence Whitehead (eds) (1986) *Transitions from Authoritarian Rule: Comparative Perspectives* (Baltimore, MD: Johns Hopkins University Press).

Ohmae, Kenichi (2005) *The Next Global Stage: Challenges and Opportunities in our Borderless World* (Upper Saddle River, NJ: Wharton School Publishing).

Ohr, Dieter and Henrik Oscarsson (2011) 'Leader Traits, Leader Image, and Vote Choice', in Kees Aarts, André Blais, and Hermann Schmitt (eds) *Political Leaders and Democratic Elections* (Oxford: Oxford University Press), pp. 187–219.

Olsen, Johan P. (1980) 'Governing Norway: Segmentation, Anticipation and Consensus Formation', in Richard Rose and Ezra N. Suleiman (eds) *Presidents and Prime Ministers* (Washington, DC: American Enterprise Institute), pp. 203–55.

Olson, David M. (1994) *Democratic Legislative Institutions: A Comparative View* (New York: M.E. Sharpe).

Olson, Mancur (1965) *The Logic of Collective Action: Public Goods and the Theory of Groups* (Cambridge, MA: Harvard University Press).

O'Neill, Jim (2001) 'Building Better Global Economic BRICs'. *Global Economics Paper No. 66*. 30 November, Goldman Sachs, New York.

Onuf, Nicholas Greenwood (1989) *World of Our Making: Rules and Rule in Social Theory and International Relations* (Columbia, SC: University of South Carolina Press).

Organisation for Economic Cooperation and Development (2011) *50th Anniversary Vision Statement,* www.oecd.org. Accessed October 2011.

Organisation for Economic Co-operation and Development (2015) *Trade Union Density* at https://stats.oecd.org. Accessed June 2015.

Organization for Economic Co-operation and Development (OECD) (2013) *Government at a Glance 2013* (Paris: OECD Publishing).

Orren, Karen and Stephen Skowronek (1995) 'Order and Time in Institutional Study: A Brief for the Historical Approach', in James Farr, John S. Dryzek and Stephen T. Leonard (eds) *Political Science in History: Research Programs and Political Traditions* (New York: Cambridge University Press), pp. 296–317.

Osborne, David and Ted Gaebler (1992) *Reinventing Government: How the Entrepreneurial Spirit Is Transforming the Public Sector* (London: Penguin).

Oscarsson, Henrik and Soren Hölmberg (2010) *Swedish Voting Behavior.* Report by Swedish Election Studies Program, Department of Political Science, University of Gothenburg, at www.valforskning.pol.gu.se.

Ostrogorski, M. (1902) *Democracy and the Organisation of Political Parties* (London: Macmillan).

Owen, Roger (1993) 'The Practice of Electoral Democracy in the Arab East and North Africa: Some Lessons from Nearly a Century's Experience', in Ellis Goldberg, Resat Kasaba, and Joel S. Migdal (eds) *Rules and Rights in the Middle East* (Seattle, WA: University of Washington Press), pp. 17–40.

P

Paine, Thomas (1791/2) [1984 edn] *Rights of Man* (Harmondsworth: Penguin).

Parel, Anthony J. (1992) 'The Comparative Study of Political Philosophy', in Anthony J. Parel and Ronald C. Keith (eds) *Comparative Political Philosophy: Studies Under the Upas Tree* (New Delhi: Sage Publications).

Parsons, Wayne (1995) *Public Policy: An Introduction to the Theory and Practice of Policy Analysis* (Aldershot: Edward Elgar).

Parsons, Craig (2010) 'Constructivism and Interpretive Theory', in David Marsh and Gerry Stoker (eds) *Theory and Methods in Political Science*, 3rd edn (Basingstoke: Palgrave Macmillan), pp. 80–98.

Pateman, Carole (2012) 'Participatory Democracy Revisited', in *Perspectives on Politics* 10:1, March, pp. 7–19.

Pedersen, Mogens (1979) 'The Dynamics of European Party Systems: Changing Patterns of Electoral Volatility', in *European Journal of Political Research* 7:1, March, pp. 1–26.

Pegg, Scott (1998) *International Society and the De Facto State* (Aldershot, Ashgate).

Pei, Minxin (2003) 'Lessons From the Past: The American Record on Nation-Building', Carnegie Endowment Policy Brief No. 24, April.

Pennings, Paul, Hans Keman, and Jan Kleinnijenhuis (2006) *Doing Research in Political Science: An Introduction to Comparative Methods and Statistics,* 2nd edn (London: Sage).

Peregudov, Sergei (2001) 'The Oligarchical Model of Russian Capitalism', in Archie Brown (ed.) *Contemporary Russian Politics: A Reader* (Oxford and New York: Oxford University Press), pp. 259–68.

Peretti, Terri Jennings (2001) *In Defense of a Political Court* (Princeton, NJ: Princeton University Press).

Peters, B. Guy (1998) *Comparative Politics: Theory and Methods* (New York: New York University Press).

Peters, B. Guy (1999) *Institutional Theory in Political Science: The 'New Institutionalism'* (London: Pinter).

Peters, B. Guy and Jon Pierre (eds) (2004) *The Politicization of the Civil Service in Comparative Perspective: A Quest for Control* (London: Routledge).

Pew Research Center (2011) 'Internet Gains on Television as Public's Main News Source', at www.people-press.org/2011. Accessed November 2012.

Pew Research Center (2012) 'Views of Leaders', at www.pewglobal.org/2012. Accessed November 2012.

Pew Research Center (2013) The State of the News Media, at www.stateofthemedia.org. Accessed July 2015.

Pew Research Center (2014) 'Public Trust in Government: 1958-2014', at www.people-press.org/2014/11/13/public-trust-in-government. Accessed June 2015.

Pew Research Center (2015) at www.people-press.org. Accessed April 2015.

Phillips, Anne (1995) *The Politics of Presence* (Oxford: Oxford University Press).

Pierson, Paul (2004) *Politics in Time: History, Institutions and Social Analysis* (Princeton, NJ: Princeton University Press).

Pilet, Jean-Benoit and William Cross (eds) (2014) *The Selection of Political Party Leaders in Contemporary Parliamentary Democracies: A Comparative Study* (Abingdon: Routledge).

Pitkin, Hanna Fenichel (1967) *The Concept of Representation* (Berkeley: University of California Press).

Pollitt, Christopher and Geert Bouckaert (2011) *Public Management Reform: A Comparative Analysis*, 3rd edn (Oxford: Oxford University Press).

Popkin, Samuel L. (1994) *The Reasoning Voter: Communication and Persuasion in Presidential Campaigns* (Chicago: University Of Chicago Press).

Popper, Karl R. (1959) [2000 edition] *The Logic of Scientific Enquiry* (London: Routledge).

Porta, Donnatella Della and Mario Diani (2006) *Social Movements: An Introduction*, 2nd edn (Oxford: Blackwell).

Powell, G. Bingham, Russell J. Dalton, and Kaare Strøm (2014) *Comparative Politics: A Theoretical Framework*, 11th edn (New York: Pearson Longman).

Powell, Jonathan M. and Clayton L. Thyne (2011) 'Global instances of coups from 1950 to 2010: A new dataset', in *Journal of Peace Research* 48:2, March, pp. 249–259.

President of Russia (2009) *President of Russia,* at www.kremlin.ru. Accessed November 2009.

Preston, Julia and Samuel Dillon (2004) *Opening Mexico: The Making of a Democracy* (New York: Farrar, Straus and Giroux).

Pryor, Kane (2003) *A National State of Confusion,* at www.salon.com (posted 6 February).

Przeworski, Adam and Henry Teune (1970) *The Logic of Comparative Social Enquiry* (New York: Wiley-Interscience).

Przeworski, Adam (1991) *Democracy and the Market: Political and Economic Reforms in Eastern Europe and Latin America* (New York: Cambridge University Press).

Przeworski, Adam, Michael E. Alvarez, José Antonio Cheibub, and Fernando Limongi (2000) *Democracy and Development: Political Institutions and Well-Being in the World, 1950–1990* (New York: Cambridge University Press).

Putnam, Robert D. (1976) *The Comparative Study of Political Elites* (Englewood Cliffs, NJ: Prentice-Hall).

Putnam, Robert D. (1993) *Making Democracy Work: Civic Traditions in Modern Italy* (Princeton, NJ: Princeton University Press).

Pye, Lucien (1995) 'Political Culture', in Seymour Martin Lipset (ed.) *The Encyclopaedia of Democracy* (London: Routledge), pp. 965–9.

Q

Qualter, T. (1991) 'Public Opinion', in Vernon Bogdanor (ed.) *The Blackwell Encyclopaedia of Political Science* (Oxford: Blackwell), p. 511.

R

Rahat, Gideon (2007) 'Candidate Selection: The Choice before the Choice', in *Journal of Democracy* 18:1, January, pp. 157–71.

Rainer, Helmut and Thomas Siedler (2009) 'Does Democracy Foster Trust?', in *Journal of Comparative Economics* 37:2, June, pp. 251–69.

Regeringskansliet (Government Offices of Sweden) (2015) *How the Government and Government Offices Function,* at www.government.se/sb/d/2856. Accessed May 2015.

Riedl, Rachel Beatty (2014) *Authoritarian Origins of Democratic Party Systems in Africa* (New York: Cambridge University Press).

Reilly, Benjamin (2007) 'Electoral Systems and Party Systems', in *Journal of East Asian Studies* 7:2, May–August, pp. 185–202.

Rein, Martin (2006) 'Reforming Problematic Policies', in Michael Moran, Martin Rein and Robert E. Goodin (eds) *The Oxford Handbook of Public Policy* (Oxford: Oxford University Press), pp. 389–405.

Remington, Thomas F. (2014) 'Parliamentary Politics in Russia', in Stephen White, Richard Sakwa and Henry E. Hale (eds) *Developments in Russian Politics 8* (Basingstoke: Palgrave Macmillan), pp. 42–59.

Renan, Ernest (1882) [1990 edn] 'What is a Nation?', in Geoff Eley and Ronald Grigor Suny (eds) *Becoming National: A Reader* (New York: Oxford University Press), pp. 42–55.

Reno, William (1997) *Warlord Politics and African States* (Boulder, CO: Lynne Rienner).

Richardson, Jeremy, Gunnel Gustafsson, and Grant Jordan (1982) 'The Concept of Policy Style', in Jeremy Richardson (ed.) *Policy Styles in Western Europe* (London: Allen & Unwin), pp. 1–16.

Rifkin, Jeremy (2004) *The European Dream: How Europe's Vision of the Future is Quietly Eclipsing the American Dream* (New York: Jeremy Tarcher/Penguin).

Riker, William H. (1996) 'European Federalism: The Lessons of Past Experience', in Joachim Hans Hesse and Vincent Wright (eds) *Federalizing Europe? The Costs, Benefits and Preconditions of Federal Political Systems* (Oxford: Oxford University Press), pp. 9–24.

Ritzer, George (2011) *The McDonaldization of Society*, 6th edn (Thousand Oaks, CA: Pine Forge Press).

Rogers, Everett M. (2003) *Diffusion of Innovations*, 5th edn (New York: Free Press).

Romero, Vidal F. (2004) 'Developing Countries', in John G. Geer (ed.) *Public Opinion and Polling Around the World: A Historical Encyclopaedia* (Santa Barbara, CA: ABC-CLIO), pp. 485–91.

Rosanvallon, Pierre (2008) *Counter-Democracy: Politics in an Age of Distrust* (Cambridge: Cambridge University Press).

Rose, Richard (1991) 'Comparing Forms of Comparative Analysis', in *Political Studies* 39:3, September, pp. 446–62.

Rose, Richard (2005) *Learning from Comparative Public Policy: A Practical Guide* (Abingdon: Routledge).

Rose, Richard and Derek Urwin (1969) 'Social Cohesion, Political Parties and Strains in Regimes', in *Comparative Political Studies* 2:1, April, pp. 7–67.

Rosenbluth, Frances and Michael F. Thies (2014) 'Politics in Japan', in G. Bingham Powell, Russell J. Dalton, and Kaare Strøm (eds) *Comparative Politics Today: A World View*, 11th edn (New York: Pearson Longman), pp. 294–333.

Ross, Cameron (2010) 'Reforming the Federation', in Stephen White, Richard Sakwa and Henry E. Hale (eds) *Developments in Russian Politics* 7 (Basingstoke: Palgrave Macmillan), pp. 152–70.

Ross, Marc Howard (2009) 'Culture and Identity in Comparative Political Analysis', in Mark Irving Lichbach and Alan S. Zuckerman (eds) *Comparative Politics: Rationality, Culture and Structure* (New York: Cambridge University Press), pp. 42–80.

Rossi, Peter H., Mark W. Lipsey, and Howard E. Freeman (2003) *Evaluation: A Systematic Approach,* 7th edn (Thousand Oaks, CA: Sage Publications).

Rotberg, Robert I. (2004) 'The Failure and Collapse of Nation-States: Breakdown, Prevention and Repair', in Robert I. Rotberg (ed.) *When States Fail: Causes and Consequences* (Princeton, NJ: Princeton University Press), pp. 1–50.

Rothstein, Bo (1996) 'Political Institutions: An Overview', in Robert E. Goodin and Hans-Dieter Klingemann (eds) *A New Handbook of Political Science* (Oxford: Oxford University Press), pp. 205–22.

Rothstein, Bo (2002) 'Sweden: Social Capital in the Social Democratic State', in Robert D. Putnam (ed.) *Democracies in Flux: The Evolution of Social Capital in Contemporary Society* (New York: Oxford University Press), pp. 289–332.

Rousseau, Jean-Jacques (1762) [1968 edn] *The Social Contract* (London: Penguin).

Roy, Olivier (1994) *The Failure of Political Islam* (London: I. B. Tauris).

Rubin, Edward L. and Malcolm M. Feeley (2008) 'Federalism and Interpretation', in *Publius* 38:2, spring, pp. 167–91.

Russell, Bertrand (1938) *Power: A New Social Analysis* (London: Allen & Unwin).

S

Saich, Tony (2015) *Governance and Politics of China*, 4th edn (Basingstoke: Palgrave Macmillan).

Said, Edward (2001) 'The Clash of Ignorance', in *The Nation*, 4 October.

Saikal, Amin (2003) *Islam and the West: Conflict or Cooperation?* (Basingstoke: Palgrave Macmillan).

Sait, Edward McChesney (1938) *Political Institutions: A Preface* (New York: Appleton-Century).

Salamon, Lester M. (2002) 'The New Governance and the Tools of Public Action: An Introduction', in Lester M. Salamon (ed.) *The Tools of Government: A Guide to the New Governance* (New York: Oxford University Press), pp. 1–47.

Sandbrook, Richard (1985) *The Politics of Africa's Economic Stagnation* (Cambridge: Cambridge University Press).

Sartori, Giovanni (1994) *Comparative Constitutional Engineering: An Inquiry into Structures, Incentives and Outcomes* (London: Macmillan).

Savoie, Donald (1999) *Governing from the Centre: The Concentration of Power in Canadian Politics* (Toronto: University of Toronto Press).

Scarrow, Susan E., and Burcu Gezgor (2010) 'Declining memberships, changing members? European political party members in a new era', in *Party Politics* 16:6, November, pp. 823–43.

Schaffer, Frederic Charles (ed.) (2007) *Elections for Sale: The Causes And Consequences of Vote Buying* (Boulder, CO: Lynne Rienner).

Schattschneider, E.E. (1960) *The Semi-sovereign People* (New York: Holt, Rinehart, Winston).

Schedler, Andreas (ed.) (2006) *Electoral Authoritarianism: The Dynamics of Unfree Competition* (Boulder, CO: Lynne Rienner).

Schedler, Andreas (2009) 'Electoral Authoritarianism', in Todd Landman and Neil Robinson (eds) *The Sage Handbook of Comparative Politics* (London: Sage), pp. 381–93.

Scherpereel, John A. (2010) 'European Culture and the European Union's "Turkey Question"', in *West European Politics* 33:4, July, pp. 810–29.

Schlozman, Kay L. (2010) 'Who Sings in the Heavenly Chorus? The Shape of the Organized Interest System', in L. Sandy Maisel and Jeffrey M. Berry (eds) *The Oxford Handbook of American Political Parties and Interest Groups* (Oxford: Oxford University Press), pp. 425–50.

Schmidt, Vivien A. (2002) *The Futures of European Capitalism* (New York: Oxford University Press).

Schmitt-Beck, Rüdiger and David M. Farrell (2002) 'Do Political Campaigns Matter? Yes, but It Depends', in David M. Farrell and Rüdiger Schmitt-Beck (eds) *Do Political Campaigns Matter? Campaign Effects in Elections and Referendums* (London: Routledge), pp. 183–93.

Schmitter, Philippe (2004) 'Neo-functionalism', in Antje Wiener and Thomas Diez (eds) *European Integration Theory* (Oxford: Oxford University Press) pp. 45–74.

Schöpflin, George (1990) 'The End of Communism in Eastern Europe', in *International Affairs* 66:1, January, pp. 3–17.

Schudson, Michael (1998) *The Good Citizen: A History of American Civic Life* (Cambridge, MA: Harvard University Press).

Schuler, Paul, and Edmund J. Malesky (2014) 'Authoritarian Legislatures', in Shane Martin, Thomas Saalfeld, and Kaare W. Strøm (eds) *The Oxford Handbook of Legislative Studies* (Oxford: Oxford University Press), pp. 676–95.

Schumpeter, Joseph (1943) *Capitalism, Socialism and Democracy* (London: Allen & Unwin).

Scott, James C. (1985) *Weapons of the Weak: Everyday Forms of Peasant Resistance* (New Haven, CT: Yale University Press).

Sharlet, Robert (2005) 'In Search of the Rule of Law', in Stephen White, Zvi Gitelman and Richard Sakwa (eds) *Developments in Russian Politics 6* (Basingstoke: Palgrave Macmillan), pp. 130–47.

Shepherd, Robin (2006) 'The Denim Revolt that Can Rid Europe of Tyranny', in *Financial Times*, 17 March, p. 19.

Shirk, Susan (ed.) (2011) *Changing Media, Changing China* (New York: Oxford University Press).

Shepsle, Kenneth A. (2006) 'Rational Choice Institutionalism', in Sarah A. Binder, R. A. W. Rhodes, and Bert A. Rockman (eds) *The Oxford Handbook of Political Institutions* (Oxford: Oxford University Press), pp. 23–38.

Shugart, Matthew Soberg and John M. Carey (1992) *Presidents and Assemblies: Constitutional Design and Electoral Dynamics* (New York: Cambridge University Press).

Silvia, Stephen J. and Wolfgang Schroeder (2007) 'Why Are German Employers' Associations Declining? Arguments and Evidence', in *Comparative Political Studies* 40:12, December, pp. 1433–59.

Simon, Herbert A. (1983) *Reason in Human Affairs* (Oxford: Blackwell).

Skocpol, Theda (1979) *States and Social Revolutions: A Comparative Analysis of France, Russia and China* (New York: Cambridge University Press).

Smith, Anthony D. (2009) *Ethno-symbolism and Nationalism: A Cultural Approach* (London: Routledge).

Smith, Anthony D. (2010) *Nationalism,* 2nd edn (Cambridge: Polity).

Smith, B. C. (2009) *Understanding Third World Politics*, 3rd edn (Basingstoke: Palgrave Macmillan).

Smith, Daniel Jordan (2007) *A Culture of Corruption: Everyday Deception and Popular Discontent in Nigeria* (Princeton, NJ: Princeton University Press).

Solomon, Peter H. (2007) 'Courts and Judges in Authoritarian Regimes', in *World Politics* 60:1, October, pp. 122–45.

Sørensen, Georg (2004) *The Transformation of the State: Beyond the Myth of Retreat* (Basingstoke: Palgrave Macmillan).

Spilchal, Slavko (2002) *Principles of Publicity and Press Freedom* (Lanham, MD: Rowman and Littlefield).

Sreberny, Annabelle and Gholam Khiabany (2010) *Blogistan: The Internet and Politics in Iran* (London: I.B. Tauris).

Steinberger, Peter J. (2004) *The Idea of the State* (Cambridge: Cambridge University Press).

Steinmo, Sven (2003) 'The Evolution of Policy Ideas: Tax Policy in the Twentieth Century', in *British Journal of Politics and International Relations* 5:2, May, pp. 206–36.

Stepan, Alfred (2001) *Arguing Comparative Politics* (Oxford: Oxford University Press).

Stevens, Anne (2007) *Women, Power and Politics* (Basingstoke: Palgrave Macmillan).

Stevens, Jacqueline (2012) 'Political scientists are lousy forecasters', in *New York Times*, 23 June.

Stimson, James A. (2004) *Tides of Consent: How Public Opinion Shapes American Politics* (New York: Oxford University Press).

Stokes, Wendy (2005) *Women in Contemporary Politics* (Cambridge: Polity).

Stone Sweet, Alec (2000) *Governing with Judges: Constitutional Politics in Europe* (Oxford: Oxford University Press).

Strange, Susan (1996) *The Retreat of the State: The Diffusion of Power in the World Economy* (Cambridge: Cambridge University Press).

Street, John (2011) *Mass Media, Politics and Democracy*, 2nd edn (Basingstoke: Palgrave Macmillan).

Strøm, Kaare and Benjamin Nyblade (2007) 'Coalition Theory and Government Formation', in Carles Boix and Susan C. Stokes (eds) *The Oxford Handbook of Comparative Politics* (Oxford: Oxford University Press), pp. 782–804.

Sundberg, Jan (2002) 'The Scandinavian Party Model at the Crossroads', in Paul Webb, David Farrell and Ian Holliday (eds) *Political Parties in Advanced Industrial Democracies* (Oxford: Oxford University Press), pp. 181–216.

Svolik, Milan W. (2008) 'Authoritarian Reversals and Democratic Consolidation', in *American Political Science Review* 102:2, May, pp. 153–68.

Svolik, Milan W. (2012) *The Politics of Authoritarian Rule* (New York: Cambridge University Press).

T

Talbot, Strobe (1992) 'America Abroad: The Birth of the Global Nation', in *Time*, July 20.

Taylor, Adam (2014) 'We treat him like he's mad, but Vladimir Putin's popularity has just hit a 3-year high', in *The Washington Post*, 13 March.

Tetlock, Philip E. (2005) *Expert Political Judgment: How Good Is It? How Can We Know?* (Princeton, NJ: Princeton University Press).

Tetlock, Philip E. and Aaron Belkin (eds) (1996) *Counterfactual Thought Experiments in World Politics* (Princeton, NJ: Princeton University Press).

Teune, Henry (1995) 'Local Government and Democratic Political Development', *Annals of the American Academy of Political and Social Sciences* 540, July, pp. 11–23.

Teune, Henry (2010) 'The Challenge of Globalization to Comparative Research', in *Journal of Comparative Politics* 3:2, July, pp. 4–19.

Thachil, Tariq (2014) *Elite Parties, Poor Voters: How Social Services Win Votes in India* (Cambridge: Cambridge University Press).

Thomas, Clive S. and Ronald J. Hrebenar (2009) 'Comparing Lobbying Across Liberal Democracies: Problems, Approaches and Initial Findings', in *Journal of Comparative Politics* 2:1, March, pp. 131–42.

Thomas, Sue (2005) 'Introduction', in Sue Thomas and Clyde Wilcox (eds) *Women and Elective Office,* 2nd edn (New York: Oxford University Press), pp. 3–25.

Tilly, Charles (1975) 'Reflections on the History of European State-Making', in Charles Tilly (ed.) *The Formation of National States in Western Europe* (Princeton, NJ: Princeton University Press), pp. 3–83.

Tilly, Charles (1997) 'Means and Ends of Comparison in Macrosociology', in *Comparative Social Research* 16, pp. 43–53.

Tilly, Charles (2004) *Social Movements, 1768–2004* (Boulder, CO: Paradigm Publishers).

Tlemcani, Rachid (2007) 'Electoral Authoritarianism', in *Al-Ahram Weekly*, 29 May, reproduced by Carnegie Endowment for International Peace at http://carnegieendowment.org.

Tocqueville, Alexis de (1835) [1966 edn] *Democracy in America* (New York: Vintage Books).

Tracey, Michael (1998) *The Decline and Fall of Public Service Broadcasting* (Oxford: Oxford University Press).

Tremewan, Christopher (1994) *The Political Economy of Social Control in Singapore* (Basingstoke: Palgrave Macmillan).

Trumbull, Gunnar (2012) *Strength in Numbers: The Political Power of Weak Interests* (Cambridge, MA: Harvard University Press).

Turner, Mark and David Hulme (1997) *Governance, Administration and Development* (London: Macmillan).

Twigg, Judy (2005) 'Social Policy in Post-Soviet Russia', in Stephen White, Zvi Gitelman and Richard Sakwa (eds) *Developments in Russian Politics 6* (Basingstoke: Palgrave Macmillan), pp. 204–20.

U

UNESCO (United Nations Educational, Scientific and Cultural Organization) (2002) *Universal Declaration on Cultural Diversity,* at www.unesco.org. Accessed April 2006.

UNHCR (United Nations High Commission for Human Rights) (1966) *United Nations Covenant on Civil and Political Rights,* at www.unhcr.ch. Accessed February 2006.

United Nations Population Fund (2015), at www.unfpa.org/migration#sthash.KQcRM22Q.dpuf. Accessed June 2015.

UN Public Administration Network (2015) at www.unpan.org. Accessed June 2015.

United States Elections Project (2012) *2012 Early Voting Statistics,* at http://elections.gmu.edu. Accessed November 2012.

V

Valentino, Benjamin (2004) *Final Solutions: Mass Killing and Genocide in the 20th Century* (Ithaca, NY: Cornell University Press).

Vanhanen, Tatu (1997) *Prospects of Democracy: A Study of 172 Countries* (London: Routledge).

Vedung, Evert Oskar (1998) 'Policy Instruments: Typologies and Theories', in Marie-Louise Bemelmans-Videc, Ray C. Rist and Evert Oskar Vedung (eds) *Carrots, Sticks, and Sermons: Policy Instruments and Their Evaluation* (New Brunswick, NJ: Transaction), pp. 21–52.

Verba, Sidney (1987) *Elites and the Idea of Equality: A Comparison of Japan, Sweden and the United States* (Cambridge, MA: Harvard University Press).

Verba, Sidney (1991) 'Comparative Politics: Where Have We Been, Where Are We Going?', in Howard J. Wiarda (ed.) *New Directions in Comparative Politics* (Boulder, CO: Westview Press).

Verba, Sidney, Norman H. Nie, and Jae-on Kim (1978) *Participation and Political Equality: A Seven-Nation Comparison* (New York: Cambridge University Press).

Verba, Sidney, Kay Lehman Schlozman, and Henry E. Brady (1995) *Voice and Equality: Civic Voluntarism in American Politics* (Cambridge, MA: Harvard University Press), pp.26–38.

Vincent, Andrew (1987) *Theories of the State* (Oxford: Blackwell).

Voerman, Gerrit, and Wijbrandt H. van Schurr (2011) 'Dutch Political Parties and their Members', in Emilie van Haute (ed.) *Party Membership in Europe: Exploration into the Anthills of Party Politics* (Brussels: Editions de l'Université de Bruxelles) pp. 57–94.

Vreese, Claes de (2010) 'Campaign Communication and Media', in Lawrence LeDuc, Richard G. Niemi and Pippa Norris (eds) *Comparing Democracies 3: Elections and Voting in the 21st Century* (Thousand Oaks, CA: Sage), pp. 118–40.

W

Waldron, Jeremy (2007) *Law and Disagreement* (Oxford: Oxford University Press).

Walker, Jack L. (1991) *Mobilizing Interest Groups in America: Patrons, Professionals and Social Movements* (Ann Arbor, MI: University of Michigan Press).

Waterbury, John (1983) *The Egypt of Nasser and Sadat: The Political Economy of Two Regimes* (Princeton, NJ: Princeton University Press).

Wattenberg, Martin P. (2000) 'The Decline of Party Mobilization', in Russell J. Dalton and Martin P. Wattenberg (eds) *Parties without Partisans* (New York: Oxford University Press), pp. 64–76.

Watts, Ronald J. (2008) *Comparing Federal Systems,* 3rd edn (Montreal: Institute of Intergovernmental Relations).

Way, Lucan (2011) 'Comparing the Arab Revolts: The Lessons of 1989', in *Journal of Democracy* 22:4, October, pp. 17–27.

Weale, Albert (2007) *Democracy,* 2nd edn (Basingstoke: Palgrave Macmillan).

Weaver, R. Kent and Bert A. Rockman (eds) (1993) *Do Institutions Matter? Government Capabilities in the United States and Abroad* (Washington, DC: Brookings Institution).

Weber, Max (1905) [1930 edn] *The Protestant Ethic and the Spirit of Capitalism* (London: Allen & Unwin).

Weber, Max (1922) [1957 edn] *The Theory of Economic and Social Organization* (Berkeley, CA: University of California Press).

Wehner, Joachim (2006) 'Assessing the Power of the Purse: An Index of Legislative Budget Institutions', in *Political Studies* 54:4, December, pp. 767–85.

Weissberg, Robert (2002) *Polling, Policy and Public Opinion: The Case Against Heeding 'The Voice of the People'* (Basingstoke: Palgrave Macmillan).

Welzel, Christian and Ronald Inglehart (2005) *Modernization, Cultural Change, and Democracy: The Human Development Sequence* (New York: Cambridge University Press).

Welzel, Christian and Ronald Inglehart (2009) 'Political Culture, Mass Beliefs, and Value Change', in Christian W. Haerpfer, Patrick Bernhagen, Ronald Inglehart and Christian Welzel (eds) *Democratization* (Oxford: Oxford University Press) pp. 127–44.

Wendt, Alexander (1999) *Social Theory of International Politics* (Cambridge: Cambridge University Press).

Wheeler, Deborah L. and Lauren Mintz (2012) 'New Media and Political Change: Lessons from Internet Users in Jordan, Egypt, and Kuwait', in Richard L. Fox and Jennifer M. Ramos (eds) *iPolitics: Citizens, Elections and Governing in the New Media Era* (New York: Cambridge University Press), pp. 259–87.

White, Stephen (2007) 'Russia's Client Party System', in Paul Webb and Stephen White (eds) *Party Politics in New Democracies* (Oxford: Oxford University Press), pp. 21–52.

Whiteley, Paul F. (2011) 'Is the Party Over? The Decline of Party Activism and Membership Across the Democratic World', in *Party Politics* 17:1, January, pp. 21–44.

Wiarda, Howard J. (1991) 'Comparative Politics Past and Present', in Howard J. Wiarda (ed.) *New Directions in Comparative Politics* (Boulder, CO: Westview Press).

Wiarda, Howard J. (ed.) (2004) *Authoritarianism and Corporatism in Latin America – Revisited* (Gainesville, FL: University Press of Florida).

Wigbold, Herman (1979) 'Holland: The Shaky Pillars of Hilversum', in Anthony Smith (ed.) *Television and Political Life: Studies in Six European Countries* (London: Macmillan), pp. 191–231.

Wildavsky, Aaron (1979) *The Art and Craft of Policy Analysis* (Boston, MA: Little, Brown).

Wilson, Woodrow (1885) *Congressional Government* (Boston, MA: Houghton Mifflin).

Wilson, Woodrow (1887) 'The Study of Administration', in *Political Science Quarterly* 2:2, June, pp. 197–222.

Wlezien, Christopher (2010) 'Election Campaigns', in Lawrence LeDuc, Richard G. Niemi and Pippa Norris (eds) *Comparing Democracies 3: Elections and Voting in the 21st Century* (Thousand Oaks, CA: Sage), pp. 98–117.

Wood, Gordon S. (1993) 'Democracy and the American Revolution', in John Dunn (ed.) *Democracy: The Unfinished Journey, 508 BC to AD 1993* (Oxford: Oxford University Press), pp. 91–106.

World Bank (1997) *World Development Report: The State in a Changing World* (Oxford: Oxford University Press).

World Bank (2015) open data at http://data.worldbank.org. Accessed June 2015.

World Association of Newspapers and News Publishers (2015) *World Press Trends*, www.wan-press.org. Accessed July 2015.

Y

Yadav, Vineeta (2011) *Political Parties, Business Groups, and Corruption in Developing Countries* (New York: Oxford University Press).

Yin, Robert K. (2013) *Case Study Research: Design and Methods*, 5th edn (Thousand Oaks, CA: Sage).

Z

Zakaria, Fareed (2003) *The Future of Freedom: Illiberal Democracy at Home and Abroad* (New York: Norton).

Zhong, Yang (2015) *Local Government and Politics in China: Challenges from Below* (Abingdon: Routledge).

Zijderveld, Anton C. (2000) *The Institutional Imperative: The Interface of Institutions and Networks* (Amsterdam: Amsterdam University Press).

Index

Concept definitions are shown in **bold**.